ST. THOMAS AQUINAS

1274-1974

COMMEMORATIVE STUDIES

PRINTED BY UNIVERSA — WETTEREN — BELGIUM

JUSTUS OF GHENT · THE LOUVRE

ST. THOMAS AQUINAS

1274-1974

COMMEMORATIVE STUDIES

Foreword
by
Etienne Gilson

PONTIFICAL INSTITUTE OF MEDIAEVAL STUDIES
TORONTO, CANADA
1974

ACKNOWLEDGMENTS

These volumes have been published with the help of a grant from the Canada Council.

Thanks are also due to the University of St. Michael's College, Toronto, for its generous support through its Varsity Fund.

CONTENTS

VOLUME ONE

Foreword by Etienne Gilson   9

I THE LIFE OF ST. THOMAS

The Legend of St. Thomas Aquinas
    Edmund Colledge, O.S.A.   13

Papst Johannes XXII. und Thomas von Aquin. Zur Geschichte der Heiligsprechung des Aquinaten   *Angelus Walz, O.P.*   29

II THE WRITINGS OF ST. THOMAS

De Substantiis Separatis: Title and Date
    Francis J. Lescoe   51

Les Sermons de Saint Thomas et la *Catena Aurea*
    L. J. Bataillon, O.P.   67

"Versus" dans les Œuvres de Saint Thomas
    C. M. Joris Vansteenkiste, O.P.   77

La Lettre de Saint Thomas à l'Abbé du Montcassin
    Antoine Dondaine, O.P.   87

III EXEGETICAL STUDIES

Quasi Definitio Substantiae   *Etienne Gilson*   111

The Separated Soul and its Nature in St. Thomas
    Anton C. Pegis   131

"Ecclesia" et "Populus (Fidelis)" dans l'Ecclésiologie de S. Thomas   *Yves Congar, O.P.*   159

Les Idées Divines dans l'Œuvre de S. Thomas
    L. B. Geiger, O.P.   175

IV ST. THOMAS AND HIS PREDECESSORS

Aquinas as Aristotelian Commentator
                              Joseph Owens, C.Ss.R.   213

The *Nicomachean Ethics* and Thomas Aquinas
                              Vernon J. Bourke   239

St. Thomas and Ulpian's Natural Law
                              Michael Bertram Crowe   261

Fatalism and Freedom according to Nemesius and Thomas Aqui-
    nas   *Gérard Verbeke*   283

The Doctrine of Filioque in Thomas Aquinas and its Patristic An-
    tecedents. An Analysis of *Summa Theologiae*, Part I, Ques-
    tion 36   *Jaroslav Pelikan*   315

Unitas, Aequalitas, Concordia vel Connexio. Recherches sur les
    Origines de la Théorie Thomiste des Appropriations
                              Jean Châtillon   337

St. Thomas and the Habitus-Theory of the Incarnation
                              Walter H. Principe, C.S.B.   381

Saint Thomas et ses Prédécesseurs Arabes   *Louis Gardet*   419

Saint Thomas d'Aquin et la *Métaphysique* d'Avicenne
                              Georges C. Anawati, O.P.   449

Motion in a Void: Aquinas and Averroes
                              James A. Weisheipl, O.P.   467

VOLUME TWO

V ST. THOMAS AND HIS CONTEMPORARIES

William of Auvergne, John of La Rochelle and St. Thomas Aquinas on the Old Law *Beryl Smalley* 11

The *Quinque Viae* and some Parisian Professors of Philosophy *William Dunphy* 73

Certitude of Reason and Faith in St. Bonaventure and St. Thomas *John Francis Quinn, C.S.B.* 105

John Pecham and the Background of Aquinas's *De Aeternitate Mundi* *Ignatius Brady, O.F.M.* 141

Un Adversaire de Saint Thomas: Petrus Ioannis Olivi *Marie-Thérèse d'Alverny* 179

Brother Thomas, the Master, and the Masters *Edward A. Synan* 219

VI ST. THOMAS IN HISTORY: 14TH TO 19TH CENTURIES

The *Summa Confessorum* of John of Freiburg and the Popularization of the Moral Teaching of St. Thomas and of some of his Contemporaries *Leonard E. Boyle, O.P.* 245

The Unity of a Science: St. Thomas and the Nominalists *Armand A. Maurer, C.S.B.* 269

Galileo and the Thomists *William A. Wallace, O.P.* 293

Documents sur les Origines et les Premières Années de la Commission Léonine *Pierre M. de Contenson, O.P.* 331

8   CONTENTS

VII ST. THOMAS IN THE 20TH CENTURY

Création et Histoire   *M. D. Chenu, O.P.*   391

St. Thomas' Doctrine of Subject and Predicate: a Possible Starting
    Point for Logical Reform and Renewal   *Henry Veatch*   401

Il Nuovo Problema dell'Essere e la Fondazione della Metafisica
                               Cornelio Fabro, C.S.S.   423

Analektik und Dialektik. Zur Methode des Thomistischen und
    Hegelschen Denkens   *Bernhard Lakebrink*   459

Guide-Lines from St. Thomas for Theology Today
                                       E. L. Mascall   489

Notes on Contributors   503

Index   511

FOREWORD

For a rather short life (1225-1274) Thomas Aquinas has had an endless posterity of disciples, historians, and commentators; and let us not forget the editors of particular works, or even of Opera Omnia, *who can hardly wait for the end of an edition before declaring it out-of-date and undertaking a new one. In this Seventh Centenary of Thomas' death, the Pontifical Institute of Mediaeval Studies in Toronto wishes to join the many institutions and learned publications which, the whole world over, are commemorating the event.*

Some of these publications will chiefly testify to the faithfulness of the Thomistic school to its master, but most of them will rather express the conviction that, like Dante, Thomas Aquinas and his work are a landmark universally recognized in the history of western culture. There are also countless private readers who have become friends of Aquinas for life through the simple reading of the Summa Theologiae. *Many years ago, while in New York, I paid a visit to the author of* The Mediaeval Mind, a History of the Development of Thought and Emotion in the Middle Ages. *I knew that H. O. Taylor was not a professional historian, but a lawyer, and I wanted to ask him how, though not a Catholic, he had acquired such an insight into the spirit of the Middle Ages. I still hear him answering in all simplicity: "You know, I have read the whole* Summa Theologiae, *and when I came to the passage of the Third Part where the work was left interrupted, I actually cried."*

Whatever their inspiration, all the homages to the memory of the Angelic Doctor will be found to have in common one paradoxical feature, namely the diversity of their subjects. That diversity is typical of this many faced man. He has been, first of all, a theologian, but also a philosopher and a scientist, as this notion is found in the Aristotelian corpus, which included the science of both nature and man. A mere glance at the titles of the essays collected in these volumes will reveal the astonishing variety of the subjects in which that theologian was interested. More remarkable still is the variety of the methods, points of view, and principles to which he resorted in handling them. To Descartes and his successors, philosophical method, scientific method, and mathematical method are one and the same; to Thomas Aquinas and his disciples, the method of each science, while respecting the common laws of logic, must adapt itself to the specific nature of its proper object: extension in geometry, number in arithmetic, motion and change in physics, life in the sciences of the soul and living things. This attitude is typical of the methodological realism of Thomas Aquinas, and the notion is easy to understand; but to see it at work and to conform to it is quite another proposition. Like Aristotle before him, and William James after him, Thomas Aquinas lived in the pluralistic universe which is that of all true realists. To them, the mind adapts itself to the native diversity of the universe instead of reducing it to the mind's own unity. The universe is far from lacking order, but its order remains that of an ordered diversity.

Etienne GILSON

Director of Studies and Professor Emeritus
of the Pontifical Institute of Mediaeval Studies
Toronto

I

THE LIFE OF ST. THOMAS

THE LEGEND OF ST. THOMAS AQUINAS

Edmund Colledge O.S.A.

TODAY it is impossible to write of the pious stories told and written about the holy men and women of old times without being influenced, knowingly or not, by the work of the Bollandists, and, in particular, of Hippolyte Delehaye. He showed that many (some would write "most") of such stories are not true, and, more importantly, that those who circulated them were offering, not scientifically verifiable fact — so far as that concept was present to mediaeval minds — but edifying and symbolizing fiction. Thanks to Delehaye and his school, we are now warned and on the watch for the circumstances which will promote such fabrications.

Delehaye cannot have been ignorant of the doctrine, which in his own lifetime became so fashionable, of the "economic interpretation of history". The money to be gained, in one place from pilgrims' offerings, or throughout the Church by the spread of a special devotion, was a powerful inducement for those who might so benefit to press claims for sanctity, to associate them with given prayers or devotional objects, to defend possession of tombs, shrines and relics. A classic example is the centuries-long warfare between the Canons Regular and the Austin Friars over Augustine's *Rule* and his remains at Pavia, which gave scandal even to the Middle Ages, hardened to such disedifying spectacles.[1]

If some organization was gaining fame or wealth through a form of prayer or veneration associated with one of its saints, rival organizations would foster competitive devotions, and claim that they had been originated by their own holy ones. Again, if some one form of vision or miracle was seen to be especially impressive on the minds of the faithful, it would soon be claimed for a wide variety of ecstatics and wonder-workers.

Standard patterns of biography evolved, strongly influenced by the Scriptures, and, in particular, by the infancy narratives concerning

---

1 In the first half of the fifteenth century, John Capgrave O. S. A. made several appeals to his own Order and the Canons Regular for peace and a mutual recognition that they were both Augustine's co-heirs.

Christ and John the Baptist. Parents, and especially mothers, were almost invariably pious, there were pre-natal prophecies of future holiness, and marvellous or miraculous events in such children's earliest years. Happenings which the unprejudiced might think purely natural were given supernatural explanations. Anecdotes first intended to show merely human qualities were moralized to indicate divine intervention.

Constantly, we shall find identical wonders told of quite different saints. The causes of this can be various. Identities could be transferred, so that many Christian saints were endowed with the attributes and deeds of their predecessors, often pagan, sometimes mythical. The causes of such transfer can often lie in iconography, always important in the evolution of any cult among the illiterate: thus, Perseus rescuing Andromeda may become a Christian warrior-saint, a heathen sage winging his way up to wisdom a doctor of the Church. The picture of one event, such as Christ's baptism in Jordan, may be taken to show something entirely different, such as the sacring of some holy king. Two or more saints of the same name may suffer fusion. But, most of all, we shall find that plagiarism was regarded as a work of piety — "if their saint X was fed by a raven, then our saint Y was fed by a dove".

Then, too, all the time one encounters human forgetfulness and inventiveness. Eye-witnesses give different accounts of the same event. Biographers assert that their subjects were alive when the records show that they were dead, that "the histories" tell us that a man's family was of one origin when in fact they say nothing of the sort.

Today, we know all this to be so; yet even when the practice of mediaeval hagiography was in full swing, there were some who thought it an inferior method of honouring the saints. When Leo and two other companions of Francis of Assisi in 1246 sent their Minister-General their reminiscences, for which he had asked, they said in their prologue that they had not written "in the manner of a *Legenda*", that they had not been "content simply to narrate miracles, which do not create but only demonstrate holiness", but that instead they had tried to show by Francis's own words what was his true holiness. But, as their latest editor has observed,[2] they were not wholly successful in their undertaking. Current fashion was too strong for them, and despite them, the miracles kept on intruding themselves.

But if we too seek for a mediaeval saint's true holiness as the Bollandists have taught us to do, we must beware of a too facile dismissal of all that the Middle Ages tell us about him as mere fiction. Delehaye

2   Rosalind B. Brooke, ed., *Scripta Leonis, Rufini et Angeli Sociorum S. Francisci* (Oxford 1970) 86-87, 5.

himself saw how dangerous his methods could be if unskilfully and un-critically applied. In his perceptive study of the cult of Ida of Toggen-burg,[3] he warns that simply to eliminate from her legend every event which seems to a twentieth-century mind incredible is to employ a system which is arbitrary, illusory, confounding the true with the probable. He reminds us that when in 1608 the Congregation of Rites forbade the recitation of Ida's office, Bellarmine, the president, remarked: "The trouble is not so much the saint as her story"; and Delehaye goes on: "The learned cardinal then defined the rule which ought to guide the critics: do not mistake the personality of a saint for the portrait imagined by the hagiographers".[4]

Though most scholars today are content to follow Delehaye's line without observing his cautions, writing, for example, of "the human personality ... lost beneath layers of legend and rhetoric, or diluted to insipidity by imagination and error",[5] there are still those not satisfied with using "hagiography" as a merely pejorative term. A few years ago Giuseppe Agnello produced a sharp attack on the "mythological school",[6] in which he observed: "The desire to discuss the personality of a saint by contradicting everything attributed to him in legends cannot give results acceptable to critics. By using such a criterion one could reduce every saint, however authentic, to a mere figure of myth".[7]

Nothing would be easier than to set about de-mythologizing Thomas Aquinas, for, as we trace the evolution of his legend, we shall find examples of every error and fault which we have listed. There was bitter conflict for the possession of his remains, and those who wanted them to stay at Fossanova, those who organized their translation to Toulouse, glossed the accounts of his last days to suit their opposing purposes. It is difficult not to see, in the legends put about to encourage devotion to his wonder-working cincture, Dominican competition with the long-established Augustinian confraternities (whose charter, it may be ad-ded, was an equally dubious story). If we wish to demolish the account of the dying man's longing for herrings, so surprisingly gratified, we may point out that a similar story was told of Francis, decades before. As a naked infant in his bath he had produced for his nurses signs of his future sanctity; but the same, many of his biographers must have

---

3 "La légende de la bienheureuse Ida de Toggenburg", repr. from *Nova et Vetera* 4, 1929, in *Mélanges d'hagiographie grecque et latine* (Brussels 1966) 347-352.

4 Ibid. 352.

5 M. D. Knowles, "Great Historical Enterprises, I: The Bollandists", *Transactions of the Royal Historical Society* V vol. 8 (1958) 149.

6 "Tradizioni Agiografiche e Alterazioni Leggendarie", in *Saggi e Ricerche in Memoria Et-tore Li Gotti* (Palermo 1962) I 25-35.

7 Ibid. 25.

known, was told of Nicholas of Bari. Supernatural influences have been
ascribed to many events of his life which can bear strictly natural interpretations, and this is especially true of his last sickness. Even today,
he is the victim of "figured histories", so that his picture can be
mistaken for Dominic or Vincent Ferrer, that of his sister for our Lady.
The few remaining and aged witnesses at the formal interrogations who
had known him in life were no more reliable than most, as we shall see
from their accounts of his arrival at Fossanova. His biographers were
prone to their own flights of fancy, so that the unkind nickname given
him by his fellow students becomes a tribute to his mythical royal stock.

All this being so, need we trouble ourselves with his legend at all?
Surely we must, and for several reasons. Though the lapse of time between his death and the collection of evidence towards his canonization
is shorter by far than is usual, we can observe in those few years the
growth of distortions, the intrusion of fictions and the preservation of
true tradition. True tradition will tell us what Thomas did; yet even the
distortions and fictions will show what his familiars thought that he
was, and what was the age in which he lived, when men expected interior sanctity to be marked by external signs and wonders.

In his lifetime and immediately thereafter, Thomas was not given
universal veneration. It is noteworthy that John Pecham, who as a
Franciscan professor at Paris had been involved in public conflict with
him, writing to the University of Oxford on 7 December 1284, calls him
merely "bonae memoriae", whereas in the next month, in letters to the
Roman curia, he refers to his predecessor as archbishop of Canterbury,
Robert Kilwardby, as "sanctae memoriae". [8] But the University of Paris,
where he had been the centre of so many storms, sent its condolences to
the Order of Preachers on his death, and asked them, and also the abbot of Fossanova, for the custody of his body, sure sign that such
veneration was already growing. [9] As we study the offices composed for
his feasts, and his popular representations, we can see how fast the
legend grew and how wide it spread. In the old Dominican church at
Maastricht there are frescoes with an inscription dated 1337 (now
barely discernible, but preserved in a drawing by Victor de Stuers). [10]
There we see, for the edification of the Dutch faithful, the hermit
"Bonus" of Roccasecca, with inscribed scroll, confronting Thomas's

8   F. Ehrle ed. F. Pelster, *Gesammelte Aufsätze zur englischen Scholastik* (Rome 1970) 67, 70.
9   P. Mandonnet, "La canonization de S. Thomas d'Aquin", *Mélanges Thomistes* (Le Saulchoir
1923) 12-13.
10 *La peinture au pays de Liège et sur les bords de la Meuse,* 2nd ed. (Liège 1903), 40-41. I owe
my knowledge of this, as of many other art-objects associated with Thomas, to the valuable collections of the Index of Christian Art at Princeton, New Jersey.

mother Theodora and prophesying the unborn child's sanctity, the infant, nimbed, holding a scroll as he is bathed, his abduction by his brothers, his temptation by the courtesan and other such legendary scenes. Beyond doubt these frescoes were of Dominican commissioning, but they do show how widely and willingly the legend was accepted.

There is, however, another iconographical tradition, equally ancient, of much more sober derivation, that of the so-called "apotheosis" paintings and miniatures. Whether we find these in service-books such as MSS Milan Coll. Hoepli XXXII and XXXIII, both of the fourteenth century,[11] in details such as that from the "Last Judgment" panel in the Philip Lehmann collection in New York[12] or in such frescoes as that in St. Catherine's church in Pisa, attributed to Francis Traini[13] and that in the Spanish Chapel of Santa Maria Novella in Florence, variously attributed to Andrew of Florence, Antony di Bonaiuto and Thaddaeus Gaddi, and, according to Künstle, inspired by the anonymous painting executed at Fossanova in 1323, the year of Thomas's canonization,[14] they show regularly recurring features. He is depicted teaching, and this is usually indicated by his holding a book or books, often inscribed with quotations from his writings — at Pisa, the opening words of *Contra Gentiles*.[15] Above, he is surrounded by a great nimbus, inhabited variously by Christ in the centre, the apostles Peter and Paul, the evangelists, or Plato and Aristotle — all the sources of his wisdom. Light emanates from him, and prostrate at his feet are Sabellius, Averroes, Arius. (Nothing in this is novel. MS Bibliothèque Nationale latin 1684, of the eleventh century, shows, fol. 1, Athanasius treading down a fallen Arius; and the frontispiece of the contemporary MS B.N. latin 2079, to illustrate *Contra Faustum* shows Augustine as a bishop, with his crozier thrusting a disputing Faustus down to the ground.)

We may ask why Thomas's Order was so relatively slow in seeking through canonization for official approbation of his cult, when devotion to him, both as wonder-worker and divinely inspired teacher, was so early and prevalent. He had lived in anything but obscurity, and his death on the way to the Council of Lyons had been mourned by the whole Western Church, and even beyond its confines. Why then did almost fifty years elapse before he was raised to the altars? It has been suggested, and with great probability,[16] that the first impetus was given

11 P. Toesca, *Miniature Italiane* (Rome 1930) 48 ff.

12 R. Offner, *Florentine Painting* III 2 (Florence 1930) pt. 1, pl. XIX (2).

13 M. D. Knowles with D. Obolensky, *The Middle Ages* (London 1969) pl. C 19.

14 K. Künstle, *Ikonographie der christlichen Kunst* (2 vols., Freiburg i. B. 1926-1928) II 559.

15 For a list of such inscriptions on surviving representations, see G. Kaftal, *Iconography of the Saints in Tuscan Painting* (Florence 1952) 979.

16 To me, by my colleague Fr. James Weisheipl, O. P.

by the establishment of an independent Sicilian Dominican province, and its need — and that of the University of Naples, founded by Frederick II in 1224 — to promote the reputation of the kingdom's greatest modern saint.

To this end the Sicilian province in 1317 commissioned two of its brethren, William of Tocco and Robert of Benevento, to collect the materials necessary for a petition to the Holy See.[17] In November of that year William was in the Abruzzi, at the home of Thomas of San Severino, son of Roger and of Theodora, Thomas's youngest sister. After a journey to Salerno, William returned the next February, and this time met Catherine of Mora, daughter of William of San Severino, Roger's elder brother, and of Mary, another sister of Thomas. Catherine said that she had learned Thomas's history from his own mother, her grandmother; and in the canonization process it is recorded that she is the source of the story of his arrest and imprisonment by his family after he joined the Dominicans.

Later in 1318 William of Tocco was in Avignon, where he met Bernard Gui; and it is probable that Bernard then sketched, from William's communications, the outlines of the *Life* which he was later to publish. In 1319 evidence was heard, in Naples from 23 July until 26 November, and at Fossanova from 10 to 26 November. In 1320-1321 William completed the second, corrected draft of his *Life*, and in 1324-1326 Bernard published a revision of his work.

These were not the first or the last of such writings. The Dominican Ptolemy of Lucca, who had been personally acquainted with Thomas, in his *Annals* reported his death, his noble birth, his learning, his studies under Albert, the part he had been meant to play at Lyons in treating with the Greeks, miracles (unspecified) at Fossanova, and the first disputes over his remains[18] — a factual and dignified account. There has been much controversy, especially between Mandonnet and Prümmer, about the respective value of these sources, but most modern scholars would agree with what Pelster wrote half a century ago: "The biography of William of Tocco is, together with the data of Ptolemy of Lucca, the life-history of Thomas which is chronologically first and in content most important".[19]

The collection of the evidence had been no easy task. Bernard Gui in his *Life* complained that the Preachers through negligence had failed to

17 This chronological account of the process investigations is derived partly from K. Foster, *The Life of St. Thomas Aquinas* (Baltimore 1959), partly from Mandonnet, *La canonization.*
18 MGH Script. NS VIII (1930) 146-147, 176-177.
19 "Die älteren Biographien des hl. Thomas von Aquino", *Zeitschrift für katholische Theologie* 44 (1920) 242-274, 366-397.

record many miracles; and during the process Bartholomew of Capua said that it was commonly and strongly asserted that the Fossanova Cistercians had concealed such miracles in their fear of losing Thomas's body. Bartholomew also stated that when Thomas's secretary and faithful companion, Reginald of Piperno (by far the most important single source of information) was dying, he had confided matters vital to Thomas's cause to John del Giudice, and that when Bartholomew met John at Anagni, he had made him bring these to the knowledge of William of Tocco, and, later, of Benedict XI, himself a Dominican. We begin to see some of the difficulties which William experienced, and of which he wrote: "A certain friar ... his mind full of anxiety, his heart full of love, was pondering how he could best construct the saint's history from all the wonderful manifestations of his sanctity and the stories in praise of him, all of them true, so that it could show what were his origins, the course of his life, his scholarly attainments and his holy end ...".[20] His problem was solved by his dream-vision of the silver net interwoven with golden chains and studded with many-coloured gems. Translated into action, this seems to have meant that he decided to exclude nothing which would serve the purposes he had here declared: he intended to make a collection of wonders to illustrate Thomas's nativity, his religious life, his theology and his saintly death. In fact, William's aim is precisely that "demonstration of holiness" which Leo and his companions had disclaimed.

Thomas's nativity had therefore to be accompanied by events which would signalize the advent of a child of extraordinary sanctity. To the canonization process, William reported that Catherine of Mora had deposed to him at Marsico that Theodora, Thomas's mother, had told her that a hermit called "Friar Bonus" (though this may mean "a hermit friar of the Order called 'Bonus'") had come to the castle of Roccasecca and had said to her: "Gaude domina quia tu es pregnans et paries filium quem vocabis Thomam ...", and that he had prophesied that the child would join the Dominicans, rather than enter Monte Cassino as his family would wish.[21] One would have thought that William's Latin here makes the Lucan allusion clear enough; but not content with this, in *Vita* 1 he adds that Theodora replied: "Non sum digna talem parere filium, faciat deus sue beneplacitum voluntatis".[22] This is the account which Bernard Gui follows, though not ad lit-

---

20 D. Prümmer ed., *Fontes Vitae Sancti Thomae Aquinatis* (Toulouse n.d.) 122-123. Angelico Ferrua, *S. Thomae Aquinatis Vitae Fontes Praecipuae* (Alba 1968) has also been consulted, but this does not provide the critical edition so much needed to supersede Prümmer's unreliable texts.
21 Ibid. 350.
22 Ibid. 67.

teram;[23] but Peter Calo can improve on it. According to him, what the hermit said was: "Letare vere o domina, filium enim paries qui vocabitur Thomas, in quo profecto erit abyssus sapientie plenioris".[24]

All that we can safely adduce from this is that William asserted that Catherine had told him that her grandmother had told her that a hermit had prophesied the sanctity of her yet unborn child. To drive this point home, St. Luke's Gospel, *Regina coeli*, Isidore of Seville have all been pressed into service ; and since we have no means of knowing what precisely Theodora told Catherine or Catherine told William, it would be idle to speculate how much hindsight or rationalization there may have been in the story's first form. But its essential point need not be doubted: that Thomas from his earliest days was formed in the shape of Christ.

Another infancy narrative, that of the young Thomas in his bath, is probably of different origin. Theodora, it would seem, made no mention of it to Catherine, or Catherine to William. Instead, Peter Caracciolo of Naples deposed at the process that Constance Fanisari had told him that she was present when his mother could not make the child part with the piece of paper on which was written "Ave Maria ...",[25] and which he swallowed. This last detail appears in William's *Vita*, with his gloss: "... ubi divinitus premonstrabatur in puero quam discreta ruminatio scripturarum in ipso debebat precedere ... et quantum saporem dulcedinis doctor sensurus erat ..."[26] Bernard Gui has the story without the moral;[27] but, once again, Peter Calo improves on William. According to him, the incident is "clare insinuans quod futurus erat armarium scripturarum".[28] The bathos of this needs no comment.

But there is reason for suspecting that here we may have to do with a "transferred identity". In MS Bibliothèque Nationale français 51 (John du Vignay's translation of Vincent de Beauvais's *Speculum Historiale*), fol. 117c, between the first and second chapters of the life of Nicholas of Bari, there is an illustrative miniature. Chapter 1 ends with the account of Nicholas's birth, chapter 2 begins: "Et quant il fu orphelin de pere et de mere il mectoit souvent vne euuangille deuant sez oeilz laquelle euuangille (fol. 117d) dist qui ne renonce a tout ce quil a il ne puet pas estre mon disciple ...". The miniature shows, in the foreground, the infant Nicholas naked in his bath attended by his nurses, in the

23 Ibid. 168.
24 Ibid. 18.
25 Ibid. 395.
26 Ibid. 68.
27 Ibid. 168-169.
28 Ibid. 18.

background the young man secretly bestowing gold upon three young girls and being received by the bishop. That we today know how wholly fictional is the received "Life" of Nicholas is irrelevant. We also know how universally it was accepted and represented in late mediaeval literature and plastic art. It would be of interest to know if any other such painting exists, showing the infant in his bath with a scroll, as in the Maastricht Thomas fresco, but reading "Qui ne renonce ..." Even on the evidence of MS B.N. français 51 alone, there is good reason for thinking that this Thomas anecdote may have been borrowed from a Nicholas life — whether through pious fraud or genuine error, one cannot say.

All the witnesses agree that Thomas's entry into the Dominican Order was a stormy one, marked by his abduction by his family and their attempts to lure him into unchastity. We have seen that it is stated that Catherine, his niece, was the prime source here; and there seem to be no grounds for doubting her. Though such events are still a part of the Southern Italian way of life, the story reflects no credit upon his family (even his mother, however reluctantly, had consented to the abduction), and William would hardly have risked offending them at a time when their good will was so much needed, had he not been satisfied that they knew the story to be true.

The account of his temptation by the harlot, whom he drove out with a burning brand, was given an appendix, which then became inalienable from it. William of Tocco said at the process that the previous year at Anagni he had been told by Robert of Sezze, O.P., who had been told by his uncle, Stephen, that after Thomas had thrown the woman out, he prayed that he might never again be assailed by such a temptation, and so fell asleep. In a vision two angels appeared to tell him that God had heard his prayer. They pressed upon his loins and said: "Ecce ex parte dei cingimus te cingulo castitatis quod nulla possit temptatione dissolvi". He cried aloud with the pain and awoke, but refused to say what had made him shout. "Postmodum vero hec et alia multa revelavit predicto socio suo pro eius consolatione".[29] The defective text presented here by Prümmer does not make it clear who is this "predictus socius"; in the lack of evidence we may guess that it was Reginald, and that this was part of his dying revelation. Later, William said this;[30] and Bernard[31] and Peter Calo[32] follow him.

---

29 Ibid. 349.
30 Ibid. 75.
31 Ibid. 175.
32 Ibid. 24.

This story regularly appears in all the popularizations of Thomas's cult. We find it in one of the matins responses for a fourteenth-century office for his feast:

Orat pressa cruce mirifica,
Renes cingit manus angelica.[33]

In MS Bibliothèque Nationale latin 9473 (French, of the fifteenth century), fol. 174v, Thomas in glory in the centre is flanked, left, by three miniatures: above, he is received as a boy by the Preachers, centre, he drives out the courtesan as his brother watches, below, he is girded by angels. All these incidents are included in a composite scene on an early fourteenth-century panel, variously attributed, in the Berlin State Museum.[34] The "cingulum castitatis" becomes one of Thomas's attributes. In the late fifteenth-century portrait by Fra Carnovale in the Poldi-Pezzoli Museum in Milan, he wears the black outdoor habit, under which a white capuche shows, and, outside, the cincture, giving him the appearance more of an Augustinian.[35]

The sources of this story are so obscure that it is useless to speculate on its authenticity; but, again, its implications were at once and universally accepted: from his youth, Thomas was of angelic purity. But the idea that veneration of a cincture would promote a like purity in the devoted is much more recent. It seems to have been originated by the Venerable Mary Villani (1584-1670), of St. John the Baptist's convent in Naples, whose Dominican biographer, Dominic Marchese, recorded that Christ and Thomas appeared to her, Thomas by Christ's command girding her with such a cincture whilst Christ promised as a further grace that the gift of chastity would be granted to anyone wearing with full faith a girdle woven by her.[36] As has been said, it is difficult not to discern in this a spirit of competition with the already established Augustinian cincture confraternities.

We have seen that in a fourteenth-century office this girding by angels with the cincture is associated with Thomas's prayer before a crucifix of miraculous properties. This collocation is, however, fortuitous, and most of the evidence suggests that this second event is to be assigned to his later days in Naples. It is, possibly, the best known and most frequently mentioned wonder of his whole life.

---

33 C. U. J. Chevalier, *Repertorium hymnologicum* (Louvain 1892-1912, Brussels 1920-1921) 6081; G. M. Dreves, *Analecta hymnica medii aevi* (Leipzig 1886-1922) V 321.
34 Kaftal, *Tuscan Painting* 982, where the earlier erroneous identification with Dominic is corrected.
35 Künstle II 558, ill. 265.
36 C. Pera, "De Sacro Cingulo S. Thomae Aquinatis", *Xenia Thomistica* III (1925) 486-487.

One Dominican prose alludes to it in general terms:

> Crucifixus commendabat
> Quod de ipso scriptitabat
> Tam venusto schemate ...[37]

Another prose quotes it more closely:

> Crucifixus hunc adfatur
> Et promittens consolatur
> Se doctori praemium ...;[38]

and a hymn gives the original anecdote almost verbatim:

> Nam cum sacrae corpus cenae
> Descripsisset fratribus
> Panis, vini substans plene
> Solis accidentibus:
> De me, Thoma, scriptum bene
> Crux afflavit auribus.[39]

The story, not in the context in which it usually appears, but otherwise in its most explicit form, is found in William of Tocco's *Vita* 34. Dominic of Caserta, the sacristan at Naples, one night after matins followed Thomas into the chapel of St. Nicholas, and found him in prayer, lifted two cubits into the air. He heard a voice speaking from the crucifix: "Thoma, bene scripsisti de me, quam recipies a me pro tuo labore mercedem? Qui respondit: Domine, non nisi te". After this he wrote the third part of the *Summa,* on Christ's Passion and Resurrection, and this was almost the last that he wrote, a sign that he had already received this reward.[40]

Bartholomew of Capua in his account of how Thomas stopped writing makes no mention, as we shall see, of this locution; and we must observe that William, in *Vita* 52, has a second version, in which, when the Paris masters were publicly contradicting each other about accidents in the Blessed Sacrament, Thomas took what he had written into the chapel, laid it upon the altar, and prayed before the crucifix to be told if it were true; whereupon suddenly he saw Christ standing upon his notes, and heard him say: "Bene de hoc mei corporis sacramento scripsisti." Remaining there in prayer, he was raised a cubit into the air. Many witnessed this and related it to others.[41]

---

37 Chevalier 28104; Dreves XLIV 27.
38 Chevalier 28938; Dreves XXXVII 270.
39 Chevalier 31449; Dreves XLIII 294.
40 *Fontes* 108.
41 Ibid. 125-126.

Later tradition seems to have associated this miracle with Naples and not with Paris. In 1595, an account of the conflict in the Naples convent between supporters and opponents of reform concluded by saying that the victors ended the day reciting the Litanies of the Name of Jesus "in the chapel of the most holy Crucified One who spoke to St. Thomas Aquinas".[42]

We should also notice that later writers — John Michael Pio[43] and Raphael Carnavali[44] — assert that Thomas received a third "Bene scripsisti" locution at Orvieto, whilst he was composing his office of the Blessed Sacrament.[45] But older traditions seem to associate the event directly with a miraculous crucifix, and only indirectly, if at all, with the Eucharist. In MS Caius College Cambridge 148, c. 1400, the prayer often attributed to Thomas, "Concede michi queso misericors deus ..." is preceded by this rubric: "Hanc oracionem fecit sanctus thomas ... quam cotidie coram crucifixo dicere solebat. A quo idem thomas hec verba audire meruit: Bene scripsisti de me thoma ...".[46] Wilmart reserved judgment on the authenticity of "Concede michi", because he had not found it in manuscripts older than the fourteenth century; but he reports one of the fifteenth century, MS Bologna University Library 1580, with a rubric with a similar incipit: "Oratio beati thomae de aquino quam dicebat quotidie cum lacrimis coram crucifixo".[47]

In considering these accounts, we must begin by conceding that this was an age of miraculous crucifixes, and that this, beyond doubt, is to be associated with the increasingly more naturalistic representations of Christ's Passion which began about the year 1200, and reached their horrifying apex with *Christi Leiden in einer Vision geschaut* and Matthias Grünewald. It became a cliché of late mediaeval painters to indicate devotion to the Passion by showing the devotee in prayer before such a crucifix. A classic example is Francis, receiving the stigmata from one borne on seraph wings;[48] and this in its turn is transferred to Catherine of Siena — e.g. in MS Bibliothèque Nationale allemand 34, fol. 1r, the initial of a Middle High German translation of the *Dialogo*.

Corresponding stories abound. The abbot of a neighbouring monastery told how a monk known to him came upon Bernard of Clair-

42 M. Miele, *La Riforma Domenicana a Napoli ... 1583-1725* (Rome 1963) 367.
43 *Delle vite degli uomini illustri di San Domenico* (Bologna 1607-1613) 226-227.
44 *Vita di S. Tommaso d'Aquino* (Foligno 1882) 150.
45 J. V. De Groot, *Het Leven van den H. Thomas van Aquino* (Utrecht 1907) 364 n. 3.
46 A. I. Doyle, "A Prayer attributed to St. Thomas Aquinas", *Dominican Studies* I (1948) 231-232.
47 A. Wilmart, *Auteurs spirituels et textes dévots du moyen âge latin* (Paris 1932) 379 n. 1, 584.
48 E.g. MS Bibliothèque Nationale latin 1288, a fourteenth-century Franciscan breviary, fol. 521v.

vaux praying alone in the church. He was prostrate before the altar, when a crucifix appeared before him, which he reverenced and kissed. The image freed its hands from the nails, and pressed and embraced him.[49] One day as Francis prayed before the wooden crucifix in St. Damian's in Assisi, it parted its lips to say: "Go and repair my house, which is falling in ruins".[50] In MS Florence Riccardiana 1489, a partly Franciscan miscellany of the fourteenth century, on fol. 3v Francis is shown embracing the foot of the cross and gesturing towards Poverty; Christ bleeds profusely from hands and side. Sister Cecilia, of the St. Agnes convent at Bologna, described for the author of *The Nine Ways of Prayer of St. Dominic* how the saint used to pray, upright, prostrate, genuflecting or before the crucifix;[51] and one manuscript of the *Nine Ways*, Vatican Ross. 3, contains three miniatures depicting this, in all of which there pour out torrents of blood.[52]

If the ecstatic is shown in Dominican habit, identification with Thomas rather than Dominic will only be certain if the crucifix is given a "Bene scripsisti" scroll. But this sometimes is transferred, as in the Thomas apotheosis by Antonello of Messina in the National Museum at Palermo, where the words are inscribed on a book held by two angels to the right of God the Father, so robbing them of their traditional context.[53]

Thomas's age was attracted by the sensational elements of this anecdote; but these do not impair its real significance — the depth of his devotion to the Passion and the Eucharist, and the intensity of prayer and self-examination which accompanied all his work. Walz wrote: "Thomas's visions are all concerned with the manifestation of truth... These divine illuminations came to him in answer to the ardent prayers and fasts by which he implored the grace of understanding in dark and difficult matters".[54]

We may however question whether this is wholly true, when we come to consider the famous accounts of the "last vision". The immediate source is the evidence to the Naples process of the chancellor and protonotary Bartholomew of Capua, who said that this was some of the information given by the dying Reginald to John del Guidice, who

---

49   *Exordium Magne Cisterciense* VII vii, PL 185 419-420.

50   O. Englebert, *St. Francis of Assisi* (7th rev. English edn., Chicago 1965) 74, quoting II Celano 10 and 11.

51   F. C. Lehner, *St. Dominic: Biographical Documents* (Washington 1964) 147.

52   *Bibliotheca Sanctorum* IV 694.

53   M. Grabmann, trans. N. Ashenbrener, *The Interior Life of St. Thomas Aquinas* (Milwaukee 1951) 19.

54   A. Walz, trans. S. Bullough, *St. Thomas Aquinas, a biographical Study* (Westminster, Md., 1951) 171-172.

repeated it to Bartholomew, who in his turn has made it known to
William of Tocco and others. According to Bartholomew, one day after
celebrating Mass in the chapel of St. Nicholas at Naples, Thomas was
strangely changed. He would write or dictate nothing more, and
"suspendit organa scriptionis" in the middle of III, *De Poenitentia*.
Reginald asked him how he could leave unfinished anything so great,
and his reply was "Raynalde, non possum". Reginald, "timens ne propter multum studium aliquam incurisset amentiam", continued to urge
him, and Thomas would only say that all that he had written seemed
now so much straw to him. They went to stay with his sister, the coun-
tess of San Severino, who was much perturbed by the change she saw,
saying to Reginald that Thomas seemed dazed, and hardly spoke to her.
Finally, imposing silence on Reginald until after his death, Thomas
told him: "Omnia que scripsi videntur michi palee respectu eorum que
vidi et revelata sunt michi".[55] Earlier in his evidence Bartholomew had
recounted how, after this incident, on the way towards Lyons, Thomas
"percussit caput in quadam arbore que ceciderat per transversum ita
quod fere stupefactus quodammodo fuit circa casum".[56]

In *Vita* 67, William gives a different version, in which it is at San
Severino that Thomas experienced ecstasy for an extraordinary length
of time, until Reginald felt obliged to recall him to himself. He then
sighed, and said: "Tibi in secreto revelo, prohibens ne in vita mea alicui
audeas revelare. Venit finis scripture mee, quia talia sunt mihi revelata
quod ea que scripsi et locui modica mihi videntur; et ex hoc spero in
deo quod sicut doctrine mee sic cito finis erit et vite".[57] This is the version repeated by Bernard Gui;[58] but either gives us the essentials.

Of the whole legend, no other incident suggests more clearly a purely
natural explanation. Several medical authorities with whom the present
writer has discussed it have independently said that it presents the standard symptoms of severe brain damage through haemorrhage: impaired
speech, manual dexterity and gait, expectation of further such attacks,
and violent mental disturbance. Yet, on the other hand, we have, in
Bartholomew's account, through, it is true, two intermediaries,
Thomas's own statement that this disturbance had taken with him the
form of a perception of divine truth clearer than had ever before been
granted to him, and totally overwhelming. These are the facts as they
are known to us; to pass further judgment on them would be
temerarious.

---

55 *Fontes* 376-378.
56 Ibid. 375.
57 Ibid. 120.
58 Ibid. 193.

From then on, we can see, Thomas lived in daily expectation of death. Obedience made him set out for Lyons, but it is plain that he did not hope to arrive there; and when he was taken to Fossanova, saying that he wished to die in a house of religion, he uttered the famous "Hec requies mea in seculum seculi, hic habitabo quoniam elegi eam" (the Vulgate version of Psalm 131.14, the first psalm of ferial Thursday vespers in the Cursus Dominicanus).[59] The Fossanova monks gave this much prominence in their evidence to the process, since they interpreted it to mean that Thomas's body was not to be taken away; but their varying accounts of where this was said show how defective is the human memory.

Octavian of Babuco said that he, Peter of Montesangiovanni and others were present at Thomas's arrival, and that the words were spoken "ante chorum ecclesie".[60] But Peter of Montesangiovanni deposed that it was "in loco parlatori";[61] and Nicholas of Fresolino said that he had heard Peter say that it was "in ingressu dicti monasterii".[62] Still other varying accounts by such as Bartholomew of Capua and William of Tocco need not be considered, as they were not eye-witnesses.

Enough has been said to show what was the temper of Thomas's first biographers — their determination to find wonders in every possible event, their enthusiastic acceptance of stories of highly dubious authenticity, and their remorseless moralizing. His fellow students in Paris had called him "the dumb ox", in unkind allusion to his taciturnity and girth; but this is for William of Tocco a peg on which to hang the tale of how, in Cologne, he one day answered so perfectly that Albert was moved by the spirit of prophecy to exclaim: "He will low so loud when he teaches that it will sound throughout the world".[63] Later the epithet is endowed with a different significance; we are told that he was called "bos sicilie" because of his great and handsome stature, "for he, King Louis of Sicily and King Peter of Aragon were the sons of three sisters, 'ut habetur in hystoriis'".[64] The lords of Aquino, it is true, were connected by marriage with the Hohenstaufen dynasty,[65] and so with the royal houses of Sicily, Aragon, Castile and France; but that Theodora had two kings for nephews is pure fiction.

---

59 W. R. Banniwell, *A History of the Dominican Liturgy* (New York 1944) 136.
60 *Fontes* 286.
61 Ibid. 332.
62 Ibid. 280.
63 Ibid. 78-79.
64 "Quedam pertinentia ad translationem corporis S. Thomae de Aquino", *Analecta Bollandiana* 58 (1940) 43.
65 E. Kantorowicz, *Kaiser Friedrich der Zweite* (2 vols., Berlin 1931) indices.

The story of the "dumb ox", in its primitive form, tells us only of Thomas's recollection, patience and humility (and that he was from his youth corpulent); and so, with every other anecdote, we must search, discarding embellishments and pruning accretions, for that basic truth which in their allusive and indirect way the biographers sought to convey.

Every saint has his own distinctive emblem. Light, and the sources of light, are Thomas's. Before his body had been washed for burial, John of Ferentino, sub-prior of Fossanova, who was blind, laid himself upon it, placing his eyes over the saint's; and at once his sight was restored.[66] When John Coppa, a Naples notary, and his Dominican brother Bonfiglio visited Thomas, who was sick in his cell in the Naples convent, both saw a very bright star enter through the window and hang over the bed "for so long as one takes to say a slow 'Hail Mary'".[67] A Preacher who saw the boy in Naples and was astounded by his knowledge three times had a vision of him, his face shining like the sun and illumining everything.[68] For the three nights before his death a star like a comet was seen over Fossanova; and as he died, one of the monks who had fallen asleep praying in the church saw another star, of extraordinary brilliance, fall to the earth, where it was followed by two more, all three presently rising again to the heavens.[69] William of Tocco in *Vita* 61 repeats this and moralizes: Thomas in this life had already seen the lumen gloriae.[70]

Seven centuries have gone by, and we live in an age suspicious not only of what hagiographers such as William of Tocco were prepared to accept as evidence, but of the pieties which they sought to inspire. Yet Thomas's holiness transcends all this; nor can it be dissociated from his learning. His entire life was a singleminded and prayerful pursuit of divine truth; and his legend, in its mediaeval fashion, tells us how richly he was given what he had sought.

---

66 *Fontes* 335.
67 Ibid. 391-392.
68 Ibid. 70.
69 Ibid. 133.
70 Ibid. 134-135.

PAPST JOHANNES XXII. UND THOMAS VON AQUIN

ZUR GESCHICHTE DER HEILIGSPRECHUNG DES AQUINATEN

Angelus Walz O.P.

SEITDEM Gregor IX. im Jahre 1234 das Recht der Heiligsprechungen ausschliesslich dem Oberhaupt der Kirche vorbehalten
hat,[1] nehmen diese unter den Amtshandlungen des Papstes einen Vor-
zugsplatz ein. Infolgedessen wird der Name des heiligsprechenden Papstes mit dem des Heiliggesprochenen innig verknüpft. Da Johannes
XXII. die Heiligsprechung des Aquinaten vornahm, so sind die Namen
dieser beiden Männer in der Geschichte der Kirche und der Kultur in
besonderer Weise verbunden.

Im Folgenden kann von einer durchgehenden Neudarstellung der
Geschichte der Heiligsprechung des Aquinaten aus Gründen der
Raumgrenze nicht die Rede sein, es werden aber einerseits die
Grundzüge des Verlaufs dieser Angelegenheit vorgeführt und an-
dererseits Berichtigungen sowie neue Teilerkenntnisse zu früheren Dar-
stellungen geboten.

DER AQUINATE IM RUF DER HEILIGKEIT UND DER WUNDER

Abseits von den grossen Verkehrsadern Westeuropas und fern von
den belebten Mittelpunkten des Handels, der Wirtschaft und des
Reichtums, des Wissens, der politischen und der Kirchenmacht hat
Thomas von Aquin das Zeitliche gesegnet. Dem Ruf Gregors X.
folgend, der seine Gegenwart beim 2. Konzil von Lyon gewünscht hatte,
starb er auf dem Weg zur Rhônestadt in der Frühe des 7. März 1274
in der an Ausläufern der Lepinerberge gelegenen Zisterzienserabtei
Fossanova.[2] Mit ihm war ein überragender Gelehrter und eine

---

1 J. Schlafke, *De competentia in causis Sanctorum decernendi a primis p. Ch. n. Saeculis ad a.
1234* (Rom 1961) 145. Belege für das Folgende bei A. Walz, "Historia canonizationis S. Thomae de
Aquino," *Xenia thomistica*, 3 (Rom 1925) 105-172. In den folgenden Anmerkungen werden nicht
alle Nachweise geboten, sondern nur neuere Quellen- und sachliche Angaben sowie Ver-
besserungen.

2 A. Walz, *Luoghi di San Tommaso* (Rom 1961) 112-122.

vielverehrte Persönlichkeit, ein Priester und Ordensmann von seltener
Geistigkeit heimgegangen. Schon im Zeugnis, das Papst Alexander IV.
am 3. März 1256 dem verhältnismässig jungen Dozenten Thomas von
Aquin ausstellte als "einem Mann, der sowohl durch den Adel der
Geburt als auch durch Ehrbarkeit der Sitten ausgezeichnet ist und den
Schatz der schriftkundigen Wissenschaft durch die Gnade Gottes er-
worben hat," kommt eine übergewöhnliche Wertschätzung zum Aus-
druck. Thomas wird als Gelehrter und als ethische Gestalt gerühmt.
Seine Selbstbeherrschung und Vornehmheit bei der akademischen Disputation in Pariser Universitätskreisen mit dem streitbaren Johannes
Peckham OFM blieb unvergessen.[3] Peckham stiess übrigens mit einem
andern Thomas, dem von Cantilupe, Bischof von Hereford zusammen,
den er als Erzbischof von Canterbury mit dem Kirchenbann belegte.[4]
Auffallende Gebetserhörungen und wunderwirkende Kräfte wurden
dem Aquinaten schon zu Lebzeiten zugeschrieben. Nach seinem Tod
betrauerte die Pariser Artistenfakultät in einem Schreiben an das in
Lyon versammelte Generalkapitel der Dominikaner den Heimgang
dieses so hervorragenden Meisters und Lehrers als einen Verlust für die
allgemeine Kirche und eine offenkundige Verarmung der Pariser
Hochschule. Aus Pariser Gelehrtenkreisen stammt das Zeugnis des
Gottfried von Fontaines († nach 1306), der Thomas persönlich gekannt
hatte: "Einige bekämpfen in manchen Punkten die überaus fruchtbare
Lehre eines gewissen berühmten Meisters, dessen Andenken Ehre verdient; sie laufen Sturm gegen seine Aussagen, indem sie sowohl ihn
persönlich herabsetzen als auch seine Lehre, allerdings mehr mit
Schmähungen als mit Gründen."[5] In Neapel, wo Thomas seine letzten
Jahre verbracht hatte, konnte die öffentliche Meinung über sein tugend-
haftes und verdienstreiches Beispiel nicht verstummen. Die Zelle im
Dominikanerkloster in Neapel galt als verehrungswürdig. Zumal Wilhelm von Tocco OP hegte grosse Andacht zum verewigten Lehrer und
sprach sich darüber mit andern aus, die ihn ebenfalls gekannt hatten.[6]
So mit Bartholomäus von Capua, der in jugendlichem Alter Thomas
schätzen gelernt hatte, und, in Wissenschaft und Gesellschaft zu hohem
Rang aufgestiegen, ihm persönliche Verehrung erwies und sich darüber
mit Papst Benedikt XI. zu dessen Freude unterhielt.[7]

---

3 *Fontes vitae S. Thomae Aquinatis*, ed. M.-H. Laurent (Saint Maximin 1934) 374, test. Bar-
tholomaeus de Capua. A. Walz - P. Novarina, *St. Thomas d'Aquin* (Louvain-Paris 1962) 156.
4 *Lex. f. Theol. u. Kirche*, 10 (1965) 138.
5 A. Walz, "Politik um Thomas von Aquin," *Religion, Wissenschaft u. Kultur*, 12 (1961) 231.
6 *Fontes vitae*, 345, 355.
7 *Lex. f. Theol. u. Kirche*, 2 (1958) 11. *Fontes vitae*, 378.

Die Abtei Fossanova ehrte Thomas mit der Beisetzung vor dem Hochaltar und auch durch Übertragungen, um sich diesen Schatz zu sichern. Denn es erhoben sich Stimmen, zumal aus Dominikanerkreisen, die die sterblichen Überreste des Aquinaten für sich beanspruchten. Bei einer der Übertragungen wurde nicht die Messe de requiem, sondern die eines Bekenners gefeiert. Hilfesuchende und fromme Beter wie Bartholomäus von Capua fanden sich am Thomasgrab ein.[8]

In den Akten dominikanischer Generalkapitel wird Thomas als *venerabilis* oder *recolende memorie* und seine Lebensführung als *laudabilis* bezeichnet. Er gilt auch sonst als *sancte memorie*.[9] Mitglieder der Hierarchie wie Marinus Erzbischof von Capua, Ägidius von Rom OSA Erzbischof von Bourges, Albert der Grosse, Franziskus OFM, Bischof von Terracina-Priverno-Sezze, der Coronensis, und andere bezeugen seine Heiligkeit und Verehrung.[10] Der selige Jakob von Viterbo OSA, Erzbischof von Neapel (†1307/08) schrieb: "Das Ansehen des Bruders Thomas hat sich, obwohl seine Schriften nach seinem Tod...angegriffen wurden, nie vermindert, sondern immer mehr gefestigt und über die ganze Erde hin verbreitet zugleich mit der Verehrung und Hochschätzung für ihn." Innige Verehrung zollte Albert von Brescia OP dem Aquinaten. Über eine Vision von ihm berichtete er im Jahre 1310 zwei Studenten. Remigius Girolami OP in Florenz preist Thomas als *doctor doctorum sanctusque cacumine morum.* Dante erwähnt die höfliche Art und das glorreiche Leben des Aquinaten und das Beispiel des "buon frate Tommaso." Historiographische Zeugnisse bei Gerhard von Frachet, Thomas von Cantimpré, Tholomäus von Lucca und Bernhard Gui trugen bei, den Ruf der Heiligkeit Thomas' weithin zu tragen. Er hatte sich verbreitet im Dominikanerorden, bei Welt- und Ordensgeistlichen bis nach Zypern, ins Heilige Land und zu den "barbarischen Nationen."[11]

---

8 *Fontes vitae*, 380 ff.; 355.

9 *Fontes vitae*, 621 ff.; 637; 655; 656. A. Dondaine, "Venerabilis doctor," *Mélanges Et. Gilson*, (Toronto-Paris 1959) 211-225.

10 Walz, "Historia canonizationis," 110. Der Coronensis, im Prozess von Neapel (*Fontes vitae*, 403; vgl. C. Eubel, *Hierarchia catholica medii aevi*, 2 (2. Aufl. Münster 1914) xix, Carm[in]en. seu Carinen. genannt, war Dominikaner. Mit Carmicensis oder Carminensis dürfte der Bischof von Corone in Böothien gemeint sein, vgl. R. J. Loenertz, "Athènes et Néopatras," *Archiv. Fratr. Praed.* 28 (1958) 32.

11 *Fontes vitae*, 385; 586-89.

DIE THOMASLEHRE ALS "DOCTRINA COMMUNIS"

Bei der edlen und heiligmässigen Lebensführung des Aquinaten liegt es nahe, aus seinem Beruf als Gelehrter und aus seiner wissenschaftlichen Betätigung auf eine besondere Gediegenheit seiner Geistesarbeit und seiner Doktrin zu schliessen. Das bezeugen schon das Schreiben der Artistenfakultät von 1274 und die Urteile von Gottfried von Fontaines, Jakob von Viterbo und anderen. Das bewahrheitet sich in dem Masse, dass in der Geschichte der Scholastik das 13. Jahrhundert "das Jahrhundert des hl. Thomas"[12] genannt wird. Bei dem Pluralismus der Lehrer und Geistesrichtungen darf es aber auch nicht verwundern, dass die wissenschaftliche Methode und Lehre des Aquinaten zu seinen Lebzeiten und nach seinem Tod nicht allseitig anerkannt und befolgt wurden. Eine ortskirchliche, in Stefan Tempier, Bischof von Paris, verkörperte Autorität verurteilte am 7. März 1277 40 theologische und 179 philosophische Sätze, im ganzen 219 Lehrpunkte, darunter einige, die als Ansichten des Aquinaten galten.[13] Am 18. März 1277 folgte eine ähnliche Verurteilung in Oxford durch Robert Kilwardby OP, Erzbischof von Canterbury. Kilwardbys Nachfolger auf dem Erzbischofsstuhl Johannes Peckham kam im Jahre 1284 wiederholt auf sie zurück.[14] Der Generalminister der Franziskaner verbot auf dem Generalkapitel zu Strassburg 1282 die Vervielfältigung der *Summa* des Bruders Thomas. Nur bemerkenswert intelligente Lektoren und diese bloss bei Benützung der *Declarationes* des Wilhelm de la Mare sollten davon ausgenommen sein. Mit Wilhelms Schrift begann der Korrektorienstreit, der sich durch zwei Jahrzehnte gegen und für die Thomaslehre hinzog.[15] Im Jahre 1302 übersiedelte Johannes Duns Scotus OFM nach Paris. In ihm trat ein gewichtiger Kämpe gegen das Lehrgebäude des Aquinaten auf.

Das dominikanische Generalkapitel von Mailand 1278 unter dem Vorsitz des seligen Johannes von Vercelli ordnete zwei Patres nach England ab, um über die Mitbrüder, die zum Ärgernis des Ordens über die Schriften des Aquinaten sich verächtlich ausgelassen haben, Erkundigungen einzuziehen. Das Generalkapitel von Paris 1279 verbot, unehrerbietig und unpassend über Thomas und seine Schriften zu sprechen; wer sich verfehle, soll gestraft werden. In Paris traten für Thomas unter anderen ein Wilhelm de Peyre de Godin, bekannt durch

---

12 F. Van Steenberghen, *La philosophie au XIIIᵉ siècle* (Louvain-Paris 1966) 540.
13 Walz, "Politk um Thomas," 231. *Fontes vitae*, 596-614.
14 *Fontes vitae*, 615-617.
15 *Lex. f. Theol. u. Kirche*, 6 (1961) 561; vgl. 10 (1965) 1138. A. Walz, "S. Tommaso d'Aquino dichiarato dottore della Chiesa nel 1567," *Angelicum*, 44 (1967) 148.

seine *Lectura thomasina* von 1300,[16] Herveus Natalis, der vielleicht
angesehenste Dominikanertheologe des beginnenden 14. Jahrhunderts,[17] und Petrus de Palude, in England Thomas von Sutton und
Richard Knapwell, in Italien Rambert von Primadizzi und Johannes
von Neapel, im deutschen Raum Johannes Picardi von Lichtenberg,
Nikolaus von Strassburg, Heinrich von Lübeck sowie Johannes und
Gerhard von Sternengassen.[17a]

Dietrich von Freiberg ging eigene Wege. Johannes Quidort und
zumal Johannes von Metz[18] wichen von Thomaslehren ab. Dem letz-
teren erwiderte (1302-1307) Herveus.[19] Grossen Anstoss erregte bei Mit-
brüdern, Augustinern, Karmeliten, dem Kanzler von Oxford, und anderen der Sentenzenkommentar des Durandus. Während zehn Jahren
(1307-1317) trat ihm Herveus entgegen.[20] Das Generalkapitel von Zara-
goza 1309 empfahl verstärkt die Thomaslehre. Durandus, der seine
Lehrtätigkeit von Paris nach Avignon verlegt hatte, wird durch die Ver-
ordnung des Generalkapitels von Metz 1313 getroffen. Man soll nicht
das Gegenteil dessen vortragen, was gemeinhin als Lehre des Aquinaten
gilt, auch keine Schriften ausserhalb des Ordens veröffentlichen ohne
vorhergehende Prüfung durch den Ordensmeister. Die Thomaslehre gilt
als "sanior et communior."[21] Der Ordensmeister Berengar von Landore
übergab wohl noch 1313 die Schriften des Durandus einer zehnköpfigen
Kommission. Ihr stand Herveus vor. Die Hauptbearbeiter der Zen-
surenliste (93 Artikel) waren Johannes von Neapel und Petrus de Palude.[22] Eine zweite Liste (235 Artikel) ist ebenfalls von ihnen verfasst
worden. In der zweiten ist ein Fortschritt des Thomismus als betonterer
Gegensatz zwischen Durandus und dem Aquinaten festzustellen.[23] Das
Generalkapitel zu London 1314 empfiehlt das Studium moralphilo-
sophischer und anderer Traktate des Aquinaten und bestätigt die
Bestimmung von Metz. Das Generalkapitel zu Bologna 1315 schärft den
Studienpräfekten die Anzeigepflicht an Obere ein, wenn Lektoren "con-

16 P. Glorieux, *Répertoire des maîtres en théologie de Paris au XIIIᵉ siècle*, I (Paris 1933), 187-
188. *Lex. f. Theol. u. Kirche*, 8 (1963) 363-4.

17 J. Koch, *Durandus de S. Pourçain O.P.: Forschungen zum Streit um Thomas von Aquin zu
Beginn des 14. Jahrhunderts, Literargeschichtliche Grundlegung* (Münster i.W. 1927) I, 211.

17a Vgl. M. Grabmann, *Mittelalterliches Geistesleben*, III (München 1956) 352.

18 L. Ullrich, *Fragen der Schöpfungslehre nach Jakob von Metz O.P.*, Eine vergleichende Untersuchung aus der Dominikanerschule um 1300 (Leipzig 1966). B. Decker, *Die Gotteslehre des
Jakob von Metz*: Untersuchungen zur Dominikanertheologie zu Beginn des 14. Jahrhunderts, hg.
von R. Haubst (Münster i.W. 1967).

19 Glorieux, *Répertoire*, I, 200. N. Valois, *Jacques Duèse (Pape Jean XXII)*, Histoire littéraire
de la France, 34 (Paris 1914) 349.

20 Koch, *Durandus*, I, 211-391; 406-7. Glorieux, *Répertoire*, I, 201-5.

21 Koch, *Durandus*, I, 410-11. *Fontes vitae*, 655-56.

22 Koch, *Durandus*, I, 412-13; 200-203.

23 Koch, *Durandus*, I, 416; 203-8.

tra communem doctrinam Thome" oder der Kirche verstossen. [24] Gegen den Dozenten Hubert Guidi in Florenz, der sich "contra sanam et sacram doctrinam doctoris fratris Thome de Aquino" erklärt hatte, schritt das Kapitel der römischen Provinz 1315 ein. [25] Das Kapitel der Toulouser Provinz zu Orthez 1316 verfügt, dass keine der allgemeinen Lehre entgegenstehenden Ansichten vorgetragen werden. Man lese nach den Werken "der ehrwürdigen Brüder Thomas und Albert und Petrus von Tarantasia." [26] Im akademischen Jahr 1316-1317 disputierte Johannes von Neapel, ob man in Paris erlaubterweise die Thomaslehre in allen Punkten vortragen könne, d.h. ob die Verurteilung von 1277 Thomaslehren betreffe und Gültigkeit habe. Er verneinte das letztere und bejahte das erstere. [27]

Der Einfluss der Thomaslehre äusserte sich auch in der Benützung und Verbreitung der Werke. Die Pariser Artistenfakultät bemühte sich um Thomasschriften. Die dominikanischen Generalkapitel von 1278 an empfehlen ihr Studium. [28] König Karl II. von Neapel schenkte seinem Sohn Ludwig, seit 1296 Franziskaner und Erzbischof von Toulouse, für seine Studien die *Summa theologiae* des Aquinaten. [29] In der Bibliothek Bonifatius' VIII. fanden sich grössere und kleinere Thomaswerke. Der Stamser und andere Kataloge bieten Verzeichnisse von ihnen. Das Generalkapitel zu Bologna 1315 verordnet, dass Thomasschriften der Konventsbibliothek zugeführt und nicht veräussert werden, ausser sie seien doppelt vorhanden; für die Konventsbibliothek sollen sämtliche Werke des Aquinaten beschafft werden. [30]

EIN ANGEBOT PAPST JOHANNES' XXII.

Bei dem Ruf der Heiligkeit des Lebens und der Erhabenheit der Lehre des Aquinaten mag der eine oder andere wie Wilhelm von Tocco, Bartholomäus von Capua oder Albert von Brescia an die Möglichkeit der Heiligsprechung für Thomas gedacht haben, aber entscheidende Schritte von ihnen oder seitens des Ordens scheinen während vier Jahrzehnten nicht unternommen worden zu sein. Nach dem Tod Klemens'

---

24 Koch, *Durandus*, I, 413. *Fontes vitae*, 658.
25 *Acta Capitulorum Provincialium Prov. Romanae*, ed. T. Kaeppeli, (Romae 1941), MOPH, 20, 197.
26 Koch, *Durandus*, I, 414. *Fontes vitae*, 658.
27 C. Jellouschek, "Quaestio magistri Ioannis de Neapoli, O. P., "Utrum licite possit doceri Parisius doctrina fratris Thomae quantum ad omnes conclusiones eius" hic primum in lucem edita," *Xenia thomistica*, 3, 73-104. Walz, "S. Tommaso dichiarato dottore," *Angelicum* 44 (1967) 149.
28 *Fontes vitae*, 594-5; 621-2, 652-4, 663, 659, 672-3, 675-777. M. Grabmann, *Die Werke des hl. Thomas von Aquin*, 3. Aufl. (Münster i. W. 1949).
29 M. R. Toynbee, *S. Louis of Toulouse and the Process of Canonization in the Fourteenth Century*, (Manchester 1929) 103, 174, 236.
30 *Fontes vitae*, 652-4; 663; 659; vgl. 672-3; 675-7.

V. (†1314) ging aus einem mühevollen über zwei Jahre sich hinziehenden Konklave am 7. August 1316 Kardinal Jakob Duèse als erwählter Papst hervor: Johannes XXII.[31] Er war der Kandidat der französischen Kardinäle, des Grafen von Poitiers und des Königs Robert von Neapel. Da das Konklave im Dominikanerkloster zu Lyon stattgefunden hatte, erbot sich der neue Papst, einen Diener Gottes aus dem Dominikanerorden heiligzusprechen, den die Obrigkeiten des Ordens vorschlügen. Wann Johannes XXII. diese Absicht geäussert hat, steht nicht fest, aber offenbar zu Beginn des Pontifikates. Ordensmeister war damals Berengar von Landore. Von Johannes XXII. sehr geschätzt, wurde er zusammen mit dem Erzbischof von Bourges zur Beilegung politischer Zwiste in Frankreich, Brabant und Flandern mit einer Legation betraut.[32] An der Leitung des Generalkapitels von Pamplona 1317 verhindert, vertrat ihn als Generalvikar Petrus de Palude. Dieser unterrichtete im Auftrag des Kapitels am 29. Mai 1317 den König Jakob von Aragonien, Sardinien und Korsika vom Angebot des Papstes. Der König unternahm sofort Schritte zugunsten der Causa Raimunds von Penyafort.[33] Sie war bereits in den Jahren 1279, 1281 und 1298 erwogen worden, aber, wie die vorhergehenden Male, sollte sie auch 1317 nicht anziehen. Erst 1601 wurde Raimund von Penyafort kanonisiert.

HEILIGSPRECHUNGEN IN VORAVIGNONISCHER UND AVIGNONISCHER ZEIT

"Heiligsprechungen sind, unter Voraussetzung der nötigen sachlichen und legalen Gegebenheiten, in der sichtbaren Kirche oft ein Politikum. Der menschliche Anteil tritt in jener Zeit stark hervor. Ludwig IX. wurde am 11. August 1297 kanonisiert in einem Augenblick der Verständigung zwischen Philipp dem Schönen und Papst Bonifaz VIII." Petrus von Murrone als Papst "Cölestin V. gelangte zur Ehre der Altäre mit einer Spitze gegen das Andenken Bonifaz' VIII. Immerhin hat Klemens V. seinen mittelbaren Vorgänger nicht als Märtyrer bezeichnet, wie der französische König gewünscht hatte. Wenn das avignonische Papsttum sowieso leicht ins Politische abglitt, so verquickte es gern das Politische mit den Heiligsprechungsfeiern und umgekehrt. Mit Ausnahme des 1320 kanonisierten Thomas von Cantilupe, Bischofs von Hereford, gestorben auf einer Romfahrt 1282, erschwang sich keiner der Päpste von Avignon zu einer Kanonisation, die nicht

---

[31] G. Mollat, *Les papes d'Avignon (1305-1378)*, 9. Aufl. (Paris 1949) 41.
[32] A. Mortier, *Histoire des maîtres généraux de l'Ordre des Frères Prêcheurs*, II (Paris 1905) 516-525.
[33] *Archivum Franciscanum Historicum*, 18 (1925) 406-7.

von französischen oder angionischen Kreisen vorgetragen worden wäre."[34]

Der Heiligsprechungsprozess für die Augustinerin Klara von Montefalco (†1308), wurde wenige Monate nach ihrem Tod eingeleitet, durch den Tod Johannes' XXII. unterbrochen und erst 1882 abgeschlossen. Hingegen kamen zum Zug Ludwig von Toulouse (†1297, heiliggesprochen 1317), Thomas von Aquin (†1274, heiliggesprochen 1323), Ivo Hélory von Tréguier (†1303, heiliggesprochen 1347), und Elzéar de Sabran, Graf von Ariano (†1323, heiliggesprochen 1369). Die Causa Karls von Blois, Herzogs von Bretagne (†1364) wurde unter Gregor XI. eingeleitet,[35] sein Kult 1904 bestätigt.

Was Johannes XXII. angeht, so mag er sich für die Causa eines Dieners Gottes — wie Raimunds von Penyafort — ebensowenig bewogen gefühlt haben, wie zur Ernennung eines Kardinals der spanischen Nation, um die er zu Beginn seines Pontifikates gebeten worden war. An den König von Aragonien ging ein bezeichnender Bericht: "Iste papa ut creditur communiter erit favorabilis regi Roberto et domino Philippo de Francia et eorum domibus." Friedrich Bock[36] und Giovanni Tabacco[37] haben die wohlwollenden Beziehungen Johannes' XXII. zu den Königen von Neapel und Frankreich aufgehellt. Wiederholte durch König Eduard III. von England unterstützte Bitten (1319-1331) um Heiligsprechung des Robert Winchelsea, Erzbischofs von Canterbury (†1316) liess Johannes XXII. unbeachtet.[38]

NEAPOLITANER FÜR DIE THOMASCAUSA

Angesichts der engen Bande, die König Robert und Papst Johannes XXII. verknüpften oder gar erst auf die Kunde vom Angebot des Papstes, einen Dominikaner heiligzusprechen, die im Sommer oder Herbst des Jahres 1316 nach Neapel gedrungen sein dürfte, traten wohl neapolitanische Kreise der Einbringung der Thomascausa näher. Im Hinblick darauf oder auf eine zu schreibende *Vita*[38a] des Aquinaten hat Wilhelm von Tocco bei Aquinern wahrscheinlich seit November 1316 abgehört, was sie von Thomas zu berichten wussten.

---

34 Walz, "Politik um Thomas." 232.

35 Toynbee, *S. Louis of Toulouse*, 244.

36 "Studien zum politischen Inquisitionsprozess Johanns XXII," *Quellen u. Forschungen aus italienischen Bibliotheken u. Archiven*, 26 (1935/6) 21-142; ders., "Kaisertum, Kurie u. Nationalstaat im Beginn des 14. Jahrhunderts," *Römische Quartalschrift*, 44 (1936) 122; 165; 167; 220.

37 "La politica italiana di Federico il Bello re dei Romani," *Archivio storico italiano*, 10 (1950) 3-77; ders., *La casa di Francia nell'azione politica di papa Giovanni XXII*, (Rom 1953) 22-42.

38 Toynbee, *S. Louis of Toulouse*, 153-4. Für Winchelsea vgl. Eubel. *Hierarchia*, I, 2. Aufl., 163.

38a Vgl. W. Eckert, "Stilisierung und Umdeutung der Persönlichkeit des hl. Thomas von Aquin durch die frühen Biographen," *Freiburger Zeitschrift für Philosophie und Theologie*, 18 (1971) 7-28.

Papst Johannes XXII. und Thomaswerke

Johannes XXII. war ein Freund des Studiums und der Bücher.[39] In den Rechnungsbüchern der Apostolischen Kammer stehen vom Februar bis zum November 1317 Ausgaben für auf Geheiss des Papstes erfolgte Anschaffungen von philosophischen und theologischen Werken des Aquinaten. Mit einer Ausnahme, die von Bruder Wilhelm de la Broue bezahlt wurde, wurden die anderen von Wilhelm Durandi, Lektor des Dominikanerkonventes in Bordeaux, angekauft.[40] Ob es sich bei diesen Erwerbungen um einen Nachholbedarf der päpstlichen Bibliothek oder um eine Bereitstellung für die gelehrten Anliegen jener Zeit oder um einen Zusammenhang mit der Thomascausa handelt, bleibe dahingestellt. Am 25. Oktober 1317 veröffentliche Papst Johannes XXII. die Clementinen, in deren Titulus XVI die Bulle Urbans IV. *Transiturus* über das Fronleichnamsfest steht. Von da ab wurde dieses Fest nicht in einzelnen Kirchen, sondern allgemein begangen. Seit 1317 wird als Verfasser des Fronleichnamsoffiziums der Aquinate genannt. Somit fällt diese Autorenangabe in den Pontifikat Johannes' XXII.[41]

Die Bittsteller von Neapel in Avignon

In einem wohl im Herbst zu Gaeta abgehaltenen Kapitel der Neapolitanischen Dominikanerprovinz ordnete Robert von San Valentino, Vikar des Ordensmeisters, mit den Definitoren an, Kommissare sollten ohne Zögern dem Papst Berichte über die Thomascausa vorlegen. Als Beauftragte werden Wilhelm von Tocco und Robert von Benevent ausersehen. Im Jahre 1317 tritt ein gewichtiger Helfer für die Thomascausa in Johannes von Neapel auf, den das Generalkapitel von Pamplona (1317) von Paris nach seiner Heimat als Dozenten und Studienleiter versetzte.[42] Tocco fuhr mit seinen Umfragen über Leben und Wunder Thomas' fort. In einem Fall sagt er, der Bericht sei vor Richter, Notar und vereidigten Zeugen gegeben worden. Auch wurden Postulationsschreiben für die Thomascausa von der Königinmutter

---

39 Valois, *Jacques Duèse*, 163.

40 *Fontes vitae*, 664-6. Grabmann, *Die Werke*, 124.

41 Vgl. A. Walz, "La presenza di S. Tommaso a Orvieto e l'ufficiatura del 'Corpus Domini'," *Studi eucaristici* (Orvieto 1966) 337; 339; 342; 345.

42 MOPH, 4 (Rom-Stuttgart 1899) 104. Koch, *Durandus*, I, 207. M. Grabmann, *Mittelalterliches Geistesleben*, I (München 1926) 374. *Lex. f. Theol. u. Kirche*, 5 (1960) 1064-5.

Maria, von Prinzen, Grafen, Adligen, der Stadt und der Universität
Neapel an den Papst gerichtet. Mit diesen Schriftstücken versehen,
schifften sich Tocco und sein Begleiter im Sommer 1318 nach Marseille
ein, um von dort über Saint-Maximin nach Avignon zu reisen. Die Zeit
war günstig. Das Generalkapitel war von Wien durch den Papst nach
Lyon verlegt worden. Damit wurde der Provinzial der französischen
Provinz Herveus Natalis Generalvikar des Ordens. Die Wähler erhoben
ihn am 10. Juni zum Ordensmeister. Johannes XXII. hatte an die
Kapitularen ein Schreiben gerichtet, in dem er unter anderem den
Glanz der Lehre, mit dem ihr Orden inmitten der Kirche leuchte, her-
vorhob und versicherte, er bringe dem Orden seit langem innige
Geneigheit entgegen und versuche mit Geist und Herz dessen geist-
lichen Fortschritt zu mehren. Die Kapitularen zusammen mit dem Ordensmeister erwiesen sich dem Papst gegenüber dankbar. Jeder Konvent soll jeden Tag eine heilige Messe für den Papst feiern.[43] Die Beziehungen des neuen Ordensmeisters zu Johannes XXII. waren die
allerbesten. Herveus weilte vom Juli bis September in Avignon.[44] Er
dürfte die Kommissare von Neapel gesprochen und ermuntert haben.
Der Chronist Caccia meldet, Herveus habe sich um die Thomascausa
verdient gemacht. Tocco und sein Begleiter trafen auch die Domini-
kanerkardinäle Nikolaus von Prato, Wilhelm de Peyre de Godin
und Nikolaus von Fréauville, den Palastmeister Wilhelm von
Laudun — sein Vorgänger Durandus war am 26. August 1317 zum
Bischof von Limoux befördert worden[45] — ebenso vielleicht den
Generalprokurator des Ordens Bernhard Gui, falls dieser, übrigens ein
Bekannter König Roberts, von seinen kirchenpolitischen Aufträgen in
Flandern und Savoyen, gelegentlich in Avignon erschien. Als
Historiker hat Gui Thomas bereits in den *Flores chronicorum* und
später im *Sanctorale* erwähnt. Tholomäus von Lucca, Thomasschüler
und Verfasser der 1317 abgeschlossenen *Historia ecclesiastica,* unterhielt
sich mit Tocco über die Thomascausa. Tholomäus weilte von 1309 bis
1319 meist in Avignon.[46] Ein dritter dominikanischer Historiker Johannes Colonna ist von 1312 bis 1332 in Avignon nachzuweisen. Tocco
erwähnt in seinem Thomasleben, Johannes XXII. habe gegen den
pestartigen Irrtum des Abtes Joachim eine bewundernswerte Dekretale
erlassen. Er meint damit offenbar die Dekretale *Sancta romana et
universalis Ecclesia* vom 30. Dezember 1317 gegen die Fratizellen. Da
gewisse Ansichten der Fratizellen auf Joachim zurückgingen, konnte

---

43 Mortier, *Histoire*, II, 525; 533; 535.
44 A. de Guimaräes, "Hervé Noel (†1323)," *Archiv. Fratr. Praed.* 8 (1938) 70.
45 Koch, *Durandus*, I, 409; 417.
46 *Lex. f. Theol. u. Kirche*, 2 (1958) 12.

man sagen, Joachim sei als geistiger Vater solcher Ansichten verurteilt worden. Toccos Nennung dieser Dekretale Johannes' XXII. ist wohl der Niederschlag von Gesprächen, die in avignonischen Kreisen gang und gäbe waren.[47]

Papst Johannes XXII. begrüsst die Thomascausa

Den Beauftragten von Neapel war eine Audienz beim Papst beschieden, gewiss nicht ohne Empfehlung ihrer Person und ihres Anliegens durch bewährte Seite. Sie trugen den Grund ihres Erscheinens vor und übergaben die Bittschriften von Neapel für die Thomascausa. Sie fanden nicht nur gütige Aufnahme bei Johannes XXII., sondern grösste Geneigtheit. "Wir glauben, hörten sie vom Papst, dass Bruder Thomas glorreich im Himmel ist, denn sein Leben war heilig und seine Lehre konnte nicht ohne Wunder sein." Zu Tocco als Postulator gewandt, bedeutete der Papst: "Wir bestimmen dir das nächste Konsistorium, in dem du vor uns und unseren Brüdern dein Anliegen vorbringen kannst." Drei Tage später trug Tocco im Konsistorium sein Gesuch vor. Nach Entlassung des Postulators wandte sich der Papst an die Kardinäle: "Brüder, wir werden es uns und unserer Kirche zu grosser Ehre anrechnen, diesen Heiligen in das Verzeichnis der Heiligen eintragen zu können, wenn nur einige Wunder von ihm erwiesen werden, denn er hat die Kirche mehr erleuchtet als alle andern Lehrer; in seinen Werken lernt der Mensch in einem Jahr mehr als in den Werken anderer Lehrer während der Dauer seines Lebens."

Es wurde nun eine Kommission von drei Kardinälen gebildet zur Untersuchung des Rufes der Heiligkeit und der Wunder des Aquinaten. Nachdem sie auf Grund berufener Zeugen den erforderlichen Ruf "im allgemeinen" festgestellt und dem Papst und dem Konsistorium darüber Bericht erstattet hatten, wurde eine Kommission zur Erkundigung über Leben und Wunder des Aquinaten ernannt, bestehend aus dem Erzbischof von Neapel Humbert von Montauro, dem Bischof von Viterbo Angelus Tignosi und dem apostolischen Notar Pandulf Savelli. Ein Schreiben Johannes' XXII. vom 18. September 1318 bestimmte, dass diese drei oder wenigstens zwei von ihnen an den ihnen als geeignet erscheinenden Orten gemäss den päpstlichen, dem Schreiben beigegebenen Anweisungen die nötigen Erkundigungen "de vita et conversatione et miraculis fratris Thomae" einziehen und dem Apostolischen

---

47 A. Walz, "Abt Joachim und der 'neue Geist der Freiheit' in Toccos Thomasleben, c. 20," *Angelicum*, 45 (1968) 314. Vgl. Mollat, *Les papes*, 46.

Stuhl unterbreiten sollten. Damit war die Thomascausa eingeleitet. Tocco und sein Begleiter dürften auf der Rückkehr nach Neapel in Viterbo den dortigen Bischof von dem päpstlichen Auftrag unterrichtet haben. Tocco ist im Dezember 1318 im Dominikanerkonvent zu Anagni nachzuweisen, wo ihm Robert von Sezze, ein Lektor und Prediger besten Rufes, manche Einzelheiten aus dem Leben des Aquinaten mitteilte. Vom Generalkapitel des Jahres 1319, zu Carcassonne, dem Geburtsort Johannes' XXII., aus empfahl der Ordensmeister den Papst dankbarst dem Gebet der Mitbrüder: "pro sanctissimo papa nostro, et vere nostro."[48]

Die Informativprozesse in Neapel und Fossanova

Es war kein leichtes die drei Untersuchungsrichter des Informativprozesses zusammenzubringen. Der Erzbischof von Neapel konnte aus Gründen der Residenzpflicht, des Alters und eines Beinleidens die Stadt nicht verlassen. Fossanova kam deshalb als Ort der Untersuchung nicht in Frage, wie Tocco und P. Robert geplant hatten. Die beiden hielten sich in der Osterzeit 1319 dort auf, liessen sich aus dem Leben des Aquinaten berichten und waren Zeugen vieler Gebetserhörungen. Der Bischof von Viterbo traf auch in Fossanova ein und reiste am 19. Juli mit Tocco, P. Robert und mehreren Zisterziensern nach Neapel. Hier konstituierte sich das Untersuchungsgericht, bestehend aus dem Erzbischof von Neapel und dem Bischof von Viterbo. Der dritte Richter konnte fehlen und fehlte auch. Das Verfahren begann am 21. Juli 1319 in der erzbischöflichen Kurie. Tocco als Postulator der Causa überreichte den von Johannes XXII. bestimmten Richtern das päpstliche Schreiben. Es wurde verlesen. Die Richter bestellten zwei Notare für die schriftlichen Aufnahmen. Zum Anlass hatten sich hohe Geistliche aus Neapel, Rom und Viterbo sowie andere Persönlichkeiten eingefunden. Vom 23. Juli bis zum 18. September zogen sich die Verhöre hin. 43 Zeugen traten auf: 17 Zisterziensermönche und Brüder, 12 Laien, 11 Dominikaner und 3 Weltgeistliche. 5 Dominikaner, 5 Zisterzienser und 3 Laien hatten Thomas persönlich gekannt.[49] Hatten für Ludwig von Toulouse mehrere Dominikaner ausgesagt, so keine Franziskaner für Thomas.[50] Die unterfertigten und

---

48 MOPH, V, 224.
49 *Fontes vitae*, 265-407. K. Foster *The Life of Saint Thomas Aquinas*, Biographical Documents (London-Baltimore 1958), 82-126. W. Eckert, *Das Leben des hl. Thomas von Aquin* (Düsseldorf 1965), 179-248. A. Ferrua, *S. Thomae Aquinatis vitae fontes praecipuae* [!], (Alba 1968), 197-350.
50 Toynbee, *S. Louis of Toulouse*, 165; 185.

versiegelten Zeugenaufnahmen wurden durch zwei Domherren, einen von Neapel und einen von Viterbo, nach Avignon gebracht und dort in einem Konsistorium geprüft. Tocco hat sich noch einmal nach Avignon begeben. Vielleicht traf er König Robert, der sich damals längere Zeit in Südfrankreich aufhielt.[51] Das im Jahre 1320 in Rouen abgehaltene Generalkapitel vermerkt, es bestehe gute Aussicht für die Thomascausa, und legte den Konventen entsprechende von den Provinzialen einzuziehende Kontributionen auf.

Papst Johannes XXII. schreibt in der Heiligsprechungsbulle, er habe über die Heiligkeit des Lebens und die Wirklichkeit der Wunder des in Frage stehenden Bekenners nicht nur einmal, sondern zweimal, nicht eilig, sondern reiflich Erkundigungen einziehen lassen. Mit der zweiten Untersuchung meint er den Informativprozess von Fossanova. Dort sollte noch über die auf Thomas' Fürbitte erfolgten Wunder ausgesagt werden. In einem Schreiben vom 1. Juni 1321 ernannte Johannes XXII. als Untersuchungsrichter Petrus Ferrin, Bischof von Anagni, Andreas, Bischof von Terracina, und den päpstlichen Notar Pandulf Savelli oder zwei von ihnen. Tocco überreichte am 10. November 1321 im Kapitelsaal zu Fossanova dem Bischof von Anagni und dem Magister Savelli die päpstlichen Ernennungsschreiben. Der Bischof von Terracina fehlte bei der feierlichen Eröffnung des Informativprozesses. Vom 10. bis zum 20. November wurden 99 Zeugen vernommen, zwei zu wiederholten Malen, sodass 101 Aussagen vorliegen. Die Zeugen kamen aus Fossanova, Priverno, Sonnino, Frosinone, Terracina, Sermoneta, San Lorenzo de Valle. Es waren Weltgeistliche, Zisterziensermönche, Laienbrüder oder Oblaten der Abtei, Eheleute, Jungmänner und Jungfrauen, Magister, Notare und Ärzte. Sie bezeugten Gebets-erhörungen durch den seligen Thomas von Aquin oder Besuch seines Grabes, die teils vor Inangriffnahme des Heiligsprechungsverfahrens teils während dieser Zeit erfolgten.[52]

Nach dem Prozess in Fossanova hört man nichts mehr von Tocco. Er hat als Postulator und als Hagiograph die Thomasverehrung hingebend gefördert. Die Schriften des Informativprozesses von Fossanova wurden in Avignon eingehend geprüft. Die Heiligsprechungsbulle Johannes' XXII. für Thomas hebt die Genauigkeit der Untersuchungen und Prüfungen des Falles vor dem zu erwartenden päpstlichen Entscheid hervor.[53]

---

51 Toynbee, *S. Louis of Toulouse*, 260.
52 *Fontes vitae*, 409-510.
53 *Fontes vitae*, 529. *Xenia thomistica*, III, 187.

Die Beurteilung der Lehre des Aquinaten

Papst Johannes hat sich sowohl gegenüber den Postulatoren als auch in einem Konsistorium über die Lehre des Aquinaten rühmend ausgesprochen. Selbst Gelehrter, hat er die Bedeutung und Gediegenheit der Thomasdoktrin aus Schriften und Diskussionen beurteilen können. Von einer amtlichen Prüfung dieser Lehre berichten die Quellen nichts. Um diese Lücke auszufüllen, konnte das im Jahre 1317 oder später verfasste Werk *Concordantiae dictorum fratris Thomae* dienen, das Benedikt von Asinago zugeschrieben wird.[54]

Eine Heiligsprechungsfeier mit Bündnisschau

Nach den Informativprozessen und den kurialen Untersuchungen hätte die Heiligsprechung des Aquinaten im Jahre 1322 erfolgen können. Es waren zu einem solchen Anlass auch andere Umstände zu berücksichtigen. Mit grosser Vielseitigkeit, Willensstärke und erstaunlicher Arbeitskraft betrieb Johannes XXII. die verschiedensten Angelegenheiten.[55] 1317 hatte er die Verwaltung Roms an König Robert von Neapel als "senator et capitaneus" übertragen und dazu das Generalvikariat Italiens *vacante imperio*. Die Ghibellinen widerstanden den päpstlichen Anordnungen auf der politischen Ebene. Es wurde inquisitorisch gegen sie vorgegangen. Ein Kreuzzug gegen die Visconti in Mailand scheiterte. Mailand und Ferrara schwörten Ludwig dem Bayern Treue. Gegen ihn gedachte der Papst nun ähnliche Mittel anzuwenden wie gegen die Ghibellingen. "Als Vorspiel zu diesem Vorgehen sollten festliche Tage zu Avignon dienen. Ludwig der Bayer, infolge seines Sieges von 1322 zu Mühldorf über Friedrich den Schönen im Besitz der Krone, verlieh seinem ältesten Sohn die Mark Brandenburg und durchkreuzte dadurch die Ostpolitik des Königs Johann von Böhmen. Dieser schwenkte deshalb politisch um und so trat ein neuer Verbündeter ins päpstlich-französisch-angioinische Lager. Des Böhmenkönigs Sohn Karl empfing die Firmung vom Papst selber und wahrscheinlich anlässlich einer glänzenden Heerschau der weltlichen Gefolgschaft Johannes' XXII., zu der gerade die Heiligsprechung Thomas' von Aquin den äusseren Rahmen geliefert haben dürfte."[56]

54 Grabmann, *Die Werke*, 164; 244; 411-12. T. Käppeli, "Benedetto di Asinago da Como (+ 1339)," *Archiv. Fratr. Praed.* 11 (1941) 83-94.
55 Valois, *Jacques Duèse*, 628 ff. Mollat, *Les papes*, 57. E. Pasztor, "Una raccolta di Sermoni di Giovanni XXII," *Archivio paleografico italiano*, 2-3 (1956/57) 277.
56 Walz, "Politik um Thomas," 234-5.

Am Donnerstag, dem 14. Juli 1323, war öffentliches Konsistorium. Einen Bericht darüber gibt der Dominikaner Benzio von Alessandria. Der Papst hielt zwei Sermones, den ersten mit dem Vorspruch *Haec dies boni nuntii* (4 Kg 7, 9), um die bevorstehende Heiligsprechung anzukündigen, den zweiten mit dem Vorspruch *Scitote quoniam Dominus mirificavit sanctum suum* (Ps 4, 4) zum Preis des Predigerordens und des neuen Heiligen.[57] Dieser habe in seinem Orden ein apostolisches Leben geführt, da dieser Orden nichts in den Einzelnen, sondern nur in der Gemeinschaft etwas besitze; diese Lebensart sei die apostolische. Dieser glorreiche Lehrer habe nach den Aposteln und den alten Lehrern die Kirche mehr als andere erleuchtet. Thomas habe viele Wunder, ja überhaupt so viele Wunder gewirkt als er Artikel geschrieben habe. Die Heiligen seien die Ehre der Kirche und, wenn Ordensleute, die besondere Ehre ihrer Ordensfamilie. Mit der Armutsauffassung im apostolischen Geist wandte sich der Papst gegen die Spiritualen. Er hatte es schon 1317 getan und wird es im November 1323 nochmals tun. König Robert und Königin Sancia, die minoritische Übertreibungen begünstigten, konnten sich die päpstliche Verlautbarung zur Armutsfrage zu Herzen nehmen. Nach dem Papst trat Petrus Canteri OP als stellvertretender Postulator auf. Johannes von Neapel, der als Postulator auf Tocco gefolgt war und einen *Sermo ad postulandam canonizationem Fr. Thomae de Aquino* verfasst hatte,[58] lag krank darnieder. Der Stellvertreter trug nun im Namen des Ordensmeisters und des Predigerordens die Bitte um Heiligsprechung des hervorragenden Lehrers Thomas von Aquin vor. Weitere Bittsteller folgten. Zunächst König Robert. Bei der Heiligsprechungsfeier für seinen Bruder Ludwig von Toulouse war er abwesend. Um so mehr wurde jetzt seine Anwesenheit beachtet. Nach der Ansprache bat er kniefällig, der so grosse, in so grosser Heiligkeit lebende Lehrer Thomas möge in das Verzeichnis der Heiligen aufgenomen werden. Denselben Antrag stellten der Patriarch von Alexandrien, ein Dominikaner, und nach anderen der Bischof von Lodève, ein Franziskaner. Papst Johannes erklärte zum Schluss Thomas von Aquin der Heiligsprechung für würdig und hob die Sitzung auf.

Am Montag, dem 18. Juli,[59] fand in der Kirche Notre-Dame-des-Doms zu Avignon die Heiligsprechung des Aquinaten statt. König Robert mit Königin Sancia, eine starke Vertretung des französischen

---

57 Valois, *Jacques Duèse*, 536.
58 Grabmann, *Mittelalterliches Geistesleben*, I, 374.
59 St. Baluzius, *Vitae paparum Avenionensium*, I (Paris 1693) 139; 165-66; 175. Vgl. Galuanus, *Chronica*, MOPH, 2 (1897) 110: "In M. CCCXXIII beatus Thomas de Aquino canonizatur die V Marcii [!], anno a transitu suo L. inchoante."

Hofes, Kardinäle — unter ihnen de Peyre de Godin—, Prälaten und Kurialen, Graf Thomas von San Severino und wahrscheinlich Karl von Luxemburg-Böhmen, Dominikaner und Scharen von Gläubigen waren versammelt. Der Kirchenraum war mit Lichtern übersät. Der Papst eröffnete den Ritus mit einem Sermo, der unter dem Vorspruch *Magnus es tu et faciens mirabilia* (Ps 85, 10) Leben und Wunder des Aquinaten vorführte. Dann wurde das *Veni creator Spiritus* gesungen. Hierauf setzte sich der Papst, um einen zweiten Sermo zu halten. Mit dem Wort aus der Gleichnisrede bei Matthäus 18, 19 *Redde quod debes* drückte er seine Verpflichtung dem seligen Thomas gegenüber aus, da diesen Gott so glänzend im Himmel geehrt hat und die Kirche auf Erden ehren möge. Kraft apostolischer Vollmacht trug er den Namen des glorreichen Lehrers in das Verzeichnis der Heiligen ein. Es folgte das *Te Deum* und dann die Messe zu Ehren des neuen Heiligen mit eigener Oration.

Johannes von Neapel hat einen *Sermo in festo canonizationis S. Thomae de Aquino* geschrieben,[60] aber wegen Krankheit offenbar nicht gehalten. Der Ordensmeister Herveus fehlte bei der Heiligsprechung. Nach dem im Mai in Barcelona beeindigten Generalkapitel lenkte er seine Schritte nach Avignon, erkrante in Narbonne, wo er am 7. August starb. Zufriedenheit erfüllte ihn, in Thomas das Licht auf den Leuchter gestellt zu sehen, das Gott bestimmt habe, um die Menschen zu erleuchten.[61]

DIE HEILIGSPRECHUNGSBULLE VOM 18. JULI 1323

Papst Johannes XXII. zeichnet in der am Tag der Heiligsprechung erlassenen Bulle den Lebenslauf voller Tugenden des Lehrers der heiligen Theologie, der Thomas war, und führt Gebetserhörungen auf dessen Fürbitte an. Er ruft zur Freude über die Thomasehrung auf die Kirche, die Heimat, den Predigerorden, die Ordensleute, die Gelehrten und die Studierenden. Der Gang der Thomascausa wird geschildert, das Fest des neuen Heiligen am 7. März zu begehen angeordnet und ein Ablass den Besuchern des Grabes des Heiligen gewährt.[62] Grabmann und Pieper weisen darauf hin, dass bei Thomas die Kirche vor dem Entschluss stand, einen Philosophen und Theologen zu kanonisieren, weil

60 Grabmann, *Mittelalterliches Geistesleben*, I, 374.
61 Valois, *Jacques Duèse*, 313. Mortier, *Histoire*, II, 570.
62 *Fontes vitae*, 519-530. *Xenia thomistica*, III, 173-18.

er in seinem wissenschaftlichen Leben und Wirken ein Heiliger gewor-
den war.[63]

NACH DER HEILIGSPRECHUNGSFEIER

Papst Johannes XXII. teilte die erfolgte Heiligsprechung mit an Karl
von Valois, Sohn des Königs von Frankreich, an Maria, Königin von
Frankreich und Navarra, an Clementine, Königinwitwe von Frankreich,
an Ludwig von Frankreich und an den französischen König Karl IV.
Die Dominikaner überreichten dem Papst als Zeichen der Erkennt-
lichkeit eine Sammlung von Thomaswerken. Sie begingen in Kirche
und Konvent eine Reihe von Festanlässen. König Robert fehlte nicht
dabei.

Die äussere Aufmachung der Kanonisation war eine gewaltige
Demonstration um den Papst. Bock[64] meint, die prunkvolle Heiligsprechung Thomas' von Aquin sei der weithin sichtbare Hintergrund,
den Johannes XXII. dem bevorstehenden Einschreiten gegen Ludwig
den Bayern gab. Im Herbst darauf wurde der erste Prozess gegen diesen
eröffnet. Fiel, was an der Heiligsprechungsfeier politisches Beiwerk
war, bald der Vergessenheit anheim, so verblieb für alle Zeiten ihr
geistiger Sinn.

VOM HEILIGEN LEHRER ZUM HEILIGEN KIRCHENLEHRER

Seit der Kanonisation wurde Thomas von Aquin in vermehrtem
Masse nicht nur als grosser Gelehrter und als Haupt einer führenden
geistesgeschichtlichen Schule, sondern auch als Heiliger verehrt. Waren
selbst Feste eines Franziskus oder Dominikus ausserhalb der eigenen
Orden nicht in allen kirchlichen Kalendarien zu finden, so noch
weniger das Fest des Aquinaten.[65] Die Dominikaner verrichteten bald
ein eigenes Offizium ihres neuen Heiligen.

Eine Thomaskapelle war seit 1322 in der Nähe des Savellipalastes auf
dem Aventin bei Santa Sabina in Rom geplant und ist nach der
Heiligsprechung errichtet worden. Der Notar Pandulf Savelli hat sie
gestiftet.[66]

Die sterblichen Überreste des Heiligen wurden nach mehrmaligen
Übertragungen in Fossanova durch den Grafen Honoratus von Fondi

---

63 "Die Kanonisation des hl. Thomas in ihrer Bedeutung für die Ausbreitung u. Verteidigung
seiner Lehre im 14. Jahrhundert," *Divus Thomas* 1 (1923) 241-2. Vgl. J. Pieper, *Hinführung zu
Thomas von Aquin*, (München 1958) 33.
64 Walz, "Politik um Thomas," 235.
65 Toynbee, *S. Louis of Toulouse*, 210.
66 V. J. Koudelka, "La cappella di S. Tommaso d'Aquino in Monte Savello a Roma," *Archiv.
Fratr. Praed.*, 32 (1962) 126-44.

für zwei Jahre in sein Schloss und am 28. Januar 1369 auf Geheiss Urbans V. nach Toulouse überführt. Die Hagiographie, die Geschichtsschreibung und die Bibliographie sowie die christliche Kunst haben sich mit der Heiligengestalt Thomas' beschäftigt. Predigten über den hl. Thomas von Aquin sind seit Johannes von San Gimignano[67] und Heinrich Tröglein[68] überliefert. Prediger erwähnen ihn ehrenvoll, wie Tauler[69] und der selige Heinrich Seuse, der sich freut, dass "das klare Licht, der liebe Sankt Thomas, der Lehrer"[70] Verborgenes entschlüssle. Katharina von Siena preist im 158. Kapitel des Dialogs den glorreichen hl. Thomas wegen seines Erfassens und Vermittelns der Wahrheit.

Die Lehrautorität Thomas' wuchs durch die Heiligsprechung. Der Bischof von Paris Stefan de Bourret hob am 14. Februar 1325 die Verurteilung von 1277 auf. Petrus de Palude verkündete diesen oberhirtlichen Entscheid am folgenden 7. März.[71] Päpstliche Verlautbarungen gegenüber Spiritualen, Ockham, Meister Eckhart und anderen gewinnen im Licht der Lehre und Heiligsprechung des Aquinaten eigene Bedeutung. Heinrich von Lübeck OP, Dozent in Köln und später (1325-1333) Provinzial der Saxonia, spricht vom *doctor communis, doctor venerabilis* und *sanctus Thomas de Aquino, qui omnibus aliis cautius et melius scripsit.*[72]

Gleichförmigkeit mit der Thomaslehre oder in ihrer Auslegung ist aber nie allgemein erreicht worden. Bei all ihrem ausserordentlichen Gewicht erstanden ihr Gegenspieler, zumal in dem auf der *via moderna* Ockhams und Gefährten aufbauenden Nominalismus. Als *Princeps thomistarum* erscheint Johannes Capreolus. Er lehrte von 1408 bis 1424 in Paris. An Universitäten wie Köln, Löwen, Wien, Prag und Krakau folgten zumal Dominikaner der Thomaslehre. Petrus von Bergamo OP (†1482) legte seine *Tabula aurea* von Thomasstellen vor, Peter Nigri (Schwarz) OP, Rektor der Universität zu Budapest, den *Clypeus thomistarum contra modernos et scotistas* (Venedig 1481) und den *Contra omnes doctrinae doctoris angelici detractores* (Venedig 1504). Johannes Kalekas, Demetrios Kydones und Gregorios Scholarios verbreiteten die Thomaslehre im griechischen Kulturraum. In Italien stiess

---

67 A. Dondaine, "La vie et les œuvres de Jean de San Gimignano," *Archiv. Fratr. Praed.*, 9 (1939) 153-4.

68 *Lex. f.Theol. u. Kirche*, 5 (1960) 202.

69 G. Hofmann, *J. Tauler Predigten*, (Freiburg 1961), 157; 180; 233; 235; 247; 331; 349; 546; 552.

70 "Leben Seuses," Kap. 51, H. Seuse, *Deutsche Schriften*, hg. v. K. Bihlmeyer (Stuttgart 1907), *Nachdruck* (Frankfurt a.M. 1961) 180. *Horologium sapientiae*, l. II, c. 1, ed. C. Richstätter (Turin 1929) 178: "inter ceteros et super ceteros doctor egregius."

71 Walz, "S. Tommaso dichiarato dottore," 150. A. Maier, "Der Widerruf der 'Articuli Parisienses' (1277) im Jahre 1325," *Archiv. Fratr. Praed.*, 38 (1968) 13-19.

72 Grabmann, *Mittelalterliches Geistesleben*, I, 424.

sie mit der Renaissancebewegung zusammen. In Cajetan meldet sich ein überragender Thomaskommentator. Thomasstudium blühte in den Dominikanerschulen zu Salamanca, Sevilla, Cordoba und Lissabon. Mit Erfolg erklärten Peter Crockaert 1512 in Paris und Konrad Koellin 1512 in Köln die *Summa theologiae* und Franz Sylvester in Bologna die *Summa contra gentiles*.[73] Silvester Mazzolini, einer der ersten Gegner Luthers, wurde gerade als Thomist von diesem abgelehnt. In der Zeit des Konziliarismus und der Glaubensspaltung wird die Thomaslehre für die papal-petrozentrische Ekklesiologie verwendet.[74] Anregend wirkten Thomisten wie Franz von Victoria (†1543), Dominikus Soto (†1560), Petrus de Soto (†1563), Dominikus Bañez (†1604) und andere. Auf dem Konzil von Trient waren die Thomisten mehr an Gewicht als an Zahl vertreten. 1564 schrieb Hieronymus Vielmi OP *De Divi Thomae Aquinatis doctrina et scriptis*.[75] In der Bulle *Mirabilis Deus* vom 11. April 1567 hat Papst Pius V. den hl. Thomas zum Kirchenlehrer erhoben, nicht ohne Erwähnung von dessen Präsenz auf dem Konzil von Trient. Leo XIII. hat den Aquinaten zum Patron aller katholischen Schulen erklärt. Der *Codex iuris canonici* hat Canones zugunsten seiner Lehre. Pius XI. preist ihn als *studiorum ducem*. Das 2. Vatikanische Konzil weist an zwei Stellen auf seine Lehre hin.[76]

Der vorbildliche Lebenswandel und die Bedeutsamkeit der Lehre des Aquinaten ist von Papst Johannes XXII. klar gesehen und anerkannt worden. Die von ihm vorgenommene Heiligsprechung des grossen Lehrmeisters zählt zu den Spitzenleistungen[77] seiner an vielseitiger Betätigung reichen Persönlichkeit und Regierung, ja zu einer der denkwürdigsten in der Geschichte der Kirche.

---

73 Walz, "S. Tommaso dichiarato dottore," 151-2. Grabmann, *Mittelalterliches Geistesleben*, I, 332-439; II (1936) 512-613; III (1956) 352-451. A. Harsanyi, *A domonkosrend magyarorszagon a reformacio elött*, (Budapest 1938), 178-225 (P. Nigri). I. W. Frank, *Hausstudium u. Universitätsstudium der Wiener Dominikaner*, (Graz-Wien-Köln 1968), 144-151. O. Kristeller, *Le thomisme et la pensée italienne de la Renaissance* (Paris 1967).

74 G. Hennig, *Cajetan u. Luther*, Ein historischer Beitrag zur Begegnung von Thomismus und der Reformation (Stuttgart 1966). A. Walz, "Von Cajetans Gedanken über Kirche und Papst," *Volk Gottes* (Freiburg 1967) 336-360.

75 A. Walz, *I domenicani al concilio di Trento*, (Rom 1961) passim, 414 Vielmi.

76 Walz, "S. Tommaso dichiarato dottore," 159-167.

77 Valois, *Jacques Duèse*, 530, die Kanonisation habe ein "retentissement immense" gehabt, vgl. 536; 628.

II

THE WRITINGS OF ST. THOMAS

DE SUBSTANTIIS SEPARATIS: TITLE AND DATE

Francis J. Lescoe

THE *Treatise on Separate Substances* is, without doubt, one of the most important shorter works of St. Thomas Aquinas. As the eminent historian of mediaeval philosophy, Etienne Gilson, has pointed out, the *Treatise on Separate Substances* "is an incomparably rich historical work."[1] Ignatius Eschmann has called it "one of the most important metaphysical writings of Aquinas,"[2] while H.-F. Dondaine in his *Préface* to the Leonine edition of the Treatise says, "Ce n'est pas le lieu d'insister davantage sur l'importance de l'ouvrage dans l'ensemble de l'œuvre de saint Thomas; elle dépasse de loin celle d'un écrit de circonstance, celle aussi que ses dimensions modestes feraient présager."[3] Vernon Bourke calls it "a very significant metaphysical treatise"[4] and R. Henle has described the first chapter of this work, *De Opinionibus antiquorum et Platonis*, as "the most elaborate synthesis of Platonic doctrine to be found in the whole Thomistic corpus."[5]

In view of the wide agreement by Thomistic scholars on the importance of the *Tractatus de substantiis separatis*, a closer examination of the title, date, and circumstances surrounding the composition of this

1 E. Gilson, *The Christian Philosophy of St. Thomas Aquinas* (New York, 1956) 166. Elsewhere Gilson writes, "Comment concevoir des substances spirituelles simples qui ne soient pas des dieux? ... Le traité de saint Thomas *De substantiis separatis*, œuvre d'une richesse historique incomparable, permet de suivre en quelque sorte pas à pas l'évolution de ce problème et de dégager les enseignements qu'impliquait son histoire." E. Gilson, *Le Thomisme*, 6th ed. (Paris, 1965) 216-217.
2 I. Eschmann, *A Catalogue of St. Thomas's Works* in E. Gilson, *The Christian Philosophy of St. Thomas Aquinas* 381.
3 H.-F. Dondaine, *Préface*, Sancti Thomae de Aquino, *Opera Omnia*, iussu Leonis XIII P. M. edita. Tomus XL, pars D-E, *De substantiis separatis* (Romae, 1968) D8.
4 V. Bourke, *Aquinas' Search for Wisdom* (Milwaukee, 1965) 155.
5 R. Henle, "A Note on Certain Textual Evidence in Fabro's 'Nozione Metafisica di Partecipazione'", *Modern Schoolman* 30 (1957) 278; cf. Sancti Thomae de Aquino. *De substantiis separatis*, ed. Leonine D41-43; F. J. Lescoe, *Saint Thomas Aquinas' Treatise on Separate Substances*, English only (West Hartford, 1959) 17-23; *Saint Thomas Aquinas' Treatise on Separate Substances*, Latin-English edition, printed face to face (West Hartford, 1963) 35-42. Henceforth our references will be to the English translation contained in the Latin-English 1963 edition.

work would seem to be extremely worthwhile. Specifically, we may ask
under what conditions was the *Treatise on Separate Substances* written — whether it is the work of a Novice, as in the case of the *De ente
et essentia*; whether it represents a middle point in the intellectual life
of the Angelic Doctor; or whether it can be considered as an example of
the work of a mature and fully developed theologian.

DE SUBSTANTIIS SEPARATIS OR DE ANGELIS?

The manuscripts variously refer to the Treatise as *Tractatus, Liber de
natura angelorum*,[6] *Liber, Tractatus de angelis*,[7] *De substantiis separatis*,[8] *De substantiis separatis ad fratrem Raynaldum*.[9] The two oldest
manuscripts, i.e., *Paris, Bibliothèque Nationale lat. 14546* and *Napoli,
Biblioteca Nazionale VII. B. 16*, attribute both titles (*De angelis* and
De substantiis separatis) equally. The Paris manuscript reads, "Incipit
libellus de angelis seu substantiis separatis,"[10] while the Naples work
contains the following heading: "De angelis seu substantiis separatis ad
fratrem Raynaldum de Piperno."[11]

As H.-F. Dondaine points out, it is not surprising that the first editors
of this posthumous work which was left unfinished by its author, should
hesitate in choosing definitively one or the other title. From the point of
view of external criticism, both titles seem to be equally valid.[12]

It is for this reason also that almost all editors of the Treatise from
the 13th century to the present have vacillated in their characterization
of the work as either definitely philosophical or theological. Century after century the Treatise has been classed now as a theological and now
as a philosophical work. Dondaine calls attention to this persistent
hesitation over the centuries and even to our time, when he writes,
"Même hésitation chez les éditeurs modernes les plus versés en la connaissance des écrits thomistes; aux XVII⁰ siècle, P. Pellican le classe
parmi les *Opuscula theologica*, et de même au XVIII⁰, B. M. de Rubeis.

---

6   *Lisboa, Biblioteca Nacional Illum. 95*, fol. 48vb-66vb; *Metz, Bibliothèque Municipale 1158*,
fol. 12va-22va; *Leipzig, Universitätsbibliothek, 581*, fol. 359ra-381rb.

7   *Firenze, Biblioteca Nazionale Centrale, Con. Sopp. J. VII, 47*, fol. 51ra-60vb; *Paris,
Bibliothèque Nationale, lat. 15814*, fol. 275ra-290ra; *Paris, Bibliothèque Nationale, lat. 15813*, fol.
180ra-191rb; *Vaticano (Città del), Biblioteca Apostolica, Vat. lat. 807*, fol. 112ra-138vb; *Venezia,
Biblioteca Nazionale Marciana, Fondo ant. lat. 128 (1518)*, fol. 263vb-284rb; *Cambridge, Corpus
Christi College 35*, fol. 131ra-144vb.

8   *Bordeaux, Bibliothèque Municipale, 131*, fol. 205rb-214va; *Bologna, Biblioteca Universitaria,
1655*, fol. 147ra-156va.

9   *Paris, Bibliothèque Sainte-Geneviève, 238*, fol. 88vb-87ra.

10   *Paris, Bibliothèque Nationale, lat. 14546*, fol. 84rb.

11   *Napoli, Biblioteca Nazionale, VII. B. 16*, fol. 50ra.

12   H.-F. Dondaine, *op. cit.*, D5.

Plus près de nous, P. Mandonnet l'a au contraire rangé parmi les *philosophica*, suivi en cela par J. Perrier et R. Spiazzi."[13]

In reality, a closer reading of St. Thomas' statement in the Prologue of the work, clearly indicates, to our mind, the character of the Treatise. We read, "Intendentes igitur sanctorum angelorum excellentiam utcumque depromere, incipiendum videtur ab his quae de angelis antiquitus humana coniectura aestimavit; ut si quid invenerimus fidei consonum accipiamus, quae vero doctrinae repugnant catholicae refutemus."[14]

St. Thomas is distinctly dividing his work into two parts: first, he is going to examine "ea quae antiquitus humana coniectura aestimavit" concerning the angels — hence we have here the contribution of the unaided human intellect (therefore philosophical). Secondly, the Angelic Doctor will then study in detail the teaching of "doctrina catholica" or "christiana religio" (hence theological).

At the beginning of Chapter XVIII, Aquinas reiterates his method: "Quia igitur ostensum est quid de substantiis spiritualibus praecipui philosophi Plato et Aristoteles senserunt quantum ad earum originem, conditionem naturae, distinctionem et gubernationis ordinem; — restat ostendere quid de singulis habeat christianae religionis assertio."[15]

The second portion of the Treatise, i.e., "quid de singulis habeat christianae religionis assertio," was never completed because, after having promised to explain what Christian religion holds about the spiritual substances concerning (1) their origin (2) the condition of their nature (3) their distinction and (4) the order of government, the Treatise ends abruptly with Chapter XX, in which the third point under discussion, i.e., the distinction of spiritual substances, is left unfinished and the fourth point, viz., the order of government is completely omitted.[16]

It would seem that we have here a typically Thomistic work. First, the Angelic Doctor examines in detail all the accumulated knowledge which philosophy has acquired over the centuries concerning the subject of spiritual substances. He is especially attentive to the rich

13 *Ibid.*, D8; P. Pellican ed., *Opuscula theologica et moralia* (Paris, 1656) which in 1660 became vol. 20 of *Opera omnia* edited by the Dominicans of S. Jacques, 454 ff.; B.M. de Rubeis, ed., *Opuscula theologica*, vol. 19 of *Opera omnia* (Venice, 1754) 202 ff.; P. Mandonnet ed., *Opuscula omnia* (Paris, 1927) I, 73-144; also *Tabula generalis* at end of *Introduction*, I, liii; J. Perrier, ed. *Opuscula philosophica* (Paris, 1949) *Preface*, xviii; R. Spiazzi ed., *Opuscula philosophica* (Turin, 1954).

14 *Prologus*, ed. Leon. D41, 5-10; F. J. Lescoe, *op.cit.*, Chap. 1, 35, no. 1.

15 *Ibid.*, Chap. XVIII, ed. Leon. D71, 3-9; F. J. Lescoe, *op. cit.*, Chap. XVII, 134, no. 91.

16 *Ibid.*, Chap. XX. ed. Leon. D80; F. Lescoe, *op. cit.*, Chap. XIX, 162, no. 114. All mss. end with the following words: "Et hoc secuti esse videntur qui posuerunt daemones, quos malos angelos dicimus, ex inferiori ordine et corporeos esse."

Platonic tradition, along with its characteristic nuances and insights which the recently discovered writings of Proclus have made available. But all this philosophic knowledge — the work of the unaided intellect — has an avowedly ancillary function. It is only secondary in importance.

As H.-F. Dondaine expresses it, "En fait, on est en présence d'un des écrits les plus typiquement thomistes; attentif à tout ce que la tradition philosophique peut lui offrir, notamment la tradition platonicienne dont l'arrivée de Proclus vient de lui fournir une nouvelle approche; mais dans le but explicite d'explorer *utcumque* le mystère des anges tel que la Bible et la tradition chrétienne l'ont révélé et transmis."[17]

While it is perfectly true that within theology certain philosophical positions may be developed, nevertheless this philosophy is always regarded as a tool to be used in the service of theology. Anton Pegis has stated this relationship with his usual perspicacity when he writes, "St. Thomas was by profession a theologian and not a philosopher ... (and he) created a philosophy within theology in order to aid and indeed to make possible the human expression of revealed truth."[18] He reasons, therefore, that we have here a Christian philosophy *in the service of theology*. He says, "This philosophy is Christian, it is Christian as a philosophy, but, more than this, it is a servant of theology ... it will remain forever a Christian philosophy ministering to a theology."[19] Elsewhere Pegis again insists that "St. Thomas never approached philosophy as if he were himself a philosopher. Knowing what philosophical principles were, and how to observe as well as respect them, he nevertheless chose to use philosophy as a theologian, rather than to formulate it directly as a philosopher."[20]

We are convinced, therefore, that first and foremost the Treatise is a theological one. Aquinas is primarily interested in expounding what Sacred Scripture and Christian tradition teach about the angels ("incipiendum videtur ab his quae... humana coniectura aestimavit; ut si quid invenerimus *fidei consonum* accipiamus, quae vero doctrinae repugnant catholicae refutemus"). Catholic faith is at all times the norm and ultimate criterion in the evaluation of any philosophical speculations concerning the subject of angels or spiritual substances. The *Treatise on Separate Substances* should therefore be classed unequivocally and without any hesitation among the theological works of St. Thomas Aquinas.

17   H.-F. Dondaine, *op. cit.*, D8.
18   A. C. Pegis, *The Middle Ages and Philosophy* (Chicago, 1963) 74.
19   *Ibid.*, 74-75, 78.
20   A. C. Pegis, *In Search of St. Thomas Aquinas*, McAuley Lecture 1966 (West Hartford, 1967) 7.

TRACTATUS OR OPUSCULUM?

In spite of the fact that the editors of the definitive Leonine edition of the *De substantiis separatis* have not chosen to include the word *Tractatus* in the official title of the work, we shall nevertheless insist on retaining this word *Treatise*. There is more than ample justification for our insistence on retaining the word in the title, since eleven of the twenty manuscripts which list the title of the work include the word *Tractatus*.[21]

Our insistence on the use of this word is more than purely academic. We are, again, making a deliberate effort to put to rest once and for all the completely pejorative and demeaning word "opusculum" which Thomistic scholars have used for centuries and still persist in doing so even today. Witness, for example, the use of the term in the new and definitive Leonine edition (1968) of the *Tractatus de substantiis separatis* on pages D5, D6, D8, D10, D12.

As Eschmann has pointed out so convincingly, "The notion of *Opusculum* i.e., minor or smaller work, in itself devoid of precise meaning, has in fact disserved the cause of Thomistic bibliography, if not even that of Thomistic studies."[22] There is a kind of demeaning and levelling anonymity which the word *opusculum* conveys, as if the *Tractatus de substantiis separatis* were merely one of a large collection of miscellaneous odds and ends left us by the Angelic Doctor. The time for according this outstanding treatise its proper place among Thomistic writings is *long overdue*. We shall therefore continue to refer to this work as *Tractatus de substantiis separatis*, the Leonine editors, to the contrary, notwithstanding.

DEDICATION "AD FRATREM RAYNALDUM"

Two manuscripts and all the earliest catalogues of St. Thomas' works explicitly state that the *Treatise on Separate Substances* was destined "ad fratrem Raynaldum". The Naples manuscript (*Napoli, Biblioteca Nazionale. VIII. B. 16*) reads, "De angelis seu substantiis separatis ad

---

21 The following mss. contain the word *Tractatus* in the title: *Bordeaux Bibliothèque Municipale, 131,* fol. 305rb; *Bologna, Biblioteca Universitaria, 1655,* fol. 147ra; *Bruxelles, Bibliothèque Royale, 2453-73 (1573),* fol. 11r; *Firenze, Biblioteca Nazionale Centrale Conv. Sopp. J. VII. 47,* fol. 51ra; *Firenze, Biblioteca Laurenziana, Fiesolano 105,* fol. 202rb; *Leipzig, Universitätsbibliothek 581,* fol. 359ra; *München, Bayerische Staatsbibliothek, Clm. 8005,* fol. 19ra; *Toledo, Biblioteca del Cabildo, 19-19,* fol. 59va; *Vaticano (Città del) Biblioteca Apostolica, Ottob. lat. 198* ("... explicit tractatus fratris Thomae de angelis"), fol. 207vb; *Vaticano, (Città del) Biblioteca Apostolica, Urb. lat. 127,* fol. 55va.

22 I. Eschmann, *op. cit.,* 381; cf. F. J. Lescoe, *op. cit.,* Introduction 2.

fratrem Raynaldum," while the Sainte-Geneviève manuscript (*Paris, Bibliothèque Sainte-Geneviève, 238*) begins as follows: "Capitulum primum. De substantiis separatis ad fratrem Raynaldum."[23]

Frater Raynaldus or *Reginaldus* of Piperno was a life-long friend and associate of St. Thomas. The fact that Raynaldus was entrusted with the editing of all the unfinished works of Aquinas, after the latter's untimely death in 1274, attests to the intimacy which obtained between the two men.[24] (A. Dondaine estimates that on the basis of available information, Raynaldus lived at least eleven years after the death of the Angelic Doctor, but not more than twenty years.)[25]

C. Vansteenkiste seems to question, or at least leave open, the validity of the manuscript and catalogue tradition concerning the dedication to *frater Raynaldus*. He writes, "La dédicace à fr. Reginald n'empêche pas que ce soit une œuvre destinée au grand public, comme d'ailleurs le *compendium theologiae*. Les deux œuvres, parce qu'incomplètes, ont pu rester assez longtemps inédites. D'ailleurs le fait que fr. Reginald ait hérité de ces papiers a pu faire naître la dédicace."[26]

We are inclined to reject Vansteenkiste's theorizing and we tend to agree with H.-F. Dondaine who maintains that this is only a conjecture

---

23 Cf. *Historia eccles. nova*, lib. xxiii, cap. 12, critical edition by A. Dondaine, "Les 'opuscula fratris Thomae' chez Ptolemée de Lucques" in *Arch. Fr. Praed.* 31 (1961) 152 which reads, "Tractatus de substantiis separatis ad eundem (i.e. fratrem Raynaldum) qui sic incipit: Quia sacris angelorum solempniis"; D. Prummer, ed., *Legenda sancti Thomae de Aquino* in *Fontes vitae S. Thomae* (Toulouse, 1911) fasc. 3, cap. 54. 220 states, "Tractatus de angelis seu substantiis separatis ad fratrem Raynaldum qui incipit: Quia sacris angelorum solemniis." The listing of the Prague ms. (before the end of the 13th cent.) *Praha, Metrop. Kapit. A XVII. 2* states "De substantiis separatis ad fratrem Reynaldum", quoted in H.-F. Dondaine, *op. cit.*, D5-6.

24 On Reginald of Piperno, cf. A. Dondaine, *Secrétaires de saint Thomas* (Rome, 1956) 16-17; 198-203; P. Mandonnet, *Des écrits authentiques de S. Thomas d'Aquin* (Fribourg. 1910) 2nd edit., 40-41; *Sancti Thomae Aquinatis Opuscula Omnia* (Paris, 1927) I, iv-v. M. Grabmann writes, "Die gegebene Persönlichkeit hierfür war ohne Zweifel Reginald von Piperno, der von 1259-1274 der unzertrennliche Begleiter des Aquinaten gewesen war, der Nachschriften *(Reportata)* mehrerer seiner Vorlesungen hergestellt hatte, dem Thomas mehrere *Opuscula* gewidmet hatte, der auch seinem heissgeliebten Lehrer und Freund auf dem Lehrstuhl und der Universität nachgefolgt war und auch das Supplementum zu der unvollendet gebliebenen *Summa theologiae* redigiert hatte." M. Grabmann, *Die Werke des hl. Thomas von Aquin* in *Beiträge zur Geschichte der Philosophie und Theologie des Mittelalters*, XXII, Heft 1-2 (Münster i Westf.). P. Mandonnet observes, "Raynald de Piperno avait été le compagnon, le *socius*, comme on disait dans la langue du temps, de Thomas d'Aquin, depuis le retour de ce dernier en Italie en 1259, jusqu'à sa mort." P. Mandonnet, *op. cit.*, iv. In another work, Mandonnet quotes the following notation made by a contemporary of Reginald, "Explicit postilla super partem Psalterii secundum Fratrem Thomam de Aquino ordinis Praedicatorum quia non invenitur plus in exemplari Fratri Raynaldi di Piperno qui fuit socius Fratris Thomae usque ad mortem, et habuit omnia scripta sua." P. Mandonnet, *Des écrits authentiques de S. Thomas d'Aquin*, 41.

25 A. Dondaine writes, "Dans l'état actuel de nos informations, nous devons penser que son décès fut postérieur à 1285 et presque certainement antérieur à 1295." A. Dondaine, *Les Sermons de Reginald de Piperno*, in *Mélanges Tisserant VII (Studi e Testi 236)* (Biblioteca Vaticana, 1964) 373, quoted in H.-F. Dondaine, *op. cit.,* D6 note 1.

26 C. Vansteenkiste, review in *Bulletin Thomiste* 8 (1947-1953) I, 29.

on Vansteenkiste's part — a surmise which can neither be apodictically affirmed nor rejected. The weight of evidence seems to be in favor of the ancient and time-honored tradition. Both the Naples manuscript and the Prague catalogue of St. Thomas' works belong to the last decade of the thirteenth century — a mere fifteen years after the death of the Angelic Doctor and both documents contain an explicit dedication "ad fratrem Raynaldum". It is, therefore, our conviction that the reading of the title should be as follows: *Tractatus de substantiis separatis seu de angelis ad fratrem Raynaldum de Piperno.*[27]

AUTHENTICITY

There is absolutely no question concerning the authenticity of the Tractate. It has always been characterized as "opus genuinum, absque dubio."[28] Six collections of manuscripts which date back to the thirteenth century contain the *Treatise on Separate Substances*. Each manuscript begins with the following incipit: "Quia sacris angelorum interesse solemniis non possumus...." The manuscripts are (1) *Koblenz; Stadtbibliothek, θ, 155;* (2) *Metz, Bibliothèque Municipale 1158,* (3) *Napoli, Biblioteca Nazionale. VII. B. 16,* (4) *Paris, Bibliothèque Nationale 14546,* (5) *Paris; Bibliothèque Nationale 15813,* (6) *Paris, Bibliothèque Nationale 15814.*

Ten other manuscript collections of the fourteenth century, likewise, contain the same treatise. The *Tractatus de substantiis separatis* also appears in eleven of twelve of the ancient collections of short works which the Leonine editors used in establishing their text. All ancient catalogues similarly list this treatise. H.-F. Dondaine very appropriately summarizes the question of authenticity when he writes, "Il n'est guère d'opuscule dont l'authenticité thomiste soit mieux attestée, d'ailleurs amplement confirmé par son contenu."[29]

DATE

The exact date of the composition of the *Treatise on Separate Sub-*

---

27 H.-F. Dondaine writes, "Il est raisonnable de faire crédit au témoignage de la liste de Prague, comme pour les 16 autres opuscules dont elle a soin de préciser le destinataire." H.-F. Dondaine, *op. cit.,* D5; cf. *Le Répertoire Codices manuscripti operum Thomae de Aquino* (Romae, 1967) nn. 2631, 1925.

28 Cf. M. Grabmann, *Die echten Schriften des hl. Thomas von Aquin* (Münster, 1949) 324-325; P. Mandonnet, *Des écrits authentiques de S. Thomas d'Aquin,* 104 no. 20; A. Michelitsch, *Thomasschriften. Untersuchungen über die Schriften Thomas von Aquino,* Band I (Graz und Wien, 1913) 185 no. 67; P. Synave, *Le Catalogue officiel des œuvres de S. Thomas d'Aquin, Critique-Origine-Valeur* in *Archives d'histoire doctrinale et littéraire du moyen âge,* 3 (1928) 25-103.

29 H.-F. Dondaine, *op. cit.,* D5.

stances in unknown. Since the Treatise is unfinished (St. Thomas promises in Chapter XVIII, 6-7 (D71) to treat of "the order of government of the spiritual substances" — which, as we have already noted is never developed), the presumption is that the work was composed just before the death of the Angelic Doctor.[30]

The early Pizzamanus incunabula of 1490, 1498 and 1508 contain the following colophon which would seem to argue for a late composition date: "Hucusque scripsit sanctus doctor de angelis sed morte praeventus, non potuit proficere hunc tractatum sicut nec plura alia quae imperfecta relinquit."[31]

In addition, Martin Grabmann reports the following notation (although in a different hand from that of the text), at the end of the treatise in the Naples manuscript (*Napoli, Biblioteca Nazionale. VII. B. 16*) which reads, "Si plus vixisset, auctor hic non tacuisset."[32]

In the absence of any meaningful and substantial research which could establish a later date for the composition of the treatise, Thomistic scholars generally accepted the year 1252 as a firm date for the writing of the treatise. For example, K. Werner in *Der hl. Thomas von Aquin* (nineteenth century) and J. Zimmermann in *Über die Schrift des hl. Thomas von Aquino "De Substantiis Separatis"* (beginning of the twentieth century), placed the treatise's composition around the year 1252. A. Tauron, in *La vie de S. Thomas* in the eighteenth century suggested the same date without, however, offering any firm evidence for his particular choice.[33]

The twentieth century has seen extensive and fruitful research into the question of the date of the composition of the *Tractatus de sub-*

---

30 F. J. Lescoe, *op. cit*, Chap. XVII. 134 no. 91.

31 *Opuscula praeclarissima eximii ac divini doctoris sancti Thomae de Aquino ordinis fratrum praedicatorum...* emendata atque correcta, ed. Antonius Pizzamanus, Impressa Venetiis ingenio ac impensa Hermanni Liechtenstein Coloniensis, 1490. The *De Substantiis separatis* is listed as *De angelis seu de substantiis separatis. Opus 15.* It is preceded by the *De natura veri* and followed by *De unitate intellectus contra Averroistas.* No foliation.

Opuscula Sancti Thomae: quibus alias impressis nuper haec addidimus, videlicet Summam totius Logicae. Tractatum celeberrimum de usuris nusquam alias impressum, ed. Antonius Pizzamanus. Impressum Venetiis mandato et expensis nobilis viri Domini Octaviani Scoti Livi Modoetiensis. Cura et ingenio Boneti Locatelli Bergomensis, 1498. The colophon appears in this edition on fol. 83v.

Opuscula Sancti Thomae: quibus alias impressis nuper haec addidimus, videlicet Summam totius Logicae. Tractatum celeberrimum de usuris nusquam alias impressum, ed. Antonius Pizzamanus. Impressum Venetiis mandato et expensis Petri Liechtenstein Coloniensis Germani. Cura et ingenio Jacobi Pentio de Leucho, 1508. The colophon is on fol. 76r.

32 M. Grabmann, *Die Werke des hl. Thomas von Aquin* 214.

33 H.-F. Dondaine, *op. cit.*, D6 note 2; cf. K. Werner, *Der hl. Thomas von Aquin* (Regensburg 1858) i, 115; J. Zimmermann, *Uber die Schrift des hl. Thomas von Aquino 'De Substantiis Sparatis'* (Zwittau, 1901) 1; A. Touron, *La vie de S. Thomas* (Paris, 1737). Of the latter, H.-F. Dondaine cautions, "Cette date proposée par A. Touron ne repose vraiment sur aucun indice ni aucun témoignage." *Ibid.*

stantiis separatis. It shall be our purpose, therefore, in the remainder of this paper, to sketch the highlights of this research.

The first significant, it not momentous, contribution in this area of research was Martin Grabmann's discovery that the *terminus a quo* for the treatise should be advanced by sixteen years, i.e., from 1252 to 1268. The basis for Grabmann's contention was the fact that the colophon appearing in the majority of manuscripts of William of Moerbeke's translation of Proclus' *Elements of Theology* places that work as having been completed on May 18, 1268. The colophon reads as follows: "Procli Diadochi Lycii Platonici Philosophi elementatio theologica explicit. Capitula 211. Completa fuit translatio hujus operis Viterbii a fratre G. de Morbecca ordinis praedicatorum, XV Kal. Iunii anno Christo 1268, pontificatus Clementis papae IV anno 4°."[34]

St. Thomas quotes two passages, i.e. Propositions 169 and 196, from the Latin translation of the *Elementatio Theologica* in the last chapter of the *Treatise on Separate Substances*. They appear in Chapter XX, 256-259, where St. Thomas writes, "Unde Proclus dicit in Libro divinarum coelementationum 'omnis anima participabilis corpore utitur primo perpetuo et habente hypostasim ingenerabilem et incorruptibilem.'" Again, in the same chapter (XX), lines 307-309, the Angelic Doctor writes, "Unde et Proclus dicit 'quod omnis intellectus in aeternitate substantiam habet et potentiam et operationem.'"[35] It is obvious therefore that we are dealing with a work composed in 1268 or later.

The next step in advancing an even later date, i.e. 1270, for the composition of the Treatise came by way of the corroborative evidence furnished by *Book Kappa* of Aristotle's *Metaphysics*. As R.-A. Gauthier, D. Salman and F. Pelster point out, it is an established fact that *Book Kappa* was first incorporated into the Latin translation of Aristotle's *Metaphysics* by William of Moerbeke in 1270.[36] The obvious conclusion is that *Book Lambda* should be cited as *Book XII* in any work written after the year 1270.[37]

---

34 M. Grabmann, *op. cit.*, 325.

35 F. J. Lescoe, *op. cit.*, Chap. XIX, 158, 161 nos. 110, 113. Proclus. *The Elements of Theology*, ed. E. R. Dodds (Oxford, 1933) 171, 147-149; cf. C. Vansteenkiste, *Procli Elementatio translata a Guilelmo de Moerbeke* (Textus ineditus) *Tijdschrift voor Philosophie* 13 (1951).

36 Cf. R.-A. Gauthier, "La date du commentaire de saint Thomas sur l'Ethique à Nicomaque" in *Recherches de théologie ancienne et médiévale* 13 (1951) 84-92; D. Salman, "Saint Thomas et les traductions latines des *Métaphysiques d'Aristote*" in *Archives d'histoire doctrinale et littéraire du moyen âge* 7 (1932) 85-120; F. Pelster, "Die griechisch-lateinischen Metaphysikübersetzungen des Mittelalters," *Beiträge zur Geschichte der Philosophie des Mittelalters*, Supp. Band II (Münster, 1923) 89-119; "Die Ubersetzungen der aristotelischen Metaphysik in den Werken des hl. Thomas von Aquin", *Gregorianum* 17 (1936) 377-406 esp. 380-389.

37 Cf. H. Saffrey, *Sancti Thomae de Aquino super Librum de Causis Expositio* (Fribourg-Louvain, 1954) xxxiv.

There are three specific citations of *Book Lambda* as *Book XII* in the *Treatise on Separate Substances*. In Chapter XIV, 16 of the *Tractatus*, St. Thomas writes, "...oportet igitur quod sicut ejus (Dei) substantia est suum esse, ita etiam ejus substantia sit suum intelligere sive intelligentia, ut etiam Philosophus concludit in *XII Metaphysicae*."[38] Again, in the same chapter (XIV, 88), Aquinas cites *Book Lambda* as *Book XII*. We read, "Sed quia occasionem errandi sumpserunt ex demonstratione Aristotelis in *XII Metaphysicae*, oportet ostendere quod Philosophi intentionem non assequuntur."[39] Finally, in Chapter XX, 261, the Angelic Doctor again appeals to the authority of the Stagirite, as found in *Lambda*, which is reckoned as *XII Metaphysics*. He says, "In substantia enim incorporea et intellectuali nullus appetitus esse videtur nisi intellectivus, quid quidem est simpliciter boni, ut per Philosophum patet in XII *Metaphysicae*."[40]

One word of caution has been sounded by Ignatius Eschmann concerning the validity of the *Book XII* citations in support of the year 1270 as the composition date. He warns, "Since this work (*Treatise on Separate Substances*) is unfinished and therefore not edited by Aquinas himself, its posthumous editor may perhaps be supposed to have interfered with details of this kind."[41]

On the other side of the scale, H.-D. Saffrey has discovered a remarkably close relationship between the *Tractatus de substantiis separatis* and the *Expositio super librum de causis*. He states, "De nombreux passages du *De substantiis* pourraient être mis en parallèle avec des textes du commentaire. Sans aucun doute, la parenté entre ces deux écrits est étroite."[42] He has also found that these two works are the only writings in the entire corpus of Thomas' works which cite passages from Proclus' *Elements of Theology*. As he points out, "Le seul endroit de l'œuvre de saint Thomas, en dehors du commentaire, où la traduction moerbekienne de l'*Elementatio* soit citée, est le traité *De substantiis separatis*."[43]

Saffrey has further found that the *Commentary on the Book of Causes* likewise cites *Book Lambda* as *Book XII*. There are four citations in the *Commentary*, i.e. Prop. III, p. 24, 1. 10; Prop. XII, p. 79, 1. 12; Prop. XIII, p. 83, 1. 12; and Prop. XVIII, p. 103, 1. 20.[44]

---

38 *Metaph*. XII, 9 (1074b 28-34); F. J. Lescoe, *op. cit.*, Chap. XIII, 111 no. 70.
39 *Metaph*. XII, 9 (1074b 15-1075a 10); F. J. Lescoe, *ibid.*, Chap. XIII, 114 no. 73.
40 *Metaph*. XII, 8 (1072b 18-19); F. J. Lescoe, *ibid.*, Chap. XIX, 159 no. 111.
41 I. Eschmann, *op. cit.*, 142.
42 H.-D. Saffrey, *op. cit.*, Introduction xxxv.
43 *Ibid*.
44 Cf. H.-D. Saffrey, *op. cit.*, (1) Prop. III, p. 24, 1. 10, "Unde et Aristoteles in XII° *Metaphysicae* signanter Deo attribuit et intelligere et vivere." (2) Prop. XII, p. 79, 1. 10 "... vivere enim viventis est ipsum esse ejus, ut dicitur in II° *De Anima* et ipsum intelligere primi intelligentis

The fact that both works contain citations from Proclus and also refer to *Book Lambda* as *Book XII* has prompted Saffrey to state that the two works are contemporaneous. He writes, "Le fait que l'*Elementatio*, dans toute l'œuvre de saint Thomas, ne soit utilisée que dans ces deux écrits, le *De substantiis separatis* et le commentaire sur le *Liber*, nous incline à croire ces deux écrits contemporains... C'est sans doute pendant qu'il etudiait l'*Elementatio* pour écrire le commentaire que saint Thomas a redigé le *De substantiis*."[45]

In résumé, both the Treatise and the Commentary cite Proclus; hence minimally, they must be dated 1268 or later. In addition, the Commentary quotes *Book Lambda* as *Book XII*. Inasmuch as the Commentary is a finished work, there can be no question of editorial interference concerning the *Book XII* citations. The Commentary's *terminus a quo* is thus 1270. Because of the strikingly close relationship between the two works and because of Saffrey's contention that they were written contemporaneously, we maintain that though the Treatise is an unfinished work, the *Book XII* citations were made by St. Thomas himself, and not by some posthumous editor. We therefore conclude that the *terminus a quo* for the *Tractatus de substantiis separatis* is the year 1270, i.e. during the second Parisian stay.

Let us now turn to further corroborative evidence in favor of the year 1270 as a point of departure in dating the composition of the *Treatise on Separate Substances*.

Some twelve years ago, while we were engaged in the preparation of a Latin text for the *Tractatus de substantiis separatis* based on twelve manuscripts, we were especially struck by the wording of a passage in Chapter XIII, D64, which is entitled "De errore quorundam circa cognitionem et providentiam substantiarum spiritualium."[46]

St. Thomas begins the chapter by telling us that "not only did some thinkers err concerning the substance and order of spiritual substances, judging of them after the manner of lower beings, but some of them fell into error concerning the knowledge and the providence of these substances."[47] He then proceeds to say; "For in wanting to judge of the in-

---

est vita ejus et esse ipsius, ut in XII° *Metaphysicae* dicitur." (3) Prop. XIII. p. 831. 12; "Unde et Aristoteles in XII° *Metaphysicae* probat quod intelligit seipsum tantum." (4) Prop. XVIII, p. 103, 1, 20 "... unde et Aristoteles in XII° *Metaphysicae* primo principio attribuit quod sit intellectus et quod suum intelligere sit vita, et secundum hoc ab eo omnia habent esse et vivere et intelligere."

45 H.-D. Saffrey, *op.cit.*, Introd. xxxv.

46 F. J. Lescoe, *op. cit.*, Introd. 5-6; Chap. XIII, 108 no. 67.

47 "Non solum autem in substantia et ordine spiritualium substantiarum aliqui erraverunt ad modum inferiorum rerum de eis aestimantes, sed hoc etiam quibusdam accidit circa cognitionem et providentiam earundem." Chap. XIII, D64, 4-8; F. J. Lescoe, *op. cit.,* Chap. XIII, 108 no. 67.

telligence and the operation of spiritual substances after the manner of human intelligence and operation, *they held that God and the other immaterial substances did not have a knowledge of singulars, nor did they exercise a providence over any lower beings and especially human acts.*"[48] The Latin of the italicized portion reads, "...posuerunt Deum et alias substantias immateriales singularium cognitionem non habere nec inferiorum et praecipue humanorum actuum providentiam gerere."[49]

Now the particular order in which Aquinas mentions the specific points and the words themselves are an almost verbatim restatement of Propositions X, XI, XII of the Condemnation of 1270 made by Bishop Etienne Tempier on December 10 against the Arts Masters of the University of Paris. The propositions read as follows: "X. Quod Deus non cognoscit singularia. XI. Quod Deus non cognoscit alia a se. XII. Quod humani actus non reguntur providentia Dei."[50]

If we bracket the phrase "et alias substantias immateriales" (which St. Thomas would naturally add in a treatise which dealt with the nature of separate substances), the similarity of the wording appears to be much more than merely coincidental.[51]

The thirteen condemned theses were most certainly the object of much discussion by the teaching masters of the various faculties. One might say that they were on the lips of the whole university community, teachers and students alike. It is not unreasonable to presume that St. Thomas, as one of the most highly respected masters on the campus, should have been asked to state his own position publicly and even to refute officially the unacceptable teachings. This particular section (Chapter XIII) of the *Treatise on Separate Substances* was Aquinas' answer. Characteristically, as a scholar who always sought to rise above personalities and partisan argumentation, St. Thomas incorporated the official wording of the condemned theses and then proceeded to a systematic and objective refutation of their positions. By suppressing the names of the proponents of these condemned theses, the Angelic Doctor was able to prescind from the atmosphere of heated controversy

48 *Ibid.*, D64, 11-15; F. J. Lescoe, *ibid.*
49 *Ibid.*
50 H. Denifle et E. Chatelain, *Chartularium Universitatis Parisiensis* (Paris, 1889-1897) I, 487. Cf. P. Mandonnet, *Siger de Brabant et l'Averroïsme latin au xiii⁰ siècle* (Louvain, 1911), 2nd ed. I, 111.
51 J. Riedl also refers to this striking similarity between the text of St. Thomas and the wording of the condemned propositions. Since Riedl was not concerned with the date of the composition of the *Tractatus de substantiis separatis*, his interest was merely one of literary dependence and hence he does not make what appears to us this valid inference. J. Riedl, *The Nature of the Angels* in R. E. Brennan ed., *Essays in Thomism* (New York, 1942) 136 and notes 86, 88. H.-F. Dondaine recognizes the point in our 1963 edition when he observes, "Autre indice pour le même *terminus a quo*: l'énoncé des erreurs combattues au chapitre 13 de l'opuscule semble faire écho aux propositions 10, 11, 12 condamnées à Paris en 1270." H.-F. Dondaine, *op. cit.*, D6.

and to evaluate the propositions with a calm and detached objectivity. There was no doubt about the identity of the opposition — their names and positions were common knowledge on the University of Paris campus. But Aquinas achieved his purpose in a masterful way.[52]

We are convinced, therefore, that while this internal evidence does not carry absolute and categorical certainty, it nevertheless is a type of corroborative testimony which cannot be ignored. Anyone who chooses to reject this evidence must assume the burden of proving apodictically that the sequence of notions, and even the order of the words themselves, is the result of pure chance. We find such an explanation extremely difficult, if not impossible, to accept. Accordingly, we maintain that an absolutely firm — if not irrefutable — *terminus a quo* for the writing of the *Treatise on Separate Substances* in December 10, 1270.

In spite of the Proclus and Lambda testimonies, C. Vansteenkiste still insists that at least the major portion of the Treatise was written much earlier, i.e. around the year 1259. Some of the reasons which he adduces for an earlier date are the following: parallelisms of style and of expressions with the *De Veritate*, the doctrine of spiritual matter, a different attitude on Aquinas' part toward the *Liber de Causis* in the *Treatise on Separate Substances* from the attitude he displayed in his *Commentary on the Book of Causes*.[53]

The Proclus citations which we found at the end of the Treatise, Vansteenkiste claims could have been used more fittingly and effectively at the beginning of the work where St. Thomas examines the opinions of the various philosophers. The fact that Proclus is completely ignored in this section is proof for Vansteenkiste that the Angelic Doctor wrote this portion of the Treatise before the translation of Proclus' *Elements* in 1268. Vansteenkiste further conjectures that St. Thomas then could have continued the Treatise after 1268, but this is not essential, since the two propositions cited by Aquinas could have been translated separately in advance of the commentaries which were not completed until 1268.[54]

---

52 On Latin Averroism and the Condemnation of 1270 and 1277, cf. E. Gilson, *The History of Christian Philosophy in the Middle Ages* (New York, 1955) 387-401; A. Maurer, *Medieval Philosophy* (New York, 1962) 192-207; V. Bourke, *Aquinas' Search for Wisdom* (Milwaukee, 1965) 159 ff.; M.-D. Chenu, *Toward Understanding St. Thomas,* transl. A. Landry and D. Hughes (Chicago, 1964) 73-75.

53 C. Vansteenkiste writes, "... il y a une foule d'indications qui favorisent une date bien plus ancienne, les parallélismes de style et d'expressions avec le *De Veritate*, la doctrine sur la *spiritualis materia*, des expressions comme: *si quis eas (animas) ponat corporibus uniri ut formas*, l'attitude envers le *Liber de causis* qui est autre que dans son Commentaire etc." C. Vansteenkiste, *op. cit.* 29.

54 C. Vansteenkiste concludes, "Nous inclinerions pour le gros de l'œuvre à une date voisine de 1259 ou de séjour en Italie. Il est à remarquer que les citations de Proclus ne se trouvent qu'à la

It seems to us that we are facing here too many hypotheses, too much theorizing and speculation. The cumulative evidence which we have just examined forces us to reject Vansteenkiste's surmises. Accordingly, we agree with Eschmann who writes, "Vansteenkiste took issue with this chronology (i.e. May 18, 1268 as a *point de départ*) but he failed to establish a convincing case."[55]

Angelus Walz, in his volume *Saint Thomas Aquinas*, places the composition date of the *Treatise on Separate Substances* in the Italian period, i.e. 1259-1269. He says, "This opusculum (*Compendium theologiae*), which is often assigned to Aquinas' last years, is probably more correctly to be placed in this period of his sojourn in Italy (1259-1269). The same may be said of the opusculum, also dedicated to Fr. Reginald and also incomplete, entitled *De Substantiis separatis seu de angelorum natura*. These works were doubtless broken off by a change of residence on the part of the author."[56] In Chapter XIII of the same book, Walz lists all the works of the Angelic Doctor. The *Treatise on Separate Substances* appears as Item no. 15 under the heading *Opuscula*, with the following title and date: "*De substantiis separatis seu de angelorum natura ad fratrem Raynaldum socium suum carissimum* (incomplete), 1261-1269."[57]

To our mind, Walz's dating must be rejected for the following reasons: on page 112, Walz writes, "After these various apostolic labors and activities, both religious and scientific which he performed in Italy, St. Thomas was in 1268 sent by his superiors once more to Paris to take up duties as professor of theology."[58] After describing Aquinas' journey from Italy to Paris, Walz concludes, "From Milan he proceeded to Christendom's great centre of studies in the French capital, probably passing through Vercelli and Aosta and so over the Pennine Alps. He will have arrived in Paris together with his Italian companions probably in January and certainly before Easter of the year 1269."[59]

As we have already seen, the Proclus citations in the *Treatise on Separate Substances* categorically demand a 1268 *terminus a quo*. The

---

fin de l'œuvre et qu'il aurait pu être utilisé d'une manière fort naturelle au début, où sont exposées les opinions des philosophes. On pourrait croire que S. Thomas a continué son écrit en 1268, mais ce n'est pas absolument nécessaire. Il cite deux 'propositions' de Proclus. Or les 'propositions' n'auraient-elles pas été traduite séparément sans les 'commentaires' avant la traduction complète de 1268?" C. Vansteenkiste, *op. cit.*, 29-30.

55 I. Eschmann, *op. cit.* 412.

56 A. Walz, *Saint Thomas Aquinas, A Biographical Study*, transl. S. Bullough (Westminster, 1951) 99.

57 *Ibid.*, 184.

58 *Ibid.*, 112.

59 *Ibid.*, 114.

Lambda citations as *Book XII* almost definitively advance the *terminus a quo* to the year 1270. Walz's proposed date of 1261-1269 becomes completely untenable. Even if we were to reject the 1270 date and adopt the incontrovertible 1268 as a starting point, it is absolutely inconceivable to us that Thomas Aquinas could have written such a highly technical metaphysical treatise during the period between May 1268 and either January or Easter of 1269, while he was making the long and arduous journey from Italy to Paris. We therefore find Walz's dating of the Treatise unacceptable.

Mandonnet, on the other hand, would advance the date of composition to the period between 1272 and 1273. The reasons he adduces for this "pin-pointing" are two: (1) the work is incomplete, (2) Aquinas' stay at Naples after Easter of 1272 would have afforded him the necessary leisure which was practically impossible during the turbulent teaching days at the University of Paris.[60]

Mandonnet and Vansteenkiste further see in the Prologue of the Treatise a reference to a specific feast day and hence have attempted to indicate a definite day on which Aquinas undertook the composition of the work. In the Prologue, the Angelic Doctor writes as follows: "Quia sacris angelorum solemniis interesse non possumus, non debet nobis devotionis tempus transire in vacuum, sed quod psallendi officio subtrahitur, scribendi studio compensetur."[61]

Mandonnet sees in the "sacris angelorum solemniis" a reference to a specific feast in honor of the holy Angels and he proposes October second as the day on which Aquinas commenced writing the Treatise.[62] But H.-F. Dondaine points out that the feast of the holy Angels goes back only to the sixteenth century. The Exemplar of Dominican liturgical books, which was compiled when Humbert de Romans was Provincial during the period of 1254-1263, contains no record of a feast of the holy Angels. The second day of October is dedicated to St. Léger.[63] B.M. de Rubeis, on the other hand, conjectures that the feast might be that of St. Michael the Archangel.[64]

H.-F. Dondaine's evaluation of these conjectures seems to be to the point, "... il est probable que sous la plume de saint Thomas — et dans

---

60 P. Mandonnet, *Opuscula Omnia* I, liii; cf. P. Glorieux, *Répertoire des maîtres en théologie de Paris au XIIIᵉ siècle (Etudes de philosophie médiévale*, Paris, 1933) 98.

61 *Chap.* I, D41; F. J. Lescoe, *op. cit.*, Chap. 1, 35, no. 1.

62 P. Mandonnet, "Chronologie sommaire de la vie et des écrits de saint Thomas" in *Revue des sc. phil. et théol.* 9 (1920) 151.

63 H.-F. Dondaine, *op. cit.*, D6, note 10; cf. F. M. Guerrini, *Ordinarium iuxta ritum S. Ordinis Fr. Praed.* (Romae, 1921) 264.

64 B. M. de Rubeis writes, "Festum indicare videtur sancti Michaelis archangeli." B. M. de Rubeis, *Dissertationes criticae et apologeticae XVIII* (Venetiis, 1750) 208, (Romae, 1882) ccxxxiv.

le contexte de cet ouvrage — l'expression *sacris angelorum solemniis interesse* désigne simplement l'Office choral en général. Cette formule fait réplique exacte à celle de saint Bernard parlant de la présence des anges mêlés au chœur des moines pour la *laus Dei*."[65]

Conclusion

After having reviewed the various dates offered by different Thomistic scholars for the composition of the *Treatise on Separate Substances*, we should like to conclude this short paper with the following points:

1. The May 18, 1268 *terminus a quo* (Proclus' translation) is absolutely incontestable.

2. The 1270 *point de départ*, because of the Book Lambda citations, as well as corroborating verbatim citations from the Condemnation of 1270, cannot be dismissed.

3. The period of 1270 to 1273 is, to our mind, the most logical time during which St. Thomas Aquinas wrote the *Tractatus de substantiis separatis seu de angelis ad fratrem Raynaldum de Piperno.*[66]

---

65   St. Bernard writes, "Doleo aliquos vestrum... nec caeli cives revereri, sed in praesentia principum tamquam mortuos apparere, cum vestra alacritate permoti. *vestris interesse solemniis* delectentur." St. Bernard, *Super Cantica.* sermo 7, no. 4, PL 183, 808C, quoted in H.-F. Dondaine, *op. cit.*, D7.

66   D. Callus dates the *Tractatus de substantiis separatis* as belonging to the year 1270. D. Callus, *Les sources de Saint Thomas* in *Aristote et Saint Thomas d'Aquin* (Louvain-Paris, 1956) 150. A. Dondaine cites the frequent use of the conjunction NAM in the *Tractatus de substantiis separatis* as proof that the work belongs to a later period in the writing activity of St. Thomas. The conjunction is never found in such inconstestably early works as *De ente et essentia, De principiis naturae, Contra impugnantes Dei cultum et religionem,* or *Quodlibet VII.* On the other hand, the conjunction appears, according to Dondaine's count, 24 times in the *De substantiis separatis.* Although Dondaine does not offer any specific date for the composition of this work, he does point out that the conjunction NAM began to appear "un peu avant la fin de son enseignement magistral parisien." A. Dondaine, *op. cit.*, 218-220.

From the feast of St. Nicholas (December 6, 1273) until the time of his death, Aquinas suddenly and inexplicably ceased all literary activity. Cf. *Proc. Can. Neap.* LXXIX (Fontes IV, 376-377); V. Bourke, *op. cit.*, 192-193; A. Walz, *op. cit.*, 156-157.

LES SERMONS DE SAINT THOMAS ET LA *CATENA AUREA**

Louis-Jacques Bataillon O.P.

E N lisant les rares sermons de saint Thomas d'Aquin dont l'authenticité soit assurée,[1] ce qui frappe d'abord est leur très grande
ressemblance avec la masse des prédications universitaires de son
époque. Alors que le style oratoire d'un saint Bonaventure est si bien

* La plupart des sermons étudiés ici ont été édités au t.32 des *Opera omnia* (Paris 1879) par les
soins de S.E. Fretté (ce tome sera cité simplement par Vivès suivi de l'indication de la page),
édition reproduite dans Divi Thomae Aquinatis... *Sermones et opuscula concionatoria*...ed. A.J.B.
Raulx (Barri-Ducis, Parisiis, Friburgi Helv., 1880) t.II (cité Raulx suivi de la page). Il existe de cet
ouvrage une réimpression de l'année suivante mais en deux volumes au lieu de quatre et avec une
pagination différente. Quant au t.24 des *Opera omnia* imprimé à Parme en 1869, il ne contient
comme sermons authentiques que *Puer Ihesus, Attendite a falsis prophetis* et *Lux orta est iusto*.
Les indications concernant les sermons qui ne figurent pas dans les éditions Vivès et Raulx seront
données au début de l'étude de chacun d'entre eux.
La *Catena aurea* sera citée par la référence au verset de l'Evangile commenté, suivie de l'indication de la page et de la colonne de l'édition P. Guarienti chez Marietti (Taurini-Romae 1953).
Les citations sont vérifiées sur les manuscrits suivants: *Catena in Matth.*, Linz 446; Parma, Pal.1;
Catena in Lucam, Linz 448; Laon 88: Roma, Vallicelliana B.18. J'ai aussi fait usage à l'occasion de
l'édition de J. Nicolai, t.XVII (Paris 1660).
1 Il faut rejeter comme inauthentiques les deux collections imprimées dans les diverses *Opera
omnia* sous le nom de *Sermones dominicales* et *Sermones festivi*; conservées dans le ms.
Vat.lat.3804, elles ont été imprimées dans l'édition dite *Piana* de 1570. Dans le ms. comme dans
l'édition, des renvois existent d'une collection à l'autre, mais il existe des témoins isolés de
chacune d'entre elles. Seuls quelques témoins relativement anciens des *festiui* portent une attribution à saint Thomas; les exemplaires présentent de fortes divergences d'un témoin à l'autre.
Dans tous une partie importante de la collection est tirée des sermons d'Aldobrandinus de
Cavalcantibus, provincial de la province romaine au temps de saint Thomas; cf. Th. Kaeppeli,
Scriptores Ordinis Praedicatorum Medii Aevi (Romae 1970) 37 (N° 125). Il faut également éliminer
toute une série de sermons édités par Uccelli et Ghilardi d'après le ms. Vat. lat. 812; on trouvera
les références à ces éditions dans A. Pelzer, *Codices Vaticani latini*, t. II, pars prior, Codices 679-
1134 (Bibl. Vaticana 1931) 153-162. Malheureusement Mgr Pelzer a été trompé par une fausse indication de Harmand, *Catalogue Général des manuscrits des Bibliothèques publiques des Dépar-
tements*, t. II (Paris 1855) 342. Harmand, décrivant le ms. Troyes 823, n'a pas vu qu'il contenait en
fait deux recueils distincts et a étendu aux *Sermones de tempore* du début l'attribution à Guibert de
Tournai des *Sermones de sanctis* qui suivent; l'autorité de Pelzer a fait étendre cette fausse attribution à d'autres exemplaires de ce recueil *Abiciamus opera tenebrarum ... Scriptum est ad
Hebreos*; en fait plusieurs manuscrits (Tarragona 1, Laon 290³, Vat. lat. 11524), appuyés par les
listes de taxation des *exemplaria* de l'Université de Paris, montrent que l'auteur en est un frère
Thomas Lebreton, inconnu jusqu'ici par ailleurs. On éliminera aussi l'*introitus* biblique *Intrauit
rex* attribué à saint Thomas par une lubie d'Uccelli, ainsi que le sermon édité par le P. G. Meersseman, "La prédication dominicaine dans les congrégations mariales en Italie," *Archivum fratrum
praedicatorum* 18 (1948) 131-161 (texte en 159-161); l'attribution marginale de ce sermon *Cecidit
sors* porte *fratris trŏphi*, que le P. Meersseman a interprété un peu trop hardiment *Thome philosophi*, alors qu'il faut plus probablement résoudre l'abréviation en *theophili* ou *theodulphi*.

caractérisé que le recours apparemment subjectif à l'*indoles bonaven-turiana* n'a que rarement induit en erreur la sagacité du P. Fidelis de Fanna et des éditeurs de Quaracchi, il est très difficile de découvrir des traits spéciaux à saint Thomas prédicateur. Sans doute quelques formules reviennent volontiers dans ses sermons, et le P. Kaeppeli a noté la fréquence chez lui d'une interrogation, souvent introduite par *sed numquid*, suivie d'une réponse débutant par *certe*,[2] mais ce trait n'a rien d'exclusif. Il en irait de même pour l'emploi fréquent de *uidete, uideamus*[3] et de quelques autres locutions. Ce sont là tournures que saint Thomas affectionne mais qu'il est loin d'être seul à utiliser; elles ne peuvent fournir tout au plus que des présomptions très légères d'authenticité.

Il est un point cependant par lequel saint Thomas se distingue assez souvent de ses contemporains. La plupart des prédicateurs du milieu du XIIIe siècle ne citent guère dans leurs sermons d'autorités patristiques, à l'exception de Bernard, très souvent invoqué, Augustin et Grégoire, parfois Jérôme ou Anselme; en revanche, dans certains des sermons les mieux attestés de saint Thomas on est frappé par la relative richesse des citations et par leur variété et notamment par l'usage fréquent de Chrysostome.

Presque tous les sermons certainement authentiques appartiennent à la période du second enseignement à Paris, ainsi que le montrent et les questions qui y sont traitées et le contexte des recueils qui les contiennent en même temps que les œuvres d'autres maîtres de cette époque. Il convient donc de se demander si cette documentation patristique des sermons n'aurait pas de rapports avec le considérable dossier recueilli par saint Thomas pour la composition de la *Glossa continua super quatuor euangelia* plus connue sous le nom de *Catena aurea*. Tel sera l'objet de cette enquête.

Celle-ci ne portera que sur un nombre restreint de sermons. Afin de permettre au lecteur de se référer à un texte, les sermons encore inédits

---

2 Th. Käppeli, "Una raccolta di prediche attribuite a S. Tommaso d'Aquino," *Archivum fratrum praedicatorum* 13 (1943) 59-94 (article qui sera cité désormais Kaeppeli, *Raccolta*); le passage sur l'emploi de l'interrogation suivie de *certe* se trouve p. 68-70. Comme exemples de la même formule chez des prédicateurs contemporains, on peut citer, un peu au hasard, des sermons de Jean de Verdy (Paris, B.N. lat. 15952, fol. 105va), Nicolas de Nonancourt (ibid. fol. 280ra), Jean de Saint-Benoît (Paris. B.N. lat. 14923, fol. 80rb). La réponse à la question est presque aussi souvent introduite par *dico* tant par saint Thomas que par les autres prédicateurs.

3 Ces expressions se rencontrent occasionnellement dans le commentaire de saint Thomas sur les Epîtres de S. Paul (*In I Cor.*, Prol.: *Videamus ergo primo textum; In I Thes.*, Prol., etc.). Le style de ce commentaire se rapproche par plusieurs autres points de celui des sermons. Ces textes reportés nous donnent sans doute l'image la plus fidèle de ce qu'était l'enseignement oral de saint Thomas.

ne seront pas pris en considération.[4] D'autre part, trois schémas squelettiques, conservés dans le ms. Milano, Ambrosiana A. 11 sup., ne peuvent être utilisés dans ce travail, puisqu'ils ne comportent plus que l'annonce des grandes divisions accompagnées chacune d'une citation biblique. Il s'agit des sermons *Celum et terra transibunt,*[5] *Abiciamus opera tenebrarum*[6] et *Ecce ego mitto angelum meum.*[7] S'ils ont comporté des citations des Pères, il n'en reste plus trace; le traitement de condensation qu'ils ont subi a été radical, comme celui qui a affecté les sermons bonaventuriens dont le même recueil nous a gardé maint schéma.[8] D'autres sermons enfin ont pour thème des passages bibliques, tirés d'autres livres que les Evangiles et ne se prêtent guère à une comparaison; ils ne comportent de fait que peu de citations patristiques; ce sont les sermons *Germinet terra,*[9] *Lux orta est iusto,*[10] *Beata gens,*[11] *Beatus uir,*[12] *Beati qui habitant.*[13] Enfin leur genre littéraire spécial invite à ne pas considérer ici le cas des *Collationes* sur l'oraison dominicale, la salutation angélique, le symbole des Apôtres et les dix commandements.

Faute de données chronologiques suffisamment sûres pour l'ensemble des sermons, nous examinerons ceux-ci dans l'ordre de l'année liturgique.

Le premier qu'il convient d'étudier est donc le sermon pour le premier dimanche de l'Avent *Ecce rex tuus uenit.*[14] Nous n'y trouverons qu'une seule citation patristique vers la fin de la *collatio*; elle est tirée

---

4   Ces sermons sont ceux qui ont été découverts et étudiés par le P. Kaeppeli, *Raccolta.*

5   Vivès, 692-693; Raulx, 219-220. Un autre exemplaire de ce sermon, amputé du prothème mais conservant la troisième partie omise dans le manuscrit de Milan, se trouve dans le ms. Paris, B.N.lat.14595, fol.175r-176r.

6   Vivès, 693; Raulx, 221-223.

7   Vivès, 815; Raulx, 223-224.

8   Les exemples abondent dans le volume des *Opera omnia* de Bonaventure consacré aux sermons (t.IX, Quaracchi 1901). Ainsi le sermon I pour Noël (p.103-106) compte 366 lignes de texte alors que le schéma correspondant (p.106) n'en a que vingt.

9   Ce sermon ne figure pas dans les éditions Vivès et Raulx; il a été publié par P.A. Uccelli sous le titre "Sermone inedi.o di S. Tommaso sulla Natività della SS. Virgine," *I Gigli a Maria* 12 (1874) 125-143. La collation traite, non de la nativité de Marie comme le sermon du matin, mais de l'exaltation de la Croix; il y a donc toutes chances pour que cette prédication ait eu lieu le 13 septembre 1271, dimanche dans l'octave de la Nativité avec premières vêpres de la Croix.

10   Vivès, 682-687; Raulx, 380-394.

11   Vivès, 797-802; Raulx, 394-411.

12   Vivès, 802-807; Raulx, 411-423.

13   Kaeppeli, *Raccolta,* 88-94.

14   Ce sermon a été édité par Dom Jean Leclercq, "Un sermon inédit de Saint Thomas sur la royauté du Christ," *Revue thomiste* 46 (1946) 152-166 et 572. Le fait que l'allusion à saint André se trouve à la fin de la *collatio* (p.166) et non dans le sermon du matin, est plus en faveur de la date du 29 novembre 1271 (avec les premières vêpres de l'Apôtre le soir du dimanche) que de celle du 30 novembre 1270 où il y avait occurrence des deux fêtes.

des *Tractatus in Iohannem* de saint Augustin[15]; ce passage figure aussi dans la *Catena aurea*, mais cette unique coïncidence ne peut être considérée comme significative.

Il en va tout autrement avec le sermon pour le premier dimanche après l'Epiphanie *Puer Iesus proficiebat.* [16] Si le sermon du matin ne comporte qu'une référence à la lettre 36 de saint Augustin,[17] passage qui ne se trouve pas dans la *Catena*, la collation des Vêpres contient plusieurs citations. La première débute ainsi: *In expositione huius uerbi dicit quidam Grecus satis notabile uerbum*[18]; or la *Catena* sur Luc nous donne sous l'indication *Grecus*[19] un passage qui correspond presque mot pour mot:

Sermon	Catena
Considera, inquit, prudentissimam mulierum Mariam et uere sapientie matrem qualiter scolaris pueri efficitur, et iam non ut puero neque ut uiro sed ut deo ei attendit; et sicut uerbum ipsum in mente conciperat, ita omnia facta eius et uerba nunc concipit corde.	Considera prudentissimam mulierum Mariam uere sapientie matrem qualiter scolaris fit pueri; non enim ei ut puero neque ut uiro sed ut deo uacabat....Sed sicut ipsum uerbum prius in uisceribus, ita nunc eiusdem modos et dicta concipiebat et in corde suo quodam modo fouebat.

La comparaison des textes montre une telle fidélité qu'elle invite à corriger dans le sermon *mente* en *uentre* d'après le *uisceribus* de la *Catena*.

Après une citation d'Augustin qui ne se retrouve pas dans la *Catena*, en vient une de Grégoire de Nysse. [20] Ici encore il est possible de mettre les deux textes en parallèle:

Sermon	Catena
Quisquis per motionem proficit obedientiam nunquam dimittit; antequam homo ad profectum conuersationis humane perueniat, necessarium est ipsum habere obedientiam tanquam ducentem ad bonum.	...quicquid per promotionem perficitur antequam ad finem perueniat obedientiam tanquam perducentem ad bonum utiliter amplexatur.

---

15 PL 35, 1649; *Corpus christianorum* 36, 307. La citation se trouve dans le sermon p.166 (cf.p.572); *Catena in Ioh.* VIII, 3; t.II, p. 444b.

16 Vivès, 663-671; Raulx, 224-243. Les passages cités sont corrigés d'après l'unique témoin manuscrit: Paris, B.N.lat.15034, fol.47vb-51vb.

17 Vivès, 666b; Raulx, 242. Augustin: PL 33, 151.

18 Vivès, 669b; Raulx, 240.

19 *Catena in Lucam* II, 51; t.II, p.43a. D'après Cordier et Nicolai, l'auteur grec serait Métaphraste ou Jean le Géomètre.

20 Dans le sermon il est appelé *Gregorius* sans plus alors que la *Catena* précise.

Un peu plus loin, la *Glossa* invoquée dans le sermon n'est nullement la Glose ordinaire, mais bien un passage de *Basilius in libro religionum*, c'est-à-dire des *Constitutiones monasticae* du pseudo-Basile, utilisé par la *Catena*[21]:

Sermon	Catena
Unde super illud *Subditus erat illis*, Glossa: et quibus illis? Dicit Glossa: Homines erant iusti et honesti, pauperes tamen et penuriam necessariorum habentes, teste presepi partus uenerandi ministro per continuos labores necessaria corporis querentes et Christus cum eis laborauit.	Cum enim homines essent honesti et iusti, egeni tamen et necessariorum penuriam patientes, teste presepi partus uenerandi ministro, manifestum quod sudores corporeos continuo frequentabant, necessaria inde sibi querentes. Ihesus autem obediens illis... etiam in sustinendo labores subiectionem plenariam ostendebat.

En plus de ces citations explicites, il semble qu'il y ait dans ce sermon des réminiscences d'autres passages de Pères grecs cités dans la *Catena*; les passages ci-dessus suffisent à montrer que dans cette prédication saint Thomas s'est souvenu de la documentation de la *Glossa continua*.

Le sermon de sexagésime *Exiit qui seminat*[22] est, comme l'ont noté les P. Kaeppeli[23] et H.-F. Dondaine,[24] une des pièces importantes de la lutte *contra Geraldinos* et les points communs abondent entre ce sermon, l'opuscule *Contra retrahentes* et la question disputée *De ingressu puerorum* éditée comme *Quodlibet IV*, a.23 et 24. Les trois ouvrages comprennent beaucoup de citations communes d'*auctoritates*. Mais, si tant l'opuscule que la question disputée utilisent largement la *Catena*,[25] il n'en est pas de même du sermon: seules une citation de Grégoire[26] et deux de Chrysostome correspondent à des passages de la *Catena*,[27] mais sous une forme telle qu'il n'y a aucune nécessité de penser à un recours direct.

---

21   Vivès, 670b; Raulx, 242. *Catena in Lucam* II, 51; t.II, p.43b. Ps.-Basile, *Regulae monasticae* IV, 6; PG 31, 1356 D-1357 A.
22   Edition: Kaeppeli, *Raccolta* 75-88.
23   Ibid. 65-68.
24   H.-F. Dondaine, "Note sur la documentation patristique de saint Thomas à Paris en 1270," *Revue des sciences philosophiques et théologiques* 47 (1963) 403-406, et préface de l'édition de l'opuscule *Contra doctrinam retrahentium a religione, Opera omnia* (ed. leonina) t.XLI (Romae 1969) p. C. 7.
25   Voir pour l'opuscule l'index de l'édition précitée, p. C. 83.
26   Kaeppeli, *Raccolta*, 83. *Catena in Matth.* XX, 16; t. I, p. 294a.
27   Kaeppeli, *Raccolta*, 84. *Catena in Matth.* XXIII, 15; t. I, p. 334b-335a.

Le sermon des rogations *Petite et accipietis*[28] est encore moins riche:
une seule citation commune tirée d'Augustin, que nos reportations appellent Grégoire. [29]

Nous trouvons en revanche une assez riche moisson dans le sermon *Attendite a falsis prophetis*:[30] dix-sept citations des Pères: sept
d'Augustin, trois de Grégoire, six de Chrysostome, une des *Similitudes*
attribuées à Anselme; or douze de ces citations coïncident avec la
Catena. Comme il s'agit de la Glose sur Matthieu qui ne contient que
des œuvres qui circulaient largement au temps de saint Thomas, on
pourrait se demander s'il n'y a pas simplement rencontre fortuite. Les
quatre extraits du *De sermone Domini in monte*, par exemple, ne nous
apprennent rien, car la *Catena* recopie presque mot pour mot le traité
d'Augustin. D'autres citations du sermon sont plus *ad sensum* qu' *ad litteram* et donc sans poids pour notre recherche. Mais un des cas est très
net: il s'agit d'un passage de l'*Opus imperfectum in Matthaeum* du
pseudo-Chrysostome. Le texte original porte:

> Deinde ut orans nihil nouum faciat quod aspiciant homines; nec quis
> uoce clamet ut audiatur ab aliis, nec expandat manus suas, ut Pharisaeus
> in templo, ut uideatur a multis, neque pectus suum percutiat, sed ab-
> sconse, sicut publicanus in templo, neque impudenter oculos tollat ad
> caelum ut notabilis fiat.[31]

---

28 Vivès, 688-691; Raulx, 279-288, d'après le ms. Paris, B.N.lat. 14923. Une meilleure édition a
été donnée par B. Hauréau, *Notices et extraits de quelques manuscrits latins de la Bibliothèque
Nationale*, t. IV (Paris 1892) 81-88 (cité désormais Hauréau, *Notices*), d'après les mss Paris,
B.N. lat. 14952, 14899 et 14923. Ces trois manuscrits portent une attribution explicite à saint
Thomas, mais un quatrième exemplaire de ce sermon dans le ms. München, Clm 23372, donne
comme auteur un Maître Guillaume Breton. Dans ce témoin le *sermo* est composé de la réunion
ensemble du sermon et de la collation des manuscrits parisiens alors que la *collatio* est toute
différente. Provisoirement j'inclinerais à attribuer cette collation de Munich à Guillaume Breton et
à laisser à saint Thomas le sermon et la collation de Paris.

29 Vivès, 689a; Raulx, 282; Hauréau, *Notices*, 84. *Catena in Lucam* XI, 9; t. II, 162b.

30 Vivès, 673-680; Raulx, 337-354. Je corrige d'après les mss Paris, B.N. lat.15034, fol. 132ra-
135rb, et Nürnberg, Stadtbibl. V.82, fol.213v-216r. Le P. Jules d'Albi, *Saint Bonaventure et les luttes doctrinales de 1266-1267* (Tamines 1922) 196-199, a prétendu que ce sermon n'était qu'un
démarquage du sermon de saint Bonaventure *Medius vestrum stetit* (Sermo II in Dom.III ad-
ventus: *Opera omnia* t.IX, 59-67; *Opera theologica selecta* t.V, 279-295). Les ressemblances sont
en fait très superficielles et tiennent au contexte historique commun des deux œuvres, mais le sujet
traité est entièrement différent et il n'y a aucune raison sérieuse pour refuser l'attribution d'*Attendite* à saint Thomas. Dans le manuscrit de Paris, ce sermon est daté: *in tertia dominica post
festum apostolorum Petri et Pauli*; l'inscription du manuscrit de Nuremberg est légèrement
mutilée, mais d'après le contexte il faut sûrement lire: *VIIIa dominica post trinitatem*, ce qui
correspond à la suite des péricopes évangéliques selon l'usage parisien et dominicain de l'époque;
la confrontation des deux façons de dater permet d'attribuer avec sécurité ce sermon au 26 juillet
1271.

31 Hom.13; PG 56, 709.

Voici maintenant la façon dont ce texte est abrégé dans le sermon et dans la *Catena*:[32]

Sermon	Catena
Orans nichil nouum faciat ut ab hominibus uideri possit, neque clamando, neque pectus percutiendo, neque manus eleuando.	Orans, ergo nichil nouum faciat quod aspiciant homines, uel clamando, uel pectus uel manus expandendo.

La dépendance du sermon à l'égard de la *Catena* et non du texte original de l'*Opus imperfectum* semble évidente; il pourrait cependant y avoir un intermédiaire, un passage de la *IIa IIae*, q.187,a.6, ad 3m, qui cite ce passage en recopiant textuellement la *Catena* de même que certains extraits du *De sermone Domini in monte* communs à la *Catena* et au sermon.[33] Toutefois le nombre des autres coïncidences fait plutôt penser à un recours direct de saint Thomas à sa chaîne.

Une situation assez analogue se remarque dans le sermon pour le IXᵉ dimanche après la Trinité *Homo quidam erat diues*.[34] Sur treize citations patristiques,[35] huit figurent également dans la *Catena*: une de Grégoire le Grand, trois d'Augustin, une de Théophylacte (sous le nom de Chrysostome), une autre réellement de ce dernier et deux de Basile. Si la seconde citation de Basile est seulement *ad sensum*, la première est suffisamment littérale pour montrer qu'elle ne vient pas de la traduction de Rufin mais bien de la *Catena aurea* où le passage a dû être traduit d'après la chaine grecque de Nicétas. Voici d'abord le texte tel qu'il a été traduit par Rufin:[36]

Nunquid iniquus est Deus ut nobis non aequaliter distribuat uitae subsidia, ut tu quidem esses affluens et abundans, aliis uero deesset et egerent? An idcirco magis quia et tibi uoluit benignitatis suae documenta

---

32 Vivès, 677b; Raulx, 348. *Catena in Matth.* VI, 5; t.I, p.101a.

33 *IIa IIae*, q.187, a.6, arg.3 et corps (même citation q.169, a.1, corps et *IIIa P.* q.41, a.4, ad 2) = Vivès, 678a; Raulx, 349 (corriger ainsi: *Augustinus: In hoc capitulo animaduertendum non in solo corporearum rerum nitore...*). Ibid. ad 1 = Vivès, 679a; Raulx, 351. Ad 3 = Vivès 679b - 680a; Raulx, 351. Le premier et le troisième passages sont tirés du *De sermone Domini in monte* II, 12 (PL 34, 1287; *Corpus christianorum* 35, 131-132); le second de II, 24 (PL 34, 1306; C.C. 35, 179).

34 Vivès, 791-797; Raulx, 354-372. Je corrige d'après les mss Venezia, Marc. fondo antico lat. 92, fol. 257ra-261ra; Salamanca, Univ. 2187, fol. 193rb-197ra; Sevilla, Cab. 83.2.15, fol.146ra-150rb.

35 Il faut éliminer une fausse citation des éditions (Vivés, 793a; Raulx, 360): au lieu d'*Augustinus*, il faut lire *uerbi gratia*.

36 Hom.III,7; PG 31, 1752, correspondant à l'homélie grecque VI (*In illud dictum...Destruam horrea mea*), PG 31, 276 C. Il semble que saint Thomas n'ait connu la traduction de Rufin, au moins pour cette homélie, que par l'intermédiaire du Décret qui la cite sous le nom d'Ambroise, *Ia P.* d.47, c.8 (éd. Friedberg, I, 171-172: voir notamment *IIa IIae*, q.66, a.8, corps, où est citée la fin du passage ici reproduit.

conferre, et alium per uirtutem patientiae coronare? Tu uero susceptis
Dei muneribus et in sinum tuum redactis, nihil te putas agere iniquum, si
tam multorum uitae subsidia solus obtineas.... Esurientium panis est quem
tu detines, nudorum uestimentum est quod tu recludis, miserorum
redemptio est et absolutio pecunia quam in terra defodis. Tantorum te
ergo scias inuadere bona, quantis possis praestare si uelis.

Le texte donné par la *Catena* et le sermon est tout différent:[37]

Sermon	Catena
An iniustus est Deus inequaliter nobis res dispensans?... Cur ergo tu habundas et ille mendicat nisi ut cibum dispensando uite premia consequaris et ille patientie brauiis coronetur?	An iniustus est Deus inequaliter res nobis distribuens? Cur tu habundas, ille uero mendicat nisi tu bone dispensationis merita consequaris? ille uero patientie brauiis coronetur?
At tu non depredator es, que tibi commissa sunt dispensanda appropriando?	An tu nonne spoliator es, que dispensanda suscepisti propria reputando?
Est egentium panis quem tu tenes, nudi tunica quam in conclaui conseruas, discalciati calceus qui penes te marcescit, indigentis argentum quod humi reconditum habes. Quo circa tot iniuriaris quot dare posses.	Est panis famelici quem tu tenes, nudi tunica quam in conclaui conseruas, discalceati calceus qui penes te marcescit, indigentis argentum quod possides inhumatum. Quo circa tot iniuriaris quot dare ualeres.

Ce texte est cité plusieurs fois également dans la *IIa IIae*.[38]

La citation de Théophylacte sous le nom de Chrysostome n'est pas *ad
litteram*.[39] Alors que la *Catena* donne, avec la vraie attribution, le texte
sous la forme suivante:

Ille ergo dicuntur opes nequicie quascumque dominus dedit ad inpendia
necessitatis fratrum ac conseruorum nostrorum, nos uero tenemus nobis,

le sermon résume ainsi:

Crisostomus dicit quod diuicie dicuntur mammona iniquitatis quia inique
eas retinuisti.

Comme il ne semble pas que Théophylacte ait pu être connu
autrement que par la *Catena* au temps de saint Thomas, nous avons ici
une quasi-certitude de l'utilisation de la chaine dans le sermon.

---

37 Vivès, 795a-796b; Raulx, 368-369. *Catena in Lucam* XII, 18; t. II, p. 181a.
38 *IIa IIae*, q.32, a.5, ad 2; q.66, a.2, ad 2; q.117, a.1, ad 1; q.118, a.4, arg. 4.
39 Théophylacte, *Enarr. in ev. Lucae*, XVI; PG 123, 926 A. *Catena in Lucam* XVI, 9; t. II, p.
224b. Sermon: Vivès, 797a; Raulx, 371.

Parmi les citations qui ne se retrouvent pas dans la *Catena*, l'une remonte presque certainement à l'une des sources principales de celle-ci, c'est-à-dire à la traduction latine de la chaine de Nicétas exécutée à la demande de saint Thomas. Il s'agit d'un passage d'une homélie sur l'économe infidèle attribuée erronément à Chrysostome.[40] Des fragments figurent dans la *Catena*, mais pas celui que transmet le sermon:[41]

> Aduena es, et transitorii et breuis usus sunt tibi iura commissa....Modo habes agrum uel fundum, considera quot dominos ante te habuit infinitos: uix habent tot glebas. Item, est de te sicut de illo qui sub umbra quiescit: recedas, et uenit alius qui quiescit ibi sicut et tu. Sic cedit tibi in mundo secundum diuinam prouidentiam, non tuam.

Or ce passage figure dans la chaine de Nicétas[42]; il y a donc toute vraisemblance pour que saint Thomas en préparant son sermon ait eu recours, non à la *Catena* elle-même, mais à la principale de ses sources.

Le dernier sermon, *Omnia parata sunt*, pour le vingtième dimanche après la Trinité, ne comporte aucune citation patristique.[43]

A la fin de cette étude, il apparait donc que saint Thomas n'avait pas une façon constante de préparer ses prédications. Dans certains cas, il n'use que peu ou point de l'autorité des Pères; dans le sermon *Exiit qui seminat* il puise sa documentation avant tout dans ses ouvrages contemporains; dans trois autres, *Puer Iesus*, *Attendite a falsis prophetis*, *Homo quidam erat dives*, il a eu recours au dossier patristique de la *Catena aurea*.[44] L'absence de rapports avec cet ouvrage ne saurait constituer une présomption suffisante pour refuser à saint Thomas la paternité de sermons que la critique externe lui attribue avec vraisemblance; par contre le recours à cette source, que frère Thomas connaissait mieux que quiconque, assure aux sermons où il est attesté une garantie supplémentaire non négligeable d'authenticité.

---

40 *Homelia de parabola villici*, PG 61, 785.
41 Vivès, 794a; Raulx, 363-364.
42 Ms. Vat.graec. 1611, f.214ra. B. Corderius, *Catena sexaginta quinque Graecorum Patrum in S. Lucam* (Antverpiae 1628) 395. Saint Thomas remonte également à la traduction de la chaîne grecque, au delà de la *Catena*, pour deux citations du *Contra retrahentes* (H.-F. Dondaine, article cité plus haut, note 24)
43 Edité par B. Hauréau, *Notices* 88-93.
44 Le sermon *Osanna filio Dauid*, dont seul un fragment a été édité (Kaeppeli, *Raccolta*, 72-75) comporte, outre les rapports notés par l'éditeur avec les opuscules *Contra impugnantes* et *Contra retrahentes*, quelques coïncidences avec la *Catena* et d'assez nombreux parallèles avec la *Lectura in Matthaeum*.

"VERSUS" DANS LES ŒUVRES DE SAINT THOMAS

C. M. Joris Vansteenkiste O.P.

IL n'est pas question, dans les pages qui suivent, des "poésies" de S. Thomas, authentiques ou supposées. On a parlé ainsi d'un (quelques-uns même de plusieurs) sonnet en italien.[1] On a parlé encore de l'épitaphe de S. Pierre Martyr et d'autres compositions religieuses.[2] On pensera surtout à l'office du S. Sacrement, dont l'authenticité s'affirme de plus en plus.[3] L'objet de ces modestes observations est donné par les "versus" que S. Thomas cite dans ses œuvres. (L'étude ne peut être que préliminaire, parce que nous ne disposons pas encore d'éditions critiques suffisantes, ni d'indices complets). On peut répartir ces citations en trois classes: les "versus" liturgiques, les "versus" classiques, les "versus" mnémotechniques. Ceux qui appartiennent à la liturgie (par exemple, "O Crux Ave..." dans *Summa Theologiae* III, 25, 4, s.c.) devraient être étudiés à part dans un travail sur S. Thomas et la liturgie.[4] Parmi les citations de poètes "classiques" on pourrait énumérer celles des "metra" du *De consolatione* de Boèce. Mais il serait nécessaire d'écrire une étude spéciale sur la présence de Boèce dans l'œuvre de S. Thomas, ainsi qu'on l'a fait pour d'autres auteurs (Denys, Avicenne, etc.). Nous notons ici quelques autres citations explicites (sans nous occuper des implicites) de "poètes" classiques.

Disticha Catonis[5]

1. "Legere et non intelligere negligere est, ut dicit Cato", *In IV Sent.* d. 24, q. 1, a. 3, ql. 2, obj. 3. Ce texte a été employé par le compilateur du Supplément à la *Somme* (q. 36, a. 2, obj. 3). Il s'agit d'un texte en prose de la *praefatio* au premier livre des *Disticha* (dans l'édition de O.

---

1 Qu'on lise, à ce propos, M. Grabmann, *Die Werke des hl. Thomas von Aquin*, 3. Auflage (Münster 1949) 413.

2 Ibid., 416.

3 Voir récemment T. Bertamini, "La Bolla 'Transiturus' di papa Urbano IV e l'Ufficio del 'Corpus Domini' secondo il codice di S. Lorenzo di Bognanco," *Aevum* 42 (1968) 29-58.

4 On sait que celle-ci était une "auctoritas" théologique pour Thomas.

5 L. Sorrento, *Medievalia. Problemi e Studi* (Brescia 1943) p. 372, dit: "le citazioni dello pseudo Catone sono 2."

Arntz, Amstelaedami 1754, p. 10). La sentence est citée comme de Caton par Humbert des Romans, *Expositio regulae Beati Augustini*, ed. J. J. Berthier (Romae 1888), p. 446, et sans nom d'auteur par Robert de Sorbon, *De conscientia (Maxima bibliotheca veterum patrum* 25, Lugduni 1677, p. 350).

2. "...secundum illud Catonis: Cole parentes", *Summa Theol.* II-II, q. 81, a. 1, obj. 4. L'édition canadienne indique les *Breves Sententiae* 2, 3, et 40. La dernière (40) ne semble pas convenir, mais on aurait une fusion de 2 et 3: "Parentes (ama, cognatos) cole."

Horatius[6]

3. "Ut ait Horatius: per mare pauperiem fugiunt, per saxa, per ignes; ut Augustinus dicit in IV L. contra Iulianum", *Summa Theol.* II-II, q. 23, a. 7, c. La source directe, S. Augustin, PL 44, 748; la source première: Horace, *Epist.* I, 46.

4. "Illud Horatii: brevis esse laboro, obscurus fio", *In Boethium de Trinitate,* Expositio prooemii, ed. B. Decker (Leiden 1955), p. 54. Le texte est du *De arte poetica*, 25.

5. "Illud Horatii: oderunt peccare mali formidine poenae; oderunt peccare boni virtutis amore", *De malo*, q. 1, a. 5, ad 11. La source première est *Epist.* I, 16.52. Le texte est cité encore, par exemple, dans Iohannes Viterbiensis, *Liber de regimine civitatum (Biblioteca iuridica medii aevi* 3, Bononiae 1901, p. 265), et par Albertano da Brescia, *Liber consolationis et consilii*, ed. T. Sundby (Havniae 1873), p. 87.

6. "Horatius: ludere qui nescit campestribus abstinet armis", *In Epist. I ad Timotheum*, cap. 3, lect. 2. Voir *De arte poetica*, 379.

Ovidius[7]

7. "Ovidius: et quacumque potes dote placere, place", *In IV Sent.* d. 49, q. 4, a. 1 (texte cité aussi par le compilateur du Supplément à la *Somme*, q. 95, a. 1). C'est un vers de l'*Ars amatoria*, I. 594.

8. "Poeta dicit: quis matrem nisi mentis inops in funere nati flere vetat", *In Iob* (ed. Léonine 1965, 2.266). C'est *Remedia amoris*, 127. Le vers est cité aussi par Albertano, op. cit. (ed. cit., p. 2), et dans le

---

6 L. Sorrento, op. cit., semble avoir relevé un plus grand nombre de citations, mais il ne donne pas de précisions: "*Arte poetica* (2 citazioni precise e dirette); *Odi* (1 citazione da Sant'Agostino); *Epodi* (1 citazione da Sant'Agostino); *Epistole* (1 citazione diretta)", p. 372.

7 Ici L. Sorrento est moins complet: "Ovidio Nasone, *Ars amatoria* (1 volta sola; non si può dire se diretta)", op. cit., p. 372. On pourrait renvoyer ici aux nombreuses études sur Ovide au Moyen Age (la plupart sont énumérées par S. Viarre, *La survie d'Ovide...*, Poitiers 1966).

Paedagogus Abbatum Ordinis Cistercii (ed. *Mediaeval Studies* 30, 1968, p. 309).

9. "Sicut dicit Sapiens: non minor est virtus quam quaerere parta tueri", *In Epist. ad Ephesios*, prologo. Voir: *Ars amatoria*, II.13; le vers était populaire au Moyen Age.

10. "Virtus enim laudata crescit in immensum pondus et immensum gloria calcar habet", *In Epist. ad Hebraeos*, c. 10, lect. 4. Le texte ne donne pas de nom d'auteur. Comparer: *Epist.* IV, 2.35.

Terentius[8]

11. "Terentius in Eunucho dicit quod in amore est bellum et rursus pax et indutiae", *Summa Theol.* II-II, q. 54, a. 6, ad 2. Comparer: Act. I, 1.59.

12. "Terentius dicit in Eunucho...: quae res in se neque consilium neque modum ullum habet, eam consilio regere non potes", *Summa Theol.* II-II, q. 153, a. 5. Voir: Act. I, 1.57.

13. "Terentius dicit in Eunucho...: haec verba una falsa lacrimula restringet", ibid. Voir: Act. I. 1.67 ss.

14. "Illud Terentii: Veritas odium parit", *De correptione fraterna*, a. 1, 19°. Voir: *Andria* I, 1.68, et Ausonius, *Ludus septem sapientium*: Bias, 3 (PL 19. 876 A).

15. "Unde Glosa: sine Cerere et Baccho friget Venus", *In Ieremiam* 5. 7. Voir: *Eunuchus* IV, 6.731, et la *Glossa interlinearis* (ed. Venetiis 1603, IV, col. 623-4).

Virgilius[9]

16. "Augustinus, XIV de Civitate Dei...inducens illud Virgilii: hinc metuunt, cupiunt, gaudentque dolentque", *Summa Theol.* I-II, q. 35, a. 1, s.c. Pour Virgile, v. *Aeneis* VI. 733; pour Augustin, PL 41. 412.

17. "Augustinus, XII de Trinitate...probat per dicta Virgilii, qui proprio nomine memoriae et oblivionis usus est", *De veritate*, q. 10, a. 2, s.c. 2. Voir: *Corpus Christianorum*, SL, La 1968, p. 442.

18. "Augustinus, XIV de Civitate Dei...ex verbis Virgilii...qui...dixit: sicut homines cupiunt, metuunt gaudentesque dolentesque...", *De veritate*, q. 26, a. 5, obj. 1. Cf. la citation n. 16.

19. "Sicut quando inducunt illud Virgilii: talia pendebat memorans fixusque manebat", *In Matthaeum*, c. 1 (n. 148). Cf. *Aeneis* II. 650.

---

8 L. Sorrento, op. cit. dit: "*L'Eunuchus* (4 citazioni dirette et precise e 1 da S. Girolamo", p. 372.

9 Selon Sorrento "*Aeneis* (4 dirette e precise, e 1 da Sant'Agostino); *Bucolica* (1 precisa e diretta)", op. cit., p. 372.

20. "Si enim, ut dicit Augustinus: trahit sua quemque voluptas", *In Iohannem*, c. 6 (n. 935). Voir: Augustin, *In Evangelium Iohannis*, tract. 36, c. 6 (PL 35, 1608) et *Bucol.* 2.65.

Nous ajoutons ici un vers pseudo-classique: "dicitur: in vultu legitur hominis secreta voluntas", *In II Sent.* d. 8, q. 1, a.5, ad 5. On lit dans le *Miles Gloriosus* 37: "in facie legitur hominum..." (*La Comédie Latine en France au* XIIe *siècle*, I, Paris 1931, p. 197). On trouvera une bibliographie supplémentaire chez Walther, cité ci-après, aux nn. 11765 et 12157.

Notre énumération n'est probablement pas complète, et il nous est impossible de donner une liste des citations implicites ou allusions.

Les poètes grecs cités par S. Thomas lui sont évidemment connus par des intermédiaires, surtout par Aristote. On peut nommer Homère, Hésiode, Aratos (*Summa Theol.* I, q. 1, a. 8, ad 2), connu par les *Actes des Apôtres*, et Ménandre (*In I Epist. ad Corinthios*, c. 15, lect. 14) connu par S. Jérome. L. Sorrento dira donc: "Non cita che indirettamente poeti greci" (op. cit, p. 370).

Il y a enfin le troisième genre, les vers mnémotechniques, dont l'usage appartenait à la technique de l'enseignement scolastique dans toutes ses branches. L. Thorndike en a étudié l'usage dans les ouvrages de sciences naturelles.[10] H. Walther a relevé la presque totalité de ces vers.[11] Nous présentons ici ce que nous avons trouvé chez S. Thomas. Il ne sera pas nécessaire, pour notre but, de relever les nombreuses variantes (les unes purement verbales, ou même des fautes, les autres de véritables variantes d'expression). Il faudrait avoir les éditions critiques et pouvoir retracer l'histoire de ces formules.

1.   "Sex in lacte dies, tres sunt in sanguine terni
            bis seni carnem, ter seni membra figurant".
            In III Sent. d. 3, q. 5, a. 2.

Ce texte se trouve ad litteram dans le *Regimen sanitatis* de l'école de Salerne (Salerno 1941, p. 302) et dans le *De secretis naturae* de Michel Scot (Lugduni 1598, p. 265). Comparer encore la *Glossa* d'Alexandre de Halés, III, d. 3 (Quaracchi 1954, p. 38), et IV, d. 6 (Quaracchi 1957, p. 110); Albert le Grand, *In IV Sent.* d. 31 (Borgnet 30.251).

2.   "Rex sedet in coena — turba cinctus duodena;
            se tenet in manibus — se cibat ipse cibus".
            In IV Sent. d. 11, q. 3, a. 1; *Summa Theol.* III, q. 81, a. 1, ad 1.

10 "Unde Versus," *Traditio* 11 (1955) 162-193.
11 *Carmina medii aevi posterioris latina* (Göttingen 1959 ss.).

Voir: Walther, op. cit., n. 16778; A. Wilmart, "Poèmes de Gautier de Châtillon dans un manuscrit de Charleville," *Revue bénédictine* 49, 1937, p. 135; J. De Ghellinck, "Les notes marginales du Liber Sententiarum," *Revue d'histoire ecclésiastique* 14, 1913, p. 515). Cité encore par Gervais de Melkley, *Ars poetica* (H.-J. Gräbener, Münster 1965, p. 206); Hugues de St-Cher, *Super Lucam* 22.19 (Venetiis 1703, VI, f. 259v); Albert le Grand, *In IV Sent.* d. 12, a. 15 (Borgnet 29.322).

3. "Pixide servato poteris copulare dolorem
    innatum, sed non illatus convenit illi".
    In IV Sent. d. 11, q. 3, a. 4, ql. 1; *Summa Theol.* III, q. 81, a. 4.

Voir: Albert le Grand, *In IV Sent.* d.12, a.14 (Borgnet 29. 320), *De sacramentis* (Coloniensis XXVI, p. 67); *Liber de sacramento eucharistiae*, III. 1.6 (Borgnet 38.263).

4. "Hostia dividitur in partes: tincta beatos
    plene, sicca notat vivos, servata sepultos".
    In IV Sent. d. 12, q. 1, a. 3, ql. 3, ad 4; *Summa Theol.* III, q. 83, a. 5, ad 8.

On retrouve ces vers chez Alexandre de Halés, *Glossa* IV, d.12 (ed. cit., p. 195); Albert le Grand, *In IV Sent.* d.13 (Borgnet 29.357); S. Bonaventure, *In IV Sent.* d.12, pars 1, a.3, q.3; dans les notes marginales au *Rotulus pugillaris* d'Augustin de Dacie (Walz, *Classica et Mediaevalia* 1955, p. 194). On trouve des vers semblables dans la *Summa totus homo* (H. Betti, Romae 1955, p. 62) où l'éditeur renvoie au pseudo-Hildebert (PL 171. 1280 A-B).

5. "Iussio, consilium, consensus, palpo, recursus,
    Participans, mutus, non obstans, non manifestans".
    In IV Sent. d. 15, q. 1, a. 5, ql. 3; *Summa Theol.* II-II, q. 62, a. 7.

On retrouve ces vers chez Albert le Grand, *In IV Sent.* d. 15, a. 42 (Borgnet 29.528), et Pierre de Tarantaise, *In IV Sent.* d. 15, q. 2, a. 3. Voir aussi Walther, op. cit., n. 9990.

6. "Visito, poto, cibo, redimo, tego, colligo, condo.
    Consule, castiga, solare, remitte, fer, ora".
    Summa Theol. II-II, q. 32, a. 2, obj. 1; le premier vers: *In IV Sent.* d. 15, q. 2, a. 3, ql. 1, et *In Matthaeum* c. 25 (n. 2098); le deuxième: *In IV Sent.* d. 15, q. 2, a. 3, ql. 2.

Pour une autre forme, voir le *Poeniteas cito* attribué à Pierre de Blois (PL 207, 1156 A).

Comparer les citations chez Alexandre de Halès, *Glossa* IV, d.15 (ed. cit., p. 232); Albert le Grand, *In IV Sent.* d. 15, a. 23 (Borgnet 29.505);

Bonaventure, *In IV Sent.* d. 14, dubium 2; Robert de Sorbon, *De conscientia* (ed. cit., p. 352; le premier vers), et *De confessione* (ibid., p. 358); Augustin de Dacie (ed. cit., p. 155). Voir aussi A. De Poorter, "Un catéchisme du XIII° siècle," *Revue d'histoire ecclésiastique* 28, 1932, p. 72; premier vers, et Walther, op. cit., n. 3222, 3225, 3235, 20647.

7.   "Praepropere, laute, nimis, ardenter, studiose".
            In IV Sent. d. 15, q. 3, a. 4, ql. 3, obj. 2; *In Isaiam* c. 5; *Summa Theol.* I-II, q. 72, a. 9, obj. 3; II-II, q. 148, a. 4; *De malo,* q. 2, a. 6, et q. 14, a. 3, obj. 1.

L'origine première de cette codification des espèces de la *gula* sera à rechercher dans la doctrine de S. Grègoire, *Moralia* XXX.13. Le "versus" devint propriété commune. Voir, par exemple: Thomas Chobham, *Summa confessorum* (F. Broomfield, Louvain-Paris 1968, p.406); la *Summa Alexandrina* (Quaracchi 1930, III, p. 579); Albert le Grand, *In IV Sent.* d. 33, a. 20 (Borgnet 30.310); Guillaume Peyraut (Peraldus), *Summa virtutum ac vitiorum* (Lugduni 1668, II, p. 12); Robert de Sorbon, *De confessione* (ed. cit., p. 357).

8.   "Quis, quid, ubi, quibus auxiliis, cur, quomodo, quando".
            In IV Sent. d. 16, q. 3, a. 1, ql. 2; *Summa Theol.* I-II, q. 7, a. 3; *De malo,* q. 2, a. 6.

Sur l'histoire de la doctrine et de la formule, voir J. Gründel, *Die Lehre von den Umständen der menschlichen Handlung im Mittelalter* (*Beiträge* 39, 5. Münster 1963). On peut y ajouter des citations semblables chez Remi d'Auxerre, *Commentum in Martianum Capellam* (C. E. Lutz, Leiden 1962, p. 65); l'*Accessus ad auctores* (R.B.C. Huygens, Berchem-Bruxelles 1954, p. 13); Bernard d'Utrecht (cité dans Conrad de Hirsau, *Dialogus super auctores*, ed. R. B. C. Huygens, Berchem-Bruxelles 1955, p. 11); Matthieu de Vendôme, *Ars versificatoria* I.116 (in E. Faral, *Les arts poétiques du XII° et du XIII° siècle*, Paris 1958, p. 150); Thomas Chobham, *Summa confessorum* (ed. cit., p. 48); le *Sermo de poenitentia* de "Romanus Cardinalis" (PL 217, 689 D); Robert de Sorbon, *De conscientia* (ed. cit., p. 352); *De confessione* (ibid., p. 354); Augustin de Dacie (nota marginalis; ed. cit., p. 194). Voir aussi le Pseudo-Célestin V, *De sacramentis* (in Maxima Bibliotheca..., ed. cit., p. 828); J. De Ghellinck (art. cit., p. 713); Walther, op. cit., n. 16103.

9.   "Sit simplex, humilis confessio, pura, fidelis
            atque frequens, nuda, discreta, libens, verecunda
            integra, secreta, lacrymabilis, accelerata,
            fortis et accusans, et sit parere parata".
            In IV Sent. d. 17, q. 3, a. 4, ql. 4; copié dans le Supplément à la *Somme*, q. 9, a. 4, obj. 1.

On trouve des formes identiques ou semblables dans le *Poeniteas cito* attribué à Pierre de Blois (PL 207.1153 C-D); chez Alexandre de Halés, *Glossa* IV, d.14 (ed. cit., p.216); Albert le Grand, *In IV Sent.* d.17, a.36 (Borgnet 29.707), et *De sacramentis* (ed. cit., p.99); Bonaventure, *In IV Sent.* d.21, pars 2, dubium 3; Hugues de Strasbourg, *Compendium theologicae veritatis*, VI.26. Voir aussi J. De Ghellinck (art. cit., p. 714) et Walther, op. cit., n.18330. Cp. le Pseudo-Célestin (ed. cit., p.828).

10. "Confessor dulcis, affabilis atque suavis,
     prudens, discretus, mitis, pius atque benignus".
     In IV Sent. d. 17, expositio textus.

Une formule voisine dans le *Poeniteas cito* (PL 207.1155 A). Voir aussi J. De Ghellinck (art. cit., p.714), et Walther, op. cit., n. 3067, 3135.

11. "Si pro delictis anathema quis efficiatur,
     Os, orare, vale, communio, mensa negatur".
     In IV Sent. d. 18, q. 2, a. 1, ql. 1; *In Epist. I ad Corinthios*, c. 5, lect. 3.

Voir Raymond de Pennafort, *Summa* (H. V. Laget, Veronae 1744, p. 398); Albert le Grand, *In IV Sent.* d. 18, a. 12 (Borgnet 29.793); Bonaventure, *In IV Sent.* d. 18, pars 2, a. 1, q. 1; le Pseudo-Célestin, *De censuris* (ed. cit., p. 820); Walther, op. cit., n. 17864.

12. "Utile, lex, humile, res ignorata, necesse".
     In IV Sent. d. 18, q. 2, a. 6, ql. 1.

Voir Raymond de Pennafort, *Summa* (ed. cit., p.400); Albert le Grand, *In IV Sent.* d.18, a.21 (Borgnet 29.799); Bonaventure, *In IV Sent.* d. 18, pars 2, a. 1, q. 5; le Pseudo-Célestin, *De censuris* (ed. cit., p. 820); la *Glossa ad decretales* (Romae 1582, V.1886).

13. "Fratres odit, apostata fit, spernitque fateri,
     poenituisse piget, pristina culpa redit".
     In IV Sent. d. 22, q. 1, a. 1; *Summa Theol.* III, q. 88, a. 2, obj. 1.

Voir Alexandre de Halés, *Glossa* IV, d.22 (ed. cit., p.376); Albert le Grand, *In IV Sent.* d.22, a.1 (Borgnet 29.887), *De sacramentis* (ed. cit., p.122); Bonaventure, *In IV Sent.* d.22, a.1, q.1; Pierre de Tarantaise, *In IV Sent.* d.22, q.1, a.4.

14. "Collige, sustenta, stimula—vaga morbida, lenta".
     In IV Sent. d. 24, q. 3, a. 3; copié dans le Supplément à la *Somme*, q. 40, a. 7.

Voir Innocent III, *De sacro altaris mysterio* (PL 217, 796 D); *Paedagogus Abbatum Ordinis Cistercii* (ed. cit., p. 279); Walther, op. cit., n. 2943, 3026, 3033.

15.   "Stupri sive status verberis atque necis".
             In IV Sent. d. 29, q. 1, a. 2, ad 2; copié par le Supplément à la
             Somme q. 47, a. 2, ad 2.

Voir Guido de Orchellis, *Tractatus de sacramentis* (D. & O. Van den
Eynde, Louvain 1953, p. 222); Raymond de Pennafort, *Summa* (ed. cit.,
p. 62).

16.   "Ecclesiae vetitum, necnon tempus feriatum,
             impediunt fieri, permittunt cuncta teneri".
             In IV Sent. d. 34, q. 1, a. 1; copié par le Supplément à la *Somme*,
             q. 50, a. 1.

Voir Raymond de Pennafort, *Summa* (ed. cit., p. 481); Albert le
Grand, *In IV Sent.* d. 34, a. 2 (Borgnet 30.328); Augustin de Dacie (ed.
cit., p. 189). Cp. aussi Walther, op. cit., n. 5214.

17.   "Error, conditio, votum, cognatio, crimen,
             cultus disparitas, vis, ordo, ligamen, honestas,
             si sis affinis, si forte coire nequibus,
             haec socianda vetant connubia, facta retractant".
             In IV Sent. d. 34, q. 1, a. 1; copié par le Supplément à la *Somme*,
             q. 50, a. 1.

Voir Raymond de Pennafort, *Summa* (ed. cit., p. 481); Albert le
Grand, *In IV Sent.* d. 34, a. 2 (Borgnet 30.327); Bonaventure, *In IV
Sent.* d. 34, a. 1, q. 2; Hugues de Strasbourg, *Compendium* VI.38; Pierre
de Tarantaise, *In IV Sent.* d. 34, a. 1; le Pseudo-Célestin, *De sacramentis* (ed. cit., p. 841); Augustin de Dacie (ed. cit., p. 185). Cp. Walther,
op. cit., n. 5520, 7175 (qui cite Vincent de Beauvais).

18.   "Mutat nupta genus, sed generata gradum".
             In IV Sent. d. 41, q. 1, a. 1, ql. 1 et ql. 5; copié par le Supplément
             à la *Somme*, q. 55, a. 1 et a. 5.

Voir Raymond de Pennafort, *Summa* (ed. cit., p. 511); Albert le
Grand, *In IV Sent.* d. 41, a. 4; Bonaventure, *In IV Sent.* d. 41
"praenotata" et q. 2; Pierre de Tarantaise, *In IV Sent.* d. 41, a. 1;
Augustin de Dacie (ed. cit., p. 188). Cp. Walther, op. cit., n. 15806 (il
cite précisément Augustin de Dacie).

19.   "Quae mihi, vel cuius, mea natum fonte levavit,
             haec mea commater, fieri mea non valet uxor.
             Si qua meae natum non ex me fonte levavit,
             hanc post fata meae non inde verebor habere".
             In IV Sent. d. 42, q. 1, a. 3, ql. 2; copié par le Supplément à la
             Somme, q. 56, a. 4.

Voir Guido de Orchellis, *Tractatus de sacramentis* (ed. cit., p. 217);
Thomas Chobham, *Summa confessorum* (ed. cit., pp. 168, 395); Raymond de Pennafort, *Summa* (ed. cit., p. 494); Albert le Grand, *In IV*

Sent. d. 42, a. 6 (Borgnet 30.478); Bonaventure, *In IV Sent.* d. 42, a. 1, q. 3. Cp. *Glossa ad decretales* (ed. cit., IV.1495).

20. "Unus semper eris compatrum spiritualis
     alter carnalis, nec fallit regula talis".
     In IV Sent. d. 42, q. 1, a. 3, ql. 2; copié par le Supplément à la *Somme*, q. 56, a. 4, ad 2.

Voir Raymond de Pennafort, *Summa* (ed. cit., p. 492); Albert le Grand, *In IV Sent.* d. 42, a. 4 (Borgnet 30.473); Augustin de Dacie (ed. cit., p. 187). Cp. Walther, op. cit., n. 19687.

Nous ajoutons encore trois "versus" qui se trouvent dans les éditions courantes des œuvres bibliques de S. Thomas.

1. "Simile, prostituens, vis, mors et credita forma,
    Si convertatur, post novit, mittere nequit".
    Super Evangelium Matthaei, c.V (n. 522).

2. "Expedit infirmis, licet absque dolo, sine lite,
    praelatisque licet, non expedit anachoritae,
    non licet ut per eum sint res in iure petitae".
    Super Evangelium Matthaei, c.V (n. 544).

3. "Est sine matre Deus, est sine patre caro".
    In Epist. ad Hebraeos, c.VII, lect. 1.

Nous ne prétendons pas que la liste des "versus" donnée dans ces pages soit complète, et encore moins que la documentation sur leur origine et leur usage soit exhaustive. Il nous suffit d'avoir attiré l'attention sur cet aspect (accidentel) de la méthode de S. Thomas, qui en ceci encore a suivi les usages de son temps.

LA LETTRE DE SAINT THOMAS
A L'ABBÉ DU MONTCASSIN

Antoine Dondaine O.P.

L A lettre de saint Thomas à Bernard Ayglier, abbé du Montcassin,
demeura longtemps ignorée; elle ne fut découverte, dans les marges
d'un manuscrit des Morales de saint Grégoire des Archives du
monastère, qu'en 1874, il y a juste un siècle. L'auteur de la découverte,
Dom Louis Tosti, lui-même abbé du Montcassin, ébloui par sa
trouvaille, avança tout de suite l'hypothèse d'une pièce authentique,
mieux encore, celle d'un document écrit par la main de son illustre
auteur. Présentant le volume où se lit la lettre, il écrivait:

> Il faut marquer d'un caillou blanc le jour de la fête de saint Grégoire le
> Grand 1874, au cours duquel ce manuscrit me passa entre les mains, dans
> le moment où l'Italie célébrait le sixième centenaire du décès de saint
> Thomas d'Aquin et honorait sa mémoire par de solennelles fonctions. En
> effet, tandis que je scrutais avec soin les feuillets du volume, arrivé aux
> pages 320-322, à l'improviste je découvris un commentaire dans leurs
> marges, celles-ci partout ailleurs libres. Les yeux et l'esprit avidement
> concentrés, il n'est pas possible d'exprimer la joie qui m'envahit lorsque
> j'identifiai en ce commentaire non pas seulement une lettre jusqu'alors in-
> connue de saint Thomas d'Aquin adressée à Bernard abbé du Montcassin,
> mais une lettre écrite de sa propre main. Ce manuscrit que saint Thomas
> a tenu entre les mains et qu'il a enrichi d'un nouveau témoignage de sa
> pensée, devrait être précieusement recouvert en bois de cèdre. [1]

Avant de publier sa découverte Tosti avait pressenti l'avis autorisé
d'un spécialiste des autographes de saint Thomas, l'abbé Pierre Antoine
Uccelli. Celui-ci appuya sans réserve l'hypothèse avancée: des planches
photographiques lui avaient été communiqués; leur confrontation avec
l'écriture de saint Thomas lui révélait une parenté suffisante des formes
pour conclure à une même origine. [2] Ainsi confirmé dans sa conviction,

---

1 L. Tosti, *Bibliotheca Casinensis II* (Montis Casini 1875) 302.
2 Dom Tosti publia trois lettres de P.A. Uccelli en rapport avec sa découverte, dans les
prolégomènes de *S. Thomae Aquinatis propria manu scripta epistola ad Bernardum abbatem*

Tosti proposa l'explication d'une telle origine. En ce temps là un doute doctrinal troublait la communauté du Montcassin. Apprenant le passage à Aquino de saint Thomas en route pour le concile de Lyon, l'abbé Bernard lui adressa un message le priant de venir au monastère; son autorité apaiserait le trouble de ses religieux. Le doute en question était né d'un passage des Morales de saint Grégoire; l'abbé joignit un manuscrit de cet ouvrage à son propre message: saint Thomas, ne pouvant monter au Montcassin, inscrivit sa réponse dans les marges du précieux volume.

L'accueil fait à cette explication et au texte de la lettre publiée dans le Florilegium Casinense fut d'abord très favorable,[3] mais avec le temps

Casinensem...in lucem prolata opera et studio Monachorum O.S.B. (entendez L. Tosti), Bibliotheca Casinensis II, Florilegium Casinense 199-220 (lettres d'Uccelli 210-213; dans le tiré-à-part, mêmes lieu et date, XIV-XVII). Dans la troisième de ces lettres Uccelli écrivait: "Mi affretto a ringraziarlo infinitamente per le due fotografie che si è compiaciuto inviarmi. In esse io non esito a riconoscervi la mano di S. Thomaso e le trovo assai somiglianti all'autografo di Napoli, e più ancora a quello di Bergamo" (Florilegium..., 212; tiré-à-part XVI). — Avant de connaître les reproductions photographiques, Uccelli avait soulevé l'hypothèse d'une transcription: "Una lettera sul margine di un manoscritto! Due supposizioni sole mi sembrano a farsi. Una che l'Ab. Bernardo abbia inviato il Codice di S. Gregorio a S. Tomaso per sentirne il parere intorno al passo indicato, e S. Tomaso vi avesse scritto sopra ad dirittura la riposta, facendo economia di carta, come era solito; l'altra che qualche monaco avesse sul codice gregoriano trascritta la lettera di S. Tomaso come un commentario di una dichiarazione...", ibid.211 (XV).

3   Voir par exemple le compte rendu, sommaire mais précis, de La Civiltà Cattolica, Ser. IX, vol. IX, fasc. 615 (1876) 336. Nous n'avons pu atteindre G. de Luca, "San Tommaso d'Aquino mirabilmente compendia la tradizione sulla infallibile prescienzia di Dio e l'umana libertà, La scienza e la fede 101 (1876) 177-191, 486-491, signalé par M. Grabmann, Die Werke des hl. Thomas von Aquin (Münster Westfalen 1949) 377 n. 195 et 441 n. 364, et par R. A. Verardo, S. Thomae Aquinatis, Opuscula theologica I (Torino 1954) 247. De même nous ont échappé V. Ingletti, Lettera autografa di S. Tommaso d'Aquino, Napoli 1876, extrait de L'Illustratore Cattolico di Milano, 10 Marzo 1876, a. I n. 7, mentionné par Dom Leccisotti, "S. Tommaso d'Aquino e Montecassino." Miscellanea Cassinese 32 (Montecassino 1965) 59, et Ianotta, Per il gran dottore S. Tommaso... (Sora 1903) — auquel fait allusion F. Scandone, "La vita, la famiglia e la patria di S. Tommaso de Aquino," dans S. Tommaso d'Aquino O.P., Miscellanea storica-artistica (Roma 1924) 31 n. 4—. Editions postérieures: 2) G. Deho, Lettera di San Tommaso d'Aquino novamente publicata a cura del Sac. Gaetano Deho... (Modena 1880), opuscule de 8 pages extrait de Opuscoli Religiosi, Letterarj e Morali, Ser. IV, t. VII, fasc. 19 (1880). M. Grabmann, l.c., et R. A. Verardo, l.c., signalent une édition donnée par le même Deho (Casini 1875); cette information nous paraît erronée.— 3) Edition Vivès, S. Thomae... Opera omnia, t. 32 (Paris 1889) 834-835.— 4) L. Tosti, Scritti varii, t. 2 (Romae 1890), même texte que celui de la première édition moins les planches: prolégomènes 19-42, texte 42-45. —5) A. M. Caplet, Regesti Bernardi I Abbatis Casinensis Fragmenta ex Archivio Casinensi (Romae 1890), Prolegomena XCIX-CI n. 92: édition nouvelle avec de nombreuses notes critiques.—6) I. Monterisi, Lettera doctrinale di S. Tommaso d'Aquino all'abbate cassinese Bernardo Ayglerio sull'accordo tra la prescienza divina e la libertà umana (Montecassino 1896), opuscule de 22 pages insérant le texte de la lettre dans un commentaire de vulgarisation (texte de Tosti, sans les parenthèses distinguant les compléments ajoutés par l'éditeur).—7) P. Mandonnet, S. Thomae Aquinatis opuscula omnia III (Paris 1927) 249-251: texte de Tosti à travers l'édition Vivès mais entaché de plusieurs fautes et mutilé de la finale (57 mots manquent).—8) D. A. Saba, "Bernardo I Ayglerio, Abbate di Montecassino," Miscellanea Cassinese 8 (Montecassino 1931) 78-80 en note 5: texte de Caplet, troublé de quelques infidélités.—9) R. A. Verardo, l.c., 249-250: texte repris de l'édition 7 avec ses défauts (cependant l'éditeur repêche la finale "Valeat...vobis" dans Grabmann, Die Werke..., 378).—10) T. Leccisotti,

des doutes furent soulevés soit sur les circonstances, soit sur la qualité autographe, soit même sur l'authenticité du document. Contre ces doutes, des savants comme Mandonnet, Inguanez soutinrent que la lettre était autographe; Grabmann, tout en refusant une telle qualité, en admettait l'authenticité.[4] Qui avait raison? Pour découvrir la vérité et atteindre une conviction ferme, nous nous proposons de reprendre l'enquête à partir du manuscrit du Montcassin et d'examiner les difficultés soulevées par le contenu de la lettre.

LA LETTRE N'EST PAS UN AUTOGRAPHE DE SAINT THOMAS

L'hypothèse d'une lettre autographe dans les marges du manuscrit du Montcassin heurte le bon sens. Est-il vraisemblable que l'abbé Bernard ait fait porter loin de son dépôt ce respectable volume infolio (360x260 mm.) de 384 pages, alors qu'il suffisait de quelques minutes pour transcrire sur un simple feuillet le passage de saint Grégoire objet de la lettre? Et moins concevable encore que saint Thomas ait pris sur lui d'écrire sa réponse sur ce précieux manuscrit dès ce moment plus que trois fois centenaire: la graphie malhabile, encombrée de ratures, est un outrage à la belle bénéventine du x-xie s. des Morales.

Uccelli attribuait deux écritures à saint Thomas, l'une calligraphique l'autre tachygraphique — celle que nous appelons la *littera illegibilis*. C'était manifestement dans les fragments de la *Summa contra gentiles* en écriture calligraphique mêlés à l'*illegibilis* qu'il découvrait quelque ressemblance avec l'écriture de la lettre à l'abbé Bernard. Il y a un siècle le jugement d'Uccelli pouvait faire autorité et emporter l'assentiment de Dom Tosti; il n'en est plus de même aujourd'hui. Nous ne pouvons attribuer avec certitude qu'une seule écriture à saint Thomas, la *littera illegibilis*; s'il a pratiqué également une écriture calligraphique, chose fort peu vraisemblable, nous ne la connaissons

S. Tommaso d'Aquino e Montecassino (l.c.), Documenta, tavole V-VII, texte revu sur le manuscrit; c'est la meilleure édition parue jusqu'à ce jour.—Traductions italiennes: 1) V. Ingletti, l.c.—2) R. Bonanni, *Uomini illustri di Aquino e Diocesi...* (Alatri 1923) 47-50, traduction par A. D'Amico.

4 **Doutes divers:** J. Didiot, *Le docteur angélique S. Thomas d'Aquin* (Tournai 1894) 88-91. Il date la lettre de 1269, d'ailleurs sans aucune justification. Il envisage la possibilité d'une copie dans le manuscrit à partir de l'original, mais s'en rapporte au jugement d'Uccelli pour admettre qu'il s'agit d'un autographe (p. 91 n. 1).—J. A. Endres, *Thomas von Aquin* (Mainz 1910) 105 n. 5, déclare qu'il tentera de démontrer ailleurs l'inauthenticité de la lettre: "Was den Brief des hl. Thomas an Abt Bernhard Ayglerius von Montecassino betrifft, so werde ich an anderer Stelle den Nachweis versuchen, dass er auf Echtheit keinen Anspruch erheben kann."—F. Scandone, "La vita..." (cf. n. 3) 31-32 et notes afférentes. Pour cet auteur, la lettre doit être traitée comme une fausse perle.—Nous verrons dans un instant la pensée du P. Mandonnet.—M. Inguanez, *Codicum Casinensium Manuscriptorum Catalogus* I, pars 1 (Montis Casini 1915) 86. Décrivant le codex 82 contenant les livres XI-XVI des Morales de saint Grégoire, Inguanez écrivait: "In marginibus pag. 320-322 legitur *Epistola* S. Thomae Aquinatis propria manu scripta ad Bernardum abbatem Casinensem."—M. Grabmann, l.c., 441-443.

pas. Les fragments calligraphiés dans l'autographe de la *Summa contra gentiles* sont de la main de Réginald de Piperno. [5]

La conviction du Père Mandonnet n'était pas motivée par une comparaison avec un étalon illusoire et, loin de s'atténuer avec le temps, elle s'est affermie de plus en plus; elle demande à être pesée avec attention.

En 1910, dans un ouvrage justement célèbre, après avoir reconnu qu'une comparaison avec l'écriture de saint Thomas était difficile, Mandonnet écrivait:

> Je suis porté à croire cependant que la lettre à l'abbé Bernard est de la main de saint Thomas. Si un scribe avait transporté sur les marges des *Morales* de saint Grégoire une copie de la lettre de saint Thomas d'Aquin, il l'eut fait avec plus de soin. Il semble bien que nous sommes ici en présence d'une écriture d'auteur. Les passages soulignés de traits irréguliers et peu sûrs, ceux dont l'encre a blanchi parce que l'écrivain n'a pas pris garde que sa plume n'avait pas assez d'encre, et quelques autres particularités indiquent une écriture d'autographe. [6]

Plus tard, après avoir vu de ses propres yeux le manuscrit au Montcassin (en revenant de Naples, en 1914), le P. Mandonnet corrigea sur un exemplaire personnel de son ouvrage les expressions dubitatives du passage qu'on vient de lire:

> Il n'y a pas de doute cependant que la lettre à l'abbé Bernard soit de la main de saint Thomas. Si un scribe avait transporté sur les marges des *Morales* de saint Grégoire une copie de la lettre de saint Thomas d'Aquin, il l'eut fait avec plus de soin. Nous sommes bien ici en présence d'une écriture d'auteur. Les passages soulignés de traits irréguliers et peu sûrs, ceux dont l'encre a blanchi parce que l'écrivain n'a pas pris garde que sa plume n'avait pas assez d'encre, et surtout le fait que bon nombre de mots ont été grattés et la place recouverte par la même écriture, ainsi que je l'ai constaté moi-même sur le manuscrit, et que l'a noté très en détail Caplet en rééditant cette lettre, indiquent une écriture autographe.

Cette conviction, le P. Mandonnet l'a affirmée encore en 1929, dans une note sur les autographes de saint Thomas:

> Quelques jours après avoir consulté le ms. de Naples j'examinai aussi au Mont-Cassin le volume des Morales de saint Grégoire qui porte en marge

---

5 L'identification de la main de Réginald de Piperno a été faite par M. G. Ouy, "Compte-rendu de 'Secrétaires de Saint Thomas', Addendum," *Bibliothèque de l'Ecole des Chartes* 116 (1958) 248-249. Sur l'activité de Réginald comme secrétaire de saint Thomas, nous renvoyons le lecteur à notre étude: "Sermons de Réginald de Piperno," *Mélanges Eugène Tisserant* VI (Biblioteca Vaticana 1964) 363-368.

6 P. Mandonnet, *Des écrits authentiques de saint Thomas d'Aquin*, 2ᵉ éd. (Fribourg 1910) 120-121; 1ʳᵉ éd. Extrait de la *Revue Thomiste* 1909-1910 (Fribourg 1910) 107. Nous citerons la 2ᵉ éd., revue et corrigée.

la lettre de saint Thomas d'Aquin à l'abbé Bernard Ayglier et qui fut jadis éditée par Dom Tosti comme autographe. Je n'avais pas émis de doute à cet égard; mais je suis encore plus rassuré aujourd'hui. Les conditions de l'écriture de la lettre me paraissent exclure toute autre main que celle de son auteur. Nous n'avons pas affaire à une écriture de scribe, c'est-à-dire de copiste. Les surcharges et les ratures de mots ne peuvent être que l'œuvre de saint Thomas, et Dom Caplet les a très soigneusement notées.[7]

Les motifs allégués en ces déclarations à l'appui d'un autographe d'auteur sont beaucoup plus pressants entendus d'une copie. Si l'auteur de la transcription a eu sous les yeux un modèle pour lui difficile à lire, il aura plus sûrement maculé son ouvrage de tous les incidents qu'il présente que ne l'aurait fait, même hésitant sur sa rédaction, l'auteur du texte. Les traits irréguliers et peu sûrs dont il est parlé devaient souligner des citations du texte de saint Grégoire incluses dans la lettre; qu'un copiste se soit trompé et sur leur étendue et sur leur place exacte est des plus vraisemblable; l'erreur le serait moins de la part de l'auteur du texte.[8] Le défaut d'encre sur la plume s'explique fort bien d'un scribe aux prises avec les difficultés de son modèle; de même les ratures, reprises et surcharges: c'est beaucoup trop dire qu'elles "ne peuvent être que l'œuvre de saint Thomas".

Pour refuser de voir dans la lettre un autographe, Grabmann alléguait en premier lieu la différence de l'écriture avec celle des autographes de saint Thomas que nous connaissons: c'est là un argument solide. En second lieu il mettait en avant la présence de l'avertissement précédant la lettre: "quod est extra non scribatis". Cette mise en garde, à l'adresse d'un copiste qui devait transcrire les Morales en prenant le manuscrit pour modèle, n'est pas absolument contemporaine de l'inscription de la

---

7 P. Mandonnet, "A propos des Autographes de saint Thomas d'Aquin," *Bulletin Thomiste* VI (1929) 523. Dans l'édition 7, publiée sous le nom du P. Mandonnet, le texte de la lettre est précédé d'une introduction (p. 249 n. 1) tirée à la lettre (il y a une omission) de l'éd. 3, p. 834 note a, où l'auteur (Fretté?) met en doute la qualité autographe du texte inscrit dans les marges du manuscrit du Montcassin. Telle quelle dans l'édition 7, cette introduction a fait hésiter Grabmann sur la pensée de Mandonnet (*Die Werke...*, 442 n. 368); elle a trompé R. A. Verardo (éd. 9, pp. 245-246) qui la croit expression d'une étape intermédiaire dans cette même pensée: l'examen du manuscrit aurait finalement convaincu Mandonnet et ramené à sa première position. Il aurait suffi de comparer les dates et de l'examen en question (en 1914) et de l'édition 7 (1927) pour mettre en garde sur l'interprétation proposée.

8 Un cas particulier mérite d'être relevé. Le texte controversé de saint Grégoire (*Morales* XVI) est cité deux fois, d'abord intégralement (lignes 23-26), puis en partie et par fragments séparés et soulignés d'un trait de plume. Or le premier de ces fragments fut d'abord souligné non pas en son lieu (28-29) mais dans l'énoncé intégral (24-25). Une telle erreur n'est pas imputable à l'auteur de la lettre qui ne peut hésiter sur sa composition, mais bien à un copiste trop peu attentif au sens de ce qu'il transcrit. Par la suite ce copiste — ou bien quelqu'un d'autre — répara la faute en effaçant au grattoir le trait inscrit sous le premier énoncé. Cette nouvelle intervention abima plusieurs lettres, notamment les hastes basses de p et q; les réparations postérieures sont dénoncées par le fait que ces hastes sont sur le grattage.

lettre; elle ne prouve donc rien contre la qualité autographe de celle-ci. Enfin Grabmann appuyait son refus sur la différence de la couleur de l'encre de certains mots; ceux que Mandonnet attribuait au défaut d'encre sur la plume, il les dits inscrits en second temps. Le copiste, ne sachant d'abord les lire, aurait laissé des espaces vides sur le parchemin; par la suite, après une étude plus attentive du modèle, lui-même — ou quelqu'un d'autre — les aurait déchiffrés et transcrits en leur lieu avec cette encre plus pâle. Ces mots, dit Grabmann, sont écrits d'une manière plus large, pour bien remplir un espace d'abord laissé vide, et il cite en exemple quelques cas particuliers: *officii, vita, ge* dans *gestum*.[9] Cette argumentation, croyons-nous, se fonde davantage sur l'examen des planches photographiques de l'édition de 1875 que sur une étude immédiate du manuscrit 82. Ces planches étaient remarquables à bien des égards; elles trahissent toutefois l'original sous le rapport des couleurs. Il nous paraît certain que les fragments et mots isolés à l'encre pâle appartiennent eux-aussi au premier temps de l'inscription; l'examen attentif du manuscrit ne prête guère à une erreur sur ce point. L'explication par le défaut d'encre sur la plume est vraisemblable. Quant à l'observation que les mots en question seraient écrits de manière à remplir un espace vide, c'est là une illusion sans fondement dans la réalité; elle ne mérite pas que l'on s'y attarde.

Il y avait mieux que ces faits fragiles pour écarter l'hypothèse d'un autographe de saint Thomas, et nous sommes surpris que les deux grands spécialistes qu'étaient le P. Mandonnet et Mgr. Grabmann n'y aient pas prêté attention. L'un et l'autre ont observé le document de l'extérieur, sans l'explorer en lui-même. Il suffira de produire trois arguments pour procurer une conviction de caractère critique.

Le premier sera pris d'une forme orthographique particulière. La consonne *s* redoublée est plusieurs fois remplacée par la lettre *x*.

necessitati[28]	*est écrit*	nec$\overline{x}$itati
expresse[28]	... .	exp$\overline{x}$e
necessitate[30]	... .	ne$\overline{x}$itate
potuisse[35]	... .	potuixe
successive[40]	... .	succexiue
successionem[42]	... .	succexion$\overline{e}$

---

9 M. Grabmann, *Die Werke*..., 442-443. Les trois exemples cités sont sur les lignes 9, 26 et 14 selon le manuscrit (éd. ci-après pp. 102-103). Par la suite toutes nos références au texte de la lettre renverront à ces lignes.

Un cas unique d'une telle substitution a pu être repéré dans la totalité des textes écrits de la main de saint Thomas parvenus jusqu'à nous; la fréquence d'une telle forme ici interdit de voir dans la lettre un autographe du même auteur.

Voici maintenant une anomalie. Dans le cours de la lettre nous lisons:

> Vt autem dubitantibus plenius satisfiat, inserenda sunt presentibus uerba beati gregorii que ignorantibus dubitationem ingerunt et errorem (19-23),

après quoi suit tout le passage intéressé (23-26). Si le document est un autographe, il faudrait justifier comment l'insertion du texte des Morales dans la marge du manuscrit pouvait en procurer une meilleure intelligence, et apaiser les religieux troublés davantage que celui inscrit tout à côté, en sa place normale, dans les colonnes 320b et 321a, en grands et beaux caractères. Pourquoi le répéter? Par contre, si la réponse était originairement un document isolé, individuel (cf. presentibus 21) et sans relation au manuscrit 82 plutôt qu'à un autre, il était naturel, disons même exigé, que saint Thomas y insère le fragment d'autorité divisant la communauté du Montcassin; le commentaire qu'il allait en proposer appelait cette présence.

Troisième argument. Le texte des Morales cité par saint Thomas n'est pas le même que celui du manuscrit 82 et appartient à une autre tradition; par conséquent il dépend d'une autre source que celle-là. Au cours de la lettre le passage disputé de saint Grégoire est cité à deux reprises, une première fois intégralement — lignes 23-26 "Sciendum...subtraxit" —, la seconde fois en partie seulement et en trois fragments séparés, selon la trame du commentaire — lignes 28-29 "quia accepta...amictunt", 33-34 "quamvis...quo moritur", 36-37 "Nam... merebatur". La recension des Morales supposée par l'explication qu'en donne saint Thomas est bien assurée par ces répétitions.

Recueillons d'abord la leçon du manuscrit 82, témoin d'un texte du xe-xie siècles:

> Sciendum tamen quia benignitas dei est peccatoribus spacium poenitencie largiri, sed quia accepta tempora non ad fructum poenitencie sed ad usum iniquitatis vertunt quod a diuina misericordia mereri potuerunt amittunt. Quamuis omnipotens deus illud tempus unius cuiusque ad mor-
> 5 tem presciat quo eius uita terminatur. nec alio in tempore quisquam mori potuit nisi ipso quo moritur. Nam si ezechie anni additi ad uitam quindecim memorantur. tempus quidem uite creuit ab illo termino quo mori ipse merebatur. Nam diuina dispositio ex tempore illum mori presciuit quo hunc post modum ex presenti uita subtraxit (320b-321a).

D'autres témoins manuscrits confirment cette recension; par exemple Montecassino, codex 72, du XVe siècle, p. 290a; cod. 74, XIe s., p. 159b; cod. 79, XIe s., p. 194a.[10]

Parmi les variantes par rapport aux leçons de cette famille, les doubles citations de saint Thomas — nommons *Th* la citation intégrale, *Th'* les citations partielles — cinq sont garanties par *Th* et *Th'*; une sixième de *Th*, en un lieu où *Th'* fait défaut, est confirmée par les éditions imprimées des Morales. Il suffira de noter ici la première et la dernière de ces variantes:

> 2-3 sed ad usum *cod.* 82] ad usum uero Th 24 Th' 29
> 8 ex tempore illum mori *cod.* 82 eius tempus tunc Th 26 (*PL* 75, 1127).

Ces deux leçons elles aussi sont anciennes; nous pouvons les appuyer par les manuscrits Montecassino 86, xie s., p. 280b, et 87, xie s., p. 313a.[11] Le témoignage est suffisant pour prouver que saint Thomas n'avait pas sous les yeux le texte du manuscrit 82 dans le temps où il rédigeait sa réponse à l'abbé Bernard; par conséquent la lettre dans les marges du volume ne peut pas être un autographe.

Authenticité de la Lettre

Les médiévistes de notre temps qui se sont penchés sur la lettre à l'abbé Bernard Ayglier sont généralement d'accord pour en reconnaître l'authenticité.[12] Le refus d'Endres, il y a plus d'un demi siècle, n'a pas été justifié, du moins à notre connaissance; seul celui de Scandone, catégorique, fut appuyé de quelques motifs, d'ailleurs sommairement formulés:

Le document présente un saint Thomas moine bénédictin du Mont-cassin et non un frère prêcheur.

Dans le temps auquel il faut rattacher la lettre, Thomas n'était plus capable d'en être l'auteur; depuis deux mois il n'avait plus écrit ni dicté.

A supposer qu'il se soit arrêté un moment pour prendre quelque nourriture et se reposer sur le parcours Teano-Maenza, comment les moines du Montcassin auraient-ils connu son passage?

---

10   Ces volumes sont décrits par M. Inguanez, *Codicum Casinensium... Catalogus* I, 1: MS 72, p. 82; MS 74, p. 83; MS 79, p. 85.

11   M. Inguanez, loc. cit., MS 86, p. 88; MS 87, p. 89. Dans ce dernier témoin le texte primitif 'ad usum uero' fut corrigé plus tard en 'sed ad usum'.

12   Cependant le P. A. Walz hésite à se prononcer, *San Tommaso d'Aquino* (Roma 1945) 183 — Adaptation française par P. Novarina, *Saint Thomas d'Aquin*, Philosophes médiévaux V (Louvain-Paris 1962) 194-195: "La lettre que nous possédons est peut-être authentique, mais non autographe."

Si le maître s'était senti la force d'écrire, aurait-il accusé la longueur de l'office divin et la durée du jeûne — lui, un saint! — et non son propre épuisement?

La comparaison du document avec les autographes manifestera sa fausseté de manière irréfragable. [13]

Ce dernier motif doit être récusé sans plus; s'il vaut pour nier la qualité autographe de la lettre, il est absolument inefficace au regard de l'authenticité. Le premier n'a guère plus de valeur: ces expressions de révérence et de soumission n'ont nullement la signification que leur attribue Scandone; elles étaient requises de la part du dominicain s'adressant au grand dignitaire ecclésiastique qu'était l'abbé du Montcassin. Saint Thomas ne pouvait avoir oublié sa première formation bénédictine; les formules de respect qu'il avait apprises jeune oblat lui étaient familières; elles traduisent ses sentiments de religieuse déférence, rien de plus. D'ailleurs, il pourrait se faire qu'il se soit introduit dans la copie des expressions plus accentuées que dans l'original. Le scribe qui a inscrit le texte dans les marges du manuscrit était sans doute moine du Montcassin; il a pu sans y prendre garde modifier les formules dans un sens qui lui était plus coutumier, comme Tosti a suppléé un (*nostri*) entre *Patris* et *Benedicti* alors qu'une correction sur le parchemin interdit un tel supplément. [14]

L'affirmation que saint Thomas n'était plus capable d'écrire au temps de la lettre dépasse, estimons-nous, le donné de la source qu'elle sup-

---

13   F. Scandone, *La vita...*, écrivait: "E facile, intanto, giudicare se, in quelle condizioni di mente e di salute, il santo dottore, proprio durante il viaggio, passando per Aquino (nessuna testimonianza, proprio nessuna, attesta ch'egli vi si sia mai fermato) avesse pensato ad inviare una lettera, autografa per giunta, all'abbate di Montecassino, Bernardo Ayglerio. La critica storica impone dei penosi doveri. Debbo additare come una perla falsa questo documento cassinese: sceverandolo dai veri, questi avranno maggior valore. Avrebbe potuto scrivere lui, che da due mesi non aveva scritto più nulla, e nemmeno dettato? E, nella brevissima sosta — (in cui avrebbe potuto prendere un po' di cibo e di riposo, mentre percorreva la via da Teano a Magenza) — in qual modo i frati avrebbero saputo del suo passaggio? E se anche il dottore si fosse sentita la forza di scrivere, perchè avrebbe accennato alla "prolixitas divini officii" (lui, un santo!), e alla "ieiunii prolungatio" (ma, non si trattava di digiuno meritorio, se dipendeva dalla malattia!), e non alla sua stremata salute? E una fortuna che i falsari non si diano la cura di ricercare minutamente il vero, cosa troppo lontana dalle loro mire, come dalle loro abitudini. L'esame comparativo degli autografi proverà l'assunto in modo irrefragabile" (pp. 31-32). — Et en note (32 n. 1), citant le début de la lettre, Scandone ajoutait: "Riferiamo le prime parole della lettera, che ci vorrebbe presentare un s. Tommaso, non già domenicano, ma benedettino, e cassinese. Ne giudichi il lettore: "Rev. do in Christo patri d. Bernardo, dei gratia ven. Abb. Casinensi, Frater Thomas de Aquino suus devotus filius [dunque, cassinese, non già "Ordinis praedicatorum"] se semper et ubique ad obedientiam promptum. [Ed eccone la conferma. "Pronto alla ubbidienza!". Ma se era il superiore di un Ordine, diverso dal suo!].

14   Texte de la lettre ligne 16. Avec raison Dom Leccisotti a éliminé cette addition non justifiée; il estime qu'elle avait dû être écrite primitivement, puis annulée par rasure du parchemin. Le fait même d'une telle annulation ancienne interdirait sa restitution.

pose, à savoir la déposition de Barthélemy de Capoue au Procès de Naples. Quand le Logothète — informé par les confidences de Réginald de Piperno parvenues jusqu'à lui — déclare que frère Thomas, à la suite d'une sorte d'extase mystique, s'était dit incapable de poursuivre ses travaux, et que de fait il avait cessé d'écrire ou de dicter, le témoignage concerne l'activité professorale et magistrale du saint, ses grandes œuvres, telles la *Somme théologique* interrompue au cours de la IIIe *Pars*, l'explication des Psaumes, les commentaires philosophiques (*De generatione*), il ne se rapporte pas, cela paraît évident, à des écrits mineurs comme une lettre privée. Le saint avait été éclairé par une lumière surnaturelle sur la fragilité de la spéculation humaine; tous ses grands ouvrages lui paraissent maintenant sans plus de valeur que la paille auprès de ce qu'il a compris, et il en demeure totalement absorbé, envahi par le souvenir de sa vision. Il ne s'agit pas d'une diminution de ses aptitudes, d'aliénation mentale comme ose l'écrire Scandone — "Sembrava un intontimento, da far pensare ad una alienazione mentale" (*La vita...*, 30) — mais d'une concentration intérieure qui le rend comme étranger aux choses sensibles. Si dès ce moment il avait été aussi gravement atteint qu'on le suppose, au point qu'il n'ait pu remplir ce léger devoir que la déférence et l'amitié lui imposaient envers l'abbé du Montcassin, se serait-il mis en route pour le long et rude voyage qui devait le conduire à Lyon? C'est seulement au château de Maenza, chez sa nièce, qu'il tombera malade,[15] et cette maladie elle-même ne paraît pas avoir atteint chez lui les facultés intellectuelles; sur son lit de mort,

---

15 Ce fait est bien attesté par le *Procès de Naples*. L'abbé de Fossanova, Nicolas, dépose devant les enquêteurs que "...dum dictus frater Thomas...infirmatus fuit in castro Magentie..., et cum infirmitate ipsa gravaretur, dixit..."Si Dominus voluerit me visitare, melius est quod reperiar in domo religiosorum quam in domibus secularium'. Et ex tunc...", *Fontes vitae sancti Thomae Aquinatis*...éd. D. Prümmer-H. M. Laurent (Toulouse 1911-ss) 276-277; éd. A. Ferrua, *S. Thomae Aquinatis vitae fontes praecipuae* (Alba 1968) 213. — Dans les citations suivantes nous référerons à ces deux éditions sous l'intitulé sommaire *Fontes vitae* et la désignation des pages, premier chiffre pour l'édition Prümmer - Laurent, chiffre entre ( ) pour l'édition Ferrua.— Fr. Octavien *de Babuco*, religieux de Fossanova, "dixit etiam quod ipse vidit ipsum fratrem Thomam venientem de castro Magentie in quo fuerat infirmatus...", *Fontes vitae* 286 (233). — Fr. Pierre de Mont Saint Jean, du même monastère, "Dixit etiam quod dum dictus frater Thomas iret ad concilium Lugduni...et faceret transitum per castrum Magentie, Terracinensis diocesis, et ibi per aliquos dies moram traheret pro eo quod erat aliquantulum discrasiatus...ivit ad visitandum dictum fratrem Thomam ad dictum castrum Magentie". — "...dictus frater Thomas dum viveret et esset in dicto castro Magentie et cepisset aliquantulum infirmari...", Ibid. 330-331 (272); 333 (274). — Barthélemy de Capoue, après avoir dit que saint Thomas se mit en route pour le concile, poursuit: "Et in itinere invasit ipsum infirmitas in castro Magentie de Campania, de qua postmodum decessit". — "Item dixit dictus testis quod quando idem frater Thomas incepit gravari infirmitate in eodem castro Magentie, petiit cum multa devotione quod portaretur ad monasterium sancte Marie de Fossanova, sicque factum est", Ibid. 377-378 (320). — Enfin témoignage de Ptolémée de Lucques: "...frater Thomas de Aquino...cum iter arripiens de Neapoli venisset apud Cicanum in Campania, ibi egritudo graviter ipsum arripuit." *Annales Lucennes*, anno 1274. — Cf. *Fontes vitae* (372).

à Fossanova, il expliquera encore le Cantique des Cantiques aux moines avides de l'entendre.[16]

Le refus de Scandone qu'un saint ait pu formuler les motifs d'excuse que l'auteur de la lettre allégue pour ne pas monter à l'abbaye — la prolixité de l'office divin et le jeûne, — prouve simplement que son auteur estimait fort mal le poids réel de cet office dans les monastères médiévaux, et de même celui du jeûne, lequel ne pouvait être rompu avant 15 heures. A monter au Montcassin, saint Thomas s'exposait à ne pas trouver libre pour l'entendre la communauté des religieux, et dans ce cas il aurait dû prolonger son arrêt, contrairement aux obligations de son voyage.

Reste l'impossibilité que le Montcassin ait été informé d'un arrêt momentané de saint Thomas au cours du trajet Teano-Maenza. Si en effet les voyageurs suivaient la voie maritime (Via Appia), celle-ci les aurait entraînés fort loin du monastère, lequel est situé à l'Est de la vallée du Liri; si au contraire ils faisaient route par la Campanie (Via Latina), leur passage au pied du Montcassin ne pouvait passer inaperçu et la démarche de l'abbé Bernard devient fort vraisemblable: son message aura atteint saint Thomas deux lieues plus loin, à Aquino. La difficulté soulevée par Scandone suppose le premier itinéraire; l'hypothèse est-elle fondée?

L'un des meilleurs connaisseurs actuels de la vie de saint Thomas, le P. A. Walz, le pense, parce que la bulle de canonisation dit expressément: Thomas "...de Neapoli veniens, ubi tunc temporis more solito famose legebat ut doctor, et *per maritimam transiens*, cum ad monasterium Fossenove...pervenisset...".[17] C'est accorder trop à un tel document de le citer à la barre pour attester un fait comme celui qui nous intéresse. La bulle appartient à un genre littéraire particulier qui n'exige pas une parfaite précision en ce domaine. Aussi bien son rédacteur ne fait aucune allusion à la halte de saint Thomas à Maenza, chez sa nièce la comtesse de Ceccano; il prépare simplement la citation du psaume 131 que le malade prononça lors de son arrivée à l'abbaye de Fossanova "Haec requies mea in saeculum saeculi...". Prenant le saint à Naples, il le conduit au. terme de son voyage par la route commune, sans ce soucier du détail des faits. La contradiction qui existe ici entre ce document et d'autres témoignages contemporains doit être résolue dans le sens de ceux-ci, précisément parce qu'ils déposent sur des faits

---

16 Guillelmus de Tocco, *Historia beati Thomae de Aquino* cp. 57, *Fontes vitae* 131 (107).
17 A. Walz, *San Tommaso...* (Adaptation Novarina) 194: "... la bulle de canonisation indique formellement la route du littoral". Bulle, *Fontes vitae* 522. Cf. A. Walz, *Bulla canonisationis S. Thomae Aquinatis...*, Xenia thomistica (Romae 1925) 179. C'est nous qui soulignons en texte *per maritimam transiens*.

particuliers, tandis que l'auteur de la bulle brosse l'histoire à grands traits, pour l'édification.

Sur le triple témoignage de Tosti, Uccelli et Inguanez proclamant la lettre autographe dans le manuscrit du Montcassin, A. Toso admet que saint Thomas se soit rendu à Aquino — on ne précise pas le moment; sans doute au temps de son séjour chez sa nièce —; il tient toutefois pour plus assuré le voyage par la route maritime et le littoral du Lazio qui était moins longue entre Teano et Maenza que celle par la Campanie.[18] Une telle raison étonne, parce que les deux voies étaient sensiblement égales, avec même un avantage non négligeable par la vallée du Liri. Certes les routes modernes peuvent abréger quelque peu, mais nous avons le témoignage de Barthélemy de Capoue qu'au moyen âge celle par la Campanie était la plus directe. Quand il se rendait à la Curie romaine pour traiter des affaires royales, il faisait le détour par Fossanova, par dévotion pour la tombe de frère Thomas, et "dimissa via Campanie breviori, ibat ad maritimam et hospitabatur in eodem monasterio".[19]

Il existe des témoignages formels que saint Thomas suivit la route de Campanie. Voici celui de Nicolas, abbé de Fossanova, déposant sous serment au Procès de Naples: "...dum dictus frater Thomas vocatus iret ad concilium Lugdunense et transitum faceret per Campaniam, infirmatus fuit in castro Magentie...".[20] Barthélemy de Capoue, lié par le même serment, précise incidemment la route suivie par saint Thomas: "Et dum ipse frater Thomas esset in via eundi ad concilium Lugduni..., descendens de civitate Theani per viam Burgi Novi percussit caput in quadam arbore que ceciderat per transversum...".[21] Une telle information suffirait à nous éclairer. Si les voyageurs ont laissé Teano en se dirigeant vers Borgo Nuovo, ils tournaient le dos à Minturno et la voie maritime; par conséquent ils s'engageaient sur la route de la vallée du Liri et Aquino.[22] Un tel itinéraire est confirmé par Guillaume de

---

18 A. Toso, *Tommaso d'Aquino e il suo tempo* (Roma 1941) 124-125, 171: "...perchè, se fosse passato da Aquino per andare poi a Maenza, avrebbe allungato notevolmente il suo cammino già così gravoso a dorso di mulo" (124). "Dopo Teano proseguendo per la *Marittima*, cioè la regione litoranea del Lazio, si fermo a Maenza presso sua nipote Francesca" (170).

19 *Fontes vitae* 379-380 (321-322).

20 Ibid. 276-277 (213).

21 Ibid. 375 (317).

22 Cette donnée précise paraît avoir échappé à Toso, *Tommaso d'Aquino...*, 170. — A. Walz, *San Tommaso...* (Adaptation Novarina) 192, ne l'ignore pas mais ne l'utilise pas comme élément déterminant de la question. — Scandone, lorqu'il écrivait "movendo da Teano verso il Lazio" (*La vita...*, l. c. 31 et n. 2) l'interprétait à rebours. Malgré les grands mérites de cette fort belle étude qu'est *La vita, la famiglia...di S. Tommaso De Aquino*, il faut la lire la plume à la main pour annoter ses erreurs. Citons un exemple: saint Thomas passa les fêtes de Noël 1272 à Molaria, chez son ami le cardinal de Saint Ange, Richard *degli Annibaldeschi*, — *Fontes vitae, Historia...* 96 (65). — Scandone, *La vita* 27 et n. 3, dit qu'en retournant à Naples, le saint s'arrêta à Fossanova

Tocco dans l'*Historia beati Thomae*: "Post hec cum predictus doctor iret ad concilium Lugduni celebrandum..., contingit autem ipsum transire per Campaniam et ad castrum Magentie quod erat domine Francisce neptis sue, debilem declinare...".[23]

Si la santé de saint Thomas était déjà ébranlée, au coeur de l'hiver, — on était à la fin de janvier ou dans les premiers jours de février — cette route de Campanie lui offrait l'avantage d'être moins exposée et moins insalubre que la voie par les marais Pontins. Et s'il avait le pressentiment de sa fin prochaine, nous consentirons sans peine au motif plusieurs fois mis en avant par ses historiens, qu'il voulut revoir les siens, le lieu de sa naissance et de ses premières années.[24]

Nous nous faisons trop souvent l'image d'un maître Thomas isolé dans un monde supérieur, tout absorbé par sa vie spéculative et contemplative, ses luttes scolaires; le portrait n'est pas complet. Le saint savait se dépenser activement, payer de sa personne pour ses amis et ses proches. Citons quelques faits des dernières années de sa vie.

Quittant Rome pour Naples vers la fin de l'été de 1272, il visite son ami le cardinal de Saint Ange, Richard *degli Annibaldeschi,* au château de Molaria, non loin de Rome. Réginald de Piperno qui l'accompagne, tombe gravement malade; il est guéri par l'imposition d'une relique de sainte Agnès que Thomas porte sur lui. En mémoire de cet événement, le saint fera une fondation au couvent de Naples pour procurer une réfection annuelle aux membres de la communauté.[25] Roger d'Aquila, comte de Traiecto et Fondi, époux d'Adelesia soeur du saint, était décédé le 26 août; Thomas fut nommé exécuteur testamentaire. Le 20 septembre, il est au château du défunt à Traiecto (Minturno); le 27, il est à Capoue, pour traiter avec les fonctionnaires de la curie royale, en faveur de son neveu, fils de Roger et nouveau comte de Fondi.[26] A

pour s'y reposer: "Ritornando, si trattenne, per riposarsi, nel monastero di Fossanova. Cf. Da Tocco, § 31, p. 670, e si aggiunge 'lectiones ubi dimiserat, cum esset Lector Neapoli, resumpsit'..." Or ce dernier texte ne concerne pas saint Thomas mais bien Réginald, lequel, après les obsèques du saint à Fossanova rentra à Naples et y reprit ses leçons: "Quod ex ore predicti fratris Raynaldi socii eius est habitum, qui, quod de ipso viderat, servavit in dicti doctoris vita secretum. Retulit autem predictus socius post prefati magistri obitum, quod cum de monasterio Fossenove redisset, et lectiones, ubi dimiserat, cum esset lector Neapoli, resumpsisset, cum ingenti fletu dixit: "Fratres, ego fui a magistro meo in vita sua prohibitus, ne miranda, que de ipso videram revelarem...", G. de Tocco, *Historia..., Fontes vitae* 104-105 (75).

23 *Fontes vitae, Historia...,* 129 (104). Ptolémée de Lucques doit évidemment être entendu dans le même sens lorqu'il écrit: "(Thomas de Aquino)...cum iter arripiens de Neapoli venisset apud Cicanum in Campania, ibi egritudo graviter ipsum arripit" (cf. supra, n. 15). Ceccano évoque la via Latina et non la via Appia.

24 Cf. A. Toso, *Tommaso d'Aquino...,* 125.

25 *Fontes vitae, Historia...,* 123-124 (98); *Procès de Naples,* ibid. 348 (290); Ptolémée de Lucques, *Historia ecclesiastica nova* XXIII, c. 10; *Fontes vitae* (363).

26 Cf. Scandone, *La vita...,* 22-26; *Fontes vitae* 374 (316).

Noël, il est de nouveau à Molaria, invité par le cardinal pour disputer avec deux juifs de ses amis; ceux-ci convaincus par le saint se font baptiser.[27] Il visite plusieurs fois sa nièce Francesca comtesse de Ceccano, au château de Maenza, où il tombera malade[28]; Pierre de Mont-Saint-Jean, ancien abbé de Fossanova, l'a vu à Marisco — à 150 kilomètres de Naples — chez sa sœur Theodora, comtesse de Marisco, auprès de laquelle Réginald le conduit encore en décembre 1273, cette fois au château de San Severino.[29]

Il est bien naturel que ce vrai Thomas d'Aquin ait suivi la route de Campanie pour se rendre une fois encore à Maenza. Ceci étant, les informations contenue dans la lettre à l'abbé Bernard ne soulèvent pas de difficulté particulière. Les circonstances de son voyage ne lui permettant pas un arrêt prolongé, le saint donna par écrit les éclaircissements souhaités. Le fit-il d'Aquino où l'atteignit le messager venu de Montcassin, de Roccasecca, ou bien même de Maenza où il demeura au moins une semaine? Nous ne savons. Mais une telle incertitude importe peu; la cohérence du document avec la pensée du docteur angélique comme ses leçons propres du texte de saint Grégoire, non présentes dans le manuscrit supposé le modèle, sont le gage de son authenticité; un faussaire se serait gardé de cette dernière maladresse.

LE TEXTE DE LA LETTRE

Le texte de la lettre est abîmé dans l'unique manuscrit par lequel il est parvenu jusqu'à nous. Cet état est dû en partie à l'inhabileté du scribe mais aussi aux pertes que les marges ont subies au moment d'une reliure du volume; quarante sept lignes sur soixante trois ont été mutilées à leur début par le tranchet du relieur. Des conjectures sont nécessaires pour suppléer autant que possible à ces pertes et restaurer un sens vraisemblable au document.

Son premier éditeur, Dom Louis Tosti, s'est ingénié avec un rare bonheur à ce travail de restitution; il sera difficile de faire mieux. Plusieurs fois cependant nous proposerons des leçons différentes, notamment là où l'espace mutilé invitera à une conjecture plus longue ou plus brève[30]; ailleurs ce sera le sens général de la phrase, une in-

---

27 *Fontes vitae, Historia...*, 96 (65); *Procès de Naples,* ibid. 389-391 (331-332).
28 Octavien *de Babuco,* moine de Fossanova, dépose au Procès de Naples qu'il conversa avec frère Thomas "in castro Magentie, ad quod castrum plerumque veniebat ad visitandum quandam dominam consanguineam suam," *Fontes vitae* 286 (223).
29 Ibid. 330 (271); 377 (319).
30 L'étendue de la perte pour chacun des cas est en quelque manière dénoncée par les conjectures nécessaires au début des lignes voisines; d'une ligne à l'autre, les suppléances doivent être, plus au moins, de même longueur, compte tenu des abréviations communes de l'écriture médiévale. Voici un exemple: ligne 4 Dom Tosti a restitué *semper et*, et ligne 6 *fratribus*, mais il ne supplée rien au début de la ligne 5. N'est-il pas des plus vraisemblables que celle-ci a perdu quelque chose de son texte, comme les lignes voisines; elle appelle donc elle aussi un complément.

correction du style, une faute grammaticale qui suggérera une autre intervention. Il est clair que nos options seront présentées à titre de suggestions et l'apparat mettra sous les yeux du lecteur les suppléances de Tosti et de Dom Leccisotti que nous laisserons de côté.

De manière assez générale le déchiffrage du texte est ardu, parce que celui-ci est encombré d'incidents divers qui en troublent la trame. Les abréviations sont inaccoutumées et plus souvent encore les signes complémentaires qui doivent les expliciter sont instables; des mots sont coupés, estropiés — in iquitatis 25,[31] ...octaueram 5, tumor 41 — certaines lettres sont déformées de telle sorte qu'elles en suggérent d'autres — ici un d voulait d'abord être lu b — abditi pour additi 25 —, là q est écrit comme un p — pre pour que 57 —; des corrections maladroites, des surcharges, des rasures du parchemin, des espaces vides augmentent la confusion. Dom A. M. Caplet a noté en détail un grand nombre de ces incidents; sans être complet, l'apparat de son édition contient quarante notes critiques dénonçant des accidents variés.

Malgré ses mérites, ce relevé est difficilement exploitable sans le manuscrit devant les yeux; il peut même induire en erreur, car il n'est pas certain, il s'en faut, que toutes les rasures signalées aient fait disparaître de premières inscriptions. Quelques cas pourtant sont indubitables mais comme tels ils sont rares; un seul d'entre eux dénonce clairement un texte effacé[32] et toujours nous ignorons s'il s'agit de réels changements de rédaction ou d'accidents de copie. Le grand nombre de mots omis au cours de la transcription et inscrits dans les interlignes, les fautes élémentaires dénoncent les maladresses et l'impéritie d'un copiste aux prises avec un modèle trop difficile pour lui et réparées tant bien que mal à seconde lecture.

Pour proposer une édition valable du document, nous procéderons comme Tosti; d'abord une image aussi proche que possible de l'état du texte dans sa source; en second lieu un texte normalisé.

La première édition respectera les lignes du manuscrit. Cette disposition permettra de distinguer les suppléances nécessaires au début des lignes mutilées où elles seront imprimées en caractères italiques. Les mots inscrits dans les interlignes seront ici inclus entre crochets

---

31 Ici la leçon vraie est d'autant plus blessée que la haste de la lettre q a été effacée par un grattage faisant disparaitre un trait de plume qui soulignait à tort le texte de saint Grégoire (cf. ci-dessus. n. 8); la graphie actuelle suggère ʽin iatatisʼ.

32 Nous avons noté comme à peu près certains: satisfiat 20, accepta tempora 24, tunc 26, determinat 27, nulla (de nullatenus) 28, necessitatem incurrunt non *en partie* 31, q *et* uis *de* quamvis, o *de* omnipotens 33, dei scientia falleretur. <secundum> 35, est² 37, assunt sicut ipse moysi fa 44, cas non signalé par Caplet et peut-être le plus assuré, parce que des traces d'une inscription précédente demeurent visibles.

aigus < >, sans notations particulières dans l'apparat critique—sauf exceptions justifiées par un autre motif. Les traits inclinés ///// signale-ront les rasures du parchemin sans inscription postérieure au grattage; les espaces limités par les traits / / signifieront les lacunes dans les lignes. L'apparat critique appellera l'attention sur les faits non dénoncés par ces artifices et dignes de notation. Il affirmera également les fautes du copiste conservées ici—à ne pas confondre avec des er-reurs de typographie. Les témoins cités dans cet apparat seront: le ma-nuscrit Montecassino 82= M (pM et sM premier état et second état), édition 1 (Tosti) = T, éd. 5 (Caplet) = C, éd. 10 (Leccisotti) = L.

Texte du Manuscrit

*Reve*rendo in Christo patri domino Bernardo dei gratia
*vene*rabili abbati casinensi frater Thomas
*de a*quino suus deuotus filius se
fatetur ubique ad obedientiam promtum
5 *Pre*octaueram pater Venerande quod conuocatis
fratribus qui ex uerbis Illustris doctoris
*Gre*gorii scandalum patiuntur satis-
*fa*cerem viva uoce Set hoc proli-
*xi*tas diuini officii et jeiunii
10 *obli*gatio impediuit. et forte fructuo-
sum erit ut quod scripture mandatur non
*sol*um presentibus prodesse ualeat set
*et pos*teris. nec absque diuina dispen-
*sati*one hoc gestum credo ut me pro-
15 *fici*scentem in galliam vestre littere comprehen-
*dere*nt
*a*quino ubi sanctissimi patris /----/////////
*be*nedictini beatus Maurus eius discipulus
ab eo transmissus in galliam recipere meruit
*lic*teras et sacra exenia tanti patris. Vt
20 *autem* dubitantibus plenius satisfiat
inserenda sunt presentibus uerba beati
gregorii que ingnorantibus dubitationem

1   Christo] x° M
4   *fatetur*] *def.* M *semper et* T C L
     promptum M C| *fortasse e* promtus pM   dicit *add.* L
5   *Pre*octaueram| |octaueram M   octaueram C L   optaveram T
10 *obli*gatio] |gatio M   prolongatio T C L
13 *et pos*teris] |teris M   futuris T C
15 comprehenderent| *pars ultima* (*dere*nt) *in spatio interlineari, supra* aquino M
16 patris| *sequitur lacuna trium vel quatuor litterarum, deinde rasura* M   nostri *add.* T C
19 exenia sM| exenia pM
20 satisfiat| *pars ultima, scil.* tisfiat *sup. ras.* M
22 ingnorantibus M

ingerunt et errorem. Sciendum inquid "quod
*b*enignitas dei peccatoribus spatium penitentis largitur set quia
    accepta tempora non ad fructum penitetie ad usum <uero> iniquitatis
    conuertunt quod ad diuina misericordia.
25 mereri poterant amictunt quamuis omnipotens deus illud tempus unius-
    cuiusque ad mortem presciat quo uita eius terminatur nec <alio> in
    tempore quisquam mori potuit nisi quo <moritur> nam si ezechie
    anni additi
26 *ad* uitam quindecim memorantur tempus uite creuit /////// illo tepere quo
    mori ipse merebatur. nam diuina dispositio eius tempus tunc presciuit
    quo hunc postmodum ex presenti uita subtraxit". In quibus
27 *uer*bis satis lucide doctor lucifluus duplicem uniuscuiusque hominis con-
    siderationem habendam determinat. unam quidem secundum se. aliam
    uero secundum quod ad diuinam prescientiam comparatur. secundum
    se quidem
28 *homo* consideratus in his scilicet que circa eum accidunt necx̄itati non
    subiacet set possibile est aliqua circa ipsum contigere que nullatenus
    sortiuntur effectum quod exp̄xe premictit de peccatoribus dicens "quia
    accepta
29 *tem*pora non ad fructum penitentie ad usum uero iniquitatis ///// conuer-
    tunt quod a diuina misericordia mereri poterant amictunt". Si ergo
    mereri
30 *poterant* non ex nex̄itate amittunt. Vnde ea que contra hominem accidunt

24-41 *longis lineis*
24 penitentis M
24-25 quia...omnipotens: *sub his verbis Gregorii lineam ducit* pM *quam postea erasit* sM
    quia accepta *sup. ras.* M
    penitetie M
    iniquitatis *scrips.*] in iquitatis pM in iatatis (*e ras. hastae litt.* q—*cf. nota ad* 24-25 quia) sM
    ad³ M
25 amictunt sM] ammictunt pM
    <moritur> *hic scrips.*] *om.* pM *sup. lin. ante* ezechie sM
    additi sm] abditi pM
26 creuit: *sequitur rasura vacua septem vel octo litterarum* M
    tepere (*pro* tempore) M
    tunc *sup. ras.* M
27 lucifluus: *syllaba* ci *sup. ras.* M
    determinat *sup. ras.* M
    secundum² *sup. ras.* M
28 in his scilicet *sup. ras.* M
    necx̄itati M
    subiacet sM] subiaceant pM
    contigere M
    nullatenus] nulla *deinde brevis ras.* tenus M
    effectum] *pars ult.* um *sup. ras.* M
    exp̄xe M
28-29 quia accepta...amictunt: *sub his verbis Gregorii linea est ducta* M
29 iniquitatis: *sequitur ras. vacua sex vel septem litterarum* M
    a sM] ad (*cf. lin.* 24) pM
    amictunt sM] ammictunt (*cf. lin.* 25) pM
30 non ex nex̄itate amittunt *sup. ras.* M
    enim diuine] ...im diuine *sup. ras.* M

non ex ne <cessi>tate eueniunt, eadem enim ratio est de morte <et> de quibuscumque aliis que homo agit aut patitur. omnia enim diuine
31 prouidentie supponuntur. Si uero consideretur homo diuine prescientie comparatus ea que agit uel patitur quandam nece <ssitatem> incurrunt. <non> quidem absolutam ut omnino secundum se considerata non possint ut dictum est aliter euenire. <set> conditionalem (p. 321)
32 quia scilicet hec condicionalis est necessaria. si deus aliquid prescit hoc erit. Non enim possunt ista duo simul stare aliquid esse a deo prescitum <et> illud non esse quia sic dei prescientia falleretur. est autem omnino
33 impossibile ut falsitatem veritas patiatur, et hoc signant uerba sequentia beati gregorii cum subdit "quamuis omnipotens deus illud tempus unuscuiusque ad mortem presciat quo uita eius terminatur nec alio <in> tempore
34 quisquam mori poterat nisi ipso quo moritur". scilicet quo a deo prescitus est mori. non enim possunt ista duo simul esse quod <deus> presciat aliquem mori quodam tempore et ipse alio tempore
35 moriatur. alioquin dei scientia falleretur. <Secundum> se autem consideratus homo potuit alio tempore mori. quid enim dubitat eum potuixe prius trasfigi gladio
36 igne comburi aut precipicio aut laqueo vitam finire. Hanc et distinccionem sapiunt eius uerba sequentia subdit enim "Nam si ezechie
37 anni additi ad vitam XV^{cim} memorantur tempus vite creuit ab illo <tempore> quo mori ipse merebatur" stultum autem est dicere quod aliquis mereatur id quod impossibile est euenire. ipse ergo
38 secundum se consideratus poterat tempore illo <mori> set diuine scientie comparatus non poterant hec simul esse ut ipse uno tempore moreretur et alio tempore deus eum presciret moriturum
39 .... (linea recisa) (p. 322)

31 prouidentie| ...uitentie potius M
quandam...<non> | quandam nece sup. ras. <ssitatem> sup. lin. currunt sup. ras. <non> sup. lin. M
32 a deo| adeo M
<et> sup. lin. sM| valde confuse pM
non² ex emendatione sM| fort. uero pM
quia legi.| confuse M
33 impossibile legi.| im^{le} (le sup. ras.) M
33-34 quamuis...moritur: sub his verbis Gregorii linea est ducta M
quamuis omnipotens| uis o sup. ras. M
33 unuscuiusque M
34 poterat| potuit Gregorius T
a deo| adeo M
simul| in forma compendiata et imul sup. ras. M
35 dei...falleretur sup. ras. M
potuixe M
trasfigi M
36-37 Nam...merebatur: sub his verbis Gregorii linea est ducta M
37 <tempore> sup. lin. sM| illo pM
est² sup. ras. M
38 moriturum| et add. T C L ante trans. ad pag.
39 linea recisa

40 doctoris exprimiunt quasi oculata fide dubitantium animis ingeramus. considerare oportet differentiam diuine cognitionis et humane <quia>
enim homo subiacet mutationi et tempori in quo prius et posterius
locum habent succexiue

41 cognoscit res quedam prius et quedam posterius et inde est quod preterita
memoramur. videmus presentia et prenosticamur futura. Set deus sicut
liber est ab omni motu secundum illud malachie "Ego dominus et non
tumor". ita omnem temporis

42 succexionē excedit nec in eo inuenitur preteritum
nec futurum set presentialiter omnia futura et
*pre*terita ei assunt sicut ipse moysi famulo

45 *suo* dicit "ego sum qui sum". Eo ergo modo
ab eterno presciuit hunc tali tempore moriturum
si modo nostro loquimur cum tamen eius modo dicendum
*esse*t videt eum mori quomodo ego
*vide*o petrum sedere cum sedet. Mani-

50 *fes*tum est autem quod ex hoc quod video aliquem
*sede*re nullam ingeritur ei necessitas sessionis
*I*mpossibile est hec duo simul esse vera. quod
ego uideam aliquem sedentem et ipse non
*sede*at. et similiter non est possibile quod deus presciat

55 *ali*quid esse futurum et illud non sit
*nec tam*en propter hoc futura ex necessitate
*eve*niunt. Hec sunt pater karissime pre vestre
*petiti*oni obediens ad errantium reductionem
scripsi. que si eis non sufficiunt

60 *ista* rescribere uobis obediens non
*des*inam Valeat paternitas
vestra diu. Frater Raynaldus
*com*mendat se uobis.

40   exprimiunt M
     differentiam| bifferentiam *potius (cf. nota ad additi* 25) M
     <quia>| quod *ut videtur* pM
41   quedam...quedam (*scil. neutr. plural., saepe apud Thomam*) M
     illud sM| id pM
     tumor M
42   inuenitur *scrips. cum* Ł| T ūetē M   inveniuntur T C
43   *nec| def.* M   et T C L
     present aliter M
44   assunt...famulo| assunt...fam *sup. ras.* sM   *illegibilis* pM
47   *si| def.* M   ut T L   ... C
     cum tamen: *conf.* (*potius* tum tum) M
     dicendum| dicen dum M
48   esset| |t M   ...t C
49   cum sM| dum pM T C L
51   nullam M| nullum *cum nota* C
53   ego| *def.* M   *om.* T C L (*cf. lin.* 48 *in fine et princ. lin.* 52 *et* 54)
56   *nec tamen*| |en M   Non tamen T L   ...en C
57   karissime M| Reverendissime C
     pre M et (*cum nota*) C| que *cett.*
58   *petiti*oni| |oni M   iussioni T C L
60   ista| |ta M   dicta T L   ita C

Texte Normalisé

L'apparat de ce texte aura pour fonction d'informer le lecteur sur la valeur respective des éditions antérieures. Toutefois, pour ne pas l'encombrer sans profit, nous ne nommerons que les éditions principales et les plus courantes: à savoir 1 Tosti = T, 3 Vivès (Fretté) = F, 7 Mandonnet = Ma, 9 Verardo = V, 10 Leccisotti = L. S'il y a lieu, la leçon de la source sera mise en parallèle = M et en exposant, le numéro de la ligne du manuscrit.

Reverendo in Christo patri domino Bernardo, Dei gratia venerabili abbati Casinensi, frater Thomas de Aquino suus devotus filius se fatetur ubique ad oboedientiam promptum. Praeoptaveram, pater venerande, quod convocatis fratribus qui ex verbis illustris doctoris Gregorii scandalum
5 patiuntur satisfacerem viva voce, sed hoc prolixitas divini officii et ieiunii obligatio impedivit; et forte fructuosum erit, ut quod scripturae mandatur non solum praesentibus prodesse valeat sed et posteris. Nec absque divina dispensatione hoc gestum credo, ut me proficiscentem in Galliam, vestrae litterae comprehenderent Aquino, ubi sanctissimi patris Benedicti beatus
10 Maurus eius discipulus ab eo transmissus in Galliam recipere meruit litteras et sacra exenia tanti patris.

Ut autem dubitantibus plenius satisfiat, inserenda sunt praesentibus verba beati Gregorii, quae ignorantibus dubitationem ingerunt et errorem.

"Sciendum, inquit, quod benignitas Dei peccatoribus spatium paeni-
15 tentiae largitur; sed quia accepta tempora non ad fructum paenitentiae, ad usum vero iniquitatis convertunt, quod a divina misericordia mereri poterant, amittunt; quamvis omnipotens Deus illud tempus uniuscuiusque ad mortem praesciat quo vita eius terminatur, nec alio in tempore quisquam mori potuit nisi ipso quo moritur. Nam si Ezechiae anni additi ad
20 vitam quindecim memorantur, tempus vitae crevit < ab > illo tempore quo mori ipse merebatur: nam divina dispositio eius tempus tunc praescivit quod hunc postmodum ex praesenti vita subtraxit."

In quibus verbis satis lucide doctor lucifluus duplicem uniuscuiusque

---

2   fatetur] *def.* M⁴   semper et T F Ma V L
3   promptum] promtum M⁴   dicit *add.* L
    Praeoptaveram] |octaueram M⁵   optaueram T F Ma V   octaveram L
5   satis facerem Ma
6   obligatio] |gatio M¹⁰   prolongatio T F Ma V L
7   et posteris L] |eris M¹³   futuris T F Ma V
9   comprehenderent] comprehendereant Ma V
    Aquino] Aquini T F Ma V
    patris] *sequuntur lacuna et rasura* M¹⁶   nostri *add.* T F Ma V
14-15   paenitentiae] penitentis M²⁴ L   poenitentis F
15   paenitentiae] penitetie M²⁴
16   a] ad M²⁴ C L
18   ad mortem *om.* F Ma V
20   < ab > *suppl.*] *rasura* M²⁶   ab *editiones*
    tempore] tepere M²⁶

hominis considerationem habendam determinat: unam quidem secundum
25 se, aliam vero secundum quod ad divinam praescientiam comparatur.
Secundum se quidem homo consideratus, in his scilicet quae circa eum accidunt necessitati non subiacet, sed possibile est aliqua circa ipsum contingere quae nullatenus sortiuntur effectum; quod expresse praemittit de
peccatoribus dicens "quia accepta tempora non ad fructum paenitentiae,
30 ad usum vero iniquitatis convertunt, quod a divina misericordia mereri
poterant, amittunt." Si ergo mereri poterant, non ex necessitate amittunt;
unde ea quae contra hominem accidunt, non ex necessitate eveniunt.
Eadem enim ratio est de morte et de quibuscumque aliis quae homo agit
aut patitur, omnia enim divinae providentiae supponuntur. Si vero consi-
35 deretur homo divinae praescientiae comparatus, ea quae agit vel patitur
quandam necessitatem incurrunt, non quidem absolutam ut omnino secundum se considerata non possint, ut dictum est, aliter evenire, sed conditionalem, quia scilicet haec conditionalis est necessaria, "Si Deus aliquid
praescit hoc erit." Non enim possunt ista duo simul stare, aliquid esse a
40 Deo praescitum et illud non esse, quia sic Dei praescientia falleretur: est
autem omnino impossibile ut falsitatem veritas patiatur. Et hoc significant
verba sequentia beati Gregorii cum subdit "Quamvis omnipotens Deus
illud tempus uniuscuiusque ad mortem praesciat quo vita eius terminatur,
nec alio in tempore quisquam mori poterat nisi ipso quo moritur," scilicet
45 quo a Deo praescitus est mori. Non enim possunt ista duo simul esse, quod
Deus praesciat aliquem mori quodam tempore et ipse alio tempore
moriatur, alioquin Dei scientia falleretur. Secundum se autem consideratus
homo potuit alio tempore mori: quis enim dubitat eum potuisse prius trans-
figi gladio, igne comburi aut praecipitio aut laqueo vitam finire? Hanc et
50 distinctionem sapiunt eius verba sequentia, subdit enim "Nam si Ezechiae
anni additi ad vitam quindecim memorantur, tempus vitae crevit ab illo
tempore quo mori ipse merebatur." Stultum autem est dicere quod aliquis
mereatur id quod impossibile est evenire. Ipse ergo secundum se consideratus, poterat tempore illo mori, sed divinae scientiae comparatus, non
55 poterant haec simul esse, ut ipse uno tempore moreretur et alio tempore

27   necessitati] necxitati M[26]
27-28   contingere] contigere M[28]
28   expresse] expxe M[28]
31   amittunt[1]...poterant *hom. om.* Ma V
      necessitate] nexitate M[30]
35   praescientiae] providentiae V
38   conditionalem/ p. 321 M/ quia
41   significant] signant M[33]
42   cum] quum T F Ma V
43   uniuscuiusque] unuscuiusque M[33]
44   poterat] *emendatur in* M[34]   potuit T F Ma V
48   potuisse] potuixe M[35]
48-49   transfigi] trasfigi M[35]
49   praecipitio] precipio L
51   additi *om.* F Ma V
55   moreretur] moretur L

Deus eum praesciret moriturum... (*defectus lineae* 39)... doctoris ex-
primunt, quasi oculata fide dubitantium animis ingeramus, considerare
oportet differentiam divinae cognitionis et humanae.

Quia enim homo subiacet mutationi et tempori, in quo prius et posterius
60 locum habent, successive cognoscit res, quaedam prius et quaedam
posterius; et inde est quod praeterita memoramur, videmus praesentia et
praenosticamur futura. Sed Deus, sicut liber est ab omni motu secundum
illud Malachiae "Ego Dominus et non mutor," ita omnem temporis suc-
cessionem excedit, nec in eo invenitur praeteritum nec futurum, sed
65 praesentialiter omnia futura et praeterita ei adsunt; sicut ipse Moysi
famulo suo dicit "Ego sum qui sum." Eo ergo modo ab aeterno praescivit
hunc tali tempore moriturum, si modo nostro loquimur cum tamen eius
modo dicendum esset 'videt eum mori quomodo ego video Petrum sedere
cum sedet' Manifestum est autem quod ex hoc quod video aliquem sedere
70 nulla ingeritur ei necessitas sessionis. Impossibile est haec duo simul esse
vera, quod ego videam aliquem sedentem et ipse non sedeat; et similiter
non est possibile quod Deus praesciat aliquid esse futurum et illud non sit,
nec tamen propter hoc futura ex necessitate eveniunt.

Haec sunt, pater carissime, quae vestrae petitioni oboediens ad erran-
75 tium reductionem scripsi. Quae si eis non sufficiunt ista, rescribere vobis
oboediens non desinam. Valeat paternitas vestra diu.

Frater Raynaldus commendat se vobis.

56   eum *om.* F Ma V
     moriturum] et *add.* T F Ma V L
     doctoris: *antea* M *transit ad p.* 322
56-57   exprimunt] exprimiunt M[40]
60   successive] succexive M[40]
     quaedam...quaedam] quedam...quedam M[41]   quasdam...quasdam T F Ma V L
62   Praenosticamur] prognosticamur T F Ma V
63   mutor *scrips. cum* Malachia 3[6]] tumor M[41]   *cum nota* L
64   invenitur *scrips. cum* L] inventem *potius* M[42]   inveniuntur T F Ma V
     nec[2]] *def.* M[43]   et T F Ma V L
65   adsunt] assunt M[44]
66   "Ego...sum": Exodi 3[14]
67   si] *def.* M[47] ut T F Ma V quo L
70   nulla] nullam M[51]
71   ego] *def.* M[53] *om.* T F Ma V L
71-77   non sedeat...se vobis *om.* Ma
71-76   non sedeat...desinam *om.* V
74   carissime] karissime M[57] L   charissime T F   *def.* Ma V
     quae] pre M[57]
     petitioni] |oni M[58]   iussioni F T L   *def.* Ma V
75   ista] |ta M[60]   dicta T F L   *def.* Ma V
76   desinam] |nam M[61]   *def.* Ma V

III

EXEGETICAL STUDIES

QUASI DEFINITIO SUBSTANTIAE

Etienne Gilson

THE origin of this essay is the surprise I felt, some twenty years ago, when I stumbled upon a rather abrupt statement in the disputed question *De potentia*, q. 7, a. 3, ad 4: "Ens per se non est definitio substantiae, ut Avicenna dicit..." At that time, although well advanced in years, I must confess that, asked for a definition of substance, my answer would probably have been that substance is *ens per se*, and that accident is *ens per aliud* or *in alio*. A second cause of surprise was that, finding in my edition of the *De potentia* a reference to Avicenna's *Metaphysics*, book 3, I failed to find there the text under discussion. Unless I am mistaken, the reference is not correct; but the main reason for my failure to find the words "Ens per se non est definitio substantiae" was that, as a matter of fact, Avicenna probably never wrote them.

Having been imbued during my school years with respect for exact quotations, I persisted for a long time in my efforts to find these exact words somewhere in Avicenna. My repeated failures made me imagine that perhaps I had misunderstood the obvious meaning of the sentence. Perhaps "Ens per se non est definitio substantiae, ut Avicenna dicit" meant something like: "as Avicenna says it is." But I could hardly believe this, for Thomas probably would have expressed this with a *quamvis* rather than an *ut*, and, above all, I could not find in Avicenna the enunciation at stake whether as the object of an affirmation or a negation.

Hope revived in my heart when I became aware of the existence of the invaluable memoir of C. Vansteenkiste on the quotations of Avicenna in the writings of Thomas Aquinas.[1] I hastened at once to look for the reference to *De potentia*, 7, 3, ad 4, and, of course, the text

---

1 "Avicenna-Citaten bij S. Thomas," *Tijdschrift voor Philosophie*, 15 (1953), 457-507. Same author, "Autori Arabi e Giudei nell'opera di San Tommaso," *Angelicum* 37 (1960), 336-401. I take pleasure in recalling the pioneer work of Aimé Forest, *La structure métaphysique du concret selon saint Thomas d'Aquin* (Paris 1931); see "Table des citations d'Avicenne dans l'œuvre de saint Thomas," in the second edition, 1956. pp. 331-360.

was there, duly listed in its proper place on p. 488, n. 299; but I realized at once that the author had not committed himself to giving references to the corresponding passages in the writings of Avicenna. Slightly disappointed, I simply concluded that to identify the precise Avicennian source of the 426 references listed by him in his memoir had seemed to C. Vansteenkiste a thankless task; and after all, having done so much for us, he was fully justified in leaving it to us to do the rest. So I accepted my lot: never to know exactly where Avicenna had said "Ens per se non est definitio substantiae."

In 1966, as I was preparing a memoir for the Rome-Florence congress on the influence of Islamic culture on the Latin Middle Ages,[2] I found myself confronted with the problem of the overall influence of Avicenna. It became necessary for me to identify at least some of Thomas' Avicennian quotations, and only then did I realize that Thomas' idea of a quotation was very different from our own. By the same token, the discretion shown by C. Vansteenkiste appeared wholly justified in my own sight. Of course, it has long been known that Thomas was very free in his quotations, but he could be strictly correct when correctness was required. In the case of Avicenna's Latin translation, he was at grips with a particular sort of Latin, so obscure that the average reader would have been puzzled by it. For that reason, it is seldom possible to find in Thomas Aquinas a literal quotation of Avicenna. The text usually is quoted *ad sensum*. Still, the original is always recognizable and it can be found, provided one accepts in its place what its involved syntax has become under the clear and pithy pen of Thomas Aquinas.

Since all our own references will be to the text of Avicenna that we think Thomas had in mind, it seems advisable to begin by reproducing it in full. Already in Avicenna, as will still be the case with several texts of Thomas Aquinas, the problem of how correctly to define substance is introduced by a more strictly theological problem: Does the name "substance" correctly apply to God? In other words, is it right to say that God is a substance? After answering the question in the negative, Avicenna goes on to say:

> Potest autem aliquis dicere, quod licet refugiamus dicere de Primo nomen substantiae, non tamen possumus refugere quin dicamus de eo intentionem substantiae, quoniam est ens |ed. et| non in subjecto, quae est intentio substantiae quam posuimus genus.

---

2 "Avicenne en occident au moyen âge," *Archives d'histoire doctrinale et littéraire du moyen âge*, 36 (1969), 89-121.

Contra quod dico quod haec non est intentio substantiae quam posuimus genus. Imo intentio ejus est, quod est res habens quidditatem stabilem, cujus esse est esse quod non est in subjecto corpore vel anima.

Cujus rei probatio haec est, quoniam nisi hoc fuerit intellectum de substantia, ipsa erit genus nullo modo. Quod enim significatur per hoc nomen ens, non judicatur esse genus. Negatio vero quae sequitur non addit ei aliquid super esse nisi occasionem discretionis. Hac vero intentione non affirmatur aliquid quod jam sit acquisitum in esse. Nec est intentio alicujus rei per se, sed est in respectu tantum. Esse igitur non in subjecto non est intentio affirmativa, nisi quod essentiae ejus hoc potest esse, ut sit ens, et deinde ipsum ens sit aliquid negative et relative, quod est extra idemptitatem quae est rei. Haec igitur intentio si accipitur hoc modo, non erit genus.

Tu autem jam plene nosti hoc in logica, et nosti etiam in logica, quod cum dicimus omnis aitas[3] non est, intelligimus omne [ed. esse] appropriatum quia non habet certitudinem aliam nisi aitatem. Tunc de hoc quod dicimus de diffinitione substantiae, quia ipsa est ens non in subjecto, intentio est quod est res de qua dicitur quod est non in subjecto, ita ut "ens non in subjecto" praedicetur de ea et habeat in seipsa quidditatem sicut homo, lapis et arbor.

Sic igitur oportet imaginare substantiam ad hoc ut sit genus. Probatio autem quod inter haec duo sit differentia et quod unum eorum sit genus et non alterum est haec, scilicet quod de individuo alicujus hominis cujus esse ignoratur, potest dici quod ipsum sine dubio modo non est in sub-

---

3 The ancient editions sometimes give *unitas*, sometimes *anitas*. The first reading is not satisfactory, but it must have been invented as an at least possible substitute for the impossible *anitas*. The sentence "anitas non est" is self-contradictory. Having consulted Mlle M.-T. d'Alverny on the possibility of reading "aitas" ("the property of being A"), I received from that charitable Guide of the Perplexed the following communication which I am reproducing in full.

"'Tu autem nosti hoc in Logica. Et nosti etiam in Logica quod cum dicimus omnis a < n > itas < non est > intelligimus omne appropriatum, quia non habet certitudinem aliam nisi a < n > itatem.'

Texte arabe, éd. Le Caire, 1960, t. II, p. 248: 'Tu as appris également en Logique, que si nous disons, par exemple: 'tout A', nous entendons: toute chose qualifiée en tant que A, même si < cette chose > avait une réalité autre que son aïté.'

La lecture 'anitas', pour 'aitas' qui a dû être forgé par le traducteur pour traduire 'alifiyya' (dérivé de alif = A) doit être une erreur des scribes, qui n'ont pas compris le terme et lui ont substitué 'anitas' qui se trouvait dans le même chapitre.

Mais il y a des différences entre le texte arabe et la traduction. D'abord, le fait que la traduction porte: 'omnis a < n > itas *non est*, paraît indiquer que le manuscrit utilisé avait une négation, ce qui n'a pas de sens. Ensuite, la substitution de 'aitas' à 'A' dans le premier membre de la phrase, s'explique difficilement. Enfin, les traducteurs n'ont pas compris la copule signifiante 'même si', et ont écrit à tort 'quia'; il faudrait 'etsi'.

Certitudo traduit *haqqiqa*, qui signifie vérité, et réalité."

This communication helps us to realize why Thomas Aquinas could not very well have quoted Avicenna *verbatim*, even if he had wanted to. Of course, he probably could have had recourse to the competence of scholars who knew Arabic and, perhaps, had a copy of the original at hand, but we do not know if such was the case. He probably was obliged to rely on his own insight most of the time and to guess the meaning of the sentences such as he found them in his own copies of the Latin Avicenna.

jecto, sed videtur sufficere quod assignavimus de hoc cum loquebamur de logica.[4]

As can be seen at once, if there is a text in which "Avicenna says" in so many words that "being through itself (*esse per se*) is not the definition of substance," it is not this one. At the same time, it cannot be denied that, in this text, Avicenna is painstakingly explaining that "ens non in subjecto... non est intentio substantiae." If "not to be in a subject" (or rather, "to be not in a subject") is taken as an equivalent for "to be through itself," the import of the two passages is the same couched in different words.

This particular text sets up a pattern that Thomas Aquinas will follow through the various passages in which the same theme is taken up, in relation to different problems, but always with reference to the teaching of Avicenna's *Metaphysics*. Thomas could not have been unaware that Avicenna had dealt with the same notion in his logic: Avicenna himself says as much in the text of the *Metaphysics* we have just cited. But Thomas would follow Averroes rather than Avicenna in matters of logic, and without precluding the possibility of an influence of certain texts of Avicenna's *Logic* on the Thomistic definition of substance, we shall leave to others the task of establishing it.

Since, however, the notion of substance is one of the Aristotelian categories, it is impossible to discuss it, even from the point of view of the metaphysician, without bearing in mind what logic says about it. Far from being indifferent to actual reality, the logic of Aristotle starts from the primary substance, which is the only actually existing reality. Its characteristic is "that it is never present in a subject" (*Cat.* V). Because substance signifies that which is individual, it is a self-subsisting unit and, by the same token, what the Scholastics will call an *ens non in alio*. As compared with it, species and genera were called by Aristotle "secondary substances." Socrates is a primary substance, his species "man" and his genus "animal" are secondary substances. They are not present in Socrates (manhood is not present in Socrates, nor in animality), but they are predicated of him. It is by stating species and genus that we correctly define individual substances, but they themselves are not substance in the full meaning of the term, they only are substances to the extent that they are predicable of it.

In the order of predication every genus, except substance, is a species with respect to a higher one, every species is a genus with respect to a lower one, but because in actual reality the concrete substance is that of

---

4 Avicenna, *Opera philosophica* (Venice 1508), *Metaphysica*, tract. VIII, cap. 4, fol. 99rC.

which all the rest can be predicated (including both species and genera), in the order of logical predication, the notion of substance is the supreme term and, as such, escapes all definition. Substance is the species of nothing, and since all definition is by genus and specific difference, the absolutely universal substance cannot be defined. As Avicenna says in his *Logic*: "substantia est genus generalissimum"; it is eminently genus because there is above it no higher genus of which it can be made the species: "ideo est genus quoniam impossibile est fieri speciem, quoniam supra illud non est aliud communius genus." In short, "substantia etenim non habet genus supra se."[5] There is no higher term in conjunction with which, as its difference, it can possibly be defined. Incidentally, this accounts for the fact that in a consistently idealistic view of the world, such as that of Spinoza, substance is at once posited as identical with God.

The special status of substance, as transcending all its differences and transcended by none, suggests at once that it is not susceptible of a definition properly so called. Hence the cautious words of Thomas Aquinas: "Sed si substantia possit habere definitionem non obstante quod est genus generalissimum...."[6] And the curious expressions he uses in connection with the would be definitions of the notion. Speaking of "per se existere," he once called it a "circumlocutio verae descriptionis,"[7] and another time, speaking of the correct description itself, he called it a "definitio, vel quasi definitio substantiae."[8] That was as much as saying: "substantia definitionem habere non potest."

I do not remember meeting the problem in the early works *De ente et essentia* and *In Boethium de Trinitate*. Thomas was already familiar with Avicenna when he wrote these two treatises. One sentence in the second work shows him already possessed of the Avicennian principle that would have enabled him to solve it: "Deus in nullo genere est, cum non habeat quod quid est aliud a suo esse, quod requiritur in omnibus generibus, ut Avicenna dicit."[9] With the commentary on Peter Lombard, however, the picture becomes different. Thomas obviously seeks every opportunity to stress the importance of the problem and to give it a technically justified answer.

---

5 Avicenna, *Logica*, pars prima; ed. cit. fol. 8r.
6 *De potentia*, q. 7, a. 3, ad 4; see Selected Texts I, 5.
7 *Quodl.* IX, q. 3, a. 5, ad 2.
8 *In IV Sent.* d. 12, q. 1, a. 1, ql. 3, ad 2; Vivès (Paris 1873) 10, pp. 293-294.
9 *In Boethium de Trinitate*, q. 6, a. 3, Resp.; ed. B. Decker (Leiden 1955), p. 222; with reference to Avicenna, *Metaphysica*, tr. VIII, c. 4, ed. cit. fol. 99rA-C, obviously the standard Avicennian text on the question.

1. IS GOD A SUBSTANCE?

Since, according to Saint Anselm, God is all that which it is better to be than not to be, God has, and is, all the perfection of substantial being, but the question is to know whether the name "substance" is fittingly said of God.

A first passage of the commentary on the *Sentences* goes straight to the core of the difficulty. (See Text I). The affirmative is argued from a commonly accepted definition of substance, as being "that which is not in a subject, but is a being through itself." In view of what is to follow in the discussion of other texts, let us note at once that, in the terminology of Thomas, "non esse in subjecto," or "esse non in subjecto," and "ens per se" are equivalent expressions. Since, therefore, it eminently befits God not to be in a subject, and to be through himself, he seems to belong in the genus substance.

Thomas answers that this is not so because, according to Avicenna, the words "that which is not in a subject" are not the definition of substance. Assuming the equivalence of "not to be in a subject" and to be an "ens per se," Avicenna and Thomas observe that "being is no genus." Their reason for saying so reaches the deepest layers of Avicenna's ontology, to wit: his very notion of being. As it is implicit in the argument of Thomas, we must first consider it in itself. According to the two philosophers (or to the philosopher and the theologian), being (*ens*) is that which first occurs to the human mind. [10] Thomas has often quoted Avicenna to that effect, but the problem is far from simple, for it already implies the way Thomas usually quotes Avicenna.

First, as a quotation, the sentence is incomplete, and it is noteworthy that this consistently is the case, a consistency suggestive of some intention on the part of Thomas. The complete Avicennian formula says: "Dicemus igitur quod *ens*, et *res* et *necesse* talia sunt quae statim imprimuntur in anima prima impressione, quae non acquiritur ex aliis notioribus se..." [11] Of these three terms, Thomas habitually leaves out the third, namely *necesse*. To find an explanation for this apparently systematic omission is easy, but to find the good one is not. One feels tempted to think that there is in *necesse* a touch of Moslem fatalism,

---

10 *In Boethium de Trinitate*, q. 1, a. 3, obj. 3; ed. cit. p. 69. The reply *ad 3m* will not question the truth of the principle; it will simply deny that God is what first occurs to the human mind. If, as is more and more commonly admitted, the exposition on Boethius' *De Trinitate* is one of the earliest works of Thomas, the quotation suggests that his attention was detained very early by the ontology of the Moslem philosopher.

11 Avicenna, *Metaphysica*, lib. II, tr. I, cap. 1 (in the 1495 ed.). In the 1508 ed., tr. I, c. 6, fol. 72rA.

but that would be to indulge in literary commentaries, for indeed being as such is no less necessary in itself to Thomas Aquinas than it is to Avicenna. Yet, for Avicenna, the proper qualification of the Prime Being is *necesse esse*. The God of Thomas Aquinas too is Necessary Being, but he is necessary because he is pure *Esse,* not conversely. So let us simply note the fact that the usual formula employed by Thomas Aquinas is a simplified one: "Ens est illud quod primo cadit in cognitione humana, ut Avicenna dicit...; Primum cadens in apprehensione intellectus est ens, ut Avicenna dicit...; Illud autem quod primo intellectus concipit quasi notissimum, et in quo omnes conceptiones resolvit, est ens, ut Avicenna dicit in principio *Metaphysicae* suae."[12]

We should not look for secret intentions beneath all the variations of a language as free as that of Thomas Aquinas, but it may be significant that his first quotation of the Avicennian formula is also the closest to the authentic thought of his predecessor: "ens autem et essentia sunt quae primo in intellectu concipiuntur, ut dicit Avicenna in *Metaphysica.*"[13] The insertion of *essentia* is meaningful and, this time, a precise passage of Avicenna's *Metaphysics* helps us to give it its precise meaning.

> Dico ergo quod intentio *entis* et intentio *rei* imaginantur in animabus duae intentiones. *Ens* vero et *aliquid* sunt nomina multivoca unius intentionis. Nec dubitabis quoniam intentio istorum non sit jam impressa in anima legentis hunc librum. Sed res et quicquid aequipollet ei, significat etiam aliquid aliud in omnibus linguis. Unaquaeque enim res habet certitudinem qua est id quod est, sicut triangulus habet certitudinem qua est triangulus, et albedo habet certitudinem qua est albedo; et hoc est quod fortasse appellamus esse proprium, nec intendimus per illud nisi intentionem esse affirmativi, quia verbum ens signat etiam multas intentiones, ex quibus est certitudo qua est unaquaeque res, et est sicut esse proprium rei.[14]

This very important passage is not immediately clear; its meaning appears quite simple, however, if one admits that it might be the source of another Avicenna "quotation" by Thomas Aquinas: "Nomen entis imponitur ab esse et nomen rei a quidditate, ut dicit Avicenna."[15] In the

---

12 *In Boethium de Trinitate*, q. 1, a. 3, obj. 3; ed. cit. p. 69; *In I Sent.*, d. 1, q. 38, a. 1, obj. 4; *De veritate,* I, 1, Resp. and 21, 1, Resp. For a typical quotation, see *In I Metaph.* lect. 2: "primo in intellectu cadit ens, ut Avicenna dicit...."

13 *De ente et essentia*, prooemium.

14 Avicenna, *Metaphysica*, tract. I, c. 6; ed. cit. fol. 72vC.

15 *In I Sent.*, d. 25, q. 1, a. 4, obj. 2 and Sol. Cf. *In II Sent.*, d. 37, q. 1, a. 1, Sol., and *De veritate,* q. 1, a. 1, Resp. Cf. *In II Sent.* d. 37, q. 1, a. 1, Sol.: "... ut dicit Avicenna distinguens entis et rei significationem."

same passage of his commentary on the *Sentences*, Thomas explains himself, and Avicenna, more at length, but what was rather obscure in the Latin Avicenna becomes both precise and clear in the school Latin of Thomas Aquinas. At the same time, the ultimate metaphysical import of what first looked like a mere question of vocabulary, appears in full:

> According to Avicenna, as has been said above, the name "being" and the name "thing" differ, inasmuch as two points must be considered in "thing," namely its quiddity and notion, and its *esse*; and it is from the quiddity that the name "thing" is taken. And because the quiddity can have *esse* in both the singular outside the soul and in the soul, inasmuch as it is apprehended by the intellect, the name "thing" applies to both: to that which is in the soul, inasmuch as *res* is derived from *reor reris*, and to that which is outside the soul, inasmuch as "thing" is said of what is confirmed and firm in nature. But the name "being" is taken from the fact that the thing is.[16]

From this text one should remember the first sentence, on which all the rest depends: "secundum Avicennam... hoc nomen ens et res differunt secundum quod est duo considerare in re, scilicet quidditatem et rationem ejus, et esse ipsius..." These words refer us to the first sentence of Avicenna in the above-quoted text: "intentio entis et intentio rei imaginantur... duae intentiones." Thus far the phrase "secundum Avicennam" is fully justified. It is less immediately evident that it also covers the ensuing development: "Et a quidditate sumitur hoc nomen res... Sed nomen entis sumitur ab esse rei." Yet, on closer inspection, such seems to be the meaning of the later part of the text. For it says that being (*ens*) and something (*aliquid*) are two different names for one single object. But thing (*res*) or any equivalent term, signifies something else in all languages, for every thing has an essence in virtue of which it is that which it is. The Latin Avicenna calls it the *certitudo* of the thing, a word that in his translator's vocabulary is synonymous with quiddity. Summing up his development, Avicenna himself will say: "Redeamus igitur et dicamus... quod unaquaeque res habet certitudinem propriam quae est ejus quidditas, et notum est quod certitudo cujusque rei quae est propria ei, est praeter esse quod multivocum est cum aliquid." So Thomas does not betray Avicenna in making him say that *ens* points out the *esse* of the thing while *res* points out its quiddity. Having thus cleared up the intention of Avicenna, Thomas will never hesitate to attribute to him the words which sum up the doctrine such as he himself correctly understood it.

16 *In I Sent.*, d. 25, q. 1, a. 4.

In such statements, however, Thomas freely used the various synonyms according to his own needs of the moment. For instance:

> Non autem invenitur aliquid affirmative dictum absolute quod possit accipi in omni ente, nisi *essentia* ejus, secundum quam esse dicitur; et sic imponitur nomen *res*, quod in hoc differt ab *ente*, secundum Avicennam in principio *Metaphysicae*, quod *ens* sumitur ab actu essendi, sed nomen *rei* exprimit quidditatem sive essentiam entis.[17]

The key to the problem of the true definition of substance and of its applicability to God, therefore, is the celebrated distinction of essence and *esse* in finite beings, each and every one of them definable as an essence that has an *esse*. It is well known that the doctrine is common to Avicenna and to Thomas, though a deep difference distinguishes their respective conceptions of *esse* and of its relation to essence.[18] But that difference does not affect their agreement on the notion of substance, which is our present concern.

From the first part of his *Logic*, Avicenna stresses the distinction between the quiddity of a thing and its actual being: a corresponding modification of the notion of substance necessarily follows from that innovation. To define it as an *ens per se* is to posit *ens* as the genus of the definition and *per se* as the difference. But this is impossible. *Ens* is not a genus. Either it is God, in which case it is above being, since it is pure absolute *esse*; or else it is *a* being, in which case it is an essence endowed with its own *esse*. To add that the particular being at stake is through itself, does not specify it as any definite being, since it only adds to it the merely negative condition of "not being in a subject." To define substance as "a being that is not in a subject" is accordingly to say nothing.

Such is the argument of Avicenna, as reported by Thomas in Text I. *Ens non in subjecto* cannot be the definition of substance because, since being is no genus, that would be a definition without a genus, which is impossible. Now, "in every genus one must signify a certain quiddity," more precisely, a quiddity which, unlike that of God, does not include *esse*.[19] As "being does not signify quiddity, but only the act of being

17 *De veritate*, q. 1, a. 1, Resp.

18 Because, for Avicenna, the necessity of the essence is the very core of being, actual existence (*esse*) is added to essence by the creative power of God as a sort of accident. Thomas was fully aware of what separated his own notion of being from that of Avicenna. Cf. *In XII Metaph.* lect. 3: "Avicenna posuit quod unum et ens sunt praedicata accidentalia, et quod significant naturam additam supra ea de quibus dicuntur."

19 The conclusion that God is no substance can be directly reached from the principle that he has no essence other than his *esse*. Cf. "Aliquis enim est, sicut Deus, cujus essentia est ipsummet suum esse; et ideo inveniuntur aliqui philosophi dicentes quod Deus non habet quidditatem vel essentiam, quia essentia sua non est aliud quam esse suum. Et ex hoc sequitur quod ipse non sit in

(*sed solum actum essendi*),"the argument does not follow:"*x* is not in a subject, hence it is in the genus substance." A correct argument would be: "*x* has a quiddity from which it follows that it is not in a subject." Now this cannot be said of God, whose quiddity is identical with his *esse*. So God is no substance: in him there is no essence, or quiddity, to stand under (*sub-stare, sub-stantia*) his *esse*. The name "substance" does not befit the pure actuality of God.

The whole point is perfectly summed up by Thomas in two lines of his commentary on the *Sentences*: "...non esse in subjecto non est definitio substantiae..., sed habere quidditatem cui tale esse competat."[20]

Thomas has several times restated his position on the problem at stake. A particularly interesting case is *Contra Gentiles*, I, 25, § 9-10, because the text of Thomas closely recalls the movement of the corresponding passage in Avicenna. After establishing that, although we may refuse to call the Primary Being a substance, he adds that we cannot refuse to attribute to him substantiality, because he is a being not in a subject, which is the meaning of substance posited as a genus. To the "Potest autem aliquis dicere quod licet refugiamus..."of Avicenna, echoes the "Potest autem alicui videri quod..." of Thomas Aquinas. It is the same movement of style and the content of the developments is the same.

Let us briefly recall the reasoning of Thomas Aquinas: 1) being is not a genus, 2) to be a being through itself is a pure negation, 3) for substance to be a genus it must be "a thing to which it belongs to be not in a subject," 4) the name "thing" is derived from the quiddity, as the name "being" is derived from "to be", 5) so substance should be defined as a quiddity to which it belongs to be not in another, 6) in no way then

genere, quia omne quod est in genere oportet quod habeat quidditatem praeter esse suum...." *De ente et essentia*, V; ed. Roland-Gosselin (Paris 1948), p. 37. Cf. "Quidam enim dicunt, ut Avicenna, lib. *De Intelligentiis*, cap. 1, et Rabbi Moyses, lib. I, cap. 57 et 58, quod res illa quae Deus est, est quoddam esse subsistens, nec aliquid aliud nisi esse, in Deo est: unde dicunt quod est esse sine essentia." *In I Sent*., d. 2, q. 1, Sol. Vivès (Paris 1873) 7, p. 37. On the apocryphal *De Intelligentiis*, cf. Reginald de Vaux, *Notes et textes sur l'avicennisme latin* (Paris 1934). Rabbi Moses and Thomas Aquinas followed Avicenna on that precise point, with only verbal differences: "Dico enim quod Necesse Esse non potest habere quidditatem quam comitetur necessitas essendi...." Avicenna, *Metaphysica*, tract. VIII, c. 4 (Venice 1508), fol. 99A. "...igitur necesse esse non habet quidditatem nisi quod est necesse esse, et haec est anitas." Ibid. AB. The principle is: "...quicquid habet quidditatem praeter anitatem causatum est." Since the Primary Being is uncaused, he can have no quiddity (other than his *Esse*), so: "...omne habens quidditatem causatum est"; "ibid. B. Hence it follows: "Primus etiam non habet genus; primus enim non habet quidditatem, sed quod non habet quidditatem non habet genus." Ibid. B. Since *ens* is no genus it cannot define substance, which is always some actually existing essence or quiddity. The two propositions are inseparable in the mind of Avicenna: "Primus enim non habet quidditatem," and "quod non habet quidditatem non habet genus,"

20 See Selected Texts, II, 1.

is God in the genus of substance, since he has no quiddity save his being.

Everything in this development is Avicennian in origin. One cannot find in it one expression to which Avicenna could not subscribe, for the simple reason that everything in it comes from him. And yet the two doctrines belong to different intelligible worlds, because *Necesse Esse* and *I Am* are not identical. *Necesse Esse* can say *I Am* and *I Am* is Necessary Being, but these dialectical equivalences hide from sight a deep metaphysical difference, which history as such is perhaps competent, if not to perceive, at least to convey.

Among the other passages of Thomas dealing with the same problem, there is perhaps not one that does not offer some noteworthy detail, but the position remains unchanged to the end. The text of the *Summa theologiae* is perfect in its concision.[21] The words *non solum* usefully remind the reader that what Thomas denies is not that substance is through itself; his precise point is that to be through itself is not the definition of substance, unless, as he says elsewhere, these words be used as an abridged formula and for the sake of brevity.

Almost equally concise and more technically complete is the passage of the disputed question *De potentia*, q. 7, a. 3, ad 4, which first called our attention to the problem.

> To be through itself is not the definition of substance, as Avicenna says. For indeed, being cannot be the genus of a thing, as Aristotle proves, because nothing can be added to being that does not participate in it, while the difference must not participate in the genus. But if substance is susceptible of definition, despite its being the *genus generalissimum*, that definition should run as follows: Substance is a thing to the quiddity of which it is due to be not in something. And thus the definition of substance will not befit God, who has no quiddity besides his *esse*. God, therefore, is not in the genus of substance, but is above all substance.[22]

2. Transsubstantiation and Accident

There is no treatise of Thomas Aquinas on substance. Being a theologian, he dealt with the notion when a theological problem made it necessary for him to do so. To decide whether the name "substance" correctly applies to God was such an occasion; another was the necessity to define the ontological status of the eucharistic species. Hence the second series of texts in which the correct definition of substance is reasserted by the theologian.

21 Selected Texts, I, 4.
22 Selected Texts, I, 5.

The difficulty to overcome was plainly visible. Among the many difficulties arising from the possibility of transsubstantiation, a particularly striking one was the fact that, after the consecration, all the "accidents" of bread and wine remain unchanged. All their qualities: color, taste, odor, figure, quantity, and weight are perceived by the senses just as they were before the consecration. It is hard to believe, therefore, that the substance of the body of Christ is there, under those accidents foreign to its nature, and that the substances of bread and wine themselves have ceased to be present.

This provides the theologian with an opportunity to approach the problem of the definition of substance from the point of view of the definition of accident. Of course, the theologian does not intend to make his reader *understand* such a miracle. Nor is it his task to make it appear like a natural possibility, but he has to answer objections taken from the very philosophical definition of accidents conceived in their relationship to substance. Now, just as the definition of substance is wrongly supposed to be "a being that is through itself," so that of accident is wrongly supposed to be "a being that is through another one." As Aristotle has said: "... for an accident to be is *to be in*."[23] To suppose that after the consecration of bread and wine, which converts their substance, their accidents still subsist, is to admit that accidents can subsist as though they themselves had become substances. But, in Thomas' own words: "Nec possunt per se subsistere, cum accidentis esse sit inesse."[24] For that and many other reasons, the teaching of Christ and the Church concerning that sacrament appears hard to accept.

Thomas has defined his own position on the problem as early as his lectures on the fourth book of the *Sentences* of Peter Lombard.[25] There again his starting point is the Avicennian definition of substance as different from the usual one. "As Avicenna proves in his *Metaphysics*," he writes, "to subsist through itself is not the definition of substance." We know the reason: that alleged definition does not point out the quiddity of the thing, but its *esse* which, in finite beings, is not their quiddity. Now, where there is no quiddity, there is no thing that subsists, no substance. Substance, then, let it be said again, is a thing having a quiddity to which it is due to be in itself and not in something else.

This time, however, the nature of the problem prompts Thomas to extend the consequence from the definition of substance to that of accident. So he goes on to say: "And, in like fashion, *to be in something*

23 *Metaph.* V, 7, 1077a19.
24 *Contra Gentiles*, IV, 62, § 12.
25 Selected Texts, II, 1.

else is not the definition of accident, but, on the contrary, the definition is, *a thing to which it is due to be in something else."*

How does this help to remove the difficulty? For this reason, that since such is its definition (*res cui debetur esse in alio*) an accident cannot possibly become something else, namely a substance. It cannot be separated from its definition, as would be the case if its definition were "to be in something else," for indeed, in that case, subsisting in themselves after the consecration, the former accidents of bread and wine would become many substances, which is contradictory and therefore impossible.

On the contrary, it is neither contradictory nor impossible that something to which to be in something else is due by reason of its quiddity, or essence, be caused by the divine power to subsist without any substance. A subsisting accident is something miraculous, which only God can cause to happen, but it is not a self-contradiction as would be an accident-become-substance. As St. Thomas writes, "To cause an accident to be without substance is not to separate the definition from the defined." And this is precisely what can happen, supposing the allpowerfullness of God, if the definition of accident is not "to be in a subject" but, rather, "to be something to which it is natural to subsist in a subject." The power of God is free with respect to nature, but it cannot achieve self-contradiction which, of itself, is nothingness.

Theology need not go farther than to demonstrate the intrinsic non-impossibility of miracles, especially in the case of the Eucharist, which is the greatest of all.

The very name "transsubstantiation" shows how great a miracle it is. It is not merely the passing of some accidents into others within one substance. It even is more than the annihilation of a substance and its replacement by another. Transsubstantiation is the passing over of a subject into another subject, what is called a *substantial conversion.* In such conversions, the substance of the first subject does not persist. The substance of the bread does not subsist after the consecration; the matter of that substance likewise ceases to exist. Since, however, something persists, this can only be the accidents of bread and wine. The substance of the bread then becomes the substance of the body of Christ under the accidents of the bread. In Thomas' own words, "the body of Christ in some way acquires the place of the bread, with the measurements of the bread, nonetheless, mediating."[26]

---

26 *Contra Gentiles*, IV, 63, § 12; transl. C. J. O'Neill, *On the Truth of the Catholic Faith* (New York 1957), p. 260. For a detailed justification of the non-impossibility of such a miracle from the point of view of the conservation of things (which is the same as that of their creation), see op. cit., IV, 65, § 3. Perhaps through my own fault, I have not been able to find in this chapter, which

A short passage of the *Summa theologiae* attests that Thomas had not altered his position at the time he was writing it. Speaking of the sacrament of the Eucharist, the theologian reaches the question: Whether in that sacrament the accidents persist without a subject. The answer is in the affirmative despite the straight philosophical objection that "the definition of a thing cannot be separated from that thing, even miraculously."[27] The second objection says that it is contradictory that a thing be separated from its definition or, (which comes to the same thing), that the definition of one thing should apply to another. For instance, even God cannot effect that a man, while remaining a man, be an irrational animal. That would be for contradictories to subsist together at one and the same time, since the definition of a thing is what the thing is. Now, it is of the definition of accident that it be in a subject, just as it is of the definition of substance that it subsist by itself, not in a subject. It cannot miraculously happen, then, in the sacrament of the Eucharist, that accidents be without a subject.

To this objection, Thomas makes his own usual answer, that since being is no genus, *esse* cannot be the essence of either substance or accident. So *ens in subjecto* is not the definition of accident: "but just as it is of the quiddity or essence of substance to have being not in a subject, so also is it of the quiddity or essence of accident to have being in a subject." Now, in the sacrament of the Eucharist, it is not given to the accidents to be not in a subject in virtue of their own essence (which would be contradictory), but to be not in a subject owing to the divine power that sustains them. "And so they do not cease to be accidents, because the definition of accident is not separated from them and the definition of substance does not apply to them." So they do not become substances; they subsist without ceasing to be accidents.

A last text worth mentioning is found in a *Quaestio quodlibetalis*[28] which proves at least that the question was of general theological interest around the middle of the thirteenth century: Whether, in the sacrament of the altar, there are accidents without a subject.

The second objection for the negative side and its reply bring into play the same set of arguments, and, naturally, the answer begins by appealing to the principle laid down by Avicenna, that *esse* cannot enter the definition of any genus or species. This time, however, Thomas justifies the rule by stressing, in more forcible terms perhaps than usual,

---

deals with the "objections regarding accidents," the argument drawn from the correct definition of accident. If it really is not there, nor anywhere else in the *Contra Gentiles,* I do not know the reason for its omission, especially in a work written specifically in view of the philosophers.

27 *Summa theologiae*, III, 77, 1, obj. 2. See Selected Texts, II, 2.

28 *Quaestiones quodlibetales, Quodl.* IX, q. 3, a. 5, ad 2. See Selected Texts, II, 3.

the metaphysical notion that underlies the doctrine. It also happens to be one of the most frequently neglected points of Thomism in its commonly taught school version.

Esse, Avicenna and Thomas say, cannot enter the definition of any genus or species, because all the individuals included in a genus or species are united by their sharing in their definitions, whereas genus and species are not found with one and the same *esse* in the individuals they contain. In other words, the species is the same for all the individuals contained in it, whereas the *esse* of each individual is proper to it. That uniqueness of individual *esse*, which makes a being to be an individual, is therefore required for the constitution of every substance, but because finite *esse* necessarily is the *esse* of something, the notion of the quiddity or essence that receives it is likewise required for a correct definition, description or quasi description of both substance and accident. Substances and accidents are beings only because they are things that are. Thomas repeatedly says of them that they are *res*, that is to say essences actualized, according to two different modalities, by their respective acts of being.

A few texts scattered through the complete works of Thomas Aquinas constitute all the information we have on what would have been a most important and fundamental chapter of his philosophy, had he written one. This accounts for the fact that so many "Thomists" substitute an incomplete, and to that extent incorrect, definition of substance for the authentic definition of it given by Thomas and his predecessor, the Moslem Avicenna.

Those who say that we have the philosophy of Thomas Aquinas in his early *De ente et essentia*, should specify that, although all the elements of the Thomistic definition of substance are found in that work, the definition itself of that fundamental notion is not there.

Those who maintain that the philosophy of Thomas Aquinas is contained in his commentaries on Aristotle, and even that, such as it is interpreted by him in those commentaries, the philosophy of Aristotle is his own philosophy, should account for the fact that, such as Thomas himself understands them, the fundamental philosophical notions of being, thing, substance, and accident are regularly related by him to the metaphysics of Avicenna, never to that of Aristotle. Inversely, of the 426 quotations of Avicenna in the complete works of Thomas Aquinas listed by C. Vansteenkiste, only twenty-five are found in the commentaries on Aristotle, eleven of which are in the commentary on Aristotle's *Metaphysics*. Between the metaphysics of Aristotle and that of Thomas Aquinas, the metaphysics of Avicenna acts as a kind of filter. The ontology of Aristotle reaches Thomas Aquinas Avicenna polarized. And, of course, Averroes knew full well the reason why the metaphysics of Avicenna could serve the purpose of a theologian better than that of Aristotle. Avicenna was always to be found half way between philosophy and theology. Since Thomas Aquinas, and before him Avicenna, had read the Old Testament, they have in common the God of Abraham, Isaac, and Jacob.

A last remark should perhaps be made, being well understood that there is nothing personal in it.

The narrow scope of the preceding observations does not authorize general conclusions concerning the doctrine of Thomas Aquinas, except perhaps this one, that it is pure intellectual dishonesty to present under the patronage of Thomas Aquinas some philosophy and theology using his vocabulary without keeping faith with the authentic meaning of his words. Thomism is an exceptional example of both liberty and precision in philosophical language. We cannot disregard one of its fundamental notions without wrecking the whole structure. Those who want to claim his authority in favor of their own philosophical and theological positions have to take his doctrine such as it is, or leave it.

To those who think that to take the doctrine as it is will impair their liberty of mind, I beg to offer two answers.

The first will be in the form of a question. Do you really know Thomism? Are you speaking of it on hearsay only? Or after a more or less rapid survey of the doctrine? Or after living with it for many years and progressively achieving a realization of the meaning of its principles? Let everyone answer for himself; personal experience cannot be communicated.

The second answer necessarily escapes the grasp of all those to whom Thomas Aquinas is but the name of, at best, an unknown theologian and, at worst, of a hopelessly outdated philosopher. For those, on the contrary, who have lived with him and in close familiarity with his thought, it will become increasingly evident that his guidance does not lead us to something that would be his own personal metaphysics and theology but, rather, to the very substance of metaphysical reality in philosophy as well as to that of the Christian faith in theology. The result of a close adherence to the authentic thought of Thomas Aquinas is completely to liberate the mind from every particular system and to leave him alone, a dangerously but a really free man, in exactly the situation in which Thomas himself was: at grips with the mysterious nature of ultimate reality. To follow him faithfully is the only safe way to go at least as far as he himself has gone. To go farther than he did is certainly not a forbidden ambition, but one first must join him where he is before undertaking to go beyond him.

SELECTED TEXTS

I. God and Substance

1. 2. Praeterea, substantia est quae non est in subjecto, sed est ens per se. Cum igitur Deo hoc maxime conveniat, videtur quod ipse sit in genere substantiae.

Ad secundum dicendum quod ista definitio secundum Avicennam (*Metaphy.*, tract. II, c. 1, et tract. III, c. 8) non potest esse substantiae: substantia est quae non est in subjecto. Ens enim non est genus. Haec autem negatio "non in subjecto" nihil ponit; unde hoc quod dico, ens non est in subjecto, non dicit aliquod genus, quia in quolibet genere oportet significare quidditatem aliquam, ut dictum est, de cujus intellectu non est esse. Ens autem non dicit quidditatem, sed solum actum essendi, cum sit principium ipsum; et ideo non sequitur: est non in subjecto, ergo est in genere substantiae; ... sed hoc dictum Deo non convenit, ut dictum est. *In I Sent.*, d. 8, q. 4, a. 2, ad 2; ed. Vivès (Paris 1873) 7, pp. 117-118.

2. Ut Avicenna dicit in sua *Metaphysica* (tract. II, c. 1, et tract. VI, c. 5), ad hoc quod aliquid sit proprie in genere substantiae requiritur quod sit res quidditatem habens, cui debeatur esse absolutum, ut per se esse dicatur vel subsistens. Et ideo duobus modis potest contingere quod aliquid ad substantiae genus pertinens, non sit in genere substantiae sicut species: vel quia res illa non habet quidditatem aliam nisi suum esse; et propter hoc Deus non est in genere substantiae sicut species, ut ipse Avicenna dicit. *In II Sent.*, d. 3, q. 1, a. 6, solutio; ed. Vivès (Paris 1873) 8, p. 55.

3. Potest autem alicui videri quod, quamvis nomen substantiae Deo proprie convenire non possit, quia Deus non substat accidentibus, res tamen significata per nomen ei conveniat, et ita sit in genere substantiae; nam substantia est ens per se, quod Deo constat convenire, ex quo probatum est ipsum non esse accidens.

Sed ad hoc dicendum est ex dictis, quod in definitione substantiae non est ens per se. Ex hoc enim quod dicitur ens, non posset esse genus, quia jam probatum est quod ens non habet rationem generis. Similiter nec ex hoc quod dicitur per se, quia hoc non videtur importare nisi negationem tantum: dicitur enim ens per se, ex hoc quod non est in alio, quod est negatio pura, quae non potest naturam vel rationem generis constituere, quia sic genus non diceret quid est res, sed quid non est. Oportet igitur quod ratio substantiae intelligatur hoc modo, quod substantia sit res cui conveniat esse non in subjecto, nomen autem rei a quidditate imponitur, sicut nomen entis ab esse; et sic in ratione substantiae intelligatur quod habeat quidditatem cui conveniat esse non in alio. Hoc autem Deo non convenit, nam non habet quidditatem nisi suum esse. Unde relinquitur quod nullo modo est in genere substantiae, et sic nec in aliquo genere, cum ostensum sit ipsum non esse in genere accidentis. *Contra Gentiles*, I, 25, §9-10; ed. Vivès (Paris 1874) 12, p. 33.

4. ... substantiae nomen non significat hoc solum quod est per se esse; quia hoc quod est esse non potest esse genus, ut ostensum est, sed significat essentiam, cui competit sic esse, id est, per se esse; quod tamen esse non sit ipsa

ejus essentia. Et sic patet quod Deus non est in genere substantiae. *Summa theologiae*, I, 3, 5, ad 1; ed. Vivès (Paris 1871) 1, p.26.

5. 4. Praeterea, cuicumque convenit ratio generis substantiae, est in genere. Sed ratio substantiae est per se existere, quod maxime convenit Deo. Ergo Deus est in genere substantiae. ...

Ens per se non est definitio substantiae, ut Avicenna dicit (*Metaphy*. tract. III, c. 8). Ens enim non potest esse alicujus genus, ut probat Philosophus, III *Metaphy*., com. 10, cum nihil possit addi ad ens quod non participat ipsum; differentia vero non debet participare genus. Sed si substantia possit habere definitionem, non obstante quod est genus generalissimum, erit ejus definitio, quod substantia est res cujus quidditati debetur esse non in aliquo. Et sic non conveniet definitio substantiae Deo, qui non habet quidditatem suam praeter suum esse. Unde Deus non est in genere substantiae, sed est supra omnem substantiam. *Q. D. De potentia*, q. 7, a. 3, ad 4; ed. Vivès (Paris 1875) 13, pp. 220-221.

II. Transsubstantiation

1. Sicut probat Avicenna in sua *Metaphysica*, per se existere non est definitio substantiae: quia per hoc non demonstratur quidditas ejus, sed ejus esse; et sua quidditas non est suum esse; alias non posset esse genus: quia esse non potest esse commune per modum generis, cum singula contenta in genere differant secundum esse. Sed definitio, vel quasi definitio substantiae est res habens quidditatem, cui acquiritur esse, vel debetur, ut non <sit> in alio. Et similiter esse in subjecto non est definitio accidentis, sed e contrario res cui debetur esse in alio. Et hoc nunquam separatur ab aliquo accidente, nec separari potest; quia illi rei quae est accidens, secundum rationem suae quidditatis semper debetur esse in alio. Sed potest esse quod illud quod debetur alicui secundum rationem suae quidditatis, ei virtute divina agente non conveniat. Et sic patet quod facere accidens esse sine substantia, non est separare definitionem a definito. Et si aliquando hoc dicatur definitio accidentis, praedicto modo intelligenda est definitio dicta, quia aliquando ab auctoribus definitiones ponuntur causa brevitatis non secundum debitum ordinem, sed tanguntur illa ex quibus potest accipi definitio. *In IV Sent*., d. 12, q. 1, a. 1, ql. 3, ad 2; ed. Vivès (Paris 1873) 10, pp. 293-294. Cf ... non esse in subjecto non est definitio substantiae, ut dictum est; sed habere quidditatem cui tale esse competat ..." Loc. cit., ad 3; ed. cit., p. 294.

2. 2. Praeterea, fieri non potest etiam miraculose quod definitio rei ab ea separetur, vel quod uni rei conveniat definitio alterius, puta quod homo manens homo sit animal irrationale. Ad hoc enim sequeretur contradictoria esse simul; *hoc* enim *quod significat nomen rei est definitio*, ut dicitur in IV *Metaph*. (text 28 [*lect. 16*]). Sed ad definitionem accidentis pertinet quod sit in subjecto, ad definitionem vero substantiae quod per se subsistat, non in subjecto. Non ergo potest miraculose fieri quod in hoc sacramento sint accidentia sine subjecto ....

Ad secundum dicendum quod, cum ens non sit genus, hoc ipsum quod est esse, non potest esse essentia substantiae vel accidentis. Non est ergo definitio substantiae, *ens per se sine subjecto*, nec definitio accidentis, *ens in subjecto*; sed quidditati seu essentiae substantiae competit habere esse non in subjecto; quidditati autem, sive essentiae accidentis competit habere esse in subjecto. In hoc autem sacramento non datur accidentibus quod ex vi suae essentiae non sint in subjecto, sed ex divina virtute sustentante. Et ideo non desinunt esse accidentia, quia nec separatur ab eis definitio accidentis, nec competit eis definitio substantiae. *Summa theologiae*, III, 77, 1; ed. Vivès (Paris 1872) 5, pp. 456-457.

3. 2. Praeterea, de eodem praedicatur definitio et definitum; sed *ens per se* est definitio vel descriptio substantiae; si ergo in sacramento altaris accidentia sunt per se non in subjecto, sequitur quod sint substantiae, quod est absurdum ....

Ad secundum dicendum, quod secundum Avicennam in sua *Metaphysica*, esse non potest poni in definitione alicujus generis et speciei, quia omnia particularia uniuntur in definitione generis vel speciei, cum tamen genus vel species non sit secundum unum esse in omnibus, et ideo haec non est vera definitio substantiae: substantia est quod per se est, vel, accidens est quod est in alio, sed est circumlocutio verae descriptionis, quae talis intelligitur: substantia est res cujus naturae debetur esse non in alio, accidens vero est res cujus naturae debetur esse in alio. Unde patet quod quamvis accidens miraculose non sit in subjecto, non tamen pertinet ad definitionem substantiae; non enim per hoc ejus natura debetur esse non in alio; nec egreditur definitionem accidentis, quia adhuc natura ejus manet talis ut ei debeatur esse in alio. *Quaest. Quodlibetales*, IX, q. 3, a. 5, ad 2.

THE SEPARATED SOUL AND ITS NATURE
IN ST. THOMAS

Anton C. Pegis

I

THE PROBLEM

THIS essay has grown out of an effort to understand the doctrine in *Summa Contra Gentiles* II, c. 81, especially paragraphs 5-7, dealing with the knowledge of the separated soul.[1] When compared with *Summa Theologiae* I, q. 89, a. 1, the *SCG* text shows marked differences in development as well as content: in doctrinal formation it is similar to *De Veritate*, q. 19, a. 1, as well as to *In III Sent.*, d. 31, q. 2, a. 4 and *In IV Sent.*, d. 50, q. 1, a. 3. On the other hand, *ST* I, q. 89, a. 1 is noticeably similar in its teaching to *Quaestiones de Anima*, q. 15.

The difference of *ST* I, q. 89, a. 1 from *SCG* II, c. 81 has three aspects, namely, a change in doctrine, a change in St. Thomas' view of the state of the question before him, and the entry of the Aristotelian notion of *nature* into the discussion of the knowledge of the separated soul. If these differences can be proved from the texts, then it is also permissible to think that *SCG* II, c. 81 belongs to an earlier stage in St. Thomas' views on the separated soul. And if, finally, it is correct to argue that as a *summa* the *SCG* had for its immediate purpose the assimilation of Aristotelianism, then it is plausible to believe that St. Thomas' use of Aristotelian teaching was not uniform or complete at the time of the *SCG*: it was absent, for example, from the problem of the knowledge of the separated soul, as compared with the fuller and even more radical application of Aristotelian notions in *ST* I, q. 89, a. 1 and *Quaestiones de Anima*, q. 15.

---

[1] Abbreviations used: *SCG = Summa Contra Gentiles; ST = Summa Theologiae.* On the purpose of the *SCG* referred to in the next paragraph, see A. C. Pegis, "Qu'est-ce que la Summa Contra Gentiles?" (in *L'homme devant dieu. Mélanges offerts au Père Henri de Lubac* [3 vols., Paris 1964], vol. II, pp. 169-182); *Saint Thomas Aquinas: On the Truth of the Catholic Faith: Summa Contra Gentiles, Book One: God* (New York 1955), pp. 19-44.

This conclusion does not directly argue for any precise chronology. But the recognition that *ST* I, q. 89, a. 1 contains a new perspective and a new doctrine on the separated soul throws serious doubt on the late dating recently proposed for the *SCG*, as well as on the accepted dating of *Quodlibet* III as being Easter, 1270.[2] *SCG* II, c. 81 and *Quodl.* III, q. 9, a. 1 were both written not only before 1269 at the latest, when St. Thomas held the *Quaestiones de Anima* in Paris, but also at an even earlier date (i.e. before 1265) if the *prima pars* of the *ST* was written in 1265-1268).[3] The main point is that *SCG* II, c. 81 and *Quodl.* III, q. 9, a. 1 belong in the intellectual climate of the *Sentences* and the *De Veritate*, not in the later and more developed Aristotelian climate of *ST* I, q. 89, a. 1.

II

a. *SCG II, c. 81,* §§ *5-7*

Before the chapter that concerns us, *SCG* II, c. 80 had recorded five arguments proving that the soul would not survive the body. Of these the fifth held that there was no substance without its operation and that, since the soul had no operation surviving its separation from the body, it would not itself survive the body. The core of the argument is the Aristotelian view of the human intellect. Though its own operation takes place without an organ, its objects of knowledge are phantasms, so that it cannot understand without phantasms. In addition, the soul needs other internal sensible powers to prepare the phantasms, namely, the cogitative power and the memory. Now, since all these powers die with the body, the intellect will not be able to understand without the body and will therefore not survive it.[4]

In reply, St. Thomas declares the argument false on the ground that operations not exercised through the body will survive its death. These are *intelligere* and *velle*.[5] But in view of the Aristotelian doctrine that

---

2   For these dates, see below, notes 35 and 39.

3   For the dating of the *Quaestiones de Anima* (January to June, 1269), see P. Glorieux, "Les questions disputées de saint Thomas et leur suite chronologique" (*Recherches de théologie ancienne et médiévale*, 4, 1933, pp. 5-33), pp. 22, 26-27; also J. H. Robb, St. Thomas Aquinas, *Quaestiones de Anima* (Toronto: Pontifical Institute of Mediaeval Studies, 1968), pp. 27-37. On the title "Quaestiones de Anima," see J. H. Robb, *ibid.,* pp. 26-27. — For the dating of *ST* I (1265-1268), see the summary in I. T. Eschmann, "A Catalogue of St. Thomas' Works" (in E. Gilson, *The Christian Philosophy of St. Thomas Aquinas,* tr. L. K. Shook [New York 1956], pp. 381-439), p. 387.

4   *SCG* II, c. 80, § 5. The Aristotelian basis of the argument is clear in the text. See *De Anima* I, 4, 408b24-25; III, 5, 430a23-24, 24-25; III, 7, 431a16-17.

5   *SCG* II, c. 81, § 5.

intelligere has phantasms for its objects, St. Thomas must explain how understanding takes place in the separated soul. He argues that the separated soul understands in a different way from the united or embodied soul because it exists in a different way. Everything *acts* according as it *is*. The being (*esse*) of the united human soul, though free and independent of the body, nevertheless has the body as its underlying subject. That is why the soul's act of understanding, though exercised without an organ, has a bodily object, phantasms. It is therefore true that *quamdiu anima est in corpore, non potest intelligere sine phantasmate*. It is also true that this kind of *intelligere* will perish with the death of the body.[6]

But the separated soul will have a being (*esse*) that belongs to it alone without the body. Its *intelligere* will consequently take place without reference to bodily objects or phantasms. The separated soul "will understand through itself, in the manner of the substances that are in their being completely separate from bodies." It will also receive their influence more richly for more perfect understanding. There are signs of this future perfection even now. The virtue of temperance, by restraining the soul from bodily pleasures, makes men more fit for understanding. Men asleep perceive the future under the influence of higher substances, and so, even more, do ecstatics. St. Thomas' point (which he has already proved) is that since the soul lives on the confines of two worlds, that of material and immaterial substances, or of time and eternity, on leaving the lowest level it approaches the highest.[7]

---

6 Ibid., § 6.

7 Ibid. See *SCG* II, c. 68, §§ 3-6. The notion of the soul as established on the horizon of two worlds came to St. Thomas from the *Liber de Causis*, § 2, lines 7-9 (ed. O. Bardenhewer, *Die pseudo-aristotelische Schrift Ueber das reine Gute, bekannt unter dem Namen Liber de Causis* [Freibourg-im-Br. 1882], p. 165).

It is to be noted that St. Thomas uses the doctrine of the horizon in more than one direction, depending on his immediate problem. For example, in *SCG* II, c. 68, § 6, St. Thomas' purpose is to emphasize that the soul is an incorporeal form of matter and to bring together two aspects of the soul, namely, its immateriality and its embodiment. Hence, the soul is called *horizon* and *confinium* because, *inquantum est substantia incorporea*, it is yet *corporis forma*. (This interpretation of *horizon* is likewise adopted in *Quaestiones de Anima*, q. 1, ed. J. H. Robb, p. 60). But in *SCG* II, c. 81, § 6 (as well as in *Quodl.* III, q. 9, a. 1), the point that St. Thomas wishes to make, in using the notion of *horizon*, is that, when it is free of the body, the soul reaches up to what is highest: *recedens ab infimo appropinquat ad summum*. There now follows St. Thomas' own position, namely, that the separated soul *perfecte assimilabitur substantiis separatis quantum ad modum intelligendi*. —In *SCG* III, c. 61, § 5 St. Thomas uses the notion of *horizon* simply to argue that the substance of an intellectual form of matter, being above matter, has an action above it. St. Thomas then adapts this use to his own point: the opening that the soul has toward eternity shows that in the vision of God the intellectual soul will share in eternal life. — Finally, in *SCG* IV, c. 55, § 5, where St. Thomas is concerned to show how it was fitting that Christ should be joined to *man* in the Incarnation, the notion of *confinium* is applied to man himself: he unites the whole universe by his spiritual and corporeal nature. Note: "homo... quasi quoddam confinium tenens utriusque naturae..." (*ibid.*).

These texts clearly suggest that at the time of writing them St. Thomas was not aware that in

Hence, pursues St. Thomas, when the soul "will be wholly separated from the body, it will be perfectly likened to separate substances in the mode of understanding, and receive their influence in abundance: *perfecte assimilabitur substantiis separatis quantum ad modum intelligendi, et abunde influentiam earum recipiet.*" St. Thomas therefore concludes that, though the mode of understanding of the present life will be corrupted when the body is corrupted, it will be followed by another and higher, mode of understanding: *sic igitur, etsi intelligere nostrum secundum modum praesentis vitae corrupto corpore corrumpatur, succedet tamen alius modus intelligendi altior.*[8]

St. Thomas does not say what this other mode of understanding will be, but he does argue that the separated mode of being will give to the soul a separated mode of understanding. What he does not in the least consider here is the nature itself of the human soul. If the separated soul will not have another *nature,* how can its separation from the body make its mode of operation to be like that of separate substances? This question of the nature of the human soul, however, dominates the discussion in *ST* I, q. 89, a. 1.

b. *ST I, q. 89, a. 1*

The question asked is whether the separated soul understands anything, and St. Thomas begins his discussion with the sore point involved, namely, that a soul united to the body understands only by turn-

---

Prop. 2 the *Liber de Causis* was referring, not to the human soul, but to a divine soul. But in his own commentary on the *Liber de Causis,* which with the *De Substantiis Separatis* very likely belongs to the year 1272, St. Thomas pointed out that for the *Liber de Causis* the soul that was said to be on the horizon of eternity and time was a divine and heavenly soul. See St. Thomas *Super Librum de Causis Expositio,* Prop. 2 (ed. H. D. Saffrey, Fribourg-Louvain 1954, p. 16). The *Elementatio Theologica* of Proclus, which was translated from Greek into Latin by William of Moerbeke in May, 1268, was the new source of St. Thomas' appreciation that the *Liber de Causis* was speaking of an *anima divina,* and not the human soul. It is possible that St. Thomas did not study the text of Proclus seriously until 1272, when he made his own meticulous exegesis of the *Liber de Causis* and showed that it was *excerptus,* as he said in his introductory comments (*ed. cit.,* p. 3), from the *Elementatio* of Proclus. In any case, the influence of Proclus can be found in the *De Substantiis Separatis,* especially in the general exposition of Platonism in c. 1 as well as in two specific citations in c. 19 (see *De Substantiis Separatis,* cc. 1 and 19 [ed. F. J. Lescoe, West Hartford 1962], pp. 38-42, 158, 161, 165, 178). *Anima divina* appears as a Platonic doctrine in St. Thomas' late Commentary on the *De Caelo,* but without mention of Proclus (*In Ar. Libros de Caelo et Mundo* [ed. R. M. Spiazzi, Turin-Rome, 1952], Lib. II, lect. 4, § 334, p. 163). For the doctrine of divine souls as the first of three classes of souls, see Proclus, *Elements of Theology,* Prop. 184, 185, § 201, 203 [ed. E. R. Dodds, 2nd ed., Oxford 1963], pp. 160, 162, 176, 178).

8   *SCG* II, c. 81, §§ 6-7. — The Leonine editors read *eorum* with the manuscripts in § 6, and St. Thomas may have written *eorum,* in which case the editors had no option; but the sense requires *earum,* which modern translators follow even when they print *eorum.* (For the reading *eorum* see *SCG* II, c. 81, § 6, in *S. Thomas Aquinatis Opera Omnia,* ed. Leonina, vol. 13 [Rome 1918], p. 506).

ing to phantasms. This turning is the crux of the matter because the turning to phantasms is *ex natura animae*: it follows from the nature of the soul. Were this not the case, and the turning were instead an accidental circumstance resulting from embodiment, as the Platonists held, then the answer would be an easy one. If the soul were by nature a separate substance and embodiment were for it an impediment, then on separation the soul would return to its nature and understand as a separate substance. In that case, however, union with the body would be a detriment for the soul, not a benefit, though it would be a benefit for the body. But this is not a reasonable position because matter exists for the sake of form, not contrariwise. Hence, we must face the main difficulty. If we hold that *its nature* requires the soul to understand by turning to phantasms, then "since the nature of the soul after death will not be changed, it seems that the soul is [then] naturally able to understand nothing since phantasms, to which it might turn, are not present to it: *cum natura animae post mortem corporis non mutetur, videtur quod anima naturaliter nihil possit intelligere, cum non sint ei praesto phantasmata ad quae convertatur.*"[9]

Nature and the *natural union* between soul and body have now entered the discussion with decisive effect on the problem of the knowledge of the separated soul. *Si autem ponamus quod anima ex natura sua habeat ut intelligat convertendo se ad phantasmata...* So St. Thomas writes, and the first effect of dealing with the soul *ex natura sua* is to confront what seemed like a principle in *SCG* II, c. 81. Nothing acts, St. Thomas recognizes, except so far as it is in act, and therefore a thing's mode of operation follows its mode of being. The soul, as united to the body and as separated from it, has indeed different modes of being. But there is more to be said: across these two modes of being the nature of the soul remains the same: *manente tamen eadem animae natura.* We are here beyond the position of the *SCG*, and St. Thomas drives the point home by emphasizing that the two modes of being (embodied and separate) are both controlled by the nature of the soul. The soul is joined to the body, not accidentally, but by the structure and character of its nature: *per rationem suae naturae corpori unitur.* This is why the soul understands by turning to phantasms. The point, then, is that the embodied mode of being and acting is natural to the soul, and St. Thomas goes on to draw the consequences for the separated soul. He does so in a surprising way. To understand by turning to phantasms is natural to the soul, and to be separated from the body and understand without phantasms (by turning to pure in-

9 *ST* I, q. 89, a. 1.

telligibles, as separate substances do) is beyond the nature of the soul (*praeter naturam*). This is indeed why the soul is joined to the body, namely, "to be and to act according to its nature: *ut sit et operetur secundum naturam suam*." Again, the nature of the soul is occupying St. Thomas' mind, and he admits, not without humor, that since the higher is always the better, perhaps God should have so established the nature of the soul that it would turn by nature to intelligibles above it and not need the body for this purpose. [10]

We are now at an impasse rather than an answer, caused entirely by the conclusion that the embodied mode of being and acting is what is natural to the soul. There is no doubt, St. Thomas proceeds, that to understand by turning to higher intelligibles is nobler than to understand by turning to phantasms. But, in fact, the higher mode of understanding would have been the more imperfect one for the soul. The power to understand comes to intellectual substances from the divine light, which, one and simple in God Himself, becomes divided and diversified as intellectual creatures are more and more distant from God. Angels have a higher intellectual power, and need fewer but more powerful universals for understanding; on the other hand, lower intellectual substances have more multiplied, less universal and less powerful forms by which to know. [11] Human souls are such lower intellectual substances, which means that, had they been established by God to know in the manner proper to separate substances, their knowledge would have been incomplete and confused or indeterminate. Hence the problem and its answer: "For souls to have a complete and proper knowledge about things, they are naturally established in such a way as to be joined to bodies, and to receive a proper knowledge of sensible things from sensible things themselves — much as uncultivated men cannot be led to knowledge except through sensible examples." Here, then, is where we are: it is for the soul's better good that it is joined to a body and knows by conversion to phantasms. Nevertheless, the soul can be separated and it can have another mode of understanding. [12] And this is the end of the article!

ST I, q. 89, a. 1 is surely a remarkable, not to say astonishing, text. Exactly how has St. Thomas answered his own question, namely, whether the separated soul knows anything? Down to the last sentence of the *Respondeo* he has systematically proved that to be embodied and to know in an embodied way are natural to the soul; and he has em-

10 *Ibid.*
11 *Ibid.*
12 *Ibid.*

phasized that the specific intellectual nature of the soul cuts across and governs its embodied and separated modes of being; so much so, that, seen in the light of the soul's nature, a separated mode of being and acting is for the soul *praeter naturam*. St. Thomas does answer, in the very last sentence, that the soul can be separated and have another mode of understanding. But, to say the least, this is a very modest answer to the question formally raised by *ST* I, q. 89, a. 1. This is so true that we can only wonder whether St. Thomas' purpose in the whole article was not to show that embodiment was more than a question of a state of existence; it was expressive of a nature, so that, just as the embodied state was natural, so the separated state was beyond the conditions of the soul's nature.

The emphasis on the role of nature in characterizing the embodied and separated states of the soul is a new — and Aristotelian — development in the teaching of St. Thomas. It is new, specifically, when compared with the teaching in *SCG* II, c. 81. Moreover, it is new when compared with the teaching in the *Sentences* and the *De Veritate*. On the other hand, the same notion of the nature of the soul is at work in the *Quaestiones de Anima*. Let us here limit our remarks to the two texts that we have examined. In *SCG* II, c. 81 St. Thomas held, without qualification, that the separated soul, existing through itself, *intelliget per seipsam ad modum substantiarum quae sunt totaliter secundum esse a corporibus separatae*; and he had not hesitated to add that, *quando totaliter erit* (scil. *anima*) *a corpore separata, perfecte assimilabitur substantiis separatis quantum ad modum intelligendi et abunde influentiam earum recipiet*. On the most generous interpretation, these remarks are rather surprising. They say that the separated soul, on the basis of its separated *esse*, will function perfectly as a separate substance. The soul will respond to its separated state by knowing as a separate substance. This is surely the view that St. Thomas denies in the *ST*, where his very way of stating the difficulty already transcends the perspective of *SCG* II, c. 81.

As St. Thomas sees the difficulty posed by the separated soul in *ST* I, q. 89, a. 1, it is both caused and dominated by the *nature* of the soul. The difficulty is that if the embodied way of knowing is natural to the soul, because union with the body is for the good of the soul, then, as a consequence, it would seem that the separated soul *naturaliter nihil possit intelligere*. The controlling word in this difficulty is *naturaliter*. The state of separation from the body is *praeter naturam*, since the soul does not have the intellectual power to function properly as a separate substance. Thus, whereas in *SCG* II, c. 81 the separated state of the soul was accepted as the basis for saying that it will have a separated mode of knowing, in *ST* I, q. 89, a. 1 such an answer is impossible; not indeed because the separated soul cannot understand, but because its *natural* understanding is defective by as much as separation, both as a mode of being and as a mode of knowing, is *praeter naturam.*

III

The introduction of the intellectual nature of the soul as the essential factor in dealing with the way in which the soul knows is a decisive change in St. Thomas' attitude toward the separated soul. From this moment on he saw the separated soul in the light of the embodied soul considered as the model of what is natural to the soul both in its mode of being and in its mode of operation. There is therefore a before and after *ST* I, q. 89, a. 1 in the sense that St. Thomas thought of the knowledge of the separated soul without, and then with, the intervention of the identity of nature in the embodied and the separated soul. The nature of the soul intervened with decisive force in *ST* I, q. 89, a. 1, and that intervention can be felt not only throughout q. 89, but also in the *Quaestiones de Anima.* But when he was thinking about the soul without such an intervention, St. Thomas could, and did, visualize it as having two modes of existence, embodied and separate, as well as two modes of knowing, namely, by conversion to phantasms and as a separate substance. This position we have seen in *SCG* II, c. 81, but it is already to be found in the *Sentences* and the *De Veritate.*

a. *The Commentary on the* Sentences

In the Commentary on the third book of the *Sentences,* d. 31, q. 2, a. 4, the question is asked whether the scientific knowledge (*scientia*) that man has in the present life will be taken away in the next. The answer is interesting because it shows that, however much St. Thomas believed and said at this time that soul and body were parts within the unity of human nature,[13] he had not yet related the nature of the human intellect and the soul's union with the body as aspects of one and the same doctrine. In our present scientific knowledge, he writes, there are three things to consider: habit, act, and mode of acting. The mode of acting is by conversion to phantasms. In this life, the soul can neither acquire nor use already acquired knowledge without phantasms, since phantasms are related to the intellect as sensibles are related to the sense. The act of scientific knowing consists in grasping conclusions by

13   St. Thomas, *In III Sent.,* d. 5, q. 3, a. 2 (ed. M. F. Moos [Paris 1933], pp. 206-207).

bringing them back to self-evident first principles, while the habit is the quality that enables a man to accomplish such an act. What is the cause of the soul's mode of acting, that is, its need to turn to phantasms?

There are two causes, says St. Thomas. First, the human soul is by nature the lowest of intellects, and its possible intellect is related to all intelligibles as prime matter is related to all sensibles: it understands them only by receiving their forms via the senses and the imagination. There is a second cause, namely, the fact that the soul is the form of the body. The soul therefore acts as part of the whole man, so that the body acts as presenting the object for the intellect to know; which is also why, without a phantasm, the soul cannot understand (i.e. actually reconsider) what it already knows. The consequences for the separated soul are as follows.

The nature of the soul will remain in the separated soul, but its actual union with the body will not. This means more than a state of fact. Since indeed the nature of the soul remains after the union with the body is dissolved, the question is to know what can be said of it on this precise basis. St. Thomas thinks that the separated soul is able to consider what it previously knew without resorting to phantasms, though it faces the need of phantasms with respect to new knowledge. As is clear from the sequel, St. Thomas is not saying exactly what he means to say. The separated soul will not need phantasms to use old knowledge (in fact, none are present); it will rely on the habit of scientific knowledge as a substitute. As for new knowledge, this it can acquire either from what it previously knew or by divine infusion. What St. Thomas does not wish to admit is that "on the basis of what the soul now contains in its nature, it cannot understand without the body in any way." This view is for him rather close to those who say that the soul will die with the body, for, given that a natural operation accompanies a nature, then, if none of the soul's present operations can exist without the body, neither can the soul itself exist without the body. We can admit that inquiry and discursiveness will pass away from scientific knowlege, but the certitude to which they lead will remain. We must therefore conclude that separated souls will have another mode of understanding, one without phantasms. After the resurrection St. Thomas will admit the use of phantasms, but then the body will be entirely under the rule of the soul. [14]

The St. Thomas who wrote the present text did not like to think that to know by turning to phantasms was more than a matter of the soul's embodied state. The fifth objector, construing the dependence of the

14 *In III Sent.*, d. 31, q. 2, a. 4; *ed. cit.*, pp. 996-997.

soul on phantasms strictly, not to say rigidly, is told that the phantasm is not the proximate and proper object of the intellect, since it is only a potential intelligible: the *species intellecta* (the form in its state of abstracted intelligibility) is the *per se* object. St. Thomas clearly wishes to cut the intellect from its dependence on phantasms — except in terms of its *status* as in the body. So, too, St. Thomas wishes to discard from *scientia* the view that to know through phantasms belongs to its nature, and to argue that this belongs to it from the condition of its subject, that is, its embodiment.[15] The embodied way of knowing does not, in these comments, represent the nature of the human intellect. What is worrying St. Thomas is not difficult to fathom: *dicere enim quod secundum id quod modo anima habet in natura sua non possit intelligere sine corpore aliquo modo, est valde familiare illis qui ponunt animam cum corpore deficere.*[16] Clearly, to say that embodiment means for the soul that it cannot in any way understand when it is separated from the body is to render the separated soul operationless and to threaten it with nonexistence. For, according to the teaching of *De Anima* I, 1. 403a10-11, if none of the soul's present operations can be without the body, then neither can the soul itself be without the body: *quia, ut dicitur I· De Anima t. 13, si nulla operationum quas habet* (scil. *anima*) *potest esse sine corpore, nec ipsa sine corpore esse possit.*[17] At this moment, at least, St. Thomas is not able to say that the separated condition of the soul is *praeter naturam.* He therefore isolates the nature of the intellectual soul from the fact of knowing with phantasms, and, having done so, he is free to agree with those who say that *in patria, quantum ad animas separatas, erit alius modus intelligendi, quia sine phantasmate considerabunt.*[18] The difficult point in this position is not the *alius modus intelligendi,* it is the grounding that this other mode has in the nature of the soul.

At the end of the Commentary on the fourth book of the *Sentences,* d. 50, q. 1, a. 3, St. Thomas asks whether the separated soul knows singulars. The issues involved are the same as those we have just left. Five objectors pose in different ways the fundamental problem to be met, namely, that only the sense powers grasp singulars directly. How, then, can the disembodied soul know singulars? St. Thomas' answer depends on distinguishing between the creative knowledge of God, which is prior to things and their cause, and the knowledge that comes

---

15   *Ibid.,* ad 5; *ed. cit.,* p. 998.
16   *Ibid., Solutio; ed. cit.,* p. 997.
17   *Ibid.* See *De Anima* I, 1. 403a5-16.
18   *In III Sent., ibid.*

from things and is caused by them. In the latter kind of knowledge, the universals, being abstracted from matter and individuation by matter, are unable to give a knowledge of singulars. That is why the soul, while joined to the body, knows singulars directly only through the sense powers; the intellect knows singulars indirectly, by returning to phantasms. When the soul is separated from the body, it will have both kinds of knowledge. It will receive the forms of things from above, and since these likenesses, being derived from the divine ideas, represent individuals, the soul will thereby know individuals. But the forms received from things will not enable it to know singulars directly.[19] St. Thomas offers no further clarification, and he sees no difficulty in replying to an objector that the form by which the separated soul knows, being received from higher substances, is of another nature and power than abstracted universals.[20] There is no questioning in the text of the natural fitness of the soul for such a means of knowing, or of its consequences — which are precisely the questions St. Thomas raises in *ST* I, q. 89, a. 1.

b. *De Veritate, q. 19*

Can the separated soul understand? Can it understand singulars? These two questions are not new. What is new in the *De Veritate* is the striking confrontation between the nature of the soul (the position set forth in many ways by the objectors) and the separated mode of existence belonging to the soul after the death of the body (the position maintained by St. Thomas himself in the *Respondeo*). The objectors are bent on emphasizing the need of the intellect to function within the embodied state of the soul, and to argue that this need is a matter of nature. Stressing the nature of the soul to be embodied and the need of the intellect to depend on the sense powers and the body for its objects, the objectors conclude that the separated soul cannot understand. That St. Thomas should oppose this radical conclusion is scarcely surprising; what is surprising is the manner in which he answers the strongly Aristotelian arguments uniting the objectors in their common conclusion. As we shall see, *De Veritate*, q. 19 is not governed by that persistent principle that will dominate *ST* I, q. 89, a. 1, namely, the identity of nature in the embodied and separated soul and the decisive role played by this identity.

---

19 *In IV Sent.*, d. 50, q. 1, a. 3 (*S. Thomae Aquinatis Opera Omnia*, ed. S. E. Fretté, vol. 11 [Paris 1874], pp. 559-560).
20 *Ibid.*, ad 5; *ed. cit.*, p. 560.

The teaching of Aristotle appears as a difficult enemy in the objections of *De Veritate,* q. 19, a. 1. The soul is tied to the body for its activity, even in its highest reaches. Its understanding cannot, therefore, survive the body (obj. 1-2). Phantasms are necessary to the intellect for its objects; after the death of the body there will be no phantasms and no understanding (obj. 4). Nor is this dependence of the soul on the body a matter of its present status; for *objectum potentiae determinatur secundum naturam ipsius potentiae,* and *eadem est natura animae intellectivae ante mortem et post.* If the soul is ordered to phantasms before death, therefore, the same is true of it after death (obj. 5). The argument is a strong one, and St. Thomas must make his way through it.

In his own answer, St. Thomas begins by locating the problem before him. The soul cannot survive the death of the body unless it has an activity of its own. Therefore, just as, according to the Catholic Faith, we hold firmly that the soul survives the body, so we must hold that it can understand without the body. *How* is, precisely, the difficulty. The mode of understanding involved is difficult to grasp because the absence of phantasms means that the separated soul will have a mode of understanding that is different from its present one. St. Thomas rehearses no less than five opinions before reaching his own view of the matter.[21]

The principle governing the answer states that each thing receives the causal influence of what is above it in accord with its own mode of being: *per modum sui esse.* The human soul stands between separate forms and material forms in the reception of its own *esse* from God. The *esse* of the angels is not received in matter, nor dependent on matter; the *esse* of material forms is received in matter and is dependent on matter. The human soul, as form of the body, receives its *esse* in matter and is joined to the body in its *esse*; but, unlike a material form, the soul does not depend on the body because the *esse* of the soul can be conserved without the body. This intermediate position of the soul has consequences. The intellectual light received by the soul is such that its intellectual knowledge is related to the body, as depending on bodily powers for the origin and the actual use of its knowledge. At the same time, the soul's intellectual light is free, as not itself functioning through a bodily organ. This last point on the freedom of the soul's light means to St. Thomas that "when the soul is separated from the body, just as it will have its being (*esse*) independent of the body and not existing in the body, so accordingly will it receive the light of its intellectual

---

21 *De Veritate,* a. 19, a. 1.

knowledge: it will be neither bound to the body as exercised through the body, nor have any order to the body whatever: *nec omnino aliquem ordinem ad corpus habeat.*"

We have our answer, but St. Thomas wishes to add a comparison between the two modes of knowing, the embodied and the separate. On being created in the body, the soul acquires an intellectual way of knowing that depends on the body, that is, it knows by abstraction from phantasms and knows only what can be known in this way (e.g. it does not thereby have a knowledge of separate substances). But when the soul is separated from the body, the situation will change radically. It will then receive the light of intellectual knowledge as do the angels, without a body. It will receive the forms of things from God, without needing to resort to phantasms for actual understanding. It will moreover be able to see separate substances themselves by a natural knowledge, though not God Himself, which no creature can do without grace:

> Sed quando habebit esse a corpore absolutum, tunc recipiet influentiam intellectualis cognitionis hoc modo quo angeli recipiunt sine aliquo ordine ad corpus, ut scilicet species rerum ab ipso Deo recipiat, ne oporteat ad intelligendum in actu per has species, vel per eas quas prius acquisivit, ad aliqua phantasmata converti. Poterit nihilominus ipsas substantias separatas, scilicet angelos vel daemones, naturali cognitione videre, quamvis non Deum, quod ulli creaturae non conceditur sine gratia.[22]

St. Thomas concludes. The separated soul will know in three ways: by the species it received in its embodied state, by infused species, and by seeing separate substances (though this last is at their discretion).

In the name of its *esse*, therefore, the soul, on separation from the body, will act as a separate substance. St. Thomas sees no problem arising from the nature itself of the soul. It is only in its embodied state that the soul knows through the body, St. Thomas tells the first two objectors. He gives the same reply to the fourth objector. To the fifth St. Thomas admits that the specific nature of the soul is the same before and after death; but, he adds, the mode of being is not the same, and therefore neither is the mode of acting: *tamen non est idem modus essendi, et per consequens nec idem modus operandi.* In the same spirit St. Thomas argues (ad 6, 8) that, while the separated soul will have the same intellectual powers that it now has, these will not be ordered to the body. The reply to objector 13 makes more precise the meaning of the infusion of species that St. Thomas had said would take place on the separation of the soul from the body. This objector had argued that God

22 *Ibid.*

would not infuse any gifts into the souls in hell, which means that they would not have understanding. In reply, St. Thomas points out that the infusion he has in mind is a matter of nature, and therefore will be received by the souls of the damned as well: *Praedicta autem specierum infusio, quae fit in separatione animae a corpore, pertinet ad con- ditionem naturae animae separatae; et ideo huiusmodi infusione nec animae damnatorum privantur* (ad 13).

The view that St. Thomas has here set down in *De Veritate*, q. 19, a. 1 carries over into the problem of the knowledge of singulars by the separated soul (a. 2). It will know in two ways: by species infused on separation, and by species acquired in the body. On infused species, St. Thomas says that *attribuenda est animae separatae cognitio similis angelicae cognitioni*: on separation, the soul will know (by nature) *as* a separate substance. It will know by means of forms which, derived from the divine ideas, are both universal and the likenesses of singulars. As for universals acquired in this life, in the state of separation the soul will not know singulars through them, though it will be able to use them in relation to singulars that it otherwise will know.

It should be clear that in *De Veritate*, q. 19 St. Thomas endows the human soul with two modes of being and two modes of natural operation, the embodied and the separate. He finds no difficulty in saying that the separated soul will be equipped with infused species enabling it to know in a new way as a separate substance. St. Thomas all but endows the separated soul with a new nature; or rather, he sees no problem in holding that the separated soul, while having the same nature and the same powers as the embodied soul, will yet be able on separation to function properly as a separate substance. But this is precisely the point that he will deny in *ST* I, q. 89, a. 1, where, as we have seen, he writes that the sort of intellectual nature possessed by human souls means that, had they been established by God as separate substances, *non haberent cognitionem perfectam, sed confusam in com- muni.* In other words, the angelic mode of knowing does not suit the *nature* of the soul. In the *De Veritate,* however, it does in the sense that the nature itself of the soul plays no role in determining the mode of knowing that is natural to it in the state of separation.

IV

Quaestiones de Anima, qq. 15-20

After proving the immortality of the soul in q. 14, St. Thomas approaches the knowledge of the separated soul by placing his finger on the source of the problem, namely, the need that the soul has in this life of sense powers and sense knowledge as the basis for intellectual understanding. As in *ST* I, q. 89, a. 1, the union of soul and body, expressive of the intellectual nature of the soul itself, commands St. Thomas' decisions about the separated soul. Moreover, in considering the life and activity of the separated soul, St. Thomas points out repeatedly and specifies that the whole issue at stake concerns the *natural* knowledge of the separated soul. The knowledge that the souls of the blessed will have through grace is not what is in question: on the basis of this supernatural knowledge, they will be equal to the angels, since they will see everything in the divine Word.[23] St. Thomas' precise concern in qq. 15-20 is the *naturalis influxus* of God, and the *naturalis cognitio* and the *capacitas naturalis* of the soul.[24]

Refusing to follow the belief of Plato and Avicenna that the senses contribute only extrinsically to the existence of intellectual knowledge in man, St. Thomas believes that the only tenable explanation of the natural union of soul and body is to hold that *potentiae sensitivae sunt necessariae animae ad intelligendum, non per accidens tamquam excitantes ut Plato posuit, neque ut disponentes tantum sicut posuit Avicenna, sed ut repraesentantes animae intellectivae proprium objectum.*[25] Phantasms are therefore intrinsically necessary to the intellectual activity of the soul. This poses the question: does the separated soul understand? Given that the soul is the least of intellectual creatures, can it function as a separate substance? It can do so only to the extent of its intellectual power. Hence, were it to receive forms for knowledge of the kind that the angels receive, the separated soul would know indeterminately and confusedly. The only forms that it can know properly are those in matter. Not that the separated soul will not understand and know. But since it cannot naturally function as a separate substance, if we limit ourselves to the *naturalis influxus* of forms from above we must say that the resulting knowledge of the

23 *Quaestiones de Anima*, a. 18 (ed. J. H. Robb, p. 240). Page references to the text are to this edition (on which see note 3).

24 *Ibid.*, q. 15, p. 214; q. 17, p. 230; q. 18, pp. 239, 240.

25 *Ibid.*, q. 15, p. 213.

separated soul will not be as complete and determinate in its grasp of singulars as the soul now has through the sense.[26] The separated soul will not have to bear the burden that the body is, but its natural knowledge will remain indeterminate in the absence of the senses and the body.

Similarly, after proving at length that the embodied soul can know only that separate substances exist and what they are not,[27] St. Thomas allows that the separated soul, as a result of influence from above, will know itself directly; but, in view of its lowly intellectuality, it will not (that is, by a natural knowledge) know separate substances as perfectly as they know themselves.[28] In the same way, the question whether the separated soul knows all natural things gives St. Thomas the opportunity to emphasize (a) that, as the lowest among intellectual substances, the soul has the *naturalis capacitas* to receive forms of the kind found in material things, and (b) that the separated soul has no greater intellectual power than is in keeping with such material forms: *nec est ei major virtus naturalis ad intelligendum quam ut secundum hujusmodi formas sic determinatas in cognitione intelligibili perficiatur.*[29] This, clearly, decides the matter. The separated soul receives forms in a less universal way than do the separate substances, but, then, it has a lesser intellectual power; as a result its knowledge (that is, its natural knowledge) is such that the separated soul knows things universally and without determination.[30] And this is our conclusion. "By means of a natural knowledge, separated souls know all natural things in a universal way; but they do not know each thing in a particular way." Of course, the souls of the saints have through grace a knowledge equal to that of the angels.[31]

The separated soul's knowledge of singulars likewise involves the principles that we have just seen. Where angels have the power to know singulars by participation in the creative ideas of God, the intellectual power of the separated soul is not equal to such infused universals which nevertheless contain a proper representation of singulars — except where, for some special reason, traces of the relations to particular singulars survive.[32] But the principle remains intact. The natural power of the separated soul, proportioned to knowing only material singulars,

26 *Ibid.,* p. 214.
27 *Ibid.,* q. 16, pp. 220-225.
28 *Ibid.,* q. 17, pp. 229-230.
29 *Ibid.,* q. 18, pp. 239-240.
30 *Ibid.,* p. 240.
31 *Ibid.*
32 *Ibid.,* q. 20, pp. 258-260.

and knowing intellectually only what is universal in them, knows singulars in its state of separation only in an indeterminate way.[33]

V

FROM *SCG II, c. 81 to ST I, q. 89, a. 1*

We can now see in some detail the change in teaching that *ST* I, q. 89, a. 1 represents. In the *Sentences*, the *De Veritate* and the *SCG*, St. Thomas had thought that the separated soul could know as a separate substance, and he had thought so because the intellectual nature of the soul played no limiting role in the teaching of these texts. Nor is there any visible influence in these same texts of the notions that will impress St. Thomas in the *ST* and the *Quaestiones de Anima,* namely, the identity of nature in the embodied and separated soul and, more particularly, the identity of intellectual power and capacity. The natural knowledge of the separated soul was not a problem for St. Thomas when he wrote the *Sentences,* the *De Veritate* and the *SCG.* However strange it may seem, the intellectual nature of the soul, on the one hand, and its relations to the body, on the other, were not seen in the *Sentences* as expressive of one and the same fact about man.[34] Hence, in the *De Veritate* and in the *SCG* St. Thomas based his conception of the knowledge of the separated soul, not on any consideration of its specific intellectual power, but on its separated mode of being: having such a mode of being, the separated soul could know as a separate substance.

This position did not say merely that the separated soul could in fact understand and know. It said that it had a separate mode of being and a separate mode of knowing. Admittedly, if this was true, it was an answer to those who argued that, since the proportioned and hence appropriate way for the soul to know was through the body, the separated soul could not have any understanding. But to make the separated soul into a separate substance in order to free it from total dependence on the body was too much of an answer. Yet it was the answer of *SCG* II, c. 81: *quando totaliter erit* (scil. *anima) a corpore separata, perfecte assimilabitur substantiis separatis quantum ad modum intelligendi, et abunde influentiam earum recipiet.* It is here — in the astonishing notion of "perfecte assimilabitur" — that St. Thomas had further thoughts in *ST* I, q. 89, a. 1.

---

33 *ST* I, q. 89, aa. 2-4.
34 See above, pp. 139-140.

To go as far as the *SCG* had gone was, however unintentionally, to create a new difficulty in the process of answering an old one. For if the soul could thus be perfectly like separate substances in its own state of separation, then, what was its nature and what was the point of its union with the body? St. Thomas had finally to come to terms with this question and to see that the nature of the soul as a lesser intellectual substance was properly expressed only in its state of embodiment, so that separation from the body was *praeter naturam*. The nature of the soul was such that, by constitution and power, it could be no more than an inadequate separate substance. The *natural* knowledge of the separated soul was imperfect by as much as there were no sense powers and organs to complete it. Seen in the light of what St. Thomas had written in the *Sentences* and the *De Veritate,* the text of *ST* I, q. 89, a. 1 can be read as a deliberate reassessment of his position. The separated mode of being and knowing in the soul is controlled by its intellectual nature and that nature is adequately realized only in its condition of embodiment. What God does for the soul through grace is not in question. The question concerns the nature of the soul to be embodied in the name of its own intellectuality.

The distance from *SCG* II, c. 81 to *ST* I, q. 89, a. 1 is remarkable. *ST* I, q. 89, a. 1, followed by *Quaestiones de Anima,* qq. 15-20, opens up a new outlook in the thought of St. Thomas. The outlook is new both as a development and as a correction of the earlier doctrine of St. Thomas. The correction involves the realization that it is not possible to infer an adequate mode of knowing for the separated soul on the basis of its survival as a separated form. St. Thomas' emphasis on the conditions of the natural knowledge of the separated soul, on its natural capacity and power, and on the natural imperfections that attend its ways of knowing in the state of separation from the body, is certainly a correction of his earlier doctrine. That same emphasis is also a development of his view of the unity of the human person, and especially the unity of intellectual nature in the composite of soul and body. Composition is to be understood as an expression of the soul's intellectual nature and therefore as a permanent need in the soul itself. Composition governs the nature of the separated soul, therefore, with all the consequences affecting its natural power and capacity that we have seen.

Some chronological comments can be added to these doctrinal results. Belonging in its teaching with the *Sentences* and the *De Veritate, SCG* II, c. 81 is to be located chronologically with them in the sense that it was written before *ST* I, q. 89, a. 1. It seems absurd to believe that, having corrected himself in *ST* I, q. 89, a. 1, St. Thomas reverted, after the correction, to his earlier opinion. This would be the effect of thinking that the *SCG* was written after the *ST*, that is, that the *SCG* was completed in 1273.[35] Some intellectual changes are not reversible, if only because they involve the clarification and maturing of ideas in a person's mind. Given the doctrinal substance of *ST* I, q. 89, a. 1, it seems more than implausible that *SCG* II, c. 81 was written after such a correction. *SCG* II, c. 81 could certainly have been drafted while St. Thomas was disputing *De Veritate*, q. 19; it could not have been written while St. Thomas was composing *ST* I, that is, during 1265-1268 in Italy. As far as a general chronology is concerned, therefore, it seems reasonable to argue that *SCG* II, c. 81 is to be associated in its teaching with *De Veritate*, q. 19. Since, moreover, in the second book of the *SCG*, St. Thomas makes use of William of Moerbeke's new Greek-Latin translation of Aristotle's writings on animals, done in 1260, this book was written in 1261 or 1262.[36] The old date of Tolomeo of Lucca, locating the *SCG* during the pontificate of Urban IV (1261-1264), fits the teaching of *SCG* II, c. 81.[37] That chapter was written very early in the 1260's, when St. Thomas was framing his Aristotelian principles but when he had still to apply them extensively in his theology. Taken together, *SCG* II, c. 68 and c. 81 make decisively clear that St. Thomas knew man in his existential unity before he meditated, with Aristotelian tools, on the unity of his intellectual nature.[38] This second knowledge belongs to the transition from *SCG* II, c. 81 to *ST* I, a. 89, a. 1.

35 I am referring to: *S. Thomae Aquinatis Doctoris Angelici Liber de Veritate Catholicae Fidei contra Errores Infidelium qui dicitur Summa Contra Gentiles, Introductio* (Marietti-Lethielleux 1967). This voluminous *Introduction* is by P. Marc, C. Pera and P. Caramello, and the general result of their work can be seen in the proposed new (and revolutionary) chronology of the writings of St. Thomas on pp. 406-424. The authors see no difficulty in loading the bulk of St. Thomas' theological writings and his Aristotelian commentaries into the last four years of his life. As for the *SCG*, which is the central concern of the *Introduction*, the conclusion is that St. Thomas began it late in 1269 and finished it in Naples in 1273 (p. 374). I find this view untenable, but it would require a long analysis to deal with the question adequately.

36 On the Arabic-Latin and Greek-Latin translations of Aristotle's works on animals, see G. Lacombe, *Aristoteles Latinus*, Pars Prior (Roma 1939), pp. 80-85. For St. Thomas' use of William of Moerbeke's Greek-Latin translations, see A. Gauthier's introduction to *Saint Thomas d'Aquin, Contra Gentiles*, Livre Premier (Paris 1961), pp. 41-47.

37 See Tolomeo's catalogue in P. Mandonnet, *Des écrits authentiques de s. Thomas d'Aquin* (2nd ed., Fribourg 1910), p. 60.

38 *SCG* II, c. 83 is an interesting witness on this point. It is directed against the Platonic doctrine of the eternity of souls and even more against its Christian adaptation by Origen and his followers. In this view, souls were created by God before the visible universe and then infused into bodies. Arguing against this position in the name of the unity of human nature, St. Thomas emphasizes from many points of view that the soul cannot be created before the body. The union of soul and body is natural, not violent or voluntary; the soul as form is completed in the matter in which it belongs; the soul naturally needs senses and organs for knowledge (including the knowledge of principles); etc. The intended point of these and similar arguments is that the soul was not created before the body. Yet the arguments also tell against the position that St. Thomas had just adopted in *SCG* II, c. 81, §§ 5-7. Clearly, if to be embodied is of the very nature of the soul, then separation must be in some sense *praeter naturam*. If *SCG* II, cc. 81 and 83 hang together, it can be only because the notion of *praeter naturam* is not here present to St. Thomas' mind.

VI

The Problem of *Quodlibet III, q. 9, a. 1*

Once it has been established that *ST* I, q. 89, a. 1 represents a new doctrine in the teaching of St. Thomas on the separated soul, two sorts of consequences follow. First, on this problem at least, there are doctrinal periods in St. Thomas' life: the teaching of *SCG* II, c. 81, §§ 5-7, is not compatible with that of the *ST* and with *Quaestiones de Anima,* qq. 15-20: the nature of the soul controls what St. Thomas says about the knowledge of the separated soul in the latter texts, while that same nature, though recognized, plays no part in determining how the separated soul knows in the *SCG*, the *De Veritate* and the Commentary on the *Sentences*. St. Thomas corrected himself in *ST* I, q. 89, a. 1 by recognizing that the separated state of the soul was *praeter naturam*, and its natural power inadequate to the state of separation. This correction, moreover, was the result of a development in doctrine, namely, the fuller application to the separated soul of the notion that to be joined to a body was of the very essence of the soul's intellectual nature. In this sense, there is a limited Aristotelianism in *SCG* II, concentrating its attention on the existential unity of the human person; in this same sense, the Aristotelianism of *ST* I is more extensive in influence: the nature of the separated soul is explicitly treated as still the nature proper to an embodied form.

The second consequence of *ST* I, q. 89, a. 1, as we have seen, is chronological. Clearly, St. Thomas could not have written the *SCG* (and specifically II, c. 81) in 1265-1269 when he was writing the *Prima Pars* and the *Quaestiones de Anima*. He could have written the *SCG* before 1265 or after 1269. Belonging doctrinally with the Commentary on the *Sentences* and the *De Veritate,* the *SCG* could have been written in 1261-1264. I have argued that it was, and I have done so, not by translating a clear doctrinal affinity into a chronological fact, but by emphasizing that the development of St. Thomas' Aristotelianism in *ST* I, q. 89, a. 1 makes the return to the teaching of *SCG* II, c. 81 an untenable hypothesis. No one, of course, can prove that, having written *ST* I, q. 89, a. 1 and *Quaestiones de Anima,* qq. 15-20, St. Thomas could not have gone on to write *SCG* II, c. 81, §§ 5-7. Anyone who allows such a possibility will not be impressed by doctrinal evidence. And yet that is the question. Is it conceivable that, once achieved, the development of the doctrine of the *nature* of the soul during 1265-1269 was thereafter reversed? To the present writer, at least, such a reversal does not seem possible. For this reason the *SCG* could not have been written after the *ST*; it was written early in the 1260's, as has traditionally been believed.

This conclusion brings us to *Quodlibet* III, q. 9, a. 1, which is dated Easter, 1270.[39] If we accept as correct the view that the *Quaestiones de Anima* were held in Paris in the first half of 1269,[40] then we are faced by a new and more aggravated form of the difficulty posed by dating the *SCG* after 1269. In doctrine, *Quodl.* III, q. 9, a. 1 is like the *De Veritate* and the *SCG*. Hence, if St. Thomas held the third *Quodlibet* at Easter, 1270, we must believe that he reversed the position of the *Quaestiones de Anima* a scant year after developing it. Were the change effected by *ST* I, q. 89, a. 1, a purely technical point or a relatively unimportant one, it is conceivable that St. Thomas held one view in the early 1260's, changed his opinion in 1265-1269, and then returned to his earlier opinion in 1270. But we are dealing with a major change in a major question. We are dealing with the knowledge of the separated soul, a natural part of the human person, and we are doing so at a moment when the notion of "part" is subject to its maximum stress, namely, the separation of the soul from the body. Is the separated soul, as separated, still *by nature* (that is, in its intellectuality) a part of the human composite? That it is, is what St. Thomas finally affirmed in *ST* I, q. 89, a. 1. He affirmed it, and he then elaborated it into a doctrine of the natural power and capacity of the separated soul that we have seen in *Quaestiones de Anima,* qq. 15-20. The question is: did St. Thomas then cancel this development less than one year after effecting it?

There is no doubt about the teaching of *Quodl.* III, q. 9, a. 1. The question asked is whether one separated soul knows another separated

---

39 See J. Destrez, "Les disputes quodlibétiques de saint Thomas d'après la tradition manuscrite" (*Mélanges Thomistes* [Le Saulchoir 1923]), pp. 73, 90, 94, 97; F. Pelster, "Literarhistorische Probleme der Quodlibeta des hl. Thomas von Aquin II" (*Gregorianum*, 29, 1948), pp. 63-69.

In view of the scribal evidence it may seem more than surprising to question the dating of the third *Quodlibet*. But if it is true that *ST* I, q. 89, a. 1 contains a new doctrine on the knowledge of the separated soul, then the question must be asked. There are three possible answers in the situation. (a) My interpretation of *ST* I, q. 89, a. 1, as compared with *SCG* II, c. 81, §§ 5-7, is not correct and therefore no problem, chronological or doctrinal, exists. But, *salvo meliori judicio*, the *ST* does contain a new doctrine on the *natural* knowledge of the separated soul, visibly expanded in the *Quaestiones de Anima*, qq. 15-20. If the *Summa* and the *Quaestiones* are dated 1265-1269, the change took place during this period. (b) If my interpretation of *ST* I, q. 89, a. 1 is correct, then a second possibility offers itself. *Quodl.* III is dated at Easter 1270 and St. Thomas simply changed his mind and returned to his earlier position. This is possible, but also so unlikely as not to be worth serious consideration. St. Thomas expanded his knowledge, and especially his use, of Aristotelianism in the transition from the *SCG* to the *ST*. How could he have reversed that process? (c) There remains a third — and difficult— alternative: *Quodl.* III does not belong to Easter 1270. This is not a proof but a question, arising from the evidence of the *ST* and the *Quaestiones de Anima.*

40 See above, note 3.

soul, but, though St. Thomas finally answers this question, the purpose of his *Respondeo* is to explain how the separated soul knows. The soul survives the death of the body, and since no substance is deprived of its own operation, St. Thomas must defend the view that the separated soul understands in some way. One of three possible ways of understanding can be attributed to the separated soul. It will understand (a) either by abstracting species from things, as it now does in its embodied state; (b) or by species acquired in the body and conserved after death; (c) or even by species that are concreated with the soul or in some way derived from above.

Some accept the first alternative, but St. Thomas does not. Abstraction needs sensible powers and the separated soul will not have corporeal organs for the exercise of such powers. There are those who not only deny the first alternative but also say that the separated soul will not understand by species acquired from sensible things in its embodied state. Following Avicenna,[41] these thinkers hold that species are not in any way conserved in the possible intellect; there are particular species in the imagination and the memory and when the possible intellect turns to them it then receives intelligible species from the agent intellect. But since the imagination and the memory will be corrupted with the death of the body, the separated soul will not understand by species received from the body: none are conserved in the intellect. How, then? The proposed answer is that separated souls understand through concreated species, as do the angels.

St. Thomas finds this second position irrational. He thinks, against Avicenna, that intelligible species are conserved in the intellect, where they are received with the immobility of the being of the intellect and share in that same immobility. He also thinks that the Avicennian view is contrary to the teaching of Aristotle, who held that intelligible species were present in the intellect not only in actually used knowledge but also in habitually possessed knowledge.[42] Nor is concreation a tenable answer, as St. Thomas shows. If we say that the embodied soul has and can use such concreated species, then we must hold that man can understand without sense experience. This would mean that a blind person will understand colors, which is false. If we say that union with the body will prevent the soul from knowing through its supposed con-

41 Avicenna's doctrine of intelligible species can be found in his *De Anima* (*VI Naturalium*), Part V, c. 6 (*Avicennae... Opera*, Venice 1508), fol. 26rb-va (C-D). St. Thomas has examined the doctrine in *SCG* II, c. 74; *ST* I, a. 84, a. 4; also, but under a different aspect, in *De Veritate*, q. 10, aa. 2 and 6 and q. 11, a. 1.

42 Aristotle, *De Anima* III, 4. 429b5; see St. Thomas' use of this text in *ST* I, q. 79, a. 6.

created species, then we are holding that the union of the soul and the body is not a natural one.

There remains the third alternative, which St. Thomas accepts. The separated soul will understand some things through species abstracted in the embodied state. But this is not a sufficient answer. Separated souls will know many things that we do not know in this life. There is the further difficulty that if abstracted species are the only source of knowledge for the separated soul, those who die before birth and perhaps have made no use of their intellects and acquired no intelligible species, will understand nothing after death. In addition to abstracted species, therefore, St. Thomas posits that, on separation from the body, the soul will receive intelligible species from God. The principle behind this view is what St. Thomas calls the natural order of the soul, which we ourselves experience in this life. According to this natural order, the more we free ourselves from the senses of the body, the more the soul can share in a higher light. We can see this in people who are asleep or who are in some state of alienation and who have even been known to foretell future events.

This conclusion enables St. Thomas to argue, by way of answer to the original question proposed, that one separated soul will be able to know another both by a knowledge it acquired in this life and by likenesses it will receive from God. That this is a natural knowledge is clear: *sive per aliquam similitudinem influxam a deo naturali influxu.*

In the main, *Quodl.* III, q. 9, a. 1 is a condensed version of *De Veritate,* q. 19, a. 1. The immediate questions raised are different and the diagnosis of various views on the way in which the separated soul knows is more elaborate and detailed in the latter text. But *Quodl.* III, q. 9, a. 1 follows the same development as *De Veritate,* q. 19, a. 1 and comes to the same conclusion: the separated soul will know by species abstracted in the embodied state and by infused species (this infusion is a matter of natural knowledge, not of supernatural grace). There is one difference between the *Quodlibet* and the *De Veritate.* In the manner of *SCG* II, c. 81, § 6, *Quodl.* III, q. 9, a. 1 argues that, on separation, the soul will be free to receive infused species. The principle of this freedom is that separation from the body will enable the soul to approach the higher world of intellectual light more perfectly. The natural order (*secundum naturalem ordinem*) of which the *Quodlibet* speaks is the doctrine of the soul as located on the horizon of eternity and time, understood both here and in *SCG* II, c. 81, § 6 as meaning that when the soul is free of the body it will also be free to live and act as a separate substance.[43]

43 See above, note 7.

Doctrinally, therefore, *Quodl.* III, q. 9, a. 1 belongs with the Commentary on the *Sentences,* the *De Veritate* and the *SCG*; it does not belong with the *ST* and the *Quaestiones de Anima.* After *ST* I, q. 89, a. 1, the *nature* of the soul assumes a controlling role in what St. Thomas says about the knowledge — and, specifically, the natural knowledge — of the separated soul. The new doctrine, far from seeing in separation a freedom for the soul, sees a condition that is *praeter naturam*: the proper mode of being for the soul is in the body. St. Thomas emphasizes this point more than once in the *Quaestiones de Anima,* qq. 15-20, where he also makes clear that the problem at issue concerns the natural capacity and power of the separated soul for knowledge. If (to repeat) the *Quaestiones de Anima* were held in Paris between January and June 1269, then, in the light of the change that took place between 1265 and 1269, we are faced by the following question: could *Quodl.* III, q. 9, a. 1, belonging in the doctrinal family of the *De Veritate* and the *SCG,* have been held at Easter, 1270?

Many things are possible, and there is no absolute proof that early in 1270 St. Thomas could not have repudiated what he had developed in 1265 to 1269. It is possible, but it is also incredible. Wishing to endow the separated soul with some intellectual knowledge, St. Thomas did not say until the *ST* that the natural knowledge of the separated soul was confused and indeterminate and that the separated soul was naturally inadequate to being — and acting as — a separate substance. In *SCG* II, c. 68, that marvelous text on the existential unity of soul and body in man, St. Thomas had said that *ipsum intelligere animae humanae indiget potentiis quae per quaedam organa corporalia operantur,* and from this he had inferred that the human soul *naturaliter unitur corpori ad complendam speciem humanam* (§ 12). Even so, this position had not prevented St. Thomas from holding, only a few chapters later, the doctrine that we have seen, namely, that *quando totaliter erit* (scil. *anima) a corpore separata, perfecte assimilabitur substantiis separatis quantum ad modum intelligendi, et abunde influentiam earum recipiet* (c. 81, § 6). This *modus intelligendi* remains as unconnected here with embodiment as it did in the Commentary on the *Sentences* (III, d. 31, q. 2, a. 4). But with *ST* I, q. 89, a. 1, the intellect of the separated soul reveals how much it needs embodiment and how much separation impedes its natural operation.

The question is: is it credible that St. Thomas reversed the *ST* and the *Quaestiones de Anima* in writing *Quodl.* III, q. 9, a. 1 and returned to the position and the perspective of the *De Veritate* and the *SCG*? The question is really a twofold one, since, as with the *SCG,* it concerns not only the position taken by St. Thomas but also his view of the problem to be solved. To repeat, St. Thomas had two such views, belonging doctrinally and chronologically to different periods in his life. One is *De Veritate,* q. 19, a. 1, the other is *Quaestiones de Anima,* q. 15. These texts represent two views of the same problem, namely, whether the separated soul can understand; and the views are different both in the answer proposed and in the way in which St. Thomas analyzed (both historically and doctrinally) the state of the question before him. It seems as untenable that in *Quodl.* III, q. 9, a. 1 (as well as in *SCG* II, c. 81, §§ 5-7) St. Thomas should have returned to the position of *De Veritate,* q. 19, a. 1 as that he should have returned to its perspective. The text of *ST* I, q. 89, a. 1 had eliminated the perspective of the *De Veritate,* and the *Quaestiones de Anima* had established a new one; the two texts together had defined what was and what was not natural to the soul. Having worked out a new perspective on the knowledge of the separated soul in 1269, could St. Thomas have silently ignored that perspective early in 1270 and as silently returned to the *De Veritate*? This is so unlikely both as procedure and as doctrine that it is much more reasonable to question the dating of *Quodl.* III, q. 9, a. 1.

VII

CONCLUSION

Given the nature and the dimensions of the doctrinal change effected in *ST* I, q. 89, a. 1, it seems impossible not to think of *SCG* II, c. 81 and *Quodl.* III, q. 9, a. 1 as early texts: they belong in the world defined by *De Veritate,* q. 19, a. 1. In comparison, the world of the *ST* is new in the sense that it achieved a purer and more authentic expression of the naturalism that is the distinctive mark of the Thomistic theology. If there is a doctrinal argument for the view advanced in the present essay, namely, that St. Thomas did not undo the teaching of *ST* I, q. 89, a. 1, it lies at this point. Embodiment is of the essence of the human soul, deriving from its intellectual nature; so much so, that, under the pressure of his own teaching, St. Thomas came to see (and even to underscore, in the *Quaestiones de Anima*) that the separated state of the soul was, in terms of its constitution as a nature, *praeter naturam.* When St. Thomas reached this point he added to his theology a remarkable precision on the doctrine of the immortality of the soul.

To say that embodiment is of the essence of the soul is to question not only the natural condition of the separated soul but also the separation itself. Up to and including *SCG* II, c. 81, §§ 5-7, St. Thomas was in some danger of endowing the separated soul with an intellectual power and mode of acting that could not be verified in the nature of the embodied soul. This danger the *ST* eliminated. As seen in I, q. 89, a. 1, separation was not a fulfillment for the soul according to its nature, it was a defect and a suffering caused by the fact of death. Death has never been an easy reality for philosophers to manage, even though Plato began his long career by thinking, in memory of Socrates, that philosophy was a meditation on death. But, then, such a Platonic meditation presupposed that the soul was a person in its own right, which was exactly the notion that St. Thomas worked to eliminate from Christian teaching. The soul was a part of man, man himself was the person, and, not the soul alone, but man the composite of soul and body was destined for immortal life.

We have only to see death and the separation of the soul from the body with the eyes of St. Thomas the theologian to realize that the doctrine of the immortality of the soul must not be identified with the fact of the separation of the soul from the body. The human soul is incorruptible and immortal, and it does survive the body; but, as we know from *ST* I, q. 89, a. 1, the condition of the separated soul, when seen in terms of its constitution, is *praeter naturam*.[44] Are we to say, then, that

44 The opinions of St. Thomas' sixteenth- and seventeenth-century commentators on the knowledge of the separated soul are outside the scope of the present essay. Yet Cajetan's reflections on *ST* I, q. 89, a. 1 are, in purely textual terms, a surprising phenomenon. See his commentary in *S. Thomae Aquinatis Opera Omnia*, ed. Leonina, vol. 5 (Rome 1889), pp. 371-374.

(a) Translating St. Thomas' *praeter naturam* into his own *praeternaturale*, and (b) interpreting *praeternaturale* as wider or more common than *contra naturam* (so that it includes under it *contra, supra* and *extra naturam*), Cajetan argues that in *ST* I, q. 89, a. 1 St. Thomas is taking *praeternaturale* in the sense of *supra naturam propriam ipsius animae* (§§ XI and XIII, p. 373). There is nothing in the text of St. Thomas to justify the decision, but, having made it, Cajetan separates himself even more from his master. The intellectual soul, he writes, *secundum propriam naturam* has *esse in corpore et intelligere per conversionem ad phantasmata*; but in the peak of its intellectuality, the soul *participat aliquid de natura substantiarum separatarum... and habet quod sit extra corpus, ut illae sunt, et intelligat per conversionem ad intelligibilia simpliciter, ut illae intelligunt* (§ XIII, p. 373).

This conclusion effectively destroys the unity of nature in the embodied and separated soul. Except for the knowledge of principles, there is no such intellectual peak in the soul for St. Thomas as Cajetan supposes. See *ST* I, q. 79, a. 8. Nor does St. Thomas' *praeter naturam* bear the interpretation that Cajetan has given it. It is remarkable that in the very text in which St. Thomas emphasizes at length the dependence *by nature* of the soul on the body for its intellectual operation, Cajetan has managed to make the soul into a separate substance. *Praeter naturam* is for St. Thomas, not a perfection, but a loss; that is why the *natural* knowledge of the separated soul has all the limitations that qq. 15-20 of the *Quaestiones de Anima* have systematically pointed out. In spite of Cajetan, the St. Thomas who could say in *SCG* IV, c. 79, § 10 that *est igitur contra naturam animae absque corpore esse* saw something of that *contra naturam* (to say the least) in the *praeter naturam* of *ST* I, q. 89, a. 1.

The terminology *praeter naturam* in *ST* I, q. 89, a. 1 and *contra naturam* in *SCG* IV, c. 79, § 10 should be distinguished from the same terminology used in another context, e.g. in *SCG* III, c. 100, § 1 where St Thomas writes: "... licet Deus interdum praeter ordinem rebus inditum aliquid operetur, nihil tamen facit contra naturam." For, St. Thomas continues, all nature is as a *quoddam artificiatum* of the divine art, so that "non est autem contra rationem artificii si artifex aliter aliquid operetur in suo artificio" (ibid., § 6). The *praeter naturam* and *contra naturam* that we

its own immortality confronts the soul with natural defects that the death of the body causes? Is not immortality, seen simply as the survival of the separated soul, the burden of living *praeter naturam*? This is certainly not what St. Thomas thought. On the contrary, we can see his position as a theologian in the fourth book of the *SCG* (c. 79) where he is face to face with the doctrine of the resurrection of the body. What has the human soul itself to say on this point?

It is appropriate that St. Thomas should first think of the teaching of St. Paul on the resurrection of the body. Death came into the world through the sin of Adam, but the resurrection of Christ has freed man from the consequences of sin just as at the end of time it will free man from death in the resurrection of his own body (§§ 2-8). This is a fulfillment of the faith of Job that after death he would rise from the earth and see his divine defender in the flesh (§ 9; *Job* 19.25-26). But St. Thomas does not stop with purely scriptural proofs of the resurrection. There is also *evidens ratio* in support of it, such as St. Thomas himself had set forth in *SCG* II. He looks back to that argumentation now, noting his overall conclusion that *anima corpori naturaliter unitur* and his sustained proof (cc. 56-68) of the philosophical formula of this conclusion, namely, that *est enim* (scil. *anima*) *secundum essentiam suam corporis forma*. This estimate in *SCG* IV, c. 79 of what he had proved with philosophical tools in *SCG* II is St. Thomas' prepared ground for saying, as he does say, that *est igitur contra naturam animae absque corpore esse*. The theologian who wrote these words was surely free of what he had written in *SCG* II, c. 81. But there is more. For, since nothing against nature can be everlasting (so Aristotle had taught St. Thomas to think[45]), and since the soul itself is everlasting, it follows that the soul "must again be joined to the body: *oportet eam corpori*

have seen concern the *internal* order of a created nature, namely, man, and it was St. Thomas' point that to be and to act in the state of separation from the body was for the soul to be *praeter naturam* in the Aristotelian sense in which a body is outside its natural place; similarly, given what St. Thomas proved in *SCG* II, cc. 56-68 on the natural union of soul and body, it can be said in *SCG* IV, c. 79, § 10 that "est igitur contra naturam animae absque corpore esse." The *constitutional* use of *praeter* and *contra naturam* is not to be confused with their *institutional* use within the perspective of the divine government: the first concerns the created nature, the second concerns the action of God in the created nature.

In his recent study of the action of God *praeter ordinem naturae,* Vladimiro Boublik ignored, even for terminological purposes, *praeter naturam* in *ST* I, q. 89, a. 1 and *contra naturam* in *SCG* IV, c. 79, § 10. (See V. Boublik, *L'Azione Divina "Praeter Ordinem Naturae" secondo S. Tommaso d'Aquino* [Rome 1968]). That such texts do not belong directly in the study of the divine action is perfectly clear; but it is just as clear that such texts exist, containing a terminology and a doctrine that are part of the Aristotelian naturalism that St. Thomas introduced into theology. Cajetan, for example, missed that naturalism in his astonishing interpretation of *praeter naturam* in *ST* I, q. 89, a. 1, although the Aristotelian doctrine of natural places was used by St. Thomas in the same text to explain the meaning of saying that the condition of the separated soul was *praeter rationem suae naturae* and *praeter naturam*.

45 See *De Caelo* II, 3. 286a17-18.

iterato coniungi." This is for the body to rise again. Hence: "The immortality of souls, therefore, seems to require the future resurrection of their bodies: *immortalitas igitur animarum exigere videtur resurrectionem corporum futuram"* (§ 10).

As a theologian St. Thomas is here giving full verification to a notion that is a distinctive part of his theology, namely, the notion that embodiment is by nature the permanently proper condition of the soul. God had even proportioned an otherwise mortal body, beyond the power of matter, to the immortality of the soul: He had endowed it, through the soul, with freedom from death. But death entered the life of man with the sin of Adam, and the innocence of paradise was succeeded by labor and death. Only, considering how God had established Adam, and how He had freed the body from its mortality in order to match the immortality of the soul, let us notice what death is. "Considering how human nature was established, death is therefore something befalling man as a sort of accident through sin: *est igitur mors quasi per accidens superveniens homini per peccatum, considerata institutione humanae naturae."* Moreover, this accident was taken away by Christ: *hoc autem accidens sublatum est per Christum.*[46]

As seen in *SCG* IV, cc. 79-81, the resurrection of the body is a religious truth that, beyond its scriptural foundation, finds support in the *evidens ratio* of *SCG* II, c. 68 that the intellectual soul is the form of the body. But if the soul is in its essence the form of the body, then for the soul to be without the body is *contra naturam.* Only, let us notice, this outcome contains more than the reinforcement of a religious truth by a rational argument; it also contains the shaping of a rational or philosophical truth by a religious truth. The future resurrection of the body will remove the *contra naturam* of the separated soul. The human soul is incorruptible, but it survives the body with the nature that it had as part of man. Immortality, therefore, cannot be centered in separation. Even if it cannot say more, philosophy can say this such; at least, the philosophy serving the theology of St. Thomas can say it: it can defend (or, at least, learn to defend) the unity of man within the immortality of the soul and thereby open that immortality to the natural need that the soul has of the body. The teaching of *ST* I, q. 89, a. 1 is a decisive moment in the development of that teaching.

---

46 *SCG* IV, c. 81, §§ 3-4. For philosophical arguments, based on the nature of the soul, leading to the doctrine of the Incarnation, see the justly famous text of *SCG* IV, c. 54. It is to be noted that the arguments for the Incarnation based on beatitude are set forth first and at some length (§§ 2-8) before the question of original sin is raised (§ 9). No doubt, this procedure is part of the apologetic structure and purpose of the *SCG* as a theological *summa.* — On how, as between the worlds of nature and grace, to read the *indicia* of the Incarnation, see *SCG* IV, c. 55, § 11. On the related question whether death and other evils are natural, see *ibid.* IV, c. 52, §§ 1-5.

"ECCLESIA" ET "POPULUS (FIDELIS)"
DANS L'ECCLÉSIOLOGIE DE S. THOMAS

Yves Congar O.P.

DANS le cadre d'un bref traité des sacrements, plus particulièrement
du Sacrement de l'Ordre, S. Thomas, en *Contra Gentiles*, livre IV,
chapitre 76, parle "de episcopali potestate et quod in ea unus sit sum-
mus". Voici le texte du deuxième paragraphe de ce chapitre:

> Manifestum est autem quod quamvis populi distinguantur per diversas
> dioeceses et civitates, tamen, sicut est una Ecclesia, ita oportet esse
> unum populum Christianum. Sicut igitur in uno speciali populo unius ec-
> clesiae requiritur unus episcopus, qui sit totius populi caput: ita in toto
> populo Christiano requiritur quod unus sit totius Ecclesiae caput.

L'argument repose sur le passage de l'idée d'*ecclesia* à celle de
populus, plus exactement de l'idée d'*una ecclesia* à celle d'*unus populus*, puis sur un retour de l'idée de *populus* à celle d'*ecclesia*, mais d'une
idée de *populus* enrichie ou précisée par cette donnée, prise comme évidente, qu'il ne peut y avoir de *populus* sans *caput*.

Ailleurs et antérieurement, Thomas avait exposé la même thèse, mais
sans distinguer les concepts de *populus* et d'*ecclesia*: dans *In IV Sent.*
d.24, q.3, a.2 sol. 3, il traitait les Eglises particulières et l'Eglise universelle de façon très sociologique, comme des corps sociaux poursuivant,
celles-là, un bien commun "spécial", objet d'un "regimen particulare",
celle-ci un bien commun "plus divin", objet d'un "regimen universale".[1]
La théologie de l'Eglise particulière redécouverte depuis une quinzaine
d'années serait peu satisfaite par cette considération sociologique: elle
part, en effet, de l'idée que tout le mystère de l'Eglise est réalisé dans

---

1 "Ubicumque sunt multa regimina ordinata in unum, oportet esse aliquod universale regimen
supra particularia regimina: quia in omnibus virtutibus et artibus, ut dicitur in 1 Ethic. (c. 1), est
ordo secundum ordinem finium. Bonum autem commune divinius est quam bonum speciale; et
ideo super potestatem regitivam quae conjectat bonum speciale, oportet esse potestatem regitivam
universalem respectu boni communis, alias non posset esse colligatio ad unum. Et ideo cum tota
Ecclesia sit unum corpus, oportet, si ista unitas debet conservari, quod sit aliqua potestas regitiva
respectu totius Ecclesiae supra potestatem episcopalem, qua unaquaeque specialis Ecclesia regitur:
et haec est potestas Papae; et ideo qui hanc potestatem negant, schismatici dicuntur, quasi
divisores ecclesiasticae unitatis..."

l'Eglise particulière, surtout en raison du fait que l'Eucharistie y est célébrée et qu'avec elle tout le bien commun spirituel de l'Eglise est là. [2] Ainsi le texte dont nous partons, et dont nous espérons qu'il nous introduira en une meilleure connaissance de la pensée de S. Thomas sur l'Eglise, suppose-t-il, entre les concepts d'*ecclesia* et de *populus*, à la fois une différence et une certaine identité. Nous examinerons d'abord l'identité, puis la différence.

A. LE THÈME D'IDENTITÉ

"Ipse populus Ecclesia dicitur". [3] L'Eglise n'est pas autre chose que le peuple de Dieu en sa condition chrétienne. C'est là un thème fondé dans l'Ecriture et familier à la Tradition. Il s'est développé selon deux lignes qui se sont souvent rapprochées, parfois mêlées, la ligne dogmatique et la ligne historique de Chrétienté.

1. *Dans la ligne dogmatique*

Sous une forme ou sous une autre — "populus Dei", "populus Christi", "Ecclesiae populus", "populus credentium" — la désignation de l'Eglise comme peuple fidèle est fréquente chez les Pères de l'époque anténicéenne. [4] Même chose chez les Pères de la fin du IVe siècle: Lucifer de Cagliari, [5] Ambroise, [6] Optat de Milev, [7] Jérôme. [8] Chez S. Augustin, les textes abondent. En voici quelques uns, sans recherche d'une succession chronologique rigoureuse qui, dans le cas, ne s'impose pas:

> Ecclesia id est populus Dei per omnes gentes, quod est corpus ejus (*De catech. rud.* 3, 6: PL 40, 313).
> Nunc quippe populus Dei censentur omnes qui portant sacramenta ejus...(*En. in Ps.* 47, 8: PL 36, 538).
> Societatem christiani populi (*De vera relig.* 17, 33: PL 34, 136).

---

2 Voir infra n. 71. Le décret Presbyterorum Ordinis, 5, cite en note les textes de *Sum. theol.*, III, q. 65, a. 3, ad 1 (et q. 79, a. 1 c et ad 1), où on lit: "Bonum commune spirituale totius Ecclesiae continetur substantialiter in ipso Eucharistiae sacramento."

3 S. Thomas, *In IV Sent.* d. 20, q. 1, a. 4, sol. 1, cité et commenté infra. Cf. n. 26.

4 Voir Vincenzo Loi, "Populus Dei-Plebs Dei. Studio storico-linguistico sulle denominazioni del 'Popolo di Dio' nel latino paleo-cristiano", *Salesianum* 27 (1966) 606-628.

5 Cf. *Pro Athanasio* II, 3 (PL 13, 885; CSEL 14, 150); *De non parcendo in Deum delinquentibus* 17 (PL 13, 969 C; CSEL 14, 244).

6 Cf. *In Ev. Luc.* III, 38 (PL 15, 1605 B; CSEL 32/3, 126): "Cui (Christo) nupsit Ecclesia, quae Verbi semine et Spiritu Dei plena, Christi corpus effudit, populum scilicet Christianum."

7 Cf. III, 1; VI, 1 (CSEL 26, 67, 10; 144, 10).

8 Cf. *Orig. Hom. in Ez.* X, 1 (PL 25, 761 D) avec, peut-être, une nuance: "Infamia est a populo Dei et ecclesia separari."

... Nullus seditiosus, nullus dividens populum Dei, nullus fatigans Ecclesiam in ministerio diaboli (*En. in Ps.* 84, 10: PL 37, 1076).
Ecclesia vero, quod est populus Dei...(*De baptismo* I, 15, 24: PL 43, 122).
In Spiritu enim Sancto, quo in unum Dei populus congregatur... (*Sermo*
71, 19: PL 38, 455).

On comprend que le Catéchisme de Trente dise, mais en ne donnant
pas une référence exacte, "Ecclesia, ut ait Augustinus, est populus
fidelis per universum orbem dispersus".[9] Du reste, nous retrouverons
encore S. Augustin plus loin, à propos de la définition qu'il a donnée
à l'idée de "peuple". La liturgie romaine emploie très fréquemment et
comme des synonymes les expressions "populum tuum" et "ecclesiam
tuam".[10] Celui qui fut en quelque sorte le précepteur du haut moyen
âge, S. Isidore de Séville, définit l'Eglise comme peuple de Dieu d'une
façon précise et intéressante.[11] Il exprime bien le sentiment tradition-
nel: l'Eglise est faite d'une multitude d'hommes et de peuples
rassemblés par la même foi et la soumission au même règne. Mais le
règne est ici celui de Dieu et du Christ, sans mention de la soumission
au *regimen* d'un unique *caput* ecclésiastique.

On ne s'étonnera pas que, durant le haut moyen âge, principalement
à l'époque carolingienne, l'Eglise ait été définie comme peuple de Dieu,
même à un plan purement théologique. Nous verrons plus loin que cela
était lié avec la réalité de la *société* chrétienne, mais sans s'identifier
totalement avec elle.[12] Que l'Eglise se définit comme étant le peuple
chrétien, qu'il y eût passage d'une expression à l'autre, nous avons de
nombreux témoignages que c'était là une idée commune. Richard
Wethershet, Chancelier de Lincoln au milieu du XIIe siècle, écrit:

9 Pars I, c. 10, q. 2. La monographie de J. Ratzinger (*Volk und Haus Gottes in Augustins
Lehre von der Kirche*. München 1954) contient de fines remarques mais n'épuise pas la matière
qu'annonce son titre.
10 Dans le Missel Romain d'avant Vatican II, 90 fois "populus", 80 fois "ecclesia", 12 fois
"familia": A. Schaut, "Die Kirche als Volk Gottes. Selbstaussagen der Kirche im römischen
Messbuch", *Benediktinische Monatschrift* 25 (1949) 187-196.
11 *De fide cathol.* II, 1 (De gentium vocatione): "3. Quam pluralitatem gentium ita declamat
adunari ad unius Dei cultum: *In conveniendo,* inquit, *populos in unum, et regna, ut serviant
Domino* (Ps 101, 23). In unum utique, id est in unum regem, ut qui diversorum ritu simulacrorum
regna multa et populi multi dicebantur, in unam conveniendo fidem unus Dei populus unumque
regnum vocetur. — 4. Hujus populi congregatio ex gentibus ipsa est Ecclesia..." (PL 83, 499-500).
12 Quelques textes: Alcuin, *Epist.* 23 et 129 (MGH Epp. IV, pp. 61 et 191); *Disputatio
puerorum,* "ecclesia, populus et domus est Dei" (PL 101, 1142 A); concile d'Aix de 836, c. III can.
25: "Quia enim ecclesia in una adque indiscreta Christi fide ac dilectione concorditer ad coelestia
tendens populus dicitur..."(MGH *Concilia* II/2, p.723); Hincmar de Reims, *De coercendo et ex-
stirpendo raptu viduarum,* c. 1: l'*ecclesia* est "una gens sancta, unus populus acquisitionis (...) Cum
ergo omnis populus Dei ... una grex sit sub uno pastore..." (PL 125, 1017-1018): il s'agit du Christ,
non du pape; Hincmar exprime sa conviction que ce peuple de Dieu qu'est l'Eglise garde son unité
sous et malgré la division des royaumes.

"Credo populum christianum esse sanctam Ecclesiam".[13] S. Bonaventure, dont nous célébrons le centenaire en même temps que celui de S. Thomas, a bien la même conviction.[14] Avant de revenir à S. Thomas lui-même, citons encore ce texte de Grégoire IX qui nous rapproche de celui du *Contra Gentiles*. Il s'agit d'une lettre adressée le 13 janvier 1240 à la reine Rusude de Géorgie et à son fils David pour les amener à reconnaître la juridiction du Pontife romain: il n'existe qu'*une* Eglise, donc un seul *caput* (les évêques sont appelés "in partem sollicitudinis, vices Dei et Apostolicae Sedis"...):

> Licet enim plures populi in cultum sint catholicae fidei congregati, omnes tamen una censentur ecclesia, dum uni capiti, Christi vicario et beati Petri successori, cervice reverentiam exhibent inclinata.[15]

Chez S. Thomas, les textes identifiant Eglise et peuple fidèle se distribuent sur trois thèmes dans chacun desquels se mêlent des éléments d'analyse sociologique et une vision dogmatique:

a) Contexte sacramentel. Thomas dit souvent que l'Eglise est construite, fondée, consacrée par la foi et les sacrements de la foi.[16] Il dit la même chose du peuple chrétien: "populus christianus per fidem et sacramenta Christi sanctificatus est, secundum illud (cit. de *1 Cor.* 6, 11 et *1 Petr.* 2, 9)".[17] La foi est absolument fondamentale. Dès la plus haute antiquité, avec de simples variations dans les expressions, on avait défini l'Eglise comme l'assemblée des croyants ou des fidèles. Sur la base d'une documentation que nous espérons pouvoir mettre en œuvre un jour, nous avons acquis la conviction que S. Thomas *a voulu* définir l'Eglise "congregatio (coetus, societas, collegium, communio) fidelium". Mais il n'y a pas de société sans que son unité soit exprimée et assurée par certains signes.[18] C'était le cas du peuple de Dieu sous

---

13 *Speculum Ecclesiae*, cité par W. Ullmann, *The Growth of Papal Government in the Middle Ages* (London 1955) 438 n. 2.

14 Dans le *De perfectione evangelica* q. 2, a. 2 n° IV (*Opera*, ed. Quaracchi, t. V p. 153a) il dit que critiquer la règle des Prêcheurs ou des Mineurs revient à prétendre que "Ecclesiam universalem errasse...quod Deus permitteret sic errare universaliter populum sanctum suum"; dans l'*Expos. super regulam Fratrum Minorum*, c. III n° 4 (VIII, p. 408a), il parle des douze patriarches "per quos multiplicatus est populus credentium carnaliter, duodecim etiam Apostoli per quos in novo testamento multiplicatus est populus credentium spiritualiter."

15 Potthast n° 10841. Texte dans Baronius-Raynaldus, *Annales ecclesiastici*, éd. A. Theiner, t. XXI (Bar-le-Duc 1870) p. 226: cette partie est omise dans *Registres de Grégoire IX*, éd. L. Auvray: t. III (Paris 1910) n° 5022, pp. 162-163.

16 "Ecclesia constituitur, fabricatur (*In IV Sent.* d. 18, q. 1, a. 1, sol. 1; III, q. 64, a. 2, ad 3) fundatur (*In IV Sent.* d. 17, q. 3, a. 1, sol. 5), instituitur (I, q. 92, a. 3), consecratur (*In Ioan.* c. 19, lect. 5, n. 4) per fidem et fidei sacramenta."

17 II-II, q. 99, a. 1, ad 2.

18 "Cum ecclesia sit sicut civitas (...) In qualibet autem civitate, ad hoc ut sit una, quatuor debent esse communia, scilicet unus gubernator, una lex, eadem insignia et idem finis (...) Tertio eadem sunt insignia ecclesiae scilicet sacramenta Christi, inter quae primum baptisma, quod est janua omnium aliorum." S. Thomas, *In Ephes.*, c. 4, lect. 2.

l'ancienne alliance auquel le signe de la circoncision a été donné avant
la Loi. [19] Sous l'alliance spirituelle de grâce, qui fait le "populus spiritualis", [20] c'est le baptême qui, par le signe spirituel indélébile du caractère, discerne les membres du peuple de Dieu parmi les autres hommes. [21] C'est la marque commune des fidèles, qui les situe à la base, par
laquelle "non adipiscitur aliquis nisi infimum gradum in populo christiano". [22] Elle distingue les fidèles des autres et les habilite à participer
aux sacrements; un autre caractère, celui de l'Ordre, discerne, dans le
peuple de Dieu, les ministres des simples fidèles. [23]

Le sacrement à la participation duquel le peuple chrétien est
suprêmement habilité est évidemment l'Eucharistie. Qu'à tel endroit le
fait que S. Thomas s'exprime à son sujet en termes de "populus
christianus" s'explique par le texte du pape Jules Ier qu'il vient de citer
d'après Gratien, [24] n'empêche pas S. Thomas de parler de la même façon
ailleurs, là où il n'est pas conditionné par une citation. [25]

b) S. Thomas identifie encore le peuple chrétien et l'Eglise dans les
textes où il parle de celle-ci comme d'une cité, d'une *polis*, en
distinguant cette forme de "vie ensemble" de celle de la famille. Il met
en œuvre ici la distinction formulée par Aristote, dont l'*Ethique à
Nicomaque* exerça sur les esprits, sur celui de Thomas en particulier, un

19 "Populus fidelium congregandus erat aliquo signo sensibili quod est necessarium ad hoc
quod homines in quadam religione adunentur, sicut Augustinus dicit, *Contra Faustum*, lib. XIX, c.
XI (PL 42, 355)." III, q. 70, a. 2, ad 2.

20 III, q. 74, a. 3, ad 1.

21 Cf. *In IV Sent*. d. 18, q. 2, a. 3, qa 3, ad 1: "Apostolus loquitur de paganis et aliis infidelibus
qui non habent characterem per quem annumerati sint in populo Dei. Sed quia character bap-
tismalis quo quis populo Dei annumeratur est indelebilis..."

22 III, q. 67, a. 2, ad 2.

23 *In IV Sent*. d. 4, q. 1, a. 4, sol. 3: "Sicut in naturalibus...ita etiam in spiritualibus est potentia
spiritualis quasi passiva per quam homo efficitur susceptivus spiritualium actionum, et talis
spiritualis potentia confertur in baptismo, quia non baptizatus effectum aliorum sacramentorum
suscipere non posset, unde et per consequens nec aliis tradere, et haec est prima distinctio qua
communiter totus populus fidelis, cujus est sacramentorum participem esse, ab aliis distinguitur.
Alia potentia est activa spiritualis ordinata ad sacramentorum dispensationem et aliarum
sacrarum hierarchicarum actionum exercitium... Et quia in ecclesiastica hierarchia non omnes
sunt agentes...ideo isti duo characteres non distinguunt populum Dei universaliter ab aliis, sed
quosdam de populo ab aliis."

24 "...effectum hujus sacramenti, qui est unio populi christiani ad Christum": III, q. 74, a. 6 c.,
après une citation du pape Jules ("cum in calice aqua vino miscetur, Christo populus adunatur")
tirée de Gratien, *De cons*. d. 2, c. 1 (Friedberg, col. 1314). Comparer q. 76, a. 7 c., "per aquam mix-
tam vino significatur populus adunatus Christo."

25 Ainsi III, q. 82, a. 3, ad 1; II-II, q. 187, a. 4 ("sacrificium altaris ubicumque agatur, commune est toti populo fidelium"); *In IV Sent*. d. 13, q. 1, a. 2, qa 3, ad 2, à propos du rite du Vendredi saint: "Ecclesia volens populum christianum circa ipsam dominicam passionem prout in
capite nostro fuit, mente occupari statuit ut illa die non consecraretur corpus Christi. Ne tamen ecclesia omnino sine corpore Christi esset, corpus Christi, praecedenti die consecratum et reser-
vatum sumitur." Dans ce texte, le mot *ecclesia* revêt deux sens: la première fois, celui de l'autorité
qui détermine ou consacre rites et discipline, sens fréquent chez S. Thomas à propos des
sacrements, la seconde fois, celui de la communauté chrétienne.

attrait d'une extraordinaire puissance. Le thème de la *civitas* comporte d'autres aspects encore chez S. Thomas: on pourrait suivre, par exemple, le destin qu'a eu chez lui l'idée augustinienne de "Civitas Dei", à laquelle il a gardé son statut théologal, en évitant de la sociologiser. Quelques textes vont nous guider ici:

> Sed cum Ecclesia sit congregatio fidelium, congregatio autem hominum sit duplex, scilicet oeconomica, ut illi qui sunt de una familia, et politica, sicut illi qui sunt de uno populo, Ecclesia similatur congregationi politicae, *quia ipse populus Ecclesia dicitur*, sed conventus diversi vel parochiae in una dioecesi similantur congregationi in diversis familiis vel in diversis officiis. [26]

La portée de ces quelques mots, apparemment banals et que nous avons soulignés, "quia ipse populus Ecclesia dicitur", s'éclaire à la lumière d'autres textes au terme desquels le *populus* apparaît comme exerçant la plénitude des actes les plus élevés de la cité:

> Collegium fidelium quandoque in scripturis vocatur domus, secundum illud 1 Tim. 3: *Ut scias quomodo in domo Dei oporteat te conversari, quae est Dei ecclesia.* Quandoque autem vocatur civitas, secundum illud Ps. CXXI: *Jerusalem quae aedificatur ut civitas.* Civitas enim habet collegium politicum: domus autem oeconomicum, inter quae quidem duplex differentia invenitur. Nam qui sunt de collegio domus communicant sibi in actibus privatis: qui vero sunt de collegio civitatis, communicant sibi in actibus publicis. Item qui sunt in collegio domus, reguntur ab uno qui vocatur paterfamilias; sed qui sunt in collegio civitatis reguntur a rege. Ita enim est paterfamilias in domo, sicut rex in regno. Sic igitur collegium fidelium aliquid habet de civitate, et aliquid de domo. Sed si consideretur rector collegii, pater est (*Pater noster, qui es in coelis*, etc. |Matth. 6|, *Patrem vocabis me, et post me ingredi non cessabis* [Jerem. 3]); et sic collegium est domus, si vero ipsos subditos consideres, sic civitas est, quia communicant sibi in actibus praecipuis, sc. fidei, spei et charitatis. Et hoc modo si fideles considerentur in se, est collegium civitatis; si vero rector collegii attendatur, est collegium domus. [27]

> Haec civitas est Ecclesia. Psal. 86: "Gloriosa dicta sunt de te, civitas Dei" etc. Tria sunt in ista civitate, quae sunt de ejus ratione. Primum est, quod sit ibi multitudo liberorum quia si est ibi unus vel pauci, non est civitas; et similiter si sunt servi. Et hoc maxime invenitur in Ecclesia. Gal. 4: non sumus ancillae filii, sed liberae." Secundum est quod habeat sufficientiam per se. In vico enim non inveniuntur omnia necessaria vitae humanae sanis et infirmis; sed in civitate oportet invenire omnia

26 *In IV Sent.* d. 20, q. 1, a. 4, sol. 1. Nous avons naguère utilisé ces thèmes pour une théologie de la paroisse sous l'angle sociologique: "Mission de la paroisse", in *Structures sociales et Pastorale paroissiale* (Paris 1948) pp. 48-68 (reproduit in *Sacerdoce et Laïcat...* [Paris 1962] pp. 175-205).

27 *In Ephes.*, c. 2, lect. 2.

necessaria ad vitam. Et haec sufficientia est in Ecclesia: quia quicquid necessarium est ad vitam spiritualem, invenitur in ea. Psal. 64: "Replebimur in bonis domus tuae." Tertium est unitas civium: quia ab hoc, scilicet ab unitate civium, civitas nominatur, quia civitas quasi civium unitas. Et haec est in Ecclesia. Joan. 17: "Ut sint unum in nobis, sicut et nos unum sumus." Haec ergo civitas laetificatur per gratiam Spiritus sancti in eam descendentem. [28]

S. Thomas caractérise l'Eglise comme cité et son régime propre par le fait que 1°) le communautaire, en elle, n'empêche pas l'intimité que ses enfants peuvent avoir avec leur père dans le rapport interpersonnel le plus direct et le plus étroit; 2°) cependant, on trouve dans l'Eglise la plénitude des biens spirituels, et c'est en cela qu'elle est *cité*; 3°) *tous* y participent; tous font ensemble les actes les plus élevés de cette cité, qui consistent dans "les trois théologales", par lesquelles nous entrons immédiatement en rapport de communion avec Dieu lui-même. Tous font évidemment aussi ensemble les actes de la prière. [29]

Pour saisir la force de cette affirmation il est bon de se rappeler que, dans la cité médiévale, il existait un "peuple d'en haut", qui seul exerçait vraiment les actes de la citoyenneté, et un "peuple d'en bas", que désignent souvent les expressions *vulgus, plebs* ou *popularis, populares*, et qui ne les exerçait pas. [30] Saint Isidore distinguait le *vulgus* ou la *plebs* du *populus*, lequel formait la *civitas*. [31] Mais Jean le Teutonique dans sa *Compilatio IV*, vers 1216, écrivait: "nomine populi comprehenduntur patricii et senatores". [32] Vers la même époque, un commentateur du *Décret* écrivait: "Nota quod ea[dem] differentia est inter populum et plebem, que est inter animalem et hominem, inter genus et speciem. Nobiles enim, et in nobiles simul collectum, sunt

28 *In Ps.* XLV, n. 3 (éd. Parme XIV, 327).

29 Dans un texte comme celui-ci "ecclesiae in quibus populus christianus ad laudem Dei congregatur" (I-II, q. 102, a. 4, ad 3), il n'y a pas de distinction entre fidèles et ministres.

30 D'une assez abondante documentation, extrayons seulement quelques références sur ce sens de *populares* à l'époque de S. Thomas: Thomas lui-même, I-II, q. 100, a. 11 c.; q. 102, a. 6, ad 8 fin; q. 105, a. 1; III, q. 47, a. 5 c ("minores id est populares"); S. Bonaventure, *Apologia pauperum* c. 9, n. 9 (Quaracchi VIII, p. 297 — les gens du peuple, distingués des rois, princes et chevaliers); Henri de Gand, Sermon d'ouverture du concile parisien de 1289, dans K. Schleyer, *Anfänge des Gallikanismus im 13. Jahrhundert* ...(Berlin 1935) p. 172 (les gens du peuple, par distinction des *magnates*).

31 *De fide cathol.* II, 1, 6: "Populus ergo tota civitas, vulgus vero plebs est. Plebs autem dicta a pluralitate, major est enim numerus minorum quam seniorum (...) Vulgus est passim inhabitans multitudo, quasi quisque quo vult" (PL 83, 500).

32 In *Antonii Augustini Opera omnia*, t. IV (Lucca 1769) 626: cité par J. Sydow, "Elemente von Einheit und Vielfalt in der mittelalterlichen Stadt (im Lichte kirchenrechtlicher Quellen)", in *Universalismus und Partikularismus im Mittelalter*, hrsg. v. P. Wilpert (Berlin 1968) 186-197: cf. pp. 191-192, qui renvoie aussi, pour ce régime hiérarchisé de la cité médiévale, à *Patriziat und andere Führungsschichten in der südwestdeutschen Städten* (Tübingen 1965).

populus. Ple[b]s est ubi non sunt senatores et viri consulares..."[33] Tout le monde n'avait pas le plein exercice des droits de citoyen dans la cité hiérarchisée du moyen âge. Dans l'Eglise, dit S. Thomas, tous participent aux activités les plus hautes: "ipse populus Ecclesia dicitur".

c) Un troisième aspect sous lequel S. Thomas identifie *ecclesia* et *populus fidelium* est celui des "mores populi christiani".[34] Il s'agit, par exemple, du remplacement du sabbat mosaïque par le dimanche: cela est venu "non ex vi praecepti legis, sed ex constitutione Ecclesiae et consuetudine populi christiani".[35] Ou bien il s'agit de jeûnes imposés "sub praecepto"; cela n'est-il pas contraire au statut de liberté qui caractérise le peuple de Dieu sous le régime de la grâce?[36] Non, répond Thomas avec un large optimisme: "Nec sunt contra libertatem populi fidelis, sed magis sunt utilia ad impediendam servitutem peccati quae repugnat libertati spirituali". Le tout est de savoir de quelle liberté il s'agit!

2. Dans la ligne historique de Chrétienté

Le fait est bien connu: l'expression *populus fidelis* (ou *christianus*), le mot même d'*ecclesia*, durant le moyen âge, mais surtout le haut moyen âge, désignent de façon indistincte ce que nous appelons Eglise et la société, car celle-ci était faite de baptisés: c'était la société chrétienne.[37] Le *populus christianus* était, d'une certaine façon, identique à l'*ecclesia*, au point que Charlemagne pouvait être appelé "rector ecclesiae".[38] L'expression, cependant, était ambivalente, car elle désignait aussi bien le peuple constituant l'Eglise sous l'autorité du Sacerdoce et l'ensemble des chrétiens qui, sous le gouvernement des princes, continuaient la *christianitas*.[39] Le thème s'annonce à partir de S. Grégoire le Grand, chez lequel "populus christianus" comporte une nuance de société soumise à la fois au Sacerdoce et aux rois.[40] Dans plusieurs textes de l'époque carolingienne, "populus Dei", "ecclesia" et "respublica"

---

33 Summa "Antiquitate et tempore", Dist. 2, c. Lex est: MS, Vat. Palat. lat., fol. 37v, cité par G. Post, *Studies in Medieval Legal Thought, Public Law and the State 1100-1322* (Princeton 1964) p. 374, n. 16.

34 Expression de I-II, q. 102, a. 2.

35 II-II, q. 122, a. 4, ad 4.

36 I-II, q. 147, a. 3, où l'objection 3 était: "sed non minus videtur libertas populi christiani impediri per multitudinem observantiarum quam per multitudinem sacramentorum."

37 Nombreuses études classiques. Nous-même avons publié *L'Ecclésiologie du Haut Moyen Age* (Paris 1968).

38 Alcuin disait aussi bien "Rector populi christiani". Voir textes et références dans notre ouvrage cité n. précédente, pp. 267, 277 s. M. Hoechstetter, *Karl der Grosse, König, Patritius und Kaiser als Rector ecclesiae* (Diss. Augsburg 1934).

39 Cf. F. Kempf, "Das Problem der Christianitas im 12. und 13. Jahrhundert", *Historisches Jahrbuch* 79 (1961) 104-123; J. Rupp, *L'idée de Chrétienté dans la pensée pontificale des Origines à Innocent III* (Paris 1939).

40 Cf. J. Rupp, op. cit., pp. 28 s.

désignent la même réalité concrète.[41] Il y a cependant une nuance qui s'annonce dans certains textes d'Alcuin[42] et qui s'explicite chez le pape Jean VIII (872-882), avec l'emploi du mot *christianitas* comme équivalent de *populus christianus* pour désigner, l'un comme l'autre, l'ensemble des chrétiens en tant que, sous le gouvernement des princes fidèles, ils avaient des intérêts religieux temporels communs, tandis que *ecclesia* désignait les chrétiens soumis à l'action du Sacerdoce.[43] On ne s'étonne pas, dès lors, de trouver "christianus populus" dans un contexte de croisade, par exemple chez Urbain II ou S. Berbard.[44] Il est normal qu'Innocent III (1198-1216) ait fait un grand usage des termes *christianitas* et *populus christianus*, puisque sa conception de sa charge pontificale, aussi cohérente qu'explicite, fait de lui le chef, non seulement de l'*ecclesia*, mais du peuple chrétien: car le pape est vicaire du Christ, prêtre et roi selon l'ordre de Melchisédech.[45] Il serait trop long de citer ici tous les textes. Nous ne nous étonnerons évidemment pas, connaissant son idéologie du pouvoir pontifical, que Boniface VIII ait qualifié Rome de "communis omnium Christiani populi nationum curia"[46]: où l'on perçoit bien l'implication temporelle de l'expression "peuple chrétien".

Chez Innocent III et Boniface VIII, cette compréhension du terme "populus Christianus (Dei)" s'inscrivait au bénéfice de l'autorité pontificale, mais elle pouvait aussi bien servir les prétentions des rois et, à la faveur de l'identité entre *populus fidelis* et *ecclesia*, appuyer leur revendication d'un droit de régir l'Eglise. Tel avait été l'enjeu du conflit entre Grégoire VII et l'empereur Henri IV. Grégoire avait voulu sortir, en quelque sorte, de l'indivision et de l'indistinction des juridictions.[47]

---

41 Nous avons déjà cité supra n. 12, le texte du concile d'Aix de 836. Voir encore, par exemple, Paschase Radbert, *Vita Walae*, lib. II, c. 17 (PL 120, 1639 C).

42 Ainsi MGH *Epp.* IV, p. 148, "Christo Deo propitiante in omni proficias bonitate ad consolationem sanctae Dei aecclesiae et gaudium populi christiani"; p. 289, "plena tibi scientia data est a Deo ut per te sancta Dei aecclesia in populo christiano regatur, exaltetur et conservetur."

43 Cf. J. Rupp, op. cit., pp. 36, 48; notre *Ecclésiologie du Haut Moyen Age*, pp. 239 s.

44 Urbain II, *Epist.* 5, "divina populum suum respiciente Clementia", à propos de la Reconquista (PL 151, 288); S. Bernard, contre ceux "qui repositas in Ierosolymis christiani populi inaestimabiles divitias tollere gestiunt" (*Ad milites Templi*, c. 3, n. 5: PL 182, 925); voir aussi la lettre adressée en 1146 à Conrad III pour l'inviter à mater la révolte des Romains qui ont forcé le pape à quitter Rome: *Epist.* 244 (PL 182, 400 D - 442 C): il parle en termes de *populus christianus*, non d'*ecclesia*.

45 Voir notre *L'Eglise de S. Augustin à l'époque moderne* (Paris 1970) 192-197. Pour l'usage de *populus christianus* et *christianitas*, parfois distingués par une nuance d'*ecclesia*, chez Innocent III, voir J. Rupp, op. cit., pp. 99-123; F. Kempf, *Papsttum und Kaisertum bei Innozenz III...* (Rome 1954) 301 s.

46 Extrav. Comm. lib. II, tit. III, c. unic. (Friedberg, col. 1256).

47 Voir G. B. Ladner, "The Concepts of 'Ecclesia' and 'christianitas' and their relation to the idea of papal 'plenitudo potestatis' from Gregory VII to Boniface VIII", *Sacerdozio e Regno da Gregorio VII a Bonifacio VIII...* (*Miscell. Hist. Pontif.*, XVIII), (Rome 1954) pp. 42-77; notre *Eglise de S. Augustin à l'époque moderne*, pp. 102-107 (Grégoire VII), 113 (les impériaux), 116-118 (l'Anonyme Normand).

On comprend la gravité de cet enjeu quand on voit l'usage du terme *populus christianus* fait par le fameux Anonyme Normand, vers l'an 1100, en faveur du droit des rois à régir l'Eglise.[48]

Christianitas n'est pas du vocabulaire de S. Thomas.[49] Il connaît, par contre, l'emploi de "populus christianus" en situation de Chrétienté: et comment eût-il pu l'ignorer, puisque le terme et la chose étaient inscrits dans les textes et dans les faits de son époque? De fait, Thomas utilise l'expression dans certains contextes guerriers de Chrétienté.[50] Il connaît la situation où les lois d'Eglise sont en même temps lois de la cité, voire où certaines prescriptions en matière de pratique religieuse sont portées également par les "principes christiani populi".[51] Mais dans le texte même où il dit cela, Thomas distingue les deux autorités et, ailleurs, deux domaines.[52] Au-delà d'une "mentalité" conditionnée par son milieu historique, c'est dans ce sens qu'allait son "esprit", pour reprendre une heureuse distinction élaborée par M. Jean Guitton.

B. Le thème de distinction

Si S. Thomas est passé d'un terme à un autre, même pour arguer de l'identité des réalités qu'ils recouvrent, il doit bien y avoir une raison. Ce ne serait pas le seul cas où deux termes désignent (comme matériellement) la même réalité, mais sous des aspects comportant chacun leur nuance propre: ainsi Eglise et Corps mystique, voire même, chez S. Augustin, Eglise et Cité de Dieu.

Or une logique assez évidente, qu'illustrent de très nombreux témoignages, montre que *populus* connote l'idée de soumission à un gouvernement et à des lois. C'est normal puisque, comme l'écrit S. Thomas, "populus est multitudo hominum sub aliquo ordine comprehensorum".[53] Déterminer l'ordre en question est l'objet de la loi

---

48   Voir *Die Texte des Normannischen Anonymus...* hrsg. von K. Pellens (Wiesbaden 1966): pp. 149, 157, 168, 198, 199, 200-201, 222-223.

49   C'est ce que remarque I. Th. Eschmann, "St. Thomas and the two Powers", *Mediaeval Studies* 20 (1958) 177-205: p. 191 n. 44.

50   Cf. II-II, q. 40, a. 2, ad 3, "bella carnalia in populo fideli"; q. 99, a. 1, ad 2, le peuple chrétien est sanctifié, "et ita id quod fit in injuriam populi christiani secundum quod infideles ei praeficiantur, pertinet ad irreverentiam sacrae rei": q. 188, a. 4 c. "corporalibus armis populum fidelium tueri."

51   Cf. *Quodl.* IV, 13, "praelatis Ecclesiae et principibus populi christiani determinanda"; comparer, en plus général, I-II, q. 108, a. 1, c. et II-II, q. 147, a. 3.

52   Cf. *In IV Sent.* d. 19, q. 1, a. 1, qa 3, ad 2. L'objection partait précisément de la situation de Chrétienté, où les rois, étant oints comme les prêtres "etiam potestatem in populum fidelem divinitus habent". La réponse distingue les pouvoirs "in temporalibus" et "in spiritualibus", et ajoute "sed excellentia potestatis ipsorum a Christo descendere significatur, ut et ipsi sub Christo in populo christiano regnent." Dans l'excercice de ce gouvernement, ils sont subordonnés aux prêtres et surtout au pape "cui omnes reges populi christiani oportet esse subditos" (*De regimine principum*, I, 14, si cette partie est encore de S. Thomas).

53   I, q. 31, a. 1, ad 2; comparer I-II, q. 17, a. 4 c.; III, q. 8, a. 1, ad 2.

Aussi "ad rationem populi pertinet ut communicatio hominum ad invicem justis praeceptis legis ordinetur".[54]

S. Thomas, comme beaucoup d'autres avant lui (Isidore, par exemple), à son époque et après lui, a plusieurs fois cité la définition du *populus* que S. Augustin avait empruntée à une traité de Cicéron: "Populus est coetus multitudinis juris consensu et utilitatis communione sociatus".[55] Si donc on passe de *populus* à *ecclesia* — et S. Thomas fait expressément l'application de cette définition au "populus Dei" — , ce sera sous l'angle où l'Eglise comporte une organisation juridique par des lois: la loi de Dieu d'abord, les lois humaines ensuite.

L'autorité publique gouverne selon les lois. La notion de *populus* implique celle de gouvernement. Depuis des siècles, le Vendredi saint, l'Eglise priait Dieu de garder le pape "incolumen ecclesiae tuae, ad regendum populum sanctum Dei".[56] Dans maints textes anciens le mot *populus (Dei)* attire la détermination: *gubernare* ou *regere*.[57] Tel est le cas aussi chez S. Thomas.[58] Il partage l'antique conviction formulée ainsi par les *Proverbes* (11, 14): "Ubi non est gubernator, populus corruet".[59]

Nous ne nous étonnerons pas que, chez S. Thomas comme très fréquemment dans les textes ecclésiastiques et jusque dans la Constitution de Vatican II sur la liturgie, *populus*, avec ou sans précision, désigne l'ensemble des fidèles en tant que distingués des ministres qui les gouvernent et qui, aussi, les président et les représentent, au sens que S. Thomas donne à ce mot "représenter", qui signifie plutôt "personnaliser".[60]

---

54 I-II, q. 105, a. 2. Comparer "omnis lex alicui populo datur": I-II, q. 90, a. 2; a. 3; q. 96, a. 1; q. 101, a. 3; III, q. 70, a. 2, ad 2.

55 Augustin, *De civitate Dei* II, 21 et XIX, 21 et 24 (PL 41, 67 et 648) = Cicéron, *De Republica* I, 25. Cité par S. Thomas I-II, q. 105, a. 2; II-II, q. 42, a. 2; *In Hebr.* c. 8, lect. 3, avec application formelle au "populus Dei". Cf. Isidore, *Etymol.* IX, 4; Vincent de Beauvais, *Speculum doctrinale* VII, 7 (éd. Douai, 1624, p. 561); un peu plus tard, Alvarez Pelayo, avec application à l'Eglise (*De planctu Ecclesiae*, c. 63, in Rocaberti, *Bibl. Max. Pontif.* III, p. 208).

56 Au Gélasien, éd. Wilson, p. 75.

57 Exemples dans mon *Ecclésiologie du haut moyen âge* (Paris 1968) p. 64, n. 15. Usages fréquents chez les canonistes, par exemple Deusdedit, "sacerdotes et levite summi pontificis cardinales... populum Dei regant" (éd. W. von Glanvell. Paderborn 1905, pp. 267-268); Gratien, "potestas gubernandi populum" (C. 16, q. 2, dict. post c. 7), etc.; S. Bernard, *Epist.* 188, "stat zelus auctoritas Romanae ecclesiae super populum Dei" (PL 182, 353 A).

58 Exemples: "Christus constitutus est rex a Deo ad populum regendum" (*In Ps* 2, n. 7: éd. Parme XIV, 154); "regimen populi" (I-II, q. 105, a. 1, c. et ad 1); "Sacerdotes et principes Iudaeorum erant illud populi seniores" (III, q. 42, a. 2, obj. 3). Voir aussi II-II, q. 87, a. 1 à propos des dîmes; q. 147, a. 3 à propos des jeûnes; *In 2 Cor.*, prol., "ministri gubernant populum Dei".

59 Cf. III, q. 65, a. 4.

60 Ainsi plusieurs fois dans *C. Gent.* IV, 75; I-II, q. 102, a. 4 et 5; III, q. 80, a. 12. Voir également I-II, q. 95, a. 4 ("sacerdotes pro populo Deum orantes"); II-II, q. 83, a. 12 ("Communis oratio est quae per ministros ecclesiae in persona totius fidelis populi Deo offertur, et ideo oportet

Si *populus* connote l'idée de gouvernement, *ecclesia* se situe de soi, à un plan de grâce et de vie théologale: là réside, à notre avis, la différence qui fonde l'emploi de deux termes dans le texte même où S. Thomas passe de l'un à l'autre en les faisant désigner la même réalité. C'était peut-être aussi le motif pour lequel, en plein régime de Chrétienté caractérisé par la symbiose de la société politique et de la communauté ecclésiale, certains textes dédoublaient les vocables, marquant ainsi une certaine distance entre eux (voir supra nn. 42 s.). S. Thomas savait bien que, sous la grâce, les fidèles ne sont plus soumis à un régime théocratique et hiérocratique comme l'était le peuple juif.[61] Il n'a pas écrit de traité de l'Eglise, mais sa pensée ecclésiologique peut, croyons-nous, être dégagée avec assez de certitude. Du moins permettra-t-on à un homme qui l'a longuement étudiée, de dire comment il la comprend.[62] La question nous semble liée au plan de la Somme sur lequel j'ai aussi publié quelques études.[63]

D'une façon générale, S. Thomas a bien distingué le moment nécessaire, essentiel, et le moment contingent, historique, du mystère surnaturel.[64] C'est ce qui explique le fait, de prime abord étonnant et presque scandaleux, qu'il ait traité de la grâce avant de parler du Christ. C'est qu'il s'agit, pour S. Thomas, d'être en communion avec le *Dieu-Triade*, ce que réalisent la grâce et les vertus théologales, et ce pour quoi le Christ, en tant que Verbe incarné (n') est (qu') un *moyen* historique, et donc accidentel par rapport à l'essentiel qui est, dans toute la vérité de l'expression, une *déification*.[65] C'est pourquoi, là où il s'est expliqué le plus formellement et le plus librement sur l'Eglise, à savoir dans son commentaire du Symbole, il en définit l'être et l'unité par les vertus théologales et par l'habitation du Saint-Esprit. C'est pourquoi, dans notre étude de 1939 (cf. supra n. 62), nous avions rat-

quod talis oratio innotescat toti populo, pro quo profertur"); q. 86, a. 2 ("sacerdos quodammodo constituitur sequester et medius inter populum et Deum"); q. 87, a. 1 et q. 108, a. 2 (il est convenable que les ministres soient sustentés par le *populus*); III, q. 65, a. 1 ("sacerdotes hostias offerunt non solum pro se, sed etiam pro populo"); q. 80, a. 12.

61   Voir I-II, q. 105, a. 1, ad 1.

62   Voir déjà "L'idée thomiste de l'Eglise", paru en anglais in *The Thomist*, oct. 1939, pp. 331-359, en français dans *Rev. Sciences philos. théol.* 29 (1940) 31-58 et dans *Esquisses du mystère de l'Eglise* (Paris 1941) 59-91, puis notre *Eglise de S. Augustin à l'époque moderne* (Paris 1970) 232-241. De la bibliographie citée là, retenons ici surtout M. Useros Carretero, *"Statuta Ecclesiae" y "Sacramenta Ecclesiae" en la eclesiologia di S. Tomas* (Rome 1962).

63   En particulier "Le moment 'économique' et le moment 'ontologique' dans la Sacra doctrina (Révélation, Théologie, Somme théologique)", *Mélanges offerts à M.-D. Chenu* (Bibl. Thomiste, XXXVII). (Paris 1967) 135-187 (bibliographie).

64   Voir en ce sens les remarques du P. A. Patfoort, "L'unité de la Ia pars et le mouvement interne de la Somme théologique de S. Thomas d'Aquin", *Rev. Sciences philos. théol.* 47 (1963) 513-544.

65   Voir à ce sujet L.-B. Gillon, "L'imitation du Christ et la morale de S. Thomas", *Angelicum* 36 (1959) 263-286.

taché d'abord la vue ecclésiologique de S. Thomas à la IIème pars et à son thème du *reditus*. C'est pourquoi aussi, même après avoir parlé du Christ et de sa "grâce capitale", S. Thomas présente l'Eglise ou le Corps mystique comme étant le domaine de la grâce, "effectus gratiae", au risque d'attirer les critiques d'un A. Mitterer qui veut le mettre en contradiction avec l'encyclique *Mystici Corporis* de Pie XII, et de pouvoir effectivement prêter à une mauvaise interprétation dans le sens d'une Eglise invisible. [66] S. Thomas n'a-t-il pas admis le thème augustinien et grégorien de l'"ecclesia ab Abel"? [67] N'a-t-il pas écrit que les anges en font partie tout comme nous? [68] Il n'aurait certainement pas appelé le pape "chef du Corps mystique": la primauté du pontife romain, que S. Thomas n'a certes pas diminuée (Harnack l'accusait d'être responsable de son élévation au plan d'un dogme!), est rattachée strictement à la juridiction.

Cela semble supposer qu'il existe deux concepts de l'Eglise: l'un répondant à la Cité de Dieu augustinienne ou à la communion des saints, l'autre à l'organisme historique, visible et juridique, dont S. Thomas a du reste abondamment et remarquablement parlé (cf. M. Useros Carretero). Par le côté essentiel des vertus théologales, de la grâce et de l'habitation du Saint-Esprit, l'Eglise est absolument une; elle n'est multiple que par le côté où elle se réalise dans un peuple de Dieu divisé en divers royaumes, provinces et cités. [69] Mais cela signifie que l'aspect d'organisation juridique, de lois et de gouvernement, celui qui est attaché au terme de *populus*, est accidentel et matériel, non essentiel ni formel pour qu'on puisse théologiquement parler d'*ecclesia*. Bien sûr, si l'on entend par Eglise celle qui existe concrètement de par la réalisation du plan de salut de Dieu par le Christ, elle englobe les deux aspects, l'essentiel-théologal et l'historique sacramentel, social et juridique!

On nous permettra de rapprocher de ce que nous croyons être la vue ecclésiologique profonde de S. Thomas, deux données ecclésiologiques récentes :

1. La lettre que la Congrégation romaine du Saint-Office adressa le 8 août 1949 à Mgr Cushing, archevêque de Boston, au sujet des errements

---

66 A. Mitterer, *Geheimnisvoller Leib Christi nach St. Thomas von Aquin und nach Papst Pius XII.* (Wien 1950). Voir notre article "Lumen Gentium n° 7, L'Eglise Corps mystique du Christ, vu au terme de huit siècles d'histoire de la théologie du Corps mystique", *Au service de la Parole de Dieu. Mélanges offerts à Mgr A.-M. Charue* (Gembloux 1969) 179-202.

67 Ainsi dans le commentaire du Symbole, art. 9. Et voir Y. Congar, "Ecclesia ab Abel", *Abhandlungen über Theologie und Kirche. Festschrift für Karl Adam* (Dusseldorf 1952) 79-108; *L'Eglise de S. Augustin à l'époque moderne*, p. 234 n. 5.

68 Voir par exemple *In III Sent.* d. 13, q. 2, a. 2, qa 2, ad 3; *In Ephes.* c. 1, lect. 8.

69 Cf. notre texte initial du *C. Gent.* IV, 76. On peut voir utilement A. Darquennes, *De juridische Structuur van de Kerk volgens Sint Thomas van Aquino*, (Leuven 1949).

théologiques du P. Léonard Feeney sur le sens de la formule "Hors de l'Eglise, pas de salut", exprime une doctrine qui repose sur une distinction entre ce qui est nécessaire par nature, c'est-à-dire essentiellement, pour entrer en communion avec Dieu et être sauvé, — c'est la foi et la charité — et ce qui est nécessaire seulement par une institution divine positive: l'Eglise, le baptême d'eau. [70] Cette distinction correspond bien à la vision thomiste des choses. Le seul point de différence est que le document romain n'aurait certainement pas donné le nom d'*ecclesia* à la pure communion spirituelle opérée sur la base de la foi et de la charité seulement. La note de visibilité rentre dans la définition de l'Eglise (cf. notre étude citée supra n. 66).

2. Le concile de Vatican II a formulé une idée de l'Eglise particulière. Si on accepte de l'identifier au diocèse, il en donne une définition digne du plus grand intérêt. Nous avons déjà évoqué ce texte (n.2): "Dioecesis est Populi Dei portio, quae Episcopo cum cooperatione presbyterii pascenda concreditur, ita ut, pastori suo adhaerens ab eoque per Evangelium et Eucharistiam in Spiritu Sancto congregata, Ecclesiam particularem constituat, in qua vere inest et operatur Una Sancta Catholica et Apostolica Christi Ecclesia." [71] L'Eglise est une. Si l'on parle en vérité d'"Eglises particulières", c'est parce qu'elles réalisent la réalité ou le mystère de l'Eglise pure et simple, que nous confessons être une, sainte, catholique et apostolique. Si on l'envisage sous l'angle de la multiplicité et même d'une certaine division, on parle de "portion du peuple de Dieu". On rejoint le vocabulaire du *C. Gentiles* IV, 76.

Nous avons commencé en citant ce texte. Pris globalement, et aussi dans le contexte de tout le chapitre, il est caractéristique de la contribution que S. Thomas, avec bien d'autres théologiens et hommes d'Eglise de son temps, a apportée à l'évolution des idées vers une ecclésiologie de l'Eglise universelle sous la primauté du Pontife romain. [72] Ce développement ecclésiologique peut être suivi dans diver-

---

70   Texte de cette lettre publiée en 1952, in *The American Ecclesiastical Rev.* 127 (1952) 307-311; en français in *Document. Cathol.* 2 nov. 1952, col. 1395-98 et notre *Sainte Eglise* (Paris 1963) pp. 427 s. et 432.

71   Décret *Christus Dominus* du 28.X.1965, n° 11. Comparer Constitution dogmatique *Lumen gentium* du 2.XI.1964, n° 23, § 2.

72   Voir nos études "Aspects ecclésiologiques de la querelle entre Mendiants et Séculiers dans la seconde moitié du XIIIe siècle et le début du XIVe", *Archives d'histoire doctrinale et littéraire du Moyen Age*, 28 (1961), 35-152; "De la communion des Eglises à une ecclésiologie de l'Eglise universelle", *L'épiscopat et l'Eglise universelle* (Paris 1962) 227-260; *L'Eglise de S. Augustin à l'époque moderne*, pp. 248-252.

ses questions, par exemple dans la théologie du schisme, que S. Thomas considère au plan de l'Eglise universelle et à l'égard de l'autorité du Pape, non dans le cadre de l'Eglise locale.[73] S'agissant du texte du *C. Gentiles* avons-nous forcé son sens? Y avons-nous introduit des subtilités arbitraires? Nous ne le croyons pas. Nous pensons avoir montré que S. Thomas a eu conscience qu'on ne peut passer d'emblée de *una ecclesia* à l'affirmation d'un *unum caput*, le pape, qui ait autorité sur toute l'Eglise: une telle démarche appelait l'usage d'un moyen terme, celui de peuple fidèle ou universalité des chrétiens et l'affirmation, difficilement contestable, de l'identité entre *Populus Dei* et *Ecclesia*. Nous trompons-nous? Il nous semble que cette démarche n'est pas sans intérêt pour comprendre la vision que Thomas a eue de l'Eglise.

73 Cf. II-II, q. 39, a. 1 et comp. le texte de *In IV Sent.* cité supra n. 1; cf. aussi notre article "Schisme", *Dict. de Théol. Cath.* 14, 1286-1312 (1939).

LES IDÉES DIVINES DANS L'ŒUVRE DE S. THOMAS

L. B. Geiger O.P.

MON intention n'est pas de traiter l'ensemble des problèmes historiques et systématiques qu'on peut soulever à propos du thème des idées divines dans l'œuvre de S. Thomas, quelque intérêt qu'offrirait un tel propos. Je voudrais seulement préciser certaines perspectives qui permettront de faire voir, je l'espère, quelle place il convient d'attribuer, dans la philosophie et la théologie de S. Thomas, aux idées en tant qu'objets de la connaissance divine.

Rappelons d'abord un point, qui ne fait d'ailleurs difficulté pour personne, à savoir la diversité des fonctions que le thème des Idées en général et celui des idées divines en particulier a été appelé à remplir au cours de l'histoire.[1] Chez Platon, les Idées sont les essences parfaites et immuables des réalités imparfaites et changeantes de notre univers, exigées par le savoir véritable dont elles sont l'objet et auquel elles fournissent les normes absolues du bien et du beau.[2] Elles n'interviennent cependant pas directement dans la formation de notre univers. Du moins Platon n'a-t-il jamais précisé, en dehors de leur statut de modèle pour le démiurge, leur rôle actif dans la participation. C'est Plotin qui les a dotées d'une énergie par laquelle elles peuvent communiquer la participation de leur similitude, leur donnant ainsi d'être à la fois objet de contemplation et cause exemplaire.[3]

Une fois qu'elles auront été placées dans un intellect divin, elles pourront assurer plus facilement cette double fonction.[4] Mais on sait que la nécessité d'admettre en Dieu la connaissance de l'univers à produire ou à gouverner s'est imposée en dehors de toute référence à la

---

1 Voir, par exemple, l'article "Idée" dans Eisler, *Wörterbuch*, 4ᵉ éd., ou celui, plus récent, d'A. Carlini, dans l'*Enciclopedia filosofica* s.v. "Idée", avec la bibliographie. Voir aussi l'exposé historique de H. Rüssimann, *Zur Ideenlehre der Hochscholastik* (Freiburg-im-Brisgau 1938).
2 Voir D. Ross, *Plato's Theory of Ideas* (Oxford 1951; réimpr. 1961).
3 Voir E. R. Dodds, *Proclus, The Elements of Theology* (Oxford 1933), pp. 215; 264 (prop. 121).
4 Pour l'histoire de ce passage des Idées dans l'intelligence divine, voir Dodds, op. cit., p. 206 (prop. 20); C. J. De Vogel, *Philosophia*, I (Assen 1970), ch. 15, spécialement, pp. 363s, 372ss.

noétique platonicienne, soit dans la révélation judéo-chrétienne par
exemple, soit dans certaines écoles philosophiques, comme le
stoïcisme,[5] encore que, très tôt, le dialogue se soit établi entre ces
courants et la tradition platonicienne des Idées.[6] Admettre la connaissance, par Dieu, de l'univers à produire ou à gouverner, ce n'est
donc pas nécessairement admettre la conception platonicienne des
Idées.[7] Aussi bien n'y-a-t-il aucune difficulté à comprendre que S.
Thomas ait toujours rejeté la noétique platonicienne ou augustinienne
des Idées, règles et normes de notre connaisssance, et retenu tout au
long de son enseignement le thème des idées divines. Il suffit que celles-
ci constituent les raisons éternelles de l'intelligence divine, raisons qui
sont comme le modèle dont s'inspire l'artisan dans son travail, sans
qu'elles soient appelées à illuminer notre connaissance intellectuelle
pour lui fournir, à défaut de l'abstraction, les principes de ses
jugements.

Mais, si un mot ne recouvre plus la réalité précise qui lui donnait sa
signification spécifique, pourquoi le conserver? Certes on peut appeler,
et on appelle en effet *idée* le modèle intérieur d'après lequel l'artisan est
censé produire son œuvre. On se trouve alors dans un domaine
totalement étranger à l'univers des Idées platoniciennes voire
augustiniennes. On s'expose donc à des malentendus. C'est un in-
convénient certain. Mais le Moyen Age était coutumier d'une certaine
indifférence à l'égard des mots, pourvu que le sens, visé en chaque cas,
fût suffisamment certain.

Il y a plus. Certains interprètes de sa pensée estiment que S. Thomas
aurait éliminé de sa théologie les développements qu'il consacre aux
idées divines s'il avait suivi la seule logique de ses positions personnelles. Ce serait "le langage platonicien en usage dans son milieu,"
ou "la reconnaissance de l'autorité théologique de S. Augustin" qui ex-
pliqueraient le maintien d'un mot et d'un ensemble de propositions que
rien, du point de vue systématique, n'invitait à conserver, que tout
devait amener, au contraire, à écarter. Leur suppression n'entraînerait
aucun changement dans l'équilibre de la doctrine. Tout à l'inverse, la
netteté de ses lignes caractéristiques n'en sortirait que plus clairement.

---

5 Voir M. Pohlenz, *Die Stoa* (Göttingen 1948), I, pp. 93-101.

6 Philon, par exemple. Voir H. A. Wolfson, *Philo* (Cambridge, Mass. 1948), I, ch. 3 et 4; C. J.
De Vogel, *Greek Philosophy*, 2nd ed. (Leiden 1964), III, n. 1294. Sur le monde intelligible, voir
ibid., n. 1293.

7 Pour la notion de la providence chrétienne et ses rapports avec la doctrine des idées divines,
voir E. Gilson, *L'esprit de la philosophie médiévale*, 2ᵉ éd. (Paris 1948), ch. 8. Pour ce qui est du
Nouveau Testament, G. Kittel fait remarquer que le sens platonicien de *eidos* ne s'y rencontre
jamais: *Theol. Wörterbuch zum N.T.*, s.v. "eidos", p. 373, 30ss.

Avec le P. Sertillanges, par exemple,[8] on peut se montrer sensible aux simplismes qu'on risque d'introduire dans la théologie de S. Thomas en traitant des idées divines, expression authentiquement thomiste, il est vrai, sans tenir compte des thèses telles que l'unité et la simplicité de Dieu, qui permettent de les comprendre correctement. Avec les idées, en effet, n'est-ce pas comme un univers intelligible, plus ou moins distinct de Dieu, qu'on introduit dans l'intelligence divine, cet univers des possibles, objet et source de tant de spéculations fallacieuses, et dont Bergson avait dénoncé le caractère illusoire, en démontant les mécanismes qui concourent à le former? N'est-ce pas aussi réduire notre univers à n'être que la reproduction d'un modèle tout fait, donc en exclure toute possibilité de nouveauté et d'invention?

D'après S. Thomas:

> L'Idée, en Dieu, s'identifie à l'essence divine considérée comme source une et simple de toute intelligibilité comme de tout être. Les idées, dans leur diversité, ne se définissent que par un rapport des réalités mêmes — j'entends des réalités concrètes, et par suite, individuelles — à cette unique Source. C'est pourquoi je dis qu'en dehors de l'exemplarité ... la doctrine des Idées est chez Saint Thomas un encombrement, non une lumière, un nid à équivoques où beaucoup de disciples ont pris occasion d'erreur. Laissé à lui-même notre auteur eût préféré sans doute suivre Aristote[9] à qui il prête, plus ou moins valablement d'ailleurs, une doctrine d'exemplarité sans Idées obsédantes. Le langage platonicien en usage dans son milieu ne le lui permit pas.[10]

On peut aussi montrer, avec M. Gilson,[11] que la thèse la plus personnelle de S. Thomas, relative à l'Etre de Dieu, *Ipsum esse subsistens,* conduit logiquement et aurait dû conduire S. Thomas à se passer de la doctrine des idées divines. Dans la perspective de l'*Esse*, en effet, le problème de la possibilité de l'univers consiste à se demander

> comment les essences peuvent émaner de l'être en qui nulle essence distinctive ne s'ajoute à l'*esse* pour composer avec lui....Sous quelque aspect qu'on envisage le problème, il semble impossible d'éviter la conclusion que l'essence est un amoindrissement, une distension et comme

---

8 A. D. Sertillanges, *Le christianisme et les philosophes* (Paris 1939), I, pp. 273-276. Voir aussi, à propos de la *Somme théologique*, I, 15, dans la traduction française de l'Edition de la Revue des Jeunes, Dieu II, les *renseignements techniques*, pp. 403-405.

9 Pour S. Thomas, on le sait, Aristote à la différence de Platon et de ses Idées subsistantes en elles-mêmes, aurait admis l'existence d'idées dans l'intellect divin. Voir par exemple *In I Sent.*, d. 36, q. 2, a. 1, ad 1. Ce n'est donc pas Aristote qui aurait pu le persuader d'abandonner les idées divines.

10 A. D. Sertillanges, ibid. I, p. 276.

11 E. Gilson, *Introduction à la philosophie chrétienne* (Paris 1960), pp. 173-183. Dans *Le Thomisme*, 6ᵉ éd. (Paris 1965), pp. 146-148, la doctrine de la *Somme théologique*, I, 15, est reproduite sans discussion.

un éparpillement de l'être...Le difficile, qui n'est peut-être qu'imparfaitement possible, est de discerner la nature de l'opération prise en quelque sorte à la source, au moment où la première essence se divise d'avec sa cause, qui est l'acte pur d'*esse*.[12]

C'est ici qu'interviennent les Idées:

La réponse à la question se tire généralement de la notion d'intellect divin, lieu des Idées qui sont elles-mêmes les archétypes des essences. Réponse correcte sans aucun doute et qui peut s'autoriser de ce que Saint Thomas lui-même, à la suite de Saint Augustin, a expressément enseigné, sur la nature des Idées divines. Pourtant, il est à peine exagéré de dire qu'au fond, tout ce que S. Thomas a dit des Idées était dans son esprit une concession de plus faite au langage d'une philosophie qui n'était pas vraiment la sienne. C'était aussi, n'en doutons pas, la reconnaissance de l'autorité théologique de Saint Augustin.[13]

La preuve en est que

l'exposé du problème et sa discussion dans le *Contra Gentiles* (I, 44-71) relègue à l'arrière plan la notion d'idée divine. Celle-ci fait de brèves apparitions aux chapitres 51 et 54, où il est question de la manière dont une pluralité d'objets connus peut être dans l'intellect divin sans en rompre l'unité, mais Saint Thomas n'en fait mention que comme d'un artifice employé par Saint Augustin pour sauver dans une certaine mesure l'opinion de Platon...La solution platonicienne du problème est donc inopérante; la *Somme contre les Gentils* ne semble pas avoir jugé nécessaire de mettre en œuvre la notion platonicienne d'Idée, entendue de quelque manière que ce soit.[14]

C'est la simplicité divine, c'est à dire la simplicité de l'*esse* divin, tel que le conçoit S. Thomas, qui rend superflu le recours aux Idées.

Intelliger est à l'intellect ce qu'être est à l'essence; mais c'est l'être qui est l'essence de Dieu; l'intellect est donc son essence, qui est son être...: *Quicquid enim est in Deo, est divina essentia, et divinum esse, et ipse Deus. Nam Deus est sua essentia et suum esse.* (CG. I, 45, § 2).[15]

On peut donc se demander à bon droit ce

qu'ont à faire les Idées dans une pareille doctrine....En effet, pourquoi poserait-on des Idées en Dieu? Pour expliquer comment, par elles, il connaît les créatures? Mais Dieu connaît par son intellect, qui est son essence, qui est son *esse*. Comme le dit Saint Thomas avec force, si l'on veut que toute connaissance se fasse par une espèce intelligible, alors, c'est l'essence de Dieu qui est en lui l'espèce intelligible.[16]

---

12 E. Gilson, *Introduction à la philosophie chrétienne*, pp. 170-173.
13 Ibid., pp. 173-174.
14 Ibid., pp. 174-175.
15 Ibid., p. 175.
16 Ibid., pp. 175-176.

Pris en somme entre ses conceptions les plus personnelles et le langage théologique de son temps avec les représentations qu'il véhiculait, S. Thomas aurait conservé les idées divines par nécessité (Sertillanges), ou par respect à l'égard de l'autorité de S. Augustin (Gilson), sans qu'on puisse leur trouver une nécessité intelligible dans sa synthèse théologique. Dépouillées de leur fonction noétique par l'abstraction aristotélicienne, difficilement conciliables avec les exigences et la simplicité de l'*Esse* divin, elles errent, telles des ombres, dans un univers qui n'est pas fait pour elles.

Personne ne contestera l'influence subie par S. Thomas, comme d'ailleurs par n'importe quel philosophe ou théologien, de la part de son milieu intellectuel et culturel, ni la déférence qu'il n'a cessé de marquer pour l'autorité de S. Augustin. On accordera aussi que les arguments fondés sur l'opposition entre la simplicité de l'*Esse* divin et le thème des idées divines ne manquent pas de valeur. On peut toutefois se demander si la conclusion s'impose. Je ne le pense pas, et j'essaierai de montrer que, si S. Thomas a conservé les idées divines tout au long de son enseignement, c'est justement pour éviter la contradiction entre la thèse de la simplicité divine et la nécessité d'affirmer la connaissance distincte, par Dieu, d'une multiplicité d'*objets* de sa connaissance.

L'idée certes, n'a plus chez lui la fonction d'objet de notre savoir théorétique ou de norme de nos jugements de valeur, comme chez Platon. Elle n'est plus liée à l'illumination divine, même si l'on consent à appeler illumination, avec S. Thomas lui-même, le don, fait par Dieu à chaque homme, de son pouvoir de connaître, participation à la lumière de Dieu. Les idées ne forment pas en Dieu un univers d'intelligibles, le monde des possibles que Dieu contemplerait et dont notre univers serait comme une reproduction. Elles ne sont pas cependant un ornement inutile, la répétition pure et simple, en d'autres mots, de ce qui a été déjà dit et bien dit. S. Thomas a en effet distingué, de plus en plus fermement, la forme qui est principe de l'acte de connaissance, en le spécifiant et en l'actualisant, et la forme qui est terme de la connaissance, parce qu'elle a été elle-même formée par l'intelligence. Les idées sont les participations de l'essence divine, connues, en tant qu'elles sont exprimées par Dieu, non pas l'essence divine en tant qu'elle est quasi forme actualisante de l'intellect de Dieu. C'est en tant que terme formé par le connaissant qu'elles permettent d'assurer la multiplicité des objets connus, donc une multiplicité d'idées, sans contredire la simplicité de l'essence divine.

Si donc l'idée, telle que S. Thomas la conçoit, ne répond ni au contenu ni aux fonctions qu'on leur attribue, en songeant à telle ou telle autre philosophie, on peut certes conclure logiquement que ce contenu ne s'y trouve pas, qu'il n'est donc pas nécessaire non plus d'en conserver le mot, dans la mesure exacte où il désigne le contenu et la fonction ainsi entendus. Mais on ne peut conclure d'une manière générale, qu'elle n'a aucun contenu utile, ni aucune nécessité, qu'elle ne représente que la fidélité à un vocabulaire et à une tradition. Si S. Thomas a donné au mot *idée* un sens qui lui est propre, il a pu en maintenir la présence pour des raisons positives et systématiques. C'est ce que nous nous proposons de montrer.

LE PROBLÈME

Que la raison d'être des idées en Dieu soit bien celle du terme formé et exprimé par le connaissant, il suffit, pour s'en convaincre, de réfléchir au prologue de *Summa Theologiae*, I, q. 14, qui donne le plan du traité consacré à "l'opération" de Dieu. L'intellection est l'une des opérations immanentes. On en traitera à la question 14. Et "puisque tout objet connu est dans le connaissant, que les raisons des choses, en tant qu'elles sont en Dieu connaissant, sont appelées idées, il faudra joindre, à la considération de la science de Dieu, celle des idées."[17] Le problème des idées concerne donc "les raisons des choses" en tant qu'elles sont *en Dieu comme connaissant*.

Or la question 14 traite des problèmes de la connaissance divine en montrant que Dieu n'a besoin que de l'identité de son intelligence avec sa propre essence pour posséder toutes les connaissances qu'on doit lui attribuer. Dans notre expérience, l'intellection, opération immanente, ne peut se produire sans l'intervention d'une forme, principe d'actuation d'ordre accidentel, qui fait passer le pouvoir de l'état de puissance à l'état actuel. En Dieu, la question 14 le montre en détail, l'unique *Esse* de Dieu, plénitude de tous les modes possibles de l'être, remplit éminemment toutes les fonctions que nous attribuons à la forme actualisante. Par son *Esse*, Dieu est en acte de tous les objets possibles de la connaissance, par l'identité entre son *Esse*, son intelligence et son acte d'intellection. Toutes les conditions sont donc remplies pour fonder la connaissance divine à l'égard de Dieu lui-même et de toutes les participations possibles de la plénitude de son être.

Tout semble donc dit au sujet de la connaissance divine. Aussi bien,

---

17 "Post considerationem eorum quae ad divinam substantiam pertinent restat considerandum de his quae pertinent ad operationem ipsius. Et quia operatio quaedam est quae manet in operante...primo agemus de scientia et voluntate (nam intelligere in intelligente est, et velle in voluntate).... Rursum, quia omne cognitum in cognoscente est, rationes autem rerum, secundum quod sunt in Deo cognoscente, ideae vocantur, cum consideratione scientiae erit etiam adjungenda consideratio de ideis." *Sum. theol.* I, 14, prol. (Ed. léonine).

quand au début de la question 15, S. Thomas déclare qu'il reste à traiter des idées, on peut se demander avec M. Gilson, pourquoi? "Ayant déjà fondé la connaissance divine du singulier sur ce qui, de toute manière, doit être l'ultime fondement — *ipsum Esse* — pourquoi ajouter à la doctrine cette sorte d'enclave consacrée aux Idées: y-a-t-il des Idées? Y en a-t-il plusieurs? Y en a-t-il de tout ce que Dieu connaît?"[18]

Dans une noétique strictement aristotélicienne, la présence de la forme intelligible suffit à faire connaître l'objet, de même que la présence de la forme sensible suffit à la connaissance sensible portant sur les êtres réels. En d'autres mots, dans la noétique aristotélicienne, il y a des formes intelligibles ou sensibles; mais elles se trouvent dans le pouvoir connaissant pour le mettre en acte, à titre de principe formel de son opération. Il y a des objets connus, mais ce ne sont pas des Idées. Ce sont les réalités elles-mêmes, sensibles ou intelligibles, ces dernières actualisées par le pouvoir appelé intellect-actif, auquel Aristote assigne une fonction analogue à celle de la lumière pour la sensation visuelle. Dans le cas de notre connaissance humaine, les pouvoirs sont d'abord réceptifs ou passifs. En tant qu'ils sont réceptifs ils ne produisent rien, si ce n'est l'acte lui-même, une fois que la forme de l'objet l'aura spécifié et, par là, actualisé.

Appliquée à Dieu, une telle noétique fonde la connaissance divine sur l'essence de Dieu, identique à son intelligence et à son acte d'intellection, et, tout ensemble, similitude éminente de toutes les participations possibles. S. Thomas ne dit-il pas, ici même (I, 14, 2, c): "Nous connaissons en acte quelque objet par nos sens ou notre intelligence du fait que notre intelligence ou notre sens sont actuellement informés par l'espèce sensible ou intelligible." La présence de la similitude de l'objet au principe de l'acte de connaissance suffit donc, semble-t-il, à assurer la connaissance de cet objet. S. Thomas conclut, d'ailleurs, immédiatement de la présence en Dieu de la quasi-forme intelligible, à la connaissance actuelle de Dieu par lui-même: *Ipsa species intelligibilis est ipse intellectus divinus et sic seipsum intelligit.* (Ibid.).

Si donc l'idée n'apportait aucune présence nouvelle de l'objet connu au sujet connaissant, aucune forme de présence surtout, qui s'impose avec quelque nécessité systématique, on ne voit pas pour quelle raison on en annonce une étude spéciale pour assurer la présence de l'objet dans le sujet connaissant (q. 14, prol.). N'aurions-nous pas affaire, très exactement, avec une de ces questions inutiles, occasionnées par les hasards de la routine scolaire, dont l'auteur de la *Somme* s'est proposé

---

18 E. Gilson, *Introduction à la philosophie chrétienne*, p. 180.

de débarrasser l'exposé ordonné de la théologie? [19] Aurait-il été si difficile de déclarer qu'on ne traitera pas des idées divines, puisque, sous
ce mot, on ne ferait que redire ce qui avait été exposé suffisamment, en
étudiant la connaissance divine et ses objets? Si S. Thomas ne l'a pas
fait, c'est croyons-nous parce que l'idée assure en effet une mode de
présence de l'objet connu dans le sujet connaissant, qui doit compléter
celui qui est assuré par la forme, principe de l'intellection. L'intellection se complète par la *dictio*, dont on ne trouve point de trace
dans la noétique de la connaissance spéculative d'Aristote. C'est
finalement, en tant que forme formée ou exprimée, non prévue par le
Stagirite, que l'idée permet de résoudre un problème qu'Aristote n'a pas
posé, et que sa noétique de la forme actualisante, transposée dans un
domaine pour lequel elle n'était pas faite, laissait sans réponse
satisfaisante, face à l'objection tirée de la multiplicité des objets à
connaître par l'intellect de Dieu.

Les rapports de notre problème des idées divines avec la pensée
d'Aristote sont en effet les suivants: d'une part, le Dieu d'Aristote, si
l'on veut appeler ainsi l'Intellect suprême, ne pose aucune difficulté au
sujet des idées, puisqu'il ne s'occupe pas de l'univers, ni pour le concevoir, ni pour le produire, ni pour le gouverner. Eternellement en acte,
il ne doit connaître que lui-même, l'intelligible le plus parfait, pour
jouir de ce fait d'une éternelle et parfaite béatitude. [20]

D'autre part, la théorie des formes, chargées de rendre présente aux
différents pouvoirs la forme de l'objet connu, était liée étroitement,
chez le Stagirite, au problème du passage de la puissance à l'acte: ou
bien le pouvoir est en acte par la forme reçue, et il peut connaître l'objet
dont il possède la similitude; ou bien il ne l'est pas, et la connaissance
ne peut pas se produire. La forme une fois reçue assure donc à un acte
immanent du pouvoir la connaissance d'objets qui en sont *réellement
distincts*, et qui, inférieurs dans certains cas au pouvoir, dans l'ordre ontologique, possèdent la priorité d'être en acte dans l'ordre de la forme et
de l'essence. La connaissance comporte donc l'assimilation du pouvoir
et de la réalité à connaître, permettant au premier de se rapporter à la
seconde, qui en est indépendante dans son être. La réalité se fait
connaître en déléguant dans le pouvoir la similitude d'elle-même sous
les espèces de la forme actualisante. [21]

---

19 "Consideravimus...huius doctrinae novitios...plurimum impediri partim quidem propter
multiplicationem inutilium quaestionum, articulorum et argumentorum. Haec igitur et alia
huiusmodi evitare studentes, tentabimus...ea quae ad sacram doctrinam pertinent, breviter ac
dilucide prosequi." *Sum. theol.*, prol.

20 Sur ce point, voir les remarques de E. Gilson, *L'esprit de la philos. médiév.*, p. 159, n. 2.

21 Voir, p.e.: *In I Sent.* d.35, q. 1, a. 1, ad 3 et 4; ed. Mandonnet (Paris 1929), I, pp. 812-813.

Un Dieu créateur, au contraire, qui produit l'univers en fonction d'une conception qu'il s'en fait, dans son ensemble comme dans le détail, et qui le produit librement, doit posséder en lui-même les formes des êtres qu'il crée, s'il est vrai que l'intellect ne connaît que les objets dont il possède la similitude. Mais il doit les posséder sans les recevoir de cet univers, qui ne peut rien lui donner, puisqu'il reçoit tout de lui, son être et son intelligibilité; et il doit les posséder de toute éternité, puisqu'il n'y a pas en lui passage de puissance à acte. Enfin, et surtout, il doit connaître l'univers en lui-même, comme *terme de connaissance*, à la manière dont l'artisan connaît le modèle, inventé ou appris, qui guide son activité, par laquelle il produira ce qui n'existe pas encore et l'amènera à sa perfection. Dieu, en effet, crée l'univers d'après un dessein de son intelligence et le gouverne par sa providence, qui prend soin, non seulement des hommes, mais encore des oiseaux du ciel et des lys des champs.

C'est dire que le rapport entre l'intelligence créatrice et son œuvre est inintelligible si, d'une manière ou d'une autre, on ne fait appel à la présence d'un terme intérieur au connaissant, forme formée librement et exprimée dans le connaissant comme terme de son acte de connaissance. Aristote, non plus que Platon d'ailleurs, n'a distingué, pour la connaissance spéculative au moins, deux formes intelligibles: l'une qui est principe, l'autre qui est terme de l'acte de connaissance. Pour Aristote, nous l'avons dit, le terme de l'acte c'est ou bien la réalité sensible, ou bien l'intelligible en puissance dans la réalité, où il est saisi, une fois actué par l'intervention de l'intellect actif.

Ne peut-on penser d'ailleurs que cette absence d'un terme produit par le connaissant tient à la conception qu'on se faisait de la connaissance spéculative? Spéculer, ce n'est pas construire a priori comme on le pensera dans la philosophie et la théologie après Kant. Spéculer, c'est regarder, contempler. Quand nous regardons, nous n'avons pas conscience d'autre chose que de la présence de notre regard à l'objet contemplé. La dignité de la connaissance spéculative tenait, non pas à la nécessité logique qui lie entre elles les moments d'un raisonnement ou les termes d'une proposition, mais à la nécessité de l'objet lui-même, éternel, immuable, manifesté à une vue, qui est justement la *saisie* intelligible. Une connaissance spéculative n'est-elle pas précisément celle qui a pour objet des réalités que nous saisissons, mais ne produisons pas? N'est-elle pas d'autant plus purement elle-même que le sujet se montre plus exclusivement réceptif, présent à un être qui se donne au connaissant, mais n'est d'aucune manière produit par lui?

La connaissance pratique comporte la production ou la conception d'un modèle que l'artisan s'applique ensuite à réaliser par son travail.

Mais on sait en quelle médiocre estime les philosophes grecs ont tenu ce genre d'activité. Il ne peut donner lieu à aucun savoir proprement dit. N'est-il pas, d'ailleurs, lié au *besoin*, à l'utile, donc aux *moyens*, destinés à accroître notre bien être, non pas notre connaissance de *ce qui est*? Il concerne le domaine des *factibilia*, dont aucun savoir théorétique ne peut consentir à s'occuper. Connaître pour connaître, et connaître ce qui vraiment est, voilà la dignité de l'homme et du philosophe. C'est aussi celle de l'Intellect suprême d'après Aristote.

Il n'est pas difficile, dès lors, de comprendre à quelles difficultés se heurteront les théologiens quand ils tenteront de traduire le mystère de la création et de la providence à l'aide de concepts philosophiques issus de Platon et d'Aristote. La métaphore de l'artisan, suggérée par l'Écriture, s'offrait tout naturellement. Elle avait d'ailleurs l'avantage de ne faire appel à aucune théorie particulière au sujet de la nature de la connaissance. Tout le monde admet facilement que l'artisan dirige son activité d'après un modèle ou une idée qu'il porte en lui-même, qu'il connaît, comme le potier, dont les doigts semblent suivre les contours d'une image intérieure, visible pour lui seul.

Mais attribuer à Dieu la connaissance pratique, c'est à dire une connaissance faite pour diriger la production d'une œuvre, n'est-ce pas le rabaisser? Certes on souligne ainsi son pouvoir absolu sur la création tout entière, la liberté du dessein créateur. Mais du même coup, n'est-ce pas la nécessité de tout l'édifice du savoir relatif à l'essence des êtres qui se trouve compromise? Concevoir un projet ou un modèle, l'exécuter ou le réaliser en inspirant chacun des gestes par ses exigences, c'est assurément une perfection qui élève l'homme au dessus des forces aveugles de la nature, et le rend indépendant, en partie du moins, de leur empire. Mais le savoir théorétique, le savoir véritable ne tient-il pas sa dignité du caractère nécessaire, éternel et immuable de son objet?

Si au contraire on tient à sauvegarder la dignité du savoir spéculatif en reconnaissant la perfection, l'éternité et l'immutabilité de son objet, ne sera-t-on pas conduit à imposer à Dieu lui-même quelque forme de nécessité: un univers de Formes qu'il contemplerait, ou qu'il formerait en lui-même par quelque processus nécessaire à partir d'un point de départ qu'il serait lui-même?

C'est donc tout le problème des rapports entre la sagesse grecque et le savoir spéculatif, d'une part, et la révélation d'une création libre, d'autre part, qu'on pourrait évoquer ici: défiance à l'égard d'Aristote, aussi longtemps du moins que sa pensée se présentait sans les changements et compléments, étrangers à son contenu original; attrait, au contraire, exercé par les différentes philosophies d'inspiration néo-platonicienne, avec le danger de céder à quelque forme d'émanatisme voire de panthéisme.[22]

Dans le problème des idées divines et leur rôle dans la création et la providence, tel que le discute S. Thomas, ces perspectives ne sont pas complètement absentes. On pourrait les évoquer facilement à la faveur de telle ou telle citation. Une étude complète se devrait de les envisager explicitement. Nous nous contenterons ici d'observer les péripéties de la rencontre entre les exigences de la connaissance du monde qui doit être celle d'un Dieu créateur et provident, et une noétique qui ne fait pas sa place à la forme formée ou exprimée par l'intelligence, en suivant, dans leur ordre chronologique, les textes majeurs qui en traitent.

LE *COMMENTAIRE SUR LES SENTENCES*

C'est au *Commentaire* sur le premier livre des *Sentences* que nous lisons le premier exposé explicite consacré au problème des idées divines. Or, remarquons le, dans le texte, le maître lui-même ne fait allusion ni aux idées, ni d'ailleurs à aucune théorie de la connaissance particulière. A la distinction 35, il précise le sens d'un certain nombre d'expressions relatives à la connaissance divine, telles que: science, préscience, providence, disposition et prédestination. Il conclut son exposé en montrant que, si des mots comme préscience, disposition, prédestination ou providence se rapportent aux réalités temporelles et seulement à elles, les mots de science ou de sagesse ont rapport non seulement aux choses temporelles mais aussi aux éternelles. "Toute la raison de la sagesse suprême et éternelle se trouve en Dieu....Son immense sagesse comprend en effet toute sagesse et toute science."[23]

---

22 Il faut donc distinguer les tentatives pour a) dire la formation de l'univers intelligible, en soi ou dans un intellect divin; b) construire l'univers réel à partir de quelques données simples, comme le fera Descartes, par exemple; c) manifester les moments par lesquels, dans les différentes philosophies émanatistes, le multiple procède d'un principe premier; d) mettre en lumière l'intelligibilité de l'univers en tenant compte explicitement de la liberté divine dans la conception et la production de la création, comme Saint Thomas le fait dans le beau chapître, *3 CG*, 97, qui a pour titre: "Quomodo dispositio providentiae habeat rationem." Pour la cause de la multiplicité et de l'inégalité des êtres, voir, p.ex. *Sum. theol.*, Ia, q. 47, a. 1 et 2. La raison de la création est la volonté de Dieu de se communiquer et de communiquer sa bonté, autant qu'il est possible, non point quelque nécessité naturelle d'émanation. La création comporte nécessairement déficience par rapport à la perfection de la bonté divine, mais elle est un don.

23 *Petri Lombardi Libri IV Sententiarum, studio et cura PP. Collegii S. Bonaventurae in lucem editi*. 2a ed. (Quaracchi, 1916), I, n. 322. J'ai traduit le texte du Lombard d'après l'éd. Mandonnet, I, 805. Il s'agit d'une citation de Saint Ambroise. Elle doit se lire ainsi: "Omnis enim ratio supernae et terrenae sapientiae, ut ait Ambrosius, in eo est, quia omnem sapientiam et essentiam capit sua immensa scientia." Ed. citée, n. 322.

"Aussi, dit-on, que toutes choses sont en Dieu et y ont été de toute éternité,"[24] comme S. Augustin l'expose dans son Commentaire sur la Genèse. Et le Lombard commente a son tour: "Par ce texte nous comprenons que ces choses visibles, avant d'exister, étaient dans la science de Dieu. C'est en ce sens qu'on dit que toutes choses sont en Dieu, et que tout ce qui a été fait est vie en lui: non point parce que la créature serait le Créateur, ou que ces réalités temporelles seraient essentiellement en Dieu, mais parce qu'elles sont toujours dans la science de Dieu, qui est vie."[25]

La distinction 36 aborde un problème, dont l'auteur nous dit qu' "on a l'habitude de la soulever ici."[26] Si en effet la connaissance ou la prescience sont en Dieu identiques à son essence, ne doit-on pas conclure que toutes les choses présentes dans la connaissance de Dieu sont présentes aussi dans son essence ou sont en Dieu par essence? L'inférence semble valide. Mais on aboutirait à cette conclusion que toutes choses sont identiques à l'essence divine, puisque être en Dieu par essence ne convient qu'à l'essence divine qui est Dieu même.

Le Lombard évite la conclusion, comme dans d'autres cas, par la simple distinction entre la présence comme objet de connaissance et présence dans la nature. La connaissance ou la prescience de Dieu sont identiques à sa nature. Il n'en suit pas qu'être présent à sa connaissance soit identiquement être présent à sa nature, comme le montre d'ailleurs un texte de S. Augustin.[27] La suite de la distinction traite spécialement de la présence du mal à la connaissance divine. On montre ensuite comment on doit entendre l'expression: toutes choses sont de Dieu, par Dieu et en Dieu. On veut dire par là, notamment, que toutes choses sont en Dieu, parce qu'il les connaît et qu'il en est l'auteur. Il faut user de distinctions analogues pour d'autres expressions qui sont examinées dans la dernière partie du texte.[28] Aucune justification, ni métaphysique, ni noétique, ne vient éclairer le débat. La discussion se tient au niveau du sens commun. Il n'est question ni d'idées, ni d'aucune donnée relevant d'un système philosophique déterminé.

---

24 Ibid., n. 323.
25 "Ecce hic habes, quia visibilia haec antequam fierent, in Dei scientia erant. Ex hoc igitur sensu omnia dicuntur esse in Deo, et omne quod *factum est* dicitur esse *vita in ipso*; non ideo, quod creatura sit Creator, vel quod ista temporalia essentialiter sint in Deo, sed quia in eius scientia semper sunt, quae vita est." Ibid., n.323 fin-324.
26 "Solet hic quaeri..." Ibid., n. 326.
27 Ibid., n. 326.
28 Ibid., n. 329-332. Présence à la connaissance divine seulement, comme objet; présence dans l'essence, cause exemplaire; présence dans l'essence et dans la connaissance sont les différentes possibilités, parmi lesquelles le Lombard aurait pu instituer une discussion. Il se contente de faire son choix parmi les deux premières, en s'appuyant sur l'autorité de Saint Augustin.

C'est dans ce contexte que, à la distinction 36, S. Thomas traite des idées. Il le fait, conformément à une tradition scolaire relativement récente.[29] A propos de cette distinction 36, S. Thomas pose deux questions. La première complète celle qui avait été développée en cinq articles, à la distinction 35. Sous le titre: *De his quae a Deo cognoscuntur*, elle traite de la connaissance des singuliers et du mal par Dieu, et de la manière dont on doit dire que se trouvent en Dieu les objets qu'il connaît. La question suivante, consacrée aux idées, ne concerne plus les objets connus par Dieu, mais ce par quoi les choses sont connues: *per quas res cognoscit*.[30]

Les idées, en effet, sont comme des "formes opératives," c'est-à-dire qu'elles sont, dans la connaissance divine, l'équivalent des modèles qui, présents dans son esprit, guident le travail de l'artisan. Les formes des objets qui sont produits par l'art ou la technique ont, en effet, "un *esse* double. D'une part elles existent en acte dans la matière; d'autre part elles existent en puissance, mais en puissance active, dans l'esprit de l'artisan....Or c'est une affirmation commune à tous les philosophes que toutes choses sont dans l'esprit de Dieu comme les produits de l'art dans l'esprit de l'artisan. Nous appelons donc idées les formes des choses existant en Dieu, qui sont comme des formes opératives." Et, après celle du Commentateur, S. Thomas fait appel à l'autorité de Denys. Il précise cependant que, le mot *idea* venant de *eidos*, il signifie la forme. Le mot *idée* peut donc s'appliquer également, en vertu de son sens propre, à la connaissance spéculative et à la connaissance pratique. Dans les deux cas, elle joue le rôle de principe de la connaissance. Dans les deux cas, elle est un objet connu.[31]

Cependant, dès le *Commentaire sur les Sentences*, S. Thomas identifie ces formes opératives avec les exemplaires, et ceux-ci avec l'essence divine en tant qu'elle est imitable par les créatures.[32] A la différence du Lombard, qui nous l'avons vu, ne veut admettre, pour les choses distinctes de Dieu, qu'une présence dans la connaissance divine, S. Thomas tient que "le mot *idée* designe l'essence divine en tant qu'elle

29 Le problème des idées divines, de leur nature et de leur multiplicité en Dieu, se trouve déjà dans les *Gloses* d'Alexandre de Halès sur les *Sentences*, à la distinction 36. Voir: *Alexandri de Hales, Glossa super quatuor libros Sententiarum Petri Lombardi* (Quaracchi 1951), I, pp. 357-358. Mais la discussion autour de ce problème est évidemment plus ancienne que son évocation à propos du texte du Lombard.

30 *In I Sent.*, ed. Mandonnet, I, p. 829.

31 Ibid., d. 36, q. 2, a. 1, sol.; p. 839.

32 A propos de la connaissance divine des singuliers, Saint Thomas rejette d'abord diverses théories. Puis il propose la solution qu'il va adopter: "Unde procedendum est per viam quam docet Dionysius...Dicit enim, quod cum Deus cognoscit res per essentiam suam quae est causa rerum..." Ibid., dist 36, q. 1, a. 1, sol.: pp. 831-832. Cf. qu. 2, a. 2, sol.; p. 841.

est l'exemplaire imité par la créature."³³ Les créatures sont donc
présentes, de quelque manière, dans l'essence divine en tant qu'elle est
imitable par elles, donc présentes aussi dans son intelligence, identique
à son essence: "Cum hoc nomen 'idea' nominet essentiam divinam
secundum quod est exemplar imitatum a creatura, divina essentia erit
propria idea istius rei secundum determinatum imitationis modum."³⁴

Pour éviter de porter atteinte à la simplicité et à l'unité de Dieu, il
faut donc distinguer les raisons de l'imitation en tant qu'elles sont
fondées dans la plénitude de l'essence divine, et en tant qu'elles sont objets de connaissance. Le mot *idée* est réservé pour exprimer la seconde
signification: "...ex hoc sunt plures rationes ideales, secundum quod
Deus intelligit essentiam suam ut imitabilem per hunc vel per illum
modum. Ipsae enim rationes imitationis intellectae, seu modi, sunt
ideae; idea enim, ut ex dictis patet, nominat formam ut intellectam, et
non prout est in natura intelligentis."³⁵ C'est cette distinction, entre
l'essence divine imitable et l'essence divine connue comme imitable, qui
est appelée, et appelée seule, à résoudre le problème de l'antinomie entre l'unité de l'intellect divin et la pluralité des idées; antinomie qui,
répétons le, ne se pose pas pour le Lombard, puisqu'il ne reconnaît
qu'une seule présence en Dieu, celle des objets de sa connaissance en
tant qu'objets, qui semble bien exclure une présence "in natura intelligentis."

Le Lombard, en somme, suit un itinéraire inverse de celui de S.
Thomas. Il développe une théologie de la science divine qui n'utilise
que de données propres au domaine de la connaissance. Il évoque ensuite une présence dans l'essence divine, mais c'est pour la rejeter. S.
Thomas, au contraire, a adopté d'emblée une présence dans l'essence
divine comme plénitude imitable, fondement de la perfection de son intellection. Dieu connaît tout, toutes choses distinctes de lui, et il connaît
tout jusque dans le détail individuel, sans recevoir sa connaissance des
êtres distincts de lui, puisque tout ce qui est est imitation de la
plénitude de sa perfection. La distinction 35 a développé ce point. Elle
a montré notamment que la connaissance d'objets multiples ne con-
tredisait point la simplicité de Dieu. Il suffit pour cela de distinguer
l'essence comme essence et l'essence comme imitable. La perfection de
la connaissance suit la perfection de l'essence et la plénitude de son
imitabilité. La présence dans la connaissance est la conséquence
logique de la présence dans l'essence à titre d'imitabilité de sa

---

33 "Hoc nomen 'idea' nominat essentiam divinam secundum quod est exemplar imitatum a
creatura." Ibid., d. 36, q. 2, a. 2, sol.; p. 842.
34 Ibid.
35 Ibid.

plénitude. Il suffit de distinguer entre un *intellectum primum* et un *intellectum secundum* pour pouvoir conclure: "Si ergo consideretur intellectum primum, nihil aliud intelligit Deus nisi se; qui non recipit species rerum, per quas cognoscat; sed per essentiam suam cognoscit, quae est similitudo omnium rerum; sed si accipiatur intellectum secundum, sic non tantum se intelligit, sed etiam alia."[36]

A cette doctrine relative à la connaissance divine, la question des idées n'ajoute rien, si ce n'est un rapport à la production des êtres, *formae operativae*, et un certaine rôle de medium de connaissance joué par ces formes à l'égard de la réalité des créatures: *per quas cognoscit*.[37] On dirait que, attentif à la *présence* des intelligibles dans la connaissance divine, S. Thomas s'est moins inquiété du problème de la *forme actualisante*. Le traité de la connaissance et celui des idées n'envisagent explicitement que la présence à titre d'objet, soit comme terme connu seulement, soit comme terme connu et medium ou quasi medium de la connaissance des êtres produits par Dieu.

C'est le rôle de forme actualisante, attribué à l'essence divine, qui va faire apparaître sous un jour nouveau l'antinomie entre la simplicité de l'essence divine et la multiplicité des objets connus.[38] Ceux-ci, en effet, ne doivent-ils pas aussi actuer en quelque sorte l'intellect divin pour être connus, comme l'exige, en principe, l'espèce intelligible selon Aristote? Si l'on veut éviter une conclusion, ruineuse pour la simplicité divine, il faudra compléter la noétique de l'espèce intelligible par une donnée nouvelle, celle de l'expression ou de la formation d'un terme connu par le connaissant. C'est ce que S. Thomas va faire quand il reprendra la discussion des idées divines et surtout le problème de leur multiplicité. L'idée, imitation de l'essence divine, identique à son essence, ne sera plus alors un objet connu seulement, présent dans son intelligence par la forme actualisante, mais aussi objet formé par le connaissant. C'est à ce titre qu'elle constituera un élément nécessaire de la synthèse théologique relative à la connaissance divine.

---

36 Ibid., d. 35, q. 1, a. 2, sol.; p. 815. Pour le vocabulaire ici employé, voir infra pp. 194-197. Sur ce point de l'essence comme similitude éminente du multiple, Dodds a cru pouvoir montrer des liens entre le néo-platonisme et la théologie chrétienne des attributs divins. Ce serait plutôt celle des idées divines qu'il faudrait évoquer, me semble-t-il. Voir, Proclus, *The Elements of Theology*, éd. citée, pp. 270-271 (prop. 112), pp. 278-279 (prop. 151-159).

37 Ce n'est pas rien. Mais c'est assurément, à propos de notre exposé du *Comm. sur les Sent.*, qu'il est légitime d'affirmer que ce sont des causes accidentelles qui expliquent la présence d'une question consacrée aux idées divines. Et l'on pourrait estimer que, sauf le rapport à la créature, considérée dans sa réalité, tout a été dit à la dist. 35 et à la qu. 1 de la dist. 36.

38 Dans notre texte, cette antinomie est envisagée à propos de la connaissance divine; d. 35, q. 1, a. 1, obj. 3; a. 2, obj. 1 et 3. Voir les réponses, et infra p. 195 s. Pour la qu. des idées, voir a. 1, obj. 2, 3, et 4. Mais il s'agit plutôt de la distinction réelle de l'intelligence et des idées et de leur fonction d'objets.

DE VERITATE, QU. 3

Nous retrouvons le problème des idées divines dans la 3ᵉ question du
De Veritate. Comme dans le *Commentaire sur les Sentences*, elle fait
suite à la discussion de la science divine. Aucun lien cependant ne la
rattache à la question précédente, ce qui est normal pour le genre
littéraire des questions disputées. Le premier article, comme dans le
Commentaire sur les Sentences, établit la nécessité d'admettre
l'existence d'idées en Dieu. Dix arguments, dont cinq sont empruntés à
S. Augustin, préparent la démonstration proposée dans le corps de l'article. Celle-ci est organisée autour de la notion de *forme*, le mot *idée*
pouvant être rendu en latin par *forma* ou *species*, au dire de S.
Augustin. Le mot *forme* comporte des sens différents. Pour définir le
sens du mot *idée*, il faut retenir celui de "forme imitée par une chose
par l'intention de l'agent qui se propose une certaine fin."[39] Cette forme
n'est rien d'autre que la forme exemplaire ou idée. C'est elle qui sert de
fin à l'artisan, c'est d'elle aussi qu'il reçoit la forme selon laquelle il
agit, si l'exemplaire est distinct de lui. Or Dieu n'agit point pour une fin
distincte de lui-même. Il ne reçoit pas d'ailleurs la forme qui lui permet
d'agir. Il n'y a donc pas d'idées en dehors de Dieu, mais seulement dans
l'esprit divin.[40]

La perspective est donc la même que dans le *Commentaire sur les
Sentences*. L'idée est le modèle d'après lequel Dieu crée, puisque la
création n'est ni l'œuvre du hasard, ni l'effet d'une nécessité naturelle.

C'est à l'article 2 que nous trouvons un nouveau développement, à
propos de la multiplicité des idées. Le problème est mis en rapport, explicitement, avec les doctrines qui voulaient limiter la connaissance
divine à une seule idée, commune à toute la création, afin de sauvegarder l'unité de Dieu. S. Thomas tient au contraire qu'"il est nécessaire
de dire que toute la distinction des choses est prédéfinie par Dieu. Il est
donc nécessaire de placer en Dieu les raisons propres de toutes choses.
Voilà pourquoi il est nécessaire de placer en Dieu plusieurs idées."[41] Il

---

39   "Haec ergo videtur esse ratio ideae, quod idea sit forma quam aliquid imitatur ex intentione
agentis qui praedeterminat sibi finem." Q. 3, a. 1; éd. léon., p. 100, ll. 221-223.
40   "Forma exemplaris vel idea habet quodam modo rationem finis et ab ea accipit artifex formam qua agit si sit extra ipsum, non est autem conveniens ponere Deum agere propter finem
alium a se et accipere aliunde unde sit sufficiens ad agendum, ideo non possumus ponere ideas
esse extra Deum sed in mente divina tantum." Q. 3, a. 1; éd. léon, p. 100, ll. 254-251.
41   "Unde necesse est dicere quod tota distinctio rerum sit praediffinita ab ipso, et ideo necesse
est in Deo ponere singulorum proprias rationes, et propter hoc necesse est ponere in eo plures
ideas." Q. 3, a. 2; éd. léon., p. 104, ll. 153-157.

faut donc montrer que cette multiplicité ne contredit pas l'unité divine.[42]

C'est ici que S. Thomas introduit une donnée dont il n'avait pas fait usage dans son exposé du *Commentaire sur les Sentences*. On a dit que l'idée était une forme, et, plus précisément "la forme exemplaire, à l'imitation de laquelle quelque chose est constitué,"[43] ou "la forme que quelque autre chose imite,"[44] qu'elle soit dans l'agent ou en dehors de lui.[45] Il suffit qu'elle soit "une forme que quelque chose imite, par l'intention d'un agent qui se propose une fin déterminée."[46]

Or

> ...une forme peut se trouver dans l'intellect de deux manières. D'une première manière elle y est en tant que principe de l'acte d'intellection, comme la forme qui appartient au connaissant en tant que connaissant; c'est la similitude, en lui, de l'objet connu. D'une autre manière, elle y est comme terme de l'acte d'intellection, quand l'artisan, par exemple, invente (*excogitat*), en connaissant, la forme de la maison. Puisque cette forme est inventée par l'acte d'intellection et, en quelque sorte, produite par lui, elle ne peut être le principe de l'acte d'intellection, constituant le premier *quo* par lequel s'effectue l'acte d'intellection. Elle est plutôt un objet connu, d'après lequel le connaissant produit quelque chose. Néanmoins cette forme est un deuxième *quo* par lequel le connaissant connaît, parce que, par la forme inventée, l'artisan connaît ce qu'il faut produire. Nous voyons de même, pour l'intellect spéculatif, que l'espèce, par laquelle l'intellect est informé pour connaître en acte, est le premier *quo*

---

42 Notons qu'au *Commentaire sur les Sentences*, Saint Thomas a marqué quelque réserve au sujet de l'expression "plures ideae." L'idée occupe comme une position intermédiaire entre l'essence, qui est une, et les "raisons," qu'on peut dire "plures." "Idea autem quasi medio modo se habet; quia essentiam et rationem imitationis, quae est secundum respectum, importat; et ideo, etsi inveniatur in nomine ideae consignificata pluralitas, ut cum pluraliter profertur, raro tamen aut nunquam invenitur significata per additionem termini numeralis, ut sic dicantur plures ideae; pluralitas enim exprimitur magis significando quam consignificando." *In I Sent.*, d. 2, ad 4; éd. Mandonnet, I, p. 843. Comparer avec le texte suivant d'Alexandre de Halès: "Idea media est secundum rationem intelligentiae inter essentiam divinam et creaturam quam facit; nihil autem est medium secundum rem. Et quia per modum medii est secundum intelligentiam, idea habet aliquem modum ex parte una, et aliquem ex parte altera. Ex parte creaturarum habet quod sit 'multa'; ex parte autem Dei, quod sit 'una'. Unde notandum quod non proprie dicitur 'multae', ut multitudo quae est in illis exprimatur per dictionem significantem multitudinem. Hoc patet ex verbis Augustini: singulorum enim rationibus erat plena est illa. Et haec est ratio: quia ex parte Dei idea propinquius se tenet, unde magis ei convenit unitas quam pluralitas; unde, si proprie exprimatur illa pluralitas, debet exprimi per multitudinem 'consignificatam' et non 'significatam'. Unde haec est propria 'ideae'; haec autem minus propria, 'multae ideae'." *Magistri Alexandri de Hales, Quaestiones disputatae "antequam esset frater"* (Quaracchi, 1960), II, pp. 799-800.

43 *De ver.*, q. 3, a. 1, c., éd. léon., p. 99, ll. 179-180.

44 Ibid l. 182.

45 "Solum hoc (ideam) dicimus quando agens propter finem determinat sibi finem, sive illa forma sit in agente sive extra agentem: dicimus enim formam artis in artifice esse exemplar vel ideam artificiati, et similiter etiam formam quae est extra artificem ad cuius imitationem artifex aliquid facit." Ibid., p. 100, ll. 214-220.

46 Ibid. ll. 220-223.

par lequel on connaît. Mais une fois en acte par une telle forme, l'intellect peut agir en formant la quiddité des choses et des jugements affirmatifs ou négatifs. La quiddité formée dans l'intellect, ou bien la proposition affirmative ou négative est donc quelque chose qui a été produit par l'intellect, mais par quoi, néanmoins, il connaît la chose extérieure, et qui constitue donc comme un deuxième *quo* de l'acte de connaissance.[47]

S. Thomas distingue donc les deux formes, qu'on appellera plus tard: espèce impresse et espèce expresse. L'artisan ou l'intellect spéculatif, qui possèdent une première forme, principe de l'acte d'intellection, peuvent en former une seconde, qui joue le rôle de terme de l'acte. On s'attend à voir cette distinction appliquée au problème des idées divines. En fait, le développement s'oriente différemment. La distinction entre la forme reçue et la forme produite, l'une et l'autre étant cependant ce par quoi (*quo*) l'intellect connaît, passe au second plan. On revient au cas de Dieu, en supposant "l'intelligence d'un artisan qui produirait une œuvre à la ressemblance de lui-même. Dans ce cas, l'intellect de l'artisan serait l'idée, non en tant qu'intellect, mais en tant que connu (*intellectum*)."[48] La conclusion sous-entendue, c'est que, dans le cas de Dieu, c'est l'intelligence, donc l'essence de Dieu, qui est l'idée, à la ressemblance de laquelle l'œuvre de la création est produite. On ne dit pas explicitement qu'une forme est conçue dans l'intellect divin, ou que nous pouvons parler d'une telle forme, par analogie avec les modèles conçus par l'artisan.

L'existence d'un modèle conçu est cependant utilisée implicitement dans la suite du texte, pour faire comprendre la possibilité d'admettre la multiplicité des idées dans l'intellect divin.

Il arrive, en effet, quand une chose est produite à l'imitation d'une autre, que l'imitation soit parfaite. Dans ce cas, l'intellect opératif, qui *conçoit d'avance* la forme de l'œuvre, a comme idée la forme même de la chose

47 "Forma enim in intellectu dupliciter esse potest. Uno modo ita quod sit principium actus intelligendi, sicut forma quae est intelligentis inquantum est intelligens, et haec est similitudo intellecti in ipso; alio modo ita quod sit terminus actus intelligendi, sicut artifex intelligendo excogitat formam domus, et cum illa forma sit excogitata per actum intelligendi et quasi per actum effecta, non potest esse principium actus intelligendi ut sit primum quo intelligatur, sed magis se habet ut intellectum quo intelligens aliquid operatur, nihilominus tamen est forma praedicta secundum quo intelligitur quia per formam excogitatam artifex intelligit quid operandum sit; sicut etiam in intellectu speculativo videmus quod species qua intellectus informatur ut intelligat actu est primum quo intelligitur, ex hoc autem quod est effectus in actu per talem formam operari iam potest formando quiditates rerum et componendo et dividendo, unde ipsa quiditas formata in intellectu vel etiam compositio et divisio est quoddam operatum ipsius, per quod tamen intellectus venit in cognitionem rei exterioris et sic est quasi secundum quo intelligitur." Q. 3. a. 2, c.; éd. léon., p. 104, ll. 159-183.
48 Ibid., p. 104. ll. 183-188.

imitée, telle qu'elle est dans la chose imitée. Il arrive aussi que l'œuvre produite à l'imitation d'autre chose n'en soit pas une imitation parfaite; en ce cas, l'intellect opératif se servirait de la forme de la chose imitée comme idée ou exemplaire de l'œuvre à produire, non pas absolument, mais dans la proportion déterminée d'après laquelle la reproduction demeure en deçà de l'exemplaire principal ou l'imite. [49]

Dans le cas de la création de l'univers par Dieu, c'est la seconde hypothèse qui se vérifie. Les créatures n'imitent la perfection divine que d'une manière déficiente. L'essence divine n'est donc pas l'idée en tant qu'essence, mais, d'une part, en tant qu'elle est connue, et, d'autre part, dans la proportion qui définit le degré selon lequel la créature imite l'essence divine ou demeure en deçà:

Je dis donc que Dieu, agissant par son intelligence, produit toutes choses à la similitude de son essence. Son essence est donc l'idée des choses, non en tant qu'essence, mais en tant qu'elle est connue. Or les choses créées n'imitent pas parfaitement l'essence divine. L'essence est donc prise par l'intellect divin comme idée, non pas absolument, mais selon la proportion de la créature à produire et de l'essence divine elle-même, selon qu'elle reste en deçà ou l'imite. Or les choses diverses imitent l'essence diversement, et chacune selon son mode propre, puisque chacune a un *esse* distinct de celui des autres. Il s'ensuit que l'essence divine elle-même, en y comprenant comme objets connus en même temps (*cointellectis*) les diverses proportions des choses à son égard, est l'idée de chaque chose. Et puisque les proportions des choses sont diverses, il est nécessaire qu'il y ait plusieurs idées, et qu'il n'y en ait qu'une de la part de l'essence, tandis que la pluralité se prend des diverses proportions des créatures par rapport à elle. [50]

49 "In his autem quae ad imitationem alterius producuntur, quandoque quidem id quod alterum imitatur perfecte imitatur ipsum, et tunc intellectus operativus praeconcipiens formam operati habet ut ideam ipsam formam rei imitatae prout est illius rei imitatae; quandoque vero quod est ad imitationem alterius non perfecte imitatur illud, et tunc intellectus operativus non acciperet formam rei absolute ut ideam vel exemplar rei operandae sed cum proportione determinata secundum quam exemplatum a principali exemplari deficeret vel imitaretur." Ibid., p. 104, ll. 187-200. Il est évident qu'il ne s'agit pas d'une inégalité qui serait l'effet de causes indépendantes de l'artisan. C'est l'artisan lui-même qui délibérément produit une œuvre dont il sait qu'elle ne représente qu'une imitation imparfaite de "l'exemplaire principal." Il doit donc connaître l'exemplaire principal, plus les diverses imitations possibles. L'œuvre à produire est donc conçue nécessairement comme un certain mode d'imitation d'un modèle qui la dépasse, c'est-à-dire que l'idée de l'œuvre à produire est elle-même relative à l'exemplaire principal, c'est-à-dire, dans le cas de la création, à l'essence divine.

50 "Dico ergo quod Deus per intellectum omnia operans omnia ad similitudinem essentiae suae producit, unde essentia sua est idea rerum non quidem ut est essentia sed ut est intellecta. Res autem creatae non perfecte imitantur divinam essentiam, unde essentia non accipitur absolute ab intellectu divino ut idea rerum sed cum proportione creaturae fiendae ad ipsam divinam essentiam secundum quod deficit ab ea vel imitatur ipsam; diversae autem res diversimode ipsam imitantur et unaquaeque secundum proprium modum suum cum unicuique sit esse distinctum ab altera. Et ideo ipsa divina essentia, cointellectis diversis proportionibus rerum ad ipsam, est idea uniuscuiusque rei: unde cum sint diversae rerum proportiones, necesse est plures esse ideas, et est quidem una ex parte essentiae sed pluralitas invenitur ex parte diversarum proportionum creaturarum ad ipsam." Ibid., p. 104, l. 200, p. 105, l. 219.

La solution, on le voit, ne reprend pas la distinction entre une forme principe de l'acte et une forme formée par l'acte. Cette distinction ne semble être intervenue que pour faire voir la possibilité d'utiliser un modèle, qui, en fait, est un objet produit par le connaissant, soit absolument, soit dans diverses proportions seulement. C'est, en tout cas, le seul aspect de la comparaison qui soit explicitement utilisé.

La forme produite par le connaissant n'intervient non plus pour résoudre la difficulté posée par la multiplicité des idées, si celles-ci sont considérées comme ce *par quoi* Dieu connaît, c'est à dire, si elles sont considérées à la fois comme une multitude d'objets connus et une multiplicité de formes actualisant l'intellect. En effet "un intellect qui connaît par plusieurs formes est un intellect composé, et il passe d'un objet à un autre, ce qui est étranger à l'intellect divin; puisque donc les idées sont des raisons des choses, par lesquelles Dieu connaît, il semble qu'il n'y ait pas plusieurs idées en Dieu."[51] S. Thomas répond:

> L'idée n'a pas raison de ce par quoi premièrement quelque chose est connu; elle a raison d'un objet existant dans l'intellect. Or l'uniformité de l'intellect suit l'unité de ce par quoi premièrement quelque chose est connu, tout de même que l'unité de l'action suit à l'unité de la forme de l'agent qui en est le principe. Bien que les rapports connus par Dieu, soient donc multiples, en quoi consiste la multiplicité des idées, son intellect n'est pas multiple, mais un, puisqu'il connaît tous ces rapports par son essence qui est une.[52]

Rien, on le voit, au sujet d'une forme-formée.

S. Thomas utilise ici, à propos du problème de la multiplicité des idées, une distinction différente de celle dont il s'était servi aux *Sentences* à propos de la multiplicité des *objets connus* par Dieu, c'est à dire à la distinction 35, non pas à la distinction 36, qu. 2, consacrée aux idées. Il ne s'agit pas formellement de l'opposition entre la multiplicité des objets et l'unité de l'intellect divin, mais plutôt de la possibilité, pour Dieu, de connaître en lui-même, et par son unique essence, les êtres *distincts* de lui, qu'il crée. Problème du même et de l'autre,

---

51   Ibid., obj. 9.

52   "Idea non habet rationem eius quo primo aliquid intelligitur, sed habet rationem intellecti in intellectu existentis; uniformitas autem intellectus sequitur unitatem eius quo primo aliquid intelligitur, sicut unitas actionis sequitur unitatem formae agentis quae est principium ipsius; unde quamvis respectus intellecti a Deo sint multi in quibus pluralitas idearum consistit, quia tamen illos omnes per unam suam essentiam intelligit, intellectus eius non est multiplex sed unus." Ibid., ad 9; éd. léon., p. 106, ll. 302-313. Saint Thomas refuse donc seulement de voir dans les idées des formes analogues à l'espèce intelligible. Il n'oppose pas un *quo primo* à un *quo secundo* mais le rôle de principe d'actuation (*quo*) à celui d'objet connu. Les idées ne sont que des objets connus, comme on l'a déjà dit dès le *Comm. sur les Sent.*; plus exactement, elles sont connues avec l'essence elle-même (*cointellecta*), comme les modes divers selon lesquels sa perfection peut être imitée.

pourrait-on dire, plutôt que problème de l'un et du multiple, bien que ce dernier entre nécessairement aussi en ligne de compte. Dieu doit connaître, en effet, les êtres qu'il crée et qu'il gouverne, qui sont donc distincts de lui (*alia a se*).

> Mais il faut savoir que l'expression *objet connu par l'intelligence*, de même que celle d'*objet vu*, s'entendent en deux sens. Il y a en effet un premier objet vu, qui est la *species* elle-même de l'objet visible, existant dans la pupille, perfection, aussi de celui qui voit, principe de vision et medium à l'égard de la chose visible; et il y a un deuxième objet vu qui est la chose elle-même en dehors de l'âme. De même le premier objet connu est la similitude de la chose qui se trouve dans l'intellect; et il y a un deuxième objet connu qui est la chose elle-même connue par cette similitude. [53]

En appliquant cette distinction à Dieu, on obtient ceci:

> Si l'on parle du premier objet connu, Dieu ne connaît que soi-même, puisqu'il ne reçoit pas les espèces des choses par lesquelles il connaîtrait, mais il connaît par son essence, qui est similitude de toutes choses. Si au contraire on parle du deuxième objet connu, Dieu ne connaît pas seulement lui-même, mais aussi les réalités distinctes de lui. [54]

C'est en pensant au premier objet connu qu'Aristote a pu dire que Dieu ne se connaît que lui-même. Et d'ailleurs, c'est le premier objet seul qui est perfection du connaissant, non le deuxième. "Ce n'est pas la pierre qui est en dehors de l'âme qui est perfection de l'intellect, mais la similitude de la pierre qui est dans l'âme." [55]

La distinction entre un *primum intellectum* et un *secundum intellectum* est donc appelée à fonder la connaissance, par Dieu, des êtres distincts de Dieu. Ceux-ci sont présents dans l'intellect divin comme objets connus, parce qu'ils ne sont rien que l'essence divine elle-même en tant qu'imitable et participable. Ils sont donc envisagés comme objets connus (*quod*), non comme principe par lequel l'intellect est en acte (*quo*). Ce dernier rôle revient à l'essence, formellement comme essence,

53 "Sciendum tamen est quod intellectum dupliciter dicitur, sicut visum etiam. Est enim primum visum quod est ipsa species rei visibilis in pupilla existens, quae est etiam perfectio videntis, et principium visionis, et medium nomen (sic: respectu?) rei visibilis: et est visum secundum, quod est ipsa res extra animam. Similiter intellectum primum est ipsa rei similitudo, quae est in intellectu; et est intellectum secundum ipsa res, quae per similitudinem illam intelligitur." *In I Sent.*, d. 35, q. 1, a. 2, sol.; éd. Mandonnet, I. pp. 814-815.

54 "Si ergo consideretur intellectum primum, nihil aliud intelligit Deus nisi se; quia non recipit species rerum, per quas congnoscat; sed per essentiam suam cognoscit, quae est similitudo omnium rerum. Sed si accipiatur intellectum secundum, sic non tantum se intelligit, sed etiam alia. Et secundum primum modum dicit Philosophus... quod Deus intelligit tantum se." Ibid., p. 815.

55 "Quod enim objicitur primo, quod intellectus est perfectio intelligentis, verum est de intellecto primo, et non de intellecto secundo. Non enim lapis, qui est extra animam, est perfectio intellectus; sed similitudo lapidis, quae est in anima." Ibid., p. 815.

"medium unique, parfaitement simple," par lequel Dieu connaît tout ce qu'il connaît, et qui est aussi le *primum intellectum*.[56]

Il n'est pas facile, assurément, de bien entendre ce vocabulaire. L'espèce de la pierre, qui est dans la pupille, n'a jamais été considerée par S. Thomas, dans ses écrits postérieurs, comme un objet vu, ni d'ailleurs l'espèce intelligible comme un objet connu par l'intelligence, si ce n'est par un acte de réflexion. Et celle-ci, justement, fait défaut aux pouvoirs sensibles. La comparaison avec le cas de Dieu suppose cependant que l'espèce, aussi bien que la réalité, soient des objets connus. L'essence divine, en effet, ne peut faire connaître les êtres distincts d'elle, comme S. Thomas veut le faire comprendre, si elle n'est pas objet connu, en tant qu'essence aussi bien qu'en tant qu'essence imitable. Il semble certain, néanmoins que par les expressions: *primum visum* et *primum intellectum*, S. Thomas désigne les espèces sensibles et intelligibles formellement comme principes d'actuation et de spécification, non comme objets connus,[57] même si, pour l'intelligence, l'espèce peut devenir un *intellectum*, au sens d'objet connu, pour l'acte de réflexion.

Quoi qu'il en soit, la difficulté est résolue uniquement par la distinction de deux "objets connus," et leur identité avec l'essence divine. Aucune mention, pour aucune forme, de sa production par l'acte d'intellection pour en être le terme. Quand, à la distinction 36, c'est non

---

56 "Scientia Dei est una numero omnium rerum, quia per unum medium simplicissimum, quod est sua essentia, omnia cognoscit." Ibid., ad 4, p. 815. Il semble donc qu'il faille comprendre ainsi l'ensemble des données; l'essence assure l'*unité* de la connaissance divine à l'égard des choses distinctes de Dieu (*alia*) en tant qu'elle contient leurs essences comme imitation (notes 54 et 55); elle est *intellectum primum*, comme essence, en tant que l'essence joue le rôle d'espèce ou de forme actualisante (note 54); elle est *intellectum secundum*, objet connu à la fois comme essence et comme similitude de toutes choses (note 54); les créatures sont seulement *intellectum secundum* nullement ce par quoi Dieu connaît (notes 54, 55); elles sont plutôt comme la pierre réelle, vue par l'œil.

57 Voici un texte, qui montre clairement que c'est bien l'espèce intelligible, en tant qu'elle actue le pouvoir, qui est *intellecta*: "Intellectus enim humanus, qui aliquando est in potentia, et aliquando in actu, quando est in potentia intelligens non est idem cum intelligibili in potentia, quod est aliqua res existens extra animam; sed ad hoc quod sit intelligens in actu oportet quod intelligibile in potentia fiat intelligibile in actu per hoc quod species ejus denudatur ab omnibus appenditiis materiae per virtutem intellectus agentis; et oportet quod haec species, quae est *intellecta in actu*, perficiat intellectum in potentia: ex quorum conjunctione efficitur unum perfectum, quod est intellectus in actu, sicut ex anima et corpore efficitur unum, quod est homo habens operationes humanas." Appliquées à Dieu, ces considérations donnent les précisions suivantes: "prout consideratur essentia ejus ut immunis a materia, sic est intelligens... sed prout consideratur essentia sua secundum quod intellectus accipit eam sine materia, sic *est intellectum*; sed prout consideratur ipsum intellectum prout non deest sibi intelligenti, sed est in seipso quodammodo, sic est intelligentia vel scientia: quia scientia nihil aliud est quam impressio vel conjunctio sciti ad scientem." Ibid., d. 35, q. 1, a. 1, ad 3; éd Mandonnet, I, p. 812. Si le texte de nos éditions est correct, Saint Thomas désigne donc par le participe *intellectum* ou *visum* à la fois ce qui fait connaître et ce qui est connu. Voir aussi les notes 55, 56, et 59.

plus l'altérité des objets connus, mais leur multiplicité qui est en cause, et leur multiplicité comme idées (*per quas intelligit*), c'est encore par l'unité de l'essence et la multiplicité de ses participations ou imitations possibles, envisagées comme objets connus, que le problème est résolu: "Ipsae enim rationes imitationis ut intellectae, seu modi, sunt ideae; idea enim...nominat formam ut intellectam, et non prout est in natura intelligentis."[58]

En résumé, nous pouvons dire que le texte du *De Veritate* développe, à propos des idées et de leur multiplicité en Dieu, la distinction entre forme principe de l'acte et forme formée par l'acte de connaissance. Les deux peuvent jouer le rôle de ce par quoi (*quo*) la réalité est connue en dehors du connaissant: l'œuvre, par exemple, connue par le modèle d'après lequel elle a été produite.[59] Mais on ne dit pas explicitement comme on pourrait s'y attendre, qu'en Dieu l'idée est comme un terme produit par le connaissant, dans lequel et par lequel la créature est connue. C'est dans la *Somme contre les Gentils* que S. Thomas va faire de l'idée en Dieu, explicitement, un terme produit par le connaissant. C'est dans cette identification de l'idée avec un terme formé qu'il voit alors la possibilité d'éviter la contradiction entre l'unité de l'intellect divin et la multiplicité des idées, contradiction à laquelle on aboutit nécessairement quand on s'en tient strictement à la notion de l'espèce intelligible, telle qu'elle est utilisée par Aristote.

LA SOMME CONTRE LES GENTILS

On a voulu voir, dans les chapitres 53 et 54 du premier livre de la *Somme contre les Gentils*, la preuve particulièrement nette que S. Thomas n'avait nul besoin de parler des idées pour traiter la question

---

58 Supra note 35.

59 Du point de vue du vocabulaire, il faut donc distinguer: a) *quo primo*, qui désigne le principe d'actualisation du connaissant comme tel, et s'oppose à *intellectum*, l'objet connu (note 52); b) *intellectum* (note 57), qui se divise en: *intellectum primum*, la forme comme forme, donc identique au *quo primo* précédent, et *intellectum secundum*, l'objet connu, qu'il soit dans le connaissant ou en dehors de lui; c) *primum quo* et *secundum quo* (note 47), le premier étant l'espèce en tant qu'elle fait connaître à titre de medium, non pas formellement en tant qu'elle actue le pouvoir; le second étant une forme produite, considérée comme objet de connaissance et medium par rapport à la réalité dont elle est la similitude. Le texte suivant montre bien les différents aspects du problème dont les multiples distinctions essaient de tenir compte: "Si ratio cognitionis accipiatur ex parte cognoscentis, Deus eadem ratione se cognoscit et alia quia et idem cognoscens et idem cognitionis actus et idem medium est cognoscendi; si autem accipiatur ratio ex parte rei cognitae sic non eadem ratione se cognoscit et alia quia non est eadem habitudo sui et aliorum ad medium quo cognoscit, quia ipse illi medio est idem per essentiam res autem aliae per assimilationem tantum, et ideo se ipsum cognoscit per essentiam alia vero per similitudinem; idem tamen est quod est eius essentia et aliorum similitudo." *De ver.*, 2, 3, ad 6; éd. léon., p. 53.

de la connaissance divine. De fait, l'ensemble des chapitres 44 à 70, si l'on excepte les chapitres 60-62, consacrés à la vérité en Dieu, forme un tout où l'on retrouve la matière traitée, dans la *Somme théologique* comme dans les *Sentences* et le *De Veritate*, sous le titre de la connaissance divine. Aucun chapitre, traitant des idées divines, ne vient le compléter. Cependant il n'est pas difficile de voir que les chapitres 51-54 forment un bloc qui interrompt l'exposé. S. Thomas vient de montrer que Dieu connaît les réalités distinctes de lui (*alia a se*) (chap. 49), et qu'il en a une connaissance propre (chap. 50). Dans la *Somme théologique*, les mêmes sujets sont traités aux articles 5 et 6 de la question 14. Ils sont suivis par des articles dont le sujet correspond, avec quelques inversions, aux chapitres 55 et suivants de la *Somme contre les Gentils*.

Les chapitres 51 et 52 introduisent, dans la séries des chapitres traitant de la connaissance divine, une discussion des doctrines selon lesquelles les multiples objets connus par Dieu, ou bien ont un *esse* distinct en Dieu, ou bien subsistent en dehors de Dieu, ou bien se trouveraient dans des intellects distincts de Dieu. Aucune n'est acceptable. D'une manière ou d'une autre. elles ruinent des thèses établies précédemment, spécialement la simplicité divine, sans parler des autres raisons qui les condamnent. Le chapitre 51 annonce qu'on va "examiner la manière dont les objets connus (*intellecta*) sont multiples," afin d'éviter de laisser s'introduire la composition dans l'intellect divin, du fait de la multitude des objets connus."[60] Le chapitre 53 se rattache à ce propos, par dessus l'exposé et la discussion des doctrines, qui occupent les chapitres 51 et 52. Or, ces doctrines, on l'a vu, sont censées transformer les intelligibles connus par Dieu en entités indépendantes de l'intellect divin, peu importe qu'elles se trouvent dans l'intellect divin lui-même ou en dehors de lui. Platon, en particulier, est longuement discuté (chap. 51).

La composition entre l'intelligence et l'intelligible peut concerner, en effet, soit l'espèce intelligible qui est principe de l'acte, soit son objet. L'espèce intelligible donne à l'intelligence d'être en acte, en lui donnant, du même coup, d'être en possession de la similitude de l'objet à connaître. Les Idées platoniciennes, au contraire, assurent la présence à titre d'objets, sans jouer le rôle d'une similitude reçue dans le pouvoir. On aurait une multitude d'objets, sans espèce intelligible correspondante dans l'intellect. S. Thomas rappelle justement, contre la con-

---

60 "Sed ne multitudo intellectorum in intellectum divinum compositionem inducat, investigandus est modus quo ista intellecta sunt multa." I *CG*, 51, init.,; éd. léon. man., pp. 48-49.

ception platonicienne, la nécessité d'une présence dans l'intellect lui-même: "Intellectum oportet esse in intelligente. Non igitur sufficit ponere formas rerum per se existentes extra intellectum divinum ad hoc quod Deus multitudinem rerum intelligat, sed oportet quod sint in ipso intellectu divino" (chap. 51 fin).

Cependant, S. Thomas a déjà montré que "l'intellect divin ne connaît par aucune autre espèce intelligible que son essence. L'espèce intelligible en effet est le principe formel de l'opération intellectuelle, tout de même que la forme de l'agent est le principe de son opération propre."[61] Il a montré que "Dieu connaît premièrement et par soi uniquement lui-même. Est en effet connue premièrement et par soi par un intellect uniquement la chose par l'espèce de laquelle il connaît. Or ce par quoi Dieu connaît n'est rien d'autre que son essence. L'objet connu par lui premièrement et par soi n'est donc que lui-même."[62] Il a montré enfin que "par le fait même que Dieu se connaît, il est nécessaire d'admettre qu'il connaît en lui-même les choses distinctes de lui."[63] Et il conclut: "En tenant ensemble ces deux conclusions (i.e. chap. 48 et 49), on voit clairement que Dieu se connaît lui-même premièrement et par soi, en quelque sorte, les autres choses comme vues dans son essence."[64] Le chapitre 50 montre ensuite longuement que Dieu doit avoir de toutes choses une connaissance propre, c'est à dire pour autant qu'elles sont distinctes les unes des autres. L'avant dernier argument est fondé sur le rapport d'imitation entre l'essence divine et les diverses formes: "Dieu connaît...selon combien de modes quelque chose peut être semblable à son essence. Or la diversité des formes tient au fait que les choses imitent diversement l'essence divine. Aussi le Philosophe appelle-t-il la forme naturelle quelque chose de divin. Dieu connaît donc les choses selon leurs formes propres."[65]

---

61 "...apparet quod intellectus divinus nulla alia specie intelligibili intelligat quam sua essentia. Species enim intelligibilis principium formale est intellectualis operationis; sicut forma cuiuslibet agentis principium est propriae operationis." Ibid., c. 46; pp. 44-45.

62 "...apparet quod Deus primo et per se solum seipsum cognoscit. Illa enim solum res est primo et per se ab intellectu cognita cuius specie intelligit: operatio enim formae quae est operationis principium proportionatur. Sed id quo Deus intelligit nihil est aliud quam sua essentia....Igitur intellectum ab ipso primo et per se nihil aliud est quam ipsemet." Ibid., c. 48, init, p. 46.

63 "Ex hoc autem quod seipsum cognoscit primo et per se, quod alia a se in seipso cognoscat ponere oportet." Ibid., c. 49, init., p. 47.

64 "Colligentes igitur has duas conclusiones (cf. cap. praec.), apparet Deum cognoscere seipsum quasi primo et per se notum, alia vero sicut in essentia sua visa." Ibid., c. 49, fin.

65 "Divina...natura communicabilis est per similitudinem. Scit ergo Deus quot modis eius essentiae aliquid simile esse potest. Sed ex hoc sunt diversitates formarum quod divinam essentiam res diversimode imitantur; unde Philosophus formam naturalem *divinum quoddam* nominat.... Deus igitur de rebus habet cognitionem secundum proprias formas." Ibid., c. 50, fin., p. 48.

Tout semble donc dit au sujet de la connaissance divine et de ses objets. La composition que "la multitude des objets connus" risque d'introduire dans l'intellect divin ne se comprend donc pleinement que si
les objets connus, en tant que tels, tenus par certains pour des intelligibles autonomes, c'est à dire des idées, entraînaient aussi une
multiplicité ou une composition du côté du pouvoir et de ses actes, c'est
à dire, si la multiplicité des objets connus exigeait une multiplicité identique du côté de l'espèce intelligible en tant que principe d'actuation.

Nous avons vu S. Thomas évoquer ce parallélisme, notamment à
propos des idées et de leur multiplicité.[66] Ici, il ne se contente pas de
distinguer entre l'espèce en tant que forme actualisante et en tant
qu'elle est objet. Pour faire voir "comment les choses connues sont dans
l'intellect,"[67] il développe, avec une ampleur remarquable, l'existence,
en plus de l'espèce intelligible, d'une *intentio*,[68] formée par l'intellect
lui-même. Il montre que cette formation est nécessaire, chez nous,
même pour la connaissance spéculative, parce que nous connaissons les
choses aussi bien présentes qu'absentes, et surtout parce que notre intelligence "connaît la chose comme séparée des conditions matérielles
sans lesquelles elle n'existe pas dans la réalité. Ceci serait impossible si
l'intellect ne formait pas pour lui-même l'*intentio* dont on vient de
parler. Mais puisque cette *intentio*, qui est objet de connaissance, est en
quelque manière le terme de l'opération intellectuelle, elle est différente
de l'espèce intelligible qui donne à l'intellect d'être en acte, et qu'il faut
considérer comme le principe de l'opération intelligible, encore que les
deux soient similitude de la chose connue."[69]

66 Voir supra, pp. 188 et n. 35; 189 et n. 36; 194 et n. 52.
67 "...ne multitudo intellectorum in intellectum divinum compositionem inducat." Voir supra,
note 60. Il s'agit donc bien de la multitude des objets, formellement comme objets connus. Or les
idées divines ne sont rien si ce n'est exactement cette multitude d'objets connus, nécessaire pour
dire le rapport de l'intelligence divine à la création. Mais au lieu de distinguer seulement l'essence
divine comme principe formel de connaissance et comme objet connu, Saint Thomas va placer les
intellecta dans le verbe produit par l'acte d'intellection. Il semble difficile de ne pas reconnaître ce
que Saint Thomas discute ailleurs sous le nom d'idées.
68 "Dico autem *intentionem intellectam* id quod intellectus in seipso concipit de re intellecta."
IV *CG*, c. 11; éd. cit., p. 445. Il faudrait citer le chapitre presqu'en entier. Sur bien des points, il
donne des définitions et des développements qui éclairent le présent chapître 53, dont on pourrait
dire, sans exagération, qu'il semble les supposer.
69 "Ulterius autem considerandum est quod intellectus, per speciem rei formatus, intelligendo
format in seipso quandam intentionem rei intellectae, quae est ratio ipsius, quam significat
definitio. Et hoc quidem necessarium est: eo quod intellectus intelligit indifferenter rem absentem
et praesentem, in quo cum intellectu imaginatio convenit; sed intellectus hoc amplius habet, quod
etiam intelligit rem ut separatam a conditionibus materialibus, sine quibus in rerum natura non
existit; et hoc non potest esse nisi intellectus sibi intentionem praedictam formaret.
Haec autem intentio intellecta, cum sit quasi terminus intelligibilis operationis, est aliud a

En appliquant ces discernements au cas de la connaissance divine, on doit dire ceci:

> L'intellect divin ne connaît par aucune autre espèce que son essence, comme on l'a montré plus haut (chap. 46). Cependant son essence est la similitude de toutes choses (chap. 29). Il s'ensuit que la conception de l'intellect divin, en tant qu'il se connaît lui-même, conception qui est son verbe, est la similitude non seulement de Dieu lui-même, objet connu, mais encore de tout ce dont l'essence divine est la similitude. Par conséquent, par une seule espèce intelligible, qui est l'essence divine, et par une seule *intentio* connue, qui est le verbe divin, une multitude d'objets peut être connue par Dieu.[70]

La composition se trouve donc éliminée. Du côté de l'espèce intelligible, comme pour la forme formée par l'intellect, c'est toujours l'unique essence divine qui est en cause. Celle-ci peut assurer la connaissance de Dieu lui-même et de toutes choses, puisque l'essence, dans sa plénitude, contient tous les modes possibles selon lesquels les êtres peuvent l'imiter. S. Thomas ne précise pas ici, comme il le fait ailleurs,[71] que la présence du verbe en Dieu n'introduit pas une composition dans l'intellect divin, comme c'est le cas pour le verbe chez nous. Il est attentif surtout à montrer, semble-t-il, que si l'on distingue l'espèce intelligible et le verbe produit, une multitude d'objets connus n'entraîne plus, logiquement, une composition dans l'intellect divin.

Il reste à faire voir explicitement, comme dans les exposés précédents, que la multiplicité peut être connue dans l'unité, puisque toute la multitude des formes ou des essences est fondée dans l'unité de la plénitude divine. Elle n'est donc pas saisie dans une sorte de vue panoramique, mais comprise dans son principe et en lui:

> L'essence divine comprend en elle les noblesses de tous les êtres, non point par mode de composition, mais par mode de perfection, comme on l'a montré plus haut (chap. 31). Or, toute forme, propre aussi bien que commune, est une certaine perfection, en tant qu'elle pose quelque chose; elle n'inclut l'imperfection que pour autant qu'elle comporte défaut par

---

specie intelligibili quae facit intellectum in actu, quam oportet considerari ut intelligibilis operationis principium; licet utrumque sit rei similitudo." I *CG*, c. 53. Comparer avec le texte cité à la note 47, et avec la première rédaction de ce chapitre, étudiée et reproduite dans notre article, cité infra note 75.

70 "Intellectus autem divinus nulla alia specie intelligit quam essentia sua, ut supra (cap. 46) ostensum est. Sed tamen essentia sua est similitudo omnium rerum (cap. 29). Per hoc ergo sequitur quod conceptio intellectus divini, prout seipsum intelligit, quae est verbum ipsius, non solum sit similitudo ipsius Dei intellecti, sed etiam omnium quorum est divina essentia similitudo. Sic ergo per unam speciem intelligibilem, quae est divina essentia, et per unam intentionem intellectam, quae est verbum divinum, multa possunt a Deo intelligi." Ibid.

71 IV *CG*, c. 11, p. 446, par exemple.

rapport à l'*esse* véritable. L'intellect divin peut donc comprendre, dans son essence, ce qui est propre à chaque être, en connaissant ce en quoi il imite son essence, et en quoi il demeure en deçà de sa perfection... Dieu peut donc avoir, par son essence, une connaissance propre de toutes choses.

Puisque d'autre part, la raison propre d'une chose se distingue de la raison propre d'une autre, et que la distinction est le principe de la pluralité, il faut admettre dans l'intellect divin une certaine distinction et une pluralité de raisons connues, pour autant que ce qui est dans l'intellect divin est la raison propre de choses diverses. Or puisque (ce qui est dans l'intellect divin) est ce par quoi Dieu connaît le rapport propre d'assimilation qui unit à lui chaque créature, il s'ensuit que les raisons des choses dans l'intellect divin ne sont plusieurs ou distinctes que dans la mesure où Dieu connaît que les choses peuvent lui être semblables selon des modes multiples et divers. [72]

C'est sur la base de cette pluralité dans l'unité, que S. Thomas accepte de dire, avec S. Augustin, que Dieu crée l'homme selon une *raison* et le cheval selon une autre, et qu'il consent à sa manière de parler des raisons des choses en Dieu selon un mode de pluralité. Il reconnaît de même la part de vérité, contenue dans l'opinion de Platon, relative à l'existence d'Idées, d'après lesquelles est formé tout ce qui existe dans les choses matérielles. [73]

Si l'on met ensemble le contenu des chapitres 53 et 54, il apparaît clairement, me semble-t-il, que S. Thomas voit, dans la formation du verbe par l'intellect, le moyen de donner une solution plus nette au problème de la multiplicité des objets connus par Dieu. Cette multiplicité soulève en effet deux difficultés: celle de la possibilité de connaître une multitude d'objets par un seul principe d'intellection; celle de la possibilité d'admettre une multitude d'objets connus, sans

---

72 "Divina autem essentia in se nobilitatem omnium entium comprehendit, non quidem per modum compositionis, sed per modum perfectionis, ut supra (cap. 31) ostensum est. Forma autem omnis, tam propria quam communis, secundum id quod aliquid ponit, est perfectio quaedam: non autem imperfectionem includit nisi secundum quod deficit a vero esse. Intellectus igitur divinus id quod est proprium unicuique in essentia sua comprehendere potest, intelligendo in quo eius essentiam imitetur, et in quo ab eius perfectione deficit unumquodque... Sic igitur patet quod essentia divina, inquantum est absolute perfecta, potest accipi ut propria ratio singulorum. Unde per eam Deus propriam cognitionem de omnibus habere potest.

Quia vero propria ratio unius distinguitur a propria ratione alterius; distinctio autem est pluralitatis principium: oportet in intellectu divino distinctionem quandam et pluralitatem rationum intellectarum considerare, secundum quod id quod est in intellectu est propria ratio diversorum. Unde, cum hoc sit secundum quod Deus intelligit proprium respectum assimilationis quam habet unaquaeque creatura ad ipsum, relinquitur quod rationes rerum in intellectu divino non sunt plures vel distinctae nisi secundum quod Deus cognoscit res pluribus et diversis modis esse assimilabiles sibi." I *CG*, c. 53. On notera que dans la *Somme théol.*, au prologue de la qu. 14, Saint Thomas écrit: "Quia...rationes rerum secundum quod sunt in Deo cognoscente ideae vocantur."

73 ibid.

multiplier du même coup les principes d'actualisation. Dès son premier enseignement, S. Thomas a vu, dans la distinction entre l'essence comme quasi forme actualisante et l'essence comme connue, le moyen de résoudre la seconde difficulté, et dans la thèse de la plénitude de l'essence divine imitable par les créatures, celle de résoudre la première. Sur ce dernier point ses exposés ne changent pas. Nous le voyons, au contraire, préciser la distinction entre l'espèce intelligible comme principe d'actualisation et comme objet connu, par la distinction de deux formes. Le chapitre 53 introduit l'expression du *verbe*, qui ne laisse plus subsister aucune équivoque.[74]

J'ai montré ailleurs[75] que la mention du verbe, et la justification de sa nécessité dans la connaissance spéculative que nous lisons actuellement dans le texte du chapitre 53, figurent seulement dans une troisième rédaction, écrite dans la marge inférieure, lors de la révision du manuscrit. Les deux premières rédactions, écrites coup sur coup, et supprimées lors de la révision, ne sont pas des ébauches, mais des exposés complets. Signalons simplement ici les analogies frappantes de la première rédaction avec *De Veritate* 3, 2, et le fait que la deuxième, plus simple, omet la mention de la forme formée par l'intellect. Le vocabulaire de la dernière rédaction offre, par contre, des ressemblances étroites avec la *Somme contre les Gentils* 4, 11, qui donne la définition des termes employés ici, au chapitre 53. Il y aurait lieu aussi d'étudier un long passage de l'autographe du chapitre 54, dont voici le début: "Ex his ulterius videri potest...(qualiter) in divina mente omnium formae vel rationes, quae ideae dicuntur, in mente divina esse possint absque aliqua intellectus divini compositione. Sunt enim in eo ut intellecta in intelligente." Aucune mention du verbe, mais seulement celle de la forme inventée par l'artisan et qui joue premièrement le rôle de *quod* et deuxièmement le rôle de *quo* dans l'acte de connaissance.[76]

Il est donc permis de conclure que, si les idées ne sont nommées qu'incidemment dans notre chapitre 53, c'est bien du problème posé par elles qu'il s'agit et de la réponse que S. Thomas a élaborée pour le résoudre. Il faut admettre une multitude d'objets connus par Dieu, si sa connaissance doit atteindre les créatures jusque dans leur diversité spécifique et même individuelle. Pour la penser, sans contradiction, il

---

74 Que le verbe dont il s'agit dans notre chapître est bien identique aux idées, il suffit, pour s'en convaincre, de comparer avec le chapitre 13 du 4e livre, où l'on retrouve, à propos du Verbe de Dieu, "omnium, quae facta sunt, ratio perfecta," la métaphore de l'artisan et du modèle, "ratio domus quam habet in mente." Ed. cit., p. 451, " Quicumque autem..." Toute la seconde partie de ce chapitre serait à citer pour compléter la doctrine de nos chap. 53 et 54.

75 "Les rédactions successives de *Contra Gentiles*, I, 53 d'après l'autographe." S. *Thomas d'Aquin aujourd'hui* (Bruges 1963) 221-240.

76 Ed. léon., XIII, 21*b, ll. 10-71.

ne suffit pas d'utiliser la notion aristotélicienne de l'espèce intelligible. Une distinction est nécessaire au moins entre le rôle de l'espèce comme forme actualisante et celui d'objet connu. Dans le texte que nous venons d'étudier, S. Thomas ajoute, de la manière la plus expresse, la distinction entre l'espèce intelligible et le verbe. La multiplicité des essences est fondée dans l'essence divine en tant que telle, donc aussi en tant qu'elle est identique à l'intellect divin et forme de son opération. Mais il ne faut parler de la pluralité des objets connus par Dieu, qui sont les raisons des êtres créés ou créables, qu'en rapport avec l'essence en tant que connue, voire en tant que verbe exprimé par le connaissant.[77]

LA *SOMME THÉOLOGIQUE*

L'étude que nous venons de faire nous autorise à affirmer que, si S. Thomas a conservé, dans la *Somme Théologique*, une question consacrée aux idées divines, ce n'est pas sans quelque raison systématique. Certes les idées ne jouent pas le même rôle que chez Platon ou S. Augustin. Mais la question 15 ne répète pas simplement la question 14. De l'une à l'autre il y a la différence entre le rôle de l'espèce intelligible et de l'objet connu. Et la question que l'on peut se poser est plutôt pourquoi on ne retrouve pas dans la *Somme Théologique* le vocabulaire si net de la *Somme contre les Gentils*, et la distinction entre *intelligere* et *dicere*. La *Somme Théologique* pourrait-elle être postérieure à la dernière rédaction du chapitre 53? La chronologie actuellement admise communément ne permet pas de le penser.

Quoi qu'il en soit, la question 14 traite formellement de l'intellection divine, donc de l'essence en tant qu'elle rend possible l'acte d'intellection, face à ses différents objets. La question 15 se limite explicitement à l'étude des *rationes rerum* appelées "idées" en tant qu'elles sont en Dieu connaissant (Qu. 14, prol.). C'est en effet la présence de ces objets là qui fait difficulté quand on admet leur multiplicité. Or il faut admettre une multiplicité d'objets connus. Il faut

---

77 Si les idées divines sont, en effet, les "rationes rerum" non seulement connues par Dieu, mais exprimées dans le Verbe ("importatur in Verbo ratio factiva eorum quae Deus facit" I, q. 34, a. 3, c.), on ne peut pas dire que "l'expressionisme bonaventurien ajoute à la doctrine thomiste des idées une sorte de génération interne de la notion des êtres réalisables. Alors qu'il suffit à Dieu de se connaître en tant que participable pour avoir, chez Saint Thomas, les idées de toutes choses, il faut encore que Dieu profère en soi, par son Verbe éternel, les notions de ces participations possibles à son essence," E. Gilson, *L'esprit de la philosophie médiévale*, 2ᵉ éd. (Paris 1948), p. 167. N'est-ce pas plutôt sur l'exemplarisme que porte la différence, comme le montre le même auteur. *La philosophie de Saint Bonaventure* 3ᵉ éd. (Paris 1953) pp. 132-134, et sans doute plus précisément encore, sur la notion de "participation possible à l'essence divine"?

donc montrer comment la concevoir sans contradiction, "ce qu'il est facile de voir, si l'on considère la manière dont l'idée de l'œuvre produite se trouve dans l'esprit de celui qui la produit. Elle y est en effet comme ce qui est connu, non pas comme l'espèce par laquelle on connaît, et qui est la forme par laquelle l'intellect est en acte."[78]

Or, "connaître une multitude d'objets, cela n'est pas contraire à la simplicité de l'intellect divin, comme serait contraire à cette même simplicité le fait pour l'intellect d'être formé (c'est-à-dire, actué) par plusieurs espèces. Il y a donc dans l'esprit divin une pluralité d'idées comme objets connus par lui.[79] L'absence de composition ainsi établie, S. Thomas passe, comme dans les autres exposés, à la démonstration de l'absence de multiplicité, en développant une fois de plus les considérations sur l'essence divine, similitude propre de chaque créature.

La présence dans le connaissant, exigée par les raisons ou idées, est donc différente de celle qui est assurée par l'espèce intelligible. Dans la réponse à la 2ᵉ objection, S. Thomas la compare à la conscience qu'aurait l'artisan de connaître, par le modèle, la maison réelle qu'il a construite.

> Les mots "sagesse" et "art" signifient ce par quoi Dieu connaît, mais l'"idée" signifie ce que Dieu connaît. Or par un seul (principe de connaissance) Dieu connaît un grand nombre de choses, non seulement en elles-mêmes, mais en tant qu'elles sont connues, ce qui revient à connaître plusieurs raisons des choses. Ainsi quand l'artisan connaît la maison (réalisée) dans la matière, on dit qu'il connaît la maison. Mais lorsqu'il connaît la forme de la maison comme contemplée par lui, du fait qu'il connaît qu'il la connaît, il connaît l'idée ou la raison de la maison. Or Dieu non seulement connaît beaucoup de choses par son essence, mais il sait aussi qu'il connaît beaucoup de choses par son essence; ce qui revient à dire que Dieu connaît plusieurs raisons des choses, ou que plusieurs idées sont dans son intelligence comme objets connus.[80]

---

78 "Ratio autem alicuius totius haberi non potest, nisi habeantur propriae rationes eorum ex quibus totum constituitur; sicut aedificator speciem domus concipere non posset, nisi apud ipsum esset propria ratio cuiuslibet partium eius. Sic igitur oportet quod in mente divina sint propriae rationes omnium rerum... Unde sequitur quod in mente divina sint plures ideae. Hoc autem quomodo divinae simplicitati non repugnet, facile est videre, si quis consideret ideam operati esse in mente operantis, sicut quod intelligitur, non autem sicut species qua intelligitur, quae est forma faciens intellectum in actu. Forma enim domus in mente aedificatoris est aliquid ab eo intellectum ad cuius similitudinem domum in materia format." *Ia*, q. 15, a. 2, c. Il s'agit donc bien d'une forme conçue par l'intelligence.

79 "Non est autem contra simplicitatem divini intellectus quod multa intelligat, sed contra simplicitatem eius esset, si per plures species eius intellectus formaretur." Ibid.

80 "Sapientia et ars significantur ut quo Deus intelligit, sed idea ut quod intelligit. Deus autem uno intellectu intelligit multa: et non solum secundum quod in seipsis sunt, sed etiam secundum quod intellecta sunt: quod est intelligere plures rationes rerum. Sicut artifex, dum intelligit formam domus in materia, dicitur intelligere domum; dum autem intelligit formam domus ut a se speculatam, ex quo intelligit se intelligere eam, intelligit ideam vel rationem domus. Deus autem

Si le mode propre de cette présence est nécessaire pour formuler correctement tous les aspects de la connaissance divine, la présence des idées est nécessaire au même titre pour l'équilibre de la synthèse doctrinale.[81]

CONCLUSION

Si nos précédentes analyses sont exactes, nous devons comprendre de la manière suivante les données historiques et systématiques du problème des idées divines dans l'œuvre de S. Thomas. Pierre Lombard, traitant de la connaissance divine, se demande si la présence des créatures dans la connaissance divine ne doit pas comporter aussi une présence dans l'essence. Il répond négativement, en s'appuyant sur S. Augustin, sans d'ailleurs faire allusion aux idées. S. Thomas, dès la distinction 35, a adopté la thèse de Denys, relative à la plénitude éminente de l'essence divine, qui contient dans son unité, toutes les perfections reçues par les créatures.[82] Il trouve, d'autre part, une question relative aux idées divines, rattachée au texte du Lombard par ses commentateurs. La thèse de Denys permet de faire comprendre que Dieu, en se connaissant lui-même, peut connaître toutes choses, si l'on fait jouer à l'essence le rôle de l'espèce intelligible, donc de la similitude, qui permet à l'acte de connaissance de se produire. Le thème des idées met en relief, non seulement la production des créatures (*formae operativae*), mais la distinction des objets connus. S. Augustin, d'ailleurs, insiste sur cette distinction: *alia ratione....* Sans elle, la connaissance distincte de l'univers par Dieu est impossible. Or il faut la maintenir, contre les doctrines qui consentent à limiter la perfection de la connaissance divine, afin d'en sauvegarder l'unité.

---

non solum intelligit multas res per essentiam suam, sed etiam intelligit se intelligere multa per essentiam. Sed hoc est inteligere plures rationes rerum; vel plures ideas esse in intellectu eius ut intellectas." Ibid., ad 2.

81   Très précisément, Saint Thomas a besoin, pour la précision de la doctrine, d'une distinction ferme entre l'essence dans sa fonction de forme de l'intelligence, et l'essence assurant la connaissance des raisons des choses comme *objets* connus, soit à titre de forme opérative ou modèle de la création, soit à titre de medium à l'égard des créatures considérées comme distinctes de Dieu. Les idées, c'est à dire ce que Saint Thomas met sous ce mot, assurent cette distinction, que la noétique de la seule espèce intelligible, sans production d'un terme par le connaissant, n'assure qu'imparfaitement, comme le montre le premier exposé de la question des idées divines, dans le *Comm. sur les Sentences.* Pour l'histoire du verbe en Saint Thomas, voir H. Paissac, O. P., *Théologie du verbe, Saint Augustin et Saint Thomas* (Paris 1951).

82   Voir supra note 32. Les objets connus par Dieu sont donc, en tant que participations, présentes dans l'essence, en ce sens du moins que Saint Thomas y voit plus qu'une présence dans la connaissance, à titre d'objets connus, plus aussi qu'une présence dans la cause, envisagée uniquement comme cause.

Dès les *Sentences*, la difficulté apparaît de bien comprendre cette multitude d'objets distincts, si tout objet connu doit être présent au principe de l'acte pour le spécifier:

> Les objets connus sont, par rapport à l'intellect, comme le dessin par rapport à une tablette; aussi le Philosophe...compare-t-il l'intellect possible, avant qu'il ne connaisse, à une tablette sur laquelle rien n'est écrit. Or il est impossible pour un même corps d'avoir en même temps et quant à la même partie diverses figures. Il est donc impossible que le même intellect puisse connaître en même temps plusieurs objets. Si donc l'intellect divin se connaît lui-même et beaucoup d'autres objets, il y aura nécessairement succession dans son intellect, et, par là, lassitude, du fait qu'il n'a pas en acte ce qu'il cherche. Et cela ne se peut.[83]

S. Thomas se contente de répondre que l'argument vaut pour tout intellect qui connaît des objets divers par des espèces diverses, ce qui n'est pas le cas de Dieu: en connaissant son essence, il connaît les autres choses.[84]

Mais dès les *Sentences* aussi, à propos de la multiplicité des idées, S. Thomas introduit la distinction entre l'essence comme essence et comme objet connu. La multiplicité des idées doit se placer du côté de l'essence en tant qu'elle est connue. Cette solution cependant ne le satisfait pas. Tout se passe comme s'il avait jugé nécessaire de distinguer non seulement l'essence en tant qu'elle assure la *présence* de l'objet, d'une part, et l'essence comme *objet connu,* mais encore l'essence comme assurant la présence de l'objet et la *manière* dont elle joue ce rôle, c'est à dire comme *forme actualisante.* La distinction entre deux formes, l'une principe, l'autre terme et produit de l'acte, va être introduite à partir du *De Veritate.* Limitée d'abord à certains actes et à certaines formes "inventées" par le connaissant, la distinction est généralisée et approfondie dans la *Somme contre les Gentils,* toujours à propos de la multiplicité des raisons que Dieu doit connaître. Elle distingue les questions 14 et 15 de la *Somme Théologique,* et on la retrouve clairement, dans la même *Ia Pars,* qu. 34, a. 3, c., ou l'on montre que le nom de Verbe, en Dieu, comporte un rapport à la créature:

> Dieu, en effet, par un acte unique, se connaît lui-même et toutes choses. Aussi son Verbe unique exprime-t-il non seulement le Père, mais aussi les créatures. Et de même que la science de Dieu est à l'égard de Dieu purement connaissante, à l'égard des créatures par contre connaissante et productrice à la fois, ainsi le Verbe de Dieu est seulement expression de

83 *In I Sent.*, d. 35, q. 1, a. 2, obj. 3; éd. Mandonnet, I, pp. 813-814.
84 Ibid., ad 3, p. 815.

ce qui est dans Dieu le Père, pour les créatures, par contre, il est à la fois expressif et opératif.

Mais

> le mot "idée" signifie principalement le rapport à la créature, et c'est pourquoi on l'emploie au pluriel en Dieu et il n'est pas personnel. Le mot "Verbe", par contre, signifie principalement le rapport à celui qui le prononce, et par voie de conséquence seulement, le rapport aux créatures, pour autant que Dieu, se connaissant lui-même, connaît toute créature. Aussi n'y a-t-il en Dieu qu'un unique Verbe et le mot désigne une personne. (Ibid. ad 4).

Je dirais donc volontiers pour conclure que poser la question de la place des idées divines dans sa théologie, c'est demander si S. Thomas aurait pu se passer des raisons multiples des choses, par lesquelles Dieu connaît en lui-même les êtres qu'il crée et gouverne. Si la réponse est négative, il faut se demander ultérieurement si, ayant fondé la multitude de ces objets connus, et leur présence dans l'intellect divin, sur la plénitude de l'essence divine, et donc ultérieurement sur son rôle d'espèce intelligible, il aurait pu aboutir à une présentation équilibrée de la doctrine, en se contentant de la seule espèce intelligible, donc en supprimant la question des idées.

S. Thomas semble avoir pensé que non. Sa conception des idées divines, en tout cas, loin de se présenter comme le résultat de causes fortuites ou extrinsèques au problème, constitue le résultat d'un effort pour trouver la synthèse entre des données, dont on peut montrer, sans doute, qu'elles viennent ou de Denys, ou d'Aristote ou de S. Augustin, mais qui apparemment, étaient pour lui les exigences objectives du problème lui-même.

Epilogue

La conclusion qui précède ne concerne directement que le problème de la connaissance divine et les textes que nous avons étudiés. Il faudrait la comparer avec les résultats d'une étude semblable d'un certain nombre de thèmes connexes, tels que: la providence, l'expression des créatures dans le Verbe, la causalité exemplaire et ses rapports avec le thème des idées, ou la création par intermédiaires.

Il y aurait lieu surtout de confronter ensuite cet ensemble avec un autre, qui, historiquement, en est largement indépendant, qui, doctrinalement, pose un problème exactement contraire, à savoir le problème des idées dans leur rapport avec la vision de l'essence divine par les esprits créés: le Christ en tant qu'homme, les anges, les bienheureux; à quoi il y aurait lieu d'ajouter certains aspects de la connaissance prophétique. Quand il s'agit de la connaissance que Dieu a du monde, la théologie chrétienne ne pouvait aller que dans le sens de la plus grande perfection possible: Dieu connaît distinctement tout objet possible de connaissance: l'ensemble et les détails, l'universel et le singulier, le passé, le présent et l'avenir, le substantiel et l'accidentel, ce que nous appelons le nécessaire et ce que nous appelons le hasard, le réel et le possible, le bien et le mal. Quand il est question, au contraire, de la vision de l'essence divine par des esprits créés, clairement affirmée par la foi, le problème se pose de maintenir une différence entre la connaissance accordée par la vision béatifique et la connaissance divine. N'y a-t-il pas danger de voir des esprits finis égaler le savoir infini de Dieu?

La difficulté devient particulièrement aigüe quand on fait intervenir les idées divines. "Le Verbe incréé en effet est un miroir qui fait connaître toutes les créatures, parce que, par lui, le Père se dit lui-même et toutes choses. En lui se trouvent donc les similitudes de toutes les choses."[85] Ces similitudes que sont elles, sinon les idées divines? Or, quiconque voit un miroir voit nécessairement tous les objets qui s'y réfléchissent. Comment dès lors ne pas conclure que la vision de l'essence divine donne en même temps la vision de tout ce que Dieu connaît? Et si l'on veut éviter la conclusion, pour assurer à Dieu un domaine privé et exclusif, en dépit de la vision de l'essence et des idées qui y sont contenues, comment y réussir sinon en estompant la netteté des idées, de certaines au moins, pour empêcher une trop grande curiosité de surprendre tout le contenu de la connaissance divine? Enfantillages, dira-t-on, matérialisations maladroites. Ce sont cependant ces difficultés qu'on trouve discutées sérieusement, à partir du moment où le thème des idées divines a été introduit dans les questions posées à propos du texte du Lombard, qui lui, ne les mentionne pas plus qu'il ne l'a fait pour la connaissance divine.

C'est dans ce contexte qu'on voit figurer notamment la distinction entre les idées divines précises et confuses,[86] distinction que S. Thomas abandonnera, avec tout le matériel des métaphores du miroir, pour montrer que les idées ne sont pas dans l'intellect comme des choses ou des images, que n'importe qui peut aller voir. Mais l'histoire de ce problème exigerait des développements qui dépassent le cadre de ce travail.

---

85 *De ver.,* q. 3, a. 1, obj. 8.
86 *In III Sent.,* d. 14, a. 2, qua 2, sol.; éd. Mandonnet, III, pp. 447-448. Comparer avec *Somme théol.,* IIIa pars, q. 10, a. 2.

IV

ST. THOMAS AND HIS PREDECESSORS

AQUINAS AS ARISTOTELIAN COMMENTATOR

Joseph Owens C.Ss.R.

I

THE role of St. Thomas Aquinas as an Aristotelian commentator still proves puzzling. Certainly his work in this respect is not the detached and theologically neutral undertaking that is found in moderns such as Bonitz, J. A. Stewart, or Sir David Ross. No matter how closely his attitude is concerned with explaining the Aristotelian text just as the text stands, it is consistently sensitive to any deviations of the teaching from the integrity of Christian faith and of orthodox theology. In fact, it does not at all give the impression that it is going out of its normal way when it corrects the Aristotelian tenets in the light of revealed doctrine. Rather, it proceeds as though correction of this type is a legitimate and integral part of its overall method.[1]

Does not this savor strongly of an out and out theological method? Should it not mean that the Aristotelian commentaries of Aquinas are to be classed as works of sacred theology rather than of philosophy? Is not the procedure in them theological through and through, in contrast to a genuinely philosophical treatment of the Aristotelian text? Does not this mean theology only?

However, hesitation arises at once in confrontation with this apparently extreme stand. The overwhelming predominance of the

---

1 E.g., *In XII Metaph.*, lect. 5, Cathala-Spiazzi nos. 2496-2499; *In VIII Phys.*, lect. 2, Angeli-Pirotta nos. 2041-2044; *In I Eth.*, lect. 9, Spiazzi no. 113; *In I Periherm.*, lect. 14, Spiazzi nos. 195-197; *In III de An.*, lect. 9, Pirotta no. 726; *In I de Cael. et Mund.*, lect. 6, Spiazzi nos. 64-66. Cf.: "Sehr beachtenswert ist die Art und Weise, wie Thomas oft ganz unauffällig an der nikomachischen Ethik Korrekturen vornimmt und auf die Ideen und Ideale des christlichen Ethos hinweist. ... Es liessen sich diese Belege von Korrekturen, die Thomas oft ganz unauffällig an Aristoteles vornimmt, noch bedeutend vermehren." Martin Grabmann, "Die Aristoteleskommentare des heiligen Thomas von Aquin," in *Mittelalterliches Geistesleben* (Munich 1926), pp. 305-306. "In the present case where the reader is the theologian Saint Thomas, the Stagirite's works are read through Christian eyes." M.-D. Chenu, *Towards Understanding Saint Thomas*, tr. A.-M. Landry and D. Hughes (Chicago 1964), p. 209. However, Grabmann (p. 282) can maintain that Aquinas was striving to present an "objective picture" of the Aristotelian doctrine. On the way a medieval commentator may claim to be giving an entirely objective interpretation, and yet not "remain within the bounds of what he had intended in principle," see Chenu, pp. 206-207, n. 9, in reference to Albert the Great.

discussion in the commentaries deals with the Aristotelian thought and not with professedly theological issues. Moreover, on the supposition of outside interference the theological interest is not the only observable intrusion into the commentaries. A partly new conception of the sciences seems to dominate the whole discussion.[2] Metaphysics seems placed in an Avicennian framework, ethics and politics in traditional Christian grooves, and logic in the setting of the three Scholastically accepted intellectual activities. Would not this new philosophical coloring have to be regarded as changing the character of the commentaries just as much as the theological concern? Or is it to be viewed as in some way connected with, and subsumed under, the theological orientation?

The above observations suggest at least that in these writings of Aquinas the task of a commentator was not understood to be a disinterested and historically exact explanation of the Aristotelian views. It was not a function to be detached from concern for revealed Christian truth. There can be little doubt that St. Thomas grasped in large part the true import and thrust of the Stagirite's tenets. He did not hesitate for a moment to acknowledge that Aristotle accepted the eternity of the world and the actuation of the heavenly bodies by spiritual souls in the sense that these tenets were strictly essential to the Aristotelian metaphysics.[3] He was continually aware that Aristotle in the *Ethics* was concerned only with this-worldly contentment. Yet he undertakes to show how the Aristotelian teachings blossom out into thoroughly Christian flora. Does not this procedure mean much more than that in the commentaries "theological considerations color his interpretations"?[4] Will it anywhere allow one to view the Aristotelian commentaries as articulating "positions which are rejected in his basically theological writings"?[5]

One may sharpen the question still further. Can the procedure in the Aristotelian commentaries be regarded as in *any* way basically philosophical, in contrast to that of the "basically theological writings"? Are the theological coloring and additions and reservations merely intruded from outside as occasion demands, in order to make the

---

2   E.g., *In Metaph.* Proem; *In I Eth.,* nos. 2-7; *In Periherm.,* Proem, no. 1; *In de Gen. et Cor.,* Proem, Spiazzi no. 2.

3   *In XII Metaph.,* lect. 5, no. 2496; cf. lect. 10, no. 2598. *In VIII Phys.,* lect. 2, no. 2043. *In I de Cael. et Mund.,* lect. 6, no. 64. On the requirement of souls for the Aristotelian heavenly bodies, see *In II de Cael. et Mund.,* lect. 13, nos. 415-419; cf. *In VIII Phys.,* lect. 21, no. 2479, and *In XII Metaph.,* lect. 4, nos. 2476 and 2536. For the *Ethics,* see infra, n. 43.

4   Victor Preller, *Divine Science and the Science of God* (Princeton 1967), p. 22.

5   Preller, *ibid.* The "articulating" of the positions rejected does not necessarily mean their acceptance by Aquinas in the commentaries. Preller's attitude is: "The closest that Aquinas comes to manifesting a purely philosophical intention is in his commentaries on Aristotle." *Ibid.*

Stagirite's doctrine palatable in a Christian milieu and safeguard it from censure-prone ecclesiastical authority? Or must these commentaries be classed as authentically theological documents? In a word, is Aquinas as an Aristotelian commentator writing as a philosopher or as a theologian?

The tendency to view the Aristotelian commentaries as basically philosophical writings is of course deep-seated. Allegedly according to the mind of St. Thomas they fill the role of a *Summa Philosophica* for beginners,[6] providing students with a complete and suitable course of philosophy,[7] presenting Thomistic philosophy in words of the Angelic Doctor himself.[8] The hermeneutical principle would be: "For Thomas interpreted Aristotle's thought not only in the light of its inner consistency, but also by taking into account the results of subsequent philosophical research."[9] Seen from this standpoint, the work is properly philosophical.

There is obviously a problem, then, in regard to the nature of the Thomistic commentaries on Aristotle. In its broadest framework, the issue is whether these commentaries are essentially philosophical or theological documents. Within the procedure proper to the one or the other discipline, as the case may be, the question has to be faced how Aquinas can so patently understand the real meaning of the Aristotelian text and yet explain it in a way that is not Aristotle's, or even opposed to Aristotle's conception of its implications. Comparatively little work has as yet been devoted to this problem. At a Scholastic congress in 1950 it was noted that the number of studies published on these commentaries was minimal, totaling less than fifty, and almost exclusively mere articles.[10] The situation has not improved notably in the intervening years. The topic is still wide open for investigation.

The meaning of the word "commentary" is practically of no help in regard to the issue. It is wide enough to cover explanation of the basic document, notes on it, reflections on it, development of questions

---

6 J. Isaac, "Saint Thomas interprète des œuvres d'Aristote," *Acta Congressus Scholastici Internationalis Romae 1950* (Rome 1951), p. 356. This would extend to present-day beginners in philosophy.

7 "... procurer à la jeunesse estudiantine un cours complet de philosophie adapté à ses besoins." Isaac, *ibid.* Against these views, see Chenu, p. 214.

8 Isaac, p. 355.

9 E. Cantore, "Critical Study: The Italian Philosophical Encyclopedia," *The Review of Metaphysics,* XXIV (1971), 515.

10 See Isaac, p. 355. Some interesting possibilities for exploration in regard to the "management" of the Aristotelian philosophy in the commentaries are suggested by A. C. Pegis, "St. Thomas and the Nicomachean Ethics," *Mediaeval Studies,* 25 (1963), 1-25.

arising from it. In the last sense it became regularly applied to works on the *Sentences* of Peter Lombard, in which the basic text served merely as a springboard for wide-ranging articles on subjects of current interest. But the word did not enter into the titles of these writings of Aquinas in their original form. Rather, they were called *Expositiones.* They were presented as explanations of the Aristotelian works. This throws the problem back to the kind of explanation found in the Thomistic undertaking. Is it philosophical or theological in character? Does it respect the original meaning scrupulously, or merely use that meaning as a springboard for its own new interests? Basically, is it explaining Aristotle or is it doing something else? Or is it in some way an amorphous combination of these possibilities?

The last suggestion does not seem to be at all acceptable, for the inspiration of the Thomistic commentaries on Aristotle seems to be unitary throughout. They do not give the impression of an amalgam of disparate elements. Rather, their procedure appears to be a self-consistent enterprise, constituting an authentic literary genre. No impression of anything amorphous or fragmentary is given in the course of these writings. The command of the situation seems firm from start to finish. The attitude shown in them is that of a man engaged in a thoroughly coherent task. He is apparently doing his work in a manner recognized and accepted in his milieu. He may embody in his technique of literal commentary a distinct improvement over his predecessors in handling the Aristotelian doctrine, but in his use of pagan thought in a Christian atmosphere he appears to be carrying on a unity of method that had been achieved through a long history of intelligent effort. The procedure has the marks of something undertaken with a well thought out and consciously adopted purpose. Prima facie, accordingly, it has every right to be approached with this assumption. It is not to be dismissed lightly on the strength of present-day formal and stereotyped norms. Rather, grass roots investigation in the commentaries themselves is indicated in order to see whether or not the above assumption will be borne out.

A close scrutiny of the commentaries, then, is the way to obtain correct answers about their nature. The Aristotelian commentaries of Aquinas are twelve in number. The earliest chronological indication for any of them is the reign of Pope Urban IV (1261-1264). This is for the commentary on the *Metaphysics,* a commentary that was not finished before 1272. The other Aristotelian commentaries are dated variously between 1266 and 1273.[11] The commentary on the *Metaphysics,* con-

---

11   See Angelus Walz, *Saint Thomas d'Aquin,* adaptation française par Paul Novarina (Louvain & Paris 1962), pp. 165-166; 221-222. Chenu, pp. 223-224.

sequently, would seem to stretch in one way or another through the whole chronological period in which Aquinas was engaged in producing these writings on Aristotle. It may therefore quite safely be approached as the proper commentary in which to begin an investigation of the procedure of Aquinas. Later the results can be tested in briefer fashion against the method shown in the other Aristotelian commentaries.

II

The commentary of Aquinas on the *Metaphysics* covers the first twelve of the fourteen books traditionally grouped under the title.[12] A short Proem introduces the study that is to be dealt with, locating it in the science that naturally dominates all the others. The Proem uses as its springboard some observations from Aristotle's *Politics*, with two explicit references. It also draws upon, but without express references, a number of characteristic Aristotelian teachings from the *De Anima*, the *Analytics*, and the *Metaphysics* itself. These various tenets are brought to bear upon the one notion "intellectual in the highest degree" (*maxime intellectualis*)[13] as the distinguishing feature of the science that is being introduced. The assembling of so many roving tenets under the one unifying principle shows a thorough mastery of the philosophical materials, and an innate ability to organize them successfully from a new and personal viewpoint. It marks Aquinas himself as the "author" of the work about to be undertaken, in the medieval sense of the *auctor*. He is the one who will be doing the thinking and passing the judgments and presenting the work as his own, no matter how liberally he is drawing upon someone else for material, help, and inspiration. Such at least is the function of the commenting writer as suggested by this Proem.

Further, there is divergence in some details from the strict Aristotelian description of the philosophical notions involved. Actuality and potentiality, for instance, are presented as consequent upon being, just as are unity and multiplicity — "ea quae consequuntur ens, ut unum

---

12 For a short survey of the general procedure in the commentary of Aquinas on the *Metaphysics*, see John P. Rowan, *St. Thomas Aquinas, Commentary on the Metaphysics of Aristotle*, 2 v. (Chicago 1961), I, viii-xxiii. The commentary will be referred to according to the numbers in the edition of M.-R. Cathala, revised by R. M. Spiazzi, *S. Thomae Aquinatis, In Duodecem Libros Metaphysicorum Aristotelis Expositio* (Turin & Rome 1964). These numbers are likewise used in Rowan's English translation of the commentary.

13 "... scientia debet esse naturaliter aliarum regulatrix, quae maxime intellectualis est. ... causarum cognitio maxime intellectualis esse videtur... Unde et illa scientia maxime est intellectualis, quae circa principia maxime universalia versatur. ... Unde scientia, quae de istis rebus considerat, maxime videtur esse intellectualis, ..." *In Metaph.*, Proem.

et multa, potentia et actus" (*In Metaph.,* Proem.). In this regard Aristotle himself gives details about the way the most general "forms" follow upon being.[14] He regards unity and multiplicity as basic, but does not mention actuality and potentiality. Rather, actuality and potentiality name original instances of being, not subsequent properties.[15]

Somewhat similarly the formal substances that in Aristotle were described as "absolutely separate" (*Metaph.,* H 1, 1042a29-31) are designated in this Proem as separate "secundum esse," in contrast to the mathematicals, which are separate "secundum rationem." This places the division in an obviously remodeled cast, for in Aristotle the mathematicals were described as things not separate, though taken in abstraction and separated by thought from movement.[16] Against an Arabian background the things that are separate "secundum esse" are distinguished as "Deus et intelligentiae," quite apparently understood in the biblical sense of God and angels. Together these separate substances are looked upon as the common and universal causes of common being — "ens commune, quod est genus, cuius sunt praedictae substantiae communes et universales causae" (*In Metaph.,* Proem).

What has happened here? There is an unmistakable effort to keep God and the angels from playing the role of subject to the science of metaphysics. Sacred theology had already appropriated God as its specifying subject.[17] This subject accordingly had to be different from the subject of any of the other sciences. The Avicennian framework was at hand to exclude God and the highest causes from the subject of metaphysics, and substitute instead the common aspect of being.[18] It

14   *Metaph., Γ* 2, 1003b28-1004a20. Actuality and potentiality had been described as attributes following upon being by Albert, *Metaph.,* I, tr. 1, c. 2; ed. Borgnet, VI, 5b. Cf. also Avicenna, *Metaph.,* I, 1D, (Venice 1508) fol. 70r2.

15   *Metaph., Δ* 7, 1017b1-9; E 2, 1026b1-2.

16   Cf. *Ph.,* II 2, 193b33-34, and *Metaph.,* E 1, 1026a9-15; K 7, 1064a32-33. The status of the mathematicals had been handed down as that of things dealt with in a science that is *sine motu inabstracta,* things that cannot be separated (*separari non possunt*) from matter and motion. Boethius, *De Trin.,* c. II; ed. Stewart and Rand (London & New York 1926), p. 8.11-14.

17   See Aquinas, *In Boeth. de Trin.,* V, 4, Resp.; ed. Bruno Decker (Leiden 1955), pp. 194.14-195.27. At p. 195.15 "God and angels" (cf. p. 165.27) is used in the context in which "God and the intelligences" occurs in the Proem to the commentary on the *Metaphysics.* In *In I Sent.,* d. 36, q. 2, a. 1, Solut. (ed. Mandonnet, I, 839) the separate movents of the spheres in Averroes seem to be entirely absorbed into the Christian notion of God. Apparently Aquinas experienced little difficulty in seeing the Aristotelian separate substances coalesce in the one Christian God, or on the contrary in regarding them as God and angels together, or in speaking of them as God and the intelligences according to the Neoplatonic tradition as found in the Arabians: "... Platonici ponebant... ordinem superiorum intellectuum separatorum, qui apud nos consueverunt *intelligentiae* vocari." *In II de Cael. et Mund.,* lect. 4, Spiazzi no. 334.

18   See Avicenna, *Metaph.,* I, 1 (Venice 1508), fol. 70rl-vl. St. Thomas seems well enough aware that the Avicennian framework has to be used as an alternate to saying that the primary philosophy treats of the separate substances and then having to add "non tamen solum ea; sed etiam de sensibilibus, inquantum sunt entia, philosophus perscrutatur. Nisi forte dicamus, ut

safeguarded the distinction between metaphysics and sacred theology. But why did not only God but also the "intellectual substances" (*Deus et intellectuales substantiae*) have to be left outside the subject of metaphysics? Surely the exclusion of God alone would have been enough to provide for the specification of sacred theology. Why, moreover, the interest in showing that in this context metaphysics bears entirely upon things separate from matter "secundum esse et rationem," not only things that can never be in matter, but also aspects that are able to be found without matter, such as common being?[19]

These preoccupations suppose a conception of metaphysics in which separate substances, apart from distinction into God and angels, functioned as the subject of metaphysics. This conception was well enough known at the time through the position of Averroes.[20] But there was enough in the Aristotelian text to substantiate it in the description of metaphysics as "theological science."[21] The title "theology" had to be accorded it, and was allowed it by Aquinas on the ground that it dealt with the separate substances in the way already explained, namely as the causes of common being.[22] The alternate Aristotelian title "first

Avicenna dicit, quod huiusmodi communia de quibus haec scientia perscrutatur, dicuntur separata secundum esse,..." *In Metaph.*, lect. 1, no. 1165. At *In I Sent.*, Prol. q. 1, a. 3, qa. 3, Solut. 1 (v. I, p. 12), metaphysics was regarded as divine from the viewpoint of subject in contrast to source of illumination: "Metaphysica autem considerat causas altissimas per rationes ex creaturis assumptas. Unde ista doctrina magis etiam divina dicenda est quam metaphysica: quia est divina quantum ad subjectum et quantum ad modum accipiendi; metaphysica autem quantum ad subjectum tantum." Here the highest causes and the divine are regarded as subject in the wide sense that they are things treated of by metaphysics, even though its source of inspiration is not divine. There is no occasion here for contrasting the subject of the science with the causes and principles of the science from the viewpoint of the science's specification, with reference to Aristotle's philosophical theology.

19   From the viewpoint of inclusion under common being, the angels as creatures have to be regarded as part of the subject of metaphysics, along with spiritual souls. This allows common aspects such as being, unity and plurality, actuality and potentiality, to be found sometimes in matter, sometimes apart from matter. When the separate intelligences are contrasted with common being as its cause or principle, then, they are viewed as coalescing in nature with the Christian God (see supra, n. 17). In the Aristotelian tradition they were called divine, and from this viewpoint would for a Christian have to coincide with the one supreme God. When on the other hand they are regarded as angels and accordingly as creatures, they are all composed of actuality and potentiality, and in this way exhibit unity and multiplicity. For Aquinas, in consequence, both actuality and potentiality are said to follow upon common being, as though by way of a property without which common being cannot be found.

20   "Et qui dicit quod prima Philosophia nititur declarare entia separabilia esse, peccat. Haec enim entia sunt subjecta primae Philosophiae." Averroes, *In I Phys.*, comm. 83G (Venice 1562), fol. 47vl. "Thus, Averroes is the permanent substrate of his commentary on the *Metaphysics*" — Chenu, p. 215. Cf. supra, n. 18.

21   Aristotle, *Metaph.*, E 1, 1026a19; K 7, 1064b3.

22   "Dicitur enim scientia divina sive *theologia,* inquantum praedictas substantias considerat." *In Metaph.*, Proem. Cf. "Sic ergo theologia sive scientia divina est duplex. Una, in qua considerantur res divinae non tamquam subiectum scientiae, sed tamquam principia subiecti, et talis est theologia, quam philosophi prosequuntur, quae alio nomine metaphysica dicitur." *In Boeth. de Trin.*, V, 4, Resp.; ed. Decker, p. 195.6-9. Cf. V, 1, Resp.; p. 166.1-6.

philosophy" was similarly admitted for the same reason, namely that it treated of these first causes of things. [23] Both these ways of expressing the nature of the science had accordingly to be accepted and the infection localized. The new standpoint would leave the divine as the specifying subject of only sacred theology, and yet acknowledge that it was studied, though in a different way, by the philosophical pursuit. This made the traditional title "metaphysics" free to designate the science from the viewpoint of its specification by its own subject, common being, which is "transphysical" insofar as it is common to material and immaterial things alike: "*Metaphysica,* inquantum considerat ens et ea quae consequuntur ipsum. Haec enim transphysica inveniuntur in via resolutionis, sicut magis communia post minus communia" (Proem). The term "metaphysics," consequently, can still imply a science of what is separate from matter, though at the cost of introducing a technical notion of "separate" that is not to be found in the Aristotelian treatises. How could any common notions be regarded in the Aristotelian context as "separata a materia secundum esse"? To be separate in the sense contrasted with "separate in notion," they would have to be substances, and for Aristotle nothing common or universal can be a substance in the setting of the *Metaphysics* (Z 13, 1038b8-35).

What is the significance of this change in location for the subject of metaphysics? If for Aristotle primary philosophy or theological science dealt with the separate substances in the sense of the divine beings, and with all other things on account of their reference to this primary instance of being, does not the change become a complete reversal in perspective? [24] For Aquinas common being, from which the divine is excluded, becomes the subject of metaphysics. The divine is treated of by the science only because of the reference it has to common being, namely in its role of the cause of common being. Yet the one formula "separata a materia secundum esse et rationem" serves for Aquinas as the means of expressing his own conception of the subject of metaphysics in words that would apply equally well to the subject of the Aristotelian theological science.

How has this change come about? In his commentary on Boethius' *De Trinitate,* Aquinas had occasion to deal with the notion of theology against both the Aristotelian and the Christian backgrounds. Boethius,

---

23 "Dicitur autem *prima philosophia,* inquantum primas rerum causas considerat." *In Metaph.,* Proem.

24 The two opposed interpretations of the *Metaphysics,* labeled the "ontological" versus the "theological" interpretation, persist through medieval into modern times. A discussion of the problem may be found in my study *The Doctrine of Being in the Aristotelian* Metaphysics, 2nd ed. (Toronto 1963), pp. 25-26; 35-67.

following Aristotle, had written that while natural philosophy and mathematics are types of non-abstract science (*inabstracta*), theology is in contrast to them abstract and separable (*abstracta atque separabilis*), since there is no matter nor movement in the substance of God.[25] In Aristotelian fashion Aquinas takes up the consideration of this subject in the plural as *res divinae* — divine things (V, 4, resp. 3; p. 194.14). The use of the plural, though taken from Aristotle, is supported by the Scriptural way of referring to the "invisible things of God" (*ibid.*, line 22 — from *Rom.*, I, 20) and "the things that are of God" (p. 195.1 — from *I Cor.*, II, 11). In this way the Aristotelian plural in referring to the divine is made to bear upon the unique Christian God.

So understood these divine things can be considered in two ways, as far as the specification of theology for Aquinas is concerned. They can be considered in their role of the common principles of all things. In this way alone can they be treated of by the philosophers, in the science that has as its subject being *qua* being and which is called by them the divine science. In the second way the divine things are considered insofar as they are things that subsist in themselves, and not as manifested through effects. Procedure in the first of these two ways gives rise to philosophical theology or metaphysics. Procedure in the second way is that of the theology of sacred scripture. Both deal with things separate from matter *secundum esse,* though separate respectively in two different ways, namely as things that can never be in matter, such as God and the angels, or as things that can be without matter though sometimes found in matter. Objects separate in the first way constitute the subject of sacred theology, while they function only as the principles of the subject of philosophical theology (pp. 194.14-195.27).

This conception of the science of metaphysics is merely repeated in the Proem to the commentary on the *Metaphysics,* without any significant addition or change. But the chronologically prior development of the doctrine, in the course of the commentary on Boethius, shows clearly enough the issue that is at stake. If God as he exists in himself is allowed to function as the subject of metaphysics, no room will be left for a further science about God arising from divine revelation.[26] The preoccupation is to make the intellectual world safe for sacred theology. The concern of the Christian theologian is crystal clear. It is allayed by making a new type of separate objects specify

---

25 Boethius, *De Trin.,* c. II.
26 See Aquinas, *In I Sent.,* Prol., q. 1, a. 1: ed. Mandonnet, I, 6-8, especially "quamvis philosophia determinet de existentibus secundum rationes a creaturis sumptas, oportet tamen esse aliam quae existentia consideret secundum rationes ex inspiratione divini luminis acceptas". *Ibid.,* ad 1m; p. 8.

metaphysics, while the divine is left free to specify sacred theology.

The task was rendered comparatively easy and the results readily acceptable in the framework already established by Avicenna. But is the
key feature in the new notion of separate object, namely separate in
being (*secundum esse*), characteristically Avicennian? It is hardly
Aristotelian. In the "Proem" to the commentary on the *Metaphysics* the
topic is introduced through contrast with the separation of the
mathematicals: "Et non solum secundum rationem, sicut mathematica,
sed etiam secundum esse, sicut Deus et intelligentiae." In this contrast,
esse can scarcely mean anything other than existence. If it had the formal sense that it would have in its regular Aristotelian use in a setting
like this, it would not set up a contrast. In the Aristotelian use of the infinitive of the verb "to be" in similar contexts, the formal aspects of a
thing were signified. For instance, the dividing and uniting by a point
or instant are the same thing but differ in εἶναι (*Ph.,* IV 13, 222a16-20).
Here and elsewhere in Aristotle[27] the infinitive is used synonymously
with *logos,* in the sense of a formal aspect. Used with "separate," it
would accordingly mean separate in notion, and not separate *secundum
esse* in the additional meaning desired here by Aquinas. *Esse* would
have to retain the Boethian meaning of *definition.*[28] The force of the
secundum esse in its present use by St. Thomas calls for considerably
more, then, than the formal Aristotelian meaning. Nor can the
Boethian text that provides the take-off point for the discussion be expected to furnish the metaphysical basis for the new concept of
separation *secundum esse et rationem.*

What new factor, then, is at work in the development of the formula
"separata a materia secundum esse et rationem" (*In Metaph.,* Proem.)
to describe the subject of metaphysics? The context strongly suggests
the meaning of existence: "... non solum illa quae nunquam in materia
esse possunt, sicut Deus et intellectuales substantiae, sed etiam illa quae
possunt sine materia esse, sicut ens commune." The prima facie
meaning suggested by these words is that objects like God and the intellectual substances can never *exist* in matter, and that an object like
common being is able to occur without matter. The reference seems
clearly enough to bear on existential status, rather than on anything
pertaining to the notions themselves. The verb is accordingly translated
as "exist" without any hesitation in the English renditions "those things
which can never exist in matter" and "those things which can exist
without matter" (tr. Rowan). In the pertinent passages in the com-

---

27 See Bonitz, *Ind. Arist.,* 221a34-61.
28 *In Isog. Porphyr.,* editio secunda, IV, 14; ed. Brandt (CSEL, vol. 48), p. 273.13-15.

mentary on Boethius the existential bearing had been expressed so strongly as to leave it beyond doubt.[29]

In the Boethian commentary the meaning of *esse* had even in the article on the specification of divine science been clearly given its sharp Thomistic force as the actuality of essence.[30] Is this notion brought into the commentary on the *Metaphysics*? Does it bear upon the presentation of the subject of the science as common being distinct from divine being, in the recognizable Avicennian framework? If so, does it mean that the notion of separation *secundum esse* gives the subject of metaphysics a status that it could not possibly have had in Avicenna?

The rejection of the Avicennian notion of being, regarded as adding something by way of accident to the essence, is explicit in the commentary on the Aristotelian *Metaphysics*. In explaining the Aristotelian tenet that the substance of a thing is unitary and existent in virtue of its own self and not in virtue of something added, Aquinas takes the occasion to note that Avicenna's view is different. But Avicenna is wrong, for the being of a thing though other than its essence is not to be understood as something superadded in the fashion of an accident. Rather, it is as it were constituted by the principles of the essence.[31]

The characteristically Thomistic view of being pervades this passage. It means that the being of a finite thing is other than the thing itself, yet is caused by the very essence of the thing, so that nothing is more essential to a thing than its being. Not other by way of subsequent accident,

29 Cf.: "Quaedam vero sunt, quae quamvis dependeant a materia secundum esse, non tamen secundum intellectum, quia in eorum diffinitionibus non ponitur materia sensibilis, sicut linea et numerus. Et de his est mathematica. Quaedam vero speculabilia sunt, quae non dependent a materia secundum esse, quia sine materia esse possunt, sive numquam sint in materia, sicut deus et angelus, sive in quibusdam sint in materia et in quibusdam non, ..." *In Boeth. de Trin.*, V, 1, Resp.; p. 165.21-27. Here the *esse* is contrasted with the definitions, and means existing in contradistinction to essence. Translation by the English term "existence" is accordingly justified: "Now there are some objects of speculation which depend on matter with respect to their existence, for they can exist only in matter ... There are some objects of speculation, however, which although depending on matter with respect to existence, do not depend on it with respect to their concept, because sensible matter is not included in their definitions." *The Division and Methods of the Sciences*, tr. Armand Maurer, 2nd ed. (Toronto 1958), pp. 7-8.
See also: "Non enim intelligit lineam esse sine materia sensibili, sed considerat lineam et eius passiones sine consideratione materiae sensibilis, ..." V, 3, ad 1m; p. 186.26-28. Cf.: V, 4, Resp.; p. 195.11-12. *Ibid.*, ad 7m; p. 199.14-21.

30 "Sed quia non habet esse a seipso angelus, ideo se habet in potentia ad esse quod accipit a deo, et sic esse a deo acceptum comparatur ad essentiam eius simplicem ut actus ad potentiam. Et hoc est quod dicitur quod sunt compositi ex 'quod est' et 'quo est,' ut ipsum esse intelligatur 'quo est,'" — *In Boeth. de Trin.*, V, 4, ad 4m; p. 198.16-20. This is exactly the same doctrine of existence as is found in *De Ente et Essentia*, c. IV (ed. Roland-Gosselin, pp. 34.4-36.3), and in *In I Sent.*, d. 8, q. 5, a. 2, Solut. (ed. Mandonnet, I, 229-230).

31 "Esse enim rei quamvis sit aliud ab eius essentia, non tamen est intelligendum quod sit aliquod superadditum ad modum accidentis, sed quasi constituitur per principia essentiae." *In IV Metaph.*, lect. 2, no. 558. Cf.: "... cum nihil sit essentialius rei quam suum esse." *In I Sent.*, d. 8, expositio Iae partis; I, 209.

the being can be other only by way of a prior actuality. [32] The disturbing feature is that this uniquely Thomistic doctrine is being used as a norm for judging in the course of a commentary on Aristotle. It is used ostensibly to defend Aristotle's tenet that the substance of a thing is existent in virtue of its own self. At the same time the tenet of the Aristotelian passage that "an existent man" (*ens homo*) is a merely verbal reduplication of what is contained in "a man" (*homo — In IV Metaph.*, lect. 2, no. 550) is waved aside by the blunt assertion that the being of a thing is other than its essence (no. 558). The assertion is made with all the assurance that it need not be defended here, and that it is accepted by the readers without argument.

This shows that the notion of being by which both Aristotle and Avicenna are being judged in the commentary is the notion developed in Aquinas' own thinking. According to that notion the nature of being is found only in a unique primary instance. It is not a nature that could be shared either univocally or in analogically ranged degrees. [33] As a nature it cannot be common. Wherever it is found outside its primary instance it is other than the nature it actuates. In consequence the nature of being cannot function as common being nor be ranged as an instance under the notion of common being. Rather, as the cause of all the things that exhibit common being it is to be regarded in this respect as the cause of common being. With the subject of metaphysics in the wake of Avicenna distinguished from God and the highest causes, and now with Aquinas designated as common being, the kind of metaphysics introduced in the Proem to the Aristotelian commentary of Aquinas becomes clear. The notion of metaphysics presented as the entry into the Aristotelian thought is that of Aquinas himself. In its light, then, one need not be surprised to find judgment passed on Aristotle and Avicenna, as well as on Averroes and any other thinker.

The frequently made assertion that Aquinas was interested only in truth and not in the author making the statements now comes into focus as regards the Aristotelian *Metaphysics*. For St. Thomas human truth consisted in the correspondence of intellect with things, [34] and his own metaphysics was the way in which his own thinking corresponded to things on the metaphysical level. It was accordingly the one truth in which he could present metaphysical tenets, no matter whose words he was using.

---

32 A discussion of this topic may be found in my article. "The Causal Proposition — Principle or Conclusion?" *The Modern Schoolman,* 32 (1955), 323-327.

33 See *In I Sent.*, Prol., q. 1, a. 2, ad 2m; I, 10.

34 E.g.: "... quae quidem correspondentia, adaequatio rei et intellectus dicitur; et in hoc formaliter ratio veri perficitur. Hoc est ergo quod addit verum supra ens, scilicet conformitatem, sive adaequationem rei et intellectus." *De Ver.*, I, 1c.

Viewed in this light, then, the kind of philosophical truth being propounded in the commentary on the *Metaphysics* should be the truth developed and expressed in the metaphysical thinking of Aquinas himself, to the extent the text of the *Metaphysics* gives occasion to do so. The care to safeguard the interests of sacred theology in the delineation of the subject of metaphysics has already shown the dominant thinking of the Christian theologian. The particular metaphysical cast into which the Proem throws the discussion that is to ensue, now indicates further the intention to present the meaning of the Aristotelian treatises in a general framework that cannot be that of Aristotle himself. How this complicated orientation works out in practice may best be seen from a study of the details that emerge as the commentary pursues its course.

The opening paragraphs (nos. 1-4) add to the thought three well-developed philosophical reasons, not found in the present passage but taken from authentic Aristotelian reasoning in other works. They substantiate the opening sentence of the *Metaphysics,* which Aristotle himself presents merely as a readily acceptable observation. This procedure does not differ in any essential way from a modern commentator's use of Aristotelian tenets from other treatises or from fragments to explain a doctrine stated succinctly in a particular sentence. In the paragraphs that follow, other Aristotelian works such as *De Anima* and the *Ethics* continue to be drawn upon to explain tenets of the present treatise, and an outside author, Cicero (no. 11) is called upon for help. All this is still standard practice among commentators today. By and large the commentary continues this presentation of the meaning found in the text, adding information judged relevant such as the names of the seven sages of ancient Greece, and representing Thales as "committing his 'disputationes' to writing" (no. 77) quite as any eminent medieval Master would do. So far things proceed as in the usual understanding of a commentary, with the virtues and the faults of its epoch.

Only at rare intervals does the alien framework imposed by the Proem make itself apparent. In this, Aquinas seems to feel himself fully in accord with Aristotle, who could make what was obscure in a preceding philosopher appear as something admirable. That was achieved by articulating "distinctly and manifestly" what the earlier philosopher wanted to say, that is, "what his intellect was tending towards, but which he was unable to express" (no. 196). In corresponding fashion Aquinas, as has just been seen (supra, nn. 31-34), explains the Aristotelian identity of being and thing in the light of his own tenet that a thing is other than its being, even though being is essential to the thing. In a severe criticism of Averroes he seems nevertheless to acquiesce in the position that knowledge of the separate substances (plural) is the goal of human intellection,[35] and in the context of the distinction of the primary philosophy from both mathematics and the philosophy of nature he continues to speak of these substances in the plural (nos. 1163-1164; 2263-2267), although apparently equating them with God as the subject matter of theological science.[36] In this setting he feels obliged to go out of the text's way to note that the primary philosophy is not concerned with separate things only, but also with sensible things. Then comes the revealing concession: "unless perhaps we may say, as Avicenna says, that these common objects of which this science treats, are called separate *secundum esse* ... because they do not of necessity have their existence in matter, as do the mathematicals."[37]

This last text can leave little doubt that Aquinas is well aware of the plain meaning of the Aristotelian passages. Separate substances, namely divine things, are the subject treated of by the primary philosophy, which is on that account theological science. One has therefore to add sensible substances, *unless* one wishes to use the Avicennian framework in which notions like common being are called separate *secundum esse*.

This conclusion is confirmed by the reference to the beginning of Book Γ for the way in which the science of the primary being is the science of common being.[38] The Aristotelian framework is clearly recognized. In it the nature of the primary instance specifies the science. The secondary instances are treated of by the science in virtue of their reference to the primary instance. In the Avicennian framework, on the contrary, the common aspect specifies the science,

---

35 "Et ratio sua, quam inducit, est valde derisibilis... Deficit enim haec ratio. *Primo* quidem in hoc, quod cognitio intellectus nostri non est finis substantiarum separatarum, sed magis e converso." *In II Metaph.*, lect. 1, no. 286.

36 "Unde sunt causa entium secundum quod sunt entia, quae inquiruntur in prima philosophia, ut in primo proposuit. Ex hoc autem apparet manifeste falsitas opinionis illorum, qui posuerunt Aristotelem sensisse, quod Deus non sit causa substantiae caeli, sed solum motus eius." *In VI Metaph.*, lect. 1, no. 1164. Cf. no. 1168, and *In XI Metaph.*, lect. 7, nos. 2264-2265.

While there need not be any doubt that for Aristotle the separate substances are the cause of being for the sublunar world, the Aristotelian text explains this in the order of final causality. Yet Aquinas, showing clear understanding of the way the influence of the separate substances reaches the sublunar world through moving the heavenly bodies, speaks in a way that would strongly suggest the exercise of efficient causality by the separate substances: "Sic enim a substantiis separatis immobilibus ponit Aristoteles procedere et fieri et esse inferiorum, inquantum illae substantiae sunt motivae caelestium corporum, quibus mediantibus causatur generatio et corruptio in istis inferioribus." *In I Metaph.*, lect. 15, no. 237.

37 *In VI Metaph.*, lect. 1, no. 1165, my translation. Text supra, n. 18.

38 "... eadem enim est scientia primi entis et entis communis, ut in principio quarti habitum est." *In VI Metaph.*, lect. 1, no. 1170. Cf. "Eadem enim est scientia quae est de primis entibus, et quae est universalis. Nam prima entia sunt principia aliorum." *In XI Metaph.*, lect. 11, no. 2267. "Et quia ad illam scientiam pertinet consideratio entis communis, ad quam pertinet consideratio entis primi, ideo ad aliam scientiam quam ad naturalem pertinet consideratio entis communis; et eius etiam erit considerare huiusmodi principia communia." *In IV Metaph.*, lect. 5, no. 593.

and the divine is treated of in the science only because of reference to the common aspect, namely as its cause.

The Thomistic metaphysics of existence, however, requires that the reference to common being be explained in terms of efficient causality. The differences of the Thomistic commentary from the original Aristotelian meaning become especially apparent when details of this reference are under consideration. Aquinas acknowledges without hesitation that in Aristotle's view the first principles in the genus of substances, the heavenly bodies, are besouled (nos. 2476 and 2536), and that the eternity of motion and time is essential in Aristotle's own procedure regarding the immaterial substances (no. 2496). These two tenets he himself rejects. Aristotle's reasons accordingly are not regarded as cogent for establishing his conclusions. Nevertheless the conclusions themselves follow with necessity when the bringing of the world into existence is the operative factor in the reasoning (no. 2499). What can this mean if not that the Aristotelian conclusions, in order to be cogent, have to be based upon the existential actuality uppermost in Aquinas' own metaphysical thinking? The shying away from the Aristotelian eternity of the world, a possible philosophical alternative, indicates also the dominance of theological motivation in this problem.

Correspondingly the *necessary* perpetuity of cosmic motion, based by Aristotle on final causality, is explained as depending in its totality upon the *will* of God. The illustration used is that artifacts are assimilated to the artisan insofar as in them the artisan's will is fulfilled.[39] The nature of the Aristotelian reference to the first causes by way of assimilation seems clearly enough recognized, but it is explained in terms of efficient causality originating from will. Further, an Avicennian and ultimately Neoplatonic consideration that a unique first principle can cause only a unitary effect is dealt with in terms of existence as an acquired actuality. It is set aside on the ground that the one efficient cause can understand a multiplicity of things and cause them accordingly (no. 2559). In the same setting the Aristotelian doctrine that a separate substance has only itself as its intelligible object, is explained as meaning that God "by understanding himself understands all other things" (no. 2614) and "by knowing himself knows all things" (no. 2615). The reason given is that as first principle he contains all things in his power. Further, the order of the universe is a working out of what is in

---

39 *In XII Metaph.,* lect. 7, no. 2535. The metaphor of "assimilation" seems to have a Neoplatonic background. On the notion of necessity dependent upon the will of the maker, see my article "'Cause of Necessity' in Aquinas' *Teria Via,*" *Mediaeval Studies,* 33 (1971), 22-23; 33-39; 44-45.

the intellect and the will of the primary movent (no. 2631), and all natural things obtain their inclinations towards their goal from the primary intelligent being (no. 2634). Against this clearly etched background of Thomistic metaphysics the explicit assertions about divine providence made in the course of the commentary (nos. 1215-1222) fall into place. The overall theological interest also comes to the fore in this regard with the statement that on account of the philosophical conclusions all things may be said according to the Catholic faith to be subject to divine providence.[40]

With the foregoing data from the survey of the commentary on the *Metaphysics*, one is in a position to formulate the questions about the kind of procedure the work involves. Quantitatively, the overwhelming percentage of the book confines itself to explanation of the Aristotelian text just as the text stands, with recourse to other Aristotelian treatises and to other writers for elucidation as the occasion demands. Taken apart as just in itself, this almost total extent of the commentary does not prima facie differ in spirit from what is understood today as a philosophical commentary or interpretation. It can accordingly be cited and used to advantage by modern commentaries on Aristotle as though it were exactly of the same literary genre as they. Any noticeable divergences can be accounted for in terms of the different literary style and approach and background of the two epochs, medieval and modern. The treatment in the Aristotelian text would from this perspective be thoroughly philosophical in character.

Even within the strictly philosophical explanation, however, at times the judgments are made and the decisions are given on the strength of the Thomistic metaphysics of existence. These occasions are few, comparatively, but they are concerned with philosophically important issues. They are not marked off by any indications that they are intrusions from the outside. Rather, they seem part of the normal flow of thought. Do they show that the whole thrust of the commentary is to propound Thomistic thought, into which the great body of Aristotelian philosophy is skilfully absorbed? Is this the bearing given it by the Proem in making common being rather than separate substance the subject of the metaphysics about to be explained?

Further, does the theological concern that is implicit in the Proem affect the general character of the treatment throughout the commentary?

---

40 "Et propter hoc secundum fidem catholicam dicitur, quod nihil fit temere sive fortuito in mundo, et quod omnia subduntur divinae providentiae." *In VI Metaph.*, lect. 3, no. 1216. This means clearly enough that on account of the reasons set forth in Aristotle one is able to apply the vocabulary of the Catholic faith to the situation that is being considered.

Does it effectively alter the rank of the Aristotelian primary philosophy as supreme among the sciences? Is it the source of the assertions about the negotiable status of the Aristotelian reasons for the eternity of the world and the besouled nature of the heavenly bodies, and of those positive claims about divine providence? Is it all-pervasive enough to change the totality of the *philosophy* in the commentary, both Aristotelian and Thomistic, into the wine of theology? Or may it be dismissed as an over-scrupulous and unjustifiable propensity of a Christian theologian to go out of his way in order to insert corrections of doctrinal error and unorthodox tendencies piecemeal wherever he finds these aberrations, no matter what happens to be the real nature of the materials with which he is dealing?

With the questions already formulated, a brief glance at the other Aristotelian commentaries of Aquinas is now in order before attempting the answers.

III

In the commentary on the *Ethics,* the subject of moral philosophy is discussed not in a Proem but at the beginning of the commentary proper. It is located in human activity directed towards a purpose. On the basis of man acting first as an individual, secondly as a member of a family or household, and thirdly as a citizen, it allows moral philosophy to be divided into three parts (no. 6). The first part is treated of in the *Ethics* (no. 7). Aristotle's concern with political philosophy in the ethical treatises in explained away by stating that "the doctrine of this book contains the first elements of political science" (no. 31), and "the reflections of the present science pertain to political science, because in this science the principles of political science are given" (no. 225). The philosophy in the Aristotelian *Ethics* is accordingly regarded as a science in some way different from the Aristotelian political science. It is placed in a framework in which a general moral science is divided into three parts, of which the first is concerned with the activities of the individual man, and the third with those of civil society. The second is left for economics, understood as the science of running a household or estate.

Can any preoccupation be recognized behind this refusal to accept Aristotle's political science as the *whole* of moral philosophy?[41] The

---

41 When the three Aristotelian *Ethics* are read strictly against their original Greek pagan background, there can be little if any doubt that they make moral and political philosophy coincide. Political science is the discipline that envisages the supreme good of man and directs to it all other human activities (*E N,* I 2, 1094a27-b7), the good of the individual and the political society

threefold division of moral philosophy has a deep background in Christian tradition, through Albert the Great and Hugh of St. Victor to Cassiodorus and Boethius. [42] In spite of the very notion of "moral," implying as it does the basis of *mores,* i.e. customs developed in a common culture, this division allows a morality to a man just as an individual. With Aquinas, moreover, care is taken to restrict the absolute dominance of political science as described in Aristotle. Political science is dominant "not absolutely, but in the order of active sciences that are concerned with things human" (no. 31). Above them all is the divine science, which envisages the ultimate end of the whole universe. The Aristotelian *Ethics,* on the other hand, deals only with the imperfect happiness attainable in the present life on earth. [43]

The preoccupation, accordingly, seems to be to safeguard the supernatural happiness of the beatific vision as the ultimate end of man. This supreme goal is something to be attained by each man as an individual. Hence there can be a morality that applies to each man as an individual, and not just as a member of political society. The Aristotelian *Ethics,* in finding that human happiness consisted essentially in in-

is one and the same (2, 1094b7-10), and moral philosophy is a political study (b10-11; *M M* I 1, 1181b28-1182a1). The *Politics* is regarded as continuing the same discipline pursued in the *Nicomachean Ethics* (X 9, 1180b28-1181b24). However, for the view that Aristotle himself broke with "cette confusion platonicienne de la morale et de la politique," see R. A. Gauthier and J. Y. Jolif, *L'Ethique à Nicomaque* (Louvain & Paris 1958-1959), II, 2.

42   See Joseph Mariétan, *Problème de la classification des sciences d'Aristote à St. Thomas* (Paris 1901), pp. 67 (on Boethius); 80-81 (Cassiodorus); 137 (Hugh of St. Victor); 172-173 (Albert the Great). With Albert the vocabulary is exactly the same as that used by Aquinas. In Hugh of St. Victor the term *solitaria* occurs instead of *monastica,* and is used as an alternate for *ethica* and *moralis* in designating the science — see *Disdasc.,* II, 19, (ed. Buttimer) pp. 37.22-38.9; VI, 14, p. 131.15-17. The focus is on the exercise of the virtues, these being regarded as the acts of individuals. Boethius, though still under the influence of Aristotle in giving political science the leading rank among the branches that deal with groups, had given the branch that deals with virtues the first place in introducing the threefold division. See texts and comment in Mariétan, pp. 66-67, nn. 3-4 and 1-2. "Virtues" and the "care of the republic" are accordingly regarded as two different objects for the specification of sciences.

43   *In I Eth.,* lect. 2, no. 31; lect. 9, n. 113; lect. 10, no. 129; lect. 15, no. 180; lect. 16, no. 202; lect. 17, no. 212; *In III Eth.,* lect. 18, no. 590; *In IX Eth.,* lect. 11, no. 1912; *In X Eth.,* lect. 12, no. 2115; lect. 13, no. 2136. The *scientia divina* at no. 31 is quite clearly meant in reference to Aristotle's assertion of the supremacy of metaphysics at *Metaph.,* A 2, 982a16-19 and b4-7, yet the wording remains open to the still higher role of sacred theology in this regard. More surprising, however, is the way Aristotle's secondary happiness, the life of the active virtues, is at no. 2115 located as happiness in this life in contrast to "separate" happiness in the only too obvious sense of happiness after death: "Et per consequens felicitas, quae in hac vita consistit, est humana. Sed vita et felicitas speculativa, quae est propria intellectus, est separata et divina." In the commentary on the *Sentences,* however, the Aristotelian happiness in this life was ranged under contemplation: "Contemplatio autem Dei est duplex. Una per creaturas, quae imperfecta est, ratione jam dicta, in qua contemplatione Philosophus, *X Ethic.,* ... felicitatem contemplativam posuit, quae tamen est felicitas viae; et ad hanc ordinatur tota cognitio philosophica, quae ex rationibus creaturarum procedit." *In I Sent.,* Prol., q. 1, a. 1, Solut.; ed. Mandonnet, I, 7-8. The same is suggested at *In X Eth.,* lect. 11, no. 2110.

tellectual activity, offered a welcome means to express the theological doctrine of the beatific vision. But what was said in the *Ethics* about the requirements for the contemplative happiness, namely, friends, good looks, affluence, full life span on earth, and so on, did not apply in any obvious sense to the Christian ultimate end. The whole of the Aristotelian happiness had therefore to be located in the imperfect happiness of the present life, subordinated entirely to a higher happiness even in its role of end for human activity. With this framework of Christian tradition made manifest, the commentary of Aquinas on the *Ethics* is able to proceed in the same way as the one on the *Metaphysics*. It occupies itself with explaining the text just as the text stands, with only the occasional indication in passing that it is placing the whole consideration in a Christian setting.[44]

The commentary on the *Physics* experiences no special difficulty in accepting mobile being as the subject for natural philosophy. It places the topic, however, in the framework of abstraction from matter, contrasting definition with existence: "... there are some things whose being depends on matter, and that cannot be defined without matter."[45] In that framework a creationist metaphysics is presupposed and freely used (nos. 2001-2008). The first cause is the efficient cause of the whole being, both matter and form.[46] Movement can accordingly be regarded as beginning in an indivisible moment, not requiring any prior movement (no. 2054).

The problem in which the creationist metaphysics surfaces so clearly is admittedly theological. It is the frankly acknowledged (nos. 2041, 2043) conflict of the Aristotelian eternal world with the Christian belief that the world began in time. The Aristotelian reasons are recognized as valid where movement has to originate through another movement, but not where things begin to exist through the production of their whole being by the first cause of being (nos. 2044-2045). The truth here held on faith cannot in consequence be efficaciously attacked by the Aristotelian arguments (no. 2044). Averroes is blamed for making oc-

---

44 E.g., the reference to the supreme God as the giver of happiness at *In I Eth.*, lect. 14, no. 167. Cf. no. 169, lect. 10, no. 120, and lect. 18, no. 223. See also the example of St. Lawrence at *In III Eth.*, lect. 2, no. 395.

45 *In I Phys.*, lect. 1, no. 3. Cf. nos. 1-6. The framework is dependence or lack of dependence on matter *secundum esse, secundum rationem. Ibid.*, no. 3.

46 "Ex hoc ergo quod omne particulare agens presupponit materiam quam non agit, non oportet opinari quod Primum Agens Universale, quod est activum *totius entis,* aliquid praesupponit quasi non creatum ab ipso." *In VIII Phys.,* lect. 2, no. 2000. This is considered to be in accord with the meaning (*intentio* — no. 2001) of Aristotle and with his knowledge of the principle of all being (*totius esse* — no. 2007). The efflux is not movement or change, but emanation from an agent who is acting voluntarily (nos. 2046-2047).

casion of these arguments to attack the faith (no. 1996), and the reader's confidence in him is softened by showing how the Arabian commentator's understanding of Aristotle's method is "ridiculous" (no. 1970). It makes everything appear confused and without order, and his basic reason is "entirely frivolous" (no. 1972).

The genre of theological polemic is unmistakable in this manner of handling the problem of the world's eternity. Nevertheless, just as in the commentaries on the *Metaphysics* and on the *Ethics,* the manifestations of sacred theology and existential metaphysics are very rare.[47] The procedure in its near entirety consists in explanation of the text just as the text stands, quite in accord with the procedure in the other two commentaries. Yet it can bring in the theological and existential considerations without any indications or feeling of an alleged change to a different type of treatment. They all seem to be integral parts of the enterprise, rather than intrusions from outside.

The Proem to the commentary on *Perihermeneias* (*De Interpretatione*) divides the science of logic according to the three activities of the intellect, namely simple apprehension, enunciation ("judgment" — nos. 31-32), and reasoning. The first two of these activities are expressly taken from an Aristotelian division, and the third is regarded as added (no. 1). Logic is without hesitation projected as a science.[48] Mention of essence or quiddity as understood "absolutely" through simple apprehension seems to presuppose the metaphysical doctrine of existence as grasped through judgment. Existence as the specifying object of judgment seems likewise understood in the explanation of truth (no. 31). Existence is explicitly presented as the actuality of every form, either substantial or accidental (nos. 71-73). Likewise unmistakable is the existential dependence of all effects on the divine will, in the explanation of God's knowledge of future contingents (nos. 195-197), and the theological motif of safeguarding the Christian notion of providence.

In the commentary on the *Posterior Analytics*[49] the theological concern does not appear, but the existential metaphysics seems back of the

---

47   E.g., the truth that God made other things on account of himself, yet without need of them for his happiness, *In VIII Phys.,* lect. 2, no. 2051; and the assertion that he can have eternal understanding of non-eternal things, no. 2047. Also the difference of the faith from the position of Anaxagoras, at lect. 3, no. 2067.

48   "Cum autem Logica dicatur rationalis scientia, necesse est quod eius consideratio versetur circa ea quae pertinent ad tres praedictas operationes rationis." *In I Periherm.,* Proem., Spiazzi no. 2. On the problem of logic and the Aristotelian division of the sciences, see Mariétan, pp. 20-25; 179-181.

49   On the bearing of the term "Analytics" for Aquinas, in the sense of bringing a judgment back to the first principles upon which its certainty rests, see *In I Post. Anal.,* Proem, Spiazzi no. 6.

contrast of definition with being (nos. 15-16) and of the distinction between being and substance in all things except in God (nos. 462-463), as well as of the requirement of a cause for the existence of all necessary beings except the one first principle (no. 480). Undoubtedly a theological interest can be detected behind this last requirement, but the language remains strictly philosophical and does not allow any theological motif to appear openly. Logic is presented as a science in the Proem (no. 2), and the Aristotelian treatises on it are located in the framework of the three activities of the human intellect (nos. 4-6).

The commentary on the *De Anima* locates its study in the framework of the sciences in which first philosophy deals with things that either are or can be without matter. [50] The existential setting is still clearer in the explanation of cognition through spiritual existence in contrast to natural existence (nos. 43, 159, 282-284, 553), and in the twofold existence to which the common nature is in this way open (nos. 378-380). Theological interests are evident in the distinction of God from the other separate substances, from the viewpoint of intellection (no. 726), and in the explanation of the two intellects as powers of the soul (734-745). On the other hand, no existential stress is here laid on the Aristotelian dictum that for living things to live is to be. [51]

The commentary on *De Sensu et Sensato* likewise uses the framework of separation *secundum esse et rationem* (no. 1), and of the twofold existence of the natures of things (nos. 213, 291). The commentaries on *De Memoria et Reminiscentia* and *Meteorologica* seem occupied solely with the explanation of the Aristotelian text. That on *De Caelo et de Mundo* invokes the Catholic faith for the creation of the world in time (nos. 64-66, 287), and in these passages and elsewhere (no. 91) repeats that God causes the heavens as an intelligent agent. The reasons given by Aristotle hold only against an original production of things by way of motion, and in no way militate against the teaching of the Catholic faith. The supreme God is distinguished from the other separate substances (nos. 295, 334), and is viewed as conserving a nature (no. 295), and as the cause that imparts existence and motion (nos. 291, 295, 299,

---

50 *In I de An.*, lect. 2, Pirotta no. 28. Though the commentary on Book I of the *De Anima* is the report of a *lectio* of Aquinas, it is accepted as authentic Thomistic doctrine; see preface in Pirotta edition (Turin 1925), pp. xi-xii.

51 *In II de An.*, lect. 7, no. 319. In the commentary on the *Sentences* a strongly existential explanation of the text had been given: "Alio modo dicitur esse ipse actus essentiae; sicut vivere, quod est esse viventibus, est animae actus; non actus secundus, qui est operatio, sed actus primus." *In I Sent.*, d. 33, q. 1, a. 1, ad 1m; ed. Mandonnet, I, 766. Similarly at *In II de Cael. et Mund.*, lect. 4, no. 334, *vivere* is explained as having two meanings, namely existence (*esse*) and operation.

A discussion of the different instances of the use of this Aristotelian passage by Aquinas may be found in A. E. Wingell, "*Vivere Viventibus Est Esse* in Aristotle and St. Thomas," *The Modern Schoolman*, 38 (1961), 85-120.

334). Aristotle is asserted to have regarded God as the maker, and not only the final cause of the heavenly bodies (no. 91). The commentary on *De Generatione et Corruptione* (Proem, no. 2) uses the framework in which as in metaphysics the common genus considered by a science is contradistinguished from the cause of that genus. In the commentary on the *Politics* (Proem, no. 6) the subject matter is regarded as contained under that of the moral sciences in general, and as the culminating point of the philosophy that is concerned with things human (no. 7). The doctrine, including the discussion on slavery (nos. 47-96), is explained just as it stands in the text. The error of the Gentiles in anthropomorphizing the separate substances created by the one supreme God (no. 30; cf. no. 154) and similarly in calling great rulers gods (no. 84), is noted. The same overwhelming quantitative predominance of explanation of the text as it stands, with occasional appearance of the already noted theological and existential considerations, is accordingly observable in these commentaries.[52]

On the whole, then, one may say that the other commentaries continue to manifest the pattern shown in the commentary on the *Metaphysics*. The sciences are made to fit into the framework in which metaphysics deals with common being as subject and separate substance as cause of the subject. The recognition of a moral science for individual actions, distinct from political philosophy, is added. The theological interests of creation, of the supremacy of God over the other separate substances, and of universal divine providence, are safeguarded wherever occasion demands. Polytheism is branded an error. Finally, the Thomistic metaphysics of existence, in the relation of existence to common nature and in the understanding of efficient causality as the bestowal of existence, seems taken for granted throughout.

IV

The above survey makes it clear that, except for quantitatively minimal proportions, the Aristotelian commentaries of Aquinas are made up of explanations of the text just as it stands, with discussions of its background and of the various opinions of others about it. In all this the Aquinas commentaries do not range outside the limits of the modern notion about what a commentary should be. But in two thirds of these commentaries on Aristotle there are passages that show an

---

52 The commentaries in this paragraph have been cited according to the numbers used in the Marietti editions.

overriding theological concern. In two thirds of them there are likewise passages that reveal a definitely existential metaphysics, something not found in the Aristotelian texts. Finally, three quarters of the commentaries have passages that locate their subject matter in a framework of the sciences rather different from that of Aristotle.

How is this situation to be assessed? May one close one's eyes to the comparatively small number of passages that introduce theological and existential considerations, as well within the percentage limit to be expected in any commentator with strong religious convictions and definite metaphysical tendencies of his own? May one regard the passages that locate the Aristotelian treatises within the then contemporary classification of the sciences as a quite normal failure to see outside the perspective of the times, much as a modern commentator is hardly blamed for putting Aristotle into frameworks like those of ontology, psychology, or philosophy of science? May all these passages as it were be mentally excised and the other ten commentaries be allowed to join the two in which no indication of theological or existential interest appears, and in which no attempt is made at science classification? In this case the Aristotelian commentaries of Aquinas would be straight philosophical explanations of the text, with all the restrictions and merits and faults of their times.

Can one, though, legitimately make this mental excision of the passages that jar with the interpretation? Do not these passages, relatively few in number as they are, set rather the whole tone of the commentaries? Certainly in their own settings they show no signs of being intrusions into the general procedure of the thought. They read as though they belong to the same original inspiration, and unable to be regarded as alien incursions except on norms that were not those of the writer. They flow forcefully from what seems to be a unitary source.

If so, what is that source? It could hardly be the metaphysical or epistemological interest. These could not be for Aquinas the inspiration of the overriding theological concern. Sacred theology, on the contrary, could be and normally would be the source of existential and epistemological inquiries for him. His most penetrating metaphysical thought is found in the commentary on the *Sentences* and other professedly theological works. His most extensive study of the classification of the sciences is in his commentary on Boethius' *De Trinitate*. For him sacred theology, as the absolutely highest wisdom, has the office of judging and orienting the results of all the other sciences.[53] It has every right, accordingly, to survey their results as occasion

---

53 *ST*, I, 1, 6c. Cf.: "Ita, cum finis totius philosophiae sit infra finem theologiae, et ordinatus

demands. Exactly that, it seems, has been done in the Aquinas commentaries on Aristotle. In these commentaries, then, may one say that Aquinas continues his dedication to the work of theological wisdom,[54] and that in them he continues to change what was water in the other sciences into the wine of theology?[55] The use of a new existential metaphysics may be taken as established. But that is still on the philosophical level. It does not just in itself prove theological motivation. Its structure is thoroughly philosophical. May the philosophical structure be regarded as remaining intact while its content functions as a part, in fact by far the greatest part quantitatively, of a colloidal theological enterprise?

The colloidal nature of wine allows the water to be extracted from it and replaced without too much difficulty. The overwhelmingly preponderant part of the commentaries may be extracted in similar fashion from the theological setting given it by the comparatively few theological passages. Extraction of philosophical statements from professed theological works such as the *Summa Theologiae* and the commentary on the *Sentences* has been standard practice for centuries. Likewise the four Aristotelian commentaries in which no theological assertions occur may be viewed in isolation from the whole work of Aquinas and be regarded as merely philosophical commentaries. But in doing so is one encountering the real St. Thomas? Is one understanding what he is doing? Is one at all in tune with the spirit of faith endeavoring to understand all the things with which it comes in contact?

A more vivid objection arises from the quantitative proportions of the theological and philosophical passages. Can a few drops of wine be expected to change into itself a chain of rather large lakes? Here the metaphor seems to break down. The biological simile of a few clusters of living cells affecting the whole medium would be more in order. At any rate, the medieval mind experienced no difficulty in seeing an author express as his own the material taken nearly one hundred per cent from other writers. Peter Lombard, for instance, could be regarded as the author of everything in his four books of *Sentences*, even though

---

ad ipsum, theologia debet omnibus aliis scientiis imperare et uti his quae in eis traduntur." *In I Sent.,* Prol., q. 1, a. 1, Solut.; ed. Mandonnet, I, 8.

54 Cf. expression of this dedication in the *Contra Gentiles*: "Assumpta igitur ex divina pietate fiducia sapientis officium prosequendi, ... propositum nostrae intentionis est veritatem quam fides Catholica profitetur, pro nostro modulo manifestare... et quomodo demonstrativa veritas fidei Christianae religionis concordet". *CG,* I, 2, Assumpta.

55 "Unde illi, qui utuntur philosophicis documentis in sacra doctrina redigendo in obsequium fidei, non miscent aquam vino, sed aquam convertunt in vinum." *In Boeth. de Trin.,* II, 3, ad 5m; ed. Decker, p. 96.18-20. On the topic, see A. C. Pegis, "*Sub Ratione Dei*: A Reply to Professor Anderson," *The New Scholasticism,* 39 (1965), 141-157.

practically all the material was taken from others.[56] As long as the writer was asserting mastery over material used and was organizing and directing it towards his own purpose, he was expressing it as his own. There is accordingly not too much difficulty in regarding St. Thomas, in taking on the duties of the wise man (*CG*, I, 2), as considering himself to be pursuing the work of sacred theology throughout the whole course of his commentaries on the Aristotelian text.

It is, of course, much easier to apply this conception of philosophy changed into theology to a work like the *Contra Gentiles*,[57] than to writings that are professedly commentaries on a pagan philosopher. Yet is the difference that crucial? The theologian is writing in the service of faith (supra, n. 55). He sees a wealth of rationally developed truth in the pagan source. What better way to bring it into the service of faith than by exploring it painstakingly word for word, presenting it as a whole, and allowing it thereby to further the understanding of the Christian conception of things? Does not this accomplish the purpose much better than a piecemeal citation of convenient passages? And will not this perspective allow the four commentaries in which there is no express mention of theological interests to be viewed as an integral part of the whole enterprise? Will they be any less theological in character than the long passages within the other commentaries in which no explicit mention of theological concern is found?

But may not the Thomistic commentaries on Aristotle be regarded as Christian philosophy, genuinely philosophical in character yet brought under Christian goals? The notion of Christian philosophy is a difficult one. It has received many interpretations in recent years.[58] If it is to be kept strictly on the philosophical level, however, it cannot use revealed truths as principles for its reasoning.[59] It cannot give them a probative function. Yet the Thomistic commentaries on Aristotle are dominated

---

56   So, for St. Bonaventure, *In I Sent.*, Proem, q. 4, the writer of the *Sentences* was exercising the function not of a scribe or of a compiler or of a commentator, but of an author: "Talis fuit Magister, qui sententias suas ponit et Patrum sententiis confirmat. Unde vere debet dici auctor huius libri". *Ibid.* Resp. This theme in Bonaventure is discussed in John Quinn, *The Historical Constitution of St. Bonaventure's Philosophy* (Toronto 1973).

57   See Pegis, art. cit., pp. 143-146.

58   See Maurice Nédoncelle, *Is There a Christian Philosophy*? tr. Illtyd Trethowan (New York 1960), pp. 85-114.

59   Aquinas states clearly the difference between the two procedures, philosophical and theological: "Vel procedunt ex principiis fidei, ... Ex his autem principiis ita probatur aliquid apud fideles sicut etiam ex principiis naturaliter notis probatur aliquid apud omnes. Unde etiam theologia scientia est". *ST*, II-II, 1, 5, ad 2m.

The work of James C. Doig, *Aquinas on Metaphysics* (The Hague 1972), appeared after this paper had been completed. Its study of the nature of Aquinas' commentary on the *Metaphysics* bears out the views of the present article, though it does not trace the reasons for the unity of Aquinas' treatment to his theological activities.

by this properly theological direction. The creation of the world in time is taught as the way the case actually is. The besouled nature of the heavenly bodies is rejected. Perfect human happiness, the first principle of ethics, is located definitely in the beatific vision. Divine providence is a "must". These considerations dominate the Thomistic interpretation of Aristotle in the commentaries. They seem to generate theology, not philosophy. The purpose is to defend revealed truth, not just Christian philosophical truth.

The distinction between "personal" works of Aquinas and commentaries is obvious and has to remain. In the "personal" works he sets his own order of discussion. In the commentaries he is bound by the order in the text before him. Correspondingly, the theological character of the works will vary. A commentary on a philosophical study will not be theological in the same way and to the same extent that the *Summae* and the *Quaestiones Disputatae* are theological. The material that is brought into theological service will manifest at far greater length its philosophical structure. The question therefore is not "theology *or* philosophy?" It concerns theology *and* philosophy found together. The question is whether the theology or the philosophy gives the work as a whole its characteristic specification. Here, just as in a colloidal solution, the issue of degrees enters. The *Summa Theologiae* is more manifestly theological than the *Summa contra Gentiles*, and both are more so than the Aristotelian commentaries. But the best philosophy in Aquinas is to be found in the most theological of his writings. Its cogency and its worth as philosophy are not at all diminished. Yet the anvil on which it was hammered into shape was theology.

This limited and selective participation in philosophy by the theologian is still a problem today. Aquinas at the height of his theological career devoted a decade to the interpretation of Aristotle. There is no indication that this was a side interest or a hobby. Rather, the theologian seemed to feel the need of philosophical guidance from Aristotle for his own theological work. Was this guidance, with all its prudential selection and its specially directed development, not incorporated into the theological enterprise? And may it not remain genuinely philosophy as material used by a theologian, while functioning on the theological level as the most apt medium for developing and expressing an overall theological conception of things?

THE *NICOMACHEAN ETHICS* AND THOMAS AQUINAS

Vernon J. Bourke

WITH the publication of the critical edition of St. Thomas' commentary on Aristotle's *Nicomachean Ethics* the time has come for an examination of what we know and what we do not know about this Thomistic work.[1] The long Latin "Preface" to the Leonine text was written by R. A. Gauthier, O.P. In spite of its thoroughness, this introduction raises many new problems and its answers to some of the old ones may not be entirely satisfactory.[2] The text of the new edition differs considerably from the vulgarized text in earlier printings of the *Commentary*. Comparison of readings in a key section, such as the explanation of prudence in Book VI, 4, reveals more than a dozen significant changes in the text, several consisting of whole clauses or phrases that are lacking in older editions.[3] This means that future studies of this commentary must be based on the Leonine text; it is probably the best edited work of St. Thomas in the Leonine edition.[4]

In what follows, we propose to examine some of the problems associated with Aquinas' exposition of the NE: the question of the Latin version used by Thomas, his utilization of preceding commentaries, the time and place of composition of his commentary, and the value of the commentary in modern Thomistic and Aristotelian studies.

---

1 Sancti Thomae de Aquino, *Opera Omnia*, iussu Leonis XIII P.M. edita, tomus XLVII: *Sententia Libri Ethicorum*, cura et studio Fratrum Praedicatorum, vol. 1, Praefatio, Libri I-III; vol. 2, Libri IV-X, Indices (Romae: Ad Sancta Sabinae 1969) pp. 275*, 193, 201-683.

A note at the bottom of p. 268* tells us what Dominican scholars worked on this edition: L. J. Bataillon, B. Guyot and M. Perrier transliterated the codices; R. A. Gauthier and M. Gils collated the MSS; Gauthier investigated the sources of the commentary (assisted by R. Gallet, A. M. Kenzeler and J. Peters) and he also "adapted" the Latin text of the *Nicomachean Ethics* (hereafter NE) to the commentary.

2 Because of its cost ($ 76 U.S.), Leonine tome XLVII will be available in only a few special libraries and there will be few reviews. The notice by B. Quelquejeu in *Revue des sciences philosophiques et théologiques* 53 (1969) 400, is a non-critical description.

3 Compare *In VI Ethicorum*, ed. R. M. Spiazzi (Turin 1964) pp. 386-389, with *Sententia Libri Ethicorum* (ed. Leon.) pp. 344-347. The Leonine editors have changed the usual title of the commentary and have deleted the paragraph nos. that were inserted in the Marietti printings.

4 Unfortunately the English translation (*Commentary on the Nicomachean Ethics*, trans. by C. I. Litzinger, 2 vols. [Chicago 1964]) was done before the Leonine text was printed. If a revised printing of the English is ever brought out, it should have a new introduction and its readings should be corrected throughout the commentary.

VERSIONS OF THE NE AVAILABLE TO AQUINAS

Concerning the Latin text of the *Ethics* that Aquinas used, some writers say that he commented on a translation made, or revised, by William of Moerbeke.[5] Other respectable scholars even claim that this Moerbeke version is found in extant manuscripts.[6] However, in 1946, Martin Grabmann reviewed the whole problem of the extent of William of Moerbeke's translations of Aristotle and showed that there is little evidence for accepting the existence of a Moerbeke text of the NE.[7] Even earlier, A. Pelzer had concluded that Moerbeke never did produce a version of Aristotle's *Ethics*.[8] Of course, Ezio Franceschini did claim that William had made a revision of Grosseteste's translation of NE but this contention was subjected to severe criticism by scholars like Leo Keeler and Antoine Dondaine.[9] The fact remains, however, that some sort of revision of the Grosseteste version was made by someone working early in the second half of the thirteenth century, and a copy of this revision was the base for Thomas Aquinas' exposition.[10]

A complete Latin translation of the NE may have been made by some unknown scholar in the twelfth century.[11] We have no evidence

5   Thus Litzinger ("Introduction," I, xii) speaks rather confidently of the version "generally attributed to William of Moerbeke, as found in the Cathala-Spiazzi edition." He adds that, "it was the basis for the Commentary, although St. Thomas at times varies from this rendition."

6   "As regards the exegesis of the *Ethics*, we are now in a position to discern the role played by the Moerbeke revision done upon the previous version of Grosseteste. In fact, as we have seen, a manuscript tradition of the Moerbeke Greco-Latin version is clearly discernible." M. D. Chenu, *Toward Understanding St. Thomas*, trans. A. M. Landry and Dominic Hughes (Chicago 1964) p. 217. Cf. I. T. Eschmann, "Catalogue of St. Thomas's Works" in E. Gilson, *The Christian Philosophy of St. Thomas Aquinas* (New York 1956) p. 404.

7   *Guglielmo di Moerbeke, O.P., il traduttore delle opere di Aristotele* (Roma 1946) pp. 103-111.

8   "Les versions latines des ouvrages de morale conservés sous le nom d'Aristote," *Revue néoscolastique de philosophie* 23 (1921) 316-341; 378-412.

9   For Franceschini's main argument see "La revisione Moerbekiana della 'Translatio Lincolniensis' dell'Etica Nicomachea," *Rivista di filosofia neoscolastica* 30 (1938) 150-162. Leo Keeler argued ("The Alleged Revision of R. Grosseteste's Translation of the Ethics," *Gregorianum* 18 [1937] 410-425) that the textual variants used by Franceschini were really derived from the *Notule* in Grosseteste's translation. See also A. Dondaine, in *Bulletin thomiste* 6 (1940-42) 90-94.

10   Gauthier, *Praefatio in Sententia Libri Ethicorum* (ed. Leon. XLVII, 1, hereafter cited as *Praefatio*) p. 232*, insists that this revision of Grosseteste was not made by Moerbeke: "nec ulla est causa cur virum doctum qui post Robertum Grosseteste *Librum Ethicorum* iterum recognovit Guillelmum de Moerbeke fuisse suspicemur." Cf. Gauthier, "Introduction," to Aristotle, *L'Ethique à Nicomaque*, 2me éd. (Louvain-Paris 1970) pp. 125-126. Hereafter cited as *Introduction E N.*

11   L. Minio-Paluello, "Iacobus Veneticus Grecus: Canonist and Translator of Aristotle," *Traditio* 8 (1952) 279. There is one MS (Cambridge, Mass., Library of Harvard University, olim Library of Philip Hofer, Typ. 233 H, f. 17ra-58ra, XIII s.) which seems to contain parts of this twelfth-century version. Cf. Gauthier, *Praefatio*, p. 204*.

that this twelfth-century version was available as a complete text at any point in the thirteenth century. Certain parts of the NE were read in Latin in the early decades of the century of St. Thomas. These may have been excerpts from the twelfth-century version, or they may have been fragmentary translations from the early thirteenth century. In any case, Books II and III (the *Ethica vetus*), plus Book I (the *Ethica nova*), plus portions of Books VII and VIII (the *Ethica Borghesiana*) were in Latin before Robert Grosseteste began to translate the NE.[12] These fragmentary translations are not unimportant. Both Albert the Great and Thomas Aquinas used them — even after they could have consulted the newer and more complete text provided by Grosseteste. It is even possible that Hermannus Alemannus translated some parts of the NE which were read in the thirteenth century.[13]

However, it is now generally accepted that the only complete thirteenth-century translation of the NE was made by Robert Grosseteste about the years 1246-1247.[14] At the time that Albert was commenting on Peter Lombard's *Sentences* (before 1245) he did not know the whole text of the NE; but in the period 1248-1252, when he was lecturing on the NE, he of course had the full text in the version of Robert Grosseteste.[15] This translation was made from the Greek and was accompanied by passages translated from Greek commentators (such as Aspasius and Eustratius) plus certain annotations (*notule*) written by Grosseteste himself.[16] It was probably in the next decade (1250-1260) that Grosseteste's translation was copied, without the comments from the Greeks and without his own *Notule*, and this constituted an *editio minor* of the *translatio Lincolniensis*.[17]

This smaller edition of Grosseteste's work was revised at some time after mid-century by a scholar who knew Greek. Many histories and reference works continue to attribute this revision to William of Moerbeke. But, as we have seen, this is probably incorrect. Gauthier lists

12 For further data consult the forthcoming vol. XXVI of *Aristoteles Latinus*; it is devoted to the mediaeval Latin translations of the NE.

13 Cf. Gauthier, *Introduction EN*, pp. 114-115.

14 D. A. Callus, "The Date of Grosseteste's Translations and Commentaries on the Ps. Dionysius and the Nicomachean Ethics," *Recherches de théologie ancienne et médiévale* 4 (1947) 201. See also O. Lottin, "Saint Albert le Grand et l'Ethique à Nicomaque," *BGPM*, Suppl. III, 1 (Münster 1935) 611-626.

15 Jean Dunbabin, "The Two Commentaries of Albertus Magnus on the Nicomachean Ethics," *RTAM* 30 (1963) 232.

16 S. H. Thomson, "The 'Notule' of Grosseteste on the *Nicomachean Ethics*," *Proceedings of the British Academy* 19 (1933) 195-218.

17 Gauthier, *Praefatio*, p. 206*, where three MSS (plus the Harvard MS mentioned above, note 11, which appears to have some parts of the Grosseteste version in contaminated form) are listed as representing the tradition of the *editio minor*.

about ten manuscripts containing this revision which are either Parisian or copied from Paris manuscripts. [18] Although the research on the catchwords and manuscript traditions conducted by Gauthier and his associates, in connection with the making of the Leonine edition, indicates that it was this revision of the Grosseteste version that was used by Thomas Aquinas, [19] it is also clear that Aquinas was acquainted with the *Ethica vetus* and *nova*, with some of the texts of the Greek commentators, and of course with the material in Albert's *Lectures* on the NE, as we shall see.

Gauthier contends that St. Thomas derived his various readings of the NE from the one manuscript prepared by the anonymous revisor mentioned above. [20] Indeed, Thomas' use of a single manuscript of the Grosseteste revision is associated by the Leonine editor with the conclusion that Aquinas was ignorant of what even mediaeval scholars knew about textual criticism. [21]

However this may be, it has not been possible to identify the manuscript that was actually used by Thomas Aquinas. In fact, there is still some doubt that it is clearly established that there was but this one manuscript at Thomas' disposal. This is the reason why the Latin text of the NE, printed in tome XLVII of the Leonine edition, is admitted to be "adapted" by R. A. Gauthier. [22] We are not yet finished with the investigation of the text and sources used by Aquinas, as a commentator on the NE. The continuing uncertainty is closely connected with the related problems of where and when he produced his commentary. [23]

---

18 Gauthier, *Praefatio,* pp. 206*-208*; this close identification of the text tradition of the revision with Paris would certainly cast doubt on its association with Moerbeke.

19 Ibid., p. 231*.

20 Ibid., p. 234*.

21 "Quin contra, si candide confitemur Thomam artis criticae, ut illis temporibus solebat, fere expertem unum solum codicem et hunc corruptum et contaminatum ad explicandam *Libri Ethicorum* sententiam adhibuisse, inanes glorias ei sane denegabimus, solidior tamen ei manebit gloria sapientis . . ." Ibid.

22 "Praefationem conscripsit P. R. A. Gauthier, qui etiam Aristotelis textum Thomae Sententiae aptavit." *Praefatio,* p. 268*.

23 G. Meersemann ("Les Manuscrits du cours inédit d'Albert le Grand sur la Morale à Nicomaque, recueilli et rédigé par saint Thomas d'Aquin," *Revue néoscolastique de philosophie* 38 [1935] 82) was overconfident in suggesting that the Grosseteste version of the N E is what is in the Marietti printings. This vulgarized text is apparently a combination of several versions.

COMMENTARIES PRIOR TO ST. THOMAS

Among the influences on St. Thomas' commentary are three types of earlier expositions of Aristotle's *Ethics*. These were commentaries in Greek, in Arabic, and in Latin. The ancient Greek commentaries included an explanation of Books I-IV, VII (in part) and VIII by the second-century A.D. scholar named Aspasius. There is also an anonymous Greek commentary on Books II-IV, dating from about the sixth century A.D. Later, Christian Greek scholarship added a commentary on Books V and IX-X, by Michael Ephesius (11th c.), a commentary on Books I and VI by Eustratius (11th c.) and an anonymous commentary on Book VII, from the twelfth or thirteenth century.

Aquinas has echoes of the views of Aspasius throughout his commentary on the eighth book.[24] The Leonine *Index Auctorum*[25] and the footnotes to Thomas' exposition of Book VIII show this dependence on Aspasius. However, Gauthier doubts that Thomas read Aspasius directly, or even in the passages included with Grosseteste's first version of the NE. Instead, Gauthier is convinced that Aquinas was indebted to Albert's *Lectura* for what is found from the Greek commentators in the Thomistic *Commentary*.[26] However it is derived, Thomas' exposition of Books I and VI shows that he knew something of Eustratius' views.[27] On the other hand, there is less evidence for a positive influence from Michael Ephesius or the anonymous Greek commentaries.[28]

In the world of mediaeval Arabic scholarship one finds paraphrases, summaries and commentaries of Aristotle's *Ethics* from the tenth century onward. Alfarabi (10th c.) commented on portions of the N E and a Latin version of his work was probably known to Albert at the time of his first *Lectura*.[29] The Tahdhib al-Akhlaq of Ibn Miskawaihi (11th c.) was the outstanding Mohammedan adaptation of Aristotelian ethics but its influence on Aquinas is not established. Such an influence would, in any case, be indirect, via twelfth-century compilations.[30] No com-

---

24 "S. Thomas a fait usage, et même de façon assez suivie, de l'œuvre d'Aspasius. La similitude frappante de plusieurs passages ne saurait trouver d'autre explication." W. Stinissen, "De commentaar van Thomas op Boek VIII en IX van de Nicomachische Ethiek. Zijn verhouding tot de Griekse commentaren," *Tijdschrift voor Philosophie* 20 (1958) p. 748 in the French Summary.

25 *Sententia Libri Ethicorum*, ed. Leon. XLVII, 2, p. 625.

26 Thus Gauthier writes: "suspectum ergo Eustratium habuit Thomas, quia Albertum, non autem Eustratium, legit." *Praefatio*, p. 247*.

27 However derived, the influence of Eustratius on Books I and VI of Thomas' *Commentary* is somewhat evident. See the footnotes of these books in the Leonine edition.

28 Cf. Stinissen, art. cit., p. 748.

29 Gauthier, *Introduction E N*, p. 109.

30 See V. J. Bourke, *History of Ethics* (New York 1968) pp. 76-77.

mentary on the NE is now attributed to Avicenna but the impact of his
development of Aristotelian psychology is evident in Thomas Aquinas'
ethics commentary.[31] It was Averroes' *Middle Commentary* on the
Ethics that was well known to Aquinas. There are more than thirty
passages in the Thomistic commentary which show some relation to the
thought of Averroes.[32] Of course, it is well known that the style of
Aquinas' *Commentary on the Ethics* is similar to that of the Averroistic
middle commentaries. In the final analysis, the most important lesson
that Thomas may have learned from the Arabs as commentators is that
Aristotelian ethics is not entirely incompatible with a strong theistic
position.

Several commentaries on the NE are found in Latin before St.
Thomas' time. At least six courses on the *Ethica vetus* and *nova*, given
by Masters in the Arts faculty at Paris, have now been identified in
manuscripts. Both Albert and Thomas knew some of these partial commentaries and used various formulae from them.[33] However, it is now
difficult to determine whether Thomas had direct access to such records
of Arts courses, at the time that he was working on his own exposition.

Another pre-thomistic Latin compilation was precisely Grosseteste's
translation of the complete text of the NE, with his own *Notule* and the
selected passages from the Greek commentators. This collection was
available in Latin before mid-century and, in fact, was used in Albert's
first course on the *Ethics*.[34] We have already discussed the possibility of
Thomas using the Greek commentaries (and it would have been through
the Grosseteste version, if the influence was direct) but the "Notes"
composed by Robert Grosseteste pose still another problem. Gauthier
has printed many of these *Notule* in the footnotes to the Leonine
edition of Thomas' *Sententia Libri Ethicorum*. They run throughout the
critical apparatus. Yet Thomas' own text does not show that he was
reading the Grosseteste "Notes" at the time that the Thomistic exposition was made. One must admit that, in some cases, Thomas uses
readings and gives explanations that would probably have been corrected, if he had had the Grosseteste "Notes" before him. It is, then, the
opinion of the Leonine editor that Thomas commented on a manuscript

---

31   The Leonine *Index* (vol. 2, 626) records more than ten resemblances to Avicenna's *De
anima (Liber VI Naturalium)*.
32   Leonine *Index*, s.v. Averroes (vol. 2, 626).
33   Gauthier, *Praefatio*, pp. 236*-246*.
34   The first two books of Grosseteste's version, plus his translation of Eustratius and the
anonymous commentary on Book II, have been critically edited by H. P. F. Mercken under the
title: *Aristoteles over de menselijke Volkomenheid* (Brussels 1964). In the same series of the
Flemish Academy of Science, Letters and Fine Arts, W. Stinissen has edited Books VIII-IX of
Grosseteste's version, under the title: *Aristoteles over de Vriendschap* (Brussels 1963).

that contained the Grosseteste version of the NE but lacked both the *Notule* and the materials from the Greek commentators.

Since the pioneering study of A. Pelzer in the early 1920's, we have known that Albert the Great lectured on the *Nicomachean Ethics*, when Aquinas was his student, and that several manuscripts of this course are extant, deriving from a *reportatio* made by Thomas Aquinas. [35] In fact, Albert produced two explanations of the NE, the first of which is closely connected with the Thomistic *Commentary*, and a second *Commentarium* which may not have been known to Aquinas. [36]

Before the mid-1240's Albert knew and cited some parts of the *Nicomachean Ethics*. [37] His early *Tractatus de natura boni* has two quotations from the NE. His *Summa de creaturis* gives evidence that Albert now knew more than the *Ethica vetus* and *nova* but his treatment of justice, at this time, depends on the first Book (rather than the more developed Book V) of the NE. The third Book of Albert's *Commentary on the Sentences* (after 1247) shows that his knowledge of the NE is growing more extensive: he now knows the treatment of liberality in NE IV and of justice in the fifth Book. When we look at Albert's comments on the fourth Book of the *Sentences*, we see that he has the full text of Grosseteste's translation of the *Ethics* in his hands. [38]

It was in the years between 1248 and 1252 that Albert headed the Dominican *studium generale* and gave the lectures that were written up by Thomas Aquinas. Albert's *Lectura in Libros Ethicorum* exists now in at least five manuscripts and a printed edition has been started. [39] Besides the analysis of the text and the commentary, this *Lectura* contains 502 Questions. It is a longer work and, in some ways, more thorough than St. Thomas' *Commentary*. [40] Comparison of Albert's work on the NE with that of Thomas Aquinas is not easy, however. For

---

35   A. Pelzer, "Le cours inédit d'Albert le Grand sur la Morale à Nicomaque recueilli et rédigé par S. Thomas d'Aquin," *Revue néoscolastique de philosophie* 24 (1922) 333-361, 479-520; reprinted in *Etudes d'histoire littéraire sur la scolastique médiévale* (Louvain 1964) pp. 272-335.

36   C. H. Lohr, "Medieval Latin Aristotle Commentaries: Authors A-F," *Traditio* 23 (1967) 344. But see Gauthier, *Introduction E N*, p. 130, where he suggests that *Sententia Libri Ethicorum* I, 1 (ed. Leon. p. 5, lines 142-155) may refer to Albert's *Commentarium*.

37   For details of these findings, see O. Lottin, "Saint Albert le Grand et l'*Ethique à Nicomaque*," *Aus der Geisteswelt des Mittelalters*, Beiträge Supplement, III (Münster 1935) 611-621.

38   Lottin's research is confirmed by D. A. Callus, "The Date of Grosseteste's Translations," *RTAM* 14 (1947) 205.

39   The two best MSS are Vat. lat. 722, and Cambridge, Gonville and Caius 510 (388). See Dunbabin, art. cit., p. 233; and Meersemann, art. cit., pp. 70-83. For the critical edition: Albertus Magnus, *Super Ethica, Commentum et Questiones, tres libros priores*, ed. Wilhelmus Kübel (*Opera Omnia*, vol. XIV, 1, 1; Köln 1968).

40   In ed. Leon. Thomas' *Commentary* runs to about 600 pages, including Aristotle's text; less than one third of Albert's *Lectura* in the Kübel ed. takes up 220 pages.

one thing, we do not know how much of the *Lectura* is due to Albert and how much to his young reporter, Thomas. Pelzer thought that Thomas reworked and completed the oral materials copied from Albert's classes.[41] Some of the *Quaestiones* in the *Lectura* have the clarity and profundity of questions in the *Secunda Pars* of St. Thomas' *Summa Theologiae*.[42] No other commentary now attributable to Albert has the complicated style or thoroughness of the *Lectura*. On the other hand, the exposition of the text and the use of added questions in the *Lectura* are reminiscent of Aquinas' *Commentary on Boethius' De Trinitate*.

No doubt the Albertine *Lectura* is an outstanding mediaeval exposition of the NE.[43] In his edition of Aristotle's *Nicomachean Ethics*, Gauthier is almost effusive in his praise of Albert's *Lectura*.[44] Now, in the "Preface" to the Leonine edition of Thomas' *Commentary*, more than twenty pages are devoted to the *Lectura*.[45] Climaxing this lengthy study is Gauthier's claim that Albert's *Lectures on the Ethics* is the main source of Thomas Aquinas' *Commentary*. This dependence is said to extend to both style and content. As far as Gauthier is concerned Aquinas used Albert as a source for the Greek commentaries, for the Latin text of the NE, and for many of the phrases (e.g. *sapientis est ordinare*) commonly considered distinctive of Thomistic terminology. We must await the printing of the complete text of Albert's *Lectura* before attempting further appraisal of these sweeping claims.

Some twenty years after giving his Cologne course on the NE, Albert returned to the text and wrote his second "commentary," a treatise of quite different character.[46] This is the *Commentarium in X Libros Ethicorum* long known in the collected works of St. Albert.[47] This work from the late 1260's is not really a commentary in the usual sense of the term. It does not contain the Latin text of the NE; nor does it include an analysis of the Aristotelian text. Divided into books, tractates and chapters, Albert's *Commentarium* is his own paraphrase of much of the thought content of the NE. The work is a semi-personal course on

---

41   "D'autre part, saint Thomas ne s'est pas contenté de mettre par écrit séance tenante, les leçons qu'il entendait chez Albert: il les a ensuite, je crois, remaniées et complétées ça et là sans recourir toutefois, lui-même, à la version de Robert Grosseteste avec son triple contenu." Pelzer, art. cit. (1922) p. 358.

42   Cf. Pelzer, art. cit. (1922) p. 348.

43   Dunbabin, art. cit. pp. 232 and 250.

44   Gauthier, *Introduction E N*, pp. 123-124.

45   *Praefatio*, pp. 235*-257*: "De Alberti Lectura."

46   Dunbabin, art. cit., p. 245, dates the second commentary in 1267-1268. It was certainly produced after Albert had resigned from the episcopate of Ratisbon (A.D. 1262).

47   *Opera Omnia*, ed. P. Jammy (Lugduni 1681) IV, 1-364; ed. A. Borgnet (Paris 1890-1899) VII, 1-611.

philosophical ethics which follows the topical order of Aristotle's ten books but does not deal with the original text, phrase by phrase. Although it uses many Greek words, the Albertine *Commentarium* contains no catch-word references.

Whether Thomas ever saw Albert's second commentary is not clear but, in any case, it played little or no part in the background of the Thomistic *Commentary*. One reason for this lack of influence may be chronological: it is quite possible that Albert's *Commentarium* post-dated Thomas' *Sententia Libri Ethicorum*. This brings us to the problem of the dating of this work of St. Thomas.

DATE AND PLACE OF COMPOSITION OF THOMAS' COMMENTARY

Thomas Aquinas seems to have known the NE throughout most of his scholarly career. Of course, we do not know that he had read any part of it during his Arts course at the University of Naples. It is probable that he studied some of Aristotle's logical and biologico-psychological writings at that time, under Masters Martin and Peter.[48] When, between 1248 and 1252, Thomas attended Albert's Cologne lectures, he must have made a thorough study of Aristotle's ethical thought. In his own lectures on the *Sentences* (A.D. 1252-1256) Thomas shows a complete mastery of the text of the NE. His *distinctio* 33, in the third book of Thomas' *Commentary on the Sentences*, is very significant on this score. Commenting on a two-page section in Peter Lombard, Aquinas now treats forty-one questions in moral theology. For the same text of Peter Lombard, Odon Rigaud used five questions, Albert four, and Bonaventure six.[49] My rapid check of this *distinctio* 33 shows Thomas making 121 explicit citations of the NE, using every book except the tenth in his commentary on this short passage. Book X of the NE is cited at the beginning of Distinction 34. There is no doubt at all, then, that as a Bachelor in Theology Aquinas was thoroughly familiar with the entire NE.

When Thomas left Paris in 1259 to spend almost a decade at various Dominican monasteries in the Papal States, he was severing his

---

48 For recent views on this early period, see Bourke, *Aquinas' Search for Wisdom* (Milwaukee 1965) pp. 20-32.

49 "Ce bachelier de 30 ans a créé ainsi 'le premier traité de théologie morale', esquisse de la seconde partie de sa Somme théologique. L'*Ethique* d'Aristote y pénètre d'une manière saisissante: alors qu'Albert, dans les mêmes circonstances, l'avait citée une douzaine de fois, Bonaventure trois fois, Thomas s'y réfère 125 fois." A. Walz, *Saint Thomas d'Aquin,* adaptation française par Paul Novarina (Louvain-Paris 1962, hereafter cited as *Walz-Novarina*) p. 86. Cf. Chenu, *Toward Understanding St. Thomas*, p. 217.

associations with university teaching. Apparently he served as Lector in Dominican houses at Anagni, Orvieto, Rome and Viterbo.[50] We know little about his actual teaching in these places but it is possible that he now devoted some time to the study of the major works of Aristotle. Indeed, as we shall see, I think he commented on the *Nicomachean Ethics* early in the 1260's. Certainly Aristotle's *Ethics* was very much in Thomas' mind at this time. If we look at the *Summa contra Gentiles* Book III, chapters 48 to 160 (a section which Aquinas wrote in Italy before 1264) we find explicit references to every book of the NE. These citations occur in every second or third chapter of this Book III.

At the University of Paris in his second professorate, from 1269 to 1272, Thomas was very busy teaching, engaging in several controversies, advising various ecclesiastical dignitaries, and writing several major works. It is the contention of R. A. Gauthier that Thomas also wrote his *Commentary on the Ethics* in Paris at this time.[51] Of course, we must admit that Thomas was making extensive use of the NE in the works written during this second Paris professorate. The second part of the *Summa of Theology* and the *Disputed Questions on Evil* show this beyond any doubt. The difficulty lies in interpreting what we know of his activities in the years 1269-1272.

Let us now turn more precisely to the problem of the time and place at which Thomas produced his ethics *Commentary*. I say "produced," because we do not really know whether it stemmed from oral lectures on the text, or was written outside the classroom in Thomas' own hand, or was dictated to secretaries. Until recently, this commentary by Aquinas was dated in the early or mid-1260's and was thought to have been done in the Papal States. The fourteenth-century historian Tolomeo of Lucca had left this account:

> isto autem tempore Thomas tenens studium Romae, quasi totam philosophiam sive moralem sive naturalem exposuit, et in scriptum seu commentum redegit; sed praecipue Ethicam et Metaphysicam, quodam singulari et novo modo tradendi.[52]

The period mentioned is the pontificate of Urban IV, from August 29, 1261 to October 2, 1264. In essence the passage says that Thomas

---

50   I have tried to summarize what can be discovered about this period, in *Aquinas' Search for Wisdom*, pp. 107-122.

51   Speaking of the origin of the archetype of the Italian MSS of Thomas' *Commentary* as stemming from this time, Gauthier concludes that it was written, "in conventum fratrum Praedicatorum parisiaco sancti Iacobi, in quo Thomas *Sententiam Libri Ethicorum* circa annos 1271-1272 scripserat..." *Praefatio*, p. 178*; see also p. 201*.

52   *Historia Ecclesiastica* XXIII, cap. 24; in L. A. Muratori, *Rerum Italicarum Scriptores* XI, col. 1162.

Aquinas commented on the *Ethics* and *Metaphysics* of Aristotle at this time. Martin Grabmann, Odon Lottin, Gérard Verbeke and others, agree that Tolomeo's report is substantially correct.[53]

On the other hand, R. A. Gauthier, A. Mansion and I. T. Eschmann have more recently suggested that Thomas' *Commentary on the Ethics* must be dated at Paris, 1271-1272.[54] The reasons proposed by Gauthier for this late date are four. First, Thomas' treatment of the virtue of magnanimity is said to show a progressive evolution from the *Commentary on the Sentences*, through the *Quaestiones de Malo*, to the *Commentary on the Ethics* and the *Summa Theologiae*, IIa-IIae.[55] Hence, the ethics commentary would appear to be contemporaneous with the writing of the second part of the *Summa of Theology*, i.e. after 1271. Second, Gauthier thinks that the *Metaphysics Lambda* test establishes that Thomas was writing his comments on the first book of the NE at the time that the Latin translation of Book *Kappa* became available: this would be in 1270-1271.[56] Third, citations of the Περὶ παθῶν of Pseudo-Andronicus are anonymous in Thomas' *Summa of Theology* up to II-II, qq. 48-49. At q. 80 this Greek writer is cited as "Andronicus Peripateticus." However, he is called Andronicus Peripateticus in the beginning of Thomas' *Commentary on the Ethics*.[57] From this Gauthier concludes that Thomas was writing his commentary at about the same time as this section of the IIa-IIae. Fourth, Gauthier suggests that the thought of Aquinas evolves on the question of the subject-powers of continence and perseverance. Early works put these virtues in the "reason," while later texts situate them in the "will."[58] The doctrine of *S.T.* II-II, qq. 143 and 155 is similar on this point to that of the *Commentary*, Book VII, 10.[59]

May I say immediately, by way of comment on these arguments, that all students of these problems are indebted to R. A. Gauthier and his

---

53 M. Grabmann, "Les Commentaires de s. Thomas sur les ouvrages d'Aristote," *Annales de l'Institut supérieur de Philosophie* (Louvain) 3 (1914) 240; *Guglielmo di Moerbeke* (1946) pp. 62-70; G. Verbeke, "La date du commentaire de s. Thomas sur l'Ethique à Nicomaque," *Revue philosophique de Louvain* 48 (1949) 207, 220; O. Lottin, *Psychologie et Morale aux xiiᵉ et xiiiᵉ siècles*, tome IV (Gembloux 1954) pp. 521-548.

54 Gauthier, "La Date du Commentaire de s. Thomas sur l'*Ethique à Nicomaque*," *RTAM* 18 (1951) 66-105; *Praefatio* (written in 1964) p. 178*; *Introduction E N*, (1970) pp. 128-129, 275; A. Mansion, "Autour de la date du commentaire de s. Thomas sur l'*Ethique à Nicomaque*," *Revue philosophique de Louvain* 50 (1952) 460-471; Eschmann, "Catalogue," p. 405.

55 Gauthier, "La Date du Commentaire," p. 76.

56 Art. cit. pp. 84-92.

57 *Sententia Libri Ethicorum* I, 6 (ed. Leon. p. 22, lines 66-67).

58 "La Date du Commentaire," pp. 102-103.

59 Gauthier (ibid. p. 103) ties in this alleged evolution of Aquinas' views with a mitigation in the later works of Thomas' "excessive intellectualism."

associates for the information on the manuscripts and sources of Thomas' *Commentary*, now found in the long "Preface" to the Leonine edition. Most of the factual data that can be uncovered are contained in this *Praefatio*. These details, particularly the tables showing the relation of the Italian manuscript tradition to that of Paris, cannot be summarized. Suffice it to say this: I think it has been established that the six or so Italian manuscripts are more or less dependent on the Paris tradition. This, in effect, is the strongest argument for the contention that Thomas commented on the NE at Paris in the early 1270's.

However, the matter is not that simple. It seems to me that we ought to distinguish between the time and place of Aquinas' initial explanation of the *Ethics* and the date of the editing, dictation or transcription of the full text of the *Commentary*, so as to provide booksellers' copies for the learned world. I think that Thomas Aquinas first commented on the *Ethics* in the early 1260's in the vicinity of Rome, quite possibly as a lecture course for young students in the Roman Province of the Order of Preachers. These young men would not do university-type studies. Some record of this course on the NE (either in Thomas' own hand, or in a *reportatio*) was then brought to Paris at the beginning of 1269 and, after some possible revision which would explain the intrusion of passages postdating the original lectures, the exposition was put into fair copies. Doubtless several of Thomas' other works were similarly handled. This interpretation of the available data means that the *composition* of the Thomistic commentary would be dated in the Papal States, 1261-1264, while the *editing* and *final copying* would occur at Paris in 1270-1272.

The first reason for this suggestion is very simple: too many of Thomas' writings are now assigned to the period 1269-1272. It would not have been humanly possible for one man to have composed all these works in three years. Remember that Thomas Aquinas was a priest who said his own Mass daily and daily served the Mass of his clerical secretary; he was engaged in giving lectures in theology at the University of Paris; he conducted academic disputations, apparently at least once a week; he was active in three time-consuming controversies; he was still consulted on numerous philosophical and theological problems by important officials in the hierarchy of the Church and of his Order; and he served on various commissions and attended regular meetings of the Order of Preachers.

To indicate what we are asked to believe about Thomas' literary production in these busy three years, I have gone to the work of Walz-Novarina which summarizes recent views, particularly of Dominican scholars.[60] Their tables assign the following works to the second Paris period:

Bible commentary:
    In Job expositio (1269-72)
    In evangelium Matthaei lectura (1271-72)
    In evangelium Joannis expositio (cap. I-V) *et lectura* (VI seq.) (1269-72)

Disputed Questions:
    De anima (1269)
    De malo (1269-72)
    De pueris (in *Quodl.* VII, art. 14-16) (1271)
    De unione Verbi Incarnati (1272-73)
    De virtutibus (1269-72)

Quodlibetal Questions:
    Quodlibeta I-VI (1269-72)
    Quodlibetum XII (1270)

Major theological writing:
    Summa theologiae, Prima Secundae et Secunda Secundae (1269-72)

Miscellaneous writings:
    Contra pestiferam doctrinam (1270)
    De aeternitate mundi (1271)
    De forma absolutionis (1270)
    De judiciis astrorum (1269-72)
    De occultis operibus naturae (1269-72)
    De perfectione vitae spiritualis (1269)
    De secreto (1269)
    De sortibus (1269-72)
    De unitate intellectus (1270)
    Responsio de articulis XLII (1271)
    Responsio de articulis VI (1271)
    Responsio de articulis XXXVI (1271)

Philosophical commentary:
    In librum De Causis expositio (1271-72)

Aristotle commentaries:
    In libros posteriorum Analyticorum (1269-72)
    In libros de Anima (lib. II et III) (1269)
    In libros de Caelo et Mundo (1272)
    In decem libros Ethicorum (1270-72)
    In libros peri Hermeneias (1269-72)
    In librum de Memoria et Reminiscentia (1271-1272)
    In XII libros Metaphysicorum (1268-72)

60 *Walz-Novarina*, pp. 221-226.

In IV libros Meteorologicorum (1269-72)
In VIII libros Physicorum (after 1268)
In libros Politicorum (1269-72)
In librum de Sensu et Sensato (1266-72)

Now, it is my contention that Thomas Aquinas could not have composed all these writings in this triennium. Given the fact that he was assisted by several scribe-secretaries, granting his scholarly dedication and genius, it was still impossible, I think, for one man to originate all this literary output in this short period. As Gauthier admits: "one may be astonished at the multitude of works that Thomas composed in this short time . . . when he was writing the Second Part of the *Summa of Theology* and other works."[61] Not only would such an output be astonishing: to my mind it would be incredible. Gauthier's position would require us to accept that about one half of all Thomas Aquinas' writings resulted from these three years! Moreover, this approach to Thomistic bibliography further demands that we accept the corollary that Aquinas produced practically no writings (apart from finishing the *Summa contra Gentiles* and doing a few miscellaneous writings) during his whole decade in the Papal States.

In place of this odd contention which rests on very indirect evidence, what I am proposing is that we accept the view that the scribes and secretaries were kept very busy at Paris in the early 1270's making clear copies of the accumulation of notes, lecture records and almost illegible personal manuscripts brought to Paris by St. Thomas in the winter of 1269. This would explain why so many manuscripts of Thomistic writings go back to copies made at this time in Paris.

A second argument for the Italian composition of Thomas' ethics *Commentary* rests on the character of the work itself. Of all his expositions of the writings of Aristotle, that on the *Ethics* is one of the simplest and least pretentious. It has comparatively few references to other authors.[62] It is stylistically the least complicated of Thomas' commentaries.[63] Because of this comparative simplicity, Grabmann and several other scholars regard the commentary on the NE as the earliest

---

61 "admirari enim solet de multitudine operum quae Thomas in parvo tempore confecit, praesertim cum *Sententiam Libri Ethicorum* Lutetiae Parisiorum circa annos 1271-1272 scripserit dum secundam partem Summae theologiae aliaque opera scribebat." *Praefatio,* p. 201*.

62 On this lack of documentation, Gauthier makes this odd comment: "Saint Thomas, au contraire de saint Albert, n'a pas eu recours de façon suivie aux multiples instruments de travail dont disposait à son époque l'exégète de l'*Ethique*: son commentaire présente tous les caractères d'une œuvre rapide, faite, si j'ose dire, 'de chic'." *Introduction EN,* p. 130.

63 Speaking of the Thomistic *Commentary on the Ethics,* Roger Guindon notes: "Comme, par ailleurs, ce commentaire est sans doute le moins développé de tous ceux que notre auteur a consacrés aux ouvrages du Stagirite." *Béatitude et théologie morale chez saint Thomas d'Aquin* (Ottawa 1956) p. 156.

of Thomas' expositions of Aristotle. [64] Remarking on this undeveloped character of the ethics commentary, Gauthier notes the view (without accepting it) that it could have been a course of lectures for young beginners in the Dominican Order. He even admits that it is not absolutely impossible that Thomas taught the NE to youthful students *at Paris* who had no previous Arts studies. [65] However, Gauthier remains convinced that it would have been out of keeping with the dignity of a Master of Theology, as Thomas was, to lecture on a philosophical text, such as the *Nicomachean Ethics*. Here again, Gauthier's view is open to criticism; he must admit that Albert, when a Master in Theology, lectured at Cologne on the NE. Indeed, whenever he did them, all of Thomas Aquinas' commentaries on Aristotle were produced after he became a Master in Theology — and portions of them (notably the first book *de Anima*) are obviously *reportationes* made from oral lectures.

In point of fact, one should ask: "Under what conditions might Thomas Aquinas have composed a commentary such as this brief exposition of the *Ethics*? Would it be at a large university center such as Paris, where books would be easily available and audiences comparatively sophisticated, or would it more likely be at some country town in Italy, where young monks would need some elementary introduction to *the* Philosopher, and where the Lector would have little more to document his course than the manuscripts that he had brought with him?" As far as I can see, the second suggestion is much preferable. One could accept the suggestion that Thomas composed this elementary exposition in the vicinity of Rome but it is difficult to think that he did it at Paris, when he was busy with the composition of the detailed moral theology of the *Pars Secunda*.

We may further ask for whom St. Thomas wrote this explanation of the NE. Gauthier seems to think it was for his own benefit, as a tool to help him with the problems that he was treating in the *Summa of Theology*.

> Saint Thomas n'a été, et n'a voulu être, qu'un théologien. Si, au moment même où il exposait dans la *IIa Pars* de la *Somme de théologie* sa théologie morale, il a commenté l'*Ethique à Nicomaque*, c'était uniquement

---

64 Grabmann speaks of "il Commento all'Etica, che io ritengo il primo commento aristotelico fatto da S. Tommaso d'Aquino." *Guglielmo di Moerbeke*, p. 64.

65 "il est possible, — mais nous n'avons aucune raison de l'affirmer, et nous en avons par contre de bonnes d'en douter, — que le commentaire de saint Thomas soit un cours, et que ce cours ait été destiné à de tout jeunes débutants, ce qui expliquerait son parti-pris de simplification et de clarté . . ." *Introduction E N*, pp. 130-131. In a footnote to this (p. 131, note 138) Gauthier adds: "il n'est pas absolument impossible que saint Thomas l'ait expliquée aux jeunes frères qui étaient entrés en religion sans avoir suivi les cours de la faculté des arts, mais c'eût été là une dérogation aux usages, le rôle du maître en théologie étant d'expliquer la Sainte Ecriture." By way of comment, it seems that only a small part of Thomas' time as a professor of theology was spent in Scripture classes!

parce qu'il voyait dans la philosophie morale d'Aristote l'instrument ra-
tionnel qui lui permettrait de rendre compte de ce que la foi nous en-
seigne sur le sens de la vie humaine.[66]

But surely it would not have been necessary or advisable for Thomas
to compose a phrase-by-phrase exposition for this purpose. At Paris in
the 1270's he would have had access to existing expositions of the NE,
notably to Grosseteste's *Notes* and Albert's *Lectura*. Nor would this
suggestion of Gauthier explain why Aquinas might have undertaken to
comment on all the other works of Aristotle at this late date. Did
Thomas think, for instance, that a commentary on the four books of the
Meteorologica, or on the eight books of the *Physics*, would help him
with problems in moral theology? It is much more likely that Thomas
composed his Aristotle commentaries at a time and place at which his
listeners or readers needed them. For most of these expositions, this
would be in Italy in the early 1260's—not in Paris in the 1270's.

A third reason for questioning the late dating of the *Commentary on
the Ethics* has to do with the alleged evolution of Thomas' thought on
key points. As we have seen, Gauthier thinks that the teaching on the
seat of continence and perseverance changed from the early works to
the later views of the *Commentary on the Ethics* and the *Secunda
Pars*.[67] Similarly, A. Mansion has argued for dating the ethics commentary after 1270, because Book I, *lectio* 17, refers to a more complete
explanation elsewhere of the state of the human soul after death. Mansion took it that this places the *Commentary* after *S.T.* I, q. 89.[68] Contrariwise, Roger Guindon argues from a study of Thomas' treatment of
final beatitude in the ethics commentary that it is an early work, having
much the same doctrinal development as the commentary on the fourth
book of the *Sentences*![69]

To my mind, arguments from doctrinal developments and comparisons are among the weakest and most deceptive devices for determining literary dates. If one looks at the whole theory that runs through

66 *Introduction EN*, p. 275.
67 See supra, note 58.
68 Mansion, "Autour de la date du commentaire," *RPL* 50 (1952) 460-471. At the end of *Sententia Libri Ethicorum* I, 17 (ed. Leon. p. 63), Thomas refuses to discuss whether the soul in a
future life knows what is going on here below and is affected by such knowledge, because Aristotle
did not treat of happiness in a future life. Thomas adds: "Alibi autem haec plenius disseruimus."
The "elsewhere" at which Thomas treated such matters could refer to several theological writings
from the *Commentary on the Sentences* and the *Summa contra Gentiles* (IV, cap. 85-95) onward.
69 Guindon (*Béatitude et théologie morale*, pp. 149-156) ranks as similar in their views of
ultimate felicity the expositions of Sacred Scripture, the *Commentary on the Sentences*, and the
Commentary on the Ethics. I am not impressed by his findings but cite the study as an example of
how misleading doctrinal comparisons for the sake of dating writings can be. For a different interpretation of Thomas' teaching on felicity in the ethics *Commentary*, see W. Kluxen,
Philosophische Ethik bei Thomas von Aquin (Mainz 1964) pp. 166-184.

Thomas' explanation of the *Ethics*, one does not get the impression that it is a well developed and mature piece of work.

Nor is the *Lambda* test of much value in this case. Book *Kappa* of the *Metaphysics* of Aristotle became available to Aquinas in 1270-1271; before that he cited the following book (*Lambda*) as XI, after that time *Lambda* becomes XII. At the beginning of the *Commentary on the Ethics*, *Lambda* is cited internally and explicitly as XI. Five *lectiones* later in the same Book I the same passage (1075a13-15) is cited internally as Book XII![70] Now Gauthier takes this to mean that Thomas was in the course of explaining the first book of the NE, when he received Moerbeke's translation of *Metaphysics Kappa*.[71] On the other hand, A. Mansion interprets this as a case of editorial correction in the second passage.[72] However, this incompatibility of references to the *Metaphysics* can be explained in several other ways, the simplest being an original error in writing or copying a Roman numeral. What is really astonishing is the fact that neither Thomas nor his secretaries detected this obvious incompatibility, or error, when the *Commentary* was being revised or copied. Even if the *Commentary* were composed in the Paris period, why would Thomas have failed to remember that he had cited *Lambda* as XI just a sheet or two earlier in the manuscript?

As for the citation of Andronicus by name in the first book of the *Commentary*,[73] his treatise Περὶ παθῶν was translated by Robert Grosseteste and could have been known by Thomas Aquinas under the name of Andronicus, from his first Paris professorate onward. It is correct that this little treatise is not attributed to Andronicus in the *Summa of Theology* until q. 80 of the II^a-II^{ae} but this does not seem to me to preclude a prior reference to Andronicus in a work from the 1260's. In any case, an editorial correction at the time of the Paris copying of the *Commentary* would have been quite possible.

My conclusion as to the place and date of composition of this commentary, then, is that it was done at Orvieto in the years 1261-1264. The testimony of Tolomeo of Lucca is roughly correct and should not be rejected on the basis of indirect and doubtful arguments. There is no convincing argument for delaying the initial composition of this *Commentary on the Ethics* to the second Paris period.

---

70 *Sententia Libri Ethicorum* I, 1 (ed. Leon. p. 4, line 12): "ut Philosophus dicit in XI Metaphysicae, ordo partium exercitus ad invicem est propter ordinem totius exercitus ad ducem." Ibid. I, 6 (ed. Leon. p. 22, line 90): "nam et ipse Aristoteles in XII Metaphysicae ponit quoddam bonum separatum a toto universo, ad quod totum universum ordinatur sicut exercitus ad bonum ducis . . ."

71 Gauthier, "La Date du Commentaire," pp. 84-88. On p. 91, he shows that 21 MSS give these readings.

72 Cf. ibid. p. 84; and Mansion, "La version médiévale de l'*Ethique à Nicomaque*," *Revue néoscolastique de philosophie* 41 (1938) 401-427.

73 *Sententia Libri Ethicorum* I, 6 (ed. Leon. p. 22, line 67).

VALUE OF THOMAS' COMMENTARY

Surprisingly, the chief editor of the Leonine text of Aquinas' *Commentary* on the NE takes a rather dim view of its value. Father Gauthier has maintained for many years that the best mediaeval commentary on Aristotle's *Ethics* is the *Lectura* of Albert the Great.[74] On the other hand, he faults Thomas Aquinas for not using the best available texts and sources for his exposition and insists that, as far as Aristotelian interpretation is concerned, the Thomistic commentary on the NE is of no help at all.[75] In fact, Gauthier finds that Thomas brought nothing new or distinctive to the mediaeval art of interpreting Aristotle.[76]

Contrasting with this severe judgment is much that has previously been written about Thomas' *Commentary*. Paul Shorey's contrary opinion has frequently been quoted:

> If I had the choice of putting into the hands of a student of Aristotle the commentary of Thomas or the book of some recent interpreter of Aristotle, I would choose the medieval schoolman as more educative in sensible methods and less likely to mislead and confuse the student.[77]

In like vein, the only complete monograph on Thomas' *Commentary on the Ethics* depicts this work as the best explanation of Aristotle's NE that we have. Professor Jaffa writes:

> Accordingly, it is not unreasonable to assume that the Aristotelian teaching is more accessible in the pages of Thomas than in the original. Certainly no one in modern times, perhaps no one since Thomas, has possessed his mastery of the Aristotelian corpus, and his marvelous capacity for relating each point in that massive edifice to every other point.[78]

---

74 Most recently (*Introduction E N*, p. 123) Gauthier has pointed to the literal exposition, plus the addition of questions, plus the utilization of the best versions and commentaries available and concluded: "Tout cela fait du premier cours d'Albert le Grand sur l'*Ethique* le meilleur, et de beaucoup, des innombrables commentaires sur l'*Ethique* que nous a légués le moyen âge." In a footnote (p. 123, note 122) Gauthier severely criticizes the manner in which the first volume of the critical edition of Albert's *Lectura* is edited.

75 "le commentaire de saint Thomas sur l'*Ethique,* envisagé du point de vue de l'exégèse aristotélicienne est une œuvre manquée et de nul secours. . ." *Introduction E N*, pp. 130-131.

76 "tempus est ut candide fateamur in interpretandis libris nil singulare, nil novum Thomam invenisse, sed contra totam interpretandi artem iam vetustate comprobatam a magistris artium Albertoque accepisse." *Praefatio,* p. 246*.

77 Shorey, *Platonism Ancient and Modern* (Berkeley, Cal. 1938) p. 90; the comment is quoted in Litzinger's "Introduction," p. XI, to *Commentary on the Nicomachean Ethics.*

78 Harry V. Jaffa, *Thomism and Aristotelianism. A Study of the Commentary by Thomas Aquinas on the Nicomachean Ethics* (Chicago 1952) p. 6. At the time this book was published, Jaffa was a professor of political science at Ohio State University.

Such diversity of scholarly opinion calls for a brief, but more detailed, appraisal of the present value of Thomas' ethics commentary.

While Jaffa and others do offer some very favorable remarks on Thomas as an interpreter of the *Ethics*, they are quick to point out areas in which Aristotle is not followed, or is distorted, by Aquinas. The following six points are said to be falsely attributed to Aristotle by Thomas:

1. Belief in divine particular providence.
2. Belief that perfect happiness is impossible in this life.
3. Belief in the necessity of personal immortality to complete the happiness intended, evidently, by nature.
4. Belief in personal immortality.
5. Belief in the special creation of individual souls.
6. Belief in a divinely implanted, 'natural' habit of the moral principles. [79]

Indeed, these beliefs are characteristic of Thomas' own outlook but he is usually rather careful to avoid saying that Aristotle so believed. Typical is his comment on a passage in the fourth book, where Aristotle gives as an example of munificence ($\mu\varepsilon\gamma\alpha\lambda o\pi\rho\acute{\varepsilon}\pi\varepsilon\iota\alpha$) expenditure for worship of the gods: "the Philosopher speaks here according to a Gentile custom which is now revoked by the obvious truth, for if anyone were to spend anything now on the worship of demons he would be sacrilegious, not munificent." [80]

We have another example of this sort of thing — where Thomas states what he considers to be the truth, not the view of Aristotle — in a remark that occurs in the last book. He has been summarizing Aristotle's conclusion that the happy man is he who is best able to contemplate truth and God (1179a30), and Thomas adds: "Supposing, as the truth of the matter has it, that God exercises care and providence over human affairs, it is reasonable for Him to take pleasure in what is best in men and most closely related and similar to God, namely understanding." [81] Here, Thomas does not assert that Aristotle believed in

79 This is Jaffa's list, *op. cit.* p. 187. He is somewhat indebted to a similar itemization of differences found in F. Copleston, *A History of Philosophy*, vol. II: *Mediaeval Philosophy: Augustine to Scotus* (Westminster, Md. 1950) chapter 39. Wolfgang Kluxen, op. cit. pp. 104-106, criticizes both Jaffa and Copleston for misunderstanding the relation of faith to reason in Thomas' thought.

80 "et loquitur hic philosophus secundum consuetudinem Gentilium, quae nunc manifestata veritate est abrogata, unde, si aliquis nunc circa cultum daemonum aliquid expenderet, non esset magnificus, sed sacrilegus." *Sententia Libri Ethicorum* IV, 7 (ed. Leon. p. 222, lines 28-32).

81 "Supposito enim, sicut rei veritas habet, quod Deus habeat curam et providentiam de rebus humanis, rationabile est quod delectetur circa homines de eo quod est optimum in eis et quod est cognatissimum, id est simillimum, Deo, quod quidem est intellectus..." *Sententia Libri Ethicorum* X, 13 (ed. Leon. p. 595, lines 116-121).

divine providence but he does say that it is true that God looks after human affairs.

Of course there are a few passages in the Thomistic *Commentary* where obviously Christian elements intrude. At one point Thomas introduces the well-known maxim of Dionysius the Pseudo-Areopagite to the effect that good stems from a cause that is one and whole, whereas evil comes from a defect in any feature of an action.[82] Again, in the third book, Thomas uses the example of the martyrdom of St. Lawrence to illustrate Aristotle's claim that it is preferable to die rather than do certain very evil deeds.[83] For a Christian audience, such as St. Thomas', this would have more meaning than an illustration from Greek mythology. It does not suggest at all that Aristotle taught anything about Christian martyrdom. Another instance of this sort of intrusion is found in the fifth book, where Thomas cites Isidore of Seville's statement that right (*ius*) means the just thing (*iustum*).[84] Apart from these few cases, there is little else in Thomas' comment on the *Ethics* to show that he is a Christian theologian; nothing other than a general attitude suggesting that he is more confident of a future life, the freedom of the human will and the presence of God to man, than is Aristotle. On the whole, Thomas as commentator is very faithful to his author and tries to get at the exact meaning of the text itself.[85]

This is not to claim that Thomas' *Sententia Libri Ethicorum* is necessarily the best mediaeval commentary on the NE. Even in the field of expositions by Christian scholars more manuscripts are coming to be known. It is possible that complete publication of Albert's *Lectura* will alter the situation. Since Thomas as "editor" may have contributed a good deal to the *Lectura*, such a finding need not diminish his reputation in the field of Aristotelian scholarship.[86]

Nor is it correct to suggest that the Thomistic *Commentary* is superior to any comparable modern work. The truth of the matter is

---

82 "Dionysius dicit in libro De divinis nominibus, quod bonum contingit ex una et integra causa, malum autem ex singularibus defectibus." *Sententia Libri Ethicorum* II, 7 (ed. Leon. p. 98, lines 10-12).

83 *Sententia Libri Ethicorum* III, 2 (ed. Leon. p. 122, line 52).

84 "nam et Ysidorus dicit in libro Ethimologiarum quod ius dicitur quasi iustum." *Sententia Libri Ethicorum* V, 12 (ed. Leon. p. 304, lines 16-17). Cf. *Libri Etymologiarum* V, 3 (PL 82, 199).

85 Thus J. Isaac suggests that Albert in his commentaries tries to philosophize himself and to use Aristotle to back up Albert's own views, whereas: "Il n'en va pas de même pour saint Thomas: il entend manifestement mettre les étudiants pour lesquels il écrit en contact direct avec Aristote et s'effacer le plus possible devant le Philosophe. Ses commentaires sont en réalité des explications de textes basées sur la critique la plus exigeante qui soit." See "Saint Thomas interprète des œuvres d'Aristote," in *Scholastica ratione historico-critica instauranda* (Roma 1951) pp. 360-361.

86 Cf. Georges Kalinowski, *Le Problème de la vérité en morale et en droit,* (Lyon 1967) pp. 129-140.

that many of the standard commentaries on the NE, done in the late nineteenth and early twentieth centuries, are of little value. This is especially so of those in English, for they were done by men who were not primarily philosophers, or by men who had little knowledge of the speculative parts of Aristotle's philosophy. But, except in humility, the French commentary by Gauthier and Jolif certainly excells the work of Thomas Aquinas on the *Ethics*.[87] Aquinas had no acquaintance with the Greek text of the NE; for most of the work he was dependent on one Latin version by Grosseteste; his awareness of previous commentaries may have been indirect (via Albert's *Lectura*) and he may have had to depend on memory of these commentaries, if he lectured on the text in the Papal States; Thomas' notion of the unity and rational structure of the NE is simplistic, when viewed in the light of the twentieth-century research on the text. There was no way in which Thomas Aquinas could have challenged the exegesis of a good modern interpreter.

When all of this has been admitted, one must add that St. Thomas still looms at the greatest ethical thinker that we can find between Aristotle and Kant.[88] The suggestion that Albert the Great is entitled to this honor is not without recent supporters.[89] No one, however, suggests that Albert's second *Commentary on the Ethics* (with which Thomas had nothing to do) is comparable in value with Thomas' work. In fact, Albert's *Commentarium* (as it appears in the printed editions) is a very inferior paraphrase of Aristotle's ethics.

It is true that a good deal of Aquinas' moral wisdom is not found in his *Commentary* but in his theological writing.[90] The problem of the relation between Thomas' moral theology and his moral philosophy is beyond the scope of this study. Perhaps it is enough to say that St. Thomas' *Commentary on the Nicomachean Ethics* is neither as valueless to Aristotelian scholarship as R. A. Gauthier implies, nor as priceless as Paul Shorey suggested.

---

87 Aristote, *L'Ethique à Nicomaque*, Introduction, traduction et commentaire, par R. A. Gauthier et J. Y. Jolif, 3 vol., (Louvain-Paris 1958-1959; 2me éd. 1970).

88 Cf. Kluxen, op. cit. p. 244: "es haben zwischen Aristoteles und Kant keinen gewichtigeren Beitrag zur praktischen Philosophie gegeben als den des Thomas von Aquin."

89 See Dunbabin, art. cit. p. 232.

90 D. J. O'Connor, for instance, remarks that, "the commentaries on Aristotle contain a higher proportion of pure philosophical discussion but are, perhaps for that reason, less important and characteristic." *Aquinas and Natural Law* (New York 1968) p. 3. He cites the *Commentary on the Ethics* only four times in his book.

ST. THOMAS AND ULPIAN'S NATURAL LAW

Michael Bertram Crowe

A NY study of the concept of the natural law, above all any historical study, must take account of the definition attributed to the Roman jurist Domitius Ulpianus (c. 170-228 A.D.): *jus naturale est quod natura omnia animalia docuit.* In the history of the natural law, notably in the Middle Ages, this definition has shown a remarkable vitality not entirely accounted for by its conspicuous adoption in that authority *par excellence*, the *Corpus Iuris Civilis* of Justinian. And while many authors expend much ingenuity in making the definition plausible, explaining it and explaining it away, St. Thomas Aquinas shows a remarkable preference for Ulpian. In this he departed from the views of his predecessors; and he found few followers. Attention has long ago been drawn to this surprising predilection — amongst others by Dom Odon Lottin over forty years ago.[1] It may be enlightening to look at it once again.

I. Ulpian and his Formulary

Ulpian's is one of the great names in Roman jurisprudence and one of those to whom the codification of the Roman law by Justinian in the sixth century was most indebted.[2] The definition of the natural law as

---

1 O. Lottin, *Le droit naturel chez saint Thomas d'Aquin et ses prédécesseurs* (Bruges 1931), pp. 61-67: "Saint Thomas et les définitions antérieures" — "par-dessus tout il affectionne (la définition) du juriste Ulpianus (*Commentary on the Sentences*)... nouvelle faveur accordée au droit romain...saint Thomas remet décidémment à l'honneur cet élément du droit romain qu'on avait trop délaissé avant lui (*Commentary on the Ethics*)...nous trouvons ici exprimé une nouvelle fois le sens strict que saint Thomas attribue au *jus naturae...quod natura omnia animalia docuit* (*Prima-Secundae*)...le fond de la pensée de saint Thomas, je veux dire ses sympathies sécrètes pour les formules du droit romain (*Prima-Secundae*)...preuve nouvelle de la sympathie de saint Thomas pour les formules du droit romain (*Secunda-Secundae*)."

2 By quantity Ulpian contributed more than any other jurist to the *Digest*, about one third of the whole. Many of the tags and aphorisms of the Roman law in the Middle Ages were attributed, not always correctly, to him; for example the definition of jurisprudence as the *ars equi et boni* and the description of justice as *constans et perpetua voluntas ius suum cuique tribuendi*; the law's precepts as *honeste vivere, alterum non laedere, suum cuique tribuere*; also the maxims *quod principi placuit legis habet vigorem* and *princeps legibus solutus*. Cf. *Dig.*, I,1,1; I,1,10; I,3,31; I,4,1, etc.

"what nature has taught all animals" was only part, but an influential part, of that debt owed by Justinian's compilers to Ulpian and to his second and third century predecessors and contemporaries. The effect of appearing in the *Corpus Iuris Civilis* was to enhance and confirm Ulpian's authority for centuries of legislators, jurists and philosophers. A definition that figured prominently in both the *Institutes* and the *Digest* (or *Pandects*) of Justinian could not fail to enjoy enormous authority. [3]

How did Ulpian arrive at his definition of the natural law — if, indeed, the definition is genuinely his? To this question there is no easy answer. But it is, in fact, a question of secondary importance; for the influence of Ulpian on the natural law thought of the Middle Ages depends neither upon the sources nor upon the genuineness of his definition. It was enough that it was adopted into the *Corpus Iuris*. [4] The context of the definition is, however, relevant. In Roman law the natural law and the *jus gentium* were not, at first, sharply distinguished. Cicero tends to identify them, particularly in passages where he appeals to universal consent; and the practice of the first century lawyers seems hardly different. [5] In the last quarter of the following century the position was unchanged. Gaius, writing about 180 A.D., distinguishes only two kinds of law, the *jus civile* and the *jus gentium*, the latter being the work of natural reason and getting its name from the fact that all peoples observed it. [6] Paulus, writing slightly later, similarly recognises no opposition between the *jus naturale* and the *jus gentium*. [7] At the end of the century, however, there is a change; for, in the writings of the jurisconsults Tryphoninus, Florentinus and, above all, Ulpian, the natural law and the *jus gentium* are clearly distinguished. [8]

---

3 *Inst.*, I,1; *Dig.*, I,1,3 (Ulpianus *Liber I Institutionum*).

4 Cf. W. Onclin, "Le droit naturel selon les romanistes des XII et XIII siècles," *Miscellanea Moralia A. Janssen* (Louvain 1948).

5 *Tusculan Disputations*, I,13,30: "Omni autem in re consensio omnium gentium lex naturae est"; I,15,35; "omnium consensus naturae vox est"; cf. F. Senn, *De la justice et du droit* (Paris 1927), Appendix, "De la distinction du jus naturale et du jus gentium," p. 77; M. Villey, *Leçons d'histoire de la philosophie du droit* (Paris, 1957), pp. 121-123.

6 *Dig.*, I,1,9: "quod quisque populus ipse sibi jus constituit id ipsius proprium civitatis est; vocaturque jus civile quasi jus proprium ipsius civitatis. Quod vero naturalis ratio inter omnes homines constituit, id apud omnes peraeque custoditur; vocaturque jus gentium, quasi quo jure omnes gentes utuntur."

7 *Dig.*, I,7,11: "Jus pluribus modis dicitur, uno modo cum id quod semper aequum et bonum est jus dicitur, ut est jus naturale..."

8 Tryphoninus and Florentinus make the distinction when they refer to slavery. *Dig.* 12,6,64 (Tryphoninus): "Ut enim libertas naturali jure continetur et dominatio ex jure gentium introducta est"; *Dig.*, 1,5,4 (Florentinus): "Servitus est constitutio juris gentium, qua quis dominio alieno contra naturam subjicitur." Cf. R. Voggensperger, *Der Begriff des "jus naturale" im Römischen Recht* (Basel 1952), pp. 17-24, 112-113.

It was Ulpian who formalised the distinction in the tripartite division of law into natural law, *jus gentium* and civil law:

> Jus naturale est quod natura omnia animalia docuit. Nam istud jus non humani generis proprium, sed omnium animalium quae in terra, quae in mari nascuntur, avium quoque commune est. Hinc descendit maris atque feminae conjunctio, quam nos matrimonium appellamus; hinc liberorum procreatio, hinc educatio; videmus enim coetera quoque animalia, feras etiam, istius juris peritia censeri. Jus gentium est quo gentes humanae utuntur; quod a naturali recedere facile intelligere licet, quia illud omnibus animalibus, hoc solis hominibus inter se commune sit..."[9]

So in the *Digest*. In the *Institutes* of Justinian the same tripartite division is retained but, while Ulpian's definition of the natural law is retained, his definition of the *jus gentium* is discarded for that of Gaius. This might seem to bring the natural law and the *jus gentium* closer together, for Gaius did not distinguish clearly between them. On the contrary, the outline given in the *Institutes* of the field of the *jus gentium* (taken this time from Hermogenianus), the consequences of war, contracts etc., brings it closer to positive law.[10] One could be critical of Justinian's compilers here; for one of the main rules laid down for them was that they were to prune the law of discrepancies and contradictions. Ulpian's division had the merit of being clean-cut; and this virtue was to stand it in good stead in later controversies about the definition of the natural law, offsetting the difficulty and implausibility of a natural law common to animals. Justinian's compilers, by their eclecticism in admitting into the *Institutes* texts which tended to assimilate the natural law and the *jus gentium*[11] forwent, doubtless unconsciously, this advantage. The result was to isolate Ulpian's definition of the natural law as what nature has taught all animals by depriving it of the support of the complementary definition of the *jus gentium* as the natural law proper to mankind.

Ulpian's definition may be an eccentric and isolated conceit in the Roman law. Whatever may be said about its sources, its genuineness or

---

9 *Dig.*, 1,1,1,3.

10 *Inst.* 1,2,2: "Jus gentium humano generi commune est. Nam usu exigente et humanis necessitatibus, gentes humanae quaedam sibi constituerunt; bella enim orta sunt et captivitates secutae et servitutes quae sunt naturali juri contrariae. Jure enim naturali omnes homines ab initio liberi nascebantur. Et ex hoc jure gentium omnes pene contractus introducti sunt ut emptio, venditio, locatio, conductio, societas, depositum et alii innumerabiles." The text of Hermogenianus is in *Dig.* 1,1,1,5.

11 Cf. *Inst.* 2,1,1: "Naturali jure communis sunt omnium haec, aer, aqua, profluens et mare et per hoc littora maris. Nemo igitur ad littus maris accedere prohibetur, dum tamen a villis et monumentis abstineat; quia non sunt juris gentium, sicut est mare" (Marcianus); also texts from Gaius in *Inst.* 2,1,11 and 2,1,41.

possible interpolation or about possible parallels in Pythagorean or Stoic philosophy, the principal fact is that it appears at the head of both the *Digest* and the *Institutes* of Justinian. To this fact rather than to any intrinsic worth must be attributed the authority it carried for so many centuries.

II. FROM ULPIAN TO ST. THOMAS

In the Middle Ages Ulpian's definition of the natural law was commonly described as the "jurists' definition" or the "definition of the law." Occasionally, however, it is attributed to Isidore of Seville. This is ironical; for while Isidore (c. 560-636) occupies a position of great importance in the transmission of the concepts of the Roman law — together with a vast accumulation of other miscellaneous learning — to the Middle Ages, he did not, in fact, transmit Ulpian's definition. His *Liber Etymologiarum*, upon which he worked during the last decade of his life, is a vast and rather uncritical encyclopaedia whose real merit is that it preserved so much of antiquity. Isidore was not always consistent in his choice of texts to preserve, and the etymologies he offers are frequently fantastic[12]; but he does deserve his place in history as one of the important educators of the Middle Ages.[13]

In Book V of the *Book of Etymologies* legal terms find their place. The trichotomy of Ulpian — natural law, *jus gentium*, civil law — appears, taken by Isidore probably from either the *Digest* or the *Institutes* of Justinian. This, indeed, is one of the indications that Isidore knew Justinian's *Corpus Iuris Civilis*.[14] But in accepting the division Isidore effectively changed the terms. He abandoned entirely Ulpian's natural law common to all animals and returned to something not unlike the law, independent of human conventions, described by Aristotle as "natural":[15]

> Jus naturale est commune omnium nationum, et quod ubique instinctu naturae, non constitutione aliqua habeatur, ut viri et feminae conjunctio,

---

12   P. Séjourné, *Le dernier Père de l'Eglise, saint Isidore de Seville* (Paris 1929), p. 62: "On a pu se demander si ce n'est pas dans les livres des juristes romains, surtout les juristes stoiciens, que notre encyclopédiste a été chercher l'idée de son ouvrage; car nulle part ailleurs on ne trouve d'aussi fréquentes et artificielles étymologies"; T. Gilby, *Law and Political Theory: Summa Theologiae 1-2ae, 90-97* (London-New York 1966), p. 110, note: "St. Isidore, a collector rather than a systematizer, salvaged what he could of the past without caring whether some of the texts he transmitted were inconsistent..."

13   Dante places him in the fourth heaven, that of the sun or light, in the excellent company of St Thomas, St Albert the Great, Gratian, Peter Lombard, Dionysius the Areopagite, Boethius and others. Cf. *Par.* X, 131.

14   P. Séjourné, op. cit., p. 65.

15   Cf. A. F. Utz, *Recht und Gerechtigkeit, Kommentar in 2-2ae, 57-79* (Deutsche Thomas-Ausgabe, Band 18), (Heidelberg 1953), p. 448.

liberorum susceptio et educatio, communis omnium possessio et omnium una libertas, acquisitio eorum quae coelo, terra, marique capiuntur. Item depositio rei vel commodatae restitutio...[16]

Another key-figure in the transmission of legal ideas and formulae to the Middle Ages was the twelfth-century canonist Gratian. Here, too, as far as Ulpian's definition is concerned, it is a matter of indirect influence. Gratian did not record Ulpian's definition but himself formulated an equally troublesome one.

The *Decretum Gratiani* (or, to give its proper title, the *Concordia discordantium canonum*) saw the light about 1140. Despite the fact that it was a "private" text, never receiving official recognition as a source of canon law, it is arguably the most important single document in the history of canon law. Gratian faced a situation in canon law not unlike that found by Justinian in the civil law six centuries before — the legislation had become a thicket through which it was next to impossible to find one's way. Gratian systematized the canons, the ecclesiastical traditions, decisions of Popes and Councils, the arguments of the Fathers and the other sources of canonical legislation. And although he never had Justinian's power to give juridical effect to his compilation, his logical categories were invaluable. It was not surprising that the *Decretum*, like the *Corpus Iuris Civilis* should attract its commentators. What Gratian says of the natural law is clearly of the greatest importance for medieval theology.[17]

Gratian relies upon Isidore for his definitions and divisions concerning the nature and varieties of law. But the issue was confused for him by the necessity of reconciling Isidore's bipartite division of law (into human and divine) with Ulpian's Roman law tripartite division of law (into natural law, *jus gentium* and civil law). Gratian's solution was unfortunate, for it confused the natural law with the divine law revealed in the Scriptures:

> Humanum genus duobus regitur, naturali videlicet jure et moribus. Jus naturae est quod in lege et Evangelio continetur quo quisque jubetur alii facere quod sibi vult fieri et prohibetur alii inferre quod sibi nolit fieri.[18]

16 *Etym.* V, 4 (PL 82, 199). Isidore similarly alters Ulpian's *jus gentium* and makes it embrace mainly war and its consequences. This may not be unconnected with the fact that Ulpian placed the *jus militare* next to the *jus gentium. Etym.* V, 6 (PL 82, 200): "Jus gentium est sedium occupatio, aedificatio, munitio, bella captivitatem, servitutes...et inde jus gentium quod eo jure omnes fere gentes utuntur."

17 Cf. B. C. Kuhlmann, *Der Gesetzbegriff beim hl. Thomas von Aquin in Licht der Rechtsstudiums seiner Zeit* (Freiburg-Bonn 1921), pp. 14-18; E. E. Hölscher, *Von römischen zum Christlichen Naturrecht* (Augsburg 1931), pp. 51-52, 63.

18 *Decretum Magistri Gratiani,* editio Lipsiensis secunda, ed. A. Friedberg (Leipzig 1879), (reprint Graz, 1959), col I (PL 187, 29, has the reading "jus naturale").

The confusion has exercised commentators from the very beginning. [19] And from the beginning Ulpian's natural law appears in the writings of the decretists who tend, as is the way of commentators, to list more or less systematically the possible meanings of the terms in their text. It was scarcely to be expected that there would be unanimity among them in their handling of Ulpian's definition. The decretists of the half century following Gratian's work present a wide variety of approach to Ulpian's definition, ranging from an unequivocal rejection, through a more or less reluctant acceptance of it as a concession to usage, to its adoption into the list of possible meanings of natural law. [20] The preference of many of the decretists was for an association of the natural law with reason. Rufinus, one of the earliest and greatest of them, speaks of it thus: *Est itaque naturale jus vis quaedam humanae creaturae a natura insita ad faciendum bonum cavendumque contrarium*, [21] a phrase that recalls Cicero.

In the last decade of the twelfth century and the first of the thirteenth there seems to have been a pause in the production of commentaries on the *Decretum Gratiani*. [22] The authoritative *Glossa ordinaria*, the work of Johannes Teutonicus (John Zimeke) about 1216-1217 and accepted as the standard commentary by subsequent students of Gratian, may be regarded as a mosaic of the current views of the canonists about the natural law. The meanings are arranged in hierarchical order. There is a natural law which is concerned with all beings, one which is limited in its application to animals, and one which takes cognisance of rational beings only. In addition, and somewhat outside the classification, there

19   O. Lottin, *Le droit naturel chez saint Thomas d'Aquin et ses prédécesseurs* (Bruges 1931), p. 11 stigmatised Gratian's definition as "une fâcheuse confusion entre le droit naturel et le droit divin." Some see the influence of St Augustine in the definition, e.g. F. Arnold, "Die Rechtslehre des Magister Gratianus," *Studia Gratiana*, 1 (1953-1954), pp. 369-370. H. E. Feine, *Kirkliche Rechtsgeschichte* (Köln-Graz, 4. Aufl., 1964), pp. 331-332, suggests that the explanation of Gratian's definition may lie partly in the distinction he makes between the natural law (i.e. the moral precepts of the Old Testament and the divinely revealed law of the New Testament) which alone binds the Holy See and other laws which do not: "Sacrosancta Romana ecclesia ius et auctoritatem sacris canonibus impertit, sed non eis alligatur." Another suggestion is that the "law" in Gratian's definition is the Roman law. Cf. C. Leitmaier, "Das Privateigentum im Gratianischen Dekret," *Studia Gratiana*, 2 (1954), pp. 369-370.

20   Rufinus (1157-1159) and Simon of Bisignano (1177-1179) wholly reject Ulpian's definition; the authors of the *Summa Monacensis* and of the *Summa Lipsiensis* (c. 1186) and Huguccio of Ferrara (c. 1188) tolerate the usage; Stephen of Tournai (c. 1160), the author of the *Summa Coloniensis* (1169-1170), Sicard of Cremona (after 1179) accept the definition each in his own way. Cf. O. Lottin, *Le droit naturel chez saint Thomas d'Aquin et ses prédécesseurs* (Bruges 1931) pp. 13-23 and Appendices I-V; Id., *Psychologie et morale aux xiiᵉ et xiiiᵉ siècles*, t. II (Louvain-Gembloux), 1948, pp. 73-75.

21   H. Singer (ed.), *Die Summa Decretorum des Magister Rufinus* (Paderborn 1902), p. 6.

22   Cf. S. Kuttner, "Bernardus Compostellanus Antiquus, A. Study in the Glossators of the Canon Law," *Traditio* 1 (1943), pp. 277-340, at pp. 279-292.

is said to be a natural law which is the equivalent of the Decalogue. This kind of hierarchical classification will be a commonplace of the theologians who, from about the time of the *Glossa ordinaria*, were beginning to write their systematic treatises on the natural law. [23]

III. St. Thomas's Immediate Sources

First of the immediate sources from which St. Thomas could have taken Ulpian's definition is, of course, the Roman law itself. Most of the glossators and post-glossators of the *Corpus Iuris Civilis* accept the definition, although some qualify it as an improper sense of the term "natural law." The first of the great medieval glossators, Irnerius (c. 1035-1125), who taught at Bologna in the last decades of the eleventh century, has no express reference to Ulpian; nor does there appear to have been much interest in the subject evinced in his twelfth century successors. [24] The thirteenth century civilians, however, following in the footsteps of Azo (who commented upon the Code of Justinian about 1210) and Accursius, the author of the *Great Gloss*, did face the question. They arrive at a list of meanings of "natural law" not unlike that of the decretists. The meanings are basically four. [25] There is, first of all, a generic natural law based upon the natural inclinations common to all animals. Azo defines it, *motus quidem instinctu naturae proveniens quo singula animalia ad aliquid faciendum inducuntur.* This, Ulpian's definition, is accepted by most of the commentators, although with qualifications by some. In the discussions some of the more paradoxical consequences are explored — the difficulty for instance, that, if Ulpian's definition is to be taken at its face value, the distinction between fornication and marriage becomes uneasy. To say that marriage is based upon contract or consent is to stress its rational character and, it seems, to remove it from the natural law conceived strictly in Ulpian's terms. [26] It is a problem that will continue to be discussed in the thirteenth century and later, and one to which there may be no answer short of the abandonment of Ulpian.

---

[23] Cf. O. Lottin, *Le droit naturel chez saint Thomas d'Aquin et ses prédécesseurs* (Bruges 1931), p. 23; M. Grabmann, "Das Naturrecht der Scholastik von Gratian bis Thomas von Aquin," *Mittelalterliche Geistesleben*, I (München 1926), p. 68.

[24] Cf. H. Kantorowicz, *Studies in the Glossators of the Roman Law* (Cambridge 1938), pp. 35-37, 146-148. One twelfth century civilian, Roger, wrote a treatise *De iure naturali, gentium et civili* in which he recorded Ulpian's definition almost without comment: "Dicitur ius naturale quasi a natura animali, quod omnium animalium sit commune." H. Kantorowicz, op. cit., p. 275.

[25] W. Onclin, "Le droit naturel selon les Romanistes des XIIᵉ et XIIIᵉ siècles; *Miscellanea Moralia A. Janssen* (Louvain 1948), II, pp. 329-338.

[26] W. Onclin, art. cit.

Of the other definitions retained by the civilians the most important
is the specifically human natural law, sometimes called *jus gentium* by
Accursius and Azo. This, and Ulpian's definition, persist with the civil
lawyers of the twelfth and thirteenth centuries in an uneasy relationship. Their reconciliation is described in a text of Cinus of Pistoia
(1270-1336), Dante's friend and a poet of the *dolce stil nuovo* as well as
a great lawyer.[27] Of the two the definition of Ulpian is the one officially
adopted by the *legistica traditio* — which is hardly surprising, given the
prominence enjoyed by it in the *Corpus Iuris Civilis*.[28] When a
theologian like St. Thomas opts for it he is, then, not making an arbitrary choice among the available juristic definitions but rather taking
the jurists' own choice.

Side by side with the lawyers, the theologians must be counted among
St. Thomas's immediate sources in the matter of Ulpian's definition.
Early medieval theology, as represented by the school of Anselm of
Laon († 1117), developed a characteristically theological teaching
about the natural law and left little room for Ulpian. The natural law is
a product of natural reason and, because men neglected it, is sup-
plemented by the Mosaic law. This view helped to point the way to
Gratian's definition of the natural law as *quod in lege et Evangelio continetur*.[29] Hugh of St. Victor holds a similar view.[30] Peter Abelard, in
his *Commentary on Romans*, speaks of the natural law as preceding the
Mosaic law; and in the *Dialogus* he adopts the Ciceronian distinction
between the *jus naturale*, prescribed by natural reason, and the *jus
positivum*, set up by men.[31] There is no room for Ulpian here either.

When, just after the mid-twelfth century, Peter Lombard wrote his
Book of Sentences, which was to have such a formative influence upon
medieval theology, he was reticent about the natural law. He refers to it
only in passing and in a context entirely in keeping with the views of
the school of Anselm of Laon; the natural law is summarised in the
prohibition of doing to others what a man would not have done to him-

27 *De justitia et jure*, i,10,3 cited by W. Onclin, art. cit. "Homo est creatus in duabus materiis,
una scilicet quam communem habet cum ceteris animalibus...et secundum hanc naturam
describitur jus naturale in legibus; altera vero quam communem habet cum angelis, scilicet
rationabilitatem, secundum quam jus definitur in canone."
28 Cf. the Gloss of Faventinus, cited in W. Ullman, *Medieval Papalism* (London 1949), p. 40:
"Hoc autem jus legistica traditio generalissime definit dicens: jus naturale est quod natura omnia
animalia docuit"; J. M. Aubert, *Le droit romain dans l'œuvre de saint Thomas* (Paris 1955), p. 95.
29 F. Bliemitzrieder, *Anselms von Laon Systematische Sentenzen* (Münster 1919), pp. 35-36;
"Contra originale peccatum sunt inventa remedia et in naturali et in scripta lege et in tempore
gratiae. Naturalem autem legem naturalis ratio tenere persuadet ut quod homo non occidatur; hanc
enim sua naturalis ratio unumquemque docet."
30 *De sacramentis legis naturalis et scriptae*, (PL 176, 39).
31 *Expositio in Epistolam Pauli ad Romanos*, (PL 178, 814-862); *Dialogus*, (PL 178, 1656).

self, and this *praeceptum juris naturalis* had to be reiterated in the Decalogue because of man's negligence of it. [32]

Peter Lombard's commentators and successors in the following century did not share his reticence about the natural law; before the middle of the thirteenth century the *Tractatus de legibus* had become an integral part of theology. And in this theological elaboration the natural law looms large and Ulpian has his say. The general development of the treatise on law in the theology of the thirteenth century has frequently been studied. Here it is necessary only to mention some of the important predecessors of St. Thomas and their attitude towards Ulpian's definition.

As with the decretists and the civilians, so with the theologians there is a tendency to list and to systematize the meanings of the natural law. Thus in the *Summa aurea* of William of Auxerre, in the first important integration of the natural law into theology, Ulpian's definition appears, described as natural law in the wide sense, as opposed to the strict sense which connects natural law with reason. [33] This general classification recurs in later writers; *ius naturale quoddam est speciale, quoddam universalius, quoddam universalissimum.* Roland of Cremona, teaching at Paris about 1229-1230, speaks of the inclination towards good in all creatures as a generic natural law under which are the more specific laws related to vegetative, animal and human nature. The *ius specialius in animalibus* he attributes to Boethius. [34]

The same ideas are also found in the important Franciscan tradition in the law-tract of the thirteenth century. The *Summa fratris Alexandri* (Book III, containing the law treatise, being the work of Alexander's collaborator, John of La Rochelle) set the tradition. [35] Here there are said to be several kinds of natural law, each derived in its own way from

---

32 Petrus Lombardus, *Liber Sententiarum*, III, D. 37 (PL 192, 832). O. Lottin, *Psychologie et morale aux xii⁰ et xiii⁰ siècles*, II (Louvain-Gembloux 1948), p. 73: "nulle part il ne parle du droit naturel", appears to have overlooked this reference; in *Le droit naturel chez saint Thomas d'Aquin et ses prédécesseurs* (Bruges 1931), p. 28, he had said more exactly: "nulle part il ne relève la moindre définition du *jus naturae*." Lombard also refers to the natural law in *Collectanea in Epistolas Divi Pauli* (PL 191, 1345).

33 Cf. O. Lottin, *Psychologie et morale aux xii⁰ et xiii⁰ siècles*, II (Louvain-Gembloux 1948), pp. 75-76.

34 O. Lottin, *Le droit naturel chez saint Thomas d'Aquin et ses prédécesseurs* (Bruges 1931), Appendix VII, p. 115: "Est aliud ius speciale magis in animalibus quod unumquodque animal coniungitur ad sibi simile, sicut dicit Boethius..."

35 V. Doucet, *Prolegomena in librum III necnon in libros I et II in Summa fratris Alexandri* (Quaracchi 1948), IV, pp. CCCLXIX, CCCVII: cf. I. Brady, "Law in the Summa fratris Alexandri," *Proceedings of the American Catholic Philosophical Association*, 24 (1950), pp. 133-136; F. Henquinet, "Ist der Traktat de legibus et praeceptis in der Summa Alexanders von Hales von Johannes von Rupella?", *Franziskanische Studien*, 26 (1930), pp. 1-22, 234-258.

the eternal law.[36] Amongst them is the natural law common to man and animal — which the *Summa fratris Alexandri* wrongly attributes to Isidore.

This is the tradition in which one would expect to find Bonaventure although, in fact, he has no special treatise on laws. A good deal can be pieced together from his various references, for example in the *Breviloquium*, to establish his views on the eternal law and the natural law.[37] But it is in his *Commentary on the Sentences* that he cites and eulogizes Ulpian's definition. He records three definitions, all of which he attributes to Isidore:

> Dicendum quod jus naturale tripliciter sumitur, scilicet communiter, proprie et magis proprie et secundum hoc tripliciter definitur...Uno modo sic: Jus naturale est quod in Lege et Evangelio continetur...Secundo modo dicitur proprie et sic definitur...jus naturale est quod est commune omnium nationum et hoc jus est quod dictat ratio recta...Tertio modo dicitur jus naturale propriissime quod natura docuit omnia animalia.[38]

Bonaventure does not give his reason for preferring Ulpian's definition. Nor is there much enlightenment to be found in his application of these notions. Fornication, he says, is against the natural law in the first sense, since it is forbidden in the Law and the Gospel; it is also against the natural law of the second definition, as being against right reason; but the natural law in Ulpian's sense neither approves nor condemns, for animals propagate in different ways.[39] Nor does Bonaventure appeal to Ulpian's definition as a way around the difficulty of the polygamy of the Old Testament Patriarchs. He might have suggested that nature has taught many animals to take a plurality of mates; instead he says that polygamy is against the animal nature of man, which inclines him towards exclusiveness in marriage, and he concedes that God could and did dispense the patriarchs from this obligation.[40]

---

36   III, pars 2, Inquis. 1, c. 7, a. 4 (Quaracchi, t. IV, n. 223, pp. 328-329): "Dicendum quod omnis lex naturalis est a lege aeterna, tamen secundum propinquius et remotius, secundum quod naturae, in quibus est, se habent secundum propinquius et remotius ad Deum."

37   *Breviloquium* I,9 (*Opera Omnia*, Quaracchi, 1889, t. V, p. 2176); cf. L. Baur, *Die lehre vom Naturrecht bei Bonaventura* (Münster 1913), p. 223 et passim.

38   *In IV Sent.*, d. 33, a. 1, q. 1 (*Opera Omnia*, Quaracchi, t. IV, pp. 747-748).

39   Centuries later supporters of Ulpian's definition still had not found a satisfactory reason for asserting that it excluded fornication. Cf. F. Suarez, *De legibus* (*Opera Omnia*, ed. Berton, Paris, 1856, t. V), II, c. 17.

40   *In IV Sent.*, d. 33, a. 1, q. 2 (*Opera Omnia*, Quaracchi, 1889, t. IV, pp. 749-750): "Si dicatur jus naturale quod natura impressit animalibus, sic dicendum quod non omnibus, sed aliquibus animalibus brutis impressit; sed tamen in natura est aliquorum animalium, et in nostra hoc natura plantavit."

Albert the Great's approach to the definition of Ulpian is in lively contrast with Bonaventure's. Albert (1206-1280) deals expressly with the natural law several times in his long career. In the *Summa de bono* (part three of his *Summa de creaturis*) and in his *Commentary on the Nicomachean Ethics* his treatment is much the same; and it includes a clear rejection of Ulpian. In the *Summa de bono* he begins with Cicero's description of the natural law as implanted by an innate force — *quod non opinio genuit sed quaedam innata vis inseruit.* In enlarging upon this *innata vis* he goes out of his way to disagree with the understanding of the natural law that would make it common to us and to animals.[41] In the following article he is even more forthright in rejecting the natural law common to animate creatures that he found in the decretists. He has little patience with the ingenuity of the doctors who made distinctions to accommodate Ulpian, forgetting that there can be a natural law in the proper sense only for man.[42] Earlier in the *Summa de creaturis*, where he is discussing the polygamy of the Old Testament patriarchs, Albert distinguishes between the nature man has in common with animals (and needs only the difference between male and female for propagation) and the nature (or *ratio*) proper to man, which demands that the act of propagation be reasonably accomplished.[43]

Some years later, when between 1248 and 1252 Albert commented at Cologne on the *Nicomachean Ethics* of Aristotle, his views had scarcely changed. He insists once again that natural law (and the natural justice of Aristotle's distinction between natural and legal justice) belongs to the specific nature of man, namely reason, and not to any nature man may share with other creatures.[44]

Finally, there is Albert's *Ethica*, composed probably later than 1260.[45] Here Albert devotes his efforts to reconciling Aristotle's and Cicero's approaches to the natural law. He does not discuss Ulpian or the jurists directly; but when he comes to the *innata vis*, the innate

41 *Summa de bono*, Tractatus V De justitia, q.1, a.1, ed. W. Kubel - F. Heyer (*Opera Omnia*, XXVIII, Münster 1951, pp. 265-266): "Non enim consentimus in distinctionem quam quidem posuerunt, scilicet quod ius naturale multis modis dicatur, et uno modo sit commune nobis cum brutis."

42 Id., q.1, a.2 (pp. 268-269): "Non erit jus naturale nisi solius hominis...Haec distinctio nec artem nec rationem habet sicut mos est decretistarum ponere distinctiones..."

43 *Summa de bono*, De Sacramentis, Tractatus IX De Matrimonio, ed. A. Ohlmeyer (*Opera Omnia*, Münster 1958, p. 165). The same teaching is found in Albert's *Commentary on the Sentences, In IV Sent.*, d. 33A, aa. 1-3 (*Opera Omnia*, ed. A. Borgnet, Paris 1890-1898, t. XXX, pp. 289-296).

44 Cf. G. Fasso, *La legge della ragione* (Bologna 1964), Appendix 19-20, pp. 268-269; G. Meersseman, "Le droit naturel chez s. Thomas d'Aquin et ses prédécesseurs," *Angelicum*, 9 (1932), pp. 63-76.

45 *Opera Omnia*, ed. A. Borgnet, t. VII.

natural force, of Cicero's conception of the natural law, he takes good care to point out that the nature in question cannot be the animal nature of man, but rather must be his rational nature. This precludes any real acceptance of Ulpian's definition and shows that Albert never wavered in his insistence upon the essentially rational character of the natural law and in his radical rejection of Ulpian. This makes it all the more curious that St. Thomas, in so many matters the faithful follower of Albert, should in this matter opt for the view of Bonaventure who, it will be recalled, adopted Ulpian's definition.

IV. St. Thomas and Ulpian

The development of the thought of St. Thomas Aquinas on the natural law presents a familiar picture. There are a number of relatively isolated discussions in the early works giving way to the systematic treatment in the *Summa theologiae* at the end of his career. In the early discussions, notably in the *Commentary on the Sentences*, a number of conceptions of the natural law appear to compete for his assent, amongst them Ulpian's. Indeed, in the most extended treatment of the natural law in the *Sentences* St. Thomas begins by making a place for Ulpian:

> Lex ergo naturalis nihil est aliud quam conceptio homini naturaliter indita qua dirigitur ad convenienter agendum in actionibus propriis, sive competant ei ex natura generis ut generare, comedere et hujusmodi, sive ex natura speciei ut ratiocinari et similia.[46]

As the discussion proceeds it becomes clear that the rational nature of man is much more important than the generic (or animal) nature. One would, therefore, expect that the emphasis upon Ulpian's definition would be correspondingly muted.[47] In the *Summa theologiae* natural law is firmly situated in the treatise on law and linked with the notion of law in general (*ordinatio rationis*) and with the eternal law of which it is said to be the rational creature's participation.[48]

This broad outline, however, calls for qualification. One of the details that does not fit is, precisely, Ulpian's definition. While it agrees somewhat uneasily with some of Aquinas's early formulations, it is certainly difficult to reconcile with his mature thought on the essence of

---

46 *In IV Sent.*, d. 33, q. 1, a. 1.

47 The cognate discussions of synderesis and conscience in the *Commentary on the Sentences* confirm the importance of rational nature as the basis of natural law. Cf. *In II Sent.*, d. 24, q. 2, a. 3; Id., d. 39, q. 3, a. 1; *De veritate*, q. 16.

48 1-2ae, q. 90; q. 94.

the natural law. Yet Ulpian's definition remains in honour throughout. This is the matter that demands closer scrutiny.

St. Thomas's first major confrontation with the natural law comes in his discussion of the polygamy of the Old Testament patriarchs: Is it or is it not against the natural law to have more than one wife? The question, as has been noted, has a peculiar acuteness for the theologian aware both of the sacramental character of marriage and of the practices, in the fields of polygamy and divorce, condoned if not actually approved in the Old Testament. St. Thomas's conclusion is that polygamy — that is to say a plurality of wives or polygyny — is against the secondary but not against the primary precepts of the natural law. But nature has clearly not taught all animals to avoid a plurality of mates. Consequently, if Ulpian's definition is to be accepted, there would seem to be no grounds for saying that polygamy is against the natural law.

St. Thomas replies to this objection[49] by distinguishing, as so many of his predecessors had done, between the senses of "natural law." Natural law, firstly, is so called because "its principle is nature"; it proceeds from or is impressed by nature. This meaning of the term is associated with Cicero's definition: *jus naturale est quod non opinio genuit sed quaedam innata vis inseruit*. Natural law, in a second sense, "proceeds from an extrinsic principle which is above nature." In this sense the "divine law" might be said to be natural because coming from God, who is above nature. Here St. Thomas accommodates Gratian's definition (which he ascribes to Isidore): *jus naturale est quod in Lege et Evangelio continetur*. The third sense is the one upon which the objection depends:

> Dicitur jus naturale non solum a principio sed a natura quia de naturalibus est.[50]

Now since nature is contrasted with reason, man's distinguishing mark, it follows that the law proper to man, even though it be dictated by natural reason, is not the natural law in the strictest meaning of the term. That strictest meaning must be reserved for the dictates of natural reason in the matters which are common to man and animals alike. Hence Ulpian's definition.

This does, perhaps, give as acceptable a sense to Ulpian's definition as is possible. But it is difficult to escape the impression that St.

---

49 *In IV Sent.*, d. 33, q. 1, a. 1 ad 4.

50 Ibid. J. M. Aubert, *Le droit romain dans l'œuvre de saint Thomas* (Paris 1955), p. 98, iabels these definitions respectively "définition suprême extrinsèque, définition par l'essence, le contenu exprimé."

Thomas is straining, as his predecessors had done, to provide a suitable
context for a definition that came to him with the weight of the Roman
law behind it. In such circumstances one looks to see if the sense of
such a definition, verbally adopted, has not been effectively changed.
And in the passage it cannot be said that the thought of St. Thomas is
unambiguous.

The objection he is answering, it will be recalled, is that a natural law
common to man and animals does not exclude polygamy. The difficulty
was how to accept the definition — because of its authority — without
accepting this consequence. In a similar context Albert the Great (who,
of course, rejected Ulpian) had pointed out that nature teaches animals
differently, each according to its species, inclining some to
monogamous unions, others to polygamy.[51] St. Thomas himself,
elsewhere in the *Sentences*, makes the same point in practically the
same terms. When speaking of the natural law status of the marriage
impediment of consanguinity he says: *conjunctio maris et feminae
dicitur esse de jure naturali quia natura hoc omnia animalia docuit; sed
hanc conjunctionem diversa animalia diversimode docuit secundum
diversas eorum conditiones.*[52] The point is more fully developed in a
discussion about the naturalness of marriage:

> Natura hominis ad aliquid inclinat dupliciter. Uno modo quia est con-
> veniens naturae generis; et hoc est commune omnibus animalibus; alio
> modo quia est conveniens naturae differentiae qua species humana abun-
> dat a genere, inquantum est rationalis, sicut actus prudentiae et tem-
> perantiae. Et sicut natura generis, quamvis sit una in omnibus animalibus,
> non tamen est eodem modo in omnibus; ita etiam non inclinat eodem
> modo in omnibus, sed secundum quod unicuique competit.[53]

One wonders why some consideration of this kind was not invoked in order to suggest that the natural law, even in Ulpian's sense, forbids
polygamy to man, the human species demanding monogamy as a pattern of marriage. But then one has departed from the literal sense of
Ulpian's definition; for monogamy is decidedly *not* what nature has
taught all animals. The dilemma seems inescapable.[54] One thing is clear

---

51   *In IV Sent.*, d. 33A, a. 1 ad 4 (*Opera Omnia*, ed. Borgnet, Paris 1890-1898, t. XXX, p. 290):
"Natura omnia animalia hoc docet, sed diversimode secundum diversitatem specierum."
52   *In IV Sent.*, d. 40, q. 1, a. 3 ad 3.
53   *In IV Sent.*, d. 26, q. 1, a. 1 ad 1.
54   J. M. Aubert, *Le droit romain dans l'œuvre de saint Thomas* (Paris 1955), pp. 98-99, offers a
benign interpretation: "Le développement de l'article insère cette...définition dans le même contexte idéologique que précédemment; la nature de l'homme est double; générique, elle s'exprime
dans la fin primaire du mariage; spécifique, dans la fin secondaire. La bigamie ne s'opposant pas à
la réalisation de la première, n'est pas contraire au droit naturel entendu au sens d'Ulpien; ce
droit, tout en portant sur des inclinations communes à tout le règne animal, n'en est pas moins
réglée par la raison; et sous cet aspect il est alors synonyme de loi naturelle dont il exprime un des
principes premiers."

— that St. Thomas does not use St. Albert's escape: outright rejection of Ulpian's definition. Was it diffidence in the face of a formidable tradition or a recognition of a genuine insight on the part of Ulpian?[55]

Certainly the tradition was a formidable one and it made its impact even upon the mature thought of St. Thomas, which might have been expected to show a departure from Ulpian's conception of the natural law. The contexts in which Ulpian's definition reappears are well-known and have been much studied. In the *Summa theologiae* Ulpian makes his appearance, both in the Prima-Secundae and in the Secunda-Secundae, although with considerably less prominence than he was accorded in the *Commentary on the Sentences*.

One does not have to rehearse the mature thought of St. Thomas in any detail in order to see that Ulpian's definition of the natural law must present a difficulty. The article on the existence of the natural law, leading up to the classical definition of the natural law as the rational creature's participation in the eternal law, says as much.[56] The third objection is a rather captious one, turning upon the proposition that the freer a thing is the less it is under law. Man, being a self-determining creature, is freer than animals, which are determined; consequently man should be less under law. This implication constitutes an objection to the conclusion of the article only on the assumption that animals do not come under the natural law; and in his explanation St. Thomas concedes the point. It seems decisive against Ulpian:

> Etiam animalia irrationalia participant rationem aeternam suo modo, sicut et rationalis creatura. Sed quia rationalis creatura participat eam intellectualiter et rationaliter, ideo participatio legis aeternae in creatura rationali proprie lex vocatur: nam lex est aliquid rationis...In creatura autem irrationali non participatur rationaliter: unde non potest dici lex nisi per similitudinem.[57]

The same point is made in a later article, where it is stated that man cannot impose a law upon irrational creatures, no matter how subject they are to him:

> Ideo rebus irrationabilibus homo legem imponere non potest quantumcumque ei subiiciantur. Rebus autem rationabilibus sibi subjectis

---

55 The point that St Thomas's fascination for Ulpian did not blind him to the essential rationality of law is made by G. Fassò, *La legge della ragione* (Bologna 1964), p. 80: "Qualche passo di opere minori o giovanili potrebbe far pensare che l'Aquinate, per verità, si sia lasciato suggestionato dalla definizione di Ulpiano. Però anche in esse la fondamentale distinzione tra esseri razionali ed esseri irrazionali — come destinatari della legge naturale — non manca mai." Cf. S. Cotta, *Il concetto della legge nella Summa Theologiae di San Tommaso d'Aquino* (Torino 1955), pp. 60-61.

56 1-2ae, q. 91, a. 2.

57 Id., ad 3.

potest imponere legem, inquantum suo praecepto vel denuntiatione quacumque imprimit menti earum quandam regulam quae est principium agendi...Alio modo creaturae irrationales subduntur legi aeternae, inquantum moventur a divina providentia, non autem per intellectum divini praecepti sicut creaturae rationales. [58]

The case against Ulpian's definition must seem to be closed; and if St. Thomas were entirely consistent, doubtless it would be. That the definition is not far from his mind emerges from a reading of the key discussion of the natural law. The question is whether the natural law contains several precepts or one only. [59] It begins with an exploration of what self-evidence may mean in relation to moral imperatives, continues with an appeal to the parallel between the procedures of the speculative and the practical intellect, and ends with an articulation of the precepts of the natural law according to the different levels of natural tendency found in man. Man's nature, considered as substance, has a tendency to persevere in being; considered as animal, it has a tendency towards the coupling of male and female and the rearing of offspring; and, as rational, it has a tendency to avoid ignorance, to cooperate with fellow-men and so on. This classification has obvious affinities with the hierarchical ordering of the senses of the natural law in St. Thomas's predecessors; it recalls, for example, the triple acceptation of the *jus naturae* in the *Glossa ordinaria* of Johannes Teutonicus. In the circumstances one would have expected a mention of Ulpian in the case of the tendencies related to the animal nature of man. Ulpian, however, is not mentioned. But, lest this be taken as an argument from silence and an indication of Aquinas's rejection of the Roman law definition, Ulpian makes an unmistakable return in the next question. The logic of Isidore's division of human law is at issue, in particular his putting of the *jus gentium* as a kind of human law "used by nearly all peoples." It might well be thought that any effort to introduce logical consistency into Isidore's divisions is an effort misplaced. And, to further complicate the matter, the particular division of human laws into *jus gentium* and *jus civile*, attributed by St. Thomas to Isidore, is not found formally in Isidore. It seems to be a conflation of two separate divisions, the division of laws into divine and human and the classical trichotomy *jus naturale, jus gentium, jus civile*. Further, there is another dictum of Isidore's that divine laws belonged to nature, human laws to custom — *divinae (leges) naturae, humanae moribus constant.* [60]

58   1-2ae, q. 93, a. 5.
59   1-2ae, q. 94, a. 2.
60   1-2ae, q. 95, a. 4 ad 1; *Etym*, V, 2-4 (PL 82, 198-199).

What is easier, then, than to assimilate *jus naturale* to divine law and *jus gentium* (together with *jus civile*) to human law? And when it is objected that the *jus gentium*, on Isidore's own showing — *quia eo omnes fere gentes utuntur* —, is more natural law than human law, Ulpian comes to the rescue:

> Jus gentium est quidem aliquo modo naturale homini, secundum quod est rationalis, inquantum derivatur a lege naturali per modum conclusionis, quae non est multum remota a principiis. Unde de facili in hujusmodi homines consenserunt. Distinguitur tamen a lege naturali, maxime ab eo quod est omnibus animalibus commune.[61]

This answer, while it meets the current difficulty, has the disadvantage of creating another; for it appears to go against what St. Thomas had said, in a previous article of the same question, about conclusions from the natural law having the force of natural law.[62]

Similar problems arise when we turn to the Secunda-Secundae. Here the topic is *jus*, the *objectum justitiae*, and the viewpoint is, as might have been expected, somewhat different from that of the law-tract in the Prima-Secundae. In concerning himself with the virtue of justice St. Thomas asks whether the division of *jus* into *jus naturale* and *jus positivum* is exhaustive, and whether *jus gentium* and *jus naturale* are distinct or identical.[63] The questions are connected; and the affirmative answer to the first leads on to the latter. And it is here that Ulpian's definition comes once more into play.

Is the *jus gentium* better assimilated to natural law or to positive law? St. Thomas, in order to answer this question, examines the element of equivalence in *jus*, the object of justice. The equivalence may be in the very nature of a given relationship — male is related to female for the purposes of generation or parent to child for the purposes of education. In such cases we have *jus naturale* absolutely speaking. But it may be that a relationship, of itself, does not give us enough information. Private property is an example; a field is no more mine than yours apart from outside considerations about efficient cultivation, peaceful possession, etc. Here we have *jus naturale*, but with a qualification. And the two kinds are reconciled for St. Thomas by the Jurisconsults — he cites Ulpian for natural law in the absolute sense and Gaius for natural law in the qualified sense:

---

61 1-2ae, q. 95, a. 4 ad 1.

62 1-2ae, q. 95, a. 2: "Derivantur ergo quaedam a principiis communibus legis naturae per modum conclusionum...quaedam vero per modum determinationis...utraque igitur inveniuntur in lege humana. Sed ea quae sunt primi modi continentur in lege humana non tamquam sint solum lege posita, sed habent etiam aliquid vigoris ex lege naturali..." Cf. L. Clément, "Le *jus gentium*", *Révue de l'Université d'Ottawa*, Section spéciale, 9-10 (1940), pp. 188-191.

63 2-2ae, q. 57, aa. 2.3.

Absolute autem apprehendere aliquid non solum convenit homini, sed etiam aliis animalibus. Et ideo jus quod dicitur naturale secundum primum modum, commune est nobis et aliis animalibus. A jure autem naturali sic dicto recedit ius gentium, ut Iurisconsultus dicit, quia illud omnibus animalibus, hoc solum hominibus inter se commune est.[64]

Ulpian is not named explicitly, although Gaius is. But Ulpian's definition plays a critical rôle in solving the present difficulty. Whether the solution, making the *jus gentium* a natural law peculiar to man, is consistent with the suggestion noticed in the Prima-Secundae that *jus gentium* belongs more to positive law, is another matter.[65]

It may be thought that too much stress is here being laid upon what are, after all, passing references to Ulpian in the *Summa theologiae*.[66] Indeed, as has already been seen, the general view of the natural law in the *Summa* is hardly reconcilable with Ulpian's definition. Yet Aquinas does appear to feel a need, not altogether explained by his habit of deference to authorities, to make provision for Ulpian. There are two considerations that should prevent too easy an acceptance of the view that the references to a law of nature common to man and animals are merely incidental in the *Summa*. One is that St. Thomas's *Commentary on the Ethics* of Aristotle, written later even than the parts of the *Summa* with which we have been concerned, is far from rejecting Ulpian. The other — which cannot here be pursued — is that for centuries after St. Thomas sporadic efforts continued to be made by disciples and followers of his to accommodate Ulpian's natural law.[67]

It is now generally accepted that St. Thomas wrote his *Commentary on the Ethics* of Aristotle very late in his career, in 1271-1272. The

---

64 2-2ae, q. 57, a. 3.

65 Further discussion of this problem would involve an examination of St. Thomas's handling of the two classical dispositions of the *jus gentium*, slavery and private property, dispositions that had already exercised the Roman jurists. Cf. R. Voggensperger, *Der Begriff des "ius naturale" im Römischen Recht* (Basel 1952), pp. 17-24, 36-39.

66 Cf. S. Cotta, *Il concetto della legge nella Summa theologiae di S. Tommaso d'Aquino* (Torino 1955), p. 64: "...gli occasionali riferimenti alla formula del *Digesto* contenuti nella *Summa* mi sembra che debbono o esser considerati elementi eterogenei, quasi meccanicamente ripetuti, o vadano meglio intesi nel quadro generale del pensiero tomista..."

67 So, for example, Peter of Tarentaise, *In IV Sent.*, d. 33, q. 1, a. 1 and other works cited in O. Lottin, *Psychologie et morale aux xiiᵉ et xiiiᵉ siècles* (Louvain 1948),II,pp.92-93; Giles of Rome, *De regimine principum*, III, pars ii, c. 25. In the "Silver Age" of scholasticism some writers continued to show a qualified acceptance of Ulpian. Domingo Bañez, for example, spoke of *jus naturale nobis et brutis commune* — cf. M. Van Overbeke, "S. Thomas et le droit," *Revue thomiste*, 55 (1955), p. 552. The more usual view was that of Francisco Suarez, who rejected Ulpian's definition as *metaphorica et valde analoga*. Cf. *De legibus*, II, c. 3, n. 9 (*Opera Omnia*, ed. Berton, Paris, 1856, t. 5). There is a useful collection of texts on this question in S. Ramirez, *El derecho de gentes* (Madrid 1955).

point is of considerable importance for studies of the development of his thought; and it is relevant to the present discussion. [68]

Aristotle's notice of "natural justice" provides St. Thomas, as it has done (and to this day still does) other commentators on the *Ethics*, with an occasion of discussing the natural law.

> Of political justice part is natural, part legal, — natural that which everywhere has the same force and does not exist by people's thinking this or that; legal that which is originally indifferent but when it has been laid down is not indifferent... [69]

The text used by St. Thomas[70] rendered Aristotle's δίκαιον φυσικόν *justum naturale*. Aristotle had divided the *justum politicum* into *justum naturale* and *justum legale*, a division that, St. Thomas suggests, is the same as the jurists' division of *jus naturale* and *jus positivum*. The reconciliation if effected by explaining the ambiguity of *justum politicum*; for Aristotle it is the general term, sub-divided into *justum naturale* and *justum legale*, whereas for the jurists the *justum politicum* is divided against the *naturale*. [71]

It is when Aquinas comes to consider the *justum naturale* at close quarters that he makes appeal to Ulpian, although without naming him explicitly. Having identified the natural law with a series of rational principles — the principles that can be related in a reasoning process as premiss and conclusion, as, for instance, the prohibition of stealing follows as a conclusion from the prohibition of injuring others,[72] he goes on to consider how such natural law judgments follow upon the inclinations of nature:

> Est autem considerandum quod iustum naturale est ad quod hominem natura inclinat. Attenditur autem in homine duplex natura: una quidem secundum quod est animal, quae est sibi aliisque animalibus communis; alia autem est natura hominis quae est propria sibi in quantum est homo, prout scilicet secundum rationem discernit turpe et honestum. Iuristae autem illud tantum dicunt ius naturale quod consequitur inclinationem

---

68 R. A. Gauthier, "La date du Commentaire de saint Thomas sur l'Ethique à Nicomaque," *Recherches de théologie ancienne et médiévale*, 18 (1951), pp. 66-105; *Sententia Libri Ethicorum (Sancti Thomae de Aquino Opera Omnia*, t. XLVII, Romae, 1969) Praefatio, p. 201: "... admirari enim solet de multitudine operum quae Thomas in parvo tempore confecit, praesertim cum *Sententiam Libri Ethicorum* Lutetiae Parisiorum circa annos 1271-1272 scripserit dum secundam partem *Summae theologiae* aliaque opera scribebat." Cotta's argument — supra note (66) — is in part based upon a mistaken chronology of St. Thomas's writings.

69 *Nic. Eth.*, V, 7, 1134b18-21.

70 Cf. R. A. Gauthier, *Sententia Libri Ethicorum*, Praefatio, III, 1, "De libri Ethicorum codice a Thoma usurpato" (*Opera Omnia*, t. XLVII, Romae, 1969), pp. 203* - 231*.

71 *In V Eth.*, lectio 12 (*Opera Omnia*, t. XLVII, Romae 1969), p. 304, 12-33.

72 Ibid., p. 305, 49-57.

naturae communis homini et aliis animalibus, sicut coniunctio maris et
feminae, educatio natorum et alia huiusmodi; illud autem ius quod consequitur propriam inclinationem naturae humanae, in quantum scilicet
homo est rationale animal, vocant ius gentium. quia eo omnes gentes
utuntur, sicut quod pacta sint servanda, quod legati etiam apud hostes
sint tuti, at alia huiusmodi. Utrumque autem horum comprehenditur sub
iusto naturali, prout hic a Philosopho accipitur.[73]

This is not an enthusiastic adoption of Ulpian's definition — St.
Thomas recognises it as a restrictive sense of natural law. But it is not
a rejection of Ulpian; and, even when it is borne in mind that St.
Thomas's preoccupation in commenting is to uncover the *sensus
Aristotelis*, this fact is significant. He does make use of Ulpian's
definition despite its incongruity with his general view.[74]

To this consideration of St. Thomas's later thought on Ulpian's
definition of the natural law one might add one or two vague passages
in the *Commentary on the Politics* of Aristotle.[75] There are no direct
references to Ulpian's natural law. There is, however, the passage,
apropos of Aristotle's saying that man is a political animal, in which St.
Thomas enlarges upon the distinction between man and animals. Man's
social or political nature is contrasted with the gregariousness of certain
animals or with the organising capacity of bees. What really
distinguishes man from the animals is his power of speech — the expression of thought; the voice of animals is sound without meaning. As
an example of the knowledge that man expresses in his speech St.
Thomas adduces the distinction between good and evil, between just
and unjust. This would seem to rule out any real acceptance of Ulpian's
definition.[76]

The same conclusion may be drawn perhaps more vaguely, from

---

73   Ibid., p. 305, 57-75.

74   S. Cotta, *Il concetto di legge nella Summa theologiae di S. Tommaso* (Torino 1955), pp. 61-
62: "Dunque i sudetti testi, lunghi dall' offrirci una univoca interpretazione naturalistica dello *ius
naturale*, ci indicano invece come essa appaia insufficiente a S. Tommaso. Tuttavia non si può
negare ch'egli sia pure in parte, la mantenga e l'accetti, e quindi il problema, per quanto ridotto a
proporzioni minori, rimane." Passages in the *Sententia Libri Ethicorum* confining law to rational
beings and implying, therefore, a rejection of Ulpian, are plentiful. Cf. *In V Eth.*, lectio 16 (*Opera
Omnia*, t. XLVII, p. 323, 103-104: "Talia sunt facta humana, de quibus dantur leges"; *In X Eth.*,
lectio 12 (Ibid., p. 592, 161-168), etc.

75   The Thomistic text ends at *In III Pol.*, lectio 6, the completion being the work of Peter of
Auvergne. The date has not yet been satisfactorily established, but there is fairly general
agreement that St. Thomas began his commentary during his second Paris period, 1269-1272. On
these matters cf. H. F. Dondaine, L. J. Bataillon, Préface, *Sententia Libri Politicorum (Opera Omnia*, t. XLVIII, Romae, 1971, pp. A5-A8).

76   *In I Pol.*, lectio 1 (*Sententia Libri Politicorum*, Lib. I, c. 1/b, 142-146, *Opera Omnia*, t.
XLVIII, Romae, 1971, p. A79): "... locutio est propria hominibus, quia hoc est proprium eis in
comparatione ad alia animalia, quod habeant cognitionem boni et mali, iusti et iniusti, et aliorum
huiusmodi que sermone significari possunt."

those passages further on in the *Commentary on the Politics* in which St. Thomas puts as good a face as he can on Aristotle's doctrine of the natural slavery of some men. Speaking of the varieties of domination, he remarks that, despite their common nature, man is naturally master of the other animals. Domesticated animals are *digniora* than wild animals precisely because they participate in the rule of reason.[77] There is nothing here about a common law, based upon the common nature of man and animals; if anything the stress upon the rule of reason excludes it. Again, one might look to the following *lectio*, in which the issue of slavery is joined expressly in terms of natural and human law. In what reads like a piece of special pleading Aquinas concedes that slavery by conquest may be injust (for the less wise may enslave their betters) and yet may be provided for in human law, on the ground that it places a premium upon valour, which is not without its use for the common good.[78] This recalls a controversy that was found already in the Roman law about the status of slavery and in which Ulpian's dictum that all men are by nature equal carried the implication that slavery must have been introduced by the *jus gentium*.[79] But St. Thomas has nothing here to say about Ulpian's natural law.

Conclusion

The conclusion to be drawn is hardly startling. It is simply that St. Thomas's complacency towards what he calls the Jurists' definition of the natural law — in fact, Ulpian's natural law common to man and animals — remains somewhat surprising, particularly in the later works. This has nothing to do with the original and highly conjectural origins of the definition. On the other hand, it does not seem to be altogether explained by the adventitious authority conferred upon the definition by its adoption in the authoritative *Corpus Iuris Civilis*; for other medieval writers, no readier than Aquinas to dispute the authority of Justinian and the Roman law, were able to relegate Ulpian's natural law to a relatively obscure rôle. Not many, admittedly, went as far as Albert the Great and rejected Ulpian out of hand, although a precedent

---

77 *In I Pol.*, lectio 3 (*Sententia Libri Politicorum*, Lib. I, c. 3, 178-185): "... similiter se habet in homine et aliis animalibus quod naturale et expediens est ut homo aliis dominetur; videmus enim quod animalia mansueta quibus homo dominatur, digniora sunt secundum naturam siluestribus in quantum participant aliqualiter regimine rationis..."

78 *In I Pol.*, lectio 4 (*Sententia Libri Politicorum*, Lib I, c. 4, 101-112).

79 Cf. R. Voggensperger, *Der Begriff des "ius naturale" im Römischen Recht* (Basel 1952), pp. 17-24.

might have been found in the Roman law, and even in Ulpian, for the denial of a law common to man and animals.[80] Most, with that penchant for lists and classifications that characterised theologians and lawyers — both civil and canon — easily enough accommodated Ulpian without having to take his definition more seriously than they took, for example, the "cosmic justice" backed by the authority of Plato in the *Timaeus*.

The trend, undoubtedly, was to develop more and more the rational aspect of the natural law and to be correspondingly less conciliatory towards Ulpian. Aquinas (and Bonaventure) go against the trend. St. Thomas's early going out of his way to approve of Ulpian's definition and his retention of it almost to the end of his career remains, in the last resort, slightly puzzling.

---

80   The consensus of Stoic philosophy, which formed such an important part of the background to the Roman law, was against a law common to man and animals. Cf. Diogenes Laertius, *Vit. Philos*, VII, 129: "Placet item illis nulla non lege naturae teneri adversus reliqua animalia ob naturae dissimilitudinem, ut Chrysippus in primo de iustitia et Poseidonius in primo de officiis tradunt." Cf. Seneca, *Ep. ad Lucil.*, 121, 124; *De ira*, ii, 26, 4; M. Pohlenz, *Die Stoa* (Göttingen, 2. Aufl. 1959), pp. 137, 228; M. Villey, *Leçons d'histoire de la philosophie du droit* (Paris 1957), pp. 144-145. In this connection Ulpian's statement that an animal cannot suffer injury *quod sensu caret* (*Liber ad Edictum* partially reproduced in *Inst.*, IV, 9) is worth recording. Perhaps the last word may be left with P. M. Van Overbeke, "S. Thomas et le droit," *Revue thomiste*, 55 (1955), p. 545: "dans une définition du droit naturel ces "animalia" ne manquent pas de rester passablement gênants."

FATALISM AND FREEDOM
ACCORDING TO NEMESIUS AND THOMAS AQUINAS

Gérard Verbeke

DURING the first centuries of the Christian era, as well as in
classical antiquity, the question of fatalism and freedom was controversial. In some currents of contemporary philosophy, the liberty of
human behaviour and the consistency of our existence are excessively
emphasized; this is one of the main reasons why some thinkers of our
time profess atheism, because the existence of God is supposed to be incompatible with the density and full value of human life. In this respect
ancient thinking and contemporary philosophy are clearly opposed:
awareness of human freedom evolved rather slowly from antiquity to
the present time. Apparently ordinary people in Greece had a keen
sense of their dependence upon the world and upon some higher, very
powerful beings, who constantly interfered with the events of human life
and the course of history.[1] This topic is one of the most recurrent
themes in Greek tragedy. Human existence is described as dominated
by higher powers; it cannot escape the grip of blind fate, as is illustrated
by the history of some famous families.[2] The original meaning of
εὐδαιμονία derives from that ancient belief: happiness is not effected
through personal activity and moral behaviour; there is an element of
chance about it, a good luck bestowed on us by the favour of divine

---

1   In a poem of Pindar (*Pyth.* 8) man is called "the dream of a shadow" (σκιᾶς ὄναρ ἄνθρωπος),
he is ἐπάμερος, which means according to H. Fränkel the uncertainty of human existence: "Denn
es ist nicht gemeint dass unsere Lage fortgesetzt wechselt, sondern vielmehr dass sie sich von
einem Tag zum andern radikal ändern kann. Je länger sich unser Leben ausdehnt, desto wahr-
scheinlicher wird es dass wir einen Tag des Umsturzes erleben." H. Fränkel, *Wege und
frühgriechischen Denkens* (Munich 1960), p. 27.
2   Speaking about Homer, H. Fränkel points to the fact that the intervention of the gods in the
Trojan war is not very evident; after all the old city is not destroyed by a heavenly fire. The intervention of the gods is for the most part integrated in the normal course of events in such a way
that the initiative of man is not entirely excluded. H. Fränkel, *Dichtung und Philosophie des
frühen Griechentums* (Munich 1962), p. 79. Still it remains true that those divine beings interfere
on the level of human events and favour some individuals rather than others. In the light of this
primitive belief the opposition of some philosophers to the notion of divine providence becomes
quite understandable.

beings. It was quite a reversal when Socrates, Plato, and Aristotle "in-teriorized" the notion of happiness: according to them, it does not depend on the arbitrary favour of divine powers but is brought about by individual behaviour. Every man is the author of his own life and the architect of his own felicity.[3] If man did not become aware of his freedom very quickly, this is explicable by the fact that he only becomes conscious of his capacities insofar as they are embodied in concrete achievements. One could hardly feel "free" unless he were able to carry out what he wants to do; the praise of man in Sophocles' *Antigone* is a marvellous piece of poetry, and yet the achievements mentioned there are hardly comparable with the discoveries and technical progress of our time. A Greek could not appreciate the capacities man bears within himself as long as they remained on the level of mere possibilities.[4]

Early Christian writers had to cope with the same situation; they also went on asking the same question, whether man may be considered the principle of his own deeds. Is man able to take free initiative, is he a being responsible for his behaviour, or is human life subject to higher powers? When the Christian message entered into history, Stoic philosophy was still widespread over the civilized world and generally accepted by intellectuals. According to philosophers of that school, human behaviour is free as far as the inner attitude is concerned; as to the course of events, man may possibly oppose it, but he is not able to change it in any way.[5] The main duty of man is to accept the events of his own life as well as the history of the world, for both are thoroughly rational. Yet, if human freedom is always stressed by Stoic philosophers, the notion of freedom they proposed is rather narrow, because it does not extend to man's creative activity in the world, but is

---

3   In this respect a sentence of Democritus should be quoted (*Vors.* 68, B 170): εὐδαιμονίη ψυχῆς καὶ κακοδαιμονίη. What does it mean that happiness, as well as its opposite, belongs to the realm of the soul? Obviously this sentence is to be understood against the background of a common belief which is discarded; happiness results from human activity and behaviour.

4   Needless to say, fatalism was accepted, even by philosophers: according to Heraclitus, whatever happens is regulated by destiny (*Vors.* 22, A 1,7: πάντα δὲ γίνεσθαι καθ' εἱμαρμένην). Similarly, the notion of Necessity plays an important role in the philosophy of Parmenides and Empedocles. As for the Stoics, their doctrine on εἱμαρμένη is quite basic in their explanation of the world: instead of denying and opposing destiny, they transformed it radically by identifying it with the divine Reason, the immanent principle of the cosmos. Consequently history in their opinion is completely "rational"; each period of the world is a masterpiece caused irresistibly by the divine Logos.

5   One of the most concise expressions of this Stoic doctrine is to be found in a prayer of Cleanthes, reported by Epictetus (*Man.*, c. 53) and Seneca (*Epist.*, 107, 10; SVF I 527). The author wants to accept willingly and without hesitation the law of destiny; otherwise, opposing the divine Reason, he will have to accept it unwillingly: "Fac nolle, comitabor gemens, malusque patiar, quod pati licuit bono. Ducunt volentem fata, nolentem trahunt."

limited to his behaviour towards the emotions.[6] Stoic philosophers acknowledged the possibility of divination: emphasizing both the unity of the world and the coherence of history, they maintained that it is possible to predict the future because everything in the world is linked with everything else.

As far as astrology is concerned, it is unnecessary to recall that it was largely recognized and practiced in the ancient world. On the other hand, Christianity too, at first glance, seemed to substantiate fatalism, because it strongly emphasizes the weakness of man without the help of God. Do we not read in the Gospel that nothing is put within the control of man? Moreover, according to Christian doctrine, God is omniscient: he knows everything, not only past and present events, but also the future. His foreknowledge extends to all future events, both contingent and necessary. Does this doctrine not entail the suppression of human freedom?[7] In any case, Celsus, as reported by Origen, advocated this doctrine against the Christians.[8] Without entering into details, we might recall that Origen firmly countered all those criticisms; he does not hesitate to acknowledge the freedom of human behaviour. His standpoint may be summarized as follows: human conduct is not regulated by the heavenly bodies, as the astrologists assume; however, the course of the heavenly bodies may be a token of some activities of man. Nor is human conduct determined by influences from outside; man may become conscious of his autonomy within the world by retiring within himself, by drawing his attention to his true self.[9]

6 According to Epictetus (*Diss.* I, 1) a wise man is able to draw a distinction between matters depending on himself and those which are independent of his individual attitude. Because he is endowed with reason, man is aware of himself, his dignity and his capacities. His behaviour is not merely the outcome of the empirical data he receives from the world, he is able to use his representations in one way or another: ἡ χρηστικὴ δύναμις ταῖς φαντασίαις. The Stoic sage accepts the divine law, because it is both rational and irresistible.

7 *De principiis*, III, 124: "Haec quidem dicunt hi qui volunt ex auctoritate divinae Scripturae disserere nihil esse positum in nostra potestate." If certain biblical texts are taken literally (v. gr. "et velle et perficere ex Deo est"), one cannot avoid the conclusion that nothing is placed within the power of man ("quod si est, liberi arbitrii non sumus"). Origen to a certain extent agrees with this doctrine: the capacity of accomplishing voluntary acts springs from God. However, it depends upon each individual to direct this power towards right or wrong deeds ("nostrum vero est motus istos quibus moveri ex Deo habemus vel ad bona vel ad mala convertere"). Cf. Hal Koch, *Pronoia und Paideusis* (Berlin-Leipzig 1932), p. 281 sqq.; E. de Faye, *Origène, sa vie, son œuvre, sa pensée*, 3 vols. (Paris 1923-28), III, pp. 179-198.

8 *Contra Celsum*, II, 17 sqq.; the same objection is to be found in *De oratione*, V, 6. According to Origen the divine foreknowledge does not cause the event; on the contrary this foreknowledge is made possible by the future event. In this context he mentions the sophism of the sick man who believes it to be useless to call a physician: everything being settled by fate, he will die or recover whatever he does. Origen replies that destiny may have settled that somebody will beget children or not; he however, will not manage to beget them without sexual intercourse.

9 According to Origen man is always able to judge whatever influence he undergoes; without his agreement, no act will be performed: εἰ μὴ εὐδόκησις καὶ συγκατάθεσις καὶ ῥοπὴ τοῦ

Finally, human acts are not the result of a mere corporeal situation; in other words, they do not simply spring out of the particular equipment of the body. Of course, Origen does not deny the importance of all these influences, but for him they do not bring about human action as a necessary consequence. [10]

Gregory of Nyssa was obliged to handle the same problem: in a public debate at Constantinople he discussed with a pagan philosopher the question of fatalism. As far as we are informed by the text of Gregory, the philosopher ascribed everything that happens to a necessity of fate; in other words, there are no free decisions. As to the notion of fate, it is conceived as an infrangible concatenation of all events according to the conjunction of the heavenly bodies. Quite in agreement with Stoicism the philosopher professes the unity of the world, comparable to the unity of a living organism; a universal sympathy links together all parts of the cosmos. [11] In his reply Gregory especially stresses the inequality of men born at about the same time; he points to the case of two men, one born shortly before the other, whereas the destiny of both is quite different. One attains the *summum* of happiness, whereas the other endures a miserable condition. [12] Gregory asks whether any reason might account plausibly for the poor and unfortunate life of this man. In Gregory's view fate is to be identified with the free choice of each man; in other words, fate is not a power compelling us from outside: it coincides with our autonomous decision. [13]

In his treatise *De migratione Abrahami*, Philo had already opposed the astrology of the Chaldeans, who also acknowledged the universal sympathy of all parts of the world. According to them the visible cosmos is the only reality; it must be identified with God, unless the soul of the world is God. [14] As one might expect, Philo discards the

---

ἡγεμονικοῦ ἐπὶ τόδε τι (*De principiis*, III, 110). As a matter of fact, it does not depend on the individual to receive some representations, but he is able to judge them by his reason: τὸ δὲ κρῖναι οὑτωσὶ χρήσασθαι τῷ γινομένῳ ἢ ἑτέρως, οὐκ ἄλλου τινος ἔργον ἢ τοῦ ἡμῖν λόγου ἐστίν (*De principiis*, III, 1, 3).

10 *De principiis*, III, 110-111.

11 *Contra fatum*, PG 45, 152 c: ἀλλ' ἐπειδὴ μία τίς ἐστιν ἐν τοῖς οὖσι συμπάθεια, καὶ συνεχές ἐστι τὸ πᾶν ἑαυτῷ, καὶ τὰ καθ' ἕκαστον ἐν τῷ παντὶ θεωρούμενα οἷον ἐπὶ σώματος ἑνὸς ἐν μιᾷ συμπνοίᾳ καταλαμβάνεται. πάντων πρὸς ἄλληλα τῶν μερῶν συννευόντων, τούτου χάριν ἀρχηγικωτέρας οὔσης τῆς ἄνω λήξεως, τὰ περίγεια πάντα τῷ προηγουμένῳ συνδιατίθεται.

12 *Contra fatum*, PG 45, 157.

13 *Contra fatum*, PG 45, 169: δῆλον ἐκ τοῦ ἀκολούθου, ὅτι μοῖρα καὶ εἱμαρμένη ἡ ἑκάστου προαίρεσις γίνεται, τὸ δοκοῦν κατ' ἐξουσίαν προαιρουμένη.

14 *De migratione Abrahami*, 178. Speaking of the Chaldeans, Philo writes: τὴν ἐμμελεστάτην συμφωνίαν τοῦ παντὸς ἐπιδεικνύμενοι τῇ τῶν μερῶν πρὸς ἄλληλα κοινωνίᾳ καὶ συμπαθείᾳ.

notion of God as it was professed by the Chaldeans: God is transcendent, he is not a merely immanent principle like the soul of the world. As far as the heavenly bodies are concerned, they are not the ultimate causes of the events occurring in human life; a prior cause has to be acknowledged, prior to all kinds of becoming and distinct from it. This cause is God, whose power pervades the whole cosmos and is the principle of its cohesion. [15]

Eusebius of Caesarea in his *Praeparatio evangelica* deals with the same question. [16] His criticism is not original: he merely borrows the arguments against Stoic determinism from the *De fato* of Alexander of Aphrodisias. According to D. Amand, these arguments have not been invented by Alexander; they stem from a source that is much earlier, namely Carneades, who initiated the debate against fatalism and whose arguments have been used by many later writers. [17] The particular kind of determinism Carneades intended to counter seems to be the extreme fatalism defended by Chrysippus. [18]

In the view of St. Augustine human freedom is an undeniably important topic, closely connected with his reflection on the problem of evil. One of his works, *De libero arbitrio*, is formally devoted to that question. Augustine endeavours to discover the origin of evil in the world. In his opinion there is no need for seeking any further cause than human freedom: [19] as our mind knows everything else and also itself, in the same way our will disposes of everything else and of itself. Hence man is able to perform right actions, but also to behave wrongly. [20] This does not, however, entail the position that the will is bad. Since it is capable of both wisdom and insanity, the human will occupies an intermediate stage between right and wrong; it belongs to the class of the "media bona." [21] In regard to divine providence, the foreknowledge of God does not suppress the liberty of our actions. That God knows beforehand the wrong actions we will perform does not imply that we

15 *De migratione Abrahami*, 181.
16 *Praeparatio evangelica*, VI, 6, 4-21.
17 *Fatalisme et liberté dans l'Antiquité grecque* (Louvain 1945).
18 D. Amand, op. cit., p. 367.
19 *De libero arbitrio*, III, 22, 63: quae peccata, ut jam diu disseruimus, nonnisi propriae voluntati earum tribuenda sunt, nec ulla ulterior peccatorum causa quaerenda. — III, 17, 48: ergo improba voluntas malorum omnium causa est.
20 *De libero arbitrio*, II, 19, 51: ut quodammodo se ipsa utatur voluntas quae utitur caeteris, sicut seipsam cognoscit ratio, quae cognoscit et caetera. According to Augustine, the same prevails in the memory: ipsa se memoria quodammodo tenet in nobis, quae non solum aliorum, sed etiam sui meminit.-I, 12, 25: quid enim tam in voluntate quam ipsa voluntas sita est?
21 *De libero arbitrio*, II, 19, 50; III, 5, 15: the capacity of free choice is always valuable even in the case of moral decay: ita est excellentior creatura quae libera voluntate peccat, quam quae propterea non peccat, quia non habet liberam voluntatem.

are necessitated to do them. [22] Augustine comes back to the same question in his *De civitate Dei*, book V (especially chapter 10), and argues that instead of talking about fate, we should rather speak of divine providence.

In order to present a general survey of Nemesius's background, I should not disregard Proclus and Boethius, both of whom face the question of fatalism and human behaviour in a neoplatonic perspective. In his treatise *De providentia et fato* Proclus does not really dismiss the doctrine of fate, he only attempts to discover its exact meaning. [23] According to him fate is to be identified with nature, whose domination extends to the whole field of corporeal beings movable by something else. [24] Consequently fate is something divine, though it does not coincide with God; it depends on divine providence and may be called its image. [25] On the other hand, Proclus opposes the doctrine of the Peripatetics and the Stoics, who claim that divine foreknowledge involves the necessity of all events. [26] In his mind the nature of knowledge does not depend upon the object but upon the knowing subject. [27] As for the freedom of human actions, it is to be located in the field of our inner choices and decisions; in other words, it does not belong to anything outside the soul. [28]

The opinion of Boethius shows at least two features akin to the doc-

---

22 *De libero arbitrio*, III, 3, 7: quamobrem, quamvis praesciat Deus nostras voluntates futuras, non ex eo tamen conficitur ut non voluntate aliquid velimis. — III, 3, 8: Non igitur per ejus praescientiam mihi potestas adimitur, quae propterea mihi certior aderit, quia ille cujus praescientia non fallitur, adfuturum mihi esse praescivit.

23 *Procli Diadochi Tria Opuscula* (De Providentia, Libertate, Malo), ed. H. Boese (Berlin 1960).

24 *De Providentia*, 10: Palam utique quod que a fato reguntur et connectuntur ab altero mobilia sunt et corporalia omnino. Si autem hoc demonstratum est, manifestum quod causam connexionis fatum ponentes ipsum presidem ab altero mobilium et corporalium esse ponemus.

25 *De Providentia*, 14: Sic igitur providentia quidem deus per se, fatum autem divina aliqua res et non deus: dependet enim a providentia et velut ymago est illius.

26 *De Providentia*, 63: Alii autem determinatam cognitionem attribuentes deo, admiserunt necessitatem in omnibus quae fiunt: Peripateticorum et Stoicorum heresum sunt haec dogmata. The reference to the peripatetics is rather astonishing. One of the criticisms often put forward in the doxographies against Aristotle concerns his negative attitude towards the doctrine on divine providence. Still, Alexander of Aphrodisias in his *De Fato* (c. 30, p. 201, 26 sqq.) wonders whether God has a determinate knowledge of the future. According to him it is questionable whether such knowledge is possible; and even if it is possible, it remains questionable whether it is to be attributed to God.

27 *De Providentia*, 65: Quare et cognoscunt dii divine et intemporaliter que in nobis et nos operamur ut apti nati sumus.

28 *De Providentia*, 35: Ubi igitur hic *le in nobis* quando quod fit connectitur cum periodo mundi, et rursum quando ex illa solummodo efficitur? Ubi autem alibi dicemus quam in nostris interius electionibus et impetibus? — Proclus asks the question whether the human soul is subject to destiny. His answer quite corresponds to the neoplatonic idea of the soul. According to its substance, the human soul ranks above fate. In its behaviour, however, it may become subject to destiny (*De Providentia*, 20).

trine of Proclus. Like him, Boethius subordinates fate to divine providence.[29] The necessity of fate is used by God to eliminate all kinds of evil from the world. For Boethius, no evil is to be found in the world itself.[30] Obviously fate does not extend to the decisions of man: these are free because man is endowed with reason.[31] In his treatment of divine foreknowledge he also criticizes the Stoics. He professes the same principle as Proclus: knowledge is not determined by the nature of the object but by the very essence of the knowing subject.[32] God knows the future because he is eternal. This knowledge, however, does not introduce any necessity into the events that follow one another in time.[33]

At the end of the fourth century, when Nemesius wrote his treatise *De natura hominis*, the question of fatalism and freedom had already been treated many times by outstanding pagan and Christian writers, apparently without arriving at a definitive answer. Was it worthwhile to face it again? Was it not a waste of time to make a new inquiry into a question on which opinions were thoroughly divided and opposed? Nemesius was convinced that the question was important, especially for the religious and moral education of the Christian community. In a different historical context we can note that the cultural climate at the University of Paris in the second half of the thirteenth century was hardly comparable to the religious condition of the Christian community in Syria at the end of the fourth century. And yet Thomas Aquinas had to cope with the same problem, especially in his struggle against Averroism. In his day Aquinas turns for his source to the authority of the bishop of Emesa, or rather to that of Gregory of Nyssa, at that time commonly supposed to be the author of the *De natura hominis*.[34] The question of fatalism and freedom is obviously one of those archetypal philosophical problems that endlessly intrude upon our attention, presenting such varied aspects that they require renewed investigation in every age.

29 *Philosophiae Consolatio*, IV, 6, 12-13: fatum vero eorum quae divina simplicitas gerenda disposuit mobilem nexum atque ordinem temporalem.

30 *Philosophiae Consolatio*, IV, 6, 55.

31 *Philosophiae Consolatio*, V, 2, 3: neque enim fuerit ulla rationalis natura quin eidem libertas adsit arbitrii.

32 *Philosophiae Consolatio*, V, 4, 24: Cujus erroris causa est quod omnia quae quisque novit ex ipsorum tantum vi atque natura cognosci aestimat quae sciuntur.

33 *Philosophiae Consolatio*, V, 6, 15.

34 In 1270 thirteen propositions were censured by Etienne Tempier, bishop of Paris. Four of them are related to the freedom of human behaviour and to the question of divine providence: (3) Quod voluntas hominis ex necessitate vult vel eligit; (4) Quod omnia que hic in inferioribus aguntur, subsunt necessitati corporum celestium; (9) Quod liberum arbitrium est potentia passiva, non activa, et quod necessitate movetur ab appetibili; (12) Quod humani actus non reguntur providentia Dei.

In the framework of the relation between Nemesius and Thomas Aquinas, we intend to investigate more closely three fundamental topics: the notion of fate or destiny, the doctrine of divine providence, and the question of human freedom.

1. Fate or Destiny

Concerning the notion of fate, five different opinions are taken into consideration by Nemesius. The most extreme fatalism maintains that whatever happens in the world is necessitated by the movements of the heavenly bodies.[35] Nemesius dismisses this view because it is not in keeping with common opinions (κοιναῖς ἐννοίαις).[36] Moreover, if it is true political organisation becomes quite useless. Blame and praise will also be meaningless. It would make no sense to pray. Divine providence and religion would have to be denied, as well as all contingency and liberty. Finally, who will be guilty of wrong deeds, such as injustice, adultery and murder? They would have to be attributed to the heavenly bodies and ultimately to God himself. Granted this opinion, how could one escape from charging God with the most execrable crimes?[37] These arguments against extreme fatalism clearly belong to the tradition originated by Carneades. They can be traced back to their origin because they occur in nearly the same fashion in the works of several pagan and Christian writers. As D. Amand has shown, they became the common way in which fatalism was attacked and discarded.[38] Even Thomas Aquinas, in his inquiry into human freedom, briefly refers to the same arguments.[39]

The names of the Stoic philosophers Chrysippus and Philopator are

---

35 *De natura hominis*, ed. C. F. Matthaei (Halle 1801), c. 34, p. 289. The correspondence of this doctrine to the fourth proposition censured by the bishop of Paris in 1270 is clear.

36 According to the Stoics, common opinions (κοιναὶ ἔννοιαι) cannot be erroneous; since they are accepted by all people, they certainly stem from nature, i.e. from the divine Reason (Alex. Aphrod., *De mixtione*, p. 216, 14 ed. Bruns; SVF II, 473). If the Logos is the immanent principle of the world, there cannot be a real agreement or a true consensus on an erroneous proposition: that would be incompatible with the rational conception of the cosmos as it was professed by the Stoics.

37 *De natura hominis*, c. 34, p. 289-290.

38 *Fatalisme et liberté dans l'Antiquité grecque*, p. 41-68. D. Amand distinguishes between two categories of arguments developed by Carneades against astrology: "Les τόποι de la seconde catégorie visent spécialement le fatalisme absolu professé par les "Chaldéens" et défendu par Chrysippe. Cette doctrine de l'εἱμαρμένη astrologique conduit nécessairement à la négation de notre liberté, à l'inaction et à l'indifférence radicale, à la suppression du mérite, à l'abrogation de la législation et des institutions judiciaires, enfin à la ruine de la morale. C'est l'argumentation "éthique" antifataliste, qui a été adoptée et répétée par quelques moralistes de l'antiquité et surtout par les théologiens chrétiens" (p. 49).

39 *S.T.*, I, q. 83, a. 1.

mentioned by Nemesius as representatives of the second group, professing a less radical form of fatalism.[40] According to these philosophers, fate must be compatible with human freedom. Every being bears within itself some particular characteristics that originate from fate, as for instance the fact that water is cold, plants yield their fruit, stones fall, and flames rise. Similarly, a living being assents to the objects it perceives and moves itself thanks to its own structure. Such a being will in fact tend to certain objects provided that it is not impeded from without and that another fate is not an obstacle.[41]

In the opinion of Nemesius this theory of fate may be reduced to the first described above. Everything is necessitated by fate. The very impulse to act springs from fate and the actual attaining of the goal may be impeded by fate. Hence freedom of action is entirely suppressed. That impulse appears to be necessitated, for the same causes always produce the same results. There is no difference whatsoever between the behaviour of men and that of animals; just as all animal activity flows necessarily from destiny, so if all the elements in human decision, including judgment and assent, are necessitated by fate, no room is left for free action.[42] Thomas Aquinas mentions Nemesius's definition of Stoic fatalism: an unchangeable concatenation of causes. In his view, as in that of Nemesius, this Stoic theory is incompatible with human freedom.[43]

The third conception of fatalism is attributed by Nemesius to certain Egyptian sages. According to them everything that happens in the world is regulated by the movements of the heavenly bodies. Yet the events are not quite immutable; some changes may be introduced through prayers and sacrifices. These may be addressed to the stars themselves or to some higher divine powers in order to propitiate them. Thus religious cult is quite justified and efficacious.[44]

---

40 About Philopator we only have limited information. He probably lived in the 2nd century A.D., wrote a treatise *On Fate* (Περὶ εἱμαρμένης) in which he tried to corroborate the point of view of Chrysippus and to save human freedom without discarding the notion of destiny. See M. Pohlenz, *Die Stoa. Geschichte einer geistigen Bewegung*, I (Göttingen 1948), p. 354; II (Göttingen 1949), p. 147. One of his pupils was the teacher of Galen (Galenus, *De cogn. an. morb.* 8, V, 41 Kühn). According to Nemesius this theory which professes the compatibility of destiny and human freedom was held not only by Chrysippus and Philopator, but also by many other outstanding thinkers (καὶ ἄλλοι πολλοὶ καὶ λαμπροί).

41 *De natura hominis*, c. 34, p. 291.

42 *De natura hominis*, c. 34, p. 291-293.

43 *Summa contra Gentiles*, III, c. 73: Per haec autem excluditur opinio Stoicorum, qui secundum ordinem quendam causarum intransgressibilem, quem Graeci ymarmenen vocabant, omnia ex necesssitate dicebant provenire.

44 *De natura hominis*, c. 35, p. 294.

Several objections against this doctrine are raised by Nemesius. First of all, in the view of the Egyptian sages the notion of fate receives a rather unusual meaning. It no longer relates to necessary events but to contingent, undetermined and unknowable facts.[45] Indeed, whatever is determined by destiny may eventually be changed through someone's prayer. Moreover, divination, and particularly astrology as it was accepted and practised, would no longer be possible. This is of course an argument *ad hominem*, since the Egyptian sages gave much value to nativity-casting.[46] As for the influence of religious cult upon the course of events, Nemesius rightly asks why prayer alone depends on human initiative. If acts of religion depend upon our free decision, why could not some other acts enjoy the same privilege?[47] On the other hand, if everybody is able to change the course of events regulated by fate, one might be able equally to transform the whole sequence of history. If only some privileged individuals are capable of doing this, how are they chosen? Was the selection also made by fate? If so, the efficacy of prayer would ultimately depend on destiny.[48] Yet even this solution is necessarily wrong; if everything depended on destiny, nobody could be righteous or unrighteous. Why do some people rule over destiny whereas others are subject to it? The selection could not be made as a reward for special merits since everything is necessitated by destiny.[49]

It is noteworthy that Nemesius examines this point of view rather carefully, presumably because it comes closer to the Christian doctrine of providence. Thomas Aquinas in turn raises a similar question: whether destiny is changeable or unchangeable? In his reply the Angelic Doctor mentions the Egyptian sages and refers to Nemesius's treatise.[50] However, he does not pay much attention to this opinion

---

45 *De natura hominis*, c. 35, p. 295: ἐροῦμεν ὅτι τῶν ἐνδεχομένων καὶ οὐχὶ τῶν ἀναγκαίων ποιοῦσι τὴν εἱμαρμένην · τὸ δὲ ἐνδεχόμενον, ἀόριστον·· τὸ δὲ ἀόριστον, ἄγνωστον. According to Nemesius the contingent future, being undetermined, is quite unknowable. This standpoint corresponds to the doctrine of Aristotle: a proposition about the contingent future is neither true nor false (*Peri Hermeneias*, c. 9, 19a7-19b4).

46 *De natura hominis*, c. 35, p. 295.

47 *De natura hominis*, c. 35, p. 295-296.

48 *De natura hominis*, c. 35, p. 296. If some people are able to change the course of events regulated by fate, they escape from the power of destiny. Accordingly, the life of some people will be regulated by fate, whereas some privileged individuals will stay outside its realm (καὶ εὑρεθήσεται, τισὶ μὲν ἀνθρώποις πάντα καθ᾽ εἱμαρμένην, τισὶ δὲ οὐδὲν καθ᾽ εἱμαρμένην, p. 297). Why are some people subject to fate whereas other people avoid it? In the opinion of Nemesius, there is no reply to that question.

49 *De natura hominis*, c. 35, p. 298.

50 *Summa contra Gentiles*, III, c. 96, n. 2717: Quidam vero e contrario divinam dispositionem orationibus vertibilem esse dicebant; sicut et Aegyptii dicebant quod fatum orationibus et quibusdam imaginibus, subfumigationibus, sive incantationibus, vertebatur.- *S. T.*, I, q. 23, a. 8 co.; q. 116, a. 3 co.

because it does not accept the immutability of divine providence. According to Thomas Aquinas destiny may have two different meanings. Insofar as it designates the orderly connection of secondary causes, destiny is changeable. On the contrary, when destiny means divine providence it is hypothetically unchangeable. If God foresees some future event, it certainly will happen.[51] Thomas Aquinas opposes the doctrine of the Egyptian sages because of its notion of destiny. For him, destiny cannot be considered completely mutable; in a way it is also immutable.

The fourth doctrine of destiny mentioned by Nemesius is professed by "the wisest of the Greeks,"[52] who apparently are the Stoics again. In the mind of these philosophers, choice itself depends upon free initiative, whereas the outcome of a man's activity is regulated by destiny. This theory indeed corresponds to the Stoic mentality: the Stoics do not consider the range of free initiative to extend to outer events, to the transformation of the external world, but confine it to inner decision, to the attitude man adopts towards the happy and unhappy events of his life. One may accept or oppose the course of history; he will never be able to change it in the slightest way because it depends on divine reason.

Nemesius to a certain extent agrees with this perspective, insofar as it acknowledges the freedom of human activity. He also accepts the conclusion that the outcome of a man's decisions is not entirely determined by the man himself.[53] Yet he disagrees with the Stoics' position that the outcome of our activity is caused by destiny. For him, it is rather entirely dependent upon divine providence.[54] In Nemesius's opinion there is an enormous difference between destiny and providence. The former is an unchangeable sequence of causes, whereas providence bestows on everybody what is really profitable for him.[55] Holding to the Stoic

---

51 *S.T.*, I, q. 116, a. 3: Et ideo dicendum est quod fatum, secundum considerationem secundarum causarum, mobile est; sed secundum quod subest divinae providentiae, immobilitatem sortitur, non quidem absolutae necessitatis, sed conditionatae; secundum quod dicimus hanc conditionem esse veram vel necessariam, *Si Deus praescivit hoc futurum, erit.* — According to Thomas the connection between secondary causes and effects is not infrangible; but whatever is foreknown by God will certainly happen, without however being necessitated by this foreknowledge.

52 *De natura hominis*, c. 36, p. 299: εἰσὶ δὲ τῶν ἑλλήνων οἱ σοφώτατοι.

53 *De natura hominis*, c. 36, p. 299: τὸ μὲν γὰρ ἐφ' ἡμῖν τιθέναι τὰς αἱρέσεις τῶν πρακτῶν, μὴ πάντως δὲ καὶ τὰς ἀποβάσεις, ὀρθότατα λέγουσι.

54 Nemesius argues against this Stoic theory which implies that fate is imperfect because the decision remains outside the realm of destiny. In a way fate is even subordinate to man because man is able to influence it through his decision (*De natura hominis*, c. 36, p. 300).

55 Nemesius refers to the Stoic definition of destiny; εἰ δὲ ἡ εἱμαρμένη εἱρμός τις οὖσα αἰτιῶν ἀπαράβατος, οὕτω γὰρ αὐτὴν οἱ στωϊκοὶ ὁρίζονται, τούτεστι τάξις καὶ ἐπισύνδεσις ἀπαράλλακτος (*De natura hominis*, c. 36, p. 301). As far as the sequence of outer events is concerned,

theory, one could not justify the fact that some people suffer from mental diseases and are thereby unable to make any free decisions. Since their disease is also caused by destiny, obviously nobody is the principle of his own decisions, because even the capacity of choosing is to be traced back to destiny.[56] Consequently this theory merges with the universal determinism it claims to avoid.

Later on, John Damascene accepted the doctrine of Nemesius on this point, although his way of formulating it is more accurate. According to Damascene, God knows our free decisions beforehand but without predetermining them.[57] According to Nemesius, however, divine providence should not be concerned with man's free choices. On this point Thomas Aquinas introduces an important improvement: our autonomous initiatives are not necessitated by divine providence, and yet they do not escape the universal ruling of God.[58]

Finally, Nemesius takes up the fifth theory, that of Plato, which was very influential in the further evolution of Christian theology. According to Plato, the notion of destiny has two different meanings. As a substance, it designates the world soul; as an activity, it refers to the unalterable divine law springing from an ineluctable cause.[59] This law has been given to the world soul by the supreme god with a view to the creation and the government of the cosmos. As such, destiny rules over everything but is also involved in divine providence as a part of it. Whatever happens according to destiny belongs to divine providence. Yet the inverse is not true: what happens according to divine providence does not always belong to the field of destiny.[60] How must we conceive the ruling function of the divine law? The answer depends on the nature of the objects concerned. Some of them are immediately related to the divine law, for instance our assents, judgments, and im-

---

everything is linked with its cause as an unavoidable result. There is no contingency. The present situation of the world is the necessary effect of the past, there is only one way which the divine Reason fashions the history of the world.

56 *De natura hominis*, c. 36, p. 301-302.

57 Joannes Damascenus, *De Fide orthodoxa*, ed. Buytaert, c. 44, p. 161: Oportet noscere quod omnia quidem praenoscit Deus, non omnia autem praedeterminat. Praenoscit enim et quae in nobis, non praedeterminat autem ea. Non enim vult malitiam fieri, neque compellit virtutem.

58 Nemesius, *De natura hominis*, c. 44, p. 349: ἡ δὲ πρόνοια τῶν οὐκ ἐφ' ἡμῖν. — Cf. ibidem, c. 44, p. 366. — Joannes Damascenus, *De Fide orthodoxa*, c. 43, p. 157: Omnia autem dico quae non in nobis: quae enim in nobis, non providentiae sunt, sed nostri liberi arbitrii. — Thomas Aquinas, *Summa contra Gentiles*, III, 90, n. 2660: Et similiter quod Gregorius Nyssenus dicit, in libro quem *de Homine* fecit, *Providentia est eorum quae non sunt in nobis, non autem eorum quae sunt in nobis*; et Damascenus eum sequens, dicit in secundo libro, quod *ea quae sunt in nobis Deus praenoscit, sed non praedeterminat*, exponenda sunt ut intelligantur ea quae sunt in nobis divinae providentiae determinationi non esse subiecta *quasi ab ea necessitatem accipientia*.

59 *De natura hominis*, c. 37, p. 303.

60 *De natura hominis*, c. 37, p. 304.

pulses. These are the starting point or basis (καθ' ὑπόθεσιν) of further events, which necessarily flow from our activity (ἐξ ὑποθέσεως).[61] Consequently the choice itself of our acts depends on our free initiative, whereas the consequences belong to the field of destiny, which partly coincides with providence. God is in no way mixed up in the wrong we eventually do, whereas moral behaviour remains free and the possibility of divination is warranted.[62]

Only on one particular does Nemesius advance an argument against Plato. According to the latter the outcome of our decisions could not belong to the field of necessity. The outcome is not necessary but contingent, for it depends on the ruling of divine providence.[63] A result of the Platonic theory is that prayer loses most of its relevance. It is limited to choice alone, whereas everything else is necessitated.[64] How could God be subject to such necessity? As a proof Nemesius mentions some special divine interventions taken from Scripture which show that God is not bound by any necessary law. The orbits of the stars have been fixed by God. Nevertheless he proved that he is not bound by his own law by making a special day and stopping the course of the sun. The same is true in the case of Enoch and Elias.[65] In this context Nemesius refers to the doctrine of ἀποκατάστασις held by the Stoics and also by Origen.[66] According to this view the history of the world would be periodical, each stage being constituted by exactly the same events. History would be the endless repeating of the same play without a definitive issue. In other words, there would be no true eschatology. Since the content of each period would be the same, the gods would be able to "predict" the future because they had witnessed the events of the past beforehand.[67] Here again God would be subject to necessity. Nemesius especially attacks the opinion of those who identify the

---

61 De natura hominis, c. 37, p. 304. According to Nemesius, divine providence is directly concerned with the constituents of our free choice, namely συγκαταθέσεις καὶ κρίσεις καὶ ὁρμαί. This conception of human decision corresponds to the doctrine of Alexander Aphrodisiensis, as it is explained in his De Fato. Cf. G. Verbeke, "Aristotélisme et Stoïcisme dans le De Fato d'Alexandre d'Aphrodisias," Archiv für Geschichte der Philosophie, 50 (1968), p. 88. It is not merely borrowed from the Nicomachean Ethics of Aristotle; some Aristotelian and Stoic elements have been combined.

62 In the opinion of Plato what happens according to fate has not been regulated eternally; it depends upon our decision and is related to them: μὴ γὰρ ἐξ ἀϊδίου ὡρίσθαι τὸ καθ' εἱμαρμένην, ἀλλ' ἐπισυμβαίνειν, προηγησαμένοις τοῖς ἐφ' ἡμῖν (De natura hominis, c. 37, p. 305). If man is truly the author of the acts he accomplishes, God does not bear any responsibility for our wrong deeds. He may not be called guilty in any way: θεὸς ἀναίτιος (op. cit., p. 306).

63 De natura hominis, c. 37, p. 306.

64 De natura hominis, c. 37, p. 306-307.

65 God is not bound by any necessary law. Related to him, even the necessary becomes contingent: πάντα δέ ἐστιν αὐτῷ ἐνδεχόμενα καὶ τὰ ἀναγκαῖα (De natura hominis, c. 37, p. 308).

66 Origenes, Contra Celsum, IV, 69; VI, 20, 25, 26. De Principiis, I, 6, 2; II, 6, 1, 3,; III, 6, 1.

67 De natura hominis, c. 37, p. 310.

Christian doctrine of resurrection and the Stoic theory of cosmic
rebirth. For him there is an essential difference between the two
because the resurrection occurred only once, being a definitive issue of
world history, whereas the Stoic "apocatastasis" is an endless process.[68]

It is noteworthy in this connection that one of the most profound
metaphysical doctrines of Thomas Aquinas is his view that God could
not be subject to necessity. In this he agrees with Nemesius. As to the
question whether God is a necessary being, Aquinas's reply is
negative: God transcends both categories of necessity and contingency
because they belong to the world of becoming. Expressing the relation
of finite beings within our evolving world, they could not be used to formulate the unique relation between the infinite and the finite. Consequently God cannot be called *Ens necessarium*. He is neither necessary
nor contingent.[69]

As a whole, the teaching of Nemesius on destiny is a truly positive
contribution to the interpretation of Christianity, insofar as it stresses
the freedom of human behaviour as well as the liberty of God. One of
the main themes of his exposition emphasizes that God cannot be subject to necessity. Nevertheless we have already pointed to a lacuna in
the theory of Nemesius, filled by Thomas Aquinas. In the opinion of
the bishop of Emesa divine providence is concerned only with things
not dependent upon our free initiative. Thomas Aquinas places even
our free behaviour under divine providence.

2. DIVINE PROVIDENCE

The second problem we have to consider in the *De natura hominis*
concerns the notion of providence. This notion is treated after the
discussion on human freedom for the reason already mentioned:
providence deals with events that are not dependent upon our choice.[70]
According to Nemesius it would not be necessary to prove divine

---

68   *De natura hominis*, c. 37, p. 311: καὶ διὰ ταύτην τὴν ἀποκατάστασιν, φασί τινες, τοὺς
Χριστιανοὺς τὴν ἀνάστασιν φαντάζεσθαι.   — Many Greek philosophers professed a cyclical
conception of time: when a period comes to an end, another starts immediately with the same
beings and the same events. There is no progress from one period to another. The trial of Socrates
will take place in each period of history and the sentence will be the same. History never comes to
a definitive end. Hence the question whether this endless repetition of the same events is
meaningful. Even Aristotle, in his theory of time, takes up a rather pessimistic point of view: being
linked with change, time is something ἐκστατικόν, pushing things out of their former condition:
"In time all things come into being and pass away; for which reason some called it the wisest of all
things, but the Pythagorean Paron called it the most stupid, because in it we also forget; and his
was the truer view. It is clear then that it must be in itself, as we said before, the condition of
destruction rather than of coming into being" (*Phys.* IV, 13, 222b16-21; transl. R. P. Hardie and R.
K. Gaye).

69   Thomas Aquinas, *Comm. in Peri Hermeneias*, I, lectio 14, n. 197: Et secundum harum conditionem causarum, effectus dicuntur vel necessarii vel contingentes, quamvis omnes dependeant a
voluntate divina, sicut a prima causa, quae transcendit ordinem necessitatis et contingentiae.

70   *De natura hominis*, c. 42, p. 332: ἀκόλουθος τοῖς ἐφ' ἡμῖν ἐστιν ὁ περὶ τῆς προνοίας
λόγος.

providence for a Jewish or Christian reader, but it would be meaningful for a Greek.[71] However, there is no special argument in Nemesius's treatise for providence as such; the proofs of the existence of God cover this ground as well. Some of these arguments receive but slight development. The author stresses the continued existence of the universe; the lasting and orderly arrangement of the world, especially the regular movements of the stars, the sequence of day and night, as well as the succession of the different seasons in a year.[72]

One topic is developed further as a particular argument in favour of providence: the disclosure and punishment even of hidden trespasses. In this connection Nemesius mentions the famous trial of Susanna and the murder of the poet Ibycus, which, according to the legend, was discovered by the help of cranes.[73] As an irrefutable sign of providence, Nemesius also points to the harmonious structure of living organisms and to the variety of colours that may be observed in animals according to their species.[74] In the same context the author refers to the common conviction of all people about the need for prayer and religious cult, as well as the common practice of beneficence and charity towards others. Furthermore, if providence is denied, prophecy and foreknowledge are ruled out.[75] Nemesius also points to the fact that each individual has his own distinguishing characteristics: an important gift of providence, for they enable him to be recognized by his friends and family. Even animals can recognize other individuals by their distinctive features.[76] Finally, speaking to the Greeks, Nemesius mentions the importance of tokens, oracles, presages, omens, all of which would be meaningless in a world without providence.[77]

It is not easy to draw a comparison between Nemesius and Thomas Aquinas on the question of providence. Nemesius's approach is rather empirical. It starts from the orderly structure of the world and from a kind of universal belief which is at least implicitly involved in human

71   In his account of providence, Nemesius will also start from what Greeks believe to be true so that he might be understood not only by Christians and Jews, but also by pagan readers (*De natura hominis*, c. 42, p. 332).
72   *De natura hominis*, c. 42, p. 334.
73   *De natura hominis*, c. 42, p. 334-335.
74   *De natura hominis* c. 42, p. 336.
75   *De natura hominis*, c. 42, p. 336: καὶ τὸ κοινῇ δὲ παρὰ πᾶσιν ἀνθρώποις ὁμολογού μενον, τὸ δεῖν εὔχεσθαι καὶ θεραπεύειν τὸ θεῖον ἀναθήμασί τε καὶ περιβόλοις, προνοίας ἐστὶ δηλωτικόν. Nemesius appeals again to the consensus of all men about the necessity of prayer; this argument often used by the Stoics could be easily accepted by a Christian, insofar as a universal mistake of all men would be incompatible with divine providence. Of course when the argument is used in order to prove divine providence, it is to be understood in its immediate significance: if everybody agrees on a particular proposition, it must be true, in other words it has been checked so many times that there cannot be a mistake.
76   *De natura hominis*, c. 42, p. 339-342.
77   *De natura hominis*, c. 42, p. 342-343.

behaviour. Thomas Aquinas takes a decidedly metaphysical standpoint. Whatever good may be found in the world, in his view, stems from God, the almighty creator of the universe. Looking at creatures, one has to distinguish between the substance of beings and their direction towards their end, especially towards their ultimate end. Whereas the substance of beings depends upon the creative causality, the orientation of beings towards their end belongs to the providence of God, who directs each creature according to a preexisting plan or *ratio* in the divine mind. Properly speaking providence means the divine idea according to which everything is related to its end.[78] In this connection Thomas mentions an objection of John Damascene, which is a quotation from Nemesius: it seems that providence, being concerned with things existing in time, would be incompatible with the eternity of God.[79] The reply of Thomas is rather summary: a distinction has to be drawn between the divine providence and its execution. The project is eternal, the carrying into effect is temporal. Thus providence is not merely temporal.[80]

In order to make his notion of providence more exact Nemesius emphasizes the distinction between the creation of things and their government after they have been brought into existence. In his opinion both are not necessarily realized by the same being. Carpenters, copyists, and modellers of clay work out projects, but they themselves do not always take care of the work they have completed. On the other hand, there are some persons (for instance herdsmen or sheperds) who perform tasks without planning them.[81] Accordingly providence may be defined as the care God takes of the beings he has created. In other words, providence is the divine project according to which all beings receive the most favourable mode of existence.[82] This leads Nemesius to a very optimistic view of the world; a more perfect arrangement of the universe would be quite impossible.[83] On the other hand, it belongs to

---

78 *S.T.*, I, q. 22, a. 1 co.: Ratio autem ordinandorum in finem, proprie providentia est.

79 *S.T.*, I, q. 22, a. 1, obj. 2: Praeterea quidquid est in Deo, est aeternum. Sed providentia non est aliquid aeternum: est enim *circa existentia*, quae non sunt aeterna, secundum Damascenum. Ergo providentia non est in Deo. — Cf. Joannes Damascenus, *De Fide orthodoxa*, c. 43, p. 155: Providentia igitur est quae ex Deo ad existentia fit cura. — Nemesius, *De natura hominis*, c. 43, p. 343: πρόνοια τοίνυν ἐστὶν ἐκ θεοῦ εἰς τὰ ὄντα γινομένη ἐπιμέλεια. According to the translation of Burgundio: Providentia igitur est ea quae a Deo ad ea quae sunt, fiens procuratio. — It might be noticed that the translations of this sentence, both made by Burgundio, nevertheless are different. According to E. M. Buytaert the translation of *De Fide orthodoxa* was made in 1153-54. The version of *De natura hominis* dates back to 1165. This later translation sticks more closely to the Greek text.

80 *S.T.*, I, q. 22, a. 1, ad 2.

81 *De natura hominis*, c. 42, p. 338-339.

82 *De natura hominis*, c. 43, p. 343: πρόνοιά ἐστι βούλησις θεοῦ δι' ἣν πάντα τὰ ὄντα τὸν πρόσφορον διεξαγωγὴν λαμβάνει.

83 *De natura hominis*, c. 43, p. 344: ... ὡς τὴν κρείττω τάξιν μὴ ἐπιδέχεσθαι. The world could not be more perfect than it is. Thus Nemesius takes up the radical optimism of the Stoics.

the creator of the world and not to any other being to take care of it. If the care of creatures were not assumed by the creator himself, it would mean that he lacked power. Hence the creator must be a God of providence, and this providence is ultimately the divine purpose or project.[84] On this topic there is a fundamental agreement between Nemesius, John Damascene (who in his chapter on providence quotes many texts from the *De natura hominis*), and Thomas Aquinas. It is worthy of note that Thomas Aquinas refers to Nemesius's definition in order to show that divine providence is not incompatible with human freedom.[85] According to him the end of each creature is to become as similar to God as possible. In the case of man this likeness involves free behaviour, because liberty also belongs to God's nature. If providence coincides with the divine project which imparts to each being the best mode of existence, man could not be deprived of his highest dignity, his capacity for free choice.[86]

One of the most important problems Nemesius deals with is whether providence is concerned only with the general ruling of the world or also with individual beings. According to Plato providence takes care of each individual but not in the same way. Three levels have to be distinguished. First, the providence of the highest god, who rules primarily over the ideas and the world as a whole, namely the heavens, the heavenly bodies, universals, such as the different kinds of things (substance, quantity, quality, and other general categories) and their subordinate forms.[87] On a lower level secondary gods are to be located; they take care of the generation of ordinary animals, plants, and all corruptible things. This providence is ascribed by Aristotle to the sun

However, the realm of providence does not extend to the free initiatives of man: these initiatives may be wrong. According to our author the world is as perfect as possible in so far as the ruling of divine providence is concerned.

84 *De natura hominis*, c. 43, p. 344.

85 *Summa contra Gentiles*, III, 73, n. 2490: unde et de providentia divina Gregorius Nyssenus dicit quod est voluntas Dei per quam omnia quae sunt convenientem deductionem accipiunt. — Apparently Thomas reproduces rather faithfully the translation of Burgundio: Providentia est voluntas Dei propter quam omnia quae sunt competentem deductionem suscipiunt.

86 *Summa contra Gentiles*, III, 73, n. 2490.

87 *De natura hominis*, c. 44, p. 345. The interpretation of Plato's doctrine on providence corresponds to the account we find in the Περὶ εἱμαρμένης, c. 9, falsely attributed to Plutarch. According to Philip H. de Lacy and B. Einarson the work was written by an unknown Platonist at the beginning of the second century A.D. The following passage should be quoted: "The highest and primary providence is the intellection or will, beneficent to all things, of the primary God: and in conformity with it all things divine are primordially arranged throughout, each as is best and most excellent. Secondary providence belongs to the secondary gods, who move in heaven, and in conformity with it all mortal things come into being in orderly fashion, together with all that is requisite to the survival and preservation of the several genera. The providence and forethought which belongs to the daemons stationed in the terrestrial regions as watchers and overseers of the actions of man would reasonably be called tertiary." (transl. de Lacy and Einarson). Cf. Calcidius, *In Timaeum commentarius*, ed. J. H. Waszink (London-Leiden 1962), 144-145, p. 182-183.

and the zodiac. [88] The third level of providence is concerned with human behaviour and some matters of lower degree, such as natural, material or instrumental things. This task is assumed by spiritual beings who are stationed around the earth as the guardians of human conduct. [89] In the opinion of Plato the second and third levels of providence are subordinate to the primary god, who rules over all the agents governing the world. Nemesius agrees with Plato insofar as the lower levels of providence are ultimately reduced to the ruling power of God, but he argues against the theory of the second level of providence being effected by the movements of heavenly bodies. In his view, such ruling cannot be called providence but destiny and necessity. [90]

Taking his information from Nemesius, Thomas Aquinas also mentions the theory of Plato and criticizes it like the bishop of Emesa. [91] As we already indicated, a distinction must be introduced between the divine plan and its exercise. The project or idea existing in the divine mind not only concerns the general government of the world but of each individual. Whatever exists and acts, God provides with the power of producing a given effect. As a result, whatever happens in the world springs from a divine project. Does this mean that the divine govern-

---

88   *De natura hominis*, c. 44, p. 345.
89   *De natura hominis*, c. 44, p. 346.
90   *De natura hominis*, c. 44, p. 347: οὐ γὰρ πρόνοια τὸ γινόμενον, ἀλλ' εἱμαρμένη καὶ ἀνάγκη.
91   *Summa contra Gentiles*, III, 76, n. 2517. Thomas's report of the theory of Plato relies on the translation of Burgundio, without being a literal quotation:

Posuit enim Plato, ut Gregorius Nyssenus dicit triplicem providentiam:

Quarum prima est summi Dei qui primo et principaliter providet propriis, idest omnibus spiritualibus et intellectualibus; consequenter vero toti mundo quantum ad genera et species, et universales causas, quae sunt corpora caelestia.

Secunda vero est qua providetur singularibus animalium et platarum et aliorum generabilium et corruptibilium, quantum ad eorum generationem et corruptionem et alias mutationes. Quam quidem providentiam Plato attribuit diis qui caelum circueunt, Aristoteles vero horum causalitatem attribuit obliquo circulo.

Tertiam vero providentiam ponit rerum quae ad humanam vitam pertinent. Quam quidem attribuit quibusdam daemonibus circa terram existentibus qui sunt, secundum ipsum, humanarum actionum custodes.

Igitur Plato quidem et universalia et singularia providentiam disponere vult dividens providentiae sermonem in tria:
Nam primam quidem esse eam quae est primi dei; providere hunc antecendenter quidem propriis, deinde vero omni universali mundo, puta caelis et astris et omnibus universalibus, hoc est generibus et substantiae et quantitati et qualitati et aliis talibus et his quae his subiectae sunt speciebus.
Generationi vero individuorum et animalium et plantarum et omnium quae in generatione et corruptione sunt, secundos deos providere qui caelum circueunt. Aristoteles vero horum generationem imponit soli et zodiaco circulo.

Deductionis vero et finis gestibilium et ordinis eorum, quae et secundum hanc vitam sunt et naturalium et materialium et organicorum vocatorum bonorum et eorum quae his sunt opposita, tertiam esse providentiam Plato enuntiat. Sed et praesistere huic quosdam ordinatos daemones custodes humanarum gestionum.

Cf. *S.T.*, I, q. 22, a. 3 co. — *S.T.*, I, q. 103 a. 6 arg. 1.

ment is exercized without intermediaries? Certainly not. God always governs lower beings by means of higher, not because he needs help but because he wants to impart his causality to his creatures. Consequently in the opinion of Thomas Aquinas providence is at once mediate and immediate. Insofar as the divine planning is concerned, it is immediate; but in the actual exercise of the divine plan lower beings are introduced and participate in the causality of God.[92]

At this point Nemesius once again mentions the Stoic theory which tried to combine human freedom and destiny. Actually this theory leaves no room for providence and suppresses liberty of choice.[93] This objection to Stoicism is rather astonishing because in the ancient doxography the Stoics are generally contrasted with Aristotle and the Epicureans on the very issue of providence. In his list of philosophers who deny general as well as individual providence Nemesius cites the names of Democritus, Heraclitus, and Epicurus. As far as Aristotle is concerned, the author refers to the sixth book of the *Nicomachean Ethics*, where according to the Stagirite everything is ruled by nature and there is no individual providence.[94] Apparently the information of Nemesius on this issue is rather poor. No connection is made with the Aristotelian doctrine of divine knowledge in the twelfth book of the *Metaphysics*. Insofar as Aristotle's metaphysical thinking is concerned, he quite obviously denies providence because it is incompatible with the purely actual character of divine knowledge. On the other hand, he does not categorically deny certain common opinions in favour of providence.

The main problem Nemesius has to face in his defense of providence is undoubtedly the existence of evil. If each particular being is ruled by divine providence, what is the source of the terrible injustices inflicted upon good people, their humiliations, and every kind of evil? Why are the wicked and violent blessed with power, wealth, and many other

92 *S.T.*, I, q. 22, a. 3 co.
93 *De natura hominis*, c. 44, p. 347.
94 Nemesius probably refers to *Eth. Nic.* VI, 13, 1144b4-17. In his doctrine of human freedom our author was certainly influenced by the *Nicomachean Ethics* of Aristotle. In the third book of this treatise can be found one of the most remarkable analyses of free choice and personal responsibility handed down to us from antiquity. The knowledge Nemesius had of the work of Aristotle is probably limited to the *Nic. Eth.*. In a work on the nature of man one could expect him to mention the Περὶ ψυχῆς of the Stagirite. Obviously Nemesius has some information about the psychological doctrine of Aristotle; however a direct knowledge of the *De Anima* is rather questionable. Eusebius in his *Praeparatio evangelica* (XV, 4, 9, ed. Mras, II, 352) also refers to the ethical treatises of Aristotle. What he writes about them could hardly depend on a direct contact with the work of the Stagirite. In his opinion the moral doctrine of Aristotle has little value, and may be profitable only for uneducated people, children, and women. About Aristotle's teaching on providence, Eusebius contrasts Plato with the Stagirite. According to the latter's view divine providence would extend only to the moon, not to the sublunary world. (*Praep. evang.* XV, 5, 1, ed. Mras, II, 355). Against Aristotle, Nemesius argues that nature does not coincide with divine providence, but is only a part of it (*De natura hominis*, c. 44, p. 350).

goods?[95] Nemesius asks whether the injustice in the world is compatible with the notion of providence extending to every particular being and event. In his reply he first draws attention to the immortality of the human soul. It would be wrong to evaluate human life taking into account only our present existence.[96] Besides, if the soul is held to be superior to the body, the good of the soul will be much more valuable than whatever promotes the well-being of the body.[97] In the mind of our author real happiness may include some bodily or material elements, but these play a very secondary role: they do not belong to the strict notion of happiness ($\varkappa\alpha\tau\grave{\alpha}$ $\pi\varepsilon\varrho\iota\gamma\varepsilon\alpha\varphi\acute{\eta}\nu$).[98] Obviously Nemesius's view on this matter is less Aristotelian than Stoic: virtue is said to be the only true and sufficient condition of happiness. Finally, Nemesius maintains that it is very difficult, if not impossible, to give a well-founded judgment of a human life: ignorant of the future, one can only take into account the present condition. From this limited viewpoint, how can a man judge whether poverty, the death of his children, or the flight of his slaves, is a good? Divine knowledge is not limited to the present situation; it also embraces the future. What seems to be an evil from our standpoint may truly be a good if human life were seen as a whole.

Some philosophers, while admitting a general providence, refuse to acknowledge any providence for particular things and events. Nemesius gives three possible arguments supporting their opinion. One could imagine a god who is unaware that he has to take care of everything. But this supposed ignorance is quite incompatible with the divine perfection. Besides, how could general providence itself be actually realized without taking care of individual beings? Indeed, if all individuals perish, nothing remains as the object of general providence.[99] Nemesius then asks whether God may eventually decline to take care of individuals. Of course, he could not refuse to do so through indolence owing to fear or desire for pleasure. The only plausible reason, at least at first glance, could be a certain unfittingness connected with the divine perfection. One may wonder indeed whether it is fitting for God to be involved in all material concerns and foolish decisions.[100] Ac-

---

95 *De natura hominis*, c. 44, p. 351.

96 *De natura hominis*, c. 44, p. 351: $\mu\acute{\alpha}\lambda\iota\sigma\tau\alpha$ $\delta\grave{\varepsilon}$ $\tau\tilde{\eta}\varsigma$ $\psi\upsilon\chi\tilde{\eta}\varsigma$ $\tau\grave{o}$ $\grave{\alpha}\theta\acute{\alpha}\nu\alpha\tau\sigma\nu$. This passage must be associated with the doctrine explained in chapter 2. Does Nemesius agree with Iamblichus on the theory of metempsychosis? Addressing his work not only to Christians but also to Greeks, our author does not discard categorically metempsychosis among human beings. On the other hand, he could hardly accept it, because he clearly envisages another life different from our existence on earth (op. cit., c. 44, pp. 359-360).

97 *De natura hominis*, c. 44, p. 352.

98 *De natura hominis*, c. 44, p. 352.

99 *De natura hominis*, c. 44, p. 355.

100 *De natura hominis*, c. 44, p. 356.

cording to Nemesius this argument does not stand up, because in this supposition we attribute to God a contempt for human affairs, as well as the danger of being defiled, both of which are incompatible with the divine nature. God does not scorn the details of human life, and his perfection cannot be sullied. Can the sun be defiled when her rays shine on mire and mud?[101]

A final question concerns God's ability to take care of all individual things. Is this not contrary to his nature? Our author draws a comparison between divine providence and political government. Those responsible for the latter take care not only of the society as a whole but also of individuals.[102] An important argument against the objection mentioned above is the spontaneous attitude of people who are in need. They immediately call in the aid of prayers and turn to divine providence. Nemesius stresses the fact that this is spontaneous and natural, and, being instilled by nature, it cannot be meaningless.[103]

Where do the objections against particular providence come from? According to our author they mainly spring from two sources. People who oppose particular providence are persuaded that the human soul is mortal, with the result that the sins committed during this life will never be punished. This is obviously contrary to the common belief not only of the Greeks but also of other people.[104] The second major reason for denying providence is our inability fully to grasp the divine ruling power: man with his finite mind cannot grasp the divine government of the world.[105] This is true, Nemesius replies, but our lack of understanding is no ground for dismissing this government. We have to accept many things beyond our grasp.[106] If providence is the project in the divine mind according to which God provides everybody with the optimum mode of existence, then it seems necessary to take into ac-

---

101 *De natura hominis*, c. 44, p. 357.

102 *De natura hominis*, c. 44, p. 358-359.

103 *De natura hominis*, c. 44, p. 359: ὡς ἂν τῆς φύσεως ἀγούσης ἡμᾶς ἀδιδάκτως ἐπὶ τὴν τοῦ Θεοῦ βοήθειαν. οὐκ ἂν δὲ ἡμᾶς ἀδιδάκτως ἦγεν ἡ φύσις ἐπὶ τὸ μὴ φύσιν ἔχον γίνεσθαι. This argument may be associated with the Aristotelian teleology: the work of nature is always purposive, a natural tendency could not be ineffectual.

104 *De natura hominis*, c. 44, p. 360: In this context Nemesius again mentions metempsychosis, yet not as his own conviction, but as a doctrine professed by outstanding Greek philosophers. In connection with this opinion he refers to the theory concerning the places where the souls stay after death, each soul getting the place it deserves with respect to its moral behaviour. This point of view corresponds to the theory of Plato about the life of the soul after death; especially in the *Gorgias* (523a sqq.) where the author emphasizes the justice of God who bestows on each soul the life it deserves. Some souls are severely punished, whereas others are admitted to perpetual happiness.

105 *De natura hominis*, c. 44, p. 360: εἰ δὲ ἀκατάληπτος ἡμῖν ἐστιν τῆς τῶν κατὰ μέρος προνοίας ὁ λόγος. It is noticeable that the term ἀκατάληπτος used by Nemesius in this context stems from the Stoics: it means a true knowledge grasping the object which is intended. It is to be located between opinion (δόξα) and science (ἐπιστήμη) and is defined as the assent (συγκατάθεσις) to a true representation, in other words, the assent to a representation capable of grasping the object (Sextus Empiricus, *Adv. Math.* VII, 151; SVF II, 90).

106 *De natura hominis*, c. 44, p. 360.

count individual differences between men and also various conditions
within the evolution of human life. As a matter of fact, particular
providence does not mean that God causes without qualification
everything that happens in the world. We must realize that many events
are only permitted by divine providence.[107] Of course there may be a
hidden reason for some things that we do not immediately grasp.
People suffer and die, and we ask why. It might be a punishment for
secret sins; it might be better for them to die; the sufferings of a martyr
might be the source of salvation of others. Many explanations might be
given. Whatever may be the case, we should not judge according to
outer appearances; we ought to be convinced that everything is as it
must be. Whatever springs from divine providence is perfect; we should
admire everything.[108] The only real evils in the world are the wrong
deeds coming from man's free decisions.

Thomas Aquinas in his turn was obliged to handle the same problem.
Referring to Nemesius and John Damascene, he wondered whether a
created free will could always do right and never wrong. Are there not
some creatures which are incorruptible whereas others are corruptible?
The human soul and the heavenly bodies are naturally incorruptible.
Why then could not a spiritual creature be naturally impeccable?[109] The
reply of Thomas Aquinas refers again to the teaching of Nemesius and
John Damascene. Having been created *ex nihilo*, man inevitably has a
changeable (and therefore peccable) nature. As long as he lives, he cannot definitively adhere to the right. It is true that a created being can be
incorruptible. But this comparison does not justify the inference
deduced from it. Man is able to come close to the absolute Good
through his free acts. Hence, to suppress the changeable character of
human nature would entail the denial of freedom and man's ability
freely to approach the absolute Good.[110]

As far as the doctrine of providence is concerned, there is an
unquestionable connection between Nemesius, John Damascene, and
Thomas Aquinas. Some passages from Nemesius and John Damascene

---

107 *De natura hominis*, c. 44, p. 362: φαμὲν γοῦν τινὰ γίνεσθαι κατὰ συγχώρησιν τοῦ
θεοῦ.

108 *De natura hominis*, c. 44, p. 366.

109 *De Veritate*, q. 24, a. 7, obj. 5: Praeterea Gregorius Nyssenus et Damascenus hanc
rationem assignant quare creatura sit mutabilis secundum liberum arbitrium quia est ex nihilo. Sed
propinquius consequitur creaturam ex hoc quod est ex nihilo posse in nihilum cedere, quam posse
malum facere. Sed invenitur aliqua creatura quae naturaliter est incorruptibilis, sicut anima et corpora caelestia. Ergo multo fortius potest inveniri aliqua creatura spiritualis quae naturaliter est im-
peccabilis. — Cf. *De natura hominis*, c. 41, p. 324: Burgundio translates as follows: Inquimus igitur
confestim rationali subintrare liberum arbitrium et generatis aptam natam esse transmutationem et
versionem maxime his quae ex subjecta materia fiunt. — Joannes Damascenus, *De Fide orthodoxa*,
c.41: Inquimus igitur rationali confestim cointrari liberum arbitrium. Omne enim generabile et
vertibile est.

110 *De Veritate*, q. 24, a. 7 co. et ad 5. Cf. ibid. q. 24, a. 1, ad 16.

are quoted by Thomas, and there is a general agreement concerning the doctrine itself. Still, the philosophical approach to the problem is different. The starting point of the inquiry in Thomas Aquinas is a metaphysical understanding of the nature of God, whereas Nemesius appeals to common opinions and empirical data.

3. HUMAN FREEDOM

Nemesius's treatment of the question of freedom is one of the most important handed down to us from that early period. We do not intend to examine the sources of the *De natura hominis*; this has already been done to a large extent. Occasionally we shall refer to thinkers who undoubtedly influenced the doctrine of Nemesius, for instance Aristotle, Carneades, Alexander, Epictetus, and Origen. Here again our main concern is the relation between Nemesius and Thomas Aquinas. It is not necessary to recall that many quotations from Nemesius have been taken over by John Damascene in his *De fide orthodoxa*.

Nemesius starts his inquiry into human freedom with an investigation concerning voluntary and involuntary acts.[111] A clear distinction must be drawn between them. Whereas involuntary acts are caused either by violence or by ignorance, voluntary deeds spring from the agent himself. The agent is truly the source of what he is doing without necessitation by outer or inner influence. He is aware of the particular circumstances of his act.[112] The question arises whether the work of nature (for instance the process of growing or digestion) is to be called voluntary or involuntary. According to our author neither of these terms applies to a natural process: it is neither voluntary nor involuntary. In other words, a natural process does not belong to the category of things depending on our initiative.[113] On the contrary, what is done under the impulse of our emotions (for example anger or lust) is to be accounted voluntary: these acts are commonly praised or blamed, their performance is accompanied by pleasure or grief, and their source resides within the agent.[114] Man is not necessarily determined by his emotions; the behaviour of each individual depends on his moral education.[115] Finally, Nemesius proceeds to the problem whether animals and children are able to perform voluntary acts. His reply is af-

111 *De natura hominis*, c. 29, p. 263 — c. 32, p. 277.
112 *De natura hominis*, c. 32, p. 275: συνθέντες οὖν ἑκάτερον ὁριζόμεθα τὸ ἑκούσιον οὖ ἡ ἀρχὴ ἐν αὐτῷ, εἰδότι τὰ καθ' ἕκαστα, ἐν οἷς ἡ πρᾶξις.
113 *De natura hominis*, c. 32, p. 275.
114 *De natura hominis*, c. 32, p. 275.
115 *De natura hominis*, c. 32, p. 276.

firmative. He bases his answer on the fact that animals and children search for food without being impelled from outside, knowing what they are doing, and carrying it out with pleasure or grief according to the circumstances. The behaviour of animals and children, then, is used to prove that acts performed under the impulse of emotions do not cease to be voluntary.[116]

In his inquiry into the notion of the voluntary act, Thomas Aquinas refers to the doctrine of Nemesius. If an act may only be termed voluntary if its source lies within the agent, the question arises whether any human action is voluntary. Is it not always caused from outside, by the desirable object?[117] According to Thomas, human activity is voluntary in the highest degree. It not only originates from the agent himself but it is purposive. In other words, man is not only aware of what he is doing, but he consciously aims at a goal he is pursuing.[118] As to the question whether animals are able to carry out voluntary acts, Thomas refers to the treatise of Nemesius, whose doctrine he tries to improve.[119] An activity is to be called voluntary insofar as the agent knows the goal that is intended. Such knowledge must take place on two levels: the mere knowledge of the object that is aimed at, or the understanding of the notion of goal. In the latter case, the agent grasps the very notion of an aim and the relation he has towards it. Hence he is able to turn it over in his mind and to deliberate about his behaviour. One could not attribute this complete awareness of the goal to animals; they possess only an imperfect knowledge of the object they pursue.[120]

Do choice and voluntary act coincide? In the mind of Nemesius the notion of voluntary is broader: a voluntary deed is not always an act of choice.[121] In order to define more accurately the notion of choice, our author compares it to other kinds of human activity. Choosing is not the

---

116 *De natura hominis*, c. 32, p. 276. In his *Eudemian Ethics* Aristotle asks whether children or animals are able to perform a πρᾶξις; in other words does the term πράττειν apply to the activity of children or animals? His reply is negative: the term πρᾶξις refers to the behaviour of a man who is able to deliberate about what he intends to do (*Eth. Eud.*, II, 6, 1222b18; II, 8, 1224a28). With respect to this question Aristotle also asserts that an animal is not capable of "eudemony" or happiness; a horse, a bird or a fish could not be called happy (*Eth. Eud.*, II, 7, 1217a26).

117 *S.T.*, I-II, q. 6, a. 1, obj. 1.

118 *S.T.*, I-II, q. 6, a. 1 co: Et ideo cum utrumque sit ab intrinseco principio, scilicet quod agunt et quod propter finem agunt, horum motus et actus dicuntur voluntarii: hoc enim importat nomen voluntarii, quod motus et actus sit a propria inclinatione. Et inde est quod voluntarium dicitur esse secundum definitionem Aristotelis et Gregorii Nysseni et Damasceni, non solum cujus principium est intra, sed cum additione scientiae. Unde cum homo maxime cognoscit finem sui operis et movet seipsum, in ejus actibus maxime voluntarium invenitur.

119 *S.T.*, I-II, q. 6, a. 2, sed contra.

120 *S.T.*, I-II, q. 6, a. 2 co: Unde soli rationali naturae competit voluntarium secundum rationem perfectam; sed secundum rationem imperfectam competit etiam brutis animalibus.

121 *De natura hominis*, c. 33, p. 277.

same as desiring.[122] Nemesius especially emphasizes the difference between choosing and wishing: whereas choice is always concerned with things depending on us, wishing may aim at something impossible.[123] Moreover, wishing is directed towards an end, whereas choice is also linked to the means leading to the end.[124] Neither is choice the same as opinion: opinion may refer to something eternal, it may be true or false, and it is related to a universal object — none of which applies to choice.[125] Finally, choice differs from deliberation; it is rather the outcome of deliberation.[126] According to Nemesius choice is a combination of three constituent elements: deliberation, judgment, and desire.[127] This corresponds to the doctrine of Alexander rather than to that of Aspasius, as E. Dobler suggests.[128]

In his study of choice Thomas Aquinas again mentions the theory of Nemesius. He agrees that choice is a combination of elements. Referring to the sixth book of the *Nicomachean Ethics*, he distinguishes two components, understanding and desire, which are related to each other as the formal and material aspects of choice. In this respect he freely quotes a passage of Nemesius stating that the combination of the constituents of choice may be compared to the composition of body and soul in man.[129] Obviously the theory of Nemesius has been somewhat distorted. First of all the combination as it is described by Nemesius embraces three elements, not just two. Besides, the relation of body and soul is not conceived by him according to the pattern of matter and form. On the other hand Thomas Aquinas agrees with Nemesius on the question whether animals are able to choose. Choice belongs only to the will, not to sensitive desire.[130] Finally, it is worth noticing that Thomas only speaks of animals and not of children.

Deliberation undeniably is an important component of choice. What

---

122 *De natura hominis*, c. 33, p. 278. On this subject Nemesius is in agreement with the *Nicomachean Ethics* of Aristotle. According to the Stagirite choice may not be identified with ὄρεξις, it is a βουλευτικὴ ὄρεξις τῶν ἐφ' ἡμῖν (III, 3, 1113a11; VI, 2, 1139a23).

123 *De natura hominis*, c. 33, p. 279. Cf. Aristoteles, *Eth. Nic.* III, 2, 1111b22.

124 *De natura hominis*, c. 33, p. 279. Cf. Aristoteles, *Eth. Nic.* III, 4, 1113a15.

125 *De natura hominis*, c. 33, p. 280. Cf. Aristoteles, *Eth. Nic.* III, 2, 1111b30.

126 *De natura hominis*, c. 33, p. 280-281. Cf. Aristoteles, *Eth. Nic.* III, 3, 1113a4.

127 *De natura hominis*, c. 33, p. 281: ἔστιν οὖν μικτόν τι ἐκ βουλῆς καὶ κρίσεως καὶ ὀρέξεως.

128 E. Dobler, *Nemesius von Emesa und die Psychologie des menschlichen Aktes bei Thomas von Aquin* (Werthenstein 1950), p. 105: "Auch hier hat Nemesius nicht ganz originell gedacht. Aehnlich lehrt nämlich auch der Aristoteliker Aspasius, mit dem Unterschied jedoch, dass er an Stelle von drei konstituierenden Faktoren nur deren 2 annahm: Ueberlegung und Wollen (βουλή und ὄρεξις)."

129 *S.T.*, I-II, q. 13, a. 1 co.: Unde Gregorius Nyssenus dicit quod electio neque est appetitus secundum seipsam, neque consilium solum, sed ex his aliquid compositum. Sicut enim dicimus animal ex anima et corpore compositum esse, neque vero corpus esse secundum seipsum, neque animam solam, sed utrumque, ita et electionem. — Thomas faithfully reproduces the translation of Burgundio.

130 *S.T.*, I-II, q. 13, a. 2 sed contra et co.

does it mean? Does deliberation coincide with inquiry? In the opinion of Nemesius it does not. We may investigate whether the sun is larger than the earth, but this is not a topic of deliberation. [131] Indeed, deliberation is always a kind of inquiry, but the reverse is not true. A man deliberates only about what depends on him, on what he is able to do, the outcome being uncertain. [132] What is at issue is always something to be done, a *prakton*. How could he really deliberate about necessary events, about what happens always in the same way, about what is effected by nature or due merely to chance? Only when something depends on our own initiative, the outcome being uncertain, does deliberation become meaningful. [133] No deliberation is required in the case of scientific knowledge and technical skill. Some arts, however, involve a certain degree of deliberation, as for instance the arts of healing, gymnastics, and navigation. [134] Moreover, deliberation is not concerned with the goal to be pursued but with the means to be used. [135] In this connection Nemesius distinguishes between different modes: some things are necessary, others are contingent; and among the latter some are more probable than their opposite, others are less probable, other again are equally probable. As a result, deliberation is concerned with contingent facts of which both alternatives are equally possible. If a man is unable to perform one of the alternatives, deliberation is meaningless. [136]

Thomas Aquinas fully agrees with Nemesius on the distinction between deliberation and inquiry. According to Aquinas deliberation is a special kind of inquiry, which is necessary because in the field of human activity so much uncertainty occurs. Our actions deal with particular and contingent matters. Consequently without an inquiry no one could ever come to a judgment. [137] For the same reason Thomas, like Nemesius, acknowledges that deliberation is concerned only with matters depending on our initiative. [138] He also wonders whether deliberation is involved in everything we are going to do. He mentions

---

131 *De natura hominis*, c. 34, p. 283; Cf. Aristoteles, *Eth. Nic.*, III, 3, 1112b21.
132 *De natura hominis*, c. 34, p. 284. Cf. Aristoteles, *Eth. Nic.*, III, 3, 1112a30.
133 *De natura hominis*, c. 34, p. 285-286. Cf. Aristoteles, *Eth. Nic.*, III, 3, 1112a18-30.
134 *De natura hominis*, c. 34, p. 286. Cf. Aristoteles, *Eth. Nic.*, III, 3 1112a34-b8.
135 *De natura hominis*, c. 34, p. 286. Cf. Aristoteles, *Eth. Nic.*, III, 3, 1112b11 ss.
136 *De natura hominis*, c. 34, p. 287-288. Cf. Aristoteles, *Eth. Nic.*, III, 3, 1112b24 ss.; *Peri Hermeneias*, c. 9.
137 *S.T.*, I-II, q. 14, a. 1, sed contra: Sed contra est quod Gregorius Nyssenus dicit: Omne quidem consilium quaestio est, non autem omnis quaestio consilium. — Here again Thomas reproduces rather faithfully the translation of Burgundio: Nam omne quidem consilium quaestio est, non omnis autem quaestio est consilium.
138 *S.T.*, I-II, q. 14, a. 3, Sed contra est quod Gregorius Nyssenus dicit: Consiliamur de his quae sunt in nobis et per nos fieri possunt. — The translation of Burgundio is worded as follows: Consiliamur igitur de his quae sunt in nobis et per nos fieri possunt.

two exceptions. One is taken from Aristotle: we do not deliberate about
unimportant matters. The other is borrowed from Nemesius: actions
depending on technical skill are not deliberated.[139] According to
Thomas Aquinas deliberation is an inquiry about the means to be used,
not about the end itself. On this issue too he is in agreement with
Nemesius, though his doctrine is more intricate than it looks at first
glance.[140] A distinction is to be made between the ultimate end and the
many subordinate goals of human activity. These subordinate goals are
not only determined by deliberation but they depend to a large extent
on moral behaviour. Everybody aims at goals that correspond to the
moral level of his life.[141]

Nemesius devotes a whole chapter to the question whether some acts
truly spring from our initiative, so that a man may be considered to be
their source. According to him many people oppose this view. He
probably refers not only to pagans but also to Christians.[142] In order to
explain human activity Nemesius advances several hypotheses which he
successively eliminates. In no way may God be called the cause of our
acts, because some of them are wrong and unrighteous. Our actions may
not be attributed to necessity either, because they are not always and invariably the same. Might they be produced by destiny? No, for in that
case all of them would be necessitated. Furthermore, they are not the
work of nature, because the field of nature is the material world of
plants and animals. Neither may they be attributed to fortune, since fortune concerns only exceptional and unexpected matters. Neither may
chance be their source, since chance belongs only to inanimate beings
and animals.[143] All other explanations eliminated, man is to be considered the principle of his acts. Besides, if man were not responsible
for his own activity, deliberation would be meaningless, and moral life

139 *S.T.*, I-II, q. 14, a. 4 sed contra: Sed contra est quod Gregorius Nyssenus dicit quod de his
quae secundum disciplinam vel artem sunt operibus non est consilium. — The passage to which
Thomas refers in the translation of Burgundio is as follows: Neque enim de his quae secundum
disciplinam vel artem sunt operibus vel gestionibus est consilium.—ibid., q. 14, a. 4 co.: Et ideo de
duobus non consiliamur quamvis ordinentur ad finem, ut Philosophus dicit, scilicet de rebus parvis
et de his quae sunt determinata qualiter fieri debent, sicut in operibus artium, praeter quasdam
conjecturales, ut Gregorius Nyssenus dicit, ut puta medicinalis, negotiativa et hujusmodi. — The
way in which Thomas reproduces the passage of Nemesius slightly departs from the original text:
Determinatae enim sunt quae harum rationes, praeter paucas artes vocatas conjecturales, puta
medicinalem et gymnasticam et gubernativam.

140 *S.T.*, I-II, q. 14, a. 2, sed contra: Sed contra est quod Gregorius Nyssenus dicit quod non de
fine, sed de his quae sunt ad finem est consilium. — The translation of Burgundio: Monstratum
autem est quod non de fine sed de his quae ad finem sunt, est consilium.

141 On this subject Thomas takes up the point of view of Aristotle, *Eth. Nic.*, III, 5, 1114a32:
ἀλλ' ὁποῖός ποθ' ἕκαστός ἐστι, τοιοῦτο καὶ τὸ τέλος φαίνεται αὐτῷ, taking into account that
everybody to a certain extent is the author of his character.

142 *De natura hominis*, c. 39, p. 311: πολλοὶ γὰρ οἱ πρὸς τοῦτο ἀντιβαίνοντες.

143 *De natura hominis*, c. 39, p. 312-314.

would no longer be possible. But man is obviously the author of his virtues, which he acquires by repeatedly performing the same acts.[144]
Moreover, warnings and exhortations as well as laws would be deprived
of value. In short, the proposed thesis is quite unacceptable, for it is
clearly against man's natural knowledge of his own activity.[145]

Which acts belong to the realm of our free initiative? Nemesius mentions in general our voluntary acts, or acts that we accomplish willingly,
and mainly those that have to do with the soul (τὰ ψυχικὰπάντα).[146] The
inner world of each individual is in the first place the province of free
initiative. In the opinion of the Stoics this was the only room left to
human liberty. Nemesius does not go that far. For him, each deed
issuing from a previous deliberation is an act of choice, which belongs
to our own initiative. This choice is made by our mind, the principle of
our behaviour.[147] What does this statement mean in the concrete life of
man? To the province of our own initiative belong the whole field of
moral action, our technical work, as well as our psychic and intellectual
activity.[148]

In his further treatment of the question Nemesius has to cope with
two important difficulties: the relationship of human activity to divine
providence and the dependence of our behaviour upon our bodily condition. Undoubtedly some interrelationship between human initiative
and divine governance has to be admitted. We may be prevented by
divine providence from making a choice. After all, human freedom is
not unlimited; it is always combined with the interference of God's
providential action in the world.[149] In regard to the second difficulty,
man is not only spiritual, he is unity of body and soul. Even our highest
activities do not escape the influence of our bodily condition. Many

144 De natura hominis, c. 39, p. 315: in this passage Nemesius explicitly refers to Aristotle: ἃ
γὰρ ποιοῦντες μανθάνομεν, ταῦτα μαθόντες ποιοῦμεν. Cf. Eth. Nic., II, 1, 1103a32.
145 De natura hominis, c. 39, p. 316: φυσικῶς ἄρα πᾶσιν ἀνθρώποις ἡ γνῶσις τοῦ ἐφ'
ἡμῖν συγκατέσπαρται. The value of this knowledge is guaranteed by its natural character.
146 De natura hominis, c. 40, p. 317: κυρίως δὲ ἐφ' ἡμῖνἐστι τὰ ψυχικὰ πάντα καὶ περὶ
ὧν βουλευόμεθα.
147 De natura hominis, c. 40, p. 318: ποιεῖται δὲ τούτου τὴν αἵρεσιν ὁ νοῦς ὁ ἡμέτερος,
καὶ οὗτός ἐστι ἀρχὴ πράξεως. Without stating explicitly that mind is the origin of our decisions,
Aristotle apparently suggested this doctrine. In the Nicomachean Ethics the Stagirite teaches that
the true self of man coincides with the mind (IX, 8, 1168b35-1169a2; X. 7, 1178a2). According to
this doctrine the true self of man (νοῦς) will be the author of all free initiatives.
148 De natura hominis, c. 40, p. 319: ἐφ' ἡμῖν ἄρα καὶ αἱ κατὰ τέχνην ἐνέργειαι καὶ ἀρεταὶ καὶ
πᾶσαι πράξεις ψυχικαί τε καὶ λογικαί.
149 De natura hominis, c. 40, p. 320. Here again Nemesius draws a clear distinction between
the free decisions of man and the action of divine providence. In the becoming of the world both
constituents are combined; therefore, what happens is a combination, and the outcome may be according to the free decision of man, according to the planning of providence or according to both
principles joined (Ibid., p. 321: μικτῶν δὲ ὄντων γινομένων).

people refer wrong actions to a defective bodily constitution, so that all responsibility is transferred to the domain of necessity. Nemesius does not agree with them. In his opinion man's behaviour is not necessitated by his bodily condition. Besides, in some cases a defective state of the body is to be attributed to the responsibility of the individuals concerned.[150]

Finally Nemesius attempts to disclose the origin itself of human freedom. Endowed with reason, man has the capacity of free choice, insofar as a reasonable creature is able to deliberate. He is not determined by a given state of things but has the possibility of stepping back and turning over in his mind the constituents of a particular situation. Thus deliberation would be useless if man were unable to act according to his own insight and decision.[151] As a matter of fact, the knowledge at issue here is not speculative but a practical intuition indicating how we must behave in each particular case.[152] Besides, human life is always changeable; it does not remain in the same condition but, as a part of the becoming of the world, it is integrated in it. In the case of man this mutability flows from the fundamental characteristics of his being. Human life has a beginning and the structure of man includes a material principle.[153] This is to be understood against the background of Aristotelian philosophy. If human existence has a beginning, it bears within itself the possibility of not being, since it did not exist before. Its generation entails its corruptibility, for it is inserted in the process of coming to be and passing away. Moreover, a material principle is indeterminate; it is a kind of openness towards further determinations. This principle is constantly present in human life, not only at the beginning but during the whole course of existence. According to Nemesius several degrees of mutability must be distinguished. Spiritual beings living close to the earth and participating in man's activity are more integrated in the becoming process than are higher spiritual beings, who are further removed from the instability of the world.[154] As a result, human liberty bears the same character of mutability: man is able to develop in one of several directions. God cannot be called the cause of

150 *De natura hominis*, c. 40, p. 321-323. Cf. Aristoteles, *Eth. Nic.*, III, 5, 1114a21-31.

151 *De natura hominis*, c. 41, p. 324-325. The same argument has been developed by Alexander of Aphrodisias in his *De Fato* (Cf. G. Verbeke, *Aristotélisme et Stoïcisme dans le De Fato d'Alexandre d'Aphrodisias*, p. 87).

152 *De natura hominis*, c. 41, p. 326. Practical wisdom is called φρόνησις, as it is in the *Nicomachean Ethics* of Aristotle.

153 *De natura hominis*, c. 41, p. 326.

154 *De natura hominis*, c. 41, p. 327. In this context Nemesius uses two characteristic terms which are to be traced to the Stoics: ἀπαλλοτριόω and προσοικειόω. Needless to say that the notion of οἰκείωσις (*conciliatio* or *commendatio* in the translation of Cicero) plays an important part in the ethical philosophy of the Stoics.

man's wrong deeds because each individual bears the responsibility of
his own behaviour. Hence the question arises whether human freedom
is to be accounted an evil. Not at all, in the opinion of Nemesius. If
man behaves badly, it is not because he has the capacity of choosing,
but because his habits acquired through free acts are wrong. Because
some people use badly their capacity of choice, human freedom in itself
is not to be accounted an evil. [155]

In his treatment of *liberum arbitrium* Thomas Aquinas refers to
Nemesius several times. According to Thomas we have to look at the
matter very closely. It is not quite accurate to claim that man's activity
is free. The heart of the question is choice or decision. That is the
meaning of *liberum arbitrium*. Our judgment is free, it is not
necessitated in any way by the object we choose. [156] In his further
metaphysical explanation the author points to the transcendental
background of each particular choice, introducing a kind of inevitable
ambiguity. Constantly uncertain and unsatisfied, man has to make
decisions; his inner tendencies always reach beyond the particular
values he attains. For this reason Thomas, like Nemesius, stresses the
fact that man is free insofar as his inner decision is concerned. He may,
however, be prevented from doing what he wants. Does a free act
originate from reason or free will? Thomas Aquinas mentions the view
of Nemesius and John Damascene, who apparently believe freedom to
be in immediate connection with reason, because it springs from
reason. [157] According to Thomas Aquinas this cannot be correct. Nevertheless, he gives a benign interpretation to the text of his predecessors:
it may mean, he says, that freedom is related to the rational soul, to
which the will belongs as a faculty; or else it may mean that the first
source of freedom is reason, though it is not the immediate principle of
choice. [158] Are animals endowed with liberty? It may seem that they are,
because they are able to move themselves, which means that they are
able to move or not to move. In this context Thomas refers to Nemesius
who, arguing against this objection, declares that although the faculty of
moving is in itself indeterminate, the judgment or *arbitrium* through
which they perform a particular movement is determinate and not

---

155 Are wrong actions to be attributed to our faculties? Certainly not according to Nemesius;
they do not belong to our faculties but to our habits and our choices, in other words to our moral
character (*De natura hominis*, c. 41, p. 329: οὐκ εἰσὶν ἄρα τῶν δυνάμεων αἱ κακίαι, ἀλλὰ τῶν
ἕξεων καὶ τῆς προαιρέσεως).

156 *De Veritate*, q. 24, a. 1, ad 1.

157 *De Veritate*, q. 24, a. 6, obj. 4: Praeterea secundum Damascenum et Gregorium Nyssenum,
secundum hoc sumus arbitrio liberi quod sumus rationales. Sed rationales sumus secundum quod
habemus rationem. Ergo secundum quod habemus rationem sumus arbitrio liberi; et ita videtur
quod liberum arbitrium sit ratio.

158 *De Veritate*, q. 24, a. 6, ad 4.

free.[159] Can animals be called free because, like man, they have been generated? Their life also has a beginning and is subject to change. According to Thomas Aquinas this question arises from a misunderstanding. Man is free because he is endowed with reason, as Nemesius, Augustine, and John Damascene teach. Besides, man is able to do wrong because his liberty is subject to change. The instability of human existence generally speaking springs from the fact that life has a beginning. Moral virtue and perversion are constantly present in human existence as possible ways of living. The freedom of man shows a frailty that can never be overcome.[160]

4. Conclusions

The following conclusions may be drawn from our inquiry:

1. Undoubtedly in its own day the contribution of Nemesius to the problem of fatalism and human freedom was important and influential. It was a very valuable attempt to replace pagan destiny by divine providence and save the liberty of man in the face of many objections and criticisms.

2. At the same time the *De natura hominis* was an attempt to initiate a fruitful dialogue between the Christian message and ancient philosophy. Many ideas and theories borrowed from Plato, Aristotle, the Stoics, Plotinus, and other philosophers are combined with Christian doctrine in order to make it understandable and acceptable by intellectuals of that time.

3. The treatise, considered to be a work of Gregory of Nyssa, was highly esteemed by Thomas Aquinas. He refers to it several times, as well as to the *De fide orthodoxa* of John Damascene. And even when he does not quote explicitly from the *De natura hominis* he is generally in agreement with its doctrine. We must acknowledge that the level of philosophical inquiry is far from being the same. Whereas Thomas Aquinas is an outstanding and original metaphysical thinker, Nemesius for the most part reproduces the opinions of previous philosophers and takes an empirical approach to the problems he tackles. The most interesting investigations of Thomas Aquinas concerning providence and freedom do not simply derive from the treatise of Nemesius; they bear the stamp of his own creative mind.

---

159 *De Veritate*, q. 24, a. 2, obj. 2 et ad 2.

160 *De Veritate*, q. 24, a. 2, obj. 4 et ad 4: Ad quartum dicendum quod incipere a versione vel esse ex nihilo non assignat Damascenus causam libertatis arbitrii, sed causam flexibilitatis liberi arbitrii in malum; causam autem liberi arbitrii assignat tam Damascenus quam Gregorius quam Augustinus rationem.

THE DOCTRINE OF FILIOQUE IN THOMAS AQUINAS
AND ITS PATRISTIC ANTECEDENTS

An Analysis of *Summa Theologiae*, Part I, Question 36

Jaroslav Pelikan

IN 1909, commenting on the thirty years that had elapsed since the *Aeterni Patris* of Leo XIII, with its emphasis on the place of the church fathers in Thomas Aquinas,[1] Martin Grabmann registered this complaint: "Leider ist in der an die Enzyklika sich anschliessenden thomistischen Bewegung diese Kontinuität zwischen Patristik und Scholastik nicht genügend beachtet worden."[2] In 1923, the dean of French patrologists, Gustave Bardy, addressed himself to the same question with the judgment: "L'étude des sources patristiques de saint Thomas d'Aquin est à peine commencée."[3] In 1938, G. Geenen was able to quote Bardy's words as still an accurate description of the situation.[4] In 1946, he quoted them again in his fine article on "Saint Thomas et les Pères" for the *Dictionnaire de théologie catholique.*[5] And in 1965, two-thirds of a century after Grabmann's comment, Ceslaus Velecky made the wry assertion: "It is strange that the research into these [patristic] sources still remains a Cinderella of Thomist studies, neglected by comparison with studies on St Thomas as an Aristotelian."[6]

In part, of course, the task is complicated by the sheer mass of the material, which makes it necessary for a scholar to confine his attention to some smaller aspects of the problem. For example, in a monograph

---

1 "Thomas Aquinas: qui, uti Caietanus animadvertit, veteres 'Doctores sacros qui summe veneratus est, ideo intellectum omnium quodammodo sortitus est.'" Denzinger 3139.

2 Martin Grabmann, *Die Geschichte der scholastischen Methode* (2 vols.; Freiburg i. Br. 1909-11) 1, 22, n. 2.

3 Gustave Bardy, "Sur les sources patristiques grecques de saint Thomas dans la Ire Partie de la *Somme Théologique,*" *Revue des sciences philosophiques et théologiques,* 12 (1923) 493.

4 G. Geenen, "L'usage des 'auctoritates' dans la doctrine du baptème chez S. Thomas d'Aquin," *Ephemerides Theologicae Lovanienses,* 15 (1938) 280; see also the same author's study, "Saint Thomas d'Aquin et ses sources pseudépigraphiques," *ibid.,* 20 (1943) 71-80.

5 G. Geenen, "Saint Thomas et les Pères," *Dictionnaire de théologie catholique,* 15, 738.

6 Ceslaus Velecky, "Appendix 3" to Volume 6 of Blackfriars edition of *Summa Theologiae* (London 1965) p. 131.

that was presented as a thesis to the faculty of theology at Toulouse in
1906, M. Duffo examined *Saint Jean Damascène, source de saint
Thomas*.[7] Duffo's work has never been published; more generally
available is the exhaustive catalogue compiled by J. Durantel, *Saint
Thomas et le Pseudo-Denis,* which makes the declaration: "S. Thomas
cite Denis fréquemment. Nous avons relevé, sauf erreur, 1.702 citations
expresses, 12 mentions générales visant l'œuvre sans citations de textes,
11 passages du commentaire de Maxime et 4 de celui de Hugues de S.
Victor."[8] A controversy whose repercussions can still be heard in the
recent publication of the Leonine edition of *Contra errores Graecorum*[9]
was that launched by F. H. Reusch's study of "Die Fälschungen in dem
Tractat des Thomas von Aquin gegen die Griechen,"[10] Thomas's relation
to the Greek patristic tradition has been the subject not only of the article by Bardy already cited, but also of the thorough monograph by
Ignaz Backes, which identified the method at work in his patristic
citations as one, "den Zusammenhang heranzuziehen, in gleicher Weise
danach strebend, den wahren Sinn eines Textes herauszustellen, wie die
Ehrfurcht vor den Vätern nicht zu verletzen.... Ganz selten und nur in
der S. th. kommt eine Erklärung zustande, die der dogmengeschicht-
lichen Lage Rechnung trägt."[11] As Backes's work shows, perhaps the
most satisfactory way of studying the relation of Thomas to the fathers
is to concentrate not on the use of one figure throughout the Thomistic
corpus, but on one theological theme. This is what Geenen did in his
study of baptism, quoted earlier. It is from such close *explication de
texte* that one can begin to evaluate such judgments as that of Michel
Riquet, that "l'œuvre de saint Thomas est tout autre chose qu'une compilation érudite mais impersonnelle,"[12] by contrast with his "milieu intellectuel," which, according to R. P. Gardeil, "est fait d'hommes qui
ont prouvé...à quel degré ils avaient le culte du document."[13]

7 See Bardy, *op. cit.*, p. 493, n. 1; Geenen, "L'usage des 'auctoritates,'" p. 281, n. 6.

8 J. Durantel, *Saint Thomas et le Pseudo-Denis* (Paris 1919) p. 60.

9 *Sancti Thomae de Aquino Opera Omnia iussu Leonis XIII p. m. edita* (Rome 1882—) 40-A,
7-8, 13. Wherever possible, I have cited Thomas according to the Leonine edition, adhering to it in
text, capitalization, orthography, and punctuation — except that in the last I have used inside
quotation marks rather than italics for quotations within quotations.

10 *Sonderdruck aus den Abhandlungen der königlichen bayerischen Akademie der Wissenschaften* (Munich 1889).

11 Ignaz Backes, *Die Christologie des hl. Thomas von Aquin und die griechischen Kir-
chenväter* (Paderborn 1931) p. 123.

12 Michel Riquet, "Saint Thomas d'Aquin et les 'auctoritates' en philosophie," *Archives de
philosophie* 3 (1926) 124.

13 R. P. Gardeil, "La réforme de la théologie catholique: la documentation de saint Thomas,"
Revue Thomiste, 11 (1903) 202.

Of all the theological themes with which Thomas dealt, the one best
suited to such an examination by a historian of the development of doctrine would appear to be the Trinity. His "Trinitarian articles" have
been called "unrivalled as precise statements of the Christian faith."[14]
In his *Commentary on the Sentences* Thomas himself defined the
"cognitio Trinitatis in unitate" as "fructus et finis totius vitae nostrae."[15]
It would be possible to examine the doctrine of the Trinity in that commentary and to compare it with his later formulation of the doctrine in
the *Summa Theologiae,* thus testing the suggestion of Chenu that in the
earlier work Thomas was "exploiting the Dionysian scheme of creative
procession," while in the latter, "in accordance with the riches he reaps
from Augustine's analyses, he brings to the fore the original relationship of subject to known and loved object in a mind capable of knowing
and loving God."[16] We have chosen instead to narrow the topic to the
most controversial issue in the trinitarian tradition received by Thomas
from the fathers, the doctrine of Filioque, as this was discussed in Part
I, Question 36 of the *Summa Theologiae.*[17] For if, as Velecky has
claimed, "the doctrine of the Trinity is the key to the whole theology of
the *Summa,*"[18] its handling of this controversial issue ought to illumine
both the trinitarianism of Thomas and his relation to his "auctoritates."
The appeal to authority, as all the monographs remind us, was regarded
by Thomas as the weakest of arguments — in philosophy.[19] But in
theology the situation was quite different. Here "quae... fidei sunt
[preeminently the Trinity], non sunt tentanda probare nisi per auctoritates, his qui auctoritates suscipiunt."[20] Among those "qui auctoritates suscipiunt" were, of course, the separated Christians of the
East; yet there were "plures" among them who read these "auctoritates"
as proof "Spiritum Sanctum non procedere a Filio," and "inter [eos] fuit
etiam Damascenus."[21]

The controversy over the Filioque is, then, a crucial test case for
Thomas's use of patristic "auctoritates." But his use of "auctoritates" is
also crucial for the history of the Filioque. It was, after all, on the way
to the Council of Lyons that Thomas died in 1274; and at that council it
was declared to have been "orthodoxorum Patrum atque Doctorum,

---

14 David Knowles, *The Evolution of Medieval Thought* (London 1962) p. 267.
15 *In I Sent.,* d. 2, exp.; ed. Mandonnet (Paris 1929) 1, 77.
16 M.-D. Chenu, *Toward Understanding Saint Thomas,* tr. A.-M. Landry and D. Hughes
(Chicago 1964) pp. 274-75.
17 *Opera,* 4, 375-86. Unless otherwise indicated, all references to the *Summa* are to Part I.
18 Velecky, *op. cit.,* p. xx.
19 Cf. Riquet, *op. cit.,* pp. 148-49; Chenu, *op. cit.,* p. 139, n. 19.
20 *S. Th.* I, q. 32, art. 1, resp.
21 *S. Th.* I, q. 36, art. 2, ad 3.

Latinorum pariter et Graecorum incommutabilis et vera sententia" that "Spiritus Sanctus aeternaliter ex Patre et Filio, non tanquam ex duobus principiis, sed tanquam ex uno principio, non duabus spirationibus, sed unica spiratione procedit."[22] These very qualifications, one "principium" and one "spiratio," were the issues whose patristic antecedents were probed with such care by Thomas, so that in some ways — leaving out of consideration the determinative influence of secular and ecclesiastical politics, both Eastern and Western[23] — we may be entitled to view the dogmatic outcome at Lyons as at least in part an achievement of Thomas Aquinas. Geenen has spoken of "quelques études non publiées," presumably his own and those of other scholars as well, among them one "sur les sources grecques et latines de la doctrine trinitaire" of Thomas.[24] From this unpublished, and hence unavailable, study he has derived the conclusion that Thomas's "théologie trinitaire... est une doctrine latino-grecque, où l'élément latin dominé par la doctrine d'Augustin, dépasse de loin l'influence grecque."[25] Other works on the subject of the Filioque, notably those of Grumel and Malet,[26] do touch on the issue of the use of the fathers, but there would still appear to be need for an analysis of Part I, Question 36 that deals with it *ex professo*.

In the treatment of the doctrine of the Holy Spirit, as in his theology generally, Thomas was obliged to come to terms with patristic tradition. Therefore he argued in Part I, Question 36 not only on the basis of what "accommodatum est ex usu Scripturae,"[27] but also from what "ex usu Ecclesiae est accommodatum"[28]; or, as he put it in the corresponding Article of the *Commentary on the Sentences*, his trinitarian authority was "tota Scriptura et totus usus Ecclesiae."[29] The source and norm in the discussion of such issues as procession (or processions) in the Godhead was the "fides catholica."[30] The witnesses to this "fides catholica" were the fathers of the church, or, as he usually denominated them, the

22   Denzinger 850.

23   Deno J. Geanakoplos, *Emperor Michael Palaeologus and the West, 1258-1282* (Cambridge, Mass. 1959); Stephan Kuttner, "Conciliar Law in the Making: The Lyonese Constitutions (1274) of Gregory X in a MS. at Washington," *Miscellanea Pio Paschini* (2 vols.; Rome 1948-49) 2, 39-81.

24   "Saint Thomas et les Pères," p. 739.

25   *Ibid.*, p. 744.

26   V. Grumel, "S. Thomas et la doctrine des Grecs sur la procession de Saint-Esprit," *Echos d'Orient*, 25 (1926) 257-80; A. Malet, *Personne et amour dans la théologie trinitaire de Saint Thomas d'Aquin* (Paris 1956) pp. 151-55, 161-87.

27   *S. Th.* I, q. 36, art. 1, resp.

28   *S. Th.* I, q. 36, art. 1, ad 1.

29   *In I Sent.* d. 10, q. 1, art. 4, s. c.; ed. Mandonnet, 1, 267.

30   *S. Th.* I, q. 27, art. 1, resp.

"doctores" or "sancti doctores."[31] For the purposes of this analysis we shall concentrate on his use only of the fathers in this Question. Therefore we shall leave out of consideration not only the intriguing quotation from the *Physics* of Aristotle in Article 2, Objection 7, but also the quotation from Anselm in the same passage and the references to "quidam."[32] Moreover, because Thomas himself made an issue of chronology as a principle of interpretation, arguing that the passage of time and the rise of controversy enabled one to make sense of the relation between "primum symbolum" and "sequens concilium,"[33] it may be beneficial to consider these "auctoritates" chronologically, that is, in the chronological sequence in which Thomas and his contemporaries believed them to have arisen historically.

The earliest authority quoted in Question 36 was the apocryphal *Acta Sancti Andreae,* in which the Holy Spirit was said to be "procedentem ex Patre, et in Filio permanentem."[34] This would seem to deny the doctrine of Filioque, for "nihil procedit ab eo in quo quiescit."[35] But this objection did not hold; for in some places "et Filius in Patre manere dicitur, cum tamen a Patre procedat."[36] This appears to have been the only quotation from any such apostolic legend anywhere in Part I of the *Summa,* although there were some in later sections of the work. Nevertheless, Thomas presumably accepted the account at face value and took the words seriously as more or less apostolic in origin. Among the apocryphal *Acta* of the various apostles, the *Acta Sancti Andreae* are generally thought to enjoy the earliest attestation and thus supposedly the most credibility.[37] It would be tempting to make something of the circumstance that Thomas refers specifically to Andrew in this context. By this time it was common among Byzantine theologians to call him πρωτόκλητος,[38] and the legend of his having had the foresight to found a church in what was eventually to be Constantinople had been connected with this title to claim a "primacy" of sorts for the Second Rome.[39] But

31 On this usage and on the entire question, see the penetrating and learned discussion of Joseph de Ghellinck, "Patristique et argument de tradition au bas moyen âge," *Aus der Geisteswelt des Mittelalters* (Münster 1935) 1, 403-26.
32 *S. Th.* I, q. 36, art. 2, ad 3; and art. 4, resp.
33 *S. Th.* I, q. 36, art. 2, ad 2.
34 *Acta apostolorum apocrypha,* ed. Constantin Tischendorf (Leipzig 1851) p. 105.
35 *S. Th.* I, q. 36, art. 2, obj. 4.
36 *S. Th.* I, q. 36, art. 2, ad 4; apparently Thomas was thinking of such biblical passages as John 15:10, although John 14:10 speaks of "Pater in me manens."
37 Tischendorf, *op. cit.,* p. xl.
38 Cf. E. A. Sophocles, *Greek Lexicon of the Roman and Byzantine Periods* (Boston 1870) p. 958, *s. v.*
39 Francis Dvornik, *The Idea of Apostolicity in Byzantium and the Legend of the Apostle Andrew* (Cambridge, Mass. 1958).

Thomas's arguments for the primacy of Peter and therefore for the primacy of Rome, even the most sharply polemical ones in *Contra errores Graecorum,* do not seem to have been concerned with this rather lame refutation of the Latin case.[40] It seems, therefore, that the function of this quotation from the *Acts of Andrew* in Thomas's exposition of the Filioque was one of classifying terminology: such terms as "quiescere" or "manere," while authenticated by scriptural and early patristic authority, were not to be treated as though they were technical terms (as, for example, "mittere" and above all "procedere" were); hence it was not valid to argue against the Filioque on the basis of such usage.

Also possessing great antiquity and high cisapostolic authority for Thomas was the Dionysian corpus. For the doctrine of Filioque it was somewhat discomfiting. In his *Commentary on the Sentences* Thomas had quoted the second chapter of *De divinis nominibus* to the effect that "Pater quidem est fontana deitas, Filius et Spiritus sanctus deigenae deitatis, si ita oportet dicere, pullulationes sunt, et sicut flores divinae naturae, et sicut divina lumina a sanctis eloquiis accepimus."[41] As Durantel has noted, all such expressions in Dionysius could be treated by Thomas as symbolic in intent and therefore "ne sont pas sans gêner quelque peu S. Thomas."[42] Unlike the quotation from the *Acts of Andrew,* this passage from Dionysius did not pass from the *Commentary on the Sentences* to the defense of the Filioque in the *Summa.* Instead, there was only one Dionysian reference: "Secundum Dionysium, 'non est audendum dicere aliquid de substantiali divinitate praeter ea quae divinitus nobis ex sacris eloquiis sunt expressa.'"[43] Since the procession of the Holy Spirit from the Son was not stated in Scripture, but only the procession from the Father, the Filioque would seem to be excluded. This passage occurred frequently in Thomas, usually as part of an Objection against the use of one or another *vox ἄγραφος*: for example, "persona" (against which a much more pungent objection could be quoted from Jerome),[44] as well as the far less common "notio."[45] Each time he quoted these words from Dionysius, Thomas replied to the effect that "licet nomen... in Scriptura... non inveniatur..., tamen id quod nomen significat, multipliciter in sacra Scriptura in-

40 Cf. *Contra errores Graecorum* II, 34.

41 *In I Sent.* d. 11, q. 1, art. 1; ed. Mandonnet, 1, 276; Dionysius the Areopagite *De divinis nominibus* 2.7, PG 3, 645 (not 635, as Mandonnet has it).

42 Durantel, *op. cit.,* pp. 141-42.

43 *S. Th.* I, q. 36, art. 2, obj. 1; Dionysius the Areopagite *De divinis nominibus* 1.1, PG 3, 588.

44 *S. Th.* I, q. 39, art. 3, obj. 1 and obj. 3.

45 *S. Th.* I, q. 32, art. 2, obj. 1.

venitur."[46] Here in Question 36, too, the reply was that "licet autem per verba non inveniatur in sacra Scriptura quod Spiritus Sanctus procedit a Filio, invenitur tamen quantum ad sensum."[47]

In another context, to be sure, Thomas argued from the absence of an explicit scriptural warrant that a Greek theologoumenon which had in it echoes of the Filioque or of its equivalent was to be avoided: "Doctores Graecorum communiter dicunt Spiritum Sanctum esse imaginem Patris et Filii. Sed doctores latini soli Filio attribuunt nomen Imaginis: non enim invenitur in canonica Scriptura nisi de Filio."[48] Basically, however, the simpleminded biblicism that could be taken to be the meaning of the words of Dionysius was to be rejected, on the same grounds on which the fathers had refused to accept the Arian objections to ὁμοούσιος.[49] From the frequency with which Thomas quoted these words of Dionysius, almost always in an Objection and for the same purpose, it would seem valid to conclude that they did not have any distinctive place in the discussion of Filioque, except to support the principle of hermeneutics that "regulariter etiam in sacra Scriptura tenendum est, quod id quod de Patre dicitur, oportet de Filio intelligi, etiam si dictio exclusiva addatur," with the important proviso, however, that this did not apply "in illis in quibus Pater et Filius secundum oppositas relationes distinguuntur."[50] Therefore if, as the East insisted and as the West conceded, there was no explicit scriptural proof text for the Filioque, it was nevertheless a valid inference, on the basis of this principle, from the procession "ex Patre." By a *reductio ad absurdum* that would have been even more harmful to theological terminology in Greek than to the vocabulary of the Latin scholastics, Thomas was arguing that such inferences had as much probative authority as verbatim quotations from Scripture. For the purposes of this *reductio ad absurdum,* the oft-repeated words of Dionysius provided a convenient foil.

There is special interest in Thomas's use of the authority of Athanasius. The treatise *Contra errores Graecorum* contained many quotations attributed to Athanasius, but even the care and erudition of the Leonine editors has failed to yield more than the admission, "non repertus," for many of these, although the ideas expressed in them are recognizable as broadly Athanasian.[51] Here in Part I of the *Summa,*

46 *S. Th.* I, q. 29, art. 3, ad 1.
47 *S. Th.* I, q. 36, art. 2, ad 1.
48 *S. Th.* I, q. 35, art. 2, resp.
49 *S. Th.* I, q. 39, art. 2, ad 2.
50 *S. Th.* I, q. 36, art. 2, ad 1.
51 See the index, *Opera,* 40-A, 158.

however, Thomas put aside all of these dubious quotations from the
Libellus. As Bardy notes, "la première partie de la Somme renvoie
treize fois à saint Athanase; mais sous ce nom illustre, c'est toujours le
symbole pseudo-athanasien qui est mentionné."[52] Thomas did, of
course, share the general Western notion that the *Quicunque vult* was
the work of the Alexandrian church father.[53] Therefore it was extremely
useful to be able to quote the great Greek-speaking theologian of the
fourth century against the Greek-speaking theologians of the thirteenth: "Sed contra est quod dicit Athanasius: 'Spiritus Sanctus a Patre
et Filio, non factus, nec creatus, nec genitus, sed procedens.'"[54] The
same passage from the *Quicunque vult* had appeared earlier, also in a
Sed contra, as proof that "generatio" was not an appropriate term for
the procession of the Holy Spirit;[55] and for this purpose it would have
been acceptable also to Eastern thought. In Question 36, however, it
served to support the Western argument for the Filioque. The use of it
as a clinching proof for this argument, together with the familiar
references to the *Quicunque vult* in Part II-II, Question 1,[56] was "une
preuve éclatante pour démontrer que les textes des Pères sont une
véritable source de la théologie."[57] Earlier Latin disputants against the
East had already made use of this passage. It appeared, for example, in
the *De haeresibus Graecorum* of Hugo Etherianus,[58] who had lived at
the court of Manuel I Comnenus, Byzantine emperor; and this book was
translated into Greek.[59] Soon after its use by Thomas, however, the
authenticity of the *Quicunque vult,* and especially of the words he had
quoted on the Filioque, came under attack from the Greeks. It is interesting to speculate, in the light of Laurent's researches into the
Eastern attitude toward this creed,[60] what the Greek reaction would
have been at Lyons if Thomas had arrived there and had used this
quotation against them as he did in *Contra errores Graecorum* and
again in the *Summa.*[61] It seems obvious that it would not have been
challenged.

When we consider the next patristic authority employed by Thomas
in defense of the Filioque, Athanasius's contemporary and indeed "the

---

52 Bardy, *op. cit.,* p. 494.
53 See J. N. D. Kelly, *The Athanasian Creed* (New York 1964) pp. 35-48.
54 *S. Th.* I, q. 36, art. 2, s. c.
55 *S. Th.* I, q. 27, art. 4, s. c.
56 *S. Th.* II-II, q. 1, art. 9-10.
57 Geenen, "Saint Thomas et les Pères," p. 739.
58 Hugo Etherianus *De haeresibus Graecorum* 3.21, PL 202, 393.
59 See PL 202, 230.
60 V. Laurent, "Le symbole Quicumque et l'Eglise byzantine. Notes et documents," *Echos
d'Orient,* 39 (1936) 385-404.
61 *Contra errores Graecorum,* II, 27.

Athanasius of the West," Hilary of Poitiers, we come to a source of the highest importance. On the one hand, as Velecky has suggested, he may be "the unacknowledged authority" to whom Thomas was indebted for some of his trinitarian thought.[62] For that matter, some of what Thomas, on this very issue, drew from Augustine was drawn by him, in turn, from Hilary; for despite Alfred Schindler's recent judgment that "tatsächlich [ist] der Einfluss des Hilarius kein sehr tiefgehender und verschwindet vor allem da, wo Augustin über die blosse [sic!] Begründung des Dogmas aus der Schrift hinausgeht,"[63] Hilary had probably provided Augustine with much of the exegetical tradition of the Greek fathers and had thus taught him to read the Bible in a trinitarian way.[64] On the other hand, Hilary occupies an influential place in the growth of the Filioque doctrine. He had not fully thought through the implications of the Arian controversies for the deity of the Holy Spirit, and his language about the relation of the Spirit to the Father was therefore vague and uncertain. But he was much clearer in his belief that if the Son was truly equal to the Father in all things, He had to be a participant in the "being sent," hence also in the "proceeding," of the Holy Spirit.[65] Consistently carried out after the full deity of the Holy Spirit had been articulated, this belief led directly to the Augustinian, and to the Western, doctrine of Filioque.

There were three quotations from Hilary in Question 36. The first occurred at the very beginning, where Hilary was cited as authority for the observation that the title "Holy Spirit" was used in Scripture for each of the three persons of the Trinity.[66] From this it seemed to follow that "hoc nomen 'Spiritus Sanctus' non sit proprium nomen alicuius divinae personae," but a name common to all three persons.[67] Without following Hilary's (and Thomas's) exegesis of the specific texts in question, one must acknowledge that the use of the term in the Old and New Testament did constitute a problem if one were insisting upon trinitarian precision. Actually, the most perplexing text of all, and one about which both Hilary and Augustine were troubled,[68] was 2 Corinthians 3:17: "Dominus [sc., Christus] autem Spiritus est." Yet this text

62 Velecky, *op. cit.*, p. 133.
63 Alfred Schindler, *Wort und Analogie in Augustins Trinitätslehre* (Tübingen 1965) p. 129.
64 There is need for further study of the exegesis of specific passages of Scripture in the Greek tradition and of the transmission of this exegesis through Hilary and Ambrose to Augustine, and through him to Western interpreters for more than a millennium.
65 Jaroslav Pelikan, *Development of Doctrine: Some Historical Prolegomena* (New Haven 1969) pp. 120-41.
66 Hilary *De Trinitate* 8.25, PL 10, 254.
67 *S. Th.* I, q. 36, art. 1, obj. 1.
68 Hilary *De Trinitate* 2.32, PL 10, 72-73; Augustine *De Trinitate* 2.10.19, CCSL 50, 105-106.

did not occur in the *Summa* until later.[69] Thomas's response to the difficulty raised by Hilary was to distinguish between "Holy Spirit" as a
common noun and as a proper noun, using a statement of Augustine as
a resolution.[70] From this it followed that the title, "prout sumitur in virtute duarum dictionum, commune est toti Trinitati."[71] The words of
Hilary thus made it possible to see the distinctions between these two
usages in the language of Scripture itself. What did not come through in
Thomas's discussion, since it was not intended to be an exercise in the
history of doctrine but a formulation of doctrine, was the ambiguity still
present in the language of Hilary, which prompted him to equivocate as
much as he did.

Some of that equivocation was visible in the passage which Thomas
next quoted from Hilary. It was taken from the closing paragraph of
Hilary's book on the Trinity, in which the author, despairing of any
conceptualization that would remove the mystery and the ambiguity of
trinitarian doctrine, broke into doxology as an appeal to a higher court.
From that doxology Thomas quoted the words: "Conserva hanc, oro,
fidei meae religionem, ut semper obtineam Patrem, scilicet te; et Filium
tuum una tecum adorem; et Spiritum Sanctum tuum, qui est per
Unigenitum tuum, promerear."[72] Now these words were quoted as the
Sed contra in the article dealing with the issue, "Utrum Spiritus Sanctus
procedat a Patre per Filium."[73] This was, of course, the Eastern alternative to the Filioque, one that seemed safer both in relation to patristic
usage and on the basis of intratrinitarian metaphysics. To Thomas, on
the other hand, its appearance in patristic usage, and in Western usage
at that, suggested that it had to be understood in a manner that could be
harmonized with the eventual Western formulation of the Filioque. He
therefore set out to determine the various ways in which the preposition
"per" could be used, showing that "ex Patre per Filium" was not inconsistent with the Western position, indeed that "potest dici quod
Pater per Filium spirat Spiritum Sanctum; vel quod Spiritus Sanctus
procedat a Patre per Filium, quod idem est"[74] — and, although he did
not add it right here, "idem" with the formula "ex Patre Filioque."
Eastern theologians provided various explanations for the formula "ex
Patre per Filium," but refused to accept the identification of this with
the Western Filioque.[75]

69 See the index, *Opera*, 16, 57.
70 See p. 329 below.
71 *S. Th.* I, q. 36, art. 1, ad 1.
72 Hilary *De Trinitate* 12.57, PL 10, 471-72.
73 *S. Th.* I, q. 36, art. 3, s. c.
74 *S. Th.* I, q. 36, art. 3, resp.
75 See Martin Jugie, *De processione Spiritus Sancti ex fontibus revelationis et secundum
Orientales dissidentes* (Rome 1936) pp. 320-36.

The reason for this refusal becomes evident when we turn to the third and most problematical of the passages quoted by Thomas from Hilary in the explication of the Filioque. At stake in the Eastern opposition to Filioque was the unity of God, which, for Eastern theology, was guaranteed in the context of the dogma of the Trinity by the insistence upon only one ἀρχή in the Godhead, that of the Father, from whom alone both Son and Holy Spirit were coeternally and equally derived. Western language about an eternal derivation of the Holy Spirit "ex Patre Filioque" appeared to compromise this unity of ἀρχή.[76] Therefore Thomas devoted Article 4 of Question 36 to the issue, "Utrum Pater et Filius sint unum principium Spiritus Sancti." Here he had to come to terms with the imprecise, perhaps even downright careless, expressions of the same Western theologians to whom the development of the doctrine of Filioque owed the most. Among these the most embarrassing were, of course, Hilary and Augustine, and in some ways the former more than the latter. For Hilary had permitted himself to say "quod Spiritus Sanctus 'a Patre et Filio auctoribus confitendus est'."[77] From this it would seem to follow that although, economically speaking, "Pater et Filius et Spiritus Sanctus, quia sunt unum principium creaturae, dicuntur esse unus Creator," the same did not hold immanently, where "Pater et Filius non sunt unus spirator, sed 'duo spiratores'" and where, consequently, "Pater et Filius non sunt unum principium Spiritus Sancti."[78] Taken as it stood, this formula of Hilary seemed to be a corroboration of the Eastern charge that the idea of Filioque necessarily implied the positing of two ἀρχαί in the Godhead and therefore jeopardized the oneness of God.

The clarification of Hilary's formula proposed by Thomas was aimed at affirming (or reaffirming) one ἀρχή and yet grasping what was correct in the formula. To do this he argued that "'spirans' adiectivum est, 'spirator' vero substantivum." Speaking adjectivally, one could refer to the Father and the Son as "'duo spirantes,' propter pluralitatem suppositorum; non autem 'duo spiratores,' propter unam spirationem."[79] Therefore Hilary was to be exonerated on the grounds that his term, "a Patre et Filio auctoribus," was intended theologically, if not grammatically, only in an adjectival sense. It is, to be sure, not at all clear that this exoneration rested upon an accurate reading of

76 Cf. Martin Jugie, *Theologia dogmatica Christianorum Orientalium ab ecclesia Catholica dissidentium* (5 vols., Paris 1926-35) 2, 296-535.

77 Hilary *De Trinitate* 2.29, PL 10, 69; it is interesting that one transmission of the text reads, "qui Patre et Filio auctoribus," without the preposition.

78 *S. Th.* I, q. 36, art. 4, obj. 7.

79 *S. Th.* I, q. 36, art. 4, ad 7.

Hilary's intent, which would appear to have been determined, at least in part, by his attitude toward the relation between the immanent and the economic in the Godhead.[80] Mandonnet has suggested, moreover, that the distinction between "duo spirantes" and "duo spiratores" was not really necessary, since even the noun "spirator" is a "nomen verbale," which is a noun in form but has adjectival force. "Si adjective sumatur spirator," Mandonnet continues, "sunt duo spiratores, si vero substantive, ut in *Summa theologiae* expresse sumitur, non est nisi unus spirator."[81] Thus Thomas's apologia for "a Patre et Filio auctoribus" would appear to be more plausible theologically than historically or even grammatically. It was nevertheless a highly revealing instance of his devotion to the fathers and of his readiness to go to considerable lengths in vindicating their essential orthodoxy.

Coming after the death of both Athanasius and Hilary and shrouded even today in considerable obscurity, the deliberations and creedal decisions of the First Council of Constantinople in 381 figured prominently in the conflicts over the doctrine of Filioque. As quoted by the *Acta* of the Council of Ephesus in 431 and by those of the Council of Chalcedon in 451, the formula of Constantinople read: "Credimus in Spiritum Sanctum, Dominum et vivificantem, ex Patre procedentem, cum Patre et Filio adorandum et glorificandum."[82] Thus the adoration and glory properly belonged to the Father and to the Son, as well as to the Holy Spirit, but the procession was from the Father. But this particular quotation demanded attention not only on material grounds, because of the seeming contradiction between the Western doctrine and the doctrinal decree of the second ecumenical council, but especially on formal or procedural grounds, because of the arbitrary and unilateral Western addition to it. For Thomas went on: "Nullo igitur modo debuit addi in symbolo nostro [i. e., the Western] quod Spiritus Sanctus procedat a Filio: sed videntur anathematis rei, qui hoc addiderunt,"[83] this latter referring to the council's condemnation of those who would tamper with the text of the creed. It would perhaps be too much to say that the East objected as vehemently to the highhandedness of the Western interpolation as to its theological content, but the East certainly did insist that even if the double procession could be explained in an orthodox manner, the Latins had no right to add it to the creed on

80 Cf. Pelikan, *op. cit.,* pp. 131-33.
81 Mandonnet, *op. cit.,* 1, 285, n (a).
82 See A. Hahn, ed., *Bibliothek der Symbole und Glaubensregeln der Alten Kirche* (3rd ed.; Breslau 1897) p. 166.
83 *S. Th.* I, q. 36, art. 2, obj. 2.

their own. The original collision over the Filioque had come not in a theological disputation about ἀρχή in the Godhead, but in a eucharistic celebration, where the divergent texts of the Nicene Creed had disturbed the peace of the liturgy. [84]

In his answer to Objection 2, Thomas was able to quote the words of the Council of Chalcedon[85] regarding the validity of later statements that had not been explicitly present in conciliar formulas but could be inferred from them. He could therefore conclude that "continebatur tamen implicite in hoc ipso quod dicebatur Spiritus Sanctus a Patre procedere" and that the Western text had merely made this explicit. [86] As for the charge of arbitrary interpolation, he dismissed this with the claim that it was entirely legitimate to add words to the creed, since "expressum fuit auctoritate Romani Pontificis; cuius auctoritate etiam antiqua concilia congregabantur et confirmabantur." In *Contra errores Graecorum* he had sought to prove that "ad dictum pontificem [Romanum] pertineat quae sunt fidei determinare,"[87] whether with or even without a council not being specified. Here in the *Summa* he answered the Eastern objection by claiming for the pope the authority to convoke and confirm universal councils and therefore also to amplify their doctrinal declarations. Needless to say, the historical proof that the ancient councils had in fact been convoked by this authority was wanting, even though it was possible to quote various Eastern theologians, as late as Maximus Confessor,[88] on the prime authority of the see of Peter.

It is not surprising that there were more quotations from Augustine in Question 36 than from any other source except Scripture. When Chenu speaks of "the innumerable texts of Augustine in the works of Saint Thomas,"[89] this is only a slight hyperbole. As Hertling has shown, Augustine was the linchpin of one Article after another in the *Summa*. [90] His doctrine of incorporation into Christ through baptism, for example, was, as Geenen has called it, "la doctrine par excellence exposée" in the tract on baptism; and it was "précisément empruntée au *De Peccat. merit. et remiss. et de remiss. et de baptismo parvulorum* de S.

84　For a convenient summary, see Steven Runciman, *The Eastern Schism* (Oxford 1955) pp. 29-32.

85　See p. 332 below.

86　*S. Th.* I, q. 36, art. 2, ad 2.

87　*Contra errores Graecorum*, II, 36.

88　Cf. Jaroslav Pelikan, "'Council or Father or Scripture': The Concept of Authority in the Theology of Maximus Confessor," in David Neiman and Margaret Schatkin (edd.), *The Heritage of the Early Church: Essays in Biblical and Patristic Studies in Honor of the Eightieth Birthday of the Very Reverend Georges Vasilievich Florovsky* (Rome 1973) pp. 266-77.

89　Chenu, *op. cit.*, p. 129.

90　G. von Hertling, "Augustinuszitate bei Thomas von Aquin," *Sitzungsberichte der bayerischen Akademie der Wissenschaften*, philos.-philol. Klasse (1914) Heft 4, 535-602.

Augustin."[91] If this was true of doctrines in general and of the doctrine of baptism in particular, it is to be expected that it be true *a fortiori* of the doctrine of the Trinity, which was transmitted to later Latin theology largely through Augustine. Here in Question 36 there were three explicit references to him, and in addition a specifically Augustinian theme in which Augustine was not cited as an authority but was nevertheless used as a source. In other parts of the treatise on the Trinity Thomas made use of various Augustinian and pseudo-Augustinian writings; but the principal writing employed there, and the only one employed here, was *De Trinitate*. With Boethius, whose significance we shall assess a little later, Thomas could have said that in his trinitarian theology "ex beati Augustini scriptis semina rationum aliquos in nos uenientia fructus extulerint."[92]

The first quotation from Augustine in Question 36 occurred in the *Sed contra* of Article 1, in combination with the *comma Johanneum*: "Sed contra est quod dicitur I Ioan. ult.: 'Tres sunt qui testimonium dant in caelo, Pater, Verbum et Spiritus Sanctus.' Ut autem Augustinus dicit, VII *de Trin.*, cum quaeritur, 'Quid tres?' dicimus, 'Tres personae.'" The words were quoted several times in the treatise on the Trinity; it is noteworthy that in most of these instances they appeared as a proof text in the *Sed contra*. From the conflation of this formula with the *comma Johanneum* not only here in Question 36 and in Question 30, Article 2, but especially in Question 29, Article 4, it seems that Thomas was quoting from memory or from the *Sentences* of Peter Lombard.[93] In Augustine they were not given as a gloss on the *comma Johanneum* — whatever his relation to this variant reading may have been[94] — and in fact did not appear in this precise form.[95] A formula as terse as this one was, of course, adaptable to many purposes.[96] Within Question 36, Article 1, it performed a rather menial role, compared with that performed by the other quotation from Augustine in the same Article. It enabled Thomas to take account of the absence of a "proprium nomen" for the "processio" and the "relationes" peculiar to the third member of the divine Triad and yet to insist that "persona" was a fitting term and that "ergo Spiritus Sanctus est nomen divinae personae."

91   Geenen, "L'usage des 'auctoritates,'" p. 316, n. 118.
92   Boethius *De Trinitate* pr., *Loeb Classical Library* (Cambridge, Mass., 1918) p. 4.
93   That is the suggestion of Velecky, *op. cit.,* p. 56, n. 3.
94   For a recent study, which changes some of the conclusions of the nineteenth century, see E. Riggenbach, *Das Comma Johanneum* (Gütersloh 1928).
95   "Quid igitur tres? Si enim tres personae..." Augustine *De Trinitate* 7.4.7, CCSL 50, 255.
96   See, for example, Etienne Gilson, *Introduction à l'étude de saint Augustin* (4th ed.; Paris 1969) p. 298, n. 2.

As we have just indicated, the other quotation from Augustine in Article 1 of Question 36 carried out a more distinctive service. The words of Hilary quoted earlier[97] emphasized the difficulty of employing "Spiritus Sanctus" as a designation for one of the Trinity, since in the usage of Scripture each of the three was called "Spiritus." Thomas used Hilary in the Objection as a means of raising this difficulty. Although there was no specific reference to Hilary in Augustine's answer, Thomas neatly provided the appropriate explanation by citing a discussion that appeared in Book V and again in Book XV of Augustine's *De Trinitate*,[98] summarizing it in a paraphrase: "Quia Spiritus Sanctus communis est ambobus, id vocatur ipse proprie quod ambo communiter: nam et Pater est Spiritus, et Filius est Spiritus; et Pater est sanctus, et Filius est sanctus"[99]. Hence "Spiritus Sanctus" could very well be used of Him who proceeded from the Father and the Son. There was a congruence between the title "Holy Spirit," with its ambiguity, and the doctrine of Filioque; and so a problem raised in the Objection became almost an indirect proof in the Response. Eventually, of course, this explanation of the title "Spiritus Sanctus" proved to be one which Thomas found to be rather more clever than convincing. In his careful elaboration of the meaning of "spiratio" he sought to provide a more fundamental explanation, which was, to be sure, not as explicitly Augustinian but which nevertheless drew upon Augustinian precedents.[100]

The most sensitive issue in the doctrine of Filioque, as we have noted, was the Eastern charge that it implied a double ἀρχή in the Godhead and thus that it compromised the monotheistic confession of the church. To meet this grave charge, Thomas had to deal with the embarrassment of Hilary's formula, "a Patre et Filio auctoribus." From Augustine, on the other hand, he drew a definition of the Filioque that could serve as a refutation of the Eastern accusation. As the *Sed contra* to the series of Objections containing Hilary's formula, therefore, Thomas could quote, though not quite verbatim, from Augustine: "Sed contra est quod Augustinus dicit, in V *de Trin.*, quod Pater et Filius non sunt duo principia, sed unum principium Spiritus Sancti."[101] Because of its prominence in Greek polemics against the doctrine of Filioque, the idea of "principium" or ἀρχή needed to be specified. Augustine's statement, "fatendum est Patrem et Filium principium esse

97   See pp. 323-24 above.
98   Augustine *De Trinitate* 5.11.12, CCSL 50, 219-20; 15.19.37, CCSL 50, 513-14.
99   *S. Th.* I, q. 36, art. 1, resp.
100 Cf. Malet, *op. cit.*, pp. 120-23.
101 *S. Th.* I, q. 36, art. 4, s. c.

Spiritus Sancti, non duo principia,"[102] provided a key to such specification.

It was likewise from Augustine's exposition of the Filioque that Thomas drew the axiom, "Pater est principium totius deitatis,"[103] the exegesis of which he worked out in Question 33, Article 1. The same axiom then appeared in a later Objection, to which Thomas replied by identifying the sense in which it was true that the Father was the "principium" both of the Son and of the Holy Spirit "generando et spirando."[104] As part of his counterattack against Greek fire, he was also able to point out an imprecision in Greek trinitarian terminology as compared with Latin: "Graeci utuntur in divinis indifferenter nomine 'causae,' sicut et nomine principii: sed latini doctores non utuntur nomine causae, sed solum nomine principii."[105] This was presumably because "causa," if applied to the relation between the Father and the Son, could not avoid the taint of subordinationism. For the same reason, while "apud Graecos invenitur de Filio vel Spiritu Sancto dici quod principientur," the Latins avoided such language, "ut vitetur omnis erroris occasio."[106] The distinction between "causa" and "prinncipium" could not, however, be maintained with utter consistency; thus in explaining the term, "a Patre per Filium," here in Question 36, Thomas asserted that "haec praepositio 'per' designat in causali aliquam causam seu principium illius actus."[107] But the Augustinian use of "principium," the common translation of ἀρχή, in the sense of "unum principium" proved to be a valuable defensive weapon nevertheless.

There was one other Augustinian element in Question 36, as well as in other Questions, which demonstrated the pervasive authority of Augustine through the very infrequency with which it was attributed to him: the identification of the Holy Spirit as "amor."[108] It helped to nail down the argument for the Filioque by analogy from the relation between word and love in human experience: "Necesse est autem quod amor a verbo procedat: non enim aliquid amamus, nisi secundum quod conceptione mentis apprehendimus. Unde et secundum hoc manifestum est quod Spiritus Sanctus procedit a Filio."[109] It is instructive to follow this analogy of the Holy Spirit as "amor" through the preceding discussion. In Question 27, Article 3, Response, he spoke of "alia

---

102 Augustine *De Trinitate* 5.14.15, CCSL 50, 223.
103 Augustine *De Trinitate* 4.20.29, CCSL 50, 200.
104 *S. Th.* I, q. 39, art. 5, obj. 6.
105 *S. Th.* I, q. 33, art. 1, ad 1.
106 *S. Th.* I, q. 33, art. 1, ad 2.
107 *S. Th.* I, q. 36, art. 3, resp.
108 Malet, *op. cit.,* pp. 28-29 and *passim.*
109 *S. Th.* I, q. 36, art. 2, resp.

processio in divinis, quae est processio amoris"; in the *Sed contra* of the next Article of the same Question, he referred without any quotation or proof to "Spiritus Sanctus, qui procedit ut amor"; in Question 28, Article 4, Response, he spoke again of a "processio amoris," again without mentioning Augustine; he did so twice in Question 30, Article 2, once in Objection 2 and again in the *Sed contra*; and the same idea was presupposed in other Articles. When he came to Question 32, Article 1, Objection 2, he made explicit reference to the origin of the analogy, pointing out that "Augustinus vero procedit ad manifestandum Trinitatem Personarum, ex processione verbi et amoris in mente nostra" and adding that he had followed Augustine in this. And then he devoted the whole of Question 37 to an exposition of the name "amor" as a designation for the Holy Spirit, quoting, almost as though in whimsy, Gregory the Great rather then Gregory's own authority, Augustine, as proof in the *Sed contra* of Article 1. But the identification of the third person of the Trinity with "amor" was, to put it mildly, far less explicit in the biblical text than was the identification of the second person with "verbum"; the latter identification was the achievement of the Gospel of John, the former the achievement largely of Augustine. Yet Thomas, together with most of the Western tradition, simply took for granted the validity of this piece of Augustinian trinitarianism, asserting that "secundum quod personaliter sumitur, [nomen amoris] est proprium nomen Spiritus Sancti; sicut Verbum est proprium nomen Filii."[110] And here in the defense of the Filioque he could use it as proof on the assumption of its validity.

As has already been mentioned in the discussion of the "Constantinopolitan" Creed, the text of this symbol, minus the Filioque, had been transmitted through its inclusion in the *Acta* of later councils, specifically those of Ephesus and Chalcedon. Yet each of these councils appeared in Thomas's discussion as something more than a witness to the text of the creed. The condemnatory decrees of Ephesus provided the basis for him to condemn the Greeks through something very much like guilt by association: "Spiritum Sanctum non procedere a Filio, primo fuit a Nestorianis introductum; ut patet in quodam symbolo Nestorianorum damnato in Ephesina Synodo."[111] This must be taken to mean that the doctrine of Filioque was present, albeit "implicite," in the teaching of the church all along, without being either denied or defended by anyone. Then in the fifth century the question was raised for the first time, when Nestorian heresy, presumably as part of the same *Ten-*

110 *S. Th.* I, q. 37, art. 1, s. c.
111 *S. Th.* I, q. 36, art. 2, ad 3.

denz that denied the idea of Theotokos, also denied the idea of Filioque. As a specific instance of a Nestorian heretic who denied the Filioque, Thomas referred to Theodoret of Cyr. Theodoret had in fact called the Filioque βλάσφημον τοῦτο,[112] so that Thomas's historical judgment about the content of Theodoret's doctrine, though not about its novelty, was accurate. In this entire question it is essential to distinguish between a theological affirmation and the historical information that formed its basis. Nevertheless, the reference to Ephesus could not have been very convincing to the Greeks, and even Thomas himself introduced it almost as an *obiter dictum.*

There is much more historical and theological sophistication in his other reference to a council of the fifth century, namely, to Chalcedon. It was, in one sense, also employed as a historical source: "In determinatione Chalcedonensis Synodi dicitur, quod illi qui fuerunt congregati in Concilio Constantinopolitano, doctrinam de Spiritu Sancto tradiderunt, 'non quod minus esset in praecedentibus (qui apud Nicaeam congregati sunt), inferentes; sed intellectum eorum adversus haereticos declarantes.'"[113] But this historical information from Chalcedon about Constantinople was intended to justify the Western interpolation; as it was legitimate for Constantinople to expand the brief formula of 325, "Et in Spiritum Sanctum," into the amplified form that was now used in both Eastern and Western liturgies, so it was legitimate for later generations to expand this, in turn, by adding the Filioque. But the comment of Chalcedon upon the use of Nicaea by Constantinople gave Thomas the occasion to elaborate a more general theory of doctrinal development: "In quolibet concilio institutum fuit symbolum aliquod, propter errorem aliquem qui in concilio damnabatur. Unde sequens concilium non faciebat aliud symbolum quam primum: sed id quod implicite continebatur in primo symbolo, per aliqua addita explanabatur contra haereses insurgentes." So it was, for example, with the Filioque. "Quia igitur in tempore antiquorum conciliorum nondum exortus fuerat error dicentium Spiritum Sanctum non procedere a Filio; non fuit necessarium quod hoc explicite poneretur.... Continebatur tamen implicite in hoc ipso quod dicebatur Spiritum Sanctum a Patre procedere."[114] By tying this theory of development to the authority of Rome, Thomas could argue that under the direction of papal authority the doctrine of the Holy Spirit had moved from its implicit state at Nicaea to a more explicit formulation at Constantinople to a still more explicit formulation in the Western text of the creed.

112 Theodoret *Confutatio XII capitum Cyrilli,* PG 76, 432.
113 *S. Th.* I, q. 36, art. 2, ad 2.
114 *S. Th.* I, q. 36, art. 2, ad 2.

Thomas had prepared for his discussion of the Trinity in the *Summa* not only by his biblical commentaries, his *Commentary on the Sentences,* and his *Contra errores Graecorum,* but also by his *Expositio super librum Boethii de Trinitate,* which seems to have been composed in the late 1250's.[115] Through the works of Grabmann and Maritain on the *Expositio,* it has acquired a well-deserved reputation as an epistemological investigation; for in it "St. Thomas treats of the division and methods of the sciences while commenting on Boethius' book on the Trinity" and in so doing "is simply taking his cue from Boethius himself."[116] Yet an examination of the quotations from Boethius, chiefly from the *De Trinitate* and from what was usually called *De duabus naturis,* in the Questions of the *Summa* on the Trinity should not prevent this valid insight from obscuring the specifically trinitarian function of Boethius in Thomas's thought. Several of the most helpful definitions in these Questions came from Boethius.[117] Here in Question 36 Boethius helped Thomas to recognize the connection between person and relation in the Trinity; for "nomina divinarum personarum ad aliquid dicuntur, ut Boethius dicit, in libro *de Trin.*"[118] Professor Pegis's translation of "ad aliquid dicuntur" with "are relative terms"[119] not only renders Thomas's sense; it may also provide an easy explanation of the origin of the earlier quotation ascribed to Boethius, "quod omne nomen ad personas pertinens, relationem significat."[120] In any event, Boethius's rule evoked from Thomas the distinction that "hoc quod dico 'Spiritus Sanctus,' relative non dicatur, tamen pro relativo ponitur, inquantum est accommodatum ad significandam personam sola relatione ab aliis distinctam";[121] from this, in turn, it would follow that the Holy Holy Spirit was distinct from the Son "sola relatione," which led in turn to the Filioque.

The last of the patristic authorities cited by Thomas in Question 36 was John of Damascus. He was also the source of the most overt rejection of the Filioque by any theologian whom Thomas and the church at large regarded as orthodox; for he had written: "Spiritum Sanctum ex Patre dicimus, et Spiritum Patris nominamus: ex Filio autem Spiritum

---

115 Cf. Bruno Decker, ed., *Sancti Thomae de Aquino Expositio super librum Boethii de Trinitate* (Leiden 1965) p. 44.

116 Armand Maurer, "Introduction" to Thomas Aquinas, *The Division and Methods of the Sciences* (3rd ed.; Toronto 1963) p. vii.

117 To mention only two examples, see *S. Th.* I, q. 29, art. 1, ad 4; and q. 30, art. 1, obj. 3.

118 *S. Th.* I, q. 36, art. 1, obj. 2; Boethius *De Trinitate* 5, *Loeb Classical Library,* p. 26.

119 Anton C. Pegis, ed., *Basic Writings of Saint Thomas Aquinas* (2 vols.; New York 1945) 1, 342.

120 *S. Th.* I, q. 29, art. 4, s. c.

121 *S. Th.* I, q. 36, art. 1, ad 2.

Sanctum non dicimus, Spiritum vero Filii nominamus."[122] The
unequivocal sound of these words had been a crux to other interpreters,[123] some of whom sought to resolve the difficulty by saying
that "Damascenus, sicut non confitetur Spiritum Sanctum esse a Filio,
ita etiam non negat."[124] Now Thomas also knew how to extricate church
fathers, including John of Damascus, from the awkwardness of their
own statements about the mysteries of trinitarian doctrine. He had, for
example, explained away the Damascene's Sabellian-sounding statement that "tres personae re idem sunt, ratione autem et cogitatione distinguuntur" by proposing that "auctoritas Damasceni sic intelligenda
est. Ratione, id est relatione."[125] But in this instance neither synonymics
nor emendation would avail. Instead, Thomas put the matter in un-
compromising terms. After citing the Nestorian origin of opposition to
the Filioque, he continued: "... et plures post ipsum; inter quos fuit
etiam Damascenus. Unde in hoc eius sententiae non est standum."[126]
There were gentler forms of reproof available to him, such as the principle that "huiusmodi locutiones non sunt extendendae, sed ex-
ponendae,"[127] or, more amply stated, that "si qua in dictis antiquorum
doctorum inveniuntur quae cum tanta cautela non dicantur quanta a
modernis servatur, non sunt contemnenda aut abicienda; sed nec etiam
ea extendere oportet sed exponere reverenter."[128] This latter "texte
suivant"[129] could conceivably have been applied here. Instead, there
came a rejection so blunt as to elicit Cajetan's explanation that Thomas
was not hereticating the Damascene, as some interpreters supposed him
to be.[130] Compared, for example, with his lenient treatment of Hilary,
this must be regarded as a severe dismissal of an orthodox "auctoritas"
whom Thomas held in high regard.

In all these ways Thomas's case for the Filioque provides data of
more than usual interest for a consideration of his use of patristic
authority. His discussion of "spiratores" and "spirantes" in Hilary and
of "principium" in Augustine indicates that he was attempting to defend
the Filioque inherited from these fathers while correcting the dangerous
implications that might be drawn from it. He saw the Eastern refusal to
equate "profluere" with "procedere" in the doctrine of the Holy Spirit

122 John of Damascus *De fide orthodoxa* 1.8, PG 94, 832-33.
123 See the long footnote, PG 94, 831-34.
124 *S. Th.* I, q. 36, art. 2, ad 3.
125 *In I Sent.* d. 2, q. 1, art. 5, ad 1; ed. Mandonnet, 1, 74-75.
126 *S. Th.* I, q. 36, art. 2, ad 3.
127 *S. Th.* I, q. 39, art. 5, ad 1.
128 *Contra errores Graecorum*, pr., *Opera*, 40-A, 71.
129 Geenen, "Saint Thomas et les Pères," p. 751.
130 *Opera*, 4, 381, par. 28.

as coming "vel ex ignorantia, vel ex protervia,"[131] but it seems fair to suggest that there was more than enough of these two commodities on both sides. Thomas insisted, for example, that "si quis consideret, inveniet 'processionis' verbum inter omnia quae ad originem qualemcumque pertinent, communissimum esse."[132] Yet if "procedere" was meant to be a translation of ἐκπορεύεσθαι, this had, according to the Greeks, to be distinguished from various other terms "quae ad originem qualemcumque pertinent," such as πέμπειν, χεῖσθαι, διαδίδοσθαι, χύσις, μετάδοσις, and others.[133] But even the Latin vocabulary of Thomas still lacked the range and the discrimination to make all of these distinctions. Quoting Durantel's conclusion that Thomas was in a position "vérifier et rectifier le texte grec,"[134] Riquet has suggested that though not "un hélleniste, il en savait assez pour lire."[135] This does not seem to have extended to the ability to read at first hand the most telling of the Greek treatises "contra errores Latinorum" in which such distinctions were set forth. It is significant that despite his direct acquaintance with some Eastern arguments,[136] the only explicit reference to these distinctions was based on a report that "quidam eorum [sc., Graecorum] dicuntur concedere quod 'sit a Filio,' vel 'profluat ab eo': non tamen quod 'procedat,'"[137] the word "dicuntur" suggesting that he had this information at second hand. And of course, his information about the Greek use of ὑπόστασις, like his information about the plural in the Hebrew name for God,[138] was also common property.

As a spokesman for the West, Thomas drew upon both dialectics and patristics to defend the Filioque and to make it defensible. He took it to be an authentic part of apostolic doctrine and of normative tradition. It does seem appropriate, nevertheless, to ask whether his doctrine of the Trinity would have led him to the Filioque if this had not been transmitted to him by what he regarded as the "fides catholica." He was hard pressed to identify what was distinctive about the third person of the Trinity, making "processio" a general term applicable both to the second person and to the third and finding "spiratio" useful but not precise. Behind this question, however, are two much more fundamental ones; their answer lies beyond the scope of the present essay, but they do arise in an analysis of the material. One needs to ask

---

131 *S. Th.* I, q. 36, art. 2, resp.
132 *S. Th.* I, q. 36, art. 2, resp.
133 Cf. Theophylact, *Liber de iis quorum Latini incusantur* 5, PG 126, 228-29.
134 Durantel, *op. cit.,* p. 65.
135 Riquet, *op. cit.,* p. 129, n. 3.
136 See, for example, *S. Th.,* I, q. 36, art. 2, resp.
137 *S. Th.* I, q. 36, art. 2, resp.
138 *S. Th.* I, q. 29, art. 2, ad 2; q. 39, art. 3, ad 2.

whether the difference underlying the Filioque was merely one of
"protervia" and "ignorantia," even merely one of differing attitudes
toward tradition and authority. Was it not ultimately a clash between
two views of the Godhead and two means of salvaging monotheism
within the framework of the trinitarian dogma? Most doctrines of the
Trinity can be characterized as tending toward either the tritheistic or
the modalistic heresy. The Cappadocians and their successors had to
strain to avoid the first, while Western theologians often manifested
some inclination toward the second. Coming where it did in the structure of the *Summa,* Question 36, as well as the rest of the treatise on the
Trinity, presupposed a doctrine of divine Being, and of the oneness of
divine Being, within whose context the Trinity and the Filioque were
articulated. There was never any need for Thomas to write a treatise
Quod non tres dii sint, as there was for Gregory of Nyssa. And if it is
contended that his system of revelation required him to have more than
a simple unqualified monotheism, one is obliged to ask why two rather
than three persons would not have been enough. In a highly revealing
passage here in Question 36, Thomas argued that without the Filioque
there would be no way to distinguish the Spirit from the Son:
"sequeretur quod persona Filii et Spiritus Sancti esset una, habens duas
relationes oppositas duabus relationibus Patris. Hoc autem est
haereticum, cum tollat fidem Trinitatis."[139] For Thomas the speculative
theologian, this seems to have been less than completely satisfying; for
Thomas the expositor of patristic tradition, it was argument enough.

139 *S. Th.* I, q. 36, art. 2, resp.

UNITAS, AEQUALITAS, CONCORDIA VEL CONNEXIO

Recherches sur les Origines de la Théorie Thomiste des Appropriations (*Sum. theol.*, I, q. 39, art. 7-8)

Jean Châtillon

L A *Summa theologiae* de saint Thomas d'Aquin revient à plusieurs reprises sur le problème des appropriations trinitaires dans la série des questions qu'elle consacre au mystère des trois personnes divines. Elle y fait très explicitement allusion, tout d'abord, dans l'article où le Docteur Angélique se demande "si la Trinité des personnes divines peut être connue par la raison naturelle" (I, q. 32, art. 1). La réponse à la question ainsi posée est évidemment négative. Saint Thomas récuse avec vigueur la légitimité de toute entreprise, d'où qu'elle vienne, qui tendrait à "prouver la Trinité" par la raison. De telles tentatives, explique-t-il, ne peuvent que compromettre "la dignité de la foi" et porter les infidèles à tourner celle-ci en dérision.[1] Il reconnaît cependant que si les philosophes n'ont pu connaître ce qui appartenait en propre à chacune des trois personnes, à savoir la paternité du Père, la filiation du Fils et la procession de l'Esprit-Saint, ils ont pu néanmoins s'élever jusqu'à la connaissance de certains attributs essentiels, et que ceux-ci peuvent être rapportés à leur tour, par appropriation, à l'une ou l'autre des trois personnes: ainsi en est-il notamment des attributs de puissance, de sagesse et de bonté qui peuvent être rapportés respectivement au Père, au Fils et au Saint-Esprit.[2] L'appropriation est donc présentée ici comme une méthode de recherche et d'exposition destinée à mettre à la disposition du théologien un langage qui lui permettra de

---

On aura recours habituellement dans cet article aux sigles suivants:

AHDLM = Archives d'histoire doctrinale et littéraire du moyen âge (Paris);
BGPTM = Beiträge zur Geschichte der Philosophie und Theologie des Mittelalters (Münster in West.);
RTAM = Recherches de théologie ancienne et médiévale (Louvain).

1 *Sum. theol.*, I, q.32, art. 1, c.
2 Ibid., ad 1.

rendre compte, jusqu'à un certain point et dans certaines conditions, de l'ineffable mystère de la distinction des personnes.

La légitimité de cette méthode et quelques unes de ses applications seront examinées par la suite en deux articles particulièrement importants (I,q.39,art.7-8). Le premier, relativement bref, se place à un point de vue très général. Saint Thomas s'y interroge sur les conditions dans lesquelles on peut approprier certains "noms essentiels" au Père, au Fils ou à l'Esprit-Saint. La position du Docteur Angélique sur ce point est connue. Son exposé ne fait d'ailleurs ici que compléter et préciser ce que l'article précédemment cité avait dit à ce sujet. Bien que les attributs essentiels soient évidemment communs aux trois personnes, leur appropriation à l'une ou l'autre d'entre elles peut être justifiée parce qu'elle contribue à "la manifestation de la foi." La raison parvient en effet à la connaissance de ces attributs à partir de la création. Ceux-ci lui sont donc plus accessibles que les propriétés personnelles connues seulement par la foi. Ils lui permettent ainsi une approche du mystère de la Trinité à laquelle, sans cela, elle ne peut atteindre. Une telle méthode d'exposition ne peut engendrer de confusion dans l'esprit, car les attributs essentiels ainsi considérés ne sont pas appropriés aux trois personnes comme s'ils leur appartenaient en propre (*non sic appropriantur personis ut eis esse propria asserantur*), mais seulement par voie de similitude ou, au contraire de dissemblance.[3] L'équivoque est ici évitée par un recours à un mode d'attribution très particulier, l'appropriation, auquel correspond la catégorie de l'"approprié," sorte de nouveau prédicable, à la fois proche et distinct du "propre" ou de la "propriété."[4]

L'article dont on vient de résumer brièvement l'enseignement ne nous dit rien encore des applications que l'on peut tirer des principes ainsi posés. Celles-ci vont faire l'objet de l'article suivant (art.8) qui entreprend l'examen de quelques unes des formules auxquelles les "saints docteurs" avaient eu recours pour distinguer les trois personnes les unes des autres en leur attribuant, par mode d'appropriation, des "noms essentiels" bien déterminés. Cet article est construit d'une manière assez particulière. Le Docteur Angélique présente bien d'abord, comme

---

3 Ibid., q. 39, art. 7, c. Sur ces deux modes d'appropriation, par similitude et par dissemblance, voir ci-dessous, n. 101 et 162.

4 Saint Thomas d'Aquin ne nous donne ici aucune définition proprement dite de l'*appropriatio* et de l'*appropriatum*. Mais saint Albert le Grand précisera en logicien la signification de ce dernier terme lorsque, faisant allusion à la manière dont il est composé (*ad-propriatum*), il écrira dans sa *Summa theologiae*, I, tr. XII, q. 48, membr. 1, éd. Borgnet, t. 31, p. 505: "Appropriatum ex modo compositionis et habitudine praepositionis, quae accessum et recessum vicinitatis consignificat, dicit accessum ad proprium. Appropriatum ergo est, quod ratione sui nominis vicinam habet rationem cum proprio."

de coutume, une série d'objections qui sont ici au nombre de cinq, mais celles-ci n'ont d'autre objet que d'introduire quelques formules patristiques ou bibliques dont saint Thomas se propose de justifier la signification trinitaire. Il n'y aura donc pas de *Sed contra*: l'origine même des textes cités leur confère une autorité sur laquelle il n'est pas nécessaire d'insister. Il n'y aura pas davantage de "réponses aux objections," à la fin de l'article: c'est en effet dans le corps de l'article que le Docteur Angélique expliquera de quelle manière il convient d'interpréter chacune de ces formules.

Si nous laissons de côté les textes allégués par la cinquième et dernière objection, où il est uniquement question des "noms" qui peuvent être attribués par appropriation à la seconde personne de la Trinité (*veritas, liber vitae, qui est*), nous constatons que saint Thomas est ainsi amené à s'expliquer principalement sur la signification trinitaire de quatre triades différentes. La première (*aeternitas, species, usus*) vient de Saint Hilaire (*De Trinitate*,II,1). La seconde (*unitas, aequalitas, concordia*) est empruntée à saint Augustin (*De doctrina christiana*,I,5,5). La troisième (*potentia, sapientia, bonitas*) viendrait également de l'évêque d'Hippone, si nous en croyons du moins saint Thomas qui ne nous donne cependant aucune référence précise.[5] La quatrième enfin (*ex ipso, per ipsum, in ipso*) vient d'un verset de l'*Epître aux Romains* (XI,36), dont Augustin encore, cité de nouveau par le Docteur Angélique, avait donné à plusieurs reprises une interprétation trinitaire.

Les témoignages patristiques et bibliques auxquels se réfère saint Thomas et dont l'explication constitue la trame même de son exposé n'ont évidemment pas été choisis au hasard. Tous avaient fait l'objet d'interprétations dont on retrouve aisément la trace chez les théologiens du XIIe et du XIIIe siècles et c'est autour d'eux que s'était organisé progressivement le traité des appropriations trinitaires. Tous cependant n'y avaient pas tenu une place égale. Faute de pouvoir les examiner ici

---

5 Cf. loc. cit., art. 8, obj. 3: "Secundum Augustinum, Patri attribuitur potentia, Filio sapientia, Spiritui sancto bonitas." Alors que tous les textes patristiques cités par les autres objections de cet art. 8 ont pu être aisément identifiés, la très vague référence à Augustin de cette obj. 3 a visiblement embarrassé les éditeurs de la *Somme*. L'édition de la Commission léonine et celle de l'Institut d'études médiévales d'Ottawa (Ottawa 1941) se contentent de renvoyer à Hugues de Saint-Victor (*De sacr.*, I, p. II, 6; PL 176, 208), où il est effectivement question de cette triple attribution, mais où Augustin n'est pas nommé. Il est vrai qu'une partie du raisonnement grâce auquel saint Thomas justifie l'interprétation trinitaire qu'il donne de cette triade (art. 8, c., à partir de *Secundum vero tertiam considerationem*...) apparaît chez Hugues de Saint-Victor (loc. cit., 8, 209-210), mais il n'y est pas davantage question d'Augustin. En fait, comme nous aurons l'occasion de le rappeler plus loin, c'est Abélard qui avait été le premier à traiter d'une manière systématique de cette triple attribution dont l'origine augustinienne avait été discutée dès le XIIe siècle (cf. ci-dessous, n. 98).

un à un, on voudrait s'en tenir dans cet article à l'histoire du texte que la seconde objection présentée par le Docteur Angélique, au seuil de son article 8, emprunte au *De doctrina christiana*, et tenter de découvrir par quels cheminements la triade *unitas, aequalitas, concordia*, a pénétré dans la théologie avant d'arriver jusqu'à saint Thomas. Cette brève enquête ne pourra pourtant pas négliger complètement d'autres formules et d'autres triades dont celle-ci est fréquemment solidaire. Ainsi rencontrera-t-elle dès l'origine la triade *ex ipso, per ipsum, in ipso*, qui est au point de départ de la réflexion théologique d'où devait sortir le traité des appropriations trinitaires.

1. Le *De Doctrina Christiana* d'Augustin

C'est en effet Augustin lui-même qui a associé l'une à l'autre la triade *unitas, aequalitas, concordia*, et la triade paulinienne *ex ipso, per ipsum, in ipso*. Pour comprendre à la fois la portée de ce rapprochement et la signification des expressions auxquelles recourt Augustin, il faut reproduire le passage du *De doctrina christiana* auquel sont empruntés les textes que cite saint Thomas, d'abord dans l'énoncé de sa seconde objection, puis dans le corps de son article 8. Augustin s'exprime de la manière suivante:[6]

> Res igitur, quibus fruendum est, pater et filius et spiritus sanctus eademque trinitas, una quaedam summa res communisque omnibus fruentibus ea, si tamen res et non rerum omnium causa, si tamen et causa. Non enim facile nomen, quod tantae excellentiae conueniat, inueniri potest, nisi quod melius ita dicitur trinitas haec unus deus, ex quo omnia, per quem omnia, in quo omnia.[7] Ita pater et filius et spiritus sanctus et singulus quisque horum deus et simul omnes unus deus, et singulus quisque horum plena substantia et simul omnes una substantia. Pater nec filius est nec spiritus sanctus, filius nec pater est nec spiritus sanctus, spiritus sanctus nec pater nec filius, sed pater tantum pater et filius tantum filius et spiritus sanctus tantum spiritus sanctus. Eadem tribus aeternitas, eadem incommutabilitas, eadem maiestas, eadem potestas. In patre unitas, in filio aequalitas, in spiritu sancto unitatis aequalitatisque concordia, et tria haec unum omnia propter patrem, aequalia omnia propter filium, conexa omnia propter spiritum sanctum.

On sait dans quel contexte s'insère ce développement. L'auteur du *De doctrina christiana* vient d'introduire sa célèbre distinction entre les

---

6   *De doctr. christ.*, I, 5, 5. Je cite ici le texte de l'édition J. Martin, *Corp. christ.*, 32 (Turnhout 1962), p. 9. Pour la traduction de quelques membres de phrase donnée plus loin entre guillemets, je me suis inspiré de celle de G. Combès-J. Farges, *Œuvres de saint Augustin*, XI, *Le magistère chrétien* (Paris 1949), pp. 185-187.

7   Cf. *Rom.*, XI, 36. Sur le texte de ce verset, tel que le cite ici Augustin, voir ci-dessous, n. 9.

choses dont il faut jouir (*frui*) et celles dont il faut seulement user (*uti*). [8] Il va maintenant parler des premières, et tout d'abord des trois personnes divines qui sont une seule et unique Trinité. Mais il constate aussitôt qu' "il n'est pas facile de trouver un nom qui convienne à une réalité aussi éminente." Peut-on en effet appeler celle-ci une "chose"? N'est-elle pas plutôt "la cause de toutes les choses"? Est-elle même d'ailleurs une "cause"? Finalement Augustin estimera que le mieux est de dire que "cette Trinité est un seul Dieu, de qui (*ex quo*) toutes choses procèdent, par qui (*per quem*) et en qui (*in quo*) toutes choses existent." Cette définition s'inspire directement d'un verset de l'*Epître aux Romains* (XI,36) dont Augustin avait déjà donné à plusieurs reprises et dont il devait donner souvent par la suite une interprétation trinitaire. [9] Pourtant, il ne s'attarde pas ici à expliciter sa pensée en rapportant d'une manière distincte à chacune des trois personnes divines l'*ex quo omnia*, le *per quem omnia* et l'*in quo omnia* [10] du texte auquel il fait allusion. Son intention semble être surtout de rappeler que ce verset de saint Paul affirme simultanément l'unité de la "substance divine" et la distinction des personnes. [11] C'est sur ce point en tout cas qu'il va

8   *De doctr. christ.*, I, 3, 3-4, éd. cit., p. 8.

9   On trouvera dans O. du Roy, *L' intelligence de la foi en la Trinité selon saint Augustin* (Paris 1966), pp. 479-483, un inventaire, par ordre chronologique, de tous les passages de l'œuvre de saint Augustin dans lequel celui-ci revient sur ce verset (*Rom.*, XI, 36). Ce tableau ne relève pas moins de quarante-six citations, du *De quantitate animae* (388) au *Contra Maximum* (428). Dans plus de la moitié des cas, le verset de l'*Epître aux Romains* fait l'objet d'une interprétation trinitaire ou apparaît au moins dans un contexte trinitaire. Cette exégèse n'était pas nouvelle. O. du Roy, ibid., pp. 483-484, en signale un certain nombre d'exemples plus anciens empruntés à Origène (*Com. in epist. ad Rom.*, VIII, 13, PG 14, 1202 AB, dans la traduction de Rufin qui date de 404, et *Com. in Cant.*, Prol., *Griech. Christ. Schriftsteller*, 33, 7, l. 4-6, également dans la trad. de Rufin), et à Ambroise (*Exam.*, I, 5, 19, CSEL 23, 1, 16, l. 1-14). On peut ajouter aussi Athanase, *Adversus Sabellianos*, 13, PG, 28, 117; Eusèbe de Verceil, *De Trinitate*, IV, 21-24, et VII, 24, *Corp. christ.*, 9, p. 62, l. 171-197, et p. 98, l. 210-211; Ambrosiaster, *In epist. ad Rom.*, XI, 36, CSEL 81, pp. 391-392.

10   Ces expressions, notons-le en passant, bien qu'elles se réfèrent certainement à *Rom.*, XI, 36, ne viennent pas de la *Vulgate*. Comme l'a en effet remarqué O. du Roy, op. cit., p. 479, Augustin, lorsqu'il cite ce verset, écrit tantôt, comme il le fait ici: *Ex quo omnia, per quem omnia, in quo omnia*, tantôt, avec la *Vulgate: Quoniam ex ipso, et per ipsum, et in ipso omnia*. O. du Roy, ibid., p. 484, pense que la première formule, dont on connaît plusieurs témoins antérieurs à Augustin et qui reparaîtra souvent dans les commentaires médiévaux, "n'est pas à proprement parler une variante scripturaire, mais un résumé doxologique" qui résulterait de la fusion de *Rom.*, XI, 36, avec *I Cor.*, VIII, 6: "Nobis tamen unus Deus, Pater ex quo omnia, et nos in illum; et unus Dominus, Jesus Christus, per quem omnia, et nos per ipsum." Quelle que soit cependant la formule adoptée, lorsqu'Augustin cite la fin du verset, il écrit toujours, avec la *Vulgate*: "Ipsi gloria in saecula saeculorum."

11   Dans les textes où Augustin interprète *Rom.*, XI, 36, d'une manière plus explicite, c'est la distinction des prépositions *ex, per, in,* qui lui permet de conclure à la distinction des personnes; c'est en revanche dans l'emploi au datif singulier du pronom *ipse*, dans la conclusion du verset (*ipsi gloria*), qu'il découvre une affirmation de l'unité de l'essence divine. Voir notamment: *Enarr. in Ps. V, 3, Corp. Christ.*, 28, p. 20, l. 18-21; *De Trinit.*, I, 6, 12, *Corp. christ.*, 50, p. 41, l. 78-41; et aussi les deux textes auxquels saint Thomas emprunte les éléments de la citation factice alléguée

revenir avec insistance dans les lignes suivantes, et lorsque, vers la fin du passage qu'on vient de citer, il en arrivera à déclarer que "dans le Père est l'unité, dans le Fils l'égalité, dans le Saint-Esprit l'harmonie (*concordia*) de l'unité et de l'égalité," ce sera pour ajouter aussitôt, comme le rappellera soigneusement saint Thomas dans le corps de son article, que "ces trois attributs (*tri haec*)[12] ne font tous qu'un à cause du Père," qu' "ils sont tous égaux à cause du Fils," qu' "ils sont tous unis entre eux (*conexa*) à cause du Saint-Esprit."

Comme on peut le constater, la triade *unitas, aequalitas, concordia*, n'est introduite ici qu'incidemment. Augustin ne s'attarde pas à la commenter. On remarquera d'ailleurs qu'elle ne reparaîtra jamais, au moins sous une forme identique, dans la série des triades, pourtant si nombreuses, à l'aide desquelles l'évêque d'Hippone devait tenter par la suite de parvenir à une certaine intelligence du mystère.[13] Pour en comprendre le sens, il faut donc revenir d'abord sur l'interprétation de la doxologie paulinienne dont le *De doctrina christiana* l'a rapprochée. Cette exégèse est en effet liée au thème de la création par la Trinité et à la méthode d'ascension intellectuelle, inspirée de *Rom.*,I,20 (*Invisibilia ipsius, a creatura mundi per ea quae facta sunt ... intellecta*) qui va chercher dans la création le vestige de la Trinité pour s'élever, à partir de là, jusqu'à la connaissance du mystère qu'il reflète. Ceci sera clairement exprimé plus tard par Augustin dans un passage bien connu du *De Trinitate* qui tiendra une grande place dans l'histoire du traité des appropriations.[14] L'interprétation trinitaire de *Rom.*,XI,36, à laquelle se référera saint Thomas dans son obj.4,[15] y sert en effet de conclusion à un long développement dans lequel l'évêque d'Hippone renvoie très explicitement à *Rom.*,I,20, et où il recourt, pour évoquer le mystère de la Trinité, à une triade qui tient une large place dans son œuvre et sa pensée: *unitas, species, ordo*. La source première de l'unité, de la beauté et de l'ordre qui se manifestent dans la création, vestige du

---

dans son obj. 4: *De Trinit.*, VI, 10, 12, ed. cit., p. 243, 1. 60-62, et *Contra Maximin.*, II, 23, 4, PL 42, 800.

12 Avec G. Combès et J. Farges, op. cit., p. 187, dont j'ai cependant modifié légèrement la traduction, j'ai rendu *tria haec*, faute de mieux et pour éviter l'emploi du mot "choses", par "ces trois attributs". Mais il faut bien souligner que le mot "attribut", étranger au texte d'Augustin, risque d'être équivoque. L'unité dont il est question ici, et surtout l'égalité et la *concordia*, ne peuvent être considérés comme des "attributs divins" au sens où la théologie classique entend ce mot. Le mot "propriété" eût été plus équivoque encore. Saint Thomas, en tout cas, évitera les mots "attribut" ou "propriété" dans le commentaire qu'il donnera de cette formule d'Augustin dans le corps de son article.

13 C'est du moins ce qui ressort d'un examen de la table des principales triades néoplatoniciennes d'Augustin, dressée par O. du Roy, op. cit., pp. 537-540.

14 *De Trinit.*, VI, 10, 12, ed. cit., pp. 242-243, 1. 37-62.

15 Ibid., 1. 60-62. Cf. ci-dessus, n. 11.

créateur, ne peut être cherchée que dans la Trinité.[16] C'est donc ici la structure même de la nature créée qui nous renvoie aux trois personnes.

Ces observations nous éclairent sur la signification de la triade *unitas, aequalitas, concordia*. Celle-ci procède de toute évidence d'une réflexion sur le nombre dont l'inspiration rejoint celle d'un ouvrage composé par Augustin quelques années seulement avant le *De doctrina christiana*: le *De musica*. Au livre VI de ce traité, on trouve en tout cas un texte qu'on ne peut manquer de rapprocher de celui qui nous occupe. "Le nombre," écrit en effet Augustin,[17] "commence par l'un, il est beau par l'égalité et la similitude, il est uni par l'ordre." Comme l'a remarqué Dom O. du Roy dans le commentaire qu'il a donné de ce texte où apparaissent déjà tous les éléments de la triade *unitas, aequalitas, concordia*, mêlés à ceux de la triade *unitas, species, ordo*, le *De musica* assigne ici "à tout nombre trois moments constitutifs: son origine qui est l'un, sa beauté qui est son égalité ou sa similitude, son lien ou sa cohésion (*copulatur*) qui est son ordre ou son rang."[18] Le *De musica* ne tardera pas d'ailleurs à préciser que ces tendances constitutives n'apparaissent pas seulement dans le nombre, mais dans toute nature, et que par conséquent "tout ce qui est, dans la mesure où il est, a été fait par l'Un, Principe (*ab uno, principio*), au moyen de la Beauté ou de la Forme (*per speciem*) égale ou semblable à lui (*aequalem ac similem*), grâce aux richesses de sa bonté, Charité pour ainsi dire la plus chère, par laquelle sont unis (*iunguntur*) l'Un et l'Un issu de l'Un."[19]

L'inspiration néo-platonicienne de ce vocabulaire et de cette théologie est encore très apparente. Peut-être faut-il y discerner l'influence de Marius Victorinus. Pour ce dernier, en effet, l'Un engendré opère un mouvement de conversion vers la source dont il procède, aussi le Saint-Esprit peut-il être considéré comme le lien ou la connexion

---

16 Ibid., 1. 37-38 et 45-49: "Haec igitur omnia quae arte diuina facta sunt et unitatem quandam in se ostendunt et speciem et ordinem... Oportet igitur ut creatorem *per ea quae facta sunt intellecta conspicientes* (cf. *Rom.*, I, 20) trinitatem intellegamus cuius in creatura quomodo dignum est apparet *uestigium* (cf. *Eccli.*, L, 31). In illa enim trinitate summa origo est rerum omnium et perfectissima pulchritudo et beatissima delectatio."

17 *De musica*, VI, 17, 56, PL 32, 1191: "Numerus autem et ab uno incipit, et aequalitate ac similitudine pulcher est, et ordine copulatur."

18 O. du Roy, op. cit., p. 290.

19 *De musica*, loc. cit.: "Quamobrem quisquis fatetur nullam esse naturam, quae non ut sit quidquid est appetat unitatem, suique similis in quantum potest esse conetur, atque ordinem proprium vel locis, vel temporibus, vel in corpore quodam libramento salutem suam teneat: debet fateri ab uno, principio, per aequalem illi ac similem speciem, divitiis bonitatis ejus qua inter se unum et de uno unum charissima, ut ita dicam, charitate junguntur, omnia facta esse atque condita quaecumque sunt, in quantumcumque sunt." Je cite ici la traduction de O. du Roy, op. cit., p. 287, qui commente ce texte ibid., p. 292.

(*conexio*) du Père et du Fils.[20] Augustin reviendra en tout cas souvent
sur cette idée que la troisième personne de la Trinité est la "communauté"[21] ou la "société"[22] du Père et du Fils, et c'est dans ce contexte qu'il
faut entendre les formules si nombreuses où il affirme que le Saint-
Esprit est Charité.[23] Mais cette théologie est inséparable chez lui d'une
vision trinitaire de la création qu'ébauchent déjà ses premiers écrits.
Les textes du *De musica* qu'on vient de citer le montrent. C'est donc
bien dans les mêmes perspectives qu'il faut comprendre le développement du *De doctrina christiana*. La triade *unitas, aequalitas, concordia*,
liée à une interprétation trinitaire de la doxologie de l'*Épître aux
Romains*, ne prend tout son sens que dans une métaphysique de la création qui découvre simultanément dans le nombre et dans la nature des
structures trinitaires propres à conduire à l'intelligence du mystère et à
la connaissance du Père, du Fils et de l'Esprit-Saint.

II. LES ANCIENS COMMENTAIRES DE L'ÉPÎTRE AUX ROMAINS: FLORUS DE LYON

Le contexte dans lequel Augustin avait mentionné la triade *unitas,
aequalitas, concordia*, nous indique que c'est sans doute dans les commentaires de l'*Épître aux Romains* que nous avons quelques chances
d'en retrouver la trace. Une rapide enquête suffit en effet à montrer que
lorsque les commentateurs médiévaux en viennent à l'explication de
Rom.,XI,36, ils s'inspirent volontiers de l'exégèse trinitaire d'Augustin
et n'hésitent pas à reproduire à ce propos tel ou tel passage de son
œuvre. C'est ainsi que la compilation augustinienne de Bède le
Vénérable[24] cite textuellement un assez long passage du *De Trinitate*

---

20   Cf. *Hymnus III*, 1. 242-247, dans Marius Victorinus, *Traités théologiques sur la Trinité*, éd.
P. Henry -P. Hadot, *Sources chrétiennes*, 68 (Paris 1960), p. 650:
  "Tu, spiritus sancte, conexio es; conexio autem est quicquid conectit duo;
  Ita ut conectas omnia, primo conectis duo;
  Esque ipsa tertia conplexio duorum atque ipsa conplexio nihil distans uno, unum cum facis duo;
  O beata trinitas."
  Cf. aussi *Hymnus I*, 1.4-6, et *Hymnus III*, 1. 48, ed. cit., p. 620 et p. 636.
21   Cf. *In Jo.*, tr. XCIX, 7, *Corp. christ.*, 36, p. 586, 1. 4-6.
22   Cf. *Sermo LXXI*, 20, 33, PL 38, 463.
23   Cf. p. ex. *De musica*, VI, 17, 56, PL 32, 1191; *De quantitate animae*, 34, 77, PL 32, 1077; *De
fide et symbolo*, 8, 19, PL 40, 191; *De agone christiano*, 16, 10, PL 40, 300. J'emprunte ces références à P. Smulders, "Esprit-Saint (Pères latins)," *Dict. de spiritualité*, t. IV, fasc. 28-29 (Paris 1960),
col. 1271.
24   Cette compilation a été étudiée naguère par A. Wilmart, "La collection de Bède le
Vénérable sur l'Apôtre," *Rev. bénédictine*, 38 (1926), pp. 16-52, puis, plus récemment par I. Fransen, "Description de la collection de Bède le Vénérable sur l'Apôtre," *ibid.*, 71, (1961), pp. 22-70,
qui a inventorié et identifié les extraits d'Augustin cités par ce florilège.

(I,6,12)[25] que nous retrouverons par la suite: l'évêque d'Hippone ne se contente pas d'y affirmer la distinction des personnes et l'unité de l'essence divine en se fondant sur le texte de saint Paul, il y fait aussi allusion à l'égalité du Père et du Fils, évoquée par un texte bien connu de l'*Epître aux Philippiens*.[26] On retrouve des interprétations analogues de *Rom.*,XI,36, toujours inspirées d'Augustin, tout au long du IXe siècle, dans les commentaires de Raban Maur[27] et de Sedulius Scotus,[28] et dans l'*Expositio in epistolas Pauli* imprimée parmi les œuvres de Haymon d'Halberstadt mais que l'on attribue communément à Haymon d'Auxerre.[29] Aucun de ces ouvrages cependant ne mentionne la triade *unitas, aequalitas, concordia*. Celle-ci va pourtant reparaître, vers le même temps, dans une autre compilation augustinienne, celle de Florus de Lyon. Le vaste florilège composé par le diacre lyonnais vers la fin de sa carrière, c'est-à-dire peu avant l'année 860, rassemble, on le sait, un nombre considérable d'extraits augustiniens se rapportant aux passages les plus importants des *Epîtres* de saint Paul et présentés dans l'ordre qu'imposait à leur regroupement le texte de l'Apôtre. A propos de *Rom.*,XI,36, Florus reproduit intégralement le paragraphe du *De doctrina christiana* (I,5,5) qu'on a cité plus haut.[30] Le succès de cette compilation, dont les manuscrits sont nombreux, donne à penser que la citation de Florus n'est pas étrangère à la réapparition, chez les commentateurs et les théologiens du XIIe siècle, de la triade qui nous occupe.

Celle-ci cependant ne semble pas avoir retenu tout de suite l'attention. Comme l'a remarqué en effet L. Ott, on n'en retrouve la trace,

---

25 Cf. I. Fransen, op. cit., p. 34, qui, à propos de *Rom.*, XI, 33-36, identifie les deux citations suivantes: 1° *Epist. ad Xystum presb.*, CSEL 57, 180, 1. 1 -181, 1.7 (comment. du v. 33); 2° *De Trinit.*, I, 6, 12, PL 42, 826, 1. 6-827, 1. 31 (= *Corp. christ.*, 50, pp. 41-42, 1. 74-106) (comment. du v. 36).

26 *Philip.*, II, 6, cité par Augustin suivant une version légèrement différente de la *Vulgate*: "Qui cum in forma Dei esset, non rapinam arbitratus est esse aequalis Deo."

27 PL 111, 1540 B - 1542 A.

28 PL 103, 109 A.

29 PL 117, 468 AB. Sur l'attribution de cette *Expositio* à Haymon d'Auxerre, voir B. Smalley, *The Study of the Bible in the Middle Ages*, 2e éd. (Oxford 1952) p. 39, n. 2, qui renvoie à E. Riggenbach, *Hist. Studien zum Hebräerbrief, Forschung. z. Gesch. des neutest. Kanons*, éd. T. Zahn, VIII (Leipzig 1907) pp. 41-201.

30 La *Patr. lat.*, qui reproduit (t. 119, 279-420) l'édition de la compilation de Florus publiée à Venise en 1543, mais sans transcire les extraits d'Augustin dont elle se contente de donner la référence, signale déjà, à propos de *Rom.*, XI, 36, cet emprunt au *De doctrina christiana* (cf. PL 119, 311). Celui-ci est identifié avec plus de précision dans la *Liste des extraits augustiniens* donnée par C. Charlier en appendice à son étude sur "La compilation augustinienne de Florus de Lyon sur l'Apôtre," *Rev. bénédictine*, 57 (1947), pp. 132-186, (*Appendice I*, p. 170). J'ai pu examiner cette citation dans un manuscrit venu de Corbie et copié en 1164 (*Paris, B. N. lat. 11575*, f° 66va). Détail qui n'est pas sans intérêt pour nous, Florus, si nous en croyons du moins ce manuscrit, comme Augustin, écrit bien *concordia*.

ni dans les collections de *Sentences* de l'école de Laon, ni chez Abélard
et ses disciples, ni dans le *De sacramentis* de Hugues de Saint-Victor ou
dans la *Summa sententiarum*.[31] Cette absence ne saurait trop nous éton-
ner. Les commentaires scripturaires du Xe, du XIe et du début du
XIIe siècle qui ont alimenté les premières spéculations des écoles, bien
qu'ils persistent à donner de *Rom.*,XI,36, une interprétation trinitaire
inspirée d'Augustin, négligent tous, autant du moins que j'ai pu voir, le
texte du *De doctrina christiana* qu'avait cité Florus.[32] Ainsi en est-il
notamment de la *Glossa* issue de l'école d'Anselme de Laon que citera
saint Thomas dans sa quatrième objection. L'examen de quelques uns
des manuscrits que l'on compte généralement parmi les témoins les plus
anciens de la *Glose* primitive[33] m'a permis de faire les constatations
suivantes: la glose interlinéaire, tout d'abord, rapporte explicitement
l'*ex ipso* de saint Paul au Père, le *per ipsum* au Fils et l'*in ipso* au Saint-
Esprit; les gloses marginales rappellent qu'il faut voir dans les trois
prépositions *ex, per, in*, une affirmation de la distinction des personnes
et dans le datif singulier *ipsi* celle de l'identité de leur substance;[34] s'inspirant ensuite d'un passage du *De natura boni* d'Augustin dont s'était
déjà souvenu Atton de Verceil, elles précisent que dans la formule *in
ipso sunt omnia* on ne peut inclure dans l'*omnia* les péchés qui naissent
en réalité de la volonté perverse de l'homme;[35] enfin, résumant
brièvement l'enseignement que nous avions remarqué dans le *De
Trinitate* (VI,10,12), elles reviennent sur cette idée que les créatures
sont le vestige de la Trinité et que celle-ci est à la fois origine de toutes
choses, beauté parfaite et bienheureuse délectation.[36]

31 Cf. L. Ott, *Untersuchungen zur theologischen Briefliteratur der Frühscholastik*, BGPTM 34
(Münster 1937), p. 569.
32 Cf. pp. ex. Atton de Verceil, *Expositio in epist. Pauli*, PL 134, 247 D- 248 B; Lanfranc, *In
Pauli epist. commentarii*, PL 150, 144; Pseudo-Bruno le Chartreux, *Expositio in epist. Pauli*, PL
153, 99 D (commentaire attribué parfois à Raoul de Laon ou à Jean de Tours: voir sur ce point A.
Landgraf, *Introducción a la historia de la literatura teológica de la escolástica incipiente*, Barcelona 1956, p. 88). Abélard, dans la brève explication qu'il nous donne de *Rom.*, XI, 36 (*Comment. in epist. Pauli ad Rom.*, éd. Buytaert, *Corp. christ., Cont. med.*, XI, Turnhout 1969, pp. 271-
272), se contente de voir dans les trois expressions du verset de saint Paul une allusion à la
création des choses, à leur conservation et à leur consommation. On retrouvera une explication
analogue dans le *Commentarius Cantabrigiensis in epist. Pauli*, éd. A. Landgraf, *Public. in
Mediaeval Studies*, II (Notre Dame 1937), p. 174, d'après lequel cependant l'*ex ipso* de saint Paul
correspond à la "cause primordiale", et l'*in ipso* à la cause finale.
33 Je me suis reporté aux mss. *Paris, B.N. lat. 2579, 12322* et *14785*, signalés par A. Landgraf,
Introducción, p. 98.
34 Cf. *Paris, B. N. lat. 14785*, f° 20v: "*Ex, per, in*, distinctionem personarum indicant; ipse
identitatem significat substantie" (texte presque identique dans *Paris, B. N. lat. 2579* et *12322*; cf.
aussi PL 114, 510 A). Sur l'origine augustinienne de ces affirmations, voir ci-dessus, n. 11.
35 Cf. ms. cit., ibid., ou PL 114, 510 B: "*Et in ipso sunt omnia* que naturaliter sunt, non peccata
que ex uoluntate nascuntur, que naturam uitiant" (cf. Augustin, *De natura boni*, 28, PL 42, 560; Atton de Verceil, op. cit., PL 134, 247 D).
36 Cf. ms. cit., ibid.: "In creaturis uestigium apparet trinitatis. In trinitate summa est omnium

III. Les Commentaires sur l'*Epître aux Romains* de Gilbert de la Porrée, de Pierre Lombard et de Guillaume de Saint-Thierry

L'influence de la *Glossa* anselmienne sera désormais perceptible dans tous les commentaires de l'*Epître aux Romains* de xiie siècle. Trois d'entre eux cependant, avant l'année 1150, vont s'enrichir d'apports nouveaux, empruntés le plus souvent à Augustin, et introduire ainsi la triade *unitas, aequalitas, concordia*, dans leur explication de *Rom.*, XI, 36.

Le premier et le plus ancien est celui que nous a laissé Gilbert de la Porrée dans sa *Glossa super epistolas Pauli.* [37] Cet ouvrage, malheureusement inédit, a dû être composé avant 1140, peut-être dès les années 1130, [38] c'est-à-dire au temps où Gilbert enseignait à Chartres. [39] Voici, établi d'après le manuscrit *Paris, B.N. lat. 2580*, f. 32v-33r, [40] le texte de

rerum [origo] et perfecta pulchritudo et beatissima delectatio" (cf. Augustin, *De Trinitate*, VI, 10, 12, *Corp. christ.*, 50, p. 242, l. 46-49, et ci-dessus, n. 14).

[37] L'authenticité de cette *Glossa* a été établie par H. Denifle, *Die abendländische Schriftausleger bis Luther über Justitia Dei (Rom., I, 17) und Justificatio* (Mayence 1905), p. 30 ss. On trouvera dans cet ouvrage une liste des manuscrits, enrichie depuis lors par A. Landgraf, *Introducción*, pp. 135-136. Ces listes ont été reproduites par H. C. van Elswijk, *Gilbert Porreta. Sa vie, son œuvre, sa pensée*, (Spicilegium sacrum Lovaniense, Etudes et documents, 33), (Louvain 1966), pp. 54-58.

[38] Cf. H. C. van Elswijk, op. cit., pp. 57-58. Les données chronologiques dont on dispose pour déterminer la date de composition de la *Glossa* de Gilbert dépendent principalement d'un texte souvent cité de Géroch de Reichersberg. Dans son *Libellus de ordine donorum sancti Spiritus* (éd. D. et O. van den Eynde, *Gerhohi Opera inedita*, I, Spicilegium Pontif. Athenaei Antoniani, 8, Rome, 1955, p. 71), composé à la fin de l'année 1141 ou au début de l'année 1142 (cf. D. van den Eynde, *L'œuvre littéraire de Géroch de Reichersberg*, Spicilegium Pontif. Ath. Antoniani, 11, Rome 1957, pp. 76-77), Géroch s'en prend avec vivacité à l'interprétation restrictive de *Philipp.*, II, 9, proposée par un certain nombre de gloses sur saint Paul composées par les maîtres de son temps, et parmi lesquels "praecipui sunt magistri Anshelmus et magister Gillibertus et novissime Petrus Longabardus", c'est-à-dire Anselme de Laon, Gilbert de la Porrée et Pierre Lombard. Il ressort de ce témoignage que la *Glossa* de Gilbert, antérieure à celle de Pierre Lombard à laquelle on donne généralement le titre de *Collectanea in epistolas Pauli* et que l'adverbe *novissime* permet de considérer comme la plus récente des trois, a dû être composée avant 1140. C'est pour des raisons de critique interne que H. C. van Elswijk (op. cit., p. 58) estime "serrer la vérité de près en proposant les environs de 1130 comme date de composition de cette glose" de Gilbert.

[39] A vrai dire, nous connaissons trop mal la chronologie exacte des déplacements de Gilbert pour être assuré qu'il ait composé sa *Glossa* à Chartres. Si nous nous en tenons cependant aux données biographiques rassemblées par H. C. van Elswijk, op. cit., pp. 15-28, Gilbert, après avoir fréquenté les écoles de Chartres, aurait séjourné à Laon jusqu'en 1117 environ, date à laquelle il serait devenu écolâtre de la cathédrale de Poitiers. Mais il serait revenu bientôt à Chartres où on le trouve en 1124 et où il sera certainement encore en 1137. Il demeurera dans cette ville jusqu'à son départ pour Paris, sans doute en 1141, avant de devenir évêque de Poitiers en 1141 ou 1142.

[40] Ce manuscrit vient de Corbie (xiie s.). J'ai collationné également les mss. *Paris, B.N. lat. 2581*, f. 26v (xiie-xiiie s.), *12028*, f. 38v-39r (Saint-Germain des Près, xiie s.), *14414*, f. 23r-v (Saint-Victor, xiiie s.), et *Mazarine 258*, f. 18r-v (Feuillants, xiiie s.), mais ces quatre volumes ne nous offrent que des variantes mineures, parfois fautives. Ce texte avait déjà été publié d'après

l'explication que la *Glossa* de Gilbert de la Porrée consacre à *Rom.*,XI,36. Les chiffres entre crochets, intercalés dans le texte, signalent les différentes triades qui y apparaissent successivement:

[1] *Quoniam omnia,* non dico peccata que nascuntur ex uoluntate peccantium et naturam uitiant, sed omnia que naturaliter fiunt,[41] sunt *ex ipso, et per ipsum, et in ipso.* Sola enim gratia nos cum nondum essemus predestinauit, aduersos uocauit, impios iustificauit, terrenos glorificauit. Ne igitur simus ingrati, dicamus quod sequitur: *Ipsi gloria in secula. Amen.* Nota quod non ait: de ipso omnia, sed: *ex ipso.* Creata namque ex ipso sunt quoniam opus eius sunt, sed non sunt de ipso, hoc est de substantia eius. Filius autem per quem illa sunt, et spiritus sanctus in quo consistunt, non solum ex ipso, sed et de ipso, id est de substantia eius sunt,[42] neuter tamen uel decisus a plenitudine, uel decedens a singularitate substantie eius, sed substantie plenitudine totus eiusdemque singularitate unus deus, prorsus idem cum ipso.[43] Unde, quamuis personarum trinitatem insinuans uerba diuiserit, dicens: *ex ipso, et per ipsum, et in ipso,* tamen uno pronomine singulari unam trium personarum singularem substantiam debere intelligi demonstrauit, maxime cum postea non nisi semel et singulariter supposuerit: *ipsi,* significationem sine dubio ad intelligendam unam substantiam dirigens.[44] Illud quoque uigilanter attende ne quia patrem uolens intelligi dixit *ex ipso,* intelligas sic ex patre esse omnia ut neges esse uel ex filio uel ex spiritu sancto. Qui forte error subrepere posset ex eo quod filium uolens intelligi non ait : *ex quo,* sed: *per quem,* et spiritum sanctum uolens intelligi non ait: *ex quo,* sed: *in quo,* tamquam scilicet auctoritas qua ex patre sunt omnia ita sit patris quod neque filii neque spiritus sancti sit. [2] Et est quidem in patre auctoritas, in filio uero natiuitas, in spiritu sancto patris filiique communitas.[45] Sed pater non habet patrem, et ideo auctoritas que in eo est non est ex aliquo. Quoniam uero filius natiuitate est patris imago, perfecte implens illum cuius imago est, coequatur eidem, non ille imagini sue,[46] et ideo quecumque in filio est auctoritas ex eo est cui ipse perfectione imaginis coequatur. In spiritu sancto uero, qui non solum ex patre sed etiam ex filio procedit ut amborum non filius sed concordia sit, que inest auctoritas non nisi ex patre et filio ex quibus procedit est. Hoc ergo apostolus uolens intelligi ait: *ex quo omnia.* Nam sicut dictum est auc-

---

un ms. de Londres (*Brit. Mus., Add. 11853,* f. 41r-v) par M. Simon, "La Glose de l'Epître aux Romains de Gilbert de la Porrée," *Rev. d'histoire ecclésiastique* 52 (1957), pp. 74-75. Mais il était nécessaire de le reproduire ici pour la clarté de l'exposé.

41   *non dico — fiunt*: cf. *Glossa marginalis* (ci-dessus, n. 35); Augustin, *De natura boni,* 28, PL 42, 560.

42   *Nota quod — sunt*: cf. Atton de Verceil, *Exp. in epist. Pauli, ad loc.,* PL 134, 247 D; Augustin, *De natura boni,* loc. cit.

43   *neuter — ipso*: comparer Augustin, *De doctr. christ.,* I, 5, 5, l. 7-10.

44   *Unde — dirigens*: comparer *Glossa marginalis* (ci-dessus, n. 34).

45   *in patre — communitas*: cf. Hilaire, *De Trinitate,* IX, 27, et XII, 51, PL 10, 302 BC et 466 B; Augustin, *In Joh.,* tr. XCIX, 7, *Corp. christ.,* 36, p. 586, l. 4-6.

46   *Quoniam — imagini sue*: cf. Augustin, *De Trinitate,* VI, 10, 11, ed. cit., p. 241, l. 10-12.

toritas omnis in patre de nullo, et que [cumque][47] in filio non nisi ex
patre, et quecumque in spiritu sancto non nisi ex patre et filio. [3] Nam in
patre unitas, in filio equalitas, in spiritu sancto unitatis equalitatisque
concordia. Et tamen hec tria unum omnia propter patrem, equalia omnia
propter filium, conexa omnia propter spiritum sanctum.[48] [4] Huius
trinitatis in creatura quomodo dignum est apparet uestigium,[49] nam omnia que arte diuina facta sunt, et unitatem quandam et speciem et ordinem in se ostendunt. Nam quicquid est, et unum aliquid est, sicut sunt
nature corporum et ingenia animarum, et specie formatur ut corpora
figuris et qualitatibus et anime artibus, et ordinem petit uel tenet ut corpora ponderibus et collocationibus et anime delectationibus.[50]
[5] Quorum omnium in trinitate est summa origo, perfectissima
pulcritudo et beatissima delectatio.[51] [6] Nam eternitas in patre, species
in imagine, usus in munere;[52] [7] unum principium ad quod recurrimus,
una forma quam sequitur, una gratia qua reconciliamur.[53] Itaque
creatorem per ea que facta sunt conspicientes,[54] digne confitemur quod
unus deus pater *ex quo omnia,* unus unigenitus christus *per quem omnia,*
unum in omnibus donum spiritus *in quo omnia. Ipsi* secundum substantiam singulariter uni sit *gloria in secula. Amen.*

Ce commentaire demeure fidèle, dans l'ensemble, à l'interprétation
trinitaire de *Rom.,* XI,36, inspirée d'Augustin, qu'on trouve dans les
commentaires plus anciens dont il dépend d'ailleurs de toute évidence.
Il reproduit cependant des formules d'Augustin et d'Hilaire qui, semble-t-il, n'avaient pas encore été citées ou ne l'avaient été que rarement.
Mais surtout il organise son explication suivant un schéma caractérisé
principalement par l'énumération d'une série de triades que les
prédécesseurs de Gilbert n'avaient pas toutes connues ou auxquelles ils
n'avaient prêté qu'une attention inégale. Ces triades sont au nombre de
sept:

1° *Ex ipso, per ipsum, in ipso,* ou *ex quo, per quem, in quo (Rom.,*
XI, 36, cité selon les deux versions utilisées déjà par Augustin et signalées ci-dessus, n. 10);

---

47 La leçon *quecumque,* plus satisfaisante pour l'équilibre de la phrase, est empruntée aux mss.
Paris, B. N. lat. 2581, 12028, 14414, et Mazarine 258.
48 *Nam — sanctum:* cf. Augustin, *De doctr. christ.,* I, 5, 5, l. 15-18.
49 *Huius — uestigium:* cf. *Glossa marginalis* (ci-dessus, n. 36); Augustin, *De Trinit.,* VI, 10, 12,
ed. cit., p. 242, l. 46-47.
50 *nam omnia — delectationibus:* cf. Augustin, ibid., l. 37-44.
51 *Quorum — delectatio:* cf. *Glossa marginalis* (ci-dessus, n. 36); Augustin, loc. cit., l. 47-49.
52 *Nam — munere:* cf. Augustin, *De Trinit.,* VI, 10, 11, ibid., p. 241, l. 2-3, citant Hilaire, *De
Trinit.,* II, 1, PL 10, 51 A.
53 *unum — reconciliamur:* cf. Augustin, *De uera religione,* LV, 113, *Corp. christ.,* 32, p. 260, l.
138-139.
54 *creatorem-conspicientes:* cf. Augustin, *De Trinit.,* VI, 10, 12, ed. cit., p. 242, l. 45-46, citant
Rom., I, 20.

2° *Auctoritas, natiuitas, communitas* (combinaison de Hilaire, *De Trinit.*, XII, 21, et Augustin, *In Joh.*, tr. XCIX, 7);

3° *Unitas, aequalitas, concordia* (Augustin, *De doctr. christ.*, 1, 5, 5);

4° *Unitas, species, ordo* (Augustin, *De Trinit.*, VI, 10, 12);

5° *Summa origo, perfectissima pulchritudo, beatissima delectatio* (Augustin, *De Trinit.*, VI, 10, 12);

6° *Aeternitas, species, usus* (Augustin, *De Trinit.*, VI, 10, 11, citant Hilaire, *De Trinit.*, 11, 1);

7° *Principium, forma, gratia* (Augustin, *De uera religione*, LV, 113).

Cette énumération appelle quelques remarques. En ce qui concerne d'abord la triade n° 1, on notera les précisions, empruntées à Augustin, relatives à la signification de l'expression *ex ipso*, et, plus encore, l'insistance avec laquelle Gilbert met en garde le théologien contre toute interprétation qui tendrait à attribuer au Père, et à lui seul, la création des choses, sous prétexte que l'*Epître aux Romains* rapporte à la première personne de la Trinité l'expression *ex ipso*, alors qu'elle dit *per ipsum* à propos du Fils, et *in ipso* à propos du Saint-Esprit. On ne peut conclure de là, explique Gilbert, que l'*auctoritas* qui appartient au Père, n'appartient pas également au Fils et au Saint-Esprit. Il n'est pas impossible que l'auteur de la *Glossa* vise ici l'enseignement d'Abélard qui, en affirmant que la puissance devait être rapportée au Père comme lui appartenant "en propre" et "spécialement"[55] tendait à attribuer à la première personne de la Trinité un pouvoir créateur que n'auraient pas également partagé les deux autres personnes.[56] On notera d'ailleurs que Gilbert ne mentionne pas la triade *potentia, sapientia, bonitas*, qu'il devait critiquer plus tard dans son commentaire sur Boèce.[57] A ces dénominations empruntées directement aux attributs essentiels de la divinité, il préfère manifestement celles que garantissait davantage l'autorité des Pères et qui cherchaient dans la nature créée des analogies apparemment moins équivoques ou plus propres à rendre compte des relations trinitaires.

Sans doute est-ce pour ce dernier motif qu'il insiste longuement sur la triade n°2 (*auctoritas, natiuitas, communitas*) que les théologiens de l'école porrétaire commenteront souvent après lui. Gilbert semble être le premier à l'avoir présentée sous cette forme. Mais il s'inspire à la fois

---

55   Voir, entre autres textes, Abélard, *Theologia christiana*, I, 25, éd. Buytaert, *Corp. christ., Cont. med.*, 12 (Turnhout 1969), p. 81, l. 290-299; *Theologia scholarium* (dans la recension publiée sous le titre d'*Introd. ad theologiam*), I, 10, PL 178, 992 A, 994 AB.

56   C'est cette attribution spéciale de la puissance au Père que devaient condamner deux propositions du Concile de Sens, en 1140 (cf. ci-dessous, n. 106).

57   Cf. ci-dessous, n. 104.

de saint Hilaire qui avait employé à plusieurs reprises les mots *auctoritas* et *natiuitas* pour désigner le Père et le Fils,[58] et de saint Augustin qui avait déjà dit, on s'en souvient, que l'Esprit-Saint était la *communitas* du Père et du Fils.[59] Gilbert va d'ailleurs s'expliquer sur le sens de ces expressions. L'*auctoritas* convient au Père, parce que celui-ci n'a pas de Père et qu'en lui l'*auctoritas,* commune cependant aux trois personnes, n'est pas *ex aliquo,* mais *de nullo,* ce qui revient à dire que l'*auctoritas* qui lui est propre correspond à son innascibilité. La notion de *natiuitas* indique en revanche que le Fils procède du Père. Reprenant ici une formule d'Augustin, Gilbert rappelle d'ailleurs que le Fils est l'image du Père et qu'il ne peut être que son égal: le Père lui communique donc une *auctoritas* égale à la sienne. Quant au Saint-Esprit, à qui Gilbert rapporte dès maintenant la notion de *concordia,* synonyme de *communitas,* il tiendra du Père et du Fils une *auctoritas* égale, elle aussi, à celle des deux premières personnes dont il procède.

Ces explications qui nous font pénétrer dès maintenant au cœur du mystère trinitaire permettent aisément à Gilbert d'introduire aussitôt la triade n° 3 (*unitas, aequalitas, concordia*) dont la signification est très voisine de celle de la triade précédente. Cette troisième triade est présentée brièvement. La *Glossa* se contente de reproduire quelques lignes du *De doctrina christiana*[60] pour rappeler notamment que les trois éléments qui la constituent "sont tous un à cause du Père, tous égaux à cause du Fils, tous unis entre eux (*conexa*) à cause du Saint-Esprit." Les quatre triades suivantes seront énumérées plus rapidement encore. Les triades 4 et 5 sont présentées dans un contexte emprunté au passage du *De Trinitate* où Augustin lui-même en avait fait mention.[61] Quant aux triades 6 et 7, Gilbert se contente de les évoquer en reproduisant des formules venues du *De Trinitate* et du *De uera religione.*[62]

Il ressort de tout ceci que l'originalité de Gilbert a consisté principalement à regrouper une série de triades empruntées à Augustin ou à Hilaire et parmi lesquelles il faut remarquer la triade *unitas, aequalitas, concordia,* dont nous n'avions retrouvé la trace, jusqu'à présent, que dans la compilation de Florus de Lyon. Le schéma dû ainsi à l'initiative et à l'érudition de cette *Glossa* n'allait pas tarder à servir de cadre à d'autres spéculations.

---

58 Cf. ci-dessus, n. 45. Le mot *communitas* n'apparaît pas dans les textes où Hilaire fait mention de l'*auctoritas* et de la *natiuitas.*
59 Cf. ci-dessus, n. 21.
60 Cf. ci-dessus, n. 48.
61 Cf. ci-dessus, n. 50-51.
62 Cf. ci-dessus, n. 52-53.

Le second commentaire de l'*Epître aux Romains* qui a fait une place à la triade du *De doctrina christiana* est celui que nous a laissé Pierre Lombard dans ses *Collectanea in epistolas Pauli,* composés vraisemblablement entre 1138-1139 et 1141.[63] Cet ouvrage dépend certainement du précédent, notamment en ce qui concerne l'explication de *Rom.,* XI,36. Nous y retrouvons ici à peu près tout ce que nous avions lu dans la *Glossa* de Gilbert. Deux exceptions notables cependant: Pierre Lombard ne fait aucune mention des deux triades *auctoritas, natiuitas, communitas,* et *aeternitas, species, usus,* inspirées principalement, l'une et l'autre, du *De Trinitate* d'Hilaire de Poitiers. Pourquoi cette double omission? Il est évidemment bien difficile de le savoir. On peut conjecturer cependant que le Lombard a négligé la première de ces deux triades parce qu'il n'a pas réussi à en découvrir l'origine composite et qu'elle lui a semblé dès lors quelque peu suspecte. Quant à la seconde, elle a dû lui paraître chargée d'obscurité, comme il le dira plus tard très explicitement dans ses *Sententiae.*[64]

Pour le reste, le commentaire de Pierre Lombard est beaucoup plus développé que celui de son prédécesseur. Les *Collectanea,* qui prennent soin d'indiquer leurs sources patristiques, citent ici *in extenso* de longs passages d'Augustin auxquels la *Glossa* de Gilbert n'avait emprunté que quelques mots ou tout au plus une ou deux phrases. Ceci est particulièrement sensible à trois reprises. Le Lombard reproduit d'abord les deux longs extraits du *De Trinitate* d'Augustin, relatifs aux triades *origo, pulchritudo, delectatio,* et *unitas, species, ordo,* dont Gilbert n'avait cité que quelques lignes;[65] il recopie intégralement la conclusion

63   Cf. D. Van den Eynde, *Essai chronologique sur l'œuvre littéraire de Pierre Lombard,* dans *Miscellanea Lombardiana* (Novare 1953), pp. 53-55. C'est grâce au témoignage de Géroch de Reichersberg qui mentionne le commentaire du Lombard sur les *Epîtres* de saint Paul dans son *Libellus de ordine donorum sancti Spiritus,* rédigé en 1141-1142 (cf. ci-dessus, n. 38), que le P. van den Eynde a pu avancer que les *Collectanea* avaient été composés avant 1141. Mais cette certitude a été récemment ébranlée par une remarque de P. Classen, *Gerhoch von Reichersberg* (Wiesbaden 1960), p. 412. Ce dernier a fait observer qu'il n'était pas absolument impossible que les mots *et novissime Petrus Longabardus* qu'on lit dans le *Libellus* aient été ajoutés par Géroch lui-même, longtemps après la publication de son traité. Nous ne possédons en effet qu'un seul manuscrit du *Libellus,* le *Reichersbergensis VIII,* que Géroch a fait transcrire vers la fin de sa vie et que P. Classen, op. cit., p. 466, date des années 1160-1166. Le R. P. D. van den Eynde, *L'œuvre littéraire de Géroch de Reichersberg* (Rome 1957), pp. 70-71, a constaté que, dans ce volume, "au moins un passage du *Libellus* porte des traces visibles d'un remaniement postérieur" à la rédaction primitile; il pense que "le cas n'est sans doute pas isolé", mais que, faute "de point de comparaisons suffisants, il n'est plus possible de faire le départ exact entre le texte original et ses remaniements."

64   Cf. *Sent.,* I, d. 31, 2 (Quaracchi 1916), pp. 192-195.

65   Cf. *Collectanea, In epist. ad Rom.,* XI,33-36, PL 191, 1493 C 1-11, qui cite Augustin, *De Trinit.,* VI,10,12, ed. cit., p. 242, l. 45-50, et p. 243, l. 54-57 et 60-61 (cf. ci-dessus, n. 49,51), et *Collectanea,* loc. cit., 1495 A 1 - C 7, qui cite Augustin, ibid., VI,10,11-12, ed. cit., pp. 241-242, l. 9-42 (cf. ci-dessus, n. 46,50).

du *De uera religione* où il est question de la triade *principium, forma, gratia,* que Gilbert n'avait fait que mentionner rapidement;[66] enfin et surtout il reproduit en entier le paragraphe du *De doctrina christiana* que Florus de Lyon avait déjà recopié dans sa compilation et que Gilbert n'avait que partiellement cité lorsqu'il avait introduit dans sa *Glossa* la triade *unitas, aequalitas, concordia.*[67] En reproduisant ce texte du *De doctrina christiana,* Pierre Lombard, comme Augustin et comme Gilbert, écrit bien *concordia.* C'est en tout cas la leçon qu'a retenue l'édition imprimée[68] et qu'on retrouve dans la plupart des manuscrits. Parmi ceux-ci, cependant, quelques uns écrivent *connexio*[69] ou *concordia uel connexio.*[70] Cette variante témoigne de l'hésitation de certains copistes. Nous ne tarderons pas à en retrouver, sinon l'explication, du moins d'autres exemples.

Un troisième commentaire antérieur à l'année 1150 a fait enfin mention de la triade *unitas, aequalitas, concordia.* Il s'agit de l'*Expositio in epistolam ad Romanos* de Guillaume de Saint-Thierry. Nous ne connaissons pas la date exacte de cet ouvrage. Nous savons cependant qu'il est antérieur à l'*Epistola ad fratres de Monte-Dei* où Guillaume lui-même le met au nombre des écrits qu'il a déjà rédigés et dont il nous donne la liste.[71] Cette indication a permis naguère à A. Wilmart de préciser que cette *Expositio* avait été certainement rédigée entre 1135 et 1145.[72] On a donc tout lieu de penser qu'elle est postérieure de quelques années à la *Glossa* de Gilbert, peut-être même aux *Collectanea* de Pierre Lombard dont elle semble bien s'inspirer. Le bref développement que Guillaume y consacre à *Rom.*, XI,36, ne fait en effet que citer des textes d'Augustin que nous avions déjà rencontrés dans le commentaire du Lombard. L'*Expositio* reproduit d'abord la plus grande partie du passage du *De uera religione* que nous avions remarqué dans les *Collectanea;*[73] aussitôt après, elle cite le paragraphe du *De doctrina christiana*

---

66   Cf. *Collectanea,* loc. cit., 1494 A 3 - C 1, qui cite Augustin, *De uera religione,* LV, 113, ed. cit., pp. 259-260, l. 123-145 (cf. ci-dessus, n. 53).

67   Cf. *Collectanea,* loc. cit., 1494 C 1 - D 8, qui cite Augustin, *De doctr. christ.,* I,5,5, ed. cit., p. 9, l. 1-18 (cf. ci-dessus, n. 48).

68   PL 191, 1494 D 5-6. L'édition de Migne reproduit celle qui avait été publiée à Paris en 1535.

69   Ainsi le ms. *Paris, B.N. Lat. 14266,* f. 78r, venu de Saint-Victor et copié au XIIᵉ s.

70   Ms. *Paris, B.N. Lat. 15238,* f. 50ra (Sorbonne, XIIIᵉ s.). J'ai examiné un grand nombre d'autres manuscrits parisiens qui conservent tous la leçon *concordia.*

71   Cf. *Epist. ad fratres de Monte-Dei,* 4, éd. M.-M.Davy (*Etudes de philosophie médiévale,* 29 (Paris 1940), p. 67.

72   Cf. A. Wilmart, "La série et la date des écrits de Guillaume de Saint-Thierry", *Revue Mabillon,* 14 (1924), pp. 157-167.

73   Cf. Guillaume de S.-T., *Exposit.,* PL 180, 669 A 6 - 670 A 5, qui cite Augustin, *De uera relig.,* LV, 113, ed. cit., pp. 259-260, l. 123-141 (cf. ci-dessus, n. 66).

relatif à la triade *unitas, aequalitas, concordia.* [74] L'édition de Migne qui reproduit celle de la *Bibliotheca Cisterciensis* de Tissier, écrit pourtant ici, non pas *concordia,* mais *connexio,* [75] et rien ne nous permet de penser que cette leçon ne vient pas de Guillaume lui-même. L'*Expositio* de l'abbé de Saint-Thierry s'achève par une courte citation du *De Trinitate* d'Augustin, présente, elle aussi, dans les *Collectanea* de Pierre Lombard. [76]

Il ressort des textes de Gilbert de la Porrée, de Pierre Lombard et de Guillaume de Saint-Thierry qu'on vient de signaler, que la triade *unitas, aequalitas, concordia* ou *connexio,* avait définitivement pris place dans les commentaires de *Rom.,* XI,36, antérieurs à 1150. Elle n'allait pas tarder à être citée et utilisée par des ouvrages plus spéculatifs ou plus systématiques.

IV. Les Maîtres Chartrains

Ce sont les maîtres chartrains qui ont été les premiers à donner de la formule du *De doctrina christiana,* isolée de son contexte, une interprétation théologique détachée de celle du verset de l'*Epître aux Romains* à laquelle elle avait été primitivement associée. Dans son *De sex dierum operibus,* [77] suivant une méthode qui s'inspirait de celle d'Anselme de Cantorbéry, [78] Thierry de Chartres avait en effet voulu chercher des "raisons" et des "preuves" qui fussent capables de le conduire à la connaissance des trois personnes. Il ne s'agissait pas pour lui, bien entendu, de proposer une démonstration rigoureuse qui aurait permis au théologien ou au philosophe de s'élever par ses seules forces jusqu'au mystère insondable de la Trinité, mais de "rejoindre, par une démarche intellectuelle, une donnée dont l'âme était déjà en possession par la foi." [79] C'est aux arts libéraux, et plus spécialement à

---

74   Cf. Guillaume de S.-T., ibid., 670 A5-B 5, qui cite Augustin, *De doctr. christ.,* I,5,5, ed. cit., p. 9, l. 1-18 (cf. ci-dessus, n. 67).

75   PL 180, 670 B 3. Je n'ai pu vérifier la présence de cette leçon dans l'unique manuscrit de l'*Expositio* (*Charleville, 172*) que signale A. Wilmart, art. cit., p. 164, n. 1.

76   Op. cit., 670 B 5-8, qui cite Augustin, *De Trinitate,* VI,10,12, ed. cit., p. 243, l. 60-62. La citation de Guillaume est ici plus fidèle à Augustin que celle de Pierre Lombard, *Collectanea,* PL 191, 1493 C 10-11.

77   Ed. N. Haring, "The Creation and Creator of the World according to Thierry of Chartres and Clarembald of Arras," *AHDLMA,* 22, 1955 (1956), 30-47, pp. 194-200.

78   La parenté indéniable de la méthode de Thiery de Chartres avec celle d'Anselme de Cantorbéry a été signalée par L. Ott, *Untersuchungen zur Briefliteratur der Frühscholatik, BGPTMA,* 34, 1937, p. 570, et par E. Jeauneau, "Mathématiques et Trinité chez Thierry de Chartres", dans *Die Metaphysik im Mittelalter; Vorträge des II. Internationalen Kongress für mittelalterliche Philosphie,* Köln 31 Aug. — 6 Sept. 1961, (Berlin 1963), pp. 291-292.

79   E. Jeauneau, op. cit., p. 291. Un passage du commentaire sur le *De Trinitate* de Boèce que nous a laissé Clarembaud d'Arras (éd. W. Jansen, *Der Kommentar des Clarenbaldus von Arras zu*

l'arithmétique, que Thierry voulut emprunter ces "raisons." L'exposé de ce qu'il appelle des *probationes arithmeticae*,[80] dont bien des éléments viennent du *De arithmetica* de Boèce, part de la relation qui existe entre "l'Un et l'autre," pour établir ensuite que, en Dieu, "l'Unité engendrée" ne peut être "inférieure ou supérieure à l'Unité qui l'engendre," mais doit lui être "en tout point égale"; cette Unité engendrée est donc "l'Egalité de l'Unité."[81] Dans la conclusion de son traité, Thierry annonce qu'il lui reste maintenant à expliquer comment la connexion (*connexio*) de l'égalité et de l'unité procède de l'une et de l'autre.[82] Le *De sex dierum principiis*, tel du moins qu'il est parvenu jusqu'à nous, ne nous a pas fourni l'explication ainsi promise. Mais les disciples de Thierry, s'inspirant selon toute vraisemblance de son enseignement, ne devaient pas tarder à nous la donner à sa place et à montrer qu'il faut admettre, entre l'Unité qui engendre et l'Egalité qui est engendrée, l'existence d'un troisième terme, relation d'amour qui n'est autre que le Saint-Esprit et à laquelle les maîtres chartrains, à la suite de Thierry lui-même, donneront le nom de *connexio*. Ce mot reparaît dans cinq commentaires chartrains du *De Trinitate* de Boèce qu'on a pris l'habitude de désigner par leur incipit (*Librum hunc, Quae sit, Aggreditur, Tria sunt, In titulo*) et qui s'étendent longuement sur la génération de l'*aequalitas* par l'*unitas* et sur la procession de la *connexio*.[83] On le trouvera, dans un contexte analogue, dans le commentaire du même *De Trinitate* que nous a laissé Clarembaud d'Arras,[84] puis

---

Boethius De Trinitate, Breslauer Studien zur historischen Theologie, 8, Breslau, 1926, p. 61*), cité et traduit par E. Jeauneau, ibid., p. 292, rend bien compte à cet égard des intentions de Thierry et des maîtres chartrains qui devaient reproduire sa démonstration: "Nous n'avons pas la prétention, écrit Clarembaud, de pouvoir atteindre pleinement à la connaissance de la génération (du Verbe) et de la procession (du Saint-Esprit), car nous croyons que cela est impossible à l'homme. Nous voulons seulement fournir aux apologistes catholiques le moyen de se défendre contre les Juifs et les hérétiques, lesquels s'en tiennent à l'unité divine avec une telle obstination, qu'ils rejettent absolument la trinité des personnes."

80 Thierry de Chartres, op. cit., 30, p. 194.

81 J'emprunte ces formules à l'exposé de E. Jeauneau, op. cit., pp. 290-291. Cf. Thierry de Chartres, op. cit., 36-41, p. 196-198.

82 Cf. Thierry de Chartres, op. cit., 47, p. 200.

83 Cf. *Librum hunc*, éd. W. Jansen, *Der Kommentar...*, p. 12*-14* ou éd. N. Haring, "Two Commentaries on Boethius (*De Trinitate* et *De hebdomadibus*) by Thierry de Chartres," *AHDLMA*, 27, 1960 (1961), 30-38, pp. 100-102; *Quae sit*, éd. Haring, "The Lectures of Thierry de Chartres on Boethius' *De Trinitate*," *AHDLMA*, 25, 1958 (1959), V, 16 et VII, 5-7, pp. 215 et 222-223; *Aggreditur populum*, éd. Haring, "A Commentary on Boethius' de Trinitate by Thierry of Chartres (Anonymus Berolinensis)," *AHDLMA*, 23, 1956 (1957), V, 17-21, pp. 319-321; *Tria sunt*, éd. Haring, "A short Treatise on the Trinity from the School of Thierry of Chartres," *Mediaeval Studies*, 18, (1956), 12, p. 131; *In titulo* (imprimé parmi les œuvres de Bède le Vénérable), PL, 95, 395 B. L'attribution à Thierry de Chartres des commentaires *Librum hunc, Quae sit* et *Aggreditur*, proposée par le R. P. Haring, a été contestée par L. Bataillon, *Rev. des sciences philosophiques et théologiques*, 43, (1959), pp. 692-693, et 46, (1962), p.508. Leur origine chartraine est néanmoins certaine.

dans un *De quinque septenis* imprimé parmi les œuvres de Jean de Salisbury.[85]

Un lien avait été certainement établi de bonne heure entre ces raisonnements mathématiques et la triade du *De doctrina christiana* dont ils retrouvaient l'inspiration et, pour une part au moins, le vocabulaire. Parmi les traités qu'on vient de signaler, cinq se réfèrent explicitement au texte d'Augustin[86] qu'ils modifient cependant en substituant *connexio* à *concordia*. Aucune tradition textuelle n'autorisait une telle substitution. Celle-ci pouvait cependant trouver une certaine justification dans le *De doctrina christiana* lui-même puisque, on s'en souvient, Augustin avait eu recours au participe passé *conexa* pour dire que l'*unitas,* l'*aequalitas* et la *concordia* étaient étroitement unies entre elles au sein de la Trinité. Est-ce à dire que la formule du *De doctrina christiana* soit à l'origine des spéculations chartraines ou même qu'elle ait été déjà présente à l'esprit de Thierry au moment où celui-ci entreprit de s'expliquer sur la génération de l'Egalité et la procession de la Connexion? Il est évidemment bien difficile de se prononcer à ce sujet. Pour ma part, cependant, je serais porté à croire que c'est seulement après avoir élaboré leurs démonstrations mathématiques et après avoir fixé leur vocabulaire que les chartrains ont remarqué et signalé à quel point la formule du *De doctrina christiana* s'accordait avec leurs propres raisonnements. S'il en était ainsi, on pourrait également penser que la *Glossa in epistolas Pauli* de Gilbert de la Porrée, élaborée en milieu chartrain, a pu contribuer à attirer l'attention de Thierry ou celle de ses disciples sur la triade du *De doctrina christiana*.

Cette dernière hypothèse pourrait trouver un appui dans la chronologie des traités qu'on vient de citer. Sans doute ne connaissons-nous pas exactement la date à laquelle chacun d'eux a été rédigé. Mais si nous rassemblons les indications fournies par W. Jansen et par le R. P. Haring, nous constatons que les premiers traités chartrains qui ont exposé les spéculations dont on vient de parler, mais sans citer la formule du *De doctrina christiana,* ont été rédigés vraisemblablement avant 1135,[87] et que ceux qui la citent datent approximativement des

84 Ed. W. Jansen, op. cit., pp. 61*-63*.

85 PL 199, 961 B.

86 A savoir les commentaires *Quae sit, Aggreditur, Tria sunt, In titulo,* et le traité *De quinque septenis.*

87 D'après W. Jansen, op. cit., pp.134-136, le *De sex dierum operibus* de Thierry de Chartres est certainement antérieur au commentaire *Librum hunc* dont N. Haring, "Two commentaries", *AHDLMA,* 27, 1960 (1961), p.75, nous dit qu'il a dû être composé aux alentours de l'année 1135, peut-être même plus tôt. Ces deux traités ne citent ni l'un ni l'autre le *De doctrina christiana.* La formule d'Augustin n'est pas citée non plus par le commentaire de Clarembaud d'Arras signalé ci-dessus (cf. n. 79 et 84), beaucoup plus tardif que les traités précédents puisqu'il a été composé après la mort de saint Bernard à laquelle il fait allusion, c'est-à-dire après août 1153 (cf. W. Jan-

années 1140-1150.[88] Puisque, comme on l'a vu, la *Glossa in epistolas Pauli* de Gilbert de la Porrée, a été rédigée avant 1140, peut-être même dès 1130, au temps où ce dernier enseignait à Chartres,[89] l'hypothèse selon laquelle la *Glose* de Gilbert ne serait pas étrangère à l'apparition, dans les commentaires chartrains, de la citation du *De doctrina christiana,* devient pour le moins vraisemblable. Les commentateurs de Boèce auraient substitué au mot *concordia* le mot *connexio,* étranger à Augustin et à la *Glossa* de Gilbert, parce qu'ils auraient eu recours à ce terme, aux résonances plus métaphysiques et moins psychologiques, avant même qu'ils eussent relu le *De doctrina christiana.* Quoi qu'il en soit, c'est sans doute sous l'influence des maîtres chartrains que le mot *connexio* a fait dans le vocabulaire théologique du XIIe siècle cette irruption que nous avons remarquée déjà dans l'*Expositio in epistolam ad Romanos* de Guillaume de Saint-Thierry et dans certains manuscrits des *Collectanea* de Pierre Lombard et dont nous retrouverons bientôt d'autres témoignages.

Les spéculations chartraines ne devaient plus trouver cependant que des échos assez rares ou au moins assourdis. Sans doute le vocabulaire du *De Trinitate* d'Achard de Saint-Victor, antérieur à l'année 1161, s'inspire-t-il encore de celui de Thierry de Chartres,[90] mais bien que cet ouvrage affirme que l'Esprit-Saint est la *connexio* du Père et du Fils,[91] il ne cite pas le texte du *De doctrina christiana.* Le mot *connexio* reparaît d'ailleurs à plusieurs reprises dans les écrits victorins, notamment dans une prose attribuée à Adam de Saint-Victor,[92] dans le *De tribus ap-*

sen, op. cit., p.11). Mais ce commentaire dépend directement du *De sex dierum operibus* de Thierry de Chartres.

88 D'après N. Haring, en effet, le commentaire *Quae sit* serait probablement plus tardif que le *Librum hunc* (cf. "The lectures...," *AHDLMA,* 25, 1958 (1959), pp. 121-122), mais serait de peu antérieur au commentaire *Aggreditur,* composé lui-même entre 1145 et 1150 (cf. ibid., et "A Commentary...", *AHDLMA,* 23, 1956 (1957), pp. 264-265). Quant au commentaire *Tria sunt,* il précéderait de peu le commentaire *In titulo,* composé après le concile de Reims, c'est-à-dire après 1148. Cf. "A short Treatise", *Med. Stud.,* 18 (1956), pp. 129 et 126.

89 Cf. ci-dessus, n. 38-39.

90 Cf. M.-T. d'Alverny, "Achard de Saint-Victor: De Trinitate — De unitate et pluralitate creaturum," *RTAM,* 21 (1954), p. 303. Ce traité a été certainement composé avant qu'Achard ne soit nommé évêque d'Avranches en 1161, probablement même avant qu'il ne soit élu abbé de Saint-Victor en 1155. Sur ce *De Trinitate,* voir aussi J. Châtillon, *Théologie, spiritualité et méthaphysique dans l'œuvre oratoire d'Achard de Saint-Victor (Etudes de philosophie médiévale,* LVIII) (Paris 1969), pp. 119-128.

91 Achard de Saint-Victor, *De Trinitate,* II, 3: "Ipse [Spiritus] siquidem Patris et Filii est connexio"; et *ibid.,* II, 4: "...ut nam ad Filium discretio, sic ad Spiritum sanctum...connexio." Je cite ici la transcription provisoire du *De Trinitate* d'Achard, établie d'après le ms. *Padoue, Anton. Scaff. V.89,* que Mlle M.-T. d'Alverny a eu l'obligeance de me communiquer et dont je la remercie vivement.

92 Cf. Prose XXII, str. 5, éd. L. Gautier, *Œuvres poétiques d'Adam de Saint-Victor,* I (Paris 1858), p.145 (PL 196, 1458), v. 25-30;
                      "Patri proles est aequalis,
                      Nec hoc tollit personalis,

propriatis de Richard sur lequel nous reviendrons plus loin,[93] et dans un sermon inédit pour la fête de la Purification du prieur Gauthier[94]; mais si ces derniers textes évoquent la triade augustinienne, celui de Gauthier de Saint-Victor est le seul qui fasse allusion à des spéculations sur les nombres susceptibles de rappeler celles des Chartrains. La triade *unitas, aequalitas, connexio*, reparaît en revanche, dans un contexte néo-platonicien dont les résonances chartraines ont été remarquées, dans les *Theologicae regulae* d'Alain de Lille.[95] On en reconnaît également les deux premiers termes (*unitas, aequalitas*) dans une curieuse définition de la vérité, inspirée à son tour des vues de Thierry de Chartres, due au Cistercien Hélinand de Froidmont.[96] Le souvenir de ces démonstrations mathématiques tendra néanmoins à s'estomper jusqu'à ce que Nicolas de Cues, au XVᵉ siècle, leur prête à nouveau attention.[97] On en redécouvrira seulement quelques échos dans un certain nombre d'écrits de la fin du XIIᵉ siècle et du début du XIIIᵉ que nous aurons bientôt l'occasion de signaler, mais dont les sources principales doivent être cherchées ailleurs.

              Amborum distinctio.
            Patri compar Filioque,
            Spiritalis ab utroque
            Procedit connexio."

93 Cf. ci-dessous, n. 119.

94 Ms. *Paris, B.N. lat. 14589*, f.28v-29r: "Per esse [homo] emulatur Patrem, per intelligere Filium, per uiuere Spiritum sanctum. Hec enim tria, etsi sint communia tribus personis, tamen singula ad singulas personas referuntur, ut potentia, sapientia, bonitas, unitas, equalitas, concordia. Unde in Patre unitas, in Filio equalitas, in Spiritu sancto unitatis equalitatis connexio... Unitas ad Patris personam respicit, quia cum ipsa sit origo omnium numerorum, non habet a quo sit... Equalitas autem ideo [Filius] dicitur, quia in ipso occurrit prima pluralitas et prima dualitas, uelut secunda unitas primaque distinctio uel discretio, quod totum nichil aliud est nisi ut ostendatur esse a solo Patre, ita quod est ei equalis... Concordia uel connexio dicitur amborum [Spiritus] ut ostendatur esse ab utroque, ita quod utrique consubstantialis." Sur les sermons de Gauthier, qui fut élu prieur de l'abbaye de Saint-Victor à la mort de Richard, en 1173, voir J. Châtillon, "Sermons et prédicateurs victorins de la seconde moitié du XIIᵉ siècle," *AHDLMA*, 32, 1965 (1966), pp. 40-44.

95 Cf. *Regula IV*, PL, 210, 625 AB, et E. Jeauneau, *Note sur l'Ecole de Chartres* (Chartres 1965), p. 6, n. 29 (extrait du *Bulletin de la Société archéologique d'Eure-et-Loir*, Mémoires, t. 23, 1964, qui reproduit une étude puliée dans *Studi mediaevali*, 3ᵉ sér., V, 2, 1964, pp. 821-865). La *Reg. IV* d'Alain de Lille renvoie à la *Reg. III* (ibid., 624 CD) qui cite elle-même un texte du Ps.-Hermes Trismegiste (*Liber XXIV philosophorum*, éd. C. Bäumker, *Abhandlungen aus dem Gebiete der Philosophie und ihrer Geschichte, Festgabe Hertling*, Fribourg en Br. 1913, p. 31): "Monas gignit monadem, et in se suum reflectit ardorem." Saint Thomas d'Aquin (*Sum. theol.*, I, q. 32, art. 1, ad 1) refusera plus tard toute signification trinitaire à cette *auctoritas*. Signalons qu'Alain de Lille se souvient également de la triade du *De doctrina christiana* dans un *Sermo de Trinitate* publié par Mˡˡᵉ M.-Th. d'Alverny, *Alain de Lille* (Etudes de philosophie médiévale, 52) (Paris 1965), p. 254.

96 Cf. *Sermo II in Natali Domini*, PL 212, 489 C - 490 D, analysé par M.-D. Chenu, "Une définition pythagoricienne de la vérité au moyen âge," *AHDLMA*, 28 (1961), pp. 7-13. Hélinand fut abbé de Froidmont au début du XIIIᵉ siècle.

97 Cf. E. Jeauneau, op. cit., p. 7, qui renvoie à Nicolas de Cues, *De docta ignorantia*, I,7-9, éd. E. Hoffmann et R. Klibansky (Leipzig 1932), pp. 14-19, et I,24, ibid., pp. 48-51, et au *De pace fidei*, ed. R. Klibansky et H. Bascour (Londres 1956), p. 21, 5-10, et p. 25, 1-6.

V. LES *SENTENTIAE* DE PIERRE LOMBARD
ET LE *DE TRIBUS APPROPRIATIS* DE RICHARD DE SAINT-VICTOR:
L'INFLUENCE D'ABÉLARD

La triade du *De doctrina christiana* va être en effet de plus en plus souvent citée dans les écrits théologiques de la seconde moitié du XII siècle. Les maîtres de ce temps considéreront le texte d'Augustin, même lorsqu'ils n'en connaîtront pas l'origine, comme une *auctoritas* qu'on ne peut négliger mais qui, en même temps, pose au théologien des problèmes d'interprétation délicats. Ils lui feront donc bien vite subir un traitement théologique nouveau. Jusqu'à présent, les commentateurs de l'*Epître aux Romains* s'étaient contenté de reproduire la formule et les brèves explications d'Augustin. Les maîtres chartrains, quant à eux, s'étaient longuement expliqué sur les rapports de l'unité, de l'égalité et de la *connexio*, mais lorsqu'ils en étaient arrivés au texte du *De doctrina christiana*, ils s'étaient borné à leur tour à affirmer, à la suite d'Augustin, que l'unité était "dans" le Père, l'égalité "dans" le Fils et la *connexio* "dans" le Saint-Esprit. Nul ne s'était interrogé vraiment sur la nature et la signification de cette présence "dans" chacune des trois personnes de l'unité, de l'égalité et de la *connexio*. Nul ne s'était encore hasardé, à propos des trois éléments de cette triade, à parler de "propriétés" ou même d'"attribution," moins encore d'"appropriation."

La problématique et le vocabulaire théologiques n'allaient pas tarder à subir une évolution. Celle-ci serait le fruit d'un rapprochement bientôt opéré entre les triades énumérées par la *Glossa* de Gilbert de la Porrée ou les *Collectanea* de Pierre Lombard, et la triade *potentia, sapientia, bonitas*, dont l'interprétation trinitaire avait provoqué, durant la première moitié du XII siècle, des conflits théologiques aigus.

L'histoire de ces controverses est bien connue. C'est Abélard qui avait été le premier, semble-t-il, à rapporter explicitement la puissance au Père, la sagesse au Fils et la bonté au Saint-Esprit, et à accumuler en faveur de sa thèse une masse assez considérable de témoignages bibliques et surtout patristiques, empruntés principalement à Augustin.[98] Bien qu'il prît soin de rappeler que ces trois attributs ap-

---

98 Cf. notamment *Theologia scholarium* (*Introd. ad theologiam*), I, 8-12, et II, 13-14, PL 178, 989-998 et 1069-1072; *Theologia christiana*, I, 4-7, 15-33, et IV, 86-91, éd. Buytaert, *Corp. christ., Cont. med.*, XI, pp. 73-75, 77-86, et 306-309; *Theologia summi boni*, éd. Ostlender, *BGPTM*, 35, 2-3 (Münster 1939), pp. 85-86; *Apologia*, éd. Ruf, dans P. Ruf — M. Grabmann, *Ein neu aufgefundenes Bruchstük der Apologia Abälards (Sitzungberichte der Bayerischen Akademie der Wissenschaften*, Philos.-hist. Abteilung, 1930, H.5), (Münich 1930), p. 22. Le problème de l'origine de cette triade s'était posé de bonne heure. Robert de Melun, défenseur d'Abélard (cf. ci-dessous, n. 107), déclare que l'attribution de ces trois noms aux trois personnes divines est professée par les

partenaient également aux trois personnes, l'auteur de la *Theologia
scholarium* n'en disait pas moins clairement que la puissance, la sagesse
et la bonté pouvaient être attribuées "spécialement" au Père, au Fils ou
à l'Esprit-Saint comme s'ils leur appartenaient "en propre."[99] L'interprétation de ces formules eût exigé qu'on s'interrogeât sur la
signification qu'elles revêtaient chez Abélard. Il n'est pas douteux que,
pour lui, les mots humains sont toujours incapables de rendre compte
d'une manière adéquate de la réalité divine et que par conséquent des
mots tels que "propre," "propriété" ou "attribution," en théologie
trinitaire, ne peuvent être entendus en leur sens original.[100] Toujours
est-il qu'un théologien aussi averti que Hugues de Saint-Victor con-
sentira lui aussi, non sans précautions, il est vrai, à rapporter la
puissance au Père, la sagesse au Fils et la bonté ou la bénignité au
Saint-Esprit.[101] Beaucoup d'autres maîtres de ce temps tiendront des

"saints docteurs" (*Sententiae*, I, p. III, c. 17, éd. R.M. Martin-R.M. Gallet, *Œuvres de Robert de
Melun*, t. III/2, Louvain 1952, p. 65, l. 8-9) et s'en prend un peu plus loin à ceux qui en contestent
l'origine augustinienne: on pourrait très facilement convaincre de mensonge, déclare-t-il,
quiconque nierait qu'elle a été enseignée par Augustin (ibid., c. 18, p. 66, l. 1-23). Mais lui-même
ne cite aucun texte à l'appui de cette affirmation catégorique, et son éditeur (op. cit., p. 65; en
note) se contente de fournir un certain nombre de références patristiques, dont quelques unes
avaient déjà été signalées par Abélard, et auxquelles il faut joindre celles que nous donne J.
Ribaillier dans Richard de Saint-Victor, *Opuscules théologiques (Textes philosophiques du moyen
âge*, 15 (Paris 1967), p. 185, n. 1. Mais si ces textes parlent parfois de la puissance du Père, de la
sagesse du Fils ou de la bonté de l'Esprit-Saint, aucun d'entre eux ne rapporte simultanément et
distinctement ces trois attributs aux trois personnes divines. Il est donc exagéré de dire, comme l'a
fait R. Baron, *Science et sagesse chez Hugues de Saint-Victor* (Paris 1957), p. 26, n. 114, que "cette
triade est tout à fait traditionnelle." Plus exact me paraît être le jugement de D. van den Eynde,
Essai sur la succession et la date des écrits de Hugues de Saint-Victor (Spicilegium Pont. Athen.
Antoniani*, 13), (Rome 1960), p. 68, n. 115, qui écrit: "Pour autant que je sache, la littérature
antérieure à Abélard ne connaît pas la triade spécifique *potentia — sapientia — -benignitas* et ne
l'applique pas, comme telle, aux trois personnes de la Trinité. Malgré l'importance qu'il lui attribue, le maître du Pallet n'a pas trouvé le moyen de l'introduire dans sa collection de textes
patristiques qui s'appelle *Sic et non*, pour la simple raison que les textes à propos font défaut."
   99   Traitant de ces diverses attributions, Abélard emploie fréquemment les deux adverbes
proprie et *specialiter* que ses adversaires lui reprocheront vivement. Voir p.ex. *Theologia
scholarium (Introd. ad theologiam)*, I, 10, PL 178, 991 CD, 992 AC, 994 AC, 995 A et D, etc.
   100   Sur les problèmes que pose à Abélard le langage humain lorsqu'on y recourt pour parler de
Dieu, et sur le sens du mot "propriété" en théologie, voir J. Jolivet, *Arts du langage et théologie
chez Abélard (Etudes de philosophie médiévale*, 57), (Paris 1969), pp. 296-300, et aussi S. Otto, *Die
Funktion des Bildbegriffes in der Theologie des 12. Jahrhunderts, BGPTM*, XI, 1, (Münster 1963),
pp. 73-77. S. Otto a bien montré notamment comment l'équivocité de la notion de propriété chez
Abélard ne permettait pas à ce dernier d'élaborer une théorie satisfaisante de l'appropriation.
   101   Cf. Hugues de Saint-Victor, *De sacramentis*, I, p. II, 6-8, et p. III, 26-27, PL 176, 208-210
et 227-230; *De amore sponsi et sponsae*, ibid., 989A; *De tribus diebus*, 1, 16, 21-23, ibid., 811-813,
823-824, 831-833; *In Hierarchiam coel. sancti Dionysii*, PL 175, 1062C, etc. Sur l'enseignement de
Hugues relatif à la triade *potentia, sapientia, benignitas*, voir J. Hofmeier, *Die Trinitätslehre des
Hugo von St. Viktor (Münchener theologische Studien*, II. Syst. Abt., 25), (Münich 1963), pp. 225-
227, et D. E. Luscombe, *The School of Peter Abelard (Cambridge Studies in Medieval Life &
Thought*, Ser. II, vol. 14), (Cambridge 1969), pp. 187-188. Il faut remarquer chez Hugues une
curieuse justification de l'utilisation trinitaire de cette triade. Ici-bas, en effet, les pères, plus âgés
que leurs fils, sont souvent aussi plus faibles; les fils, en revanche, sont moins expérimentés que

positions analogues, tout en les nuançant diversement. [102]

L'enseignement d'Abélard s'était pourtant heurté bien vite à l'opposition de maîtres tels que Gauthier de Mortagne[103] ou Gilbert de la Porrée, [104] et surtout à l'hostilité de Guillaume de Saint-Thierry[105] et de saint Bernard. [106] La thèse d'Abélard, précisée et nuancée, devait pourtant s'imposer grâce à l'intervention de théologiens parmi lesquels, outre Pierre Lombard et Richard de Saint-Victor que nous allons retrouver, il faut compter surtout Robert de Melun dont le plaidoyer devait jouer un rôle décisif. [107]

leurs pères; quant à l'esprit humain, il est souvent rempli d'orgueil et de suffisance. Il est donc fort utile de rapporter la puissance au Père, la sagesse au Fils et la bonté à l'Esprit-Saint, afin de prévenir les interprétations défavorables dont les noms de Père, de Fils et d'Esprit-Saint pourraient faire l'objet (cf. *De sacramentis*, I, p. II, 8, PL 176, 209-210). Cette justification singulière devait connaître un grand succès et être reprise par la plupart des théologiens qui traiteront par la suite de la triade en question. Saint Thomas d'Aquin s'en souviendra également et parlera à ce propos d'appropriation *per viam dissimilitudinis*, par opposition à l'appropriation *per viam similitudinis* (cf. *Sum. theol.*, I, q. 39, art. 7, c., et art. 8, c.). Il retrouvera ainsi, dans son vocabulaire, le thème dionysien qui semble bien être à l'origine de l'explication de Hugues. Ce dernier avait en effet longuement commenté dans son *In Hierarchiam coelestem sancti Dionysii* (PL 175, 960-990) le chapitre de la *Hiérarchie céleste* (II, PG 3, 163-165) dans lequel le Ps.-Denys traite des symboles sembables et des symboles dissemblables et de la supériorité de ceux-ci sur ceux-là. Cf. R. Roques, *Connaissance de Dieu et théologie symbolique d'après l'In Hierarchiam coelestem sancti Dionysii de Hugues de S.-V.*, dans *Recherches de Philosophie*, III-IV (Paris 1958), pp. 232-245, et S. Otto, op. cit., pp. 133-134.

102   Voir notamment, et parmi beaucoup d'autres, Guillaume de Conches, *Philosophia mundi*, I, 5, PL 172, 44 D — 45 A; *Summa sententiarum*, I, 10, PL 176, 56 D — 58 D; *Sententiae divinitatis*, éd. B. Geyer, *BGPTM*, VII, 2-3 (Münster 1909), p. 170*; maître Herman, *Sententiae*, 6-7, PL 178, 1702-1703; *Sententiae Florianenses*, 8-9, éd. H. Ostlender, dans *Florilegium patristicum*, 19 (Bonn 1929), p. 4; Roland Bandinelli, *Sententiae*, éd. Gietl (Fribourg-en-Br. 1891), pp. 21-22; maître Omnebene, cité par Gietl, ibid., p. 21; *Sententiae Parisienses*, éd. A. Landgraf, *Ecrits théologiques de l'école d'Abélard* (Louvain 1934), pp. 7-9; *Ysagoge in theologiam*, 3, éd. A. Landgraf, ibid., pp. 241-242, 257, 263; *Sententiae divinae paginae*, éd. F. Bliemetzrieder, *BGPTM*, 18, 2-3 (Münster 1919), p. 7; etc.

103   *De Trinitate*, 8 et 13, PL 209, 583-584 et 588-590.

104   *In Boecii De Trinitate*, I, 2, 16, et II, 1, 30, éd. N. Haring, *The Commentaries on Boethius by Gilbert of Poitiers* (Pont. Instit. of Med. Stud., Studies and Texts, 13), (Toronto 1966), pp. 61 et 169. Voir aussi, parmi les disciples de Gilbert, Clarembaud d'Arras, *In Boethium De Trinitate*, éd. W. Jansen, op. cit., pp. 48*-49*.

105   *Disputatio adversus Abaelardum*, 2, PL 180, 250 A - 251 C; *De erroribus Guillelmi a Conchis*, ibid., 333-334; *Epist. ad Bernardum*, 3, PL 182, 532 B. Voir aussi la *Disputatio adversus dogmata Petri Abaelardi*, I, égarée parmi les œuvres de Guillaume (PL 180, 285-298), mais qui n'est pas de lui et pourrait être de Thomas de Morigny d'après M.-B. Carra de Vaux Saint-Cyr, "Disputatio catholicorum patrum adversus dogmata Petri Abaelardi," dans *Rev. des Sciences philos. et théol.*, 47 (1963), pp. 205-220. On remarquera cependant que dans son *Aenigma fidei*, 56-60, éd. M.-M. Davy, *Guillaume de S.-T.: Deux traités sur la foi* (Paris 1959), pp. 140-145 (PL 180, 421-432), Guillaume avait admis, à certaines conditions et non sans précautions, la légitimité de l'attribution de la puissance au Père, de la sagesse au Fils et de la bonté au Saint-Esprit.

106   Voir surtout *Epist. CXC*, ou *Tractatus de erroribus Abaelardi*, 1, 3, PL 182, 1056 A, 1058 D-1059 A, et les n°⁵ 1 et 13 des *Capitula Abaelardi* qui devaient être condamnés en 1140 au Concile de Sens et dont une nouvelle édition critique vient d'être publiée par Dom J. Leclercq, "Les formes successives de la lettre-traité de saint Bernard contre Abélard," *Rev. bénédictine*, 78 (1968), pp. 103-104. On trouvera d'abondantes indications sur l'histoire de cette controverse dans D. E. Luscombe, op. cit., pp. 115-119.

107   Cf. Robert de Melun, *Sententiae*, I, p. III, c. 17-29, éd. R. M. Martin - R. M. Gallet,

Ces controverses avaient été ainsi à l'origine d'un effort d'élaboration doctrinale dont les résultats n'allaient pas tarder à se manifester. Les théologiens allaient être amenés à étudier dans toute leur ampleur les problèmes posés par la distinction des personnes et à examiner avec plus d'attention tous les "noms" susceptibles d'être attribués à chacune d'entre elles. Avant même que Robert de Melun n'intervienne dans les conflits dont on vient de rappeler brièvement les principales étapes, Pierre Lombard s'était déjà occupé de ces questions dans les longs développements que ses *Sententiae* (I, d.26-36) consacrent à la distinction des personnes, à leurs propriétés et aux problèmes posés par leur attribution éventuelle à l'une ou l'autre des trois personnes. Dans ces pages, le Lombard s'interroge aussi bien sur la signification des noms personnels qui viennent de l'Ecriture que sur celle de plusieurs triades d'origine patristique. Ainsi examine-t-il d'abord la triade d'Hilaire de Poitiers (*aeternitas, species, usus*) qu'il avait négligée dans ses *Collectanea* et qu'il déclare ici obscure et équivoque,[108] puis celle du *De doctrina christiana* d'Augustin;[109] il traitera plus loin, et en des termes favorables empruntés à Hugues de Saint-Victor, de celle qu'Abélard avait introduite dans la théologie (*potentia, sapientia, bonitas*);[110] plus loin encore il s'occupera de celle de l'*Epître aux Romains*.[111] Tout au long de ces exposés, Pierre Lombard recourt fréquemment aux notions de "propriété" et d'attribution. A propos de la triade *unitas, aequalitas, concordia*, notamment, il se pose la question de savoir pourquoi on peut ainsi "attribuer" l'unité au Père et l'égalité au Fils.[112] Sa réponse, qui ne doit rien à l'enseignement chartrain,[113] ne fait que reprendre, à vrai dire, ce que Gilbert de la Porrée avait déjà laissé entendre. Le Lombard se borne à expliquer que l'unité est attribuée (*attribuitur*) au Père parce que celui-ci ne procède de nul autre et qu'il n'est donc pas *ab alio*, étant

Œuvres de Robert de Melun, t. III/2 (Louvain 1952), pp. 65-90, et aussi *Questiones [theologice] de epistolis Pauli*, ed. cit., t. II (Louvain 1938), pp. 27-28. Sur le rôle de Robert de Melun dans cette affaire et sa dépendance à l'égard d'Abélard, voir R. M. Martin, "Pro Petro Abaelardo," *Rev. des sciences philos. et théol.*, 12 (1923), pp. 308-333; U. Horst, "Beiträge zum Einfluss Abaelards auf Robert von Melun," *RTAM*, 26 (1959), pp. 314-333; D. E. Luscombe, op. cit., pp. 286-290.

108   Cf. Pierre Lombard, *Sententiae*, I, d. 31, c. 2, éd. Quaracchi, pp. 192-195.

109   Ibid., c. 2-6, ed. cit., pp. 195-199. Pierre Lombard reproduit ici (c. 2, p. 195) le texte du *De doctrina christiana* qu'il avait cité auparavant dans ses *Collectanea* (cf. ci-dessus, n. 67). Il en néglige cependant les premières lignes (1. 1-7); il intervertit d'autre part l'ordre des phrases et cite les lignes 15-18 avant les lignes 7-15, de façon à mettre en évidence la phrase concernant la triade *unitas, aequalitas, concordia*.

110   Ibid., d. 34, c. 3-4, pp. 217-218.

111   Ibid., d. 36, c. 3-5, pp. 227-229.

112   Ibid., d. 31, c. 3, p. 196: "*Quare Patri attribuitur unitas*: Sed plurimos movet, quod Patri attribuit [Augustinus] unitatem, Filio aequalitatem ... Cur ergo Patri attribuitur unitas et Filio aequalitas?"

113   Comme l'avait déjà remarqué L. Ott, *Untersuchungen*, pp. 571-572.

bien entendu que le Fils et l'Esprit-Saint sont un avec le Père.[114] Pour le reste, il en revient au vocabulaire d'Augustin: l'égalité est "dans" le Fils parce que celui-ci ne peut être que l'égal du Père qui l'a engendré et l'égal de l'Esprit-Saint qui procède des deux premières personnes[115]; et la *concordia*, appelée aussi *connexio*, est "dans" l'Esprit-Saint parce que celui-ci, qui est amour, unit à la fois le Père au Fils et le Fils au Père, et que par lui toutes choses sont harmonieusement unies (*per eum omnia connexa*).[116]

L'intérêt de ces développements ne réside pas dans la nature des réponses, dépourvues d'originalité, que Pierre Lombard apporte aux questions posées, mais dans le recours à la notion d'attribution qu'on y remarque, et dans le rapprochement, encore assez vague et lointain, établi entre les triades anciennes et celle d'Abélard. On s'achemine ainsi vers une théologie des appropriations, qu'avaient ébauchée les théologiens à l'occasion des controverses relatives à la triade *potentia, sapientia, bonitas*, et qui va tendre à prendre en considération la série complète des triades patristiques dont les commentateurs de l'*Epître aux Romains* avaient entrepris de dresser l'inventaire.

C'est le témoignage d'une évolution analogue, mais plus avancée encore parce que plus tardive, que nous trouvons dans l'opuscule de Richard de Saint-Victor auquel on devait donner par la suite le titre, quelque peu trompeur ou au moins anachronique, de *De tribus appropriatis*.[117] Ce court traité a pour objet de répondre aux questions d'un certain Bernard, dont l'identité n'a jamais pu être établie,[118] qui désirait connaître le sentiment du théologien victorin sur l'interprétation trinitaire des triades *unitas, aequalitas, concordia*, et *potentia, sapientia, bonitas*. Le rapprochement opéré entre ces deux triades

---

114 Loc. cit.

115 Ibid., c. 5, pp. 198-199.

116 Ibid., c. 6, p. 199: "*Quare in Spiritu sancto dicitur esse virtus, concordia vel connexio.*" L'interprétation que Pierre Lombard donne de la triade du *De doctrina christiana* dans ses *Sententiae* a été exposée naguère par L. Ott, op. cit., pp. 571-572; elle a été évoquée brièvement par J. Schneider, *Die Lehre von Dreieinigen Gott in der Schule des Petrus Lombardus (Münchener theologische Studien*, II. Syst. Abt., 22), (München 1961), p. 112.

117 Ed. J. Ribaillier, dans Richard de Saint-Victor, *Opuscules théologiques (Textes philosophiques du moyen âge*, 15), (Paris 1967), pp. 182-187. "Ce titre n'est pas primitif," écrit le R.P. Ribaillier dans son introduction (op. cit., p. 174). Le verbe *appropriare* et le substantif *appropriatio* sont d'ailleurs étrangers au vocabulaire de cet opuscule composé sans doute aux alentours de l'année 1160 (ibid., p. 174). La *Table idéologique des principaux mots latins* de ces *Opuscules théologiques* (ibid., pp. 355-375) nous révèle que le verbe *appropriare* n'apparaît que dans le court traité intitulé *De spiritu blashemiae* (VI, ed. cit., p. 129), lequel, selon toute vraisemblance, est postérieur au *De tribus appropriatis* (cf. J. Ribaillier, ibid., pp. 114-115).

118 On a longtemps identifié ce correspondant de Richard avec saint Bernard, mais L. Ott, op. cit., pp. 567-568, et J. Ribaillier, op. cit., pp. 18-21, ont montré que cette hypothèse ne résistait pas à l'examen. D'après le R. P. Ribaillier (ibid., p. 21), cet énigmatique Bernard serait un chanoine régulier, peut-être un ancien disciple de Richard.

par Bernard est à lui seul déjà significatif. L'exposé de Richard l'est davantage encore. Dans sa réponse, ce dernier recourt en effet parfois à la notion de propriété, plus souvent à celle d'attribution, aussi bien d'ailleurs pour la première triade que pour la seconde, mais avec plus d'insistance encore que Pierre Lombard, notamment en ce qui concerne la *concordia*, appelée aussi, à plusieurs reprises, *connexio*.[119] Il était donc admis, dès maintenant, que les deux triades posaient des problèmes analogues, sinon même identiques. Comme l'a d'ailleurs remarqué le R. P. Ribaillier dans la suggestive étude qu'il a consacrée à l'opuscule en question,[120] celui-ci a dû être rédigé à une époque où les controverses relatives à l'interprétation trinitaire de la triade *potentia, sapientia, bonitas*, s'étaient apaisées. La voie était désormais ouverte. Les théologiens allaient pouvoir s'enquérir librement des conditions dans lesquelles les attributs ou les noms essentiels de la divinité pouvaient être rapportés à l'une ou l'autre des trois personnes.

VI. LES THÉOLOGIENS PORRÉTAINS.

Avec la *Glossa in epistolas Pauli* de Gilbert de la Porrée, les *Collectanea* et les *Sententiae* de Pierre Lombard, et aussi, jusqu'à un certain point, les commentaires sur Boèce de Thierry de Chartres et de ses disciples, nous disposons des sources principales dont allaient désormais s'inspirer, directement ou indirectement, tous les théologiens qui citeraient et commenteraient la triade du *De doctrina christiana*.

C'est d'abord dans une série d'ouvrages qui ont largement subi l'influence de Gilbert de la Porrée et qui ont contribué directement à l'élaboration définitive du traité des appropriations trinitaires que nous allons la retrouver. Si nous nous en tenons aux indications chronologiques généralement admises, il faut citer ici en premier lieu la *Summa Quoniam homines* d'Alain de Lille, composée, nous dit son éditeur, "entre 1155 et 1165, très probablement vers 1160."[121] Cet ouvrage a pour premier mérite de présenter des divisions d'une remarquable clarté. Le livre I, qui traite de la *théologia apothetica* ou *supercelestis*, par opposition à la *theologia ypothetica* ou *subcelestis* qui fait l'objet du livre II, est tout entier consacré à la Trinité. Il est lui-même divisé en deux parties: la première traite de l'unité de l'essence divine, la seconde de la pluralité des personnes. Cette seconde partie, subdivisée à son tour en six *tractatus*, s'occupe successivement des

---

119 Cf. op. cit., pp. 184-185.
120 Ibid., pp. 172-174.
121 Cf. P. Glorieux, "La Somme 'Quoniam homines' d'Alain de Lille," *AHDLMA*, 20, 1953 (1954), p. 116.

notions d'essence et de personne (*tr.I*), puis des "noms essentiels" de la divinité (*tr.II*), avant d'en arriver aux "noms personnels." A propos de ceux-ci, Alain de Lille introduit une distinction nouvelle entre les *nomina quae appropriantur nomine et re* ou *nomine et significatione*, c'est-à-dire les noms relatifs tels que Père, Fils et Saint-Esprit (*tr.III*), et les *nomina quae appropriantur nomine et non re:*[122] c'est à cette dernière catégorie qu'appartiennent les noms personnels énumérés par les trois triades qui font l'objet des trois derniers *tractatus:*

1° *Potentia, sapientia, bonitas* (tr. IV. éd. Glorieux, 80-113, p. 226-248);

2° *Unitas, aequalitas, communitas* (tr. V. ibid., 114-121, p. 248-255);

3° *Aeternitas, species, usus* (tr. VI, ibid., 122-131, p. 255-269).

Ce qui frappe tout d'abord ici, c'est l'effort accompli par la *Summa Quoniam homines* pour regrouper et mettre en quelque sorte en parallèle les trois triades venues d'Abélard, du *De doctrina christiana* d'Augustin et du *De Trinitate* d'Hilaire. Les *Sententiae* de Pierre Lombard les avait sans doute déjà étudiées, mais d'une manière qui n'avait rien de systématique et qui ne semblait pas se soucier de leur faire subir un traitement théologique identique, ni même de les comparer les unes aux autres. Mais il faut remarquer surtout qu'Alain de Lille recourt maintenant à un vocabulaire nouveau. Il ne parle plus de "propriétés," mais de "noms personnels," ce qui lui permet d'éviter beaucoup plus aisément les équivoques que d'autres, avant lui, avaient eu tant de peine à surmonter. Sa principale innovation, cependant, consiste à introduire dans son exposé le verbe *appropriare* qui revient constamment sous sa plume, et dont pourtant ses prédécesseurs, semble-t-il, n'avaient jamais fait usage en théologie trinitaire. Sans doute ne peut-on affirmer que l'auteur de la *Summa Quoniam homines* soit vraiment le créateur de ce terme.[123] On ne peut douter en revanche qu'il ait contribué à lui donner le sens nouveau qu'il allait désormais revêtir.

---

122 Ed. P. Glorieux, op. cit., tract III, 62, p. 210: "Sciendum igitur quod nominum que attribuuntur personis, alia appropriantur personis nomine et significatione, alia nomine tantum"; 80, p. 226: "Pertractatis hiis que de nominibus personalibus dicenda erant que personis appropriantur nomine et re, agendum est de illis que appropriantur nomine et non re."

123 Grâce à l'obligeance de M. Pierre Michaud-Quantin, j'ai pu consulter le fichier du *Glossaire du latin philosophique médiéval* de la Sorbonne. Je n'y ai trouvé aucun texte relatif aux mots *appropriare* ou *appropriatio*, entendus au sens qui nous intéresse ici, antérieur à un commentaire de la *Glossa in epistolas Pauli* de Gilbert de la Porrée (ms. *Paris, B. N. lat. 686*, f. 39v et 54v, cité par A. Landgraf, *Dogmengeschichte der Frühscholastik*, IV/1, Ratisbonne 1955, p. 30, n. 7 et p. 31, n. 9). Mais ce commentaire, qui date de la fin du XIIe siècle et sur lequel nous reviendrons plus loin, dépend lui-même, sinon d'Alain de Lille, du moins de Simon de Tournai qui dépend d'Alain de Lille (cf. ci-dessous, n. 143-144). Le *Glossaire* ayant déjà inventorié le vocabulaire philosophique et théologique d'un grand nombre d'ouvrages du XIIe siècle, et le *De*

Pour le reste, il faut reconnaître qu'Alain de Lille est encore largement tributaire des théologiens qui l'avaient précédé. En ce qui concerne la triade *potentia, sapientia, bonitas*, notamment, il établit entre les deux manières opposées dont on peut "approprier" ces noms aux trois personnes une distinction qui deviendra, chez saint Thomas d'Aquin, la distinction entre appropriation par ressemblance et appropriation par dissemblance, mais dont l'origine doit être cherchée chez Hugues de Saint-Victor.[124] Peut-être faut-il également considérer comme un lointain écho des spéculations chartraines les brèves indications relatives aux notions d'unité, d'égalité et de pluralité que nous donne la *Summa Quoniam homines* à propos de la triade *unitas, aequalitas, communitas*.[125] Une telle dépendance ne saurait nous surprendre de la part de l'auteur des *Theologicae regulae*. Il faut reconnaître cependant qu'elle demeure ici incertaine et peu visible.

Mais un autre ouvrage d'inspiration porrétaine, rédigé sans doute peu de temps après la *Summa Quoniam homines* qu'il a certainement connue et utilisée, doit retenir notre attention. Il s'agit des *Sententiae* ou *Institutiones in sacram paginam* de Simon de Tournai, qui ont dû être composées entre 1160 et 1165 et dont M. Schmaus a publié naguère tout ce qui se rapporte à la théologie trinitaire.[126] On y remarque en effet un long exposé relatif à la notion de personne et aux appropriations que Simon devait d'ailleurs reproduire dans son *Expositio symboli Athanasii*.[127] L'auteur des *Institutiones* ne recourt plus seulement au verbe *appropriare* mais aussi au substantif *appropriatio*. Il reprend à son compte les distinctions proposées précédemment par Alain de Lille, notamment celle des deux modes opposés d'appropriation qui venait de Hugues de Saint-Victor,[128] et surtout la distinction entre *appropriatio*

---

spiritu blasphemiae de Richard de Saint-Victor où nous avons remarqué la présence du mot *appropriare* (cf. ci-dessus, n. 117) étant lui-même, selon toute vraisemblance, postérieur à la *Summa Quoniam homines*, il y a tout lieu de penser qu'Alain de Lille est un des premiers, sinon même le premier, à avoir introduit ce mot dans la langue théologique.

124   *Summa Quoniam homines,* ed. cit., tr. IV, 80, pp. 226-227. Cf. ci-dessus, n. 101.

125   Ed. cit., tr. V, 114, p. 248.

126   Cf. M. Schmaus, "Die Texte der Trinitätslehre in den Sententiae des Simon von Tournai," *RTAM*, 4 (1932), pp. 59-72, 187-198, 294-307. D'après P. Glorieux, op. cit., p. 116, qui renvoie à O. Lottin, "Alain de Lille, une des sources des Disputationes de Simon de Tournai," *RTAM*, 17 (1950), pp. 175-186, "on ne peut douter...que...Simon de Tournai se soit inspiré d'Alain et de sa Somme dans ses *Disputationes* et déjà même dans ses *Institutiones*. D'autre part, ajoute P. Glorieux, ces *Institutiones*, "antérieures à Pierre de Poitiers, ont utilisé, comme l'a démontré le P. van den Eynde ("Deux sources de la Somme théologique de Simon de Tournai," *Antonianum*, 24, 1949, pp. 19-42), deux écrits des environs de 1160, à savoir la Glose de Rufin sur le Décret de Gratien et le *Speculum ecclesiae*. Il faut donc les dater de 1160-1165."

127   Cet ouvrage a été publié d'après un manuscrit du Mont-Cassin dans la *Bibliotheca Casinensis*, t. IV (Mont-Cassin 1880), pp. 322-346 de la seconde partie du volume (*Florilegium patristicum*). Les développements relatifs à la notion de personne et aux appropriations trinitaires, empruntés aux *Institutiones*, occupent, dans cette édition, les pp. 327-332.

128   Cf. *Institutiones*, éd. M. Schmaus, loc. cit., 6, pp. 63-64, et ci-dessus, n. 124 et 101.

nominum et rerum et *appropriatio nominum et non rerum.*[129] C'est de ce second type d'appropriation que relèvent les "noms" énumérés par une série de triades, beaucoup plus nombreuses que celles dont avait traité la *Summa Quoniam homines*, et que Simon de Tournai examine tour à tour, dans l'ordre suivant:

1° *Potentia, sapientia, bonitas* (éd. Schmaus, 5, p. 63-64);
2° *Operatio, dispositio, conservatio* (ibid., 6, p. 65);
3° *Auctoritas, nativitas, communitas* (ibid., 7, p. 65);
4° *Unitas, aequalitas, concordia* (ibid., 8, p. 66-67);
5° *Unitas, species, ordo* (ibid., 9, p. 67);
6° *Summa origo, perfectissima pulchritudo, beatissima delectatio* (ibid., 9, p. 67-68);
7° *Aeternitas, species, usus* (ibid., 9, p. 67-68);
8° *Ex quo, per quem, in quo* (ibid., 10, p. 68).

Ce schéma, dans ses grandes lignes, coïncide d'une manière frappante avec celui que nous avions remarqué dans la *Glossa in epistolas Pauli* de Gilbert de la Porrée. On ne peut douter qu'il en dépende. Simon de Tournai, il est vrai, y a ajouté la triade *potentia, sapientia, bonitas* (n°1) que Gilbert avait contestée ailleurs;[130] mais cette triade, qu'Alain de Lille avait commentée, avait acquis maintenant droit de cité en théologie depuis les interventions de Pierre Lombard et de Robert de Melun. Il y ajoute également une triade nouvelle, *operatio, dispositio, conservatio* (n°2), mais celle-ci n'a d'autre objet que d'approprier aux trois personnes divines trois opérations *ad extra* mises en relation avec les trois attributs opératifs de puissance, de sagesse et de bonté. En revanche, Simon de Tournai néglige la triade *principium, forma, gratia*, qui venait du *De uera religione* d'Augustin, mais cette omission est dépourvue de signification car Gilbert n'avait mentionné cette triade qu'en passant et sans la commenter. La dépendance de Simon de Tournai à l'égard de la *Glossa* de Gilbert de la Porrée apparaît d'ailleurs avec évidence si l'on met en parallèle les textes où ces deux théologiens énumèrent les triades 5-7 qu'on vient de signaler. L'exposé de Gilbert était fait presque uniquement de phrases ou de lambeaux de phrases empruntés au *De doctrina christiana* (I,5,5) et au *De Trinitate* (VI,10,11-12) d'Augustin, mais disposés suivant un ordre très différent de celui où ils se présentaient dans ces deux ouvrages de l'évêque d'Hippone. Simon de Tournai reproduit ces brefs extraits dans l'ordre qu'avait adopté Gilbert, en y ajoutant simplement quelques com-

129 Ibid., 4, 1. 1-3, p. 63; 5, 1. 1, p. 63; 7, 1. 1, p. 65.
130 Cf. ci-dessus, n. 104.

mentaires; une confrontation des textes montre bien d'autre part qu'il ne s'est pas reporté à Augustin, mais qu'il s'est contenté de suivre de très près la *Glossa* de son illustre prédécesseur.[131] Avec Simon de Tournai, en tout cas, le dossier patristique relatif aux appropriations trinitaires est maintenant constitué. Nous en retrouverons les éléments chez la plupart des théologiens qui viendront par la suite. La triade *unitas, aequalitas, concordia*, que Simon attribue d'ailleurs à Hilaire[132] et dont il nous donne une interprétation où il faut peut-être encore reconnaître un lointain écho de l'enseignement chartrain,[133] y occupe une place qu'elle ne perdra plus.

Des ces *Institutiones* de Simon de Tournai, et donc aussi de son *Expositio symboli Athanasii*, il faut rapprocher une *Glossa* anonyme sur les *Sententiae* de Pierre Lombard, attribuée longtemps, mais à tort, à Pierre de Poitiers,[134] et dont la rédaction est antérieure à l'année 1175.[135] On y retrouve une version courte de l'exposé consacré à la

---

131   Voici les deux passages de Simon de Tournai (*Institutiones*, ed. cit., 9, 1. 1-11 et 28-32, pp. 67-68), relatifs aux triades 5-7. On pourra les comparer aux paragraphes [4]-[6] du commentaire de *Rom.*, XI, 36, de la *Glossa* de Gilbert de la Porrée reproduit plus haut; les mots imprimés en italiques correspondent aux emprunts de Simon de Tournai à la *Glossa* dont tous les éléments reparaissent ici: "*Huius* autem *Trinitatis in creatura* quoquomodo *apparet vestigium. Nam omnia quae arte divina facta sunt, et unitatem quandam et speciem et ordinem in se ostendunt. Nam quidquid est, et unum aliquid est, sicut sunt* corpora vel spiritus, *et specie* formantur, *ut corpora figuris et qualitatibus et animae a[r]tibus, et* petunt *vel* tenent *ordinem, ut corpora ponderibus, ut quae* minus sunt affinia terrae, minus sunt gravia et econverso, *et collocationibus*, ut quanto sunt graviora, tanto deprimantur inferius, et quanto leviora, tanto extollantur altius, *et animae delectationibus*. Delectantur enim in eo, ut exemplar coelestis, ad quod creatae sunt, ordinis imitentur. *Quorum omnium*, scilicet unitatis, speciei et ordinis, *in Trinitate est summa origo, perfectissima pulchritudo et beatissima delectatio... Nam aeternitas in Patre*, et ei nomine, non re appropriatur aeternitas sicut supra auctoritas. Species autem creaturarum ad perfectissimam pulchritudinem Filium. *Species* enim *in imagine*. Ordo verso eorum refertur ad beatissimam delectationem Spiritus sanctum. *Usus* enim *in munere*."
132   Cf. ed. cit., 8, 1. 10, p. 66: "In Patre ergo ab Hilario dicitur esse unitas, in Filio vero aequalitas." De même, ibid., 1. 14: "... ideo adiectum est ab Hilario: in filio vero aequalitas."
133   Ibid., 1, 2-4, 6-7, 10-12. Les allusions aux propriétés des nombres sont en réalité moins apparentes encore chez Simon de Tournai que chez Alain de Lille. Les *Institutiones* se bornent à rappeler que l'unité est le principe de tous les nombres, et à dire quelques mots des notions d'unité, d'altérité et d'égalité.
134   C'est Casimir Oudin, *Comment. de scriptoribus ecclesiasticis* (Leipzig 1722), II, 1501, qui avait fait don de cette *Glossa* à Pierre de Poitiers. Cette attribution, déjà contestée par O. Lottin, *RTAM*, 2 (1930), pp. 81-82, a été rejectée par P. S. Moore, *The Works of Peter of Poitiers* (*Publications in Mediaeval Studies*, I), (Notre Dame 1936), pp. 153-162.
135   La date de cette *Glossa* a fait l'objet de nombreuses recherches. P. S. Moore, op. cit., pp. 151-153, a établi qu'elle était antérieure aux *Sententiae* de Pierre de Poitiers, composées vers 1175. O. Lottin, "Le premier commentaire connu des Sentences de Pierre Lombard," *RTAM*, 11 (1939), pp. 64-71, a montré à son tour qu'elle devait être également antérieure au livre VI des *Allegoriae super Novum Testamentum* (PL 175, 879-904) qu'il croit pouvoir attribuer à Richard de Saint-Victor en se référant à une étude P. S. Moore, "The Authorship of the Allegoriae super Vetus et Novum Testamentum," *New Scholasticism*, 9 (1935), pp. 209-225; ainsi la *Glossa* aurait-elle été composée avant 1173, date de la mort de Richard. C'est à partir de ces observations que A. Landgraf, *Introducción a la historia de la literatura teológica de la escolástica incipiente* (Barcelone

notion de personne et aux appropriations trinitaires par Simon de Tournai. Ce texte, publié récemment par M. Hödl,[136] reproduit de longs passages des *Institutiones*, le plus souvent presque mot pour mot. On y retrouve donc le même vocabulaire, les mêmes distinctions, les mêmes triades, à l'exception cependant de la triade *ex quo, per quem, in quo*, qui, chez Simon de Tournai, venait en dernière position. On peut évidemment s'interroger sur le sens de la relation qui unit l'exposé de la *Glossa* du Pseudo-Pierre de Poitiers à celui de Simon de Tournai. Comme il arrive toujours en pareil cas, il est difficile de savoir si c'est la version courte qui recopie la version longue en l'abrégeant, ou si c'est la version longue qui développe et amplifie une version courte plus ancienne. C'est à cette seconde explication que se rallie M. Hödl. Selon lui, le texte de la *Glossa* correspondrait à une première rédaction que Simon de Tournai aurait ensuite reprise, développée et améliorée dans ses *Institutiones* et dans son *Expositio symboli Athanasii*.[137] Quoi qu'on pense de la solution apportée ainsi à un problème d'histoire littéraire

---

1956), p. 172, a pu avancer que la *Glossa* du Pseudo-Pierre de Poitiers aurait été rédigée, au moins partiellement, avant 1173, probablement même vers 1160-1165. Mais si les livres I-IV des *Allegoriae super Novum Testamentum* font bien partie du *Liber exceptionum* de Richard et sont donc son œuvre comme l'avait montré P. S. Moore, il n'en va pas de même des livres V-VII, et donc aussi du livre VI, qui doivent en être séparés et ne peuvent donc être attribués à Richard, comme l'avaient d'ailleurs remarqué L. Ott (*Untersuchungen zur Briefliteratur der Frühscholastik*, BGPTM, 34, 1936, p. 652) et A. Landgraf lui-même ("Familienbildung bei Paulinenkommentaren des 12. Jahrhunderts," *Biblica*, 13, 1932, pp. 170 ss.). L. Hödl, *Von der Wirklichkeit und Wirksamkeit des dreieinigen Gottes nach der appropriativen Trinitätstheologie des 12. Jahrhunderts* (Münich 1965), p. 19, pour sa part, situe la composition de la *Glossa* du Pseudo-Pierre de Poitiers entre 1160 et 1170. Mais son opinion est fondée sur cette conviction que le texte trinitaire inséré dans la *Glossa* et qu'il publie dans son étude (cf. ci-dessous, n. 136) est antérieur aux *Institutiones* de Simon de Tournai, ce qui ne me semble pas absolument certain (cf. ci-dessous, n. 137). Il faut donc s'en tenir, jusqu'à plus ample informé, au *terminus ad quem* indiqué par P. S. Moore: 1175.

136 Op. cit., pp. 19-22.

137 Ibid., pp. 19-22. Les arguments que présente M. Hödl en faveur de sa thèse ne manquent pas de solidité. Sa démonstration ne m'a pourtant pas entièrement convaincu, et cela pour deux raisons: 1° L'exposé des *Institutiones* de Simon de Tournai (éd. Schmaus, pp. 60-68) me semble s'intégrer d'une façon tout à fait cohérente dans son ouvrage; en revanche, la version abrégée fait un peu figure de hors d'œuvre dans la *Glossa* du Pseudo-Pierre de Poitiers où elle apparaît (au moins dans le ms. *Paris, B. N. lat. 14423*, f. 49ra-50ra, que j'ai pu examiner) à la suite des gloses relatives à *Sent.*, I, d. 8, avec lesquelles elle n'a apparemment rien à voir. 2° Si la version longue, telle qu'on la trouve dans les *Institutiones* ou dans l'*Expositio symboli Athanasii* de Simon de Tournai est certainement mieux venue et plus satisfaisante, dans l'ensemble, que la version courte de la *Glossa* du Pseudo-Pierre de Poitiers, ce qui encourage M. Hödl à voir dans la rédaction longue un texte amélioré et plus tardif, il n'en va pas toujours ainsi: les *Institutiones* attribuent notamment à Hilaire la triade *unitas, aequalitas, concordia* (cf. ci-dessus, n. 132), alors que la *Glossa* la restitue à juste titre à Augustin (éd. Hödl, p. 18, o). Si la *Glossa* était antérieure aux *Institutiones* et à l'*Explanatio symboli*, Simon de Tournai n'aurait pas commis dans ces deux ouvrages une erreur qu'il avait précédemment évitée et dans laquelle retomberont d'ailleurs ceux qui s'inspireront de son traité. Cela dit, il reste que, quelle que soit la solution de ce petit problème, les opinions exprimées dans ces différents ouvrages sont bien celles de Simon de Tournai, comme nous l'apprend ce *secundum meam sententiam* (*Institutiones*, ed. cit., 4, p. 63, l. 57-58) sur lequel M. Hödl a justement attiré notre attention (op. cit., p. 20-21).

dont M. Hödl est le premier à reconnaître qu'il ne présente qu'un intérêt secondaire,[138] la *Glossa* du Pseudo-Pierre de Poitiers témoigne de la place que commençait à prendre, durant le troisième quart du xiie siècle, un traité des appropriations, solidement structuré autour du schèma de Gilbert de la Porrée, et dû certainement à Simon de Tournai, dont le succès n'allait pas tarder à s'affirmer.

On va en effet le retrouver déjà dans les *Sententiae* de Pierre de Poitiers, composées vraisemblablement peu avant 1170,[139] et qui recopient tout simplement le long développement de Simon de Tournai relatif aux appropriations.[140] Tous les éléments de cet exposé reparaîtront bientôt, vers la fin du xiie siècle, dans deux autres ouvrages d'inspiration porrétaine, les *Quaestiones theologicae* de maître Martin[141] et le *Speculum universale* de Raoul Ardent,[142] qui font l'un et l'autre de larges emprunts, sur ce point, à Simon de Tournai. On ne sera évidemment pas surpris de retrouver, vers le même temps, la série des triades énumérées par Gilbert de la Porrée dans un commentaire inédit de la *Glossa in epistolas Pauli* de Gilbert qui en reprend tous les éléments dans son explication de *Rom.*,XI,36,[143] et y reproduit à son tour de nombreux extraits des *Institutiones* de Simon de Tournai.[144]

138   Op. cit., p. 22.

139   Cf. P. S. Moore, *The Works of Peter of Poitiers* (Notre Dame 1936), pp. 39-41.

140   Cf. Pierre de Poitiers, *Sententiae*, I, 22, éd. P. S. Moore — M. Dulong (*Publicat. of Med. Stud.*, VII), (Notre Dame 1943), pp. 183-193, qui reproduisent mot à mot, sauf quelques lignes d'introduction (p. 183, l. 1-4) et de conclusion (p. 193, l. 265-267), le texte de Simon de Tournai, *Institutiones*, éd. M. Schmaus, loc. cit., 4-10, pp. 63-68. Pierre de Poitiers reviendra plus loin sur la triade *unitas, aequalitas, concordia* (op. cit., 29, p. 234, l. 105-124) et l'attribuera alors à Augustin, alors que dans le ch. 22 (p. 188, l. 132 et 137), à la suite de Simon de Tournai (cf. ci-dessus, n. 132), il en avait fait don à Hilaire.

141   Dans la question *De distinctione personarum*, ms. *Paris, B. N. lat. 14556*, f. 287r.

142   Ms. *Paris, Mazarine 709*, f. 112v-113r. Raoul Ardent et maître Martin, comme Pierre de Poitiers, dépendent l'un et l'autre, de toute évidence, des *Institutiones* ou peut-être de l'*Expositio symboli Athanasii*, mais non de la *Glossa* du Pseudo-Pierre de Poitiers. Eux aussi attribuent la triade du *De doctrina christiana* à Hilaire et non à Augustin.

143   Ms. *Paris, B. N. lat. 686*, f. 47va-48vb. A cet ouvrage sont apparentés des commentaires analogues contenus dans le ms. *Boulogne 24* (comment. de l'*Epître aux Romains* seulement), et *Rome, Vallicelliana C. 57*, signalés par A. Landgraf, *Introducción*, p. 138. Nous ne connaissons malheureusement ni les auteurs ni les dates de ces commentaires. Celui du ms. *Paris, B.N. lat. 686* a été attribué autrefois à Nicolas d'Amiens († après 1203) par H. Denifle (*Die abendländische Schriftausleger bis Luther*, Mayence, 1905, p. 40 ss.), mais A. Landgraf, op. cit., p. 138, estime que les arguments proposés par le savant Dominicain sont insuffisants.

144   La dépendance de ce commentaire à l'égard des *Institutiones* de Simon de Tournai est moins étroite que celle des ouvrages de maître Martin et de Raoul Ardent. Elle est cependant évidente et souvent très apparente, comme on pourra en juger par la brève comparaison suivante, donnée à titre d'exemple:

Simon de Tournai, *Institutiones*, éd. Schmaus, 10, l. 5-12, p. 68:	*Commentarium in Gilberti Glossam, Paris, B.N. lat. 686*, f. 47vb:
Hae enim *praepositiones, scilicet de et ex, cum sint* causales, *tamen,* sumuntur *in diversa*	"Nota quod non ait, etc." *He prepositiones, scilicet de et ex, cum sint causales, in diuersa*

Une parenté étroite unit entre eux tous ces écrits porrétains qui
témoignent du progrès accompli par la théologie des appropriations
durant cette période.

VII. Les Théologiens de la Fin du XII° Siècle et du Début du XIII°

Il ne serait pas difficile, désormais, de suivre à la trace la triade *unitas,
aequalitas, concordia* ou *connexio* dans la littérature théologique, et de
recueillir à ce sujet une ample moisson de textes. Sans doute faudrait-il
prêter attention à quelques témoignages isolés, tels que celui de sainte
Hildegarde de Bingen. En réponse à une lettre de l'évêque Eberhard de
Bamberg qui l'avait interrogée à ce propos, la célèbre visionnaire s'emploie à donner à son correspondant une explication mystique de la
triade du *De doctrina christiana*.[145] Mais une enquête de ce genre
devrait surtout suivre les deux pistes privilégiées dans lesquelles les
ouvrages précédemment cités l'invitent à s'engager: les commentaires
de l'*Epître aux Romains* d'une part, les gloses et les commentaires sur
les *Sententiae* de Pierre Lombard d'autre part.

A partir du milieu du XII° siècle, en effet, tous les commentateurs
des *Epîtres* de saint Paul s'inspirent, soit de la *Glossa* de Gilbert de la
Porrée, soit surtout des *Collectanea* de Pierre Lombard. Quelques sondages m'ont permis de constater que ces commentaires demeuraient
fidèles à l'interprétation trinitaire de *Rom.*, XI, 36, qui s'était
définitivement imposée, et que la plupart d'entre eux continuaient à
prêter attention à la triade *unitas, aequalitas, concordia* ou *connexio*.
Beaucoup sans doute n'ajoutent pas grand chose à ce qu'avaient dit

---

ratione causae. De enim *significat materialem
causam,* sed *ex dat auctoritatis et causae ef-
ficientis intelligentiam. Si enim dicam: annulus
est de auro, significo aurum esse materiam. Si
dicam: ex hoc patre est filius ille, significo* efficientem *causam. Quare cum non simus de
Deo* Patre *tanquam materia, sed simus ex eo
tanquam efficiente causa, non dixit Apostolus:
de ipso* sunt omnia, sed: *ex ipso sunt omnia,
significans omnium auctorem et causam efficientem.*

tamen accipiuntur *ratione cause.* Altera *enim,*
id est *de, significat materialem causam,*
reliqua, id est *ex, dat auctoritatis et cause ef-
ficientis intelligentiam. Si enim dicam: anulus
est de auro, significo aurum esse materiam. Si
dicam: ex hoc patre est ille filius, significo* ef-
ficientie *causam. Quare, cum non simus de deo
tanquam de materia, sed simus ex eo tanquam
efficiente causa, non dixit apostolus: de ipso,
sed: ex ipso sunt omnia, significans* eum
omnium esse auctorem et causam efficientem.

---

145 Sur cette correspondance, voir L. Ott, *Untersuchungen,* p. 576. La lettre d'Eberhard, qui
fut évêque de Bamberg de 1146 à 1172, et la réponse de sainte Hildegarde, qui, comme le
remarque L. Ott, ne doit rien à la théologie des appropriations trinitaires alors en cours, ont été
imprimées dans PL 197, 167-171. Dans sa requête relative à la signification de cette triade, dont il
ne semble pas connaître l'origine augustinienne, l'évêque s'en tient à une formulation différente de
celle du *De doctrina christiana* et écrit: "In Patre manet aeternitas, in Filio aequalitas, in Spiritu
sancto aeternitatis aequalitatisque connexio" (op. cit., 168 AB).

leurs prédécesseurs. [146] Plusieurs d'entre eux cependant persistent à introduire dans leurs exposés des considérations arithmétiques plus ou moins développées, dans lesquelles il faut voir encore un lointain souvenir des spéculations chartraines. [147] Fait remarquable cependant, les commentaires que j'ai pu examiner ne semblent pas connaître les précisions et les distinctions relatives aux appropriations trinitaires dont la théologie était pourtant redevable aux maîtres porrétains. [148]

Une exploration systématique des commentaires sur les *Sententiae* de Pierre Lombard nous permettrait de rassembler une quantité de textes beaucoup plus considérable encore. Ces ouvrages rencontrent tous, inévitablement, les quatre triades dont le maître des *Sentences* avait traité avant eux et qu'il avait présentées dans un ordre qui devait bientôt s'imposer définitivement:

1° *Aeternitas, species, usus (Sententiae*, I, dist. 31, c. 2);
2° *Unitas, aequalitas, concordia* ou *connexio* (ibid., c. 2-6);
3° *Potentia, sapientia, bonitas* (ibid., dist. 34, c. 3-4);
4° *Ex ipso, per ipsum, in ipso* (ibid., dist. 36, c. 3-5).

La triade du *De doctrina christiana*, que Pierre Lombard avait examinée avec attention, tient ici une place qui est loin d'être négligeable. Elle fera donc l'objet de développements relativement abondants dans tous les ouvrages qui suivent le texte ou au moins le plan du Lombard, et parmi lesquels on peut citer, à titre d'exemple, les *Sententiae* de Gandulphe de Bologne, [149] la *Glossa* du Pseudo-Pierre de

146   Ainsi p. ex. l'explication de *Rom.*, XI, 36, que nous trouvons dans le ms. *Paris, Mazarine 176*, f. 176vb-177ra, ne nous apprend rien de plus que celle de la *Glossa* de Gilbert de la Porrée dont elle dépend visiblement. Sur ce commentaire anonyme du ms. *Mazarine 176*, voir A. Landgraf, *Introducción*, p. 205.

147   Des considérations de ce genre, très proches de celles que nous avions remarquées dans le *Sermo in Purificatione*, probablement plus tardif, de Gauthier de Saint-Victor (cf. ci-dessus, n. 94) apparaissent dans les anonymes *Quaestiones in epist. Pauli, In epist. ad Rom.*, q. 283, PL 175, 501 BC (sur cet ouvrage, imprimé parmi les œuvres de Hugues de Saint-Victor, mais qui ne peut être antérieur aux années 1160 ou 1170, voir P. Glorieux, "Essai sur les Quaestiones in epist. Pauli du Pseudo-Hugues de Saint-Victor," *RTAM*, 19 (1952), pp. 48-59). Des justifications arithmétiques analogues, souvent même plus développées, se retrouvent dans le commentaire sur l'*Epître aux Romains* d'Etienne Langton, ms. *Paris, B. N. lat. 14443*, f. 284rb-va, et surtout dans celui de Hugues de Saint-Cher, éd. Paris, 1538, f. LVv, dont le goût pour les spéculations numériques a été remarqué par C. Spicq, *Esquisse d'une histoire de l'exégèse latine au moyen âge* (Paris 1944), p. 292.

148   A l'exception cependant du commentaire sur la *Glossa in epist. Pauli* de Gilbert de la Porrée, dont il a été question plus haut (cf. ci-dessus, n. 143-144) et qui dépend ici de Simon de Tournai.

149   Cf. *Magistri Gandulphi Bononiensis Sententiarum libri quatuor*, éd. J. de Walter (Vienne-Bratislava 1924), I, 47, pp. 34-36.

Poitiers dont il a été question précédemment,[150] une autre *Glossa* anonyme, d'origine porrétaine également, conservée dans le manuscrit *Paris, Mazarine 758*,[151] puis, plus tard, dans les commentaires sur les *Sentences* de Hugues de Saint-Cher,[152] d'Alexandre de Halès,[153] de saint Albert le Grand,[154] de saint Bonaventure[155] et de saint Thomas d'Aquin,[156] pour ne citer que les plus connus et les plus accessibles.

L'extrême abondance de ces ouvrages, qui se recopient d'ailleurs souvent les uns les autres, ne nous permet pas d'en entreprendre ici l'examen. Celui-ci risquerait d'ailleurs d'être assez décevant. Contraints de s'en tenir à l'ordre des distinctions et des chapitres du premier livre des *Sentences* qui leur servait de guide, et donc d'examiner séparément les triades dont avait traité cet ouvrage sans pouvoir les regrouper systématiquement comme l'avaient fait les porrétains, ces commentateurs se trouvaient dans l'impossibilité de constituer un véritable traité des appropriations. Leur fidélité au texte et au plan du Lombard devait avoir cependant une conséquence qui mérite d'être signalée. Elle allait en effet conduire les théologiens à effectuer un choix parmi les trop nombreuses triades dont le XIIe siècle s'était occupé et à concentrer leur attention sur celles qu'avaient retenues les *Sententiae*.

Ce sont finalement les auteurs des *Sommes* du XIIIe siècle qui recueilleront le fruit du labeur de ces commentateurs. Déjà la *Summa aurea* de Guillaume d'Auxerre, dont le plan s'inspire encore de très près de celui des *Sententiae* de Pierre Lombard, s'était efforcée de rapprocher les unes des autres les quatre triades que nous avons rencontrées tout à l'heure.[157] Mais la disposition générale des questions qui leur sont consacrées dans cet ouvrage reste encore imparfaite et maladroite. Dans la *Summa theologica* d'Alexandre de Halès, en revanche, nous trouvons un traité des appropriations trinitaires bien organisé,

150   Cf. ms. *Paris, B. N. lat. 14423*, f. 58vb-59ra. Cet exposé, qui se rapporte à *Sent.*, d. 31, est évidemment distinct du développement consacré aux appropriations trinitaires que le même ouvrage introduit à la suite des gloses relatives à la dist. 8, et dont il a été question plus haut (cf. ci-dessus, n. 137).

151   Cf. ms. *Paris, Mazarine 758*, f. 35rb-36vb. Sur le porrétanisme de cette glose et sur sa dépendance à l'égard de la *Glossa* du Pseudo-Pierre de Poitiers, voir A. Landgraf, *Introducción*, pp. 139 et 174.

152   Cf. *Sent.*, I, d. 31, ms. *Paris, B. N. lat. 3073*, f. 17vb. Hugues de Saint-Cher introduit ici des considérations qui ne sont plus seulement empruntées à l'arithmétique, mais aussi à la géométrie.

153   Cf. *Glossa in quatuor libros Sententiarum*, I, d. 31, 23-35 (Quaracchi 1951) I, pp. 309-318. Voir aussi d. 19, 27, ibid., pp. 205-206.

154   Cf. *In I Sent.*, d. 31, art. 9-14, éd. Borgnet (Paris 1893) 26, pp. 110-119.

155   *In I Sent.*, p. II, art. 2 (Quaracchi 1882,) I, pp. 545-549.

156   Cf. *In I Sent.*, d. 31, q. 3, art. 1-2.

157   Cf. Guillaume d'Auxerre, *Summa aurea*, éd. Pigouchet (Paris 1500) I, 8, f. XIX-XXI, mais les quatre triades dont avaient fait mention les *Sententiae* de Pierre Lombard sont présentés ici dans un ordre différent. C'est à l'obligeance du R.P. Ribaillier que je dois d'avoir pu retrouver ces références à la *Summa aurea*.

divisé en quatre questions qui examinent successivement, et fort longuement, les quatre triades des *Sentences*.[158] C'est un plan identique que suivra plus tard la *Summa theologiae* de saint Albert le Grand dans son *Tractatus de appropriatis*, divisé également en quatre questions qui traitent des mêmes triades et dans le même ordre.[159] Saint Thomas d'Aquin procéde d'une manière semblable dans l'article de la *Summa theologiae* (I,q.39,art.8) qui avait été au point de départ de notre enquête. Le Docteur Angélique y examine en effet, dans un ordre inchangé, les quatre triades des *Sententiae* de Pierre Lombard qui font l'objet, avant lui dans la *Summa* d'Alexandre de Halès, et après lui dans celle d'Albert le Grand, de quatre questions beaucoup plus développées.

VIII. Le Traité des Appropriations Trinitaires
de Saint Thomas d'Aquin

Le court traité des appropriations trinitaires constitué par les deux articles de la *Summa theologiae* de saint Thomas d'Aquin (I,q.39,art.7-8) est donc issu d'une longue maturation théologique dont nous connaissons maintenant les étapes principales. C'est évidemment aux *Sententiae* de Pierre Lombard, aux commentaires que ses contemporains avaient donné de cet ouvrage, à leurs commentaires de l'*Epître aux Romains* et aux premières *Sommes* du XIIIᵉ siècle que le Docteur Angélique a emprunté la plus grande partie des matériaux qu'il met en œuvre dans sa propre synthèse. C'est sans doute par leur intermédiaire que sont parvenues jusqu'à lui les justifications augustiniennes qu'il nous donne de la triade d'Hilaire,[160] ou encore le lointain souvenir des spéculations chartraines dont on retrouve la trace dans son bref com-

---

158 Cf. Alexandre de Halès, *Summa theologica*, Lib. I, p. II, Inq. II, tract. II, sect. II: *De nominibus personalibus appropriatis*, (Quaracchi 1924) I, pp. 640-658. Alexandre de Halès annonce lui-même en ces termes les divisions de cette sect. II (op. cit., p. 640): "Quaeritur ergo primo de appropriatione aeternitatis, speciei et usus; secundo, de appropriatione unitatis, aequalitatis, concordiae; tertio, de appropriatione potentiae, sapientiae, bonitatis; quarto, de appropriatione verborum Apostoli: *Ex ipso et per ipsum et in ipso.*" On reconnaît bien là les quatre triades des *Sententiae* de Pierre Lombard énumérées précédemment.

159 Cf. Albert le Grand, *Summa theologiae*, I, Tract. XII: *De appropriatis*, q. 48-50, éd. Borgnet (Paris 1895) 31, pp. 504-525. Un sommaire analogue à celui d'Alexandre de Halès annonce l'examen successif, dans le tract. XII, des quatre triades de Pierre Lombard. En fait, les triades *aeternitas, species, usus*, et *unitas, aequalitas, concordia sive connexio*, font l'objet des q. 48 et 49. C'est dans la q. 50 qu'Albert le Grand traite successivement de la triade *potentia, sapientia, bonitas* (membr. I) et de la triade *ex ipso, per ipsum, in ipso* (membr. IV).

160 Cf. *Sum. theol.*, I, q. 39, art. 8, c. On notera cependant le soin avec lequel saint Thomas, dans cet article, justifie l'appropriation de la *species* au Fils. C'est dans ce passage, cité souvent par les commentateurs qui traitent de l'esthétique du Docteur Angélique, que ce dernier énumère les trois caractères du beau: l'intégrité ou la perfection, la proportion et l'éclat. Cf. aussi *In I Sent.*, I, d. 31, q. 2, art. 1, c.

mentaire de la triade du *De doctrina christiana*,[161] ou enfin la distinction, inspirée de Hugues de Saint-Victor, mais indéfiniment reprise par les théologiens du XIIe et du XIIIe siècle, relative aux deux manières opposées dont on peut approprier aux trois personnes les attributs de puissance, de sagesse et de bonté.[162] Pourtant, bien que nous ne sachions pas dans quelle mesure saint Thomas d'Aquin a pu fréquenter Alain de Lille, Simon de Tournai et les maîtres porrétains, c'est de leur enseignement qu'il demeure pour une large part l'héritier. Ce sont en effet les théologiens porrétains qui avaient été les premiers à rassembler les éléments du dossier patristique dont la *Summa theologiae* reproduit l'essentiel et à les organiser dans un traité solidement structuré. Ce sont eux aussi qui avaient eu systématiquement recours aux mots *appropriare* et *appropriatio*, et qui avaient réussi, grâce à ce vocabulaire nouveau, à surmonter les ambiguïtés et les équivoques où s'étaient embarrassés leurs prédécesseurs.

Le Docteur Angélique présente cependant d'une manière nouvelle les quatre triades patristiques dont il entreprend l'examen. Il se méfie visiblement d'une théorie des appropriations qui ne serait que déductive et partirait d'un certain nombre de notions abstraites pour conclure de là à la distinction des personnes. Il rappelle donc avec insistance que notre intelligence ne parvient à la connaissance de Dieu qu'à partir des créatures.[163] Mais il s'efforce surtout de distinguer les différentes espèces d'appropriations auxquelles correspondent les quatre triades traditionnelles, afin d'opérer entre elles un classement systématique, fondé sur les diverses manières dont chacune d'elles considère la réalité divine. Il précise donc que les deux premières triades considèrent Dieu absolument, tel qu'il est en lui-même, en tant qu'il est (*aeternitas, species, usus*), ou en tant qu'il est un (*unitas, aequalitas, connexio*), sans se préoccuper encore de son activité causale ou de ses opérations *ad extra*. Les deux autres triades, en revanche, considèrent Dieu en tant qu'il est cause des choses (*potentia, sapientia, bonitas*), ou dans ses relations avec les effets dont il est la cause (*ex ipso, per ipsum, in ipso*). Ces deux points de vue sont en réalité complémentaires, aussi les deux triades qui s'y rapportent sont elles étroitement associées l'une à l'autre et ex-

---

161 Ibid. Saint Thomas se borne ici à énoncer quelques affirmations concernant les notions d'unité, d'altérité et d'égalité, et leurs rapports réciproques dans la *connexio*. Mais il ne faut pas oublier qu'il avait formulé auparavant les plus expresses réserves à l'égard des spéculations, d'origine platonicienne, relatives au nombre trois, ou à l'Un, principe des choses (cf. *Sum. theol.*, q. 32, art. 1, ad 1).

162 Ibid., et aussi art. 7, c. Cf. ci-dessus, n. 101, et Pierre Lombard, *Sent.*, I, d. 34, 4, ed. cit., p. 218; Alain de Lille, *Summa Quoniam homines*, ed. cit., 80, pp. 226-227; Simon de Tournai, *Institutiones*, ed. cit., 5, p. 64, etc.

163 *Sum. theol.*, I, q. 39, art. 8, c.

pliquées l'une par l'autre dans les exposés que saint Thomas leur consacre.[164] Leur rapprochement permettra d'ailleurs au Docteur
Angélique de justifier une nouvelle appropriation qui rapporte désormais la cause efficiente au Père, la cause formelle au Fils et la cause
finale au Saint-Esprit.[165]

Cette interprétation, à vrai dire, ne faisait que prolonger, dans le
cadre de la théorie aristotélicienne des quatre causes, une réflexion
dont les origines remontaient fort loin. Dès les premières lignes du
paragraphe du *De doctrina christiana* (I,5,5) qu'on a reproduit au début
de cet article, Augustin s'était en effet demandé si la Trinité, au lieu
d'être une chose (*res*) comme il l'avait dit d'abord, n'était pas plutôt "la
cause de toutes les choses", et ce recours à la notion de cause l'avait
amené à évoquer aussitôt la triade paulinienne *ex quo, per quem, in
quo*. L'expression *in quo* demeurait cependant obscure, aussi Augustin
avait-il pris soin, quelques années plus tard, dans son *De natura boni*,[166]
d'expliquer pourquoi l'Apôtre avait écrit *ex ipso* et non *de ipso*. Tout ce
qui est *de ipso*, avait-il précisé, est également *ex ipso*, mais non l'inverse. Le ciel et la terre sont effet *ex ipso*, parce qu'ils ont été créés par
Dieu, mais ils ne sont pas *de ipso* parce qu'ils ne sont pas "de sa substance" (*de substantia eius*). Si un homme engendre un fils et s'il bâtit
une maison, on peut dire que le fils et la maison sont *ex ipso*, mais seul
son fils est *de ipso*; la maison, elle, est de terre et de bois (*de terra et
ligno*). Ces explications avaient été reprises par certains exégètes
médiévaux;[167] elles devaient reparaître dans la *Glossa in epistolas Pauli*
de Gilbert de la Porrée[168] puis dans les *Collectanea*[169] et les *Sententiae*[170] de Pierre Lombard. Les théologiens porrétains, qui n'avaient pas
tardé à attribuer à leur tour une signification causale aux prépositions
ex et *de*, avaient pu ainsi rapporter plus explicitement encore la préposition *de* à la cause matérielle et la préposition *ex* à la cause efficiente: c'est parce que nous ne venons pas de Dieu comme d'une
matière, mais que nous dépendons de lui comme d'une cause efficiente,
que l'Apôtre n'a pas écrit *de ipso*, mais *ex ipso omnia*.[171] Saint Thomas

---

164 Ibid., et q. 45, art. 6, ad 2. C'est également en mettant en relation ces deux triades que
saint Thomas explique le texte de *Rom.*, XI, 36, dans son *Commentaire de l'Epître aux Romains,
ad loc.*, qui ne mentionne ni la triade d'Hilaire, ni celle du *De doctrina christiana*.
165 *Sum. theol.*, I, q. 39, art. 8, c.
166 27, PL 42, 560.
167 Cf. p. ex. Atton de Verceil, *Exp. in epist. Pauli, In Rom.*, XI, 36, PL 134, 247D.
168 Voir le texte de Gilbert cité plus haut, [1], et n. 42.
169 PL 191, 1493 B.
170 I, d. 36, ed. cit., p. 227.
171 Voir entre autres les textes empruntés aux *Institutiones* de Simon de Tournai et au commentaire anonyme de la *Glossa* de Gilbert de la Porrée, cités ci-dessus, n. 144.

d'Aquin semble bien se souvenir de ces explications, qu'il présente cependant d'une manière un peu différente, lorsqu'il précise que la préposition *ex* peut être entendue aussi bien de la cause matérielle que de la cause efficiente, mais que, comme il ne peut y avoir en Dieu de causalité matérielle, c'est bien la causalité efficiente qu'il faut rapporter au Père à qui a déjà été approprié l'attribut de puissance[172] et à qui sera bientôt appropriée l'œuvre de la création.[173]

La relation établie par le Docteur Angélique entre le *per ipsum* de saint Paul et la cause formelle trouvait à son tour de nombreuses justifications dans la tradition. Tout ce que saint Augustin avait dit de la *species*, de la *pulchritudo* ou de l'art divin, rapportés à la sagesse et à la seconde personne de la Trinité, allait en ce sens.[174] La triade du *De uera religione (principium, forma, gratia)* qu'avaient citée Gilbert de la Porrée et Pierre Lombard,[175] avait d'ailleurs fait une place, dans la théologie des appropriations, à la notion de forme qui conduisait tout naturellement à celle de cause formelle.[176]

Le rapport entre l'*in ipso* de saint Paul et la cause finale était sans doute moins immédiatement suggéré par les textes anciens dont s'inspirait le Docteur Angélique. Pourtant il était déjà affirmé par le *Commentarius Cantabrigiensis in epistolas Pauli*, issu de l'école d'Abélard, qu'on a rencontré plus haut.[177] Le lien métaphysique qui unit entre elles les notions de bien et de fin était d'autre part trop familier à saint Thomas pour qu'après avoir approprié à l'Esprit-Saint l'attribut de bonté, il pût hésiter à lui approprier également la causalité finale.[178]

---

172 *Sum. theol.*, I, q. 39, art. 8, c.

173 Ibid., q. 45, art. 6, ad 2.

174 Saint Thomas s'inspire visiblement de ces thèmes augustiniens lorsque, toujours dans son art. 8, il approprie la cause formelle à la seconde personne de la Trinité. Il note cependant que la préposition *per* désigne parfois ce qui appartient en propre au Fils, et ne lui est donc pas simplement approprié; c'est de cette manière notamment qu'il faut interpréter le *per* de *Jo.*, 1, 3: "Omnia per ipsum facta sunt."

175 Cf. ci-dessus, n. 53 et 66.

176 Dans la q. 46, art. 3, c., où il revient sur l'appropriation de la puissance au Père et de la sagesse au Fils, saint Thomas substitue cependant aux notions de cause efficiente et de cause formelle de la q. 39, celles de *principium effectivum* et de *principium exemplare*.

177 Cf. ci-dessus, n. 32, *in fine*.

178 Cette appropriation des trois causes débouche, chez saint Thomas, sur une appropriation des opérations *ad extra*. Le Docteur Angélique s'explique surtout à ce sujet dans la q. 45, art. 6, ad 2, où il approprie au Père la *creatio* et au Saint-Esprit la *gubernatio* et la *vivificatio* (cf. aussi q. 39, art. 8, c., où il est dit, à propos du Saint-Esprit: "sua bonitate eas [*sc.* res] conservat et gubernat.") L'opération appropriée au Fils est moins clairement définie par la q. 45, art. 6, ad 2, qui se contente d'écrire: "Filio autem appropriatur sapientia, per quam agens per intellectum operatur." Faisant écho à cette doctrine, tout en la précisant, la théologie classique, à l'époque moderne, appropriera généralement au Père la *creatio*, au Fils la *dispositio* et au Saint-Esprit la *gubernatio* (cf. p. ex. A. Chollet, art. "Appropriations aux personnes de la sainte Trinité," *Dict. de théol. cathol.*,

Le Docteur Angélique est-il le premier à avoir approprié simultanément et d'une manière aussi explicite la cause efficiente au Père, la cause formelle au Fils et la cause finale au Saint-Esprit? La nécessité où l'on est de mettre un point final à cet article ne nous permet pas d'entreprendre ici l'enquête qui serait nécessaire pour apporter une réponse à cette question. Pourtant, quelques sondages rapides me donnent à penser qu'on trouverait sans trop de peine un certain nombre d'antécédents à cette triple appropriation. Dans un texte qui n'a aucun rapport avec les spéculations arithmétiques évoquées plus haut, Thierry de Chartres avait déjà rapproché la cause efficiente de Dieu, la cause formelle de sa Sagesse et la cause finale de sa Bénignité. [179] Deux commentaires inédits de l'*Epître aux Romains*, attribués respectivement au Dominicain Guerric de Saint-Quentin[180] et au Franciscain Jean de la Rochelle,[181] approprient explicitement ces trois causes aux trois personnes de la Trinité dans leur explication de *Rom.*, XI,36. Si

---

I (3ᵉ tirage), Paris, 1923, col. 1712.) Cette triade rappelle celle que nous avions remarquée précédemment chez Simon de Tournai, *Institutiones*, éd. Schmaus, *RTAM*, 4 (1932), 6, p. 65 (*operatio, dispositio, conservatio*) qui reparaît, par exemple, dans le commentaire de l'*Epître aux Romains* attribué à Guerric de Saint-Quentin et signalé ci-dessous, n. 180.

179   Cf. Thierry de Chartres, *De sex dierum operibus*, éd. N. Haring, *AHDLMA*, 22, 1955 (1956), 2, pp. 184-185.

180   Cf. ms. *Paris. B. N. lat. 15603*, f. 6vb. Ce commentaire, attribué à Guerric de Saint-Quentin par P. Glorieux, *Répertoire des maîtres en théologie de Paris au XIIIᵉ siècle* (Paris 1933), p. 55, approprie simultanément la cause efficiente et l'*operatio* au Père, la cause formelle et la *dispositio* au Fils, la cause finale et la *conservatio* au Saint-Esprit.

181   Cf. ms. *Paris. B. N. lat. 15536*, f. 190r. "*Quoniam in ipso*, etc. Quod exponit beatus b. sic: Quid est deus ex quo omnia creabiliter et non seminabiliter, et li ex dicit causam efficientem; *per ipsum sunt omnia*, ne alium actorem uel alium opificem arbitremur, et li per notat causam formalem extrinsecam, quod notatur per hoc quod dicit opificem; *in ipso sunt omnia*, non quasi in loco, sed quasi in uirtute, et li in notat causam finalem. Demum subiungit idem b.: *ex quo omnia*, tanquam uno actore, principio omnium; *per quem omnia*, ne alterum inducatur principium; *in quo omnia*, ne inducatur locus alter. Sic ergo patet quod deus est causa efficiens, finalis et formalis omnium rerum, et ideo in ipso est omnis ratio operum eius. Dicit ergo quoniam *in ipso est*, suple potentia que est causa efficiens omnium, et *per ipsum* est sapientia qui est causa formalis omnium rerum, et *in ipso* est bonitas que est causa finalis omnium rerum." D'après L. Delisle, *Inventaire des manuscrits de la Sorbonne* (Paris 1874), p. 14, ce commentaire serait la suite de celui qui nous est transmis par le ms. *Paris. B. N. lat. 15602*, lequel, toujours d'après L. Delisle (ibid., p. 16), serait l'œuvre de Jean de la Rochelle. P. Glorieux, op. cit., ne mentionne pas le commentaire du ms. *15536*, et dit simplement de celui du ms. *15602* qu'il est "probablement l'œuvre de Jean de la Rochelle" (op. cit., pp. 22-23). Le *beatus b.* auquel se réfère le texte cité ci-dessus ne peut évidemment être que saint Bernard, qui avait effectivement écrit, dans son *De consideratione (V, 6, 14,* PL 182, 793 C, ou *S. Bernardi Opera*, éd. J. Leclercq - H. M. Rochais, t. III, Rome 1963, p. 478, l. 11-17): "*Ex quo omnia*, creabiliter, non seminabiliter; *per quem omnia*, ne alium auctorem atque alium opificem arbitreris; *in quo omnia*, non quasi in loco, sed quasi in virtute. *Ex quo omnia*, tanquam uno principio, auctore omnium; *per quem omnia*, ne alterum inducatur principium, artifex; *in quo omnia*, ne tertium inducatur, locus. *Ex quo omnia*, non de quo, quia non est materia Deus: efficiens causa est, non materialis." Saint Bernard, qui ne parle ici ni de la cause formelle, ni de la cause finale, se souvient du *De natura boni* d'Augustin (cf. ci-dessus, n. 166); la distinction qu'il établit entre la cause matérielle et la cause efficiente, représentées par les prépositions *de* et *ex*, est identique à celle des maîtres porrétains (cf. ci-dessus, n. 171).

ces ouvrages appartiennent bien aux deux théologiens à qui on les a donnés, il faut en conclure que cette triple appropriation était couramment admise par les maîtres parisiens de la première moitié du XIIIᵉ siècle. En toute hypothèse, saint Thomas d'Aquin aura eu le grand mérite de rassembler en une synthèse de quelques pages dont il faut admirer à la fois la précision, la densité et la clarté, tous les éléments d'une théologie des appropriations trinitaires que ses prédécesseurs avaient mis plus d'un siècle à élaborer.

ST. THOMAS ON THE HABITUS-THEORY
OF THE INCARNATION

Walter H. Principe C.S.B.

IN his theology of the Incarnation Thomas Aquinas frequently refers to the three famous opinions on how God became man that are outlined by Peter Lombard in Book III of his *Sentences*.[1] In Thomas, as in most of his contemporaries, the theology of the Incarnation is so intertwined with interpretation of these opinions that the one cannot be understood apart from the other. The valuable insights to be gained from examining Aquinas' interpretation of these opinions can be seen from a study that has been made of Thomas' changing views about the first opinion or "assumptus-homo theory."[2] The present study will

Sigla

Haring, *Gilbert* — N. M. Haring, "The Case of Gilbert de la Porrée Bishop of Poitiers (1142-1154)," *Mediaeval Studies* 13 (1950) 1-40.

Hypostatic Union I; II; III — Walter H. Principe, *The Theology of the Hypostatic Union in the Early Thirteenth Century*, Vol. I: *William of Auxerre's Theology of the Hypostatic Union* (Toronto 1963); Vol. II: *Alexander of Hales' Theology of the Hypostatic Union* (Toronto 1967); Vol. III: *Hugh of Saint-Cher's Theology of the Hypostatic Union* (Toronto 1970).

Lombard, *Sent.* III, 6, 1; p. 573 — Peter Lombard, *Libri IV Sententiarum*, Liber III, distinctio 6, caput 1; edd. PP. Collegii S. Bonaventurae, 2nd ed. (Quaracchi 1916) p. 573.

Thomas Aquinas:

> *Comp. th.*, 209; 403, p. 95 — *Compendium theologiae*, caput 209; in *S. Thomae Aquinatis opuscula theologica*, Vol. I, ed. R. A. Verardo (Rome 1954) no. 403, p. 95.
>
> *In Philip.* 2, 2; 60, p. 102 — *S. Thomae Aquinatis super epistolam ad Philippenses lectura*, caput 2, lectio 2; ed. R. Cai, *Super epistolas S. Pauli lectura*, 8th ed., Vol. II (Rome 1953) no. 60, p. 102.
>
> *In III Sent.* d. 2, q. 1, a. 1, qla. 1, resp. [sol.; exp. text.; arg.]; 21, p. 56 — *Scriptum super Sententiis*, Liber III, distinctio 2, quaestio 1, articulus 1, quaestiuncula 1, responsio [solutio; expositio textus; argumentum]; ed. M. F. Moos (Paris 1933) no. 21, p. 56.

---

1 See *Sent.* III, 6-7; pp. 573-89. Cf. *Sent.* III, 10 (pp. 593-97) and III, 21-22 (pp. 644-54).

2 H.-F. Dondaine, "Qualifications dogmatiques de la théorie de l'*Assumptus-homo* dans les œuvres de s. Thomas," *Les sciences philosophiques et théologiques* (Paris: Vrin, 1941-42: the only volume to appear) 163-68. As the title suggests, this study is limited to Thomas' judgment about the dogmatic tenability of the opinion and does not go into the theological issues.

The names "assumptus-homo theory" or "assumptus-theory" for the first of Lombard's opinions, "subsistence-theory" for the second and "habitus-theory" for the third originated with B. Barth, "Ein neues Dokument zur Geschichte der frühscholastischen Christologie," *Theologische Quartalschrift* [Tübingen] 100 (1919) 400-26; 101 (1920) 235-62; see esp. p. 423. The names have proved useful not only because they focus on the most characteristic feature of each opinion but also because they help to avoid the confusion introduced by some medieval theologians who changed the numbering of the opinions: see Dondaine, p. 163, n. 2, and *Hypostatic Union* I, 196, n. 28, and 201-02, n. 53.

For bibliography on the three opinions see ibid. I, 197-198, n. 31. Thomas' attitude towards the opinions is discussed in some detail by P. Galtier, *L'unité du Christ* (Paris 1939) 176-99 passim, but Galtier's understanding of the habitus-theory is defective.

examine Thomas Aquinas' presentation of the third opinion or "habitus-theory," and will then investigate the historical accuracy of his presentation as well as the role played by his reaction to this opinion in his own theology of the Incarnation.

1. THOMAS AQUINAS' PRESENTATION OF THE HABITUS-THEORY

Among Thomas Aquinas' most important expositions of the habitus-theory are those found in his commentary on Book III of the *Sentences*, in the *Contra Gentiles*, the *Summa theologiae*, and the *Compendium theologiae*. Shorter accounts of the theory are given in a *quaestio quodlibetalis*, the *Lectura super epistolam S. Pauli ad Philippenses*, and the *Quaestio disputata de unione Verbi Incarnati*.

Scriptum super Sententiis

In the *Scriptum super Sententiis* Thomas' main presentation of the habitus-theory is found, as one would expect, in his discussion of the questions regularly debated in the context of distinctions 6 and 7 of Book III of Lombard's work. Before that, only a few explicit allusions to one or other of the opinions are to be found.[3] Two of these earlier texts describe the positions of the third opinion. In one Thomas says that some interpret a text of Lombard as referring to "the opinion of those who said that Christ, according as he is man, is not something but is having himself in a qualitative way."[4] Here Thomas links the habitus-theory with the teachings that Christ as man is not *quid* or *aliquid* and that the human nature is to be understood according to the category of quality rather than substance.

In the second text Thomas speaks of those who deny that the conjunction of body and soul in Christ resulted in "some humanity." For Thomas this opinion is akin to those of various heretics, for it destroys the truth of Christ's humanity and the dignity of his body. For if Christ's soul were not united to his body as its form so that one *quid* resulted from them, then Christ could not be a true man nor could his body be truly living.[5]

---

3 *In III Sent.* d. 1, q. 2, a. 4, resp.; 130, p. 41 (second opinion on union in hypostasis or supposit as well as in person). Ibid., d. 4, q. 1, a. 2, q1a. 1, resp.; 41, p. 165 (identity of *suppositum, individuum hominis* and *persona Filii Dei* according to the second opinion). Ibid.; 43, p. 165 (*unum esse Christi* taught by the second opinion).

4 " 'Errant igitur qui nomine humanitatis etc.' ...vel tangit [Lombardus], ut quidam dicunt, opinionem eorum qui dicebant Christum, secundum quod est homo, non esse quid, sed qualiter se habens: quod infra tangetur, d. 6." *In III Sent.* d. 2, exp. text.; 158, pp. 87, 88.

5 "Ad tertiam quaestionem sciendum est quod quidam posuerunt Deum assumpsisse animam et corpus, non ita quod ex eorum conjunctione aliqua humanitas resultaret. Et haec opinio similiter veritatem humanitatis tollit et dignitatem corporis Christi. Non enim Christus verus homo esse potuit, nec corpus ejus vere vivum, nisi anima corpori unita fuisset ut forma ejus, ita quod ex eis unum quid efficeretur. Sed de hac opinione infra dicetur, 3 d." Ibid., d. 2, q. 1, a. 3, q1a. 3, sol; 79, p. 69.

When Aquinas comes to Lombard's exposition of the three opinions and their supporting authoritative texts, he undertakes an unusually lengthy summary and analysis of Lombard's text. He first describes very accurately Lombard's procedure and then examines the tenets of each of the opinions, indicating their points of agreement and disagreement. This, his most detailed exposition of the habitus-theory, deserves careful examination. [6]

First comes a statement of the points on which all three opinions agree and which distinguish the opinions from heresies of the past. All three opinions hold for only one person, the divine person, in Christ, and thereby avoid the heresy of Nestorius. All posit in Christ two natures and three substances (divinity, soul, and body, the latter two constituting human nature according to all the opinions); thereby they avoid the error of Eutyches with his doctrine of one nature in Christ. All agree that these two substances in which human nature consists were assumed by the Word; thereby they avoid the Manichean error denying the assumption of flesh. All hold that what was assumed did not exist prior in time (but only in nature) to the union; thereby they avoid an error, mentioned by John Damascene, that the divine person first assumed an intellect and afterwards became man. Thomas remarks that this seems to be the error of Origen when he posited the creation of souls before bodies. [7]

Next follows a long discussion as to how each opinion differs from the other two. Each opinion will be seen to differ, Thomas says, according to two basic comparisons of the three substances in Christ, first, according to the comparison of soul and body with each other, in that human nature consists in them, and, second, according to the comparison of soul and body to the divine person, in that these two were assumed by the divine person. [8]

The third opinion differs from the first two according to each of these comparisons. As for the relation of soul to body in Christ, the first two opinions posit something (*aliquid*) composed from soul and body, and this is assumed, whereas the third opinion maintains that these two substances are divided from one another and are assumed by the Word without being composed with each other in any way. Thus when the third opinion says that human nature is assumed by the Word, it takes human nature in a material sense as referring to the parts of human nature, just as the parts of a house are called a house. [9] With respect to

6   For his summary of Lombard's procedure see ibid., d. 6, divisio textus; 8, p. 217. For this analysis of the opinions see ibid., 9-11, pp. 217-21.

7   Ibid.; 9, pp. 217-18.

8   Ibid.; 10, p. 218.

9   "Differt autem tertia opinio a primis duabus quantum ad comparationem animae et corporis

the second comparison, that of Christ's soul and body to the divine person, the third opinion differs from the first two by positing an accidental conjoining or union of these two substances to the Word in the way that a garment is joined to a man or that an angel assumes a body in order to be seen in the body. The first and second opinions, on the other hand, say that soul and body were conjoined to the Word not accidentally but substantially as to personal *esse*.[10]

These, then, are the unique positions of the third opinion according to Thomas Aquinas: a denial of the union of soul and body in Christ; a denial of any composition of soul and body in Christ; a denial of any human *aliquid*; human nature in Christ means simply his body and soul, the parts of human nature; the union of body and soul to the Word is not substantial or personal, but accidental.

Thomas is manifestly more concerned with the differences between the first and second opinions, for he examines these differences in much greater detail than he does those of the third opinion with respect to the others.[11] Only after this extensive contrast and comparison of the first two opinions does he return to the third in order to show some of the consequences of its unique basic positions. According to Thomas' analysis, because this opinion denies the union of soul and body in Christ, it holds first of all that "man" does not predicate something composed of body and soul concerning Christ; it predicates only the parts of human nature, so that when Christ is said to be "man," this means that Christ has a soul and body united to him accidentally.[12]

The second position of the third opinion is that "man" is predicated of Christ accidentally, not in the category of substance (*quid*) but in that of quality or habit (*in quomodo se habet*), as when a man is said to be clothed. A third consequence of the denial of a union of soul and flesh in Christ is that the two substances do not belong to the personality of the Son of God, but are related to him extrinsically. Many other consequences follow from these positions, Thomas adds, if one considers

---

quia primae duae opiniones ponunt aliquid compositum ex anima et corpore, quod est assumptum; tertia vero ponit has duas substantias esse divisas ad invicem, et sine aliqua compositione a parte Verbi assumptas esse. Unde cum dicitur natura humana assumpta a Verbo, sumit naturam humanam materialiter, id est partes humanae naturae, sicut partes domus dicuntur domus." Loc. cit.

10 "Differt etiam a primis duabus quantum ad comparationem harum duarum substantiarum ad tertiam; quia ponit has duas substantias conjunctas Verbo accidentaliter, sicut vestis conjungitur homini, et sicut Angelus assumit corpus, ut in eo videatur; primae vero duae opiniones dicunt, non accidentaliter, sed substantialiter quantum ad esse personale Verbo conjunctas esse." Loc. cit.

11 Ibid.; 10-11, pp. 218-20.

12 "Tertia vero opinio, quia negat unionem animae ad carnem in Christo, ideo primo ponit quod homo non praedicat de Christo aliquid compositum ex anima et corpore, sed partes humanae naturae; ut sit sensus: *est homo*; id est habet animam et corpus sibi unita accidentaliter." Ibid.; 11, p. 221.

the root of the opinion.[13] Later on in his own commentary Thomas will draw out some of these consequences.

In a final section Thomas shows different ways in which the various opinions pair together in agreement against the remaining opinion. The first and second opinions agree that man predicates *quid* of Christ, whereas the third denies this.[14] Against the first opinion, which holds for two supposits in Christ, the second and third agree that there is only one supposit, but they assert this for different reasons. The second opinion says that the divine person stands under each nature substantially, the third that the divine person stands under the divine nature substantially but under the human nature accidentally. Thomas gives the example of one supposit for "man" and "white": because the same person is both man and white, he means, there are not two supposits or persons.[15] Again, the first and third opinions agree that the human nature does not pertain to the personality of the divine person, the first opinion because it holds that the human nature is made substantial (*substantificatur*) through itself, the third because it holds that the human nature is in no way a substance. Both therefore can agree, but for different reasons, that the divine person remained as simple after the Incarnation as before, a position contrary to the second opinion's teaching that there was after the Incarnation a "composed person."[16]

Although Thomas spends much more time comparing the first and second opinions in his questions within the distinctions of Book III, he alludes often enough to the third opinion and devotes the entire question 3 of distinction 6 to its teachings. In most cases he repeats in different contexts his basic interpretation of this opinion: soul and body are not united in Christ;[17] they fail to form some composite or composed person except in a broad sense of "composed" as "placed with another."[18] One reason why this opinion teaches a lack of composition

13 "Et ideo secundo ponit quod homo praedicatur de Christo accidentaliter, non in quid, sed in quomodo se habet; ut cum dicitur homo indutus. Et ideo tertio ponit quod duae substantiae non pertinent ad personalitatem Filii Dei, sed extrinsecus se habent ad ipsam. Et multa alia ex his opinionibus sequuntur, si quis radicem opinionum considerat." Loc. cit.

14 "Primae enim duae opiniones conveniunt in hoc quod utraque ponit quod homo de Christo praedicatur in quid: in quo differunt a tertia quae hoc negat." Loc. cit.

15 "Similiter tertia convenit cum secunda in hoc quod ponit quod in Christo non sunt duo supposita, quamvis differenter; quia secunda ponit quod supponitur utrique naturae substantialiter, tertia vero quod divinae substantialiter et humanae accidentaliter; sicut album et homo non est aliud et aliud suppositum, sed idem quod supponit homo copulat album: in quo differunt a prima quae ponit in Christo duo supposita." Loc. cit.

16 "Similiter prima et tertia conveniunt in hoc quod humana natura non pertinet ad personalitatem divinae personae, quamvis differenter; quia prima ponit quod substantificatur per se, tertia autem quod nullo modo. Unde utraque ponit quod divina persona sicut fuit simplex ante incarnationem, ita est simplex post incarnationem: in quo differunt a secunda." Loc. cit.

17 *In III Sent.* d. 6, q. 3, a. 1, resp.; 107-08, pp. 244-45. Cf. ibid., d. 6, exp. text.; 125, p. 248.

18 Ibid., d. 6, q. 2, a. 3, resp.; 94-95, pp. 241-42. Cf. ibid., d. 6, exp. text.; 129, p. 250.

is that for it the union of soul and body to the Word is accidental.[19] Throughout his commentary on distinction 6 Thomas' constant refrain is that the habitus-theory teaches such an accidental union;[20] because this opinion holds that the union of body and soul to the Word is accidental, it says that *homo* does not predicate *quid* or *aliquid* concerning Christ but rather a habitus or a having itself in a certain way (*aliquo modo se habens*).[21]

A few additional doctrines are presented by Thomas Aquinas as consequences of this opinion's basic teaching. In agreement with the second opinion and in opposition to the first, he says, it denies two supposits in Christ and maintains that Christ is only one; this unity, however, is for it not a unity *per se* as it is for the second opinion, but an accidental unity like that of a white man.[22] Later on Thomas remarks that this view of the union as accidental leads to the conclusion that Christ has a twofold *esse*, one substantial and the other accidental.[23]

Can it be said that man became God? The third opinion, not holding for a human supposit, agrees with the second, Thomas says, that it is false to say this in the proper sense.[24] With respect to the predestination of Christ, the third opinion in his view also agrees with the second: this predestination of Christ as to its source in grace and as to its effects is

---

19 "Similiter tertia opinio dicit quod est esse superadditum ad esse divinae personae accidentaliter; unde anima et corpus non dicuntur partes personae, sicut nec accidentia subjecti. Unde neutra [opinio, sc. prima vel tertia] ponit personam Verbi compositam." Ibid., d. 6, q. 2, a. 3, resp.; 94, p. 241.

20 "...sic non diceret quod praedicaret quid, sed quod esset accidentaliter unitum, sicut dicit tertia opinio." Ibid., q. 1, a. 1, qla. 1, ad sed contra; 29, p. 227. "Quod autem habet esse completum in quo subsistit, non potest uniri alteri nisi tribus modis: vel accidentaliter, sicut tunica homini, et hunc modum unionis ponit tertia opinio." Ibid., q. 1, a. 2, resp.; 45, p. 230. "...tertia vero [dicit] quod [Christus] est unum per accidens, sicut homo albus." Ibid., q. 2, a. 1, resp.; 66, p. 235. "Opinio tertia...ponit quod partes humanae naturae adveniunt divinae personae accidentaliter...." Ibid., q. 2, a. 2, resp.; 81, p. 239. "...tertia [opinio] ponit quod non subsistit assumptum, nec persona in eo, sed est esse accidentale superadditum." Ibid., q. 3, a. 2, resp.; 119, p. 247: this article (nos. 113-23, pp. 245-47) gives the main discussion of whether the union is accidental within the context of the third opinion. See also ibid., exp. text.; 129, p. 250.

21 "...secundum vero tertiam [homo] non praedicat aliquid, sed aliquo modo se habens." Ibid., exp. text.; 124, p. 247. "Quarta, quod homo de Deo non praedicat quid, sed habitum...." Ibid.; 129, p. 250. See also the first text in n. 20.

22 "Et quia plurale est geminatum singulare, ideo Christus non posset dici aliqua, nisi essent in eo duo supposita naturarum: quod negat secunda opinio et similiter tertia. Et ideo utraque opinio dicit quod Christus est unum; sed secunda dicit quod est unum per se; tertia vero, quod est unum per accidens, sicut homo albus." Ibid., q. 2, a. 1, resp.; 66, p. 235.

23 "Similiter opinio tertia, quia ponit quod partes humanae naturae adveniunt divinae personae accidentaliter, ponit duo esse, unum substantiale et aliud accidentale." Ibid., q. 2, a. 2, resp.; 81, p. 239.

24 "Secunda autem opinio et tertia ponunt quod homo, prout de Christo praedicatur, non habet aliud suppositum quam suppositum aeternum. Sed secunda dicit quod homo supponit suppositum aeternum; tertia autem, quod homo copulat ipsum, sicut termini accidentales. Et quia illud suppositum nunquam non fuit Deus, ideo haec est falsa secundum hoc: *Homo factus est Deus*." Ibid., d. 7, q. 2, a. 2, resp.; 73, pp. 270-71. See also ibid., d. 6, exp. text.; 124, p. 248.

not by reason of the one supposit of the Son of God but rather by reason of the assumed nature which is united to the Son of God and which did not always exist; because it did not always exist, the effects of grace were foreseen in it and this constitutes its predestination.[25] Thomas seems to imply, finally, that the third opinion holds that even in his death Christ remained a man because, as he says, it maintained that even before his death he was a man not by a union of soul and body but only by a union of each to the Word. Since these latter unions continued in the triduum of death, he would for them still be a man.[26]

What, according to Thomas, are the reasons behind the special teachings of the third opinion or habitus-theory? Those who held this opinion, he says, believed that every composite of body and soul has the *ratio* of a man. But since they refused to agree with the first opinion that a man was assumed or that Christ was two, they developed the teaching that the assumed soul and body were not united to each other.[27] Another root of this opinion was that it held that the human nature was not assumed to the *esse* of the divine person; from this it concluded that an accidental *esse* is added by reason of the human nature in the Incarnation.[28] A still further reason for the development of this theory, Thomas adds, was its desire to show that there is no change in the divine person in the Incarnation and no increase in the number of persons in the Trinity; this led to its denial of a human *quid* in Christ.[29] This is the nearest Thomas comes in the *Sentences* to saying that the third opinion denied a human *quid* in Christ in order to avoid seeing a human person in Christ; he will bring out this point more clearly in later works. Important as a source of this theory's use of the category of habitus, Thomas realizes, is the number of patristic texts authorizing such use; many of these are quoted by Lombard at this point.[30]

---

25 Ibid., d. 7, q. 3, a. 1, resp.; 85-89, pp. 273-74.

26 " 'Et ipse forte ante mortem...' Hoc dicit propter tertiam opinionem quae nondum erat suo tempore damnata quae dicebat quod etiam ante mortem erat hoc modo homo." Ibid., d. 22, exp. text.; 168, p. 690. The words quoted are those of Lombard's text (*Sent.* III, 22, 1; p. 651). See also Thomas' discussion of Lombard's position, *In III Sent.* d. 22, q. 1, a. 1, resp.; 14-17, pp. 663-64.

27 "Tamen ista opinio videtur ex eodem fonte processisse cum prima, scilicet ex hoc quod credebant omne compositum ex anima et corpore habere rationem hominis. Et ideo, quia prima opinio posuit animam et corpus unita ad invicem esse assumpta, coacta fuit ponere hominem esse assumptum et Christum esse duo. Haec autem opinio, ut hoc negaret, posuit animam et corpus esse assumpta non unita." Ibid., d. 6, q. 3, a. 1; 108, pp. 244-45.

28 "Tamen etiam quantum ad hanc positionem procedit ab eodem fonte cum prima [opinione], scilicet ex hoc quod humana natura non assumeretur ad esse divinae personae. Unde prima ponebat quod assumptum esse habebat per se, in quo subsistebat; haec autem tertia ponit quod non subsistit assumptum, nec persona in eo, sed est esse accidentale superadditum." Ibid., q. 3, a. 2, resp.; 119, p. 247.

29 Ibid., exp. text.; 129-30, p. 250.

30 Ibid.; 130, p. 251. Cf. ibid., q. 3, a. 2, arg. 1; 113, p. 245.

Here it may be asked how Thomas Aquinas judges the third opinion or habitus-theory with respect to the teaching of faith. Attacking its teachings both by reasoning and by quotations from authority, he names it a heresy on two counts. A union of body and soul is necessary for the notion of man and of all his parts, he argues, whereas a lack of this union would mean that man or flesh would be such only equivocally, as when one calls a portrait a man. The third opinion, by denying the union of Christ's soul to his flesh, cannot escape the conclusion that Christ is not a true man or that his flesh is not true flesh. Such a conclusion, Thomas continues, is against an article of faith, and therefore this opinion is not only false but heretical and was condemned by Pope Alexander in a council.[31]

Thomas' second reason for judging this theory heretical is found in his discussion of its use of habitus within the question whether the human nature is accidentally united to the Word. In a *sed contra* argument he quotes a decretal of Pope Alexander III, "Cum Christus," which condemns those who say "Christus secundum quod homo non est aliquid." Thomas, that is, identifies this statement with the third opinion's use of habitus and sees both as equivalent to an accidental union, even though in the answer to the first argument he shows how habitus can be understood of Christ in a non-accidental way.[32] Using the decretal's condemnation of the *non est aliquid* doctrine, Thomas says that accidental predication does not predicate *aliquid* but only *aliqualiter se habens*, so that if the decretal is to be followed, man cannot be an accidental predicate.[33]

The same argument is pursued further in the main reply at this point. The only way that a substance can be accidentally united to

---

31 "Responsio. Dicendum quod unio animae ad carnem constituit rationem hominis et omnium partium ejus. Unde remota anima, non dicitur homo neque oculus neque caro nisi aequivoce, sicut homo pictus. Et ideo si tollatur unio animae Christi ad carnem ejus, sequitur quod non sit verus homo, neque caro ejus vera: quod est contra articulum fidei. Et ideo haec opinio tertia non solum est falsa, sed haeretica et in Concilio a Papa Alexandro condemnata." Ibid., q. 3, a. 1, resp.; 107, p. 244. Thomas is evidently alluding to the decretal, *Cum Christus*, of Alexander III, which he quotes in the following article and which we shall see next. Thomas uses the argument about the need for union of body and soul for a true man or true flesh several times, e.g., ibid., exp. text.; 129 & 130, pp. 250 & 251. In discussing whether Christ during the three days of his death was a man, Thomas uses the same argument (ibid., d. 22, q. 1, a. 1, resp.; 14-15, p. 663): in fact, for him Christ's state in the triduum is the same as that taught by the third opinion — a union of body and soul to the divine person without their union to each other.

32 Ibid., d. 6, q. 3, a. 2, sc 1 & ad 1; 114 & 120, pp. 246 & 247. On the various condemnations issued by Alexander III see *Hypostatic Union* I, 201, n. 52. The text, which Thomas quotes with insignificant variations, is most readily available in H. Denzinger and A. Schönmetzer, eds., *Enchiridion Symbolorum...*, 34th ed. (Barcelona 1967) no. 750.

33 "Sed contra est Decretalis Alexandri Papae: 'Cum,' inquit, 'Christus sit perfectus Deus et perfectus homo; qua temeritate audent quidam dicere quod Christus, secundum quod homo, non est aliquid?' Sed praedicatum accidentale non praedicat aliquid, sed aliqualiter se habens. Ergo homo non est praedicatum accidentale." Ibid., d. 6, q. 3, a. 2, sc 1; 114, p. 246.

another substance is either through bodily contact or through movement of one substance by the other. Since bodily contact with the divine person is impossible, to hold that the union in Christ is accidental, as this opinion does in his view, means that the union in Christ is seen as that of the divine person moving the human nature as an angel does in assuming a body in order to be seen, or as the Holy Spirit did when he was seen in a dove.[34] This type of assumption, however, does not allow what is assumed to be predicated of the one assuming it, nor can the the properties of the former be transferred to the latter. Therefore, Thomas concludes, "this opinion cannot say that the Son of God is truly man or that he truly suffered; and therefore, since it denies a truth of the articles of faith, it was condemned as heretical."[35]

It is interesting to note that this is the only place in the *Sentences* where Thomas Aquinas attacks the doctrine that Christ as man is not *aliquid*. We shall see later that at this period he was not ready to affirm *aliquid* of the human nature of Christ without precise qualification,[36] so that he found some difficulty with the decretal. His reduction of the doctrine that Christ as man is not *aliquid* to an accidental union made it easier for him to attack it; this reduction may be significant in assessing his own position.

Thomas Aquinas also attacks the third opinion for its imprecision in theological method when it uses the authoritative texts employing habitus with respect to the union in Christ. These texts, he says, are only comparisons and should not be taken properly: "...Sed haec omnia per similitudinem dicuntur, et non per proprietatem."[37] Thus he criticizes the habitus-theory for moving from metaphor or comparison to proper or strict predication of the category of habitus, a method that in theology leads to error.[38]

---

34 "...quod est in se substantia, non potest esse accidens alicujus, quamvis conjunctio unius substantiae ad alteram possit esse accidens, ut sic una substantia alteri accidentaliter advenire dicatur, sicut vestis homini. Sed hoc non potest esse nisi dupliciter: vel quod conjungatur ei secundum contactum, sicut vestis homini vel sicut dolium vino; aut sicut mobile motori, sicut Angelus conjungitur corpori quod assumit. Et cum contactus non sit nisi corporum, oportet dicere, quod humana natura non potest advenire divinae personae nisi sicut mobile motori, ut dicatur Christus hoc modo assumpsisse naturam humanam, sicut Angelus corpus assumit, ut oculis mortalium videatur, sicut in *Littera* dicitur; et sic Spiritus sanctus visus est in columba." Ibid., resp.; 117, p. 246.

35 "Haec autem assumptio non vere facit praedicari assumpta de assumente, neque proprietates assumpti vere transfert in assumentem; non enim Angelus assumens corpus ad hominis similitudinem vere est homo, neque vere habet aliquas proprietates hominis....Unde patet quod haec opinio non potest dicere quod Filius Dei vere sit homo vel vere sit passus; et ideo cum negat veritatem articulorum, condemnata est quasi haeretica." Ibid.; 118, pp. 246-47.

36 See below, p. 413.

37 *In III Sent.* d. 6, exp. text.; 130, p. 251.

38 A final point in the *Sentences*: Peter Lombard summarizes an argument made by supporters

Thus the *Scriptum super Sententiis* provides considerable material showing Thomas' views about the teaching and worth of the habitus-theory. In his later works he returns from time to time to this theory and although his analyses are less detailed than those seen above, some noteworthy developments occur.

Quaestio quodlibetalis 9

The ninth quodlibetal question adds nothing of importance to what has already been seen in the *Sentences*. The third opinion, Thomas says, maintains no union in Christ of soul and body either to constitute a man, as the first opinion held, or to constitute a human nature, as the second opinion held. It said that human nature is to be understood "multipliciter, id est pro partibus eius, scilicet anima et corpore, cum dicamus humanam naturam assumptam a Verbo." For Thomas this makes it clear that Christ would not be truly said to be a man and that his human nature would not be a true human nature. Therefore, he concludes, it was condemned as heretical.[39]

Lectura super epistolam S. Pauli ad Philippenses

In commenting on Philippians 2, 7: *Habitu inventus ut homo*, a text constantly quoted in this area, Thomas gives two possible explanations of *habitu*. It may refer to Christ's exterior way of life and in particular to his acceptance of all the defects and properties of human nature except sin.[40] It may also refer to Christ's taking humanity itself as a habit, that is, the fourth kind of habitus in which the habitus itself is changed but does not change the one having it. An example of this kind of habitus is clothing. Human nature in Christ may be likened to this kind of habitus for it came to the divine person in such a way that it did not change the person but was itself changed and made better by being filled with grace and truth.[41]

---

of the habitus-theory against their opponents saying that if God were man essentially or man were God essentially, then, if God had assumed man in the female sex, a woman would have been God essentially and God would have been a woman essentially (*Sent.* III, 6, 4; p. 579). Nothing more is added — apparently for them this was so absurd as to need no comment! Thomas remarks quite simply about this possibility: "...patet non esse inconveniens" (*In III Sent.* d. 6, exp. text.; 129, p. 250). He qualifies this, however, when he says further on: "Et tamen simpliciter concedendum est quod potuit assumere sexum femineum de potentia absoluta loquendo, quamvis non fuisset ita congruum" (Ibid., d. 12, exp. text.; 86, p. 390).

39   *Quaestiones quodlibetales*, q. 9, q. 2, a. 1, ad 1.

40   "Tertio naturae humanae conditiones ponit, dicens *et habitu inventus ut homo*, quia defectus omnes et proprietates continentes speciem, praeter peccatum, suscepit. Et ideo habitu inventus ut homo, scilicet in exteriori conversatione, quia esuriit ut homo, fatigatus fuit, et hujusmodi." *In Philip.* 2, 2; 60, p. 102.

41   "Vel habitu, quia ipsam humanitatem accepit quasi habitum. Est autem habitus quadruplex.

Referring to the threefold opinions given by Lombard, Thomas remarks that some have used this text erroneously by saying that Christ's humanity came to him accidentally. This is false because the supposit of divine nature became a supposit of human nature and therefore came to it not accidentally, but substantially. Aquinas adds that this does not mean that the divinity did not come naturally to Christ, but that it is predicated substantially of him.[42] This adds little new to what has been seen. The positive statement of Thomas himself, however, is important; it shows how Thomas' discussion of this opinion leads him to formulate his own position more clearly. We shall see this in more detail in the third section of this study.

Summa contra Gentiles

The discussion of the habitus-theory in the *Contra Gentiles* opens with a rather sympathetic approach to the intentions of its adherents but ends with a more severe and detailed condemnation of it as a heresy than has been seen thus far. More clearly than in the *Sentences*, Thomas states that proponents of this theory sought to avoid, on the side of the humanity, a human person and, on the side of the Word, a change in the divine person. After first stating the teaching of Catholic faith against Nestorius and Eutyches, Thomas explains that because this teaching seems foreign to what human reason experiences, some "later persons" asserted the following position concerning the union: because "man" is constituted from the union of soul and body and "this man" from "this" soul and "this" body, and because "this man" designates a hypostasis or person, they sought to avoid positing in Christ some hypostasis or person other than that of the Word. They did so by maintaining that Christ's soul and body were not united with each other and that there was not some substance made from them: this they did to avoid the error of Nestorius.[43]

Unus mutat habentem, et ipse non mutatur, ut stultus per sapientiam. Alius mutatur et mutat, ut cibus. Alius, qui nec mutat, nec mutatur, ut annulus adveniens digito. Alius, qui mutatur, et non mutat, ut vestimentum. Et per hanc similitudinem natura humana in Christo dicitur habitus, qui sic advenit divinae personae, quod non mutavit ipsum; sed mutata est in melius, quia impleta est gratia et veritate....Dicit ergo *in similitudinem hominum factus*, ita tamen quod non mutatur, *quia habitu inventus est ut homo.*" Ibid.; 61, p. 102. One recognizes the divisions of habitus given by Augustine, *De Diversis Quaestionibus LXXXIII*, 73, 1 (PL 40, 84), and summarized by Lombard, *Sent.* III, 6, 6 (pp. 580-81).

42 "Sed advertendum est quod ex hoc verbo *habitu*, etc., aliqui erraverunt. Unde tangitur triplex opinio VI distinct. III *Sentent.* Prima est quod humanitas Christi advenit ei accidentaliter, quod est falsum: quia suppositum divinae naturae factum est suppositum humanae naturae; et ideo accidentaliter non advenit ei, sed substantialiter, non quod divinitas naturaliter non advenit ei, sed substantialiter praedicetur de ipso." Ibid., 62, p. 102.

43 "Sed quia hoc alienum videtur ab his quae naturalis ratio experitur, fuerunt quidam posteriores talem de unione positionem asserentes. Quia enim ex unione animae et corporis con-

Those holding this opinion, Thomas goes on, also sought to avoid the error of Eutyches. For them, he says, the only way a subject could have something substantial to it which it did not have by nature would be by a change in that subject. But in the Incarnation the Word is entirely unchangeable. They were left with two alternatives, either to posit that the assumed soul and body pertained to the nature of the Word which he had from eternity, that is, the divinity, or to say that the Word assumed a human soul and body accidentally rather than substantially. In order to avoid the heresy of Eutyches, they rejected the first alternative and chose the second, comparing the Word's assumption of body and soul to a man's clothing himself.[44]

As will be seen later, Thomas Aquinas is historically more accurate in discerning the roots of the habitus-theory than he is in stating its positive teaching. It is against this positive teaching as he views it, that is, the denial of an union of body and soul in Christ and an accidental union of the soul and body with the Word, that he directs the force of his arguments and his accusation of heresy. Some of these arguments have already been seen; some are new. As in the *Sentences*, Thomas states that this opinion is entirely opposed to the teaching of faith because a lack of union of body and soul in Christ would mean that he is not truly in the species man, that he is called man only equivocally, that his body is not a true human body because it is not vivified by union to a rational soul.[45] A new argument along these lines adds that his soul would not be a truly human soul, and so there would not be a truly human nature, because the human soul is naturally able to be united to a body, and if a soul is never united to a body to constitute something (*aliquid*) it is not a human soul.[46]

As for the attempts of the habitus-theory to avoid Eutyches' heresy by positing an accidental union like that of clothing, Thomas asserts

stituitur homo, sed ex hac anima et ex hoc corpore hic homo, quod hypostasim et personam designat; volentes evitare ne cogerentur in Christo ponere aliquam hypostasim vel personam praeter hypostasim vel personam Verbi, dixerunt quod anima et corpus non fuerunt unita in Christo, nec ex eis aliqua substantia facta est, et per hoc Nestorii haeresim vitare volebant." *Contra Gentiles* IV, 37, [1].

44 "Rursus, quia hoc impossibile videtur quod aliquid sit substantiale alicui et non sit de natura eius quam prius habuit, absque mutatione ipsius; Verbum autem omnino immutabile est: ne cogerentur ponere animam et corpus assumpta pertinere ad naturam Verbi quam habuit ab aeterno, posuerunt quod Verbum assumpsit animam humanam et corpus modo accidentali, sicut homo assumit indumentum; per hoc errorem Eutychetis excludere volentes." Loc. cit.

45 Ibid., [2]-[4].

46 "Amplius. Anima humana naturaliter unibilis est corpori. Anima igitur quae nunquam corpori unitur ad aliquid constituendum, non est anima humana: quia *quod est praeter naturam, non potest esse semper*. Si igitur anima Christi non est unita corpori eius ad aliquid constituendum, relinquitur quod non sit anima humana. Et sic in Christo non fuit humana natura." Ibid., [5].

that this attempt not only fails but indeed ends in Eutychianism. If the Word is united only in that way, the human nature was not the nature of the Word. Therefore, the Word did not subsist in two natures just as a clothed man does not subsist in two natures. But Eutyches was condemned for this very teaching that the Word does not subsist in two natures.[47] Another argument new to this work, and not without a touch of humour, states that if the Word assumed human nature only as a kind of clothing by which he could be seen by human eyes, it would have been useless for him to assume a human soul because it is by nature invisible.[48]

After these arguments, Aquinas now takes up the cudgels and rains blow after blow on this theory by reducing it in one way or another to the following heresies: that of Nestorius because it posits an accidental union;[49] that of Eutyches because its teachings would mean that the Word did not subsist in two natures; that of Arius and Apollinaris, in part at least, because it held that the body of Christ lacked animation by a rational soul; that of Manes, in part, because its views would make the body of Christ to be an imaginary body in that the soul would not be united to the flesh to constitute something.[50] Rather more mercifully he concludes the chapter by saying that the theory arose from a literal reading of Paul's words, *Habitu inventus ut homo*, which those supporting the theory should have understood as metaphorical and not as an exact likeness in every detail. Christ's human nature is like a garment in so far as the Word was seen through visible flesh as a man is seen through his garment. But if the union of a man and his apparel is accidental, that of the Word and human nature is not.[51]

---

47 "Praeterea. Si Verbum unitum est animae et corpori accidentaliter sicut indumento, natura humana non fuit natura Verbi. Verbum igitur, post unionem, non fuit subsistens in duabus naturis: sicut neque homo indutus dicitur in duabus naturis subsistere. Quod quia Eutyches dixit, in Chalcedonensi Synodo est damnatus." Ibid., [6]. In the following paragraph Thomas repeats an argument against this opinion that has been seen in the *Sentences*: What happens to clothing is not referred to the clothed man; according to this view, therefore, it could not be said that God was born or suffered by reason of the assumed body. A further argument in the same chapter [par.9] develops an argument similar to that in the *Sentences* about the Holy Spirit's assuming a dove's appearance to be seen: the communication of idioms is not possible between the dove and the Holy Spirit as it is between the two natures of the Son of God. But the habitus-theory would make the Son's assumption of human nature like that of the Holy Spirit's assuming the appearance of a dove. For the arguments in the *Sentences* see above, p. 389.

48 "Adhuc. Si Verbum assumpsit humanam naturam solum ut indumentum, quo posset hominum oculis apparere, frustra animam assumpsisset, quae secundum suam naturam invisibilis est." *Contra Gentiles* IV, 37, [8].

49 Ibid., [10]. A similar reduction of the habitus-theory to Nestorianism occurs ibid., IV, 41, [7].

50 Ibid. IV, 37, [10].

51 Ibid., [11], quoted below, n. 117.

Expositio super epistolam S. Pauli ad Romanos.
Lectura super Johannem.

Although Thomas Aquinas' commentaries on Romans and on John mention the first opinion or assumptus-theory briefly,[52] I have found no direct discussion in them of the third opinion or habitus-theory. The commentary on Romans contains a brief discussion of the correctness of such sentences as "Christus secundum quod homo est Filius Dei," and "Christus secundum quod homo est persona," but these are discussed independently of any reference to the opinions.[53] The sentence, "Christus secundum quod homo est aliquid," is not mentioned. In the commentary on John, Thomas explains the meaning of the statement, "Verbum est homo," by saying that the Word is said to be man in the same way anyone else is man, that is, as "having human nature," and this not by being human nature itself, but as a divine supposit united to human nature.[54] It is interesting to note in this text his introduction of the concept of relation in order to show how the human nature can be united to the Word without change on the part of the Word. Where the third opinion introduced the category of habitus to understand this lack of change, Thomas invokes the category of relation: in fact, he uses the very phrase *se habere ad Deum* concerning the creature's relation to God.[55]

Quaestio disputata de unione Verbi Incarnati

A brief paragraph in this disputed question summarizes the habitus-theory in terms like those found in the *Contra Gentiles*. Thomas says that supporters of this opinion were trying to avoid Nestorius' position of a duality of persons in Christ. Therefore they maintained that the Word assumed a soul and body without their being united to each other, so that no human person would be constituted from the soul and body. Thomas labels this an accidental union. He argues that its position gives rise to an even greater inconvenience than Nestorius' position

---

52 *See Expositio super epistolam S. Pauli ad Romanos*, cap. 1, lect. 2 (ed. R. Cai, *Super espistolas S. Pauli lectura*, 8th ed., Vol. I [Rome 1953] no. 36, pp. 8-9), and *Lectura super Johannem*, cap. 1, lect. 7 (ed. R. Cai [Rome 1952] no. 171, p. 34).

53 Cap. 1, lect. 3; Cai, nos. 53-54, p. 12.

54 "Si vero quaeris quomodo Verbum est homo, dicendum quod eo modo est homo quo quicumque alius est homo, scilicet habens humanam naturam. Non quod Verbum sit ipsa humana natura, sed est divinum suppositum unitum humanae naturae." Cap. 1, lect. 7; Cai, no. 172, p. 34.

55 "Hoc autem quod dicitur *Verbum caro factum est*, non aliquam mutationem in Verbo, sed solum in natura assumpta de novo in unitatem personae divinae dicit. *Et Verbum caro factum est*, per unionem ad carnem. Unio autem relatio quaedam est. Relationes autem de novo dictae de Deo in respectu ad creaturas, non important mutationem ex parte Dei, sed ex parte creaturae novo modo se habentis ad Deum." Ibid.; pp. 34-35.

because it would mean that Christ was not truly a man, since the notion of man consists in a union of soul and body. For this reason, he adds once more, this error was condemned under Alexander III in the Council of Tours.[56] One has the impression that in this question Thomas is giving a stereotyped presentation of the opinion without having reflected once again on its positions.

Summa theologiae

The same impression is given by the relatively few references to the third opinion in the *Summa theologiae*. After asserting the need for Christ's soul to be united to his body if he is to be a man in the same sense as other men, Aquinas declares that to deny this union of body and soul in Christ is heretical in that it derogates from the truth of Christ's humanity.[57] That he has the third opinion in mind is clear from his reply to the first argument. The argument had said that a union of soul and body in Christ would result in a human person or hypostasis other than that of the Word of God; Thomas' reply begins by saying that this was the reasoning motivating "those who denied the union of soul and body in Christ."[58] Thomas' reply is important in its own right:

> This happens in those who are simply men and nothing more (*in puris hominibus*) because the soul and body are joined in them in such a way that they exist *per se*. But in Christ they are united to each other as linked to something more principal which subsists in the nature composed from them. And for this reason there is not constituted from the union of soul and body in Christ a new hypostasis or person, but that very conjoined reality comes to the person or hypostasis that exists prior to it.[59]

In a long article rejecting an accidental union of natures in Christ, Thomas again alludes briefly to the habitus-theory. He first repeats what he has just said about the desire of its proponents to preserve a

---

56 "Quidam vero cum Nestorio sustinentes humanam naturam accidentaliter Verbo advenisse, voluerunt evitare dualitatem personarum quam ponebat Nestorius, ponentes quod Verbum assumpsit animam et corpus sibi invicem non unita; ut sic non constitueretur persona humana ex anima et corpore. Sed ex hoc sequitur maius inconveniens, quod Christus non vere fuerit homo; cum ratio hominis consistat in unione animae et corporis. Et ideo etiam hic error damnatus est sub Alexandro III in Concilio Turonensi." A. 1c.

57 III, q. 2, a. 5c.

58 "...ex hac ratione moti videntur illi qui negaverunt unionem animae et corporis in Christo; ne per hoc scilicet cogerentur personam novam aut hypostasim in Christo inducere, quia videbant quod in puris hominibus ex unione animae ad corpus constituitur persona." Ibid., ad 1.

59 "Sed hoc ideo in puris hominibus accidit quia anima et corpus sic in eis coniunguntur ut per se existant. Sed in Christo uniuntur ad invicem ut adiuncta alteri principaliori quod subsistit in natura ex eis composita. Et propter hoc ex unione animae et corporis in Christo non constituitur nova hypostasis seu persona, sed advenit ipsum coniunctum personae seu hypostasi praeexistenti." Loc. cit.

unity of person through their denial of a union of body and soul. He
then adds that they went on to say that the separated soul and body
"were united to the Word accidentally so that in this way the number of
persons would not be increased. And this is the third opinion which the
Master gives...."[60] That "the Word of God was united to man according
to a putting on as of clothing, as the third opinion says," is no different
from the Nestorian position that "the Word of God was united to Christ
the man according to indwelling as in his temple." This means an accidental union, and the third opinion is even worse than the Nestorian
doctrine because "it says something worse than Nestorius did, namely,
that the soul and body are not united." Because it teaches an accidental
union, the third opinion should not in fact be called an opinion but
rather a heresy condemned by the Church in her councils.[61]

The *sed contra* argument of this same article makes the same link
between a denial of a human *quid* in Christ and the teaching of an accidental union of natures in him as has been seen in earlier works.[62]
What is accidentally predicated, Thomas argues, does not predicate a
quid, but rather "quantum vel quale vel aliquo modo se habens." If the
human nature in Christ came to the divine person only accidentally, the
statement that Christ is man would not predicate a *quid* but only a
quale or *quantum* or *aliquo modo se habens*. But this would be against
the decretal of Pope Alexander rejecting the temerity of those daring to
say that Christ as man is not *quid*.[63]

I have found no other direct references to the third opinion in the
Summa theologiae except for a passing allusion to it in the discussion of
the statement, "Deus est homo." Those who deny a union of body and
soul in Christ, Thomas says, "did not maintain that God is true man but
held that he is said to be man figuratively, by reason of the parts" of

---

60 "Alii vero, volentes servare unitatem personae, posuerunt Christi animam non esse corpori
unitam, sed haec duo, separata ab invicem, esse unita Verbo accidentaliter, ut sic non cresceret
numerus personarum. Et haec est tertia opinio quam Magister ibidem [in sexta distinctione tertii
libri *Sent.*] ponit." III, q. 2, a. 6c.

61 "Alia vero opinio incidit in errorem Nestorii quantum ad hoc quod posuit unionem accidentalem. Non enim differt dicere quod Verbum Dei unitum est homini Christo secundum
inhabitationem sicut in templo suo, sicut dicebat Nestorius; et dicere quod unitum fuit Verbum Dei
homini secundum induitionem sicut vestimento, sicut dicit tertia opinio. Quae etiam peius dicit
aliquid quam Nestorius, scilicet quod anima et corpus non sunt unita....Similiter etiam prima
opinio, quae ponit duas hypostases, et tertia, quae ponit unionem accidentalem, non sunt dicendae
opiniones, sed haereses in Conciliis ab Ecclesia damnatae." Loc. cit.

62 See above, pp. 386, 388-89, 391-92.

63 "...illud quod accidentaliter praedicatur, non praedicat quid, sed quantum vel quale vel
aliquo modo se habens. Si ergo humana natura accidentaliter adveniret, cum dicitur: Christus est
homo, non praedicaretur quid, sed quale aut quantum aut aliquo modo se habens. Quod est contra
decretalem Alexandri Papae...." III, q. 2, a. 6 sc.

human nature.[64] Indirectly, the third opinion is involved in Thomas' discussion as to whether Christ was a man in the three days of his death. Here he recalls Lombard's position that at that time Christ was still a man because it sufficed for him to be a man that the Word have or be united to a body and soul: whether the body and soul were united or not made no difference to the essential constitution of man. Thomas at this point does no more than allude to his previous discussion about the union of soul and body in Christ, where he had identified such a position about Christ as man with the third opinion.[65] By doing so, however, he appears to link Peter Lombard with those who held the third opinion, at least on this particular point.

Although these are the only references to the habitus-theory in the *Summa theologiae*, we shall see that Thomas Aquinas, in his own responses to various arguments in other questions, comes to grips with a number of problems that the theory had raised in the history of the theology of Christ.

Compendium theologiae

Although the *Compendium theologiae* gives basically the same presentation of the habitus-theory as the works already seen, it introduces slight refinements that are worth noticing. Thomas links the teaching of this theory on a union according to habitus, seen as an accidental union, with the principle that everything coming to something already complete in *esse* must be joined to it accidentally.[66] In the *Summa theologiae* Thomas makes the latter principle the source of a separate argument concluding to an accidental union, but he does not link it with the example of habitus as he does here.[67] In the *Compendium* he once again notes this opinion's attempt to avoid a human person in Christ through its teaching a lack of union of body and soul.[68]

---

64 "...illi qui posuerunt quod in Christo anima et corpus non fuerunt unita, non posuerunt quod Deus sit verus homo, sed quod dicatur homo figurative, ratione partium." III, q. 16, a. 1c.

65 "Magister etiam *Sent.* in XXII dist. III libri, posuit quod Christus in triduo mortis fuit homo alia ratione: quia credidit quod unio animae et carnis non esset de ratione hominis, sed sufficit ad hoc quod aliquid sit homo, quod habeat animam humanam et corpus, sive coniuncta, sive non coniuncta. Quod etiam patet esse falsum ex his quae dicta sunt in Prima Parte, et ex his quae supra dicta sunt circa modum unionis." III, q. 50, a. 4c. Thomas' judgment of Lombard's position is more severe here than earlier, *In III Sent.* d. 22, q. 1, a. 1, resp.; 17, p. 664.

66 "Considerantes enim quidam, quod omne quod advenit alicui post esse completum, accidentaliter ei adiungitur, ut homini vestis, posuerunt quod humanitas accidentali unione fuerit in persona Filii Divinitati coniuncta, ita scilicet quod natura assumpta se haberet ad personam Filii Dei sicut vestis ad hominem." 209; 403, pp. 94-95.

67 See *Summa theologiae* III, q. 2, a. 6, arg. 2.

68 209; 403-404, p. 95.

Here again there is a certain compression and linking of arguments kept separate before, because this doctrine is now linked with the example of clothing in an unusual way.[69]

Some of Thomas' arguments against this opinion are familiar from his other writings, for they bear on the truth of Christ's humanity.[70] As for the example of habitus, the judgment is almost verbally the same as in the *Summa theologiae*: The use of this example by them is no better than Nestorius' example of indwelling in a temple and it is worse because it cannot profess Christ to be a true man.[71] The communication of idioms is also pressed against this theory. A clothed man cannot be a person of the clothing and cannot be in the species of clothing; but the Son of God must be said to be a person of human nature and to be of the same species as other men.[72]

The preceding survey of Thomas Aquinas' presentation of the third opinion or habitus-theory shows a firm continuity in his basic understanding of its unique positions. At the same time certain new refinements or emphases appear in works written after the *Scriptum super Sententiis*. These refinements are most evident concerning Thomas' explanation of the motivations leading to the development of the opinion and his own arguments against the opinion.

2. THE HISTORICAL ACCURACY OF THOMAS AQUINAS' PRESENTATION OF THE HABITUS-THEORY

Recent research on the three opinions has given a clearer picture both of the motivations and of the actual teaching of supporters of the third opinion.[73] It is in the light of this research that one can form a judgment on Thomas Aquinas' historical accuracy in his exposition of the habitus-theory. Since Thomas lacked the twelfth-century texts

---

69 "Si igitur anima in Christo fuisset corpori unita, videre non poterant quin sequeretur quod ex tali unione constitueretur persona. Sequeretur ergo in Christo duas esse personas, scilicet personam assumentem, et personam assumptam: in homine enim induto non sunt duae personae, quia indumentum rationem personae non habet. Si autem vestis esset persona, sequeretur in homine vestito duas esse personas. Ad hoc igitur excludendum, posuerunt quidam animam Christi unitam nunquam fuisse corpori, sed quod persona Filii Dei animam et corpus separatim assumpsit." Loc. cit.

70 See 209; 404, p. 95.

71 Loc. cit. For the *Summa theologiae* see above, p. 396.

72 209; 404, p. 95.

73 The assessment of the opinions which follows is based mainly on Haring, *Gilbert*, pp. 26-39, and *Hypostatic Union* I, 64-70, 196-208. Both studies give many texts from the twelfth century, together with references to other studies.

enabling modern scholars to understand this opinion but rather had to rely on Lombard's text and on the accounts of his more immediate predecessors, it is understandable that he falls short of complete accuracy in his presentation of the habitus-theory. What this recent research also reveals, however, is the rather surprising fact that the third opinion or habitus-theory, in its relatively unsophisticated approach, comes closer to some of Thomas' views on the Incarnation than might have been expected if one were to judge from Thomas' own statements about the opinion.

Thomas Aquinas is historically accurate when he repeats so often that proponents of the habitus-theory were motivated by the desire to avoid asserting a human person in Christ. This was indeed the fundamental problem faced by supporters of each of the three opinions; their differences came precisely in the way in which they tried to solve this problem.[74]

Thomas Aquinas is also historically accurate in saying that the third opinion, in order to avoid a human person in Christ, made the statement, "Christus secundum quod homo non est aliquid." He is inaccurate, however, when he identifies the statement with the teaching of the third opinion because this statement in fact was accepted as well by those who professed the second opinion or subsistence-theory. This can be seen from careful analysis of the second opinion, and it is stated clearly by a well-informed author of the twelfth century, John of Cornwall, who says: "It should also be observed that this third opinion holds in common with the second that Christ is not some substance consisting of flesh and soul and that Christ as man is not something."[75] The second and third opinions differed not concerning this expression and the doctrine it implied but rather in their positive explanation of the mode of union in Christ and in their attitude towards the question whether the person of Christ is composed or not. "[The third opinion] differs [from the second] on this," John continues, in that it holds "that the person of Christ is not composed of two natures or three substances."[76]

Thomas would undoubtedly have been surprised to know that the second opinion, which he views as the correct, orthodox position,[77] held

74 See Haring, *Gilbert*, pp. 28, 34, and *Hypostatic Union* I, 67-68, 199-204.

75 "Notandum etiam quod hec tertia sententia commune habet cum secunda quod Christus non est aliqua substantia constans ex carne et anima et quod Christus secundum quod homo non est aliquid." *Eulogium ad Alexandrum Papam tertium*, 1; ed. N. M. Haring, *Mediaeval Studies*, 13 (1951) 261.

76 "Hoc habet diuersum quod persona Christi non est ex duabus naturis siue tribus substantiis composita." Loc. cit.

77 "Sic ergo patet quod secunda trium opinionum quas Magister ponit, quae asserit unam hypostasim Dei et hominis, non est dicenda opinio, sed sententia catholicae fidei. Similiter etiam

that Christ as man is not *aliquid*. Both opinions held this view because they could not see how Christ as man could be an individual substance (an *aliquid*) and not be a human person. After the double condemnation of this teaching in 1170 and 1177 by Pope Alexander III, who as a professor had taught the opinion he now condemned,[78] theologians had to adjust their teachings on Christ as *aliquid*, but they did not have to give up their positive teachings on the mode of union in terms of subsistence or habitus because these addressed themselves to a different aspect of the question. That is why the first opinion or assumptus-theory did not win the day and why the second opinion or subsistence-theory was still able to develop in such a way as to become the common opinion in the thirteenth century.[79]

Again, Thomas Aquinas is historically accurate when he says that the habitus-theory had a special teaching about the union of body and soul in Christ, but he misinterprets this teaching when he says the theory denied any kind of union between soul and body and held that they were united only to the Word. It is clear from many texts of the twelfth and even of the early thirteenth century that the habitus-theory did not deny a union of body and soul in Christ. What it denied was a union of body and soul in such a way as to produce of itself a human substance, *aliquid*, or person, independently of the union with the Word. A theologian by the name of Udo, whose *Sententiae* were written about 1160 to 1165 and who supports the habitus-theory, writes:

> The notion of conjoining is different in Christ from that in an ordinary man: for in a man there is only one union, namely, of soul and flesh, which suffices to make a man: but in Christ there is a twofold union, that is, one of the soul and flesh, which does not suffice to make Christ to be a man... There is also another union, namely, that of the soul and flesh to the divinity, and this suffices to make Christ to be a man....[80]

---

prima opinio, quae ponit duas hypostases, et tertia, quae ponit unionem accidentalem, non sunt dicendae opiniones, sed haereses in Conciliis ab Ecclesia damnatae." *Summa Theologiae* III, q. 2, a. 6c. Thomas was less severe towards the first opinion in his earlier works; see the article by Dondaine referred to in n. 1.

78 "Ad hec dicimus, Christum terciam personam esse in Trinitate, sed secundum quod Deus, nec secundum quod homo, presertim cum secundum quod homo non sit persona, et ut verius loquamur nec menciamur, nec aliquid; non enim ex eo, quod Christus homo est, aliquid, sed potius, si fas est, dici potest alicuius modi." Rolandus Bandinelli, *Sententiae*; ed. A. M. Gietl, *Die Sentenzen Rolands nachmals Papstes Alexander III* (Freiburg im Br. 1891; reprint, Amsterdam 1969) 175-77.

79 See *Hypostatic Union* I, 67-70, 201-08, on the development and adjustments of the various opinions.

80 "Alia est ratio conjunctionis in Christo et alia in puro homine: in homine enim tantum est una unio, scilicet animae et carnis, quae sufficit ad hominem faciendum: in Christo autem duplex est unio, una videlicet animae et carnis, quae non sufficit ad faciendum Christum esse hominem....Est et alia unio, scilicet animae et carnis ad divinitatem, quae sufficit ad faciendum Christum esse hominem...." Text from the critical edition being prepared by Rev. J. N. Garvin,

Supporters of the habitus-theory were simply trying to point out that the union of body and soul in Christ failed to have the same result as in other men, that is, a human person. Thomas himself makes the same point frequently with respect to the question of a human person distinct from the divine person. And, as will be seen in the third part of this study, Thomas himself finds that he must make careful distinctions when it comes to the question of asserting the existence of a human substance or *aliquid* in the united body and soul of Christ.

Where did Thomas Aquinas acquire this inaccurate view of the third opinion's teaching about the relationship of soul and body in Christ? It is not contained in Peter Lombard's description of the third opinion, even though his discussion of whether Christ was a man in the triduum of his death could furnish some grounds for such an interpretation of his own views on the union of body and soul.[81] It is more likely that Thomas took his interpretation from his immediate predecessors. It is true that in the late twelfth century, several decades after the appearance of the habitus-theory, some presentations of its views on the manner of union of soul and body in Christ could give the impression that it denied any union at all. But influential theologians of the early thirteenth century such as Godfrey of Poitiers and William of Auxerre clearly stated that the habitus-theory taught a union of body and soul with each other, and others such as Alexander of Hales make no association of the habitus-theory with a denial of union of body and soul with each other in Christ.[82]

It seems to have been Hugh of Saint-Cher, a Dominican master writing between 1230 and 1232, who introduced the idea that the

C.S.C., of the Medieval Institute of the University of Notre Dame, to whom I am grateful for the loan of the text. For further remarks and texts on the habitus-theory's teaching on the union of soul and body in Christ, see *Hypostatic Union* I, 68, 204-206.

81 "Cum ergo illa susceptio per mortem non defecerit, sed Deus homini et homo Deo, sicut ante, unitus erat vere; et tunc Deus erat homo et e converso, quia unitus animae et carni; et homo mortuus erat, quia anima a carne divisa erat. Propter separationem animae a carne mortuus, sed propter utriusque secum unionem, homo. Non autem sic erat homo, ut ex anima et carne simul iunctis subsisteret, ex qua ratione dicitur aliquis alius homo. Et ipse forte ante mortem hoc etiam modo erat homo, et post resurrectionem fuit; in morte vero homo erat tantum propter animae et carnis secum unionem, et mortuus propter inter illa duo divisionem." Lombard, *Sent.* III, 22, 1; pp. 650-51. Cf. Thomas Aquinas' commentary on Lombard's text, *In III Sent.*, d. 22, q. 1, a. 1, resp.; 14-17, pp. 663-64, and in the text above, n. 65. The words of Thomas in the *Sentences* at this point show that he did not interpret Lombard as holding the position of the habitus-theory, as he understood it, on the lack of union of body and soul in the Incarnation.

82 For the twelfth-century presentations see *Hypostatic Union* I, 205-06. For Godfrey and William see William of Auxerre, *Summa aurea* III, tr. 1, q. 1, cap. 9; no. 7, in *Hypostatic Union* I, 282. The text is really Godfrey of Poitier's, but it was copied into at least some MSS of William's *Summa* and circulated as William's views. On this see ibid., pp. 242-45. For Alexander of Hales' authentic works see *Hypostatic Union* II, 203. I have found no statements in the *Summa Fratris Alexandri* or in the *Commentary on the Sentences* by Bonaventure ascribing to the third opinion the teaching that there was no union of body and soul in Christ in the Incarnation.

habitus-theory denied a union of body and soul with each other in Christ. Arguing against this theory, he says: "Again, if in Christ there was not one thing conjoined from body and soul, therefore there was never a separation of soul and body. Therefore Christ was never dead."[83] He adds an argument that will be used later by Thomas Aquinas: "In what way, therefore, is he said to be truly dead? But they say that the soul gave life to the body. But I think it unintelligible that a soul that is not conjoined should give life."[84]

Thomas Aquinas' immediate source for his interpretation may have been Albert the Great, although Albert does not ascribe to the habitus-theory an outright denial of union of body and soul in Christ. Introducing the third opinion as an "error," Albert begins his summary of its seven positions as follows: "The first [position] is that although there is a twofold natural union, namely that of soul to flesh and of flesh and soul with the deity, neither of these [unions] made some one thing: for neither did the soul and flesh, when united, make one man, nor did the nature of man and the Son of God, when united, make one person..."[85] Albert's reply also seems to recognize that this opinion held for some kind of union, but he finds its idea of the union insufficient: "There are three reasons against the first [position]: because the body of man does not sense or live with natural life by being joined to the soul by any kind of conjoining whatsoever, but [only] by being conjoined to it as to its perfection and act. Therefore, either Christ's body did not sense or live by natural life and with natural sensation, or it was necessary that his soul be united to his body as act to potency or to its proper matter."[86] Albert is thus, even while opposing this position, more nuanced and somewhat closer to the original opinion than was

---

83 "Item, si in Christo non fuit unum conjunctum ex corpore et anima, ergo numquam fuit separatio animae et corporis. Ergo Christus numquam fuit mortuus." *Scriptum super III Sent.* d. 6; no. 108, in *Hypostatic Union* III, 201.

84 "Quomodo ergo dicitur vere mortuus? Sed dicunt quod anima vivificabat corpus. Sed credo quod non est intelligibile quod anima non conjuncta vivificet." Ibid.; no. 110, ibid. III, 201. See also ibid., pp. 62-63.

85 "Ex primo capitulo trahunt septem positiones hujus erroris, quae omnes falsae sunt. Prima est, quod cum duplex sit unio naturalis, scilicet animae ad carnem, et carnis et animae cum deitate, quod in Christo neutra illarum fecit unum aliquod: nec enim anima et caro fecerunt unum hominem unita, nec natura hominis et Filius Dei fecerunt unam personam unita..." *In III Sent.* d. 6, G, exp. text.; ed. S. Borgnet, *B. Alberti Magni...opera omnia* (Paris 1894) XXVIII, 139.

86 "Sunt autem tres contra primam [positionem]: quia corpus hominis non sentit nec vivit vita naturae, per hoc quod conjungitur animae quacumque conjunctione: sed per hoc quod conjungitur ei ut perfectioni et actui: aut igitur Christi corpus nec sentiit, nec vixit vita naturali et naturali sensu: aut oportuit, quod corpori esset unita anima ut actus potentiae vel materiae propriae." Ibid.; XXVIII, 140.

Thomas Aquinas, who interpreted the third opinion's view as an absolute denial of union of soul and body.[87]

It has been seen that Thomas Aquinas constantly interprets the third opinion's use of habitus to mean that it taught an accidental union of the human nature to the Word. In this respect also he has only partially grasped the motivation of the opinion and has misinterpreted its teaching on the mode of union.[88] He is partially correct when he says that its supporters, in appealing to the category of habitus, wanted to avoid a human substance in the sense of a human person in Christ.[89] What was equally and perhaps more important to them in their use of habitus was their desire, when explaining the statement that God *became* man, to eliminate any change in the person of the Word by reason of the Incarnation. Rejecting the category of substance and wishing to understand the union according to one of the categories, they thought that authoritative texts of scripture, Augustine, and others gave them a basis for likening the human nature to a habitus that comes to a person without changing him. As Lombard says in describing the opinion:

> He is said to become true man because he took the truth of flesh and soul. We read that he is said to have taken these two into the singularity and unity of his person not because those two or anything composed of them is one person with the Word or is the Word, but because by the coming of these two to the Word the number of persons was not increased so that there came to be a quaternity in the Trinity, and because the very person of the Word, which previously was without a garment, was not divided or changed by taking up [this] garment, but remains one and the same unchanged [person]. They say that God became man according to habitus.[90]

This insistence on a lack of change was directed especially against the second opinion's teaching that in the Incarnation the person of the

---

87 Thomas' first statement on this subject (in n. 5 above) might be interpreted as similar to Albert's more nuanced position, but he soon speaks of the lack of union of body and soul in absolute terms (see text in n. 9 above).

88 See Haring, *Gilbert*, pp. 35-36, esp. n. 84.

89 See ibid., pp. 28-29, 34.

90 "Qui ideo dicitur factus verus homo, quia veritatem carnis et animae accepit. Quae duo etiam in singularitatem vel unitatem suae personae accepisse legitur, non quia illa duo, vel aliqua res ex illis composita, sit una persona cum Verbo, vel sit Verbum, sed quia, illis duobus accedentibus Verbo, non est personarum numerus auctus, ut fieret quaternitas in Trinitate; et quia ipsa persona Verbi, quae prius erat sine indumento, assumtione indumenti non est divisa vel mutata, sed una eademque immutata permansit. Qui secundum habitum Deum hominem factum dicunt." *Sent.* III, 6, 4; p. 579.

Word was "factam *compositam* ex divinitate et humanitate."[91] Although Thomas Aquinas, on the authority of John Damascene, will
accept the notion of a "composed person" in Christ,[92] he would agree
with this concern of the habitus-theory to avoid any change on the part
of the Word. Moreover, with the same concern, he himself makes use of
a category with an affinity to the category of habitus when he says that
the union is a *quaedam relatio*; he does so for the same reason as those
using habitus, that is, because it gave him a way of understanding the
union of the human nature to the divine person in which all newness or
"change" is on the part of the human nature that is assumed whereas
the divine person, terminus of the relation, remains unchanged.[93] It is
true that Thomas acknowledges the third opinion's concern to eliminate
change in the divine person,[94] but it is unfortunate that he saw it as
taking the category of habitus and the example of clothing to be so
literally applicable to the union that, in his view, it taught an accidental
union. An accidental union was not included in this theory's use of
habitus any more than in Thomas' own use of the category of relation or
of a term even more closely related to habitus, *habitudo*: "...Secundum
humanam naturam non adveniat sibi [Filio Dei] novum esse personale,
sed solum nova habitudo esse personalis praeexistentis ad naturam
humanam."[95]

Thus it must be concluded that although Thomas Aquinas perceives
the underlying motivation of the third opinion or habitus-theory, he
fails on several counts to interpret its teachings accurately. He thereby
passes over some points in it that are quite close to his own positions.
Moreover, because of his own historical influence, he left later authors,
some in our own day, with a false impression on the teachings of this
opinion. At this point, however, one must recall the remarks of M.-D.
Chenu that Thomas Aquinas, in reporting, analyzing and discussing
opinions of the past does not proceed "in the manner of a pure
historian," but rather seeks to extract from positions he judges
erroneous whatever illumination they can give both by the elements of
truth they contain and by the consequences implied by their errors.[96] If

---

91 Lombard, *Sent.* III, 6, 3; p. 576.
92 *Summa theologiae* III, q. 2, a. 4. In his *Sentences* he is more cautious about using the expression: see *In III Sent.* d. 6, q. 2, a. 3, resp. (95, p. 242), and ibid., d. 11, a. 3, resp. (50, p. 367).
93 See *Summa theologiae* III, q. 2, a. 7c, and the text from his commentary on John's gospel
quoted above, n. 55.
94 See *In III Sent.* d. 6, exp. text. (130, p. 250), and the text from *Contra Gentiles* quoted
above, n. 44.
95 *Summa theologiae* III, q. 17, a. 2c. In this text, the *nova habitudo* would be real on the part
of the nature assumed rather than on the part of the person: this is clear from one of the replies in
the same article (ad 4m). See also the text in n. 55.
96 *Introduction à l'étude de saint Thomas d'Aquin* (Montreal-Paris 1950) 162-167; trans. A.-M.
Landry and D. Hughes, *Toward Understanding Saint Thomas* (Chicago 1964) 191-196.

Thomas was less successful in seeing all the positive elements in the habitus-theory, it was because as teacher or apologist he was using the opinions on the Incarnation not so much as descriptions of the past but rather as models of typical positions that were possible concerning the Incarnation. As teacher or apologist he wished to bring out the inner coherence of such typical positions and to show more clearly where each position, as he interpreted it, could lead if it were followed to its logical conclusions. In any case, in reacting to these opinions, even only partially understood, he was led to emphasize or develop certain positions of his own on the Incarnation. It is to his emphases and developments made in reaction to the habitus-theory that we now turn.

3. THOMAS AQUINAS' THEOLOGY OF THE INCARNATION IN REACTION TO HIS UNDERSTANDING OF THE HABITUS-THEORY

Given the method of disputation and discussion so prevalent in medieval theology, one may expect to find that even a theory judged erroneous would provide an opportunity for an author to embark upon fruitful new developments or at least to lay stress on certain aspects of his own thought. Thomas Aquinas undoubtedly develops most of his theology on the Incarnation independently of his reactions to the habitus-theory, but his response to it does shed light on his doctrine in this area.

For Thomas, as we have seen, the habitus-theory denied a union of body and soul in Christ. In rejecting this position Thomas is led to insist strongly and constantly not only on their union but also on the necessity of such a union in all men, and in Christ as well, if Christ is to be a true man like other men. Some of his responses have already been seen. Here we need only recall the varieties they take: this lack of union would mean that the *ratio* of man is found in Christ only equivocally; Christ is not a true man; he does not have a true human nature; he is not in the same species "man" as other men. The same lack of reality would have to be affirmed of the parts of Christ — his flesh especially, or his eyes or his bones: these would be said of him only equivocally or metaphorically if his soul were not united to his flesh.[97] The same principle is applied to the soul: it would not be a true soul if it were not united to his flesh.[98] Christ would not have true human sensation

---

97   See the texts quoted above, nn. 5, 31, 56, 64, and 65. See also *Quaestiones quodlibetales*, q. 9, q. 2, a. 1, ad 1; *Summa theologiae* III, q. 2, a. 5; *Comp. th.*, 209; 404, p. 95.
98   See *Contra Gentiles* IV, 37, [5] quoted above, n. 46.

without a union of body and soul.[99] Indeed, he would be a phantasm only appearing to be like other men.[100]

A closely-related and important doctrine emerges in Aquinas' rebuttal of a lack of union of soul and body in Christ, that is, his affirmation that the flesh of Christ is not vivified by the Word but by the soul of Christ acting as a formal cause. In the *Sentences*, while discussing the third opinion, he faces an argument saying that the Word suffices to give life to the flesh of Christ so that there is no need for the soul to be united to the flesh. Thomas replies that "the Word gives life to the flesh of Christ actively but not formally, and therefore there is required a soul to give life formally."[101] The same argument and reply, both developed more fully, recur in the *Summa theologiae* in a question whose first argument shows that Thomas has the habitus-theory in mind. His reply to the problem is as follows:

> The principle of bodily life is twofold. One is effective, and in this way the Word of God is the principle of all life. The other way in which something is a principle of life is formally. For since "for living things to be is to live," as the Philosopher says in II *De Anima*, just as anything is formally through its form, so a body is and lives through its soul. And in this way the body could not live through the Word, which cannot be the form of a body.[102]

Because Thomas Aquinas interprets the habitus-theory as teaching an accidental union in Christ, he opposes it by emphasizing certain doctrines about the Incarnation. Although in this respect his arguments against Nestorianism are more developed, those opposed to the habitus-theory are also worth noting.

We have already seen one of his responses in which, after discussing the example of clothing in terms of an accidental union, he eliminates any possibility of an accidental union in Christ and sees the habitus-theory as leading logically to a heresy denying the communication of

---

99 "Sequeretur etiam ulterius quod Christi corpus sentire non potuit, non enim sentit corpus nisi per animam sibi coniunctam." *Comp. th.*, 209; 404, p. 95.

100 "Si enim anima non est unita carni ad alicuius constitutionem, phantasticum erat quod videbatur Christus similis aliis hominibus ex unione animae et corporis constitutis." *Contra Gentiles* IV, 37, [10].

101 "Ad quartum dicendum quod Verbum vivificat carnem Christi active, non autem formaliter; et ideo requiritur anima quae formaliter vivificet." *In III Sent.* d. 6, q. 3, a. 1 ad 4; 112, p. 245.

102 "...duplex est principium vitae corporalis. Unum quidem effectivum. Et hoc modo Verbum Dei est principium omnis vitae. Alio modo est aliquid principium vitae formaliter. Cum enim 'vivere viventibus sit esse', ut dicit Philosophus, II *De An.*; sicut unumquodque formaliter est per formam suam, ita corpus est et vivit per animam. Et hoc modo non potuit corpus vivere per Verbum, quod non potest esse corporis forma." III, q. 2, a. 5, ad 3. Cf. the following: "Sequeretur etiam quod Christus vere mortuus non fuerit [if there were no union of soul and body]. Mors enim est privatio vitae. Manifestum est enim quod Divinitatis vita per mortem privari non potuit, corpus autem vivum esse non potuit, si ei anima coniuncta non fuit." *Comp. th.*, 209; 404, p. 95.

idioms in Christ.[103] Within the same discussion Thomas introduces an argument that recurs in several of his works, that is, what comes to something after its *esse* is complete is an accident, so that the human nature in Christ, coming to the Son of God after his *esse* is complete, must come accidentally.[104] Thomas' reply agrees that Christ's human nature comes to the Son of God after his *esse* is complete, but he denies that it comes accidentally because it is drawn into union in that very *esse* of the Son of God, just as the body will come to the soul in the resurrection.[105] This reply, which is important for the questions of the unity of *esse* in Christ and for the unity of man, receives a very full and important elaboration when the same argument is met in the *Summa theologiae*.[106] Although in this work the argument and reply are not so directly related to the habitus-theory as in the *Sentences*, its entry in the *Sentences* in the discussion of this theory shows that the third opinion's position is the origin of the argument and the occasion for Thomas' important responses throughout his works.

Elsewhere the accidentality of the union seen by Thomas in the teaching of the habitus-theory is opposed by the doctrine of the communication of idioms. This has already been seen in one text from the *Sentences*,[107] and it recurs at least twice in the same work. Speaking of the statement, "God is man," Thomas says that the third opinion, by espousing an accidental union, holds that this statement involves predication by way of inherence, as when a man is said to be white. This is most improper, he replies, because this opinion, which holds that the body and soul come to the Son of God like a garment, could predicate man of God only denominatively, that is, it would say that God is humanized in the way a man is said to be clothed.[108]

103 See above, p. 389.

104 "Omne quod advenit post esse completum est accidens. Sed humana natura advenit Filio Dei post esse completum ipsius. Ergo advenit ei accidentaliter." *In III Sent.* d. 6, q. 3, a. 2, arg. 2; 113, p. 245. This argument is repeated, with slight variations, in *Contra Gentiles* IV, 40, |13|, and in *Summa theologiae* III, 2, 6, arg. 2.

105 "Ad secundum dicendum quod quamvis adveniat post esse completum, non tamen est accidentaliter adveniens; quia trahitur ad unionem in illo esse, sicut corpus adveniet animae in resurrectione." *In III Sent.* q. 3, a. 2, ad 2; 121, p. 247.

106 "...illud quod advenit post esse completum, accidentaliter advenit, nisi trahatur in communionem illius esse completi. Sicut in resurrectione corpus adveniet animae praeexistenti; non tamen accidentaliter, quia ad idem esse assumetur, ut scilicet corpus habeat esse vitale per animam. Non est autem sic de albedine, quia aliud est esse albi, et aliud est esse hominis cui advenit albedo. Verbum autem Dei ab aeterno esse completum habuit secundum hypostasim sive personam; ex tempore autem advenit ei natura humana, non quasi assumpta ad unum esse prout est naturae, sicut corpus assumitur ad esse animae, sed ad unum esse prout est hypostasis vel personae. Et ideo humana natura non unitur accidentaliter Filio Dei." III, q. 2, a. 6, ad 2.

107 See above, p. 389.

108 "...cum haec duo [anima et corpus] secundum hanc opinionem adveniant Filio Dei quasi habitus, non potest homo proprie praedicari de eo nisi denominative; sicut nec vestis de homine, sed dicitur homo vestitus." III, d. 7, q. 1, a. 1, resp.; 29, p. 261. A similar statement recurs in a later discussion of the expression *homo dominicus*; see ibid., q. 1, a. 2, resp.; 48, p. 265.

The *Contra Gentiles* likewise invokes the communication of idioms several times in order to oppose this theory: if the Word assumed a soul and body as a man does a garment, it could not be said that God was born or suffered because of the assumed body,[109] nor could the Son of God be said to have become man or to be less than the Father according to the assumed nature.[110] A similar argument occurs briefly in the *Lecture on Philippians*.[111]

Still in opposition to this theory's supposed teaching of an accidental union, Thomas makes several important statements about the subsistence of the Word in two natures. In a chapter of the *Contra Gentiles* devoted exclusively to the habitus-theory, he argues that its teaching would mean that "after the union, the Word did not subsist in two natures, just as a clothed man is not said to subsist in two natures. Because Eutyches said this, he was condemned in the Council of Chalcedon."[112] The reason for this deduction is slightly amplified in a subsequent paragraph: "Nothing subsists in that which is accidentally united to itself."[113]

An interesting variation of this statement occurs in the *Lecture on Philippians*, again in a discussion of the habitus-theory. This opinion, Aquinas says, erred by holding that "the humanity of Christ came to him accidentally, which is false because the supposit of divine nature became a supposit of human nature, and therefore it did not come to him accidentally but substantially."[114] A similarly striking statement in the *Summa theologiae* about the subsistence of the Word in human nature has already been seen.[115]

Thus, although Thomas Aquinas is historically inaccurate in saying that the habitus-theory taught an accidental union, his responses to it on this score serve to bring out his own positive positions on the union in several different directions and in formulas that are both clarifying and striking.

Closely related to these developments are Aquinas' explanations of the meaning of habitus when he meets it in authoritative texts as an

---

109 See IV, 37, [7].
110 See ibid., [9]; cf. ibid., IV, 39, [1].
111 See text above, n. 42.
112 See text above, n. 47.
113 "Ex hoc etiam quod dixit accidentalem unionem Verbi ad animam et carnem humanam, sequitur quod Verbum post unionem non fuit subsistens in duabus naturis, quod Eutyches dixit: nihil enim subsistit in eo quod sibi accidentaliter unitur." *Contra Gentiles* IV, 37, [10].
114 See text above, n. 42.
115 See above, p. 395. In discussing the habitus-theory, Thomas also speaks forcefully of Christ as a "person of human nature": "Adhuc autem homo vestitus non potest esse persona vestis aut indumenti, nec aliquo modo dici potest quod sit in specie indumenti. Si igitur Filius Dei humanam naturam ut vestimentum assumpsit, nullo modo dici poterit persona humanae naturae, nec etiam dici poterit quod Filius Dei sit eiusdem speciei cum aliis hominibus...." *Comp. th.*, 209; 404, p. 95.

example of the Incarnation. In each case Thomas' concern is to avoid seeing in the example an indication of an accidental union. After denying that the union in Christ is accidental, Thomas admits that the human nature in Christ has some likeness to an accident: first, because it comes to the divine person after his *esse* is complete, just as clothing and all other accidents come to their subject; second, because the human nature in Christ is a substance in itself and comes to another as clothing does to a man; third, because the human nature is bettered by its union with the Word and does not change the Word, just as clothing takes the form of the one wearing it without changing the wearer.[116] Finally, just as a man is seen through his clothing, so the Word of God appeared visibly to men through the "clothing" of human nature.[117] Through such comparisons Thomas seeks to exploit the positive values of the example of habitus without opening the way to an accidental union in Christ. As has been suggested earlier, this was in part the intent of proponents of the habitus-theory themselves.[118]

The most important reaction of Thomas Aquinas to the third opinion, and the most important clarification of his own theology of the Incarnation, occurs when he meets the doctrine, thought by him to be identical with this opinion, which said: "Christus secundum quod homo non est aliquid." Although, as has been seen, Thomas refers several times to the ecclesiastical condemnation of this statement,[119] he accepts the positive statement that Christ according as he is man is *aliquid* only with certain important qualifications that illuminate his own theology of the union in Christ.

To understand Aquinas' response to the third (and indeed to the second) opinion on this point, one must situate his statements within a broader context, that is, within his statements about the individual human nature of Christ. At least twice in the *Sentences* he speaks of the

116 "Ad primum ergo dicendum quod natura humana in Christo habet aliquam similitudinem cum accidente, et praecipue cum habitu, quantum ad tria. Primo, quia advenit personae divinae post esse completum, sicut habitus et omnia alia accidentia. Secundo, quia est in se substantia et advenit alteri, sicut vestis homini. Tertio, quia melioratur ex unione ad Verbum et non mutat Verbum; sicut vestis formatur secundum formam vestientis et non mutat vestientem." *In III Sent.* d. 6, q. 3, a. 2, ad 1; 120, p. 247. The third of these comparisons is made again in *In Philip.* 2, 2 (text above, n. 41) and in *Summa Theologiae* III, q. 2, a. 6, ad 1. An alternative interpretation, one likely closer to the true one, is also given in *In Philip.* 2, 2 (text above, n. 40).

117 "Habet igitur natura humana assumpta quandam indumenti similitudinem, inquantum Verbum per carnem visibilem videbatur, sicut homo videtur per indumentum: non autem quantum ad hoc quod unio Verbi ad humanam naturam in Christo fuerit modo accidentali." *Contra Gentiles* IV, 37, [11]. Cf. *Summa theologiae* III, q. 2, a. 6 ad 1.

118 See above, pp. 403-404.

119 See above, pp. 388, 389, 390, 395, 396. In three places he says that the condemnation referred to the teaching on a lack of union of body and soul, which is not the same thing as a denial of *aliquid*. See the texts above, nn. 31, 56, and *De unione Verbi Incarnati*, a. 1c.

human nature of Christ as a substance in itself: *in se substantia*.[120]
Within the same distinction, however, he says that Christ's human
nature is not directly contained in the genus of substance because it is
not a thing subsisting completely through itself; it is called a substance
in the same way one speaks of the human hand as a substance, that is,
by contrast with an accident.[121] For the same reasons he says that Christ
as man (*homo*) is a substance of rational nature, but only as *this* man
(*iste homo*) is he an individual substance of rational nature and
therefore a person; only *iste homo* designates the subsistent of human
nature, that is, the divine person.[122]

In the *Contra Gentiles* the meaning of Christ's human nature is further clarified. After having explained that *hic homo* designates a particular substance, and therefore a hypostasis (that of the Word) in
Christ, he says that it would be incorrect to apply the same argument
that had been made about *hic homo* to Christ's human nature: "If
anyone should transfer the same objection to human nature, saying it is
a certain substance that is not universal but particular and hence a
hypostasis, he is evidently deceived. For even in Socrates or Plato
human nature is not a hypostasis, but that which subsists in it is a hypostasis."[123] If Christ's human nature is said to be a substance, it is not as
hypostasis is a particular substance: "But that [the human nature of
Christ] is a substance and is particular is not said in that sense in which
a hypostasis is a particular substance. For a substance, according to the
Philosopher, is spoken of in two ways, namely, with reference to a supposit in the genus of substance, which is called a hypostasis, and with
reference to a quiddity, which is the nature of the thing."[124] Thomas
then indicates that the human nature of Christ is a part subsisting in the
whole that is Christ: "But the parts of any substance are not called par-

120 See *In III Sent*. d. 6, q. 3, a. 2, ad 1; 120, p. 247 (quoted above, n. 116). Cf. ibid., resp.; 117,
p. 246.
121 "Ad primum ergo dicendum quod substantia, secundum quod est genus, non proprie
praedicatur de parte. Manus enim si esset substantia, cum sit animata, esset animal — nihil enim
est in genere quasi directe contentum sub eo, nisi quod habet naturam aliquam complete — tamen
dicitur manus esse substantia, secundum quod substantia divi[di]tur contra accidens; et similiter
dico de natura humana in Christo." Ibid., q. 1, a. 1, qla. 1, ad 1; 26, p. 226.
122 "Ad primum ergo dicendum quod Christus, secundum quod homo, est substantia rationalis
naturae. Sed secundum quod iste homo, est individua substantia rationalis naturae. Unde secundum quod iste homo, est persona; sicut secundum quod iste homo, est Deus." Ibid., d. 10, q. 1, a. 2,
qla. 1, ad 1; 50, p. 338.
123 "Sed si quis eandem obiectionem ad humanam naturam transferat, dicens eam esse substantiam quandam non universalem sed particularem, et per consequens hypostasim: — manifeste
decipitur. Nam humana natura etiam in Sorte vel Platone non est hypostasis: sed id quod in ea subsistit, hypostasis est." IV, 49, [ad 10].
124 "Quod autem substantia sit et particularis, non secundum illam significationem dicitur qua
hypostasis est particularis substantia. Substantia enim, secundum Philosophum, dicitur dupliciter:
scilicet pro supposito in genere substantiae, quod dicitur hypostasis, et de eo quod quid est, quod
est natura rei." Loc. cit.

ticular substances in this way as if they were subsisting through themselves; rather, they subsist in the whole."[125] From this text it is clear
that for Aquinas Christ's human nature, when spoken of as a substance,
refers to the quiddity rather than to a hypostasis, and this quiddity is
that of a part of the whole rather than the subsisting whole.

Can the human nature of Christ be called an individual, a singular, a
particular? Yes, Thomas replies within a long grammatical analysis in
the *Sentences*: these are names of "second imposition," that is, names
signifying logical entities rather than realities, and they signify the particular in any genus and not only in the genus of substance. On the
other hand, names such as "a thing of nature," "supposit," "hypostasis,"
and "person" cannot be used of the human nature of Christ because,
signifying the particular as found only in the genus of substance, they
always refer to something complete and subsisting through itself.[126] But
just as this hand can be called "individual," "singular," and "particular," so can the human nature of Christ.[127] The same doctrine is expressed with greater clarity in the disputed question *De unione Verbi
Incarnati*, within the same kind of grammatical analysis and with the
same conclusion. Human nature in Christ can be called a *certain* individual or particular or singular, but it cannot be called a hypostasis or
supposit or person.[128]

In the *Summa theologiae*, the human nature of Christ is referred to as
"a certain individual in the genus of substance," like the human hand,
which is not a complete substance but only part of substance. Because
Christ's human nature does not exist separately through itself but rather
in something more perfect, that is, in the person of the Word of God, it
does not have its own personality.[129] Later on in the same work Thomas

---

125 "Sed neque partes alicuius substantiae sic dicuntur particulares substantiae quasi sint per
se subsistentes, sed subsistunt in toto." Loc. cit.

126 "...omne nomen designans particulare secundum respectum ad proprietates, designat
etiam ipsum per respectum ad naturam communem. Hoc ergo potest fieri dupliciter: — vel per
nomen primae impositionis: et sic est hypostasis communiter in omnibus substantiis, persona vero
in rationalibus substantiis; — vel per nomen secundae impositionis; et sic est individuum inquantum est indivisum in se, singulare vero inquantum est divisum ab aliis, unde singulare est idem
quod divisum. Est etiam alia differentia attendenda inter ista; quia quaedam istorum significant
communiter particulare in quolibet genere, sicut particulare, individuum et singulare; quaedam
vero tantum particulare in genere substantiae, sicut res naturae, suppositum, hypostasis et persona.
Quia vero ratio substantiae est quod per se subsistat, inde est quod nullum istorum dicitur nisi de
re completa per se subsistenti. Unde non dicuntur neque de parte neque de accidente, de quibus
alia dici possunt quae in omnibus generibus inveniuntur. Quamvis enim haec albedo vel haec
manus dicatur individuum vel singulare, non tamen potest dici hypostasis vel suppositum vel res
naturae." In III Sent. d. 6, q. 1, a. 1, resp.; 22-23, p. 225.

127 "Sicut enim haec manus dicitur individuum vel singulare vel particulare; ita humana
natura in Christo est individuum, singulare et particulare." Ibid.; 24; p. 226.

128 A. 2c.

129 "Sciendum est tamen quod non quodlibet individuum in genere substantiae etiam in

implies by his example of the hand that the human nature of Christ can be called "a certain kind (*quaedam*) of individual substance" but not a person, and he says it may be called "a certain kind (*quoddam*) of individual or singular."[130] Here as always in Aquinas the qualifications *quaedam* and *quoddam* show that he uses the word thus qualified in an analogical and not univocal sense; human nature in Christ is not an individual substance, individual, or singular in exactly the same sense as are other substances. *A fortiori*, it is not a human hypostasis or person.

With this background in mind, we may approach Thomas Aquinas' discussion of the statement, "Christus secundum quod homo non est aliquid." What for him does *aliquid* mean with reference to Christ's human nature and how may it be applied to him? The most direct treatment of this problem is found, as would be expected, in distinction 10 of Book III of the *Sentences*, for this is where Lombard raises the issue most clearly. The discussion of *aliquid*, however, is surprisingly brief: there is no question explicitly on this point; what there is occurs within discussion of the question whether Christ as man is *individuum*.[131] Here in distinction 10 Thomas repeats what he has said in distinction 6, that is, that although *individuum* is found in both substances and accidents, it is only in substance and not in accidents that *individuum* has the notion of something subsisting. "Christ's human nature," Thomas continues, "is a certain kind of individual, but Christ is not that individual; rather he is a subsisting individual. Taking "individual" in this way, which is the way it is predicated of Christ, there is in Christ only one individual, just as there is only one person. Hence just as Christ is not a person as man, so is he not an individual."[132]

rationali natura habet rationem personae, sed solum illud quod per se existit, non autem quod existit in alio perfectiori. Unde manus Socratis, quamvis sit quoddam individuum, non tamen est persona, quia non per se existit, sed in quodam perfectiori, scilicet in suo toto. Et hoc etiam potest significare in hoc quod persona dicitur substantia individua; non enim manus est substantia completa, sed pars substantiae. Licet ergo haec humana natura sit quoddam individuum in genere substantiae, quia tamen non per se separatim existit, sed in quodam perfectiori, scilicet in persona Dei Verbi, consequens est quod non habeat personalitatem propriam." III, q. 2, a. 2, ad 3.

130 "...substantia individua quae ponitur in definitione personae, importat substantiam completam per se subsistentem separatim ab aliis. Alioquin manus hominis posset dici persona, cum sit substantia quaedam individua; quia tamen est substantia individua sicut in alio existens, non potest dici persona. Et eadem ratione nec humana natura in Christo, quae tamen potest dici individuum vel singulare quoddam." Ibid., III, q. 16, a. 12, ad 2.

131 Q. 1, a. 2, q1a. 2; 44-45, 53-56, pp. 336-37, 338-39.

132 "...individuum invenitur et in substantiis et in accidentibus. Secundum autem quod in substantiis est, habet de ratione sui quod sit subsistens: non autem secundum quod in accidentibus invenitur. Et utroque modo invenitur in Christo; tamen altero tantum modo praedicatur. Humana enim natura in Christo est quoddam individuum; sed Christus non est illud individuum, sed est individuum subsistens. Et hoc modo accipiendo individuum, secundum quod de Christo praedicatur, est in Christo unum tantum individuum sicut et una persona. Unde sicut Christus non est persona secundum quod homo, ita nec individuum." Ibid.; 53, p. 338.

It is one of the arguments in this question about *individuum* that raises the problem of *aliquid*. "Christ as man is *aliquid*," it says. "But he is not something universal; therefore he is something particular. Therefore as man he is an individual."[133] Thomas agrees that Christ as man is *aliquid*, but he denies that one can conclude that as man he is therefore something universal or particular because, he says, it is accidental to man (*homo*) to be universal and particular. Therefore it is accidental to say, "Man is something (*aliquid*) particular." *Per se* predication would involve saying, "This man (*iste homo*) is something (*aliquid*) particular." "Consequently," Thomas concludes, "Christ is not something (*aliquid*) particular as man, but only as *this* man."[134]

Let us observe carefully the implications of this reply. Thomas Aquinas is saying in fact that he does not accept the statement, "Christus secundum quod homo est aliquid" if *aliquid* means *aliquid particulare*. Only if *iste* is added to *homo*, *iste homo* designating "a determinate supposit of human nature, which is the eternal supposit,"[135] will he accept such a phrase according to *per se* predication. The only way he might accept the phrase without the *iste* would be by viewing it as an example of predication *per accidens*. Thomas reinforces his judgments on *aliquid* by making exactly the same distinctions with respect to the expression, "Christus secundum quod homo est individuum." Christ, he says, is not an individual as man, but only as this man (*hic homo*), the latter term again standing for the subsisting subject, the divine person.[136] All that he will say about Christ as man is that he has an individual *nature* according as he is man.[137]

133 "Videtur quod sit, secundum quod homo, individuum. Christus enim, secundum quod homo, est aliquid. Sed non est aliquid universale. Ergo est aliquid particulare. Ergo secundum quod homo, est individuum." Ibid., arg. 1; 44, pp. 336-37.

134 "Ad primum ergo dicendum quod Christus, secundum quod homo, est aliquid; non tamen sequitur: ergo secundum quod homo, est aliquid universale vel aliquid particulare; quia homini accidit esse universale et particulare. Unde haec est per accidens: *Homo est aliquid particulare*; haec autem per se: *Iste homo est aliquid particulare*. Unde Christus non est aliquid particulare secundum quod homo, sed secundum quod iste homo." Ibid., ad 1; 54, p. 339. Behind this distinction lies a principle about *per se* predication implied in the reduplicative phrase, *secundum quod*. Thomas had explained earlier that "id quod in aliqua propositione reduplicatur cum hoc quod dico, *secundum quod*, est illud per quod praedicatum convenit subjecto. Unde oportet quod aliquo modo sit idem cum subjecto et aliquo modo idem cum praedicato." Ibid., d. 10, q. 1, resp.; 23, pp. 331-32. Cf. ibid., qla. 2, sol.; 32-33, pp. 333-34.

135 "Cum autem dicitur: *Iste homo*, demonstrato Christo, includitur ex vi demonstrationis determinatum suppositum humanae naturae, quod est suppositum aeternum, secundum secundam opinionem: cui supposito per se convenit Deum." Ibid.; 33, p. 334.

136 "Ad secundum dicendum quod de ratione individui, secundum quod de Christo praedicatur, est quod sit per se subsistens. Et hoc non convenit Christo secundum quod homo, sed secundum quod hic homo. Unde non oportet quod sit individuum secundum quod homo." Ibid., d. 10, q. 1, a. 2, qla. 2, ad 2; 55, p. 339.

137 "Unde non sequitur, si humana natura est individuum, quod Christus, secundum quod homo, sit individuum; sed quod habeat individuam naturam." Ibid., ad 3; 56, p. 339.

Does Thomas Aquinas maintain this position concerning Christ as man in his later works? In the *Summa theologiae* he does not treat the phrase explicitly, but, from what he says about *aliquid* and about similar expressions speaking of Christ as man, one may conclude that he would affirm in one way that Christ as man is *aliquid* and would deny it in another way. The final articles of question 16 of Part III examine phrases such as "Christ as man is a creature," "Christ as man is God," "Christ as man is a person."[138] In these articles the same grammatical principle is applied throughout: in the phrase, *Christus secundum quod homo*, the word *homo* can be referred back to the subject, *Christus*, by the reduplicative phrase *secundum quod* either by reason of the eternal uncreated supposit or by reason of the human nature.[139] Thomas adds that in such referral by reduplication *homo* is more properly taken for the nature than for the supposit since it is referred back to the subject by reason of the predicate, which is taken formally.[140] Applying these principles, he concludes regarding the first two expressions that one should concede more than deny that Christ *secundum quod homo* is a creature, and should deny more than concede that Christ *secundum quod homo* is God.[141]

Can anything be concluded from these principles about the statement, "Christus secundum quod homo est aliquid"? Thomas' application of these principles to the third expression examined in question 16, "Christus secundum quod homo est persona," will provide an indirect aid to answering this question. But before examining it, we must look at Aquinas' discussion of the term *aliquid* in this context, that is, in the following question on the unity of Christ. An argument, traditional in debates on the three opinions and on the question of Christ as man being *aliquid*, says that "Christ is something that the Father is and something that the Father is not. Therefore Christ is something and something. Therefore Christ is two."[142] The debate turns on the meaning of *aliquid quod non est Pater*, for *aliquid quod est Pater*

---

138 Aa. 10-12.

139 "Respondeo dicendum quod cum dicitur: Christus secundum quod homo, hoc nomen homo potest resumi in reduplicatione vel ratione suppositi, vel ratione naturae." III, q. 16, a. 10c. Cf. aa. 11c, 12c.

140 "Sciendum tamen quod nomen sic resumptum in reduplicatione magis proprie tenetur pro natura quam pro supposito; resumitur enim in vi praedicati, quod tenetur formaliter; idem enim est dictu: Christus secundum quod homo, ac si diceretur: Christus secundum quod est homo." Ibid., a. 10c. Cf. the second text quoted above in n. 134.

141 For the first of these see a. 10c, and for the second a. 11c.

142 "Christus est aliquid quod est Pater, et est aliquid quod non est Pater. Ergo Christus est aliquid et aliquid. Ergo Christus est duo." Ibid., q. 17, a. 1, arg. 4. On the growth of the question of the unity or duality of Christ within the discussion of the question of Christ as *aliquid*, see *Hypostatic Union* I, 68-70, 206-08. For an example of the argument in the early thirteenth century see William of Auxerre, *Summa aurea* III, tr. 1, q. 1, cap. 3; nos. 5 & 10, in *Hypostatic Union* I, 257 & 258.

refers to the divine nature, which even in the abstract is predicated of the Father and the Son. Thomas goes on:

> But when it is said: "Christ is something that the Father is not," the "something" is taken not for human nature itself as signified in the abstract, but as signified in the concrete — yet not according to a distinct supposit, but according to an indistinct supposit, that is, in so far as it stands under the nature but not under the individuating properties.[143]

That is, Thomas refers *aliquid*, when it designates Christ's human nature, to the one supposit, the divine person, although it fails to designate this supposit as distinctly as would, for example, the name "Jesus," since the term *aliquid* does not point out individuating properties of the human nature in which the supposit is found.

This differentiation between indistinct and distinct supposits is already present in the body of the article. Here Thomas says that in the statement, "Christus est homo," the word *homo* signifies the one having the humanity (*habens humanitatem*), but it does so only indistinctly; by contrast, the name "Jesus" signifies distinctly the one having the humanity because it signifies him under the determinate individual properties of Jesus.[144] Can these remarks be applied similarly to the sentence, "Christus secundum quod homo est aliquid"? The import of Thomas' teaching is clear: *aliquid* refers to the supposit having the human nature, that is, to the divine person, and not to the nature taken in itself apart from the supposit or person. Because of the equivalence of supposit and person, it seems legitimate to apply to the sentence, "Christus secundum quod homo est *aliquid*," the same principles as he applies to the sentence, "Christus secundum quod homo est *persona*."

This latter sentence is discussed in article 12 of question 16, that is, just before this discussion of *aliquid*. There the rules of articles 10 and 11 about *homo* in reduplication are applied again, but with a slight nuance. "As has been said above," Thomas begins, "this term 'homo' when placed in reduplication can be accepted either by reason of the supposit or by reason of the nature. Therefore, when it is said, 'Christ as man is a person,' if [homo] is accepted by reason of the supposit, it is

---

143 "...cum dicitur: Christus est aliquid quod est Pater, ly aliquid tenetur pro natura divina, quae etiam in abstracto praedicatur de Patre et Filio. Sed cum dicitur: Christus est aliquid quod non est Pater, ly aliquid tenetur non pro ipsa natura humana secundum quod significatur in abstracto, sed secundum quod significatur in concreto; non quidem secundum suppositum distinctum, sed secundum suppositum indistinctum; prout scilicet substat naturae, non autem proprietatibus individuantibus." *Summa theologiae* III, q. 17, a. 1, ad 4.

144 "Aliter tamen habens humanitatem significatur per hoc nomen homo; et aliter per hoc nomen Iesus, vel Petrus. Nam hoc nomen homo importat habentem humanitatem indistincte, sicut et hoc nomen Deus indistincte importat habentem deitatem. Hoc autem nomen Petrus, vel Iesus, importat distincte habentem humanitatem, scilicet sub determinatis individualibus proprietatibus...." Ibid., c.

clear that Christ as man is a person, because the supposit of human nature is nothing other than the person of the Son of God."[145] Now if the analysis of *aliquid* already seen is applicable in a parallel fashion, it would mean that if *secundum quod homo* refers to the supposit in Christ, then Christ as man is *aliquid* because *aliquid* refers to the supposit of human nature, even if indistinctly (this, incidentally would be true of *persona*, which refers to the supposit or person indistinctly). The sentence would really mean that Christ as man is some indistinctly designated supposit of human nature, a supposit that is not a human supposit but rather a divine supposit or person.

Thomas continues his analysis of the sentence, "Christus secundum quod homo est persona," by saying that if *secundum quod homo* refers to nature rather than to supposit, the sentence is true in one way and false in another. If *secundum quod homo* refers to nature in the sense that it belongs to human nature to be in some person, the sentence is again true "because everything that subsists in human nature is a person. But [*secundum quod homo*] can be understood such that there is owed to human nature in Christ its proper personality, caused from the principles of human nature. And in this way Christ as man is not a person because human nature does not exist through itself separately from the divine nature, which is required by the notion of person."[146]

Again, since *aliquid* refers to the divine supposit or person, it seems justified to draw parallel conclusions about the sentence, "Christus secundum quod homo est aliquid," when *secundum quod homo* is taken to refer to the nature rather than to the supposit. In that it belongs to human nature to be in some supposit, it would be true to say that Christ as man is *aliquid* because everything that subsists in human nature is a supposit, which the term *aliquid* designates. But if *secundum quod homo* is taken to refer to nature in the sense that there is owed to human nature in Christ its proper supposit, caused from the principles of human nature, then it is untrue to say that Christ as man is *aliquid* because human nature does not subsist through itself separately from the divine nature, which is required by the notion of supposit.

---

145 "...sicut supra dictum est, iste terminus homo, in reduplicatione positus, potest accipi vel ratione suppositi, vel ratione naturae. Cum ergo dicitur: Christus, secundum quod homo, est persona, si accipiatur ratione suppositi, manifestum est quod Christus, secundum quod homo, est persona, quia suppositum humanae naturae nihil est aliud quam persona Filii Dei." Ibid., q. 16, a. 12c.

146 "Si autem accipiatur ratione naturae, sic potest intelligi dupliciter. Uno modo, ut intelligatur quod naturae humanae competat esse in aliqua persona. Et hoc etiam modo verum est; omne enim quod subsistit in humana natura, est persona. Alio modo potest intelligi ut naturae humanae in Christo propria personalitas debeatur, causata ex principiis humanae naturae. Et sic Christus, secundum quod homo, non est persona, quia humana natura non est per se seorsum existens a divina natura, quod requirit ratio personae." Loc. cit.

If our interpretation is correct, Thomas Aquinas has introduced nuances into his position by comparison with that in the *Sentences*. There he had required that *iste* be added to *homo* so that it would be clear that *homo* in the sentence refers to a supposit; only with this addition would he accept the sentence, "Christus secundum quod homo est aliquid (particulare)." Without *iste*, he would reject the sentence if one were judging it as predication *per se* and not *per accidens*. In the *Summa theologiae*, on the other hand, just as under certain conditions he accepts the sentence, "Christus secundum quod homo est persona," without requiring the addition of *iste* to *homo*, so, it seems, he would accept the sentence, "Christus secundum quod homo est aliquid,"again without requiring the addition of *iste* to *homo*. He would, however, reject the sentence, "Christus secundum quod homo est aliquid," if *secundum quod homo* referred to a human supposit caused by principles of human nature as if the human nature subsisted by itself and by its own principles.

Now it is a striking historical fact that it is precisely this last understanding of "Christus secundum quod homo est aliquid" that was rejected by supporters of the second and third opinions in the twelfth century and that led them to say: "Christus secundum quod homo *non* est aliquid."[147] They were insistent, against those who held the first opinion with its doctrine that "hominem quendam ex anima rationali et humana carne constitutum" was "assumptum a Verbo et unitum Verbo,"[148] that Christ's human nature, taken precisely as human nature, was not a supposit or person: in this sense they said that Christ as man is not *aliquid*. Thus by a strange quirk of history an opinion, perhaps misunderstood and certainly condemned in the twelfth century — a condemnation upheld by Thomas Aquinas — was in fact the position of Thomas Aquinas both in his *Sentences* and, if our interpretation is correct, in the *Summa theologiae*—in the latter, at least so far as the logic of his statements is concerned. The positive meaning of all this for Thomas' own doctrine is that these intricate analyses show once again how strong is his insistence on the unity of person and supposit in Christ, and how persistently he seeks to eliminate a human supposit in Christ's human nature.

That such a turnabout concerning *aliquid* could happen derived from the fact that Thomas Aquinas was not close enough to the twelfth-century proponents of this position to have their texts at hand so as to know their position exactly. The opinions, and the teaching on *aliquid*,

147 See above, pp. 399-401.
148 Lombard, *Sent.* III, 6, 2; p. 574.

evolved throughout the later twelfth and early thirteenth century, so that Thomas, who was generally quite careful in his historical analyses, failed to see how much the habitus-theory, and the related but not identical teaching about Christ as man not being *aliquid*, were in their fundamental intuitions in accord with his own clearer and more profound doctrine of the mode of union in Christ.

In a reply to his Master General seeking his opinion about a series of articles, Thomas Aquinas said: "It would have been easier for me to make a reply if it had been your pleasure to write down the reasons for which the aforesaid articles were either asserted or attacked. For in that way I could have made a reply better [directed] toward the intention of those who are in doubt. Nevertheless I have tried, so far as I could grasp the matters, to reply in each case to that which gave rise to the doubt...."[149] Lacking the original texts and faithful reports concerning "the reasons for which" the positions of the habitus-theory "were either asserted or attacked," Thomas Aquinas' replies were not always exactly directed to these positions as they were actually held in the twelfth century. Nevertheless, the responses he did make to what he saw its positions to be were frequent enough and significant enough that to follow his presentation of this theory and his responses leads to a fuller understanding of his own theology of the Incarnation.

---

149   "Fuisset tamen mihi facilius respondere, si vobis scribere placuisset rationes, quibus dicti articuli vel asseruntur vel impugnantur. Sic enim potuissem magis ad intentionem dubitantium respondere. Nihilominus tamen, quantum percipere potui, in singulis ad id quod dubitationem facit, respondere curavi...." *Responsio ad Fr. Ioannem Vercellensem de articulis XLII*, Prooemium; in *S. Thomae Aquinatis opuscula theologica*, Vol. I, ed. R. A. Verardo (Rome 1954) no. 772, p. 211.

SAINT THOMAS ET SES PRÉDÉCESSEURS ARABES

Louis Gardet

I

VUE D'ENSEMBLE

DEPUIS les études précises de MM. Et. Gilson et A. Forest, pour ne citer que les plus suggestives,[1] l'apport des philosophes de langue arabe et d'influences musulmanes à la synthèse philosophico-théologique de Thomas d'Aquin est bien connu.[2] Non qu'il soit pleinement explicité encore. Et peut-être les citations d'Avicenne ont-elles été analysées de plus près que celles du *Commentator*, non moins décisives cependant. On ne peut que souhaiter que soit établie un jour une liste exhaustive des références à Averroès, parallèle à la liste des références avicenniennes dressée par A. Forest d'abord, et C. Vansteenkiste ensuite[3]: sans omettre d'ailleurs les autres docteurs musulmans moins fréquemment cités.

On peut répartir les "sources arabes" de saint Thomas sous trois chefs principaux: a) les *mutakallimûn*, "loquentes in lege Maurorum," — très approximativement les "théologiens"; b) Abû Hâmid al-Ghazzâlî, appelé "la preuve de l'Islam" (*hujjat al-islâm*), et qui sera l'Algazel latin; c) l'ensemble des *falâsifa* ou "philosophes hellénistiques de l'Islam," se répartissant à leur tour en deux groupes bien distincts: les "Orientaux," principalement Ibn Sînâ (Avicenne), et les "Occidentaux" ou Maghribins, principalement Ibn Rushd (Averroès). Peut-être conviendrait-il d'y joindre Ibn Hazm, le strict zâhirite andalou.

Il serait fort utile que des spécialistes du moyen âge latin poursuivissent une recension complète et analytique de ces diverses "sour-

---

1 Sans oublier les travaux qui firent date des PP. Mandonnet, Chenu, Roland-Gosselin, et de bien d'autres.

2 L'expression "philosophes arabes" (d'où "prédécesseurs arabes") est courante et commode. Il s'agit en fait de philosophes qui, à une exception près, n'appartenaient point à l'ethnie arabe. Ils écrivaient en arabe (parfois en persan) et illustrèrent l'aire culturelle arabo-musulmane (et irano-musulmane).

3 Voir A. Forest, *La Structure métaphysique du concret selon saint Thomas d'Aquin* (Paris 1931), Appendice, 331-360; C. Vansteenkiste, "Avicenna-citaten bij S. Thomas", *Tijdschrift voor Philosophie, Het Spectrum* (Utrecht 1953), 437-507.

ces" à travers toutes les œuvres de saint Thomas. Mais c'est selon une autre perspective que nous voudrions proposer aujourd'hui quelques remarques. Pouvons-nous situer ces divers emprunts, discussions ou réfutations, à la fois par rapport à la pensée de saint Thomas et par rapport à la pensée arabo-musulmane prise en son contexte propre? Nous avons là, dans l'histoire des idées, un exemple assez rare de "dialogue" spontané à travers la variété de deux cultures et climats religieux, monothéistes l'un et l'autre, mais fort différents. C'est du point de vue de l'islamisant, un peu restreint sans doute, mais que nous ne croyons pas sans intérêt eu égard à la synthèse thomiste, que nous nous placerons d'abord.

Faut-il revenir sur les grandes entreprises de traductions arabo-latines qui marquèrent les XIIᵉ et XIIIᵉ siècles, et qui sont comme le deuxième panneau du diptyque ouvert à Bagdad (IXᵉ-Xᵉ siècle) par les traductions gréco-arabes?[4] Nous en connaissons non seulement les données essentielles, mais les circonstances historiques. Il suffit de renvoyer aux travaux qui virent le jour voici quelques décennies,[5] et aux abondantes discussions auxquelles l'averroïsme latin donna lieu. L'"arrivée des Arabes" (et d'Aristote à travers eux) enrichit singulièrement l'Occident chrétien, mais non point toujours sans luttes ni dommages. La suite des condamnations de 1210, 1215, 1231, 1270, 1277, visaient premièrement à assurer une défense de la théologie chrétienne en sa spécificité.[6] Elles n'allèrent pas sans de nombreuses et peut-être inévitables confusions, et l'on sait les interprétations fallacieuses auxquelles les deux dernières, la dernière surtout, soumirent la pensée thomiste.

Comment donc saint Thomas en usa-t-il à l'égard des "Arabes"? Il nous donne ici un exemple remarquable de sa façon de procéder, de son ouverture d'esprit à toute recherche du vrai, quel qu'en soit le climat de pensée. Ce n'est pas à *une* école qu'il se réfère, mais à toute ligne

---

4 Voir à ce sujet nos résumés ap. *Introduction à la théologie musulmane* (en collaboration avec M. M. Anawati, 2ᵉ éd. Paris 1970), 195-200, 244-248 et réf.

5 Par exemple, R. de Vaux,"La première entrée d'Averroès chez les latins", *RSPT* (Paris 1933); le même, *Notes et textes sur l'avicennisme latin* (Paris 1934); Manuel Alonso, "Notas sobre les traductores toledanos, Domingo Gundisalvi y Juan Hispano", *Al-Andalus* 1943; le même, *Averroès, textos y documientos* (Madrid-Grenade 1948); Ugo Monneret de Villard, *Lo Studio dell'Islam in Europa nel XII e nel XIII secolo* (Città del Vaticano 1944); G. Théry, *Tolède, grande ville de la renaissance médiévale* (Oran 1944); M.-Th. d'Alverny, "L'Introduction d'Avicenne en Occident", *Revue du Caire* 141 (1951), 130-139, etc.

6 "La pointe tournée contre Saint Thomas, dans cette fameuse condamnation de 1277, ne doit pas distraire notre attention de sa teneur générale et du champ chrétien qu'elle recouvre et défend", M. D. Chenu, *La Théologie comme science au xiiᵉ siècle* (2ᵉ éd. 1943, p. 118; 3ᵉ éd. Paris 1957).

philosophique ou philosophico-théologique susceptible d'éclairer ses propres investigations. Il s'appuie sur les Pères — et pas seulement sur Augustin — autant qu'il les peut connaître. Nous pouvons dire de même qu'il en appelle au témoignage des "philosophes arabes," — tantôt pour l'agréer, tantôt pour le critiquer ou réfuter, — dans toute la mesure où il lui est accessible. Au temps de ses premiers écrits, il y eut, en Occident latin, un fort courant avicennisant. Plus tard, l'influence d'Averroès dominera. Saint Thomas ne fut ni avicennisant ni averroïste, mais il sut dégager les axes du système avicennien ou de la pensée rushdienne qui se croisaient avec sa propre élaboration de théologie chrétienne. Et non seulement il ne fut ni avicennisant — encore moins avicenniste — ni averroïste, mais on peut dire qu'il contribua grandement à "digérer" et canaliser les influences d'Ibn Sînâ et d'Ibn Rushd qui risquèrent plus d'une fois d'infléchir la pensée médiévale.[7]

A coup sûr, il ne put guère les situer par rapport à leur propre climat socio-culturel. D'un point de vue historique, ce reste infiniment regrettable. Quand l'Aquinate rencontre telle ou telle opinion des "Arabes", il l'accueille pour elle-même, pour la part qu'elle draine de vérité ou d'erreur objectives. Cela se vérifie d'abord à propos des références "mineures": *mutakallimûn*, Kindî, Fârâbî, Ghazzâlî (Algazel), Ibn Bâjja (Avenpace), Ibn Tufayl (Abubacer)... C'est parfois comme au second degré qu'il les rencontre et utilise: ainsi Avenpace à travers Averroès.[8] Les seuls "Arabes" vraiment personnalisés à ses yeux sont le "platonisant" Avicenne et l'aristotélicien Averroès: encore que lui échappaient les raisons précises qui commandaient par exemple certains jugements sévères du second sur le premier.

Dans une récente et riche étude, M. Et. Gilson souligne que c'est à l'ontologie d'Avicenne et à la "physique" d'Averroès que se réfère le plus volontiers l'Aquinate.[9] Si bien que les positions avicenniennes "intéressent toute la métaphysique de saint Thomas, et par conséquent sa théologie"[10]; tandis qu'il citera Averroès avec abondance par exemple dans ses commentaires des *Physiques* d'Aristote, et en accueillera l'apport sur un plan plus strictement philosophique. — Sans doute cette répartition éclairante pourrait-elle être nuancée ici ou là. Dans la mesure où des principes de psychologie rationnelle animent des conclusions théologiques, Averroès, lui aussi, sera écouté: dans les traités

---

7 Voir *Introduction à la théologie musulmane*, 264-273 et réf.
8 V.g. *Sum. theol.*, I, 88, 2, c.
9 "Avicenne en Occident au Moyen Age", *Archives d'histoire doctrinale et littéraire du moyen âge*, 1969 (1970), 89-121.
10 *Ibid.*, 109.

de la *Somme Théologique* sur l'âme humaine et la pensée humaine, l'importance des renvois à l'un et l'autre philosophe arabe s'équivalent à peu près. La précision apportée par M. Gilson n'en reste pas moins éclairante quant à l'œuvre et aux procédés de saint Thomas.[11] Mais qu'en est-il eu égard à Ibn Sînâ et à Ibn Rushd eux-mêmes? Le premier se présenterait-il en climat musulman comme un quasi-"théologien", le second comme un pur philosophe? Il ne nous semble pas sans intérêt de cerner la question de plus près; elle intéresse au premier chef ce dialogue des cultures qu'illustra le XIIIe siècle latin.

II

LE CLIMAT CULTUREL MUSULMAN

Nous nous excusons de rappeler brièvement une courbe historique bien connue, et que ne peut pas ne pas évoquer tout manuel de philosophie ou de théologie musulmanes.

A de rares exceptions près, ce sont les textes de cette discipline appelée en arabe *falsafa* qui sollicitèrent l'intérêt des grandes entreprises de traductions médiévales. *Falsafa* est la transcription très probable de philosophia; elle fut l'œuvre des *falâsifa* (sg. *faylasûf*). Le terme peut se rendre bien sûr par "philosophie".[12] Il serait plus juste de préciser cependant qu'il s'agit là d'*une* école philosophique, école très brillante d'ailleurs, et aux tendances fort diverses, mais où se retrouvent un certain nombre d'attitudes communes. Au contraire de l'exégèse coranique (*tafsîr*), du droit (*fiqh*), et de la défense des données de foi ('*ilm al-kalâm*), la *falsafa* n'est pas en Islam une "science religieuse." Bien plutôt serait-elle considérée comme "science étrangère," ou du moins marginale. Ce n'est en effet qu'au IIIe-IVe siècle de l'hégire qu'elle prit naissance, sous l'influence massive de ces traductions du grec en arabe[13] que patronaient les Califes: Platon et surtout Aristote (et Plotin et Proclus confondus avec Aristote); les grands commentateurs grecs d'Aristote; des textes de la Stoa, ou ces traités apocryphes du pseudo-Empédocle et du pseudo-Pythagore qui exercèrent tant d'influences.[14]

Très vite, à partir du moins de Fârâbî, les *falâsifa* considérèrent cet apport grec comme un acquis irrécusable de la raison en recherche du

---

11 Voir ci-après, 440-441, la position adverse d'Asin Palacios et son "averroïsme théologique de S. Thomas d'Aquin".

12 "Philosophie" au sens large se dit *hikma* en arabe, mot-à-mot: "sagesse".

13 Tout d'abord par l'intermédiaire du syriaque; par la suite directement du grec.

14 Il faut y joindre les traités scientifiques de Galien et de Ptolémée, qui commanderont toute la physiologie et toute la cosmologie des *falâsifa*.

vrai. Ils ne l'opposèrent point à la foi coranique, et se donnèrent toujours comme musulmans. La *falsafa* et la Loi religieuse seront pour eux comme deux données également valables et dont il s'agira d'établir l'accord. Ils y revinrent maintes fois, et Ibn Rushd tout autant, sinon plus que ses prédécesseurs orientaux. La foi, pour les *falâsifa*, est bien demandée au peuple; mais les sages, eux, doivent s'élever aux hautes vérités intelligibles. Le problème majeur et sans cesse évoqué ne sera donc pas celui de la raison et de la foi, mais de l'harmonie à établir entre une vision du monde philosophique et la Loi révélée (*shar'*). Et sans doute les explications cosmologiques, noétiques, métaphysiques, se nuanceront au gré tantôt des influences reçues ou choisies, tantôt du génie de chaque auteur. Mais toujours elles considèreront comme acquises la production des choses par émanation (au sens strict) de l'Etre premier, l'éternité de la création ainsi entendue (Kindî excepté), l'existence des Intelligences séparées, et l'unicité de l'Intellect agent (*al-'aql al-fa''âl*), "donateur des formes" du monde sublunaire, illuminateur des intellects humains et source de toute connaissance.

La *falsafa* connut deux moments historiques privilégiés: du IXe siècle au début du XIe, au temps de la *falsafa* orientale des Kindî, Fârâbî, Ibn Sînâ; et de la fin du XIe à la fin du XIIe siècle, au temps de la *falsafa* occidentale (ou maghribine) des Ibn Bâjja, Ibn Tufayl, Ibn Rushd. Or, la fin du XIe siècle et le début du XIIe furent marqués par une violente réaction de l'orthodoxie sunnite contre Fârâbî et surtout Ibn Sînâ. Ce fut d'une part la très célèbre attaque de Ghazzâlî (Algazel) dans le *Tahâfut al-falâsifa* ("L'effondrement des *falâsifa*"), d'autre part les sévères condamnations du "théologien" (*mutakallim*) et hérésiographe Sharastânî, surnommé "le tombeur des *falâsifa*."

Il faut avoir cette histoire culturelle présente à l'esprit si l'on veut apprécier les diverses tendances des "philosophes hellénistiques de l'Islam," et mesurer par exemple la portée de l'opposition, faut-il dire de la mauvaise humeur d'Ibn Rushd à l'égard d'Ibn Sînâ. Tous subirent l'influence directe d'Aristote, et S.Y. Suhrawardî[15] appelle Kindî, Fârâbî et Ibn Sînâ "péripatéticiens (*mashshâ'yûn*) récents." Tous étudièrent de près le Stagirite et ses commentateurs. Ibn Sînâ lut quarante fois les *Métaphysiques* d'Aristote avant que le commentaire de Fârâbî lui en ouvrît le sens...Mais les *falâsifa* orientaux subirent plus encore l'influence de Platon et surtout de Plotin. Ou plutôt, c'est à Plotin confondu avec Aristote[16] qu'ils durent leur inspiration la plus

15 Philosophie et sûfî iranien, condamné à mort et exécuté à Alep sur l'ordre de Salâh al-Dîn (Saladin), en 587 H./1191, à l'âge de 36 ans.
16 Deux textes célèbres: a) la pseudo-*Théologie d'Aristote*, extraits des *Ennéades* IV-VI, légèrement glosés en un sens monothéiste par le traducteur syriaque Ibn Nâ'ima de Hims; b) le

L. GARDET

profonde. Or, la pensée sunnite dominante et le *kalâm* officiel ne virent aucunement en cette ligne plotinisante une possibilité d'accord avec la foi musulmane.

Ici, une distinction supplémentaire. Le cas d'Abû Ya' qûb al-Kindî[17] mériterait d'être traité à part. Le moyen âge latin connut surtout de lui son *De Intellectu* (*Risâla fî l-'aql*) et quelques autres petits traités. Il est peut-être dommage que soit restée ignorée sa position même à l'égard des données de foi. Il est, semble-t-il bien, le seul des *falâsifa* qui ait établi un rapport de subordination entre la recherche philosophique et la Loi religieuse. Et peut-être le dut-il à l'influence de Jean Philopon, si bien mise en lumière par le Pr. Walzer.[18] Il est le seul en tout cas qui, au terme de sa démarche philosophique, ait accepté la possibilité ("prouvée" par la Loi) d'une création *ex nihilo* commencée dans le temps et de la résurrection des corps. Il est également le seul *faylasûf* dont on ait fait parfois un "théologien," plus exactement un "docteur en *kalâm*," du tout premier *kalâm* constitué, celui des écoles mu'tazilites. Il fut en fait à la charnière de la *falsafa* et du mu'-tazilisme, reprenant et défendant mainte thèse du second, mais se-lon des procédés apodictiques directement influencés par la logique et la pensée grecques. L'œuvre de Kindî était prégnante d'une "philo-sophie musulmane" au sens strict des termes. Il reste que sa pénétration d'Aristote, de Platon et de Plotin n'eut point la force déductive de celle de ses grands successeurs, — et que par ailleurs des événements histo-riques (socio-culturels) bloquèrent les perspectives par lui ouvertes.

Kindî vivait à la cour de Bagdad. Il fut contemporain de la réaction du Calife Mutawakkil, menée au nom de l'orthodoxie sunnite[19] contre les mu'tazilites. Quelques années plus tard, un nouveau *kalâm* devait prendre son essor, centré sur la défense de la Transcendance et de l'absolue Liberté divines. La réalité ontologique de la liberté humaine, dont les mu'tazilites avaient été les défenseurs, se résorbera en la toute-puissante et indépendante Volonté du Très Haut "que l'on n'interroge pas." Ce fut l'école ash'arite. Elle dominera l'enseignement officiel jusqu'à l'aube du xxe siècle.

Livre de l'explication d'Aristote au sujet du Bien pur, extraits de l'*Elementatio theologica* de Proclus, connu au moyen âge latin comme le *Liber de Causis*.— Sur les bases de ces confusions historiques, Fârâbî écrira son *Accord de Platon et d'Aristote*.

17 Le seul parmi les *falâsifa* à appartenir à l'ethnie arabe; appelé volontiers "le philosophe des Arabes."

18 *Greek into Arabic* (Oxford 1962), v. "New Studies on Al-Kindî", 175-205.

19 Les sunnites (*ahl al-sunna*), qui entendent demeurer fidèles à la tradition (*sunna*) du Prophète, peuvent être considérés comme les tenants de la foi musulmane en ses dominantes of-ficielles.

Si opposés qu'ils puissent être les uns aux autres, mu'tazilites et ash'arites sont bien des "théologiens," si l'on veut traduire par "théologie" cette "science religieuse" que fut et demeure le *'ilm al-kalâm*. En fait, il s'agit moins d'une théologie intelligence de la foi (au sens de saint Augustin) que d'une apologie défensive des valeurs de foi. Si la *falsafa* dut son existence aux traductions des philosophes grecs, c'est dès la bataille de Siffîn (37 H./655) que commencèrent les discussions du *kalâm*. L'influence grecque s'exercera sans doute sur le vocabulaire, et plus tard sur les modes d'argumenter; en son fonds cependant, la problématique est d'inspiration directement musulmane.

Les rapports de la *falsafa* et du *kalâm* ne sont aucunement ce que seront les rapports philosophie-théologie en chrétienté. Fârâbî déjà est fort réticent sur la valeur du *kalâm*[20]; Ibn Sînâ l'ignore; Ibn Rushd le condamne sans rémission.[21] En réplique, les docteurs en *kalâm* des écoles ash'arite et hanafite-mâturîdite, — écoles officielles en Islam sunnite,—ne cessèrent, à partir du xi⁰ siècle, d'attaquer la *falsafa*. Dans son *Tahâfut*, Ghazzâlî relève trois thèses des *falâsifa* (entendons Fârâbî et surtout Avicenne) qu'il déclare entachées d'impiété (*takfîr*): éternité du monde, non connaissance divine des singuliers, interprétation allégorique de la résurrection des corps. Avicenne n'était, ni de près ni de loin, un "docteur en *kalâm*" (*mutakallim*).

De leur vivant il est vrai, l'"orthodoxie" musulmane de Fârâbî et d'Ibn Sînâ ne fut point mise en question. C'est qu'ils appartenaient à un milieu fortement imprégné de shî'isme, voire délibérément shî'ite.[22] Or, les gnoses shî'ites, et leurs interprétations des textes du Coran, allaient dans un sens plus volontiers émanatiste que créationiste, et permettaient toutes les audaces du "sens caché." A partir du xi⁰ siècle, le shî'isme recula devant la résurgence sunnite.[23] Au temps d'Ibn Rushd, l'Islam officiel, en Andalus et au Maroc, était activement et même combativement sunnite.

Ibn Bâjja et Ibn Tufayl furent, eux aussi, néoplatonisants. Il n'en alla plus de même pour Ibn Rushd qui est certainement le plus aristotélicien de tous les *falâsifa*, le seul vraiment aristotélicien peut-

20 Voir son *Ihsâ' al-'ulûm* ("Catalogue des Sciences", éd. Palencia, Madrid, 1932).
21 Dans ses deux petits traités d'auto-défense (cf. ci-après), *Fasl al-maqâl* et *Kashf 'an manâhij al-adilla*.
22 Le shî'isme ou "parti de 'Alî" (*shî'at 'Alî*) se sépara du sunnisme dès l'an 37 de l'hégire. L'opposition, d'abord politique (plus exactement politico-religieuse), et centrée sur les conditions de validité de l'*Imâma* ou Califat, en vint à susciter des attitudes de foi et des climats de pensée qui divergeront profondément.
23 A l'heure actuelle, les shî'ites sont, en Islam, très fortement minoritaires (moins du dixième de l'ensemble des musulmans).

être. Son opposition à l'égard d'Avicenne? Elle relève, nous semble-t-il, d'un triple motif.

Le premier, et le plus décisif en un sens, est d'ordre historique. Au contraire d'Avicenne, Ibn Rushd dut défendre son orthodoxie musulmane contre les juristes (*fuqahâ'*) de son temps et de son milieu.[24] Il partait avec le handicap du *Tahâfut* de Ghazzâlî et des attaques de Shahrastânî. Or, c'est essentiellement Avicenne qui était visé par l'un et par l'autre. Aux yeux du moyen âge latin, Averroès fut par antonomase le Commentateur, et l'on peut dire que ses commentaires d'Aristote restent l'œuvre capitale de sa vie. Mais dans l'obligation où il était de défendre son "orthodoxie," il nous laissa trois petits traités et tout un ouvrage d'*apologia sua*. L'ouvrage en question, *Tahâfut al-tahâfut* ("L'effondrement de l'effondrement") entend être une réplique directe à Ghazzâlî. Et puisque ce dernier dénonçait la *falsafa* sur des thèses avicenniennes, c'est, dira Ibn Rushd, qu'Ibn Sînâ l'y avait incité de par la faiblesses de certains de ses arguments et de certaines de ses positions.[25]

Le deuxième motif est la fidélité d'Ibn Rushd envers le Stagirite, s'opposant à l'inspiration plotinienne d'Ibn Sînâ. Dans la mesure où l'augustinisme médiéval avait intégré des influences néoplatonisantes, on comprend la séduction que put exercer sur lui un certain avicennisme. Mais il ne s'agit aucunement, dans la vue du monde avicennienne, d'une primauté reconnue à des valeurs de foi, il ne s'agit aucunement d'une théologie fondée sur un donné révélé (et il s'agit moins encore d'une apologie défensive du type *'ilm al-kalâm*). Si la métaphysique d'Ibn Sînâ, dans ses chapitres concernant les choses divines (*ilâhiyyât*), intègre des thèmes tels que la prophétie, la prière, la vie future, c'est que, selon lui, la connaissance du sage peut s'élever, sous la lumière de l'Intellect agent, aussi loin en valeurs intelligibles que la révélation reçue par le prophète. Mais le prophète, de par la perfection de sa puissance imaginative, et la spéciale illumination en elle reçue, peut enseigner ces mêmes vérités au peuple, sous mode de symboles et d'allégories,—ce que ne saurait faire le sage. Et le rôle et même

24 Il avait bénéficié, au début de sa carrière, du soutien du Sultân almohade. C'est à la demande du Sultân Abû Ya'qùb Yùsuf qu'il avait entrepris de commenter Aristote. Plus tard, sous le successeur de Abû Ya'qùb, les *fuqahâ'* andalous obtinrent son exil au Maroc et condamnèrent ses œuvres au bûcher. Il mourut à Marrakech.

25 Si l'on reprend les trois thèses marquées par Ghazzâlî de la note d'"impiété": Ibn Rushd maintient l'éternité du monde, et entend prouver qu'une interprétation "profonde" des textes coraniques n'y est point opposée; pour la résurrection des corps, il se borne à affirmer sa révérence à l'égard de l'enseignement prophétique, sans traiter vraiment la question. Sa notion de connaissance divine des singuliers par contre est certainement plus conforme au Coran que ne l'était la notion avicennienne.

l'existence du prophète s'inscrit dans le déterminisme universel des choses. Rien de commun ici avec la foi musulmane comme telle, et la libre disposition par laquelle Dieu se choisit ses prophètes et envoyés. Sur ce point précis, nous verrons Ibn Rushd reprendre les thèses de son prédécesseur oriental, les corrigeant et modifiant sans doute, mais selon une problématique toute semblable. La différence majeure entre Ibn Rushd et Ibn Sînâ ne se situe point dans un rapport entre philosophie et théologie; elle est liée à cette mystique intellectualiste inhérente à toute influence plotinienne, et qu'Ibn Rushd récusait.[26]

Le troisième motif est la minutie des analyses du *Commentator*, son souci d'exactitude et de révérence à l'égard du texte d'Aristote, opposés aux vues plus larges et plus élaborées d'Ibn Sînâ. Ce sont des commentaires qui se veulent très près des textes que nous avons du premier; ce sont des œuvres de synthèse personnelle que nous a laissées le second. Certes, il est difficile d'entériner d'un trait de plume cette opposition-là. C'est parfois Ibn Rushd qui, en métaphysique, s'avance dans une ligne assez proche des conclusions de saint Thomas: ainsi sa notion de création directe par la Science divine, et donc la connaissance divine des singuliers.[27] C'est parfois Ibn Sînâ qui, en noétique et anthropologie par exemple, maintient, au contraire d'Ibn Rushd, l'individualité *post mortem* de l'intellect possible, fondant ainsi la survie personnelle de l'âme séparée. Mais l'un comme l'autre, ne l'oublions pas, affirment l'éternité (nécessaire et voulue) du monde, et le rôle illuminateur de l'Intellect agent, unique et séparé.

L'auto-défense d'Ibn Rushd ne consista aucunement à se replier sur un plan "philosophique." Elle vise à montrer l'harmonie de la *falsafa* et de la Loi religieuse. Les rapports qu'il établit entre la saisie intelligible du sage et la connaissance du prophète sont peut-être plus nuancés que chez Ibn Sînâ; ils ne sont pas radicalement autres. Pour Ibn Rushd, les ennemis des sages comme des prophètes sont les accusateurs de la *falsafa*, les "dialecticiens," c'est-à-dire les docteurs en *kalâm* (*mutakallimûn*), "esprits malades" qui, par leur méthode et leurs discussions, ont "mis en pièce la Loi religieuse et ont divisé les gens complètement."[28] La réplique d'Ibn Rushd aux "théologiens," c'est de mettre en cause la légitimité même de leur discipline. Et soit dans le *Fasl al-maqâl*, soit dans le *Tahâfut al-tahâfut*, il n'hésite pas à aborder à

---

26 Alors qu'Avicenne, comme le dit très bien le Père Chenu (*Introduction à l'étude de Saint Thomas*, Paris 1950, p. 176) "avait comme transsubstantié l'aristotélisme en une mystique néoplatonisante": grâce aux extraits des *Ennéades* et de Proclus, attribués à Aristote.
27 Thèse explicitement traitée dans un bref écrit traduit en latin *Epistola ad amicum*, et cité dans le *Pugio Fidei* de Raymond Martin.
28 *Fasl al-maqâl*, éd. et trad. franç. de L. Gauthier (Alger 1942), 29.

son tour, tout comme Ibn Sînâ, des thèmes "théologiques" tels que l'éternité du monde, le rôle du prophète, le miracle, etc.

On voit donc la portée de son accusation quand il stigmatise l'œuvre d'Avicenne comme "une sorte de moyen terme entre les Péripatéticiens et les docteurs en *kalâm*"[29]..."Il ne pouvait rien dire de plus dur contre son prédécesseur," souligne à juste titre M. Gilson.[30] Faire d'un *faylasûf* un quasi-*mutakallim*, c'était avant tout, pour Ibn Rushd, lui reprocher la faiblesse de ses arguments philosophiques, le comparer à ces "dialecticiens" (*jadaliyyûn*) du *kalâm* aux interprétations fragiles ou fallacieuses. Disons que c'est là un argument *ad hominem* du péripatéticien contre le néoplatonisant. Ibn Rushd voit bien en Avicenne un "philosophe,"[31] mais l'accuse, parce que platonisant, de se contenter, sur le plan philosophique, d'arguments aussi peu probants que ceux du *kalâm*.

III

Les *Mutakallimûn* ("Loquentes in Lege Maurorum")

Cette incursion dans la pensée musulmane va nous permettre de préciser jusqu'à quel point les "Arabes" furent connus du moyen âge latin, et plus précisément de saint Thomas; et de signaler en cours de route certains contresens historiques dont ils furent victimes.

Dans quelle mesure le *kalâm* lui-même, et ses rapports avec la *falsafa* furent-ils connus? Quand saint Thomas discute et réfute les *mutakallimûn* dans la *Somme Contre les Gentiles*,[32] il ne vise guère que les positions philosophiques de l'atomisme mu'tazilite ou ash'arite,— il serait plus juste de dire: de *certaines lignes* mu'tazilites ou ash'arites. Que sont pour lui ces *loquentes* (traduction littérale de *mutakallimûn*)? Le "in lege Maurorum" (ou *"Saracenorum"*) ajouté par les traductions latines devait lui donner une idée assez juste de leur position de "défen-

---

29   Et. Gilson, art. cit., 113, à propos du commentaire sur *Physiques* II, 3, t. comm. 225 (cité, ibid., 95), où Averroès récuse la preuve avicennienne de l'existence de Dieu par la causalité efficiente: "Via autem qua processit Avicenna in probando Primum Principium est via Loquentium, et sermo ejus semper invenitur quasi medius inter Peripateticos et Loquentes". — Nous verrons ci-après (p. 442-443) que cette preuve d'Ibn Sînâ est en réalité fort différente de la *via Loquentium*.
30   Art. cit., ibid.
31   Dans le *Fasl al-maqâl* (éd. cit., 11) Ibn Rushd fait explicitement de Fârâbî et d'Ibn Sînâ des *falâsifa*, et entreprend de les laver de l'accusation d'impiété portée contre eux par Ghazzâlî.
32   Voir à ce sujet l'analyse de M. Et. Gilson, "Pourquoi Saint Thomas a critiqué Saint Augustin" (*Archives*, 1926-1927), § 1 "critique thomiste des motecallemin", 13 et ss. M. Gilson a dressé un tableau de 6 thèses "atomistiques" critiquées par saint Thomas. Deux autres peuvent leur être jointes, en référence à *Sum. cont. Gent.*, III, 69 et 97. Voir *Intr. theol. musul.*, 285 et notes.

seurs des croyances religieuses." Mais il en parle toujours collectivement, sans distinction ni d'auteurs, ni d'écoles.

Miguel Asin Palacios entreprit, il est vrai, de prouver que saint Thomas avait des docteurs en *kalâm* une connaissance quasi-directe, à travers des textes traduits par Raymond Martin. Selon lui, l'article de la *Sum. cont. Gent.* (II, 29) qui réfute les deux positions contraires du pur volontarisme divin et d'un Dieu "nécessité" renverrait à l'opposition, à l'intérieur du *kalâm*, entre ash'arites et mu'tazilites.[33] Rien ne nous semble moins sûr. Certes, pour les mu'tazilites, Dieu est "tenu" de faire le bien, selon une obligation "morale" (non une "nécessité" physique ou ontologique) qui vient de la perfection même de son Etre et de sa toute Justice. Mais dans son acte créateur, il est absolument libre, comme l'homme à son tour est libre en ses actes, de par le "pouvoir contingent" créé en lui par Dieu. Les mu'tazilites affirment la liberté humaine au nom de la Justice divine, — les ash'arites en nient le fondement ontologique au nom de la Toute Puissance du Très Haut; le bien et le mal, selon eux la récompense et le châtiment, n'ont d'autre raison d'être que le libre Vouloir de Dieu, qui en décide à son gré. — Mais pour les uns comme pour les autres, mu'tazilites comme ash'arites, Dieu Un, Créateur absolu et Juge des juges, n'est aucunement "nécessité" selon un déterminisme de l'existence. De pouvoir absolu, la création, commencée dans le temps, eût pu ne pas être.

C'est là peut-être ce qui sépare le plus radicalement d'une part les tendances, même opposées, du *kalâm*, de l'autre la *falsafa*. Pour les *falâsifa*, maghribins ou orientaux, l'Etre premier ne peut pas ne pas produire le monde de toute éternité. Pour Averroès comme pour Avicenne, tout s'inscrit selon un déterminisme existentiel, aussi bien le "libre choix" (*ikhtiyâr*) de l'homme que les actes nécessaires des êtres non doués d'intelligence. Or c'est bien cette théorie-là (et non "l'obligation morale" mu'tazilite) que saint Thomas semble avoir en vue quand il s'élève contre l'erreur de ceux "qui divinam potentiam limitantes dicebant Deum non posse facere nisi quae facit...."[34]

Un texte parallèle l'indiquerait mieux encore.[35] Les deux erreurs à écarter sont d'une part celle des *mutakallimûn* (nommément désignés, en référence à Maïmonide) pour qui il ne saurait y avoir de loi naturelle, le feu produisant chaleur ou froid au gré de la Volonté divine, et d'autre part l'affirmation (anonyme) que "l'ordre des causes vient de la divine Providence selon un mode de nécessité." Or, nous avons ici

33 Cf. "Los origenes de la teologia escolastica", *Mélanges Mandonnet II* (Paris 1930).
34 *Sum. cont. Gent.*, II, 29 in fine.
35 Ibid., III, 97.

presque mot pour mot la définition avicennienne de la Providence
('inâya),[36] et selon une problématique étrangère au mu'tazilisme comme
à l'ash'arisme.

Comment saint Thomas connut-il l'atomisme du *kalâm* et sa négation
des causes secondes? Fidèle à son souci de multiplier des équivalences-
filières, Asin Palacios s'efforce d'établir deux sources possibles: a) certains développements de l'hérésiographe-polémiste Ibn Hazm, extraits
de son *Fisal* et traduits en latin: mais en fait, c'est le problème de la
nécessité de la révélation et de son utilité pour la race des hommes qui,
selon Palacios lui-même, serait ici en jeu[37] (nous y reviendrons); b) des
textes de Ghazzâlî traduits par Raymond Martin.[38] Certains passages
du *Tahâfut al-falâsifa* (connu de Maïmonide et de Raymond Martin)?
Ce reste possible, voire probable. Mais si le *Tahâfut* expose en effet le
volontarisme divin ash'arite, c'est pour réfuter les *falâsifa*, non point les
mu'tazilites. N'oublions pas, au surplus, que l'atomisme du *kalâm*
s'origine chez Abû l-Hudhayl al-'Allâf, l'un des plus notables
mu'tazilites de Basra. — L'*Iqtisâd*, traité de *kalâm* de Ghazzâlî? Cela
nous semble beaucoup plus douteux. Et à supposer même que des extraits de l'*Iqtisâd* aient été traduits par Raymond Martin (?), il reste que
la théorie atomistique du *kalâm* n'y apparaît qu'en *obiter dictum*, à
propos seulement de la résurrection des corps.[39]

Si quelques textes de Ghazzâlî cités dans l'*Explanatio Symboli* de
Raymond Martin purent guider saint Thomas dans sa connaissance du
kalâm, sa source principale n'en demeure pas moins indirecte, à travers
Maïmonide. Le texte ci-dessus noté de *Sum. contr. Gent.* III, 97, renvoie explicitement à Rabbi Moyses. Et les pertinentes analyses
proposées par ailleurs de l'atomisme ash'arite[40] peuvent toujours s'expliquer, semble-t-il, par des références au *Guide des Egarés*.[41] Un
changement de perspective cependant: Maïmonide, lui, connaissait
l'évolution de la pensée musulmane et son milieu socio-culturel; aussi
rattache-t-il cet atomisme à la "preuve" du commencement temporel du
monde, et il a historiquement raison. Saint Thomas, sans se soucier de
l'évolution de la problématique musulmane, va directement au nœud

---

36 Voir réf. ap. Louis Gardet, *La Pensée religieuse d'Avicenne* (Paris 1951), 131-132.
37 Voir son grand ouvrage (5 vol.) *Abenhazam de Cordoba* (Madrid 1927-1932).
38 Cf. *Los origines*, art. cit.
39 *Iqtisâd* (Le Caire, s.d.), 87.
40 *Sum. cont. Gent.*, I, 87 in fine; II, 24 (*id.*), III, 65, 69, etc. Voir Et. Gilson, "Pourquoi Saint
Thomas a critiqué Saint Augustin", art. cit.
41 *Dalâlat al-Hâ'irîn*, trad. de l'arabe par S. Munk, nouvelle ed. (Paris 1960), I, 185-189, 342,
et surtout 377-419, où Maïmonide résume en "douze propositions" les thèses philosophiques du
kalâm.

philosophique du problème, à la vue discontinue du monde et à la non densité ontologique du créé que postulaient les thèses du *kalâm*. Mais il n'est pas jusqu'au jugement d'ensemble porté (un peu vite) par saint Thomas sur la *stultitia* des *loquentes in lege Maurorum* qui ne rejoigne les appréciations dédaigneuses de Maïmonide.[42] Une meilleure et plus directe connaissance du *kalâm* eût évité sans doute cette condamnation sommaire.

En conclusion de ce paragraphe: a) pour saint Thomas, les *mutakallimûn* sont bien des docteurs "in lege Maurorum," nettement distingués par là même des "philosophes" qui se recommandaient de la pensée grecque; b) il ne semble pas avoir vraiment distingué mu'tazilisme et ash'arisme, ni situé les raisons profondes de leur opposition à l'intérieur de la "science du *kalâm*"; c) à travers Maïmonide (et quelques textes peut-être de Ghazzâlî), il a suffisamment connu les thèses cosmologiques de l'atomisme ash'arite pour les résumer avec pertinence, mais non pour en marquer les limites historiques: thèse dominante de certaines lignes mu'tazilites et du premier ash'arisme, cette vue atomistique du monde, à partir du XIe siècle, sera souvent écartée au profit du semi-conceptualisme des "modes" (d'origine mu'tazilite aussi) par l'ash'arisme dit "des modernes."

Les *loquentes in lege Maurorum* n'intéressèrent saint Thomas que dans la mesure où leur négation de toute efficace des causes secondes concrétisait — face au déterminisme existentiel des *falâsifa* — l'une des erreurs à combattre en toute question touchant à la toute Puissance divine dans ses rapports avec le monde. Evanescence du créé et déterminisme existentiel sont les "corrélatifs d'opposition" (*muqâbal*) entre lesquels la pensée musulmane ne cessa d'osciller. Nous ne croyons pas exagéré de dire que la solution de saint Thomas — Dieu fait agir nécessairement les causes nécessaires, et librement les causes libres, car la création est une libre et réelle participation d'être et d'agir, — nous ne croyons exagéré de dire que cette solution-là fut parfois comme postulée par certaines vues mu'tazilites ou mâturîdites, et certaines analyses d'un Ghazzâlî ou d'un Fakhr al-Dîn Râzî. Peut-être est-ce en prolongeant ces tentatives de jadis, dans la perspective universalisante de telle ou telle réponse thomiste, que pourrait s'opérer une rencontre entre '*ilm al-kalâm* et théologie chrétienne, que certaines ignorances ou erreurs historiques de la pensée médiévale ne permirent pas de poursuivre vraiment.

---

42 V. g. *Guide*, I, 187.

IV

A PROPOS D'ALGAZEL

On connaît de reste le contresens dont fut victime Ghazzâlî.[43] Il était, nous l'avons rappelé ci-dessus, le grand pourfendeur des *falâsifa* orientaux: beaucoup moins au nom du *'ilm al-kalâm* comme tel[44] qu'au nom des exigences de la foi coranique. Dans son autobiographie du *Munqidh*, il répartit l'héritage du Stagirite en trois parts bien distinctes: la logique et les mathématiques, qui peuvent et même doivent être acceptées; la physique (à la fois sciences physiques et philosophie de la nature) qui peut être gardée, à la condition toutefois qu'elle ne contredise pas l'enseignement du Coran; la métaphysique enfin ou "science des choses divines" (*ilâhiyyât*), qui, elle, s'avère fort dangereuse. Sous la forme que lui ont donnée Fârâbî et Ibn Sînâ "l'ensemble des erreurs qui s'y trouvent peut se ramener à vingt: dont trois doivent être taxées d'impiété (*takfîr*),[45] et dix-sept d'innovation blâmable (*bid'a*). C'est pour détruire le système par eux bâti sur ces vingt questions que nous avons écrit notre *Tahâfut*."[46]

Or, comme toutes les fois qu'il entreprenait de réfuter des erreurs à ses yeux contraires à la foi, Ghazzâlî, en un premier ouvrage, résuma très objectivement le système de ses adversaires. Le *Tahâfut* fut donc précédé de tout un traité, intitulé *Maqâsid al-falâsifa* ("Les buts des *falâsifa*"). Le style de Ghazzâlî est clair et précis, et d'une éloquence plus arabe que celui d'Ibn Sînâ. Il faut reconnaître que les *Maqâsid* sont parfois d'un abord plus aisé que les grandes œuvres avicenniennes ou que les traités de Fârâbî. On comprend l'intérêt qu'ils éveillèrent chez les traducteurs médiévaux. Dès la première moitié du XII° siècle, l'équipe Ibn Dâwûd-Gundisalvi, le premier rendant oralement le texte arabe en langue romane, le second passant du roman au latin, devait traduire les *Maqâsid*. Cette "première vague de traductions" apporta les *De Intellectu* de Kindî et de Fârâbî (et quelques autres de leurs traités), et seulement deux sections du *Shifâ'* d'Avicenne. Ce fut peut-être bien

---

43   Pour la connaissance de Ghazzâlî au moyen âge latin, voir D. Salman, "Algazel et les latins", *Archives* (1935-1936), 103-127.

44   Tout comme Maïmonide un siècle plus tard, Ghazzâlî en blâme la faiblesse argumentative. Il écrivit lui-même un traité de *kalâm*, l'*Iqtisâd*, mais prit grand soin, dans les "préambules", d'en limiter la portée à un rôle purement médicinal: pour "guérir les douteurs de leurs doutes." Ghazzâlî est avant tout un "spirituel". S'il fallait caractériser d'un mot son attitude intellectuelle, nous dirions qu'il ne fut ni *mutakallim*, ni *faylasûf*, mais "réformateur" (*islâhî*).

45   Cf. ci-dessus, p. 426.

46   *Munqidh min al-dalâl* (éd. du Caire 1372 H./1952), 68. (Le *Munqidh* a été traduit en français, aux éd, Budé, par le P. Fârîd Jabre sous le titre "Erreur et Délivrance").

par les *Maqâsid* que la *falsafa* (orientale) fut d'abord connue en son ensemble.

C'est donc tout normalement que Ghazzâlî fut considéré par le moyen âge latin comme un fervent disciple d'Aristote. Il est à noter par ailleurs que les citations d'Algazel le plus fréquemment tirées des *Maqâsid* se rapportent à des points discutés en *falsafa*. Pour nous borner à cet exemple: il semble bien qu'Algazel ait passé spécialement aux yeux de saint Thomas pour le "philosophe arabe" qui soutient la possibilité d'une infinité actuelle d'âmes séparées. La thèse est attribuée tantôt à Avicenne et Algazel à la fois,[47] tantôt à Algazel seul.[48] Saint Thomas précise qu'elle est soutenue par "les Arabes" en raison de leur affirmation de l'éternité du monde; et qu'ils estiment possible cette infinité actuelle parce qu'il ne s'agit là que d'un infini accidentel (*infinitum per accidens*). Il réfute en détail cette opinion d'un point de vue proprement philosophique dans la *Somme Théologique*, I, 7, 4, et conclut: "impossibile est igitur esse multitudinem infinitam in actu, etiam per accidens. Sed esse multitudinem infinitam in potentia possibile est."

Or, cette possibilité d'une "multitude infinie en acte *per accidens*" est effectivement soutenue par Avicenne. Mais telle n'est point la vraie pensée de Ghazzâlî. Il ne la mentionne qu'en résumant la *falsafa*, au maximum à titre d'argument *ad hominem* ("et même en ce cas-là..."), non pour la faire sienne. Quand il la rencontre dans la XXe question du *Tahâfut* (résurrection des corps), c'est pour l'écarter en fait "dès lors que l'on repousse l'éternité du monde." Son attitude est ici assez semblable à celle de saint Thomas dans la *Somme contre les Gentils*, II, 81. Saint Thomas reconnaît que si Aristote écarte un infini en acte dans les corps matériels, il n'en va plus de même pour les substances immatérielles, mais ajoute: "certum tamen est circa hoc nullam difficultatem pati catholicae fidei professores, qui aeternitatem mundi non ponunt." Si nous remplaçons "foi catholique" par "foi musulmane," nous retrouvons le Ghazzâlî du *Tahâfut*.

Sommes-nous donc en présence d'un cas précis où l'Aquinate se serait, sans le dire, référé au *Tahâfut*? A notre sens, rien ne permet de l'affirmer. Si saint Thomas avait connu la vraie position d'Algazel, tout porte à croire qu'il l'aurait mentionnée, au lieu d'en faire sur ce point un disciple d'Avicenne... Les textes parallèles relevés par Asin Palacios chez Ghazzâlî et la *Somme contre les Gentils* sont certainement suggestifs. Mais n'est-ce pas extrapoler que de conclure chaque fois à une filière historique? Il est vrai, l'*Explanatio Symboli* précéda de

---

47 V. g. *Sum. cont. Gent.*, II, 81, 3e, et *Sum. theol.*, I, 7, 4, c.
48 Ainsi *Sum. Theol.*, I, 43, 2, ad 8.

quelques années la *Somme contre les Gentils* (le *Pugio Fidei*, au contraire, lui est nettement postérieur); et Raymond Martin y évoque des traités où Ghazzâlî expose sa pensée personnelle.[49] Saint Thomas connut-il par ce biais un Algazel négateur des causes secondes et professant un pur volontarisme divin? Et la difficulté de faire cadrer de telles thèses avec les développements des *Maqâsid* expliquerait-elle son silence? Nous sommes ici dans un domaine tout hypothétique. Ce qui est sûr, en tout cas, c'est que les parallèles établis, s'ils suggèrent des rencontres possibles, ne prouvent aucunement une filière ou une influence. Il suffit de revenir à l'exemple ci-dessus proposé. Pour réfuter l'existence d'une multitude infinie actuelle *per accidens*, nous avons bien la "rencontre" du *Tahâfut* et de la *Somme contre les Gentils*, se référant l'un et l'autre au commencement temporel du monde enseigné par la foi. Mais nous avons dans la *Somme Théologique* (I, 7, 4) une réfutation par des arguments philosophiques détaillés, qui n'appartient qu'à saint Thomas.

Faut-il signaler une autre hypothèse de recherche d'Asin Palacios?[50] Il suggère que le plan de la *Somme Théologique* fut inspiré par le plan de l'*Iqtisâd*, le traité de *kalâm* de Ghazzâlî. Il faut avouer que la comparaison reste bien générale et superficielle. En premier lieu, nous n'avons aucune preuve que l'*Iqtisâd* fût vraiment connu du moyen âge latin. Mais surtout: le plan de la *Somme* ne se dégagera-t-il pas bien plus clairement à travers une courbe historique qui part du *De Fide orthodoxa* du Dasmascène, passe par les *Summae* du XIIe siècle et l'évolution des *Questiones disputatae*? Par ailleurs, rien dans l'*Iqtisâd* ne saurait évoquer le fameux "cercle d'or" de la *Somme*[51]; et le plan de tout traité de *kalâm* ne se peut justifier sans recourir aux discussions des premiers temps de l'Islam, dont la portée est moins spécifiquement théologique que politique (politico-religieuse).

Pour saint Thomas, Ghazzâlî reste bien Algazel, l'aristotélisant auteur des *Maqâsid*. Plus encore que pour les docteurs en *kalâm*, on peut regretter que le *Tahâfut* et surtout maint développement de l'*Ihyâ' 'ulûm al-dîn*[52] n'aient pas été connus ou mieux connus des latins. Car

---

49 Précisons cependant que c'est le *Pugio* qui se réfère nettement au *Tahâfut*, à l'*Ihyâ'*, au *Maqsad al-asnâ*, au *Mîzân al-a'mal*, au *Mishkat al-anwâr*, au *Munqidh*: Raymond Martin connaissait donc non seulement le Ghazzâli adversaire des *falâsifa (Tahâfut)*, mais l'auteur spirituel, soucieux d'"orthodoxie" certes, ouvert cependant à des influences néoplatonisantes.

50 Dans l'article déjà cité, "Los origines..."

51 Si, vers la fin de sa vie, les écrits "spirituels" de Ghazzâli accueillent certaines vues plotiniennes (empruntées à ses adversaires *falâsifa*), aucune influence de cette sorte ne se manifeste dans l'*Iqtisâd*, traité de *kalâm* au demeurant fort classique.

52 "Revivification des sciences de la religion": c'est le grand œuvre de Ghazzâli, qui lui assurera une gloire durable dans la culture arabo-musulmane.

fréquemment l'ash'arisme évolué de Ghazzâlî vient buter sur d'apparentes antinomies qui furent au cœur des débats du moyen âge chrétien, et spécialement des analyses thomistes: unité ou pluralité de la forme substantielle dans le composé humain; unité ou pluralité de l'âme humaine[53]; la toute Puissance divine en son absolue indépendance et l'acte de libre-choix de la créature...Nous songeons par exemple aux analyses de l'*Ihyâ'* où Ghazzâlî s'efforce de préciser les rapports de l'intelligence et de la volonté dans l'acte libre. Elles se situaient, il est vrai, dans le contexte "volontariste" des traditions ash'arites, où tout "motif" de l'intellect devient "détermination".[54] Combien éclairante eût été une discussion de ces textes ghazzâliens par saint Thomas, — et plus encore peut-être de certains textes de Fakhr al-Dîn Râzî (XIIᵉ-XIIIᵉ siècle), qui s'essaya à une vue plus large où s'unissent Volonté et Sagesse divines.[55] L'ignorance mutuelle des latins et de ces ash'arites "modernes" fut certainement, de part et d'autre, dommageable.

V

AVICENNE ET AVERROÈS

Qu'il s'agisse des docteurs en *kalâm* en leur ensemble, ou de Ghazzâlî plus spécialement, il ne faut donc ni traiter par prétérition, ni valoriser indûment la connaissance qu'en put avoir l'Aquinate. Elle resta limitée. L'atomisme du *kalâm* ash'arite retint l'attention de saint Thomas dans la mesure où il typifiait une vision des choses opposée au déterminisme des *falâsifa*; et, à travers les *Maqâsid*, s'établit une confusion jamais dénoncée explicitement entre les "Péripatéticiens" de l'Islam et Ghazzâlî.

En fait, les grandes "sources arabes" de saint Thomas, ce furent les *falâsifa*, et plus précisément Avicenne et Averroès. On peut distinguer deux vagues de traductions au XIIᵉ siècle: la première (Ibn Dâwûd-Gundisalvi), déjà signalée à propos des *Maqâsid*, la deuxième, faite directement sur l'arabe par Gérard de Crémone. A nous en tenir aux *falâsifa*, elles apportèrent maints traités de Kindî et de Fârâbî, le début du *Shifâ'* d'Avicenne, et son *Qânûn fî l-tibb*.[56] La troisième vague de

---

53 Avicenne affirme l'unité substantielle de l'âme; Ghazzâlî semble au contraire maintenir la distinction tripartite: âme végétative, âme sensitive, âme raisonnable.
54 Dieu seul dira encore Ghazzâlî dans l'*Ihyâ'* (éd. du Caire 1325 H./1933), t. IV, 219-220, peut vraiment être appelé "libre", car il agit "sans motif". L'absolu volontarisme divin des ash'arites ne serait pas sans évoquer ici la notion cartésienne de liberté.
55 Dans son traité de *kalâm*, le *Muhassal*, Fakhr al-Dîn Râzî reste fidèle à la critique ash'arite du "motif déterminant"; mais la problématique s'élargit dans son *Grand Commentaire* du Coran.
56 Qui exerça une telle influence sur les médecines arabe et latine.

traductions fut décisive. Elle se situe au début du XIIIe siècle. Michel
Scot à Tolède et en Italie, Hermann l'Allemand de Tolède, et les
traducteurs de Burgos, pour ne citer que les plus notables, revinrent à la
méthode en deux temps, arabe-roman-latin: ainsi devinrent accessibles
la seconde partie du *Shifâ'* (Burgos), des commentaires de Fârâbî,
Avicenne, Averroès sur l'*Ethique à Nicomaque*, la *Rhétorique*, la
Poétique (Hermann l'Allemand), quelques traités d'Avicenne et surtout
les Commentaires d'Averroès (par les soins de Michel Scot et de son
équipe). Ce n'est guère qu'en 1170, à la demande du Sultân almohade,
qu'Ibn Rushd avait entrepris de commenter Aristote. La traduction de
cette œuvre capitale verra le jour dès 1220, et se répandra dans le
monde latin à partir de 1230. [57]

Elle avait été précédée par la connaissance, non point exhaustive,
mais du moins assez large des *falâsifa* orientaux. Telle est sans doute la
raison la plus obvie des abondantes citations d'Avicenne dans le *Commentaire des Sentences* et les premières œuvres de saint Thomas. Certes, le *Commentator* était connu déjà, [58] mais c'était alors l'avicennisme
qui marquait la pensée médiévale. Par la suite, à partir en tout cas de la
Somme contre les Gentils, saint Thomas citera Averroès plus fréquemment qu'Avicenne. Ici, nous croyons très opportune la remarque de M.
Gilson: cela ne signifie point, comme on a pu le dire, une diminution de
l'influence d'Avicenne,— "saint Thomas citera moins Avicenne (...),
mais il l'aura assimilé une fois pour toutes." [59] Et dans la mesure où
Averroès représentait la pensée d'Aristote d'une part, où s'esquissait
d'autre part le drame de l'averroïsme latin, c'est le Commentateur qu'il
s'agissait maintenant de discuter et situer. [60]

Saint Thomas fut certainement très sensible au "platonisme" (il serait
plus juste de dire néoplatonisme) d'Ibn Sînâ. "Et ideo tam Plato quam
Avicenna, in aliquo ipsum sequens...." [61] Ce membre de phrase, qui appartient au traité *Du Gouvernement divin*, pourrait illustrer bien

---

57 La chronologie de Michel Scot reste incertaine. Selon le P. de Vaux (cf. "La première
entrée d'Averroès", art. cit., 199 et ss. et 219): "la première entreprise importante de traduction
d'Averroès doit se placer à la cour de Frédéric II, un peu avant 1210", et "Michel Scot y eut sinon
un rôle exclusif, au moins une part prépondérante". Selon le P. Théry, ce serait à Tolède, non en
Italie, que Michel Scot aurait mené à bien "la plupart" de ses traductions, et aux alentours de 1220
(op. cit., 63).
58 La rédaction du *Commentaires des Sentences* date de 1254-1256, donc vingt-cinq ans environ après l'"arrivée" d'Averroès. Saint Thomas déjà l'y utilise.
59 "Avicenne en Occident au Moyen Age", 105.
60 On doit dater la crise averroïste (Siger de Brabant) en 1266-1270, la rédaction de la *Somme
théologique* en 1267-1273, et la première condamnation de l'averroïsme en 1270. (Voir l'éclairant
tableau dressé par le P. Chenu à la fin de *Saint Thomas d'Aquin et la Théologie*, Paris 1959).
61 *Sum. theol.*, I, 115, 1, c.

d'autres remarques de l'Aquinate.[62] Averroès, en comparaison, sera le péripatéticien, et cela est parfaitement conforme à la réalité des faits. L'utilisation diverse que fit saint Thomas d'Avicenne et d'Averroès trouve là son explication. Ce sont deux "philosophes" auxquels il s'adresse, et nourris l'un comme l'autre d'Aristote. Mais l'Aristote très néoplatonisé d'Avicenne s'ouvrait à des problématiques nouvelles, liées sans doute au monothéisme musulman, mais selon une ligne de mystique intellectualiste issue de Plotin, et sans référence à des valeurs de foi comme telles. Ghazzâlî et Shahrastânî ne s'y sont point trompés. Redisons-le: en dépit de l'attaque *ad hominem* d'Ibn Rushd,[63] rien dans la démarche d'Avicenne, alors même qu'il traite des "choses divines," ne le rapproche des *loquentes in lege Maurorum.* C'est, il est vrai, le théologien Thomas d'Aquin qu'intéressaient ces problématiques nouvelles. Pour reprendre une distinction de Jacques Maritain, nous dirions volontiers que la démarche philosophique avicennienne fut non seulement sur ce point une "servante" de la théologie thomiste, mais une *research worker*, une découvreuse de domaines nouveaux: nous en donnerons ci-après quelques exemples.

Ce que demanda au contraire saint Thomas aux précisions d'analyse du Commentateur, et à son aristotélisme de base, ce fut, plus directement, un perfectionnement d'outillage philosophique. Sans aucune servilité, certes! On connaît la rapide et globale sévérité du *De Unitate Intellectus*: "Averroes qui non tam fuit peripateticus quam peripateticae philosophiae depravator."[64] Face en effet à ce qu'on pourrait appeler le monisme matérialiste d'Amaury de Bène, voici que surgissait une nouvelle interprétation d'Aristote, qui, à la suite de toute une lignée de commentateurs grecs et arabes, aboutit à un émanatisme à la fois spiritualiste et déterministe. Création éternelle, découlant nécessairement de la Science divine, Intellect agent unique, et intellect possible se résorbant en l'Intellect agent dans l'acte ultime de connaissance, distinction de l'essence et de l'existence dans la créature n'étant qu'une

---

62 Saint Thomas sut déceler le "platonisme" (néoplatonisme) d'Avicenne à travers la traduction latin du *Shifâ'*.—Avicenne cependant considérait cette "somme" comme un ouvrage destiné au "vulgaire philosophant", et la maintenait par là même en des cadres aristotéliciens éprouvés (cf. son introduction au *Mantiq al-mashriqiyyîn*, "La logique des Orientaux", éd. du Caire 1328 H./1910, p. 3). Sa "vraie pensée", il entreprendra de la révéler dans le *Hikma al-mashriqiyya* ("La Sagesse orientale") dont il annonce la rédaction. Nous n'avons point l'ouvrage lui-même, mais de nombreux écrits peuvent en être rapprochés, ou peut-être le constituer déjà en partie: *Ishârât, Gloses sur la "Théologie d'Aristote", al-Risâla al-adhawiyya fî amr al-ma'âd*, et les divers traités dits "mystiques". Ce n'est plus exactement l'Avicenne que connut saint Thomas, mais c'est un Avicenne que certaines analyses de saint Thomas semblent avoir entrevu.

63 Cf. ci-dessus, p. 428 et réf.

64 Cf. M. D. Chenu, *Introduction à l'étude de Saint Thomas d'Aquin*, 163.

distinction de raison.[65] Saint Thomas ne cessera de réfuter ces thèses rushdiennes, sur le plan philosophique même. Et sur bien des points,— individualité de l'âme séparée, distinction réelle de l'essence et de l'existence,— il sera plus près d'Avicenne que d'Averroès. Mais peut-être les critiques de ce dernier lui furent-elles un appoint dans sa révision et correction de l'extrincécisme avicennien, pour qui l'existence "arrive" (*accidit*) à l'essence.[66]

Aussi bien, ce jugement sévère qui voyait dans le *Commentator* un *depravator* reste-t-il isolé. Saint Thomas critiqua et réfuta Averroès[67]; il n'en marqua pas moins une haute estime pour nombre de ses analyses,[68] — et lors même qu'il n'en adopte pas les conclusions.[69] Remarquable est sa liberté à l'égard d'Avicenne et d'Averroès. Maintes fois, il les corrige l'un par l'autre. Il ne leur doit, ni à l'un ni à l'autre l'éclairement philosophique qui sous-tend sa théologie; mais il se sert de leurs arguments, parfois en prise directe, parfois à travers la réfutation même qu'il en propose, pour mettre au point le revêtement conceptuel des intuitions de base.

VI

LE CAS D'IBN RUSHD

Avant d'illustrer ces propos par quelques exemples, nous nous permettrons un dernier ensemble de remarques. Averroès fut certainement pour saint Thomas le Commentateur par excellence. Ce sont ses Grands, Moyens et Petits Commentaires d'Aristote qui furent traduits, et sur lesquels s'appuya d'abord l'averroïsme latin. Mais nous avons rappelé ci-dessus qu'Ibn Rushd fut en outre l'auteur d'un certain nombre de "textes de circonstance," où il défendait contre Ghazzâlî, et, à travers lui, contre les docteurs de la Loi (*fuqahâ'*) andalous, l'orthodoxie musulmane de la *falsafa*. Ce faisant, il fut "théologien,"—à tout le moins apologète,— et tout aussi "théologien" qu'Ibn Sînâ. Si l'on

---

65 Voir sur ce dernier point la critique d'Avicenne par Ibn Rushd dans son *Abrégé de la Métaphysique*, commentant Aristote, *Metaph.*, V, 7.

66 "On sait que l'existence est un accident survenu à ce qui existe, dit encore Maïmonide (très avicennien en cela); c'est pourquoi elle est quelque chose d'accessoire à la *quiddité* de ce qui existe. Ceci est une chose évidente et nécessaire dans tout ce dont l'existence a une cause", *Guide des Egarés*, I, 57 (trad. Munk, I, 230-231).

67 V. g. *Sum. theol.*, I, 66, 2, C.; 117, 1, C. et ad 2, etc.

68 V. g. Ibid., I, 54, 5, C.; 87, 1, ad 3; II-II, 171, 2, sed contra, etc.

69 V. g. Ibid., I, 88, 1, C (opinion très longuement analysée et discutée), etc. Nous nous bornons à quelques références prises dans la *Somme Théologique*; bien d'autres pourraient être glanées, entre autres dans la *Sum. cont. Gent.* ou les *Quaest. disp.*

tient compte du souci très vif d'auto-défense que les circonstances exigèrent de lui, on peut dire que sa problématique est sur ce point assez proche de celle de son prédécesseur oriental: toute centrée sur les rapports de la *falsafa* et de la Loi religieuse révélée (*shar'*), et sur l'interprétation (*ta'wîl*) du sens réel (*haqîqa*) de la Loi à la lumière de la *falsafa* et de ses certitudes apodictiques.

Et voici qu'Ibn Rushd connut ce paradoxal destin: a) Au contraire d'Avicenne, sa pensée philosophique n'eut guère d'audience dans le monde musulman.[70] Il y fut connu surtout comme juriste, et jusqu'au début du XXᵉ siècle, c'est sa *Bidâya*, son traité de droit (*fiqh*), qui seul était lu dans les Grandes Mosquées-Universités. C'est à travers l'Occident que l'Islam contemporain a redécouvert Ibn Rushd philosophe. b) Cette audience réduite fut compensée par une énorme influence dans le monde latin. Les querelles autour de l'averroïsme furent loin d'être dirimées par les condamnations de 1270 et 1277. Faut-il rappeler les débats suscités à Padoue jusqu'à l'aube de la Renaissance? Sans doute est-ce d'abord le commentateur d'Aristote qui fut étudié, discuté, écouté, non l'apologète de la *falsafa*. Il semble cependant que les "œuvres de circonstance," dont on ne trouve aucune mention explicite chez saint Thomas, aient été suffisamment connues par ailleurs pour alimenter — non sans confusion — la fameuse thèse des "deux vérités." c) A l'époque contemporaine, c'est au contraire à l'auto-défense d'Ibn Rushd que s'intéressent principalement les islamisants occidentaux,[71] et, à leur suite, divers penseurs musulmans. Les commentaires sur Aristote ne se trouvent point en édition arabe courante, au contraire du *Tahâfut al-tahâfut*,[72] et de trois petits traités apologétiques réunis à l'ordinaire sous le titre *Falsafat Ibn Rushd*, "la philosophie d'Ibn Rushd."[73]

C'est donc par son œuvre objective de commentateur qu'il marqua d'abord le moyen âge latin; et c'est à son œuvre "apologétique", tout orientée par des thèmes touchant aux valeurs de foi, qu'il doit de nos jours une audience recouvrée. Faut-il ajouter que de part et d'autre les perspectives risquent d'en être faussées? Pour connaître l'Ibn Rushd

---

[70] Les causes en sont mutiples. Nous ne pouvons songer à les résumer ici, cela nous conduirait à trop de références à l'histoire arabo-musulmane. En bref: elles tiennent avant tout aux climats religieux et culturels très différents où vécurent les deux "philosophes".

[71] Ainsi les travaux de Asin Palacios, A. F. Mehren, M. Horten, L. Gauthier, S. van den Bergh, M. Alonso, H. A. Wolfson, etc. Un effort est accompli, certes, pour intégrer le Commentateur, mais c'est avant tout sur ses œuvres "apologétiques" qu'Ibn Rushd est jugé.

[72] Editions courantes au Caire (heureusement corrigées par l'édition critique du Père Bouyges). Excellente traduction anglaise annotée de S. van den Bergh, 2 vol., (Oxford-Londres 1954).

[73] Ce sont les traités déjà mentionnés ci-dessus, note 21, et l'*Epistola ad amicum*.

historique, c'est à la fois le commentateur et l'apologète qu'il faut étudier de près; et ce sont peut-être bien les commentaires, malgré leur genre impersonnel, qui nous donneraient sa vraie pensée.

Saint Thomas eut-il accès aux "œuvres de circonstance"? Asin Palacios s'est efforcé de le prouver. Ses arguments sont parallèles à ceux qu'il mit en avant au sujet de Ghazzâlî. Là aussi, la source de saint Thomas serait Raymond Martin. De fait, le *Pugio Fidei* témoigne de la connaissance non seulement des commentaires d'Ibn Rushd, mais aussi du *Tahâfut al-tahâfut*, du petit traité sur la Science divine, et peut-être du *Fasl al-maqâl*. Mais le *Pugio* doit être daté, très probablement, de 1278[74]; il est donc postérieur à la mort de saint Thomas. Et si Maïmonide par ailleurs connaissait ces œuvres "rushdiennes", il ne les cite pas explicitement dans le *Guide des Egarés*. A nous en tenir à ces arguments de critique externe, rien ne prouve que saint Thomas eut conscience de cette "dimension apologétique" d'Averroès. Compte tenu de ses habitudes de travail, nous restons persuadé qu'il eût mentionné ces textes, au moins par référence globale, s'il les avait utilisés comme il utilisa les commentaires.

Critique interne? C'est très précisément au sujet de la révélation, de sa nécessité et de son utilité pour les hommes, qu'Asin Palacios entend établir une filière Ibn Rushd - saint Thomas.[75] Quand il parle de "l'averroïsme de saint Thomas d'Aquin," c'est bien un "averroïsme *théologique*" qu'il entend désigner. Nous ne reviendrons pas en détail sur ce point que nous avons discuté ailleurs.[76] Nous ne pouvons que redire ici: une "rencontre" sur tel aspect d'une question ne signifie nullement filière historique, surtout quand le *lumen sub quo* qui commande le débat est fort différent de part et d'autre. Sans doute les raisons mises en avant pour la révélation de vérités de soi accessibles à la raison se recoupent. Mais les "sources" de saint Thomas ne seraient-elles pas saint Augustin et Maïmonide[77] bien plus qu'Ibn Rushd? Quant aux vérités dont la raison peut connaître l'existence, mais non l'essence, il suffit de rappeler qu'elles sont pour Ibn Rushd ou bien des vérités contingentes, présentes ou futures, ou bien des prescriptions positives et

---

74   Cf. (avec réf.) U. Monneret de Villard, *Studio dell'Islam*, 37, n. 5 et 55.
75   En son étude devenue célèbre "El Averroismo teologico de Santo Tomas de Aquino", *Homenaje à D. Francisco Codera* (Saragosse 1904), 271-331.
76   Voir *Intr. theol. musulm.*, 283, n. 3, et *Les grands problèmes de la théologie musulmane: Dieu et la destinée de l'homme* (Paris 1967), 172-175.
77   Pour Maïmonide, voir P. Synave, "La révélation des vérités divines naturelles d'après Saint Thomas d'Aquin", *Mélanges Mandonnet I*, 327-370. La mise au point philosophique du P. Synave concernant les rapports Maïmonide - saint Thomas nous semble beaucoup plus pertinente que la thèse de M. Asin concernant Averroès - saint Thomas.

cultuelles: le tout fondé sur une notion de prophétisme situé comme tel dans l'universel déterminisme de l'existence.

En fait, la position d'Ibn Rushd "théologien" ne diffère point substantiellement ici de celle d'Ibn Sînâ. Peut-être insiste-t-il plus que son prédécesseur sur la supériorité du prophète par rapport au sage. Il reste que pour lui, comme pour les *falâsifa* orientaux, prophètes et sages s'élèvent aux mêmes vérités suprêmes. Mais les prophètes seuls y atteignent sans effort. Ils reçoivent, dans leur intelligence et leur imaginative, une illumination de l'Intellect agent si parfaite[78] qu'eux seuls sont capables d'enseigner le peuple (*al-'awâmm*) par mode de symboles et d'allégories, et de discerner les prescriptions positives qu'il convient d'impérer. Le sage ou philosophe reconnaît cette supériorité. Il se soumet aux obligations cultuelles, et retrouve dans la Loi religieuse, sous forme symbolique, l'expression des vérités intelligibles auxquelles l'a conduit sa recherche.[79] Il ne s'agit donc point de "deux vérités"; il s'agit d'une seule vérité, mais atteinte sous deux modes différents.[80] Dès lors, le sage ou philosophe (et lui seul) sera justifié à traiter la Loi religieuse selon une herméneutique interprétative (*ta'wîl*), où il retrouvera, par l'ésotérisme du sens caché, toutes les grandes lignes de sa propre vision du monde. Obligation stricte lui est faite de ne point communiquer cette herméneutique au peuple.

Est-il besoin de souligner que nous sommes aussi loin que possible ici de la problématique de saint Thomas sur la révélation des "vérités surnaturelles" et les rapports de la raison et de la foi?

VII

TROIS EXEMPLES

Nous proposerons, pour conclure, trois exemples susceptibles d'illustrer comment et par quels procédés saint Thomas utilise des apports avicenniens ou rushdiens. Ils éclairent, nous semble-t-il, cette attitude faite à la fois de respect pour la pensée des "prédécesseurs

---

78 Pour Kindî et Ibn Sînâ, l'intellect possible est illuminé par l'Intellect agent (et l'ensemble des Intellects séparés), et l'imaginative par les Ames célestes; pour Fârâbî et Ibn Rushd, l'Intellect agent illumine et l'intellect possible et l'imaginative. Avoir admis l'intermédiaire des Ames célestes sera l'un des reproches d'Averroès à l'égard d'Avicenne.

79 Ce fut le thème central du fameux "roman philosophique" d'Ibn Tufayl (Abubacer), *Hayy Ibn Yaqzân* (traduit en latin par Pococke sous le titre *Philosophus Autodidactus*). Ibn Tufayl présenta au Sultân almohade le jeune Ibn Rushd, et fut (ainsi) à l'origine des commentaires sur Aristote.

80 Léon Gauthier a insisté avec raison sur ce point. Voir *La théorie d'Ibn Rochd sur les rapports de la religion et de la philosophie* (thèse de doctorat 1909), et *Ibn Rochd (Averroès)* (Paris 1948).

arabes," et de liberté à leur égard, que nous avons signalée en cours de route.

1. *La saisie de l'être dans le jugement d'existence.* M. Et. Gilson souligne à bon droit[81] l'abondance des citations littérales d'Avicenne dès que saint Thomas veut préciser que l'être est *id quod primum cadit in conceptione mentis.* Il n'y a pas de doute que des textes avicenniens ont servi ici d'aiguillon au réalisme critique de l'Aquinate et à l'accent mis par lui sur l'acte d'être. De même, et en conséquence, pour les distinctions entre être et chose d'une part, entre essence et existence dans l'être créé d'autre part. Mais c'est immédiatement dans une vue créationiste (libre création *ex nihilo*), et donc selon une participation d'être intrinsèquement analogique, que saint Thomas resitue les analyses du *faylasûf.*

Cela est particulièrement sensible dans cet "approfondissement de la cause efficiente" que signale encore M. Gilson.[82] A la suite d'Aristote,[83] la notion de cause efficiente (*al-'illa al-fâ'ila*) fut couramment analysée en *falsafa* et en philosophie shî'ite. En raison même de l'émanatisme plotinien qui dominait les horizons de pensée, elle fut considérée, en sa notion première appliquée à Dieu, comme productrice de l'être et de tout l'être, *dans esse* dit fort bien saint Thomas citant Avicenne.[84] Elle fut mise en regard de la cause finale (*al-'illa al-ghâ'iyya*) appelée "cause des causes,"[85] et même "cause efficiente des causes efficientes."[86] Un texte des *Ishârât* précise l'interaction des deux causes extrinsèques: c'est "par le moyen de sa quiddité que la cause finale est cause," mais "l'idée qu'elle représente appartient à la causalité de la cause efficiente."[87] Dès lors, la preuve de l'existence de Dieu sera précédée par une double démonstration: a) impossibilité d'un nombre infini en acte de causes efficientes et matérielles; b) impossibilité d'un nombre infini de causes finales.[88] Et Dieu sera "la Cause première absolue," "Cause de toutes les autres causes." Cause efficiente suprême sans doute, puisque Principe de tout être et de tout l'être possible, mais transcendant toute distinction efficience-finalité dans l'"innovation absolue" (*ibdâ' mutlaq*).[89]

81   "Avicenne en Occident au Moyen Age", 108.
82   Ibid., 109.
83   *Physiques*, II, 3 et *Métaphysiques*, V, 2.
84   *In II Sent.*, d. 1, q. 2, ad 1 (cf. Et. Gilson, ibid.).
85   *Shifâ', Ilâhiyyât* (Le Caire 1380 H./1960), II, 292.
86   *Ishârât* (éd. Forget, Leyde 1892), 139. L'expression se trouve déjà dans Kindî, v. g. *Rasâ'il* (éd. Abû Ridâ, Le Caire 1369 H./1950), I, 248.
87   *Ishârât*, 140 (trad. franç. de A. M. Goichon, *Livre des Directives et Remarques*, Paris 1951, 356).
88   Cf. *Shifâ'*, ibid., 327-343; *Ishârât*, 141-142.
89   Voir analyses et références dans notre article "'Illa", *Encyclopédie de l'Islam*, 2ᵉ éd., 1970, 1158-1160.

Pour saisir toutes les coordonnées d'une telle preuve, il faut garder présent à l'esprit l'émanatisme "nécessaire et voulu" qui préside à l'idée de "création," la production des êtres s'opérant par une descente dialectique d'Intellects, (d'Ames), de Corps célestes. Ibn Rushd, en récusant la preuve avicennienne, entendit-il récuser également ce recours à une création non immédiate?[90] Ou fut-il guidé, plus simplement, par sa fidélité aux *Physiques* d'Aristote?[91] — Nous voyons en tout cas que la causalité efficiente de saint Thomas, si elle dépasse et approfondit la causalité motrice aristotélico-rushdienne, ne se confond point avec la causalité efficiente au sens d'Ibn Sînâ. Car cette dernière, en rigueur de termes, est "émanatrice" plutôt qu'"efficiente"; elle ne pouvait dès lors qu'écarter une authentique analogie de l'être, dans une sur-univocité "où l'être peut s'affirmer de tout selon le même genre, mais non pas immédiatement de tous les êtres."[92]

Ajoutons pour mémoire que la preuve avicennienne, quoi qu'en dise Ibn Rushd, *n'est pas* la preuve du *kalâm*.[93] Celle-ci, en effet, est *a novitate* (non *a contingentia*) *mundi*. En outre, elle relève, en ses premières formulations, d'une "logique à deux termes" mettant en rapports mutuels (corrélatif d'opposition, *muqâbal*) Dieu seul Réel, et la créature évanescente, *Haqq-khalq*.[94] Plus tard, et précisément sous l'influence des *falâsifa* orientaux qu'ils combattaient, les ash'arites "modernes" (à partir du XIe-XIIe s.) organiseront leur preuve sous mode syllogistique. Il y eut ici influence d'Avicenne sur les *mutakallimûn*, non l'inverse. Il reste que la notion de cause efficiente jouera différemment. Avicenne, par delà l'analogie limitée du "nécessaire par soi" et "nécessaire par autrui," tend à l'univocité de l'être; le *kalâm* tend à une équivocité pure entre le Créateur et la créature. Au XIVe-XVe siècles encore, Jurjânî, dans les "préambules philosophiques" de son grand traité de *kalâm*, récusera l'efficace des causes secondes sur leur effet.

Revenons à Ibn Sînâ et à la "première saisie" de l'intellect. Il ne s'agit pas chez lui d'une intuition abstractive fondée sur un jugement, comme chez saint Thomas. Il s'agit d'un concept d'être, d'un "état de l'être" (*hâl al-mawjûd*), existant d'une sorte d'existence logique qui se prend en opposition au non-être. Aussi bien, la vraie preuve de l'existence de Dieu, celle réservée aux "privilégiés" (*al-khawâss*), ne se-

---

90 Qu'il combat explicitement dans le *Tahâfut al-tahâfut* et l'*Epistola ad amicum*.
91 Cf. ci-dessus, p. 427.
92 Et. Gilson, "Avicenne et le point de départ de Duns Scot", *Archives* (1927), 110-111.
93 Nous trouvons cette dernière telle que saint Thomas put la connaître, dans Maïmonide, *Guide des Egarés*, I, 74 (trad. Munk, I, 421-435).
94 Cf. Louis Gardet, "Dieu — le Réel (*Allâh al-Haqq*)", *Studia Missionalia*, (Rome 1968), 57-61.

ra point, pour Ibn Sînâ, la preuve par la cause efficiente. Ce sera la
preuve "par l'idée d'être,"[95] selon une univocité de l'être comme tel,
considéré comme tel, indépendamment de son existence concrète. Cet
essentialisme radical, aboutissement du monisme avicennien, c'est peut-
être cela qu'Averroès visait déjà à travers sa critique de la preuve par la
cause efficiente. Et nous voyons avec quelle indépendance les formules
avicenniennes sur l'être objet de la pensée, même reprises *ad litteram*,
ont été utilisées par saint Thomas selon la perspective tout autre du
primat de l'*acte* d'être. En ontologie comme en noétique, saint Thomas
reprend à son compte certaines questions ouvertes, et certaines expressions élaborées par le *faylasûf* oriental. Mais il les situe selon des
lignes de synthèse qui n'appartiennent qu'à lui. L'influence exercée par
la vision du monde avicennienne, ce n'est pas, au moyen âge latin,
chez l'Aquinate que nous la trouverons; mais d'une part (noétique) dans
le courant de l'"augustinisme avicennisant," et d'autre part (notion de la
"nature commune," sur-univocité de l'être) chez Jean Duns Scot. M.
Gilson l'a montré avec force[96]: les oppositions de Duns Scot à saint
Thomas s'originent chez Avicenne.

2. *La notion de prophétie.* Ce n'est aucunement la notion même de
prophétie que saint Thomas emprunte à son devancier. La prophétie,
dit-il, ne requiert aucune disposition ou qualité préalable dans le sujet.
C'est Dieu qui dispose l'âme à en recevoir le don, puis le lui ac-
corde.[97] Les seules dispositions requises regardent l'*usage* de la
prophétie, qui reste, lui, *in potestate prophetae*.[98] Seul, peut-être, l'accent mis sur l'intermédiaire "habituel" d'un ministère angélique[99]
pourrait évoquer (rencontre ou emprunt) l'enseignement des *falâsifa*.[100]
    La foi musulmane est centrée sur la notion de prophétie. Dans leur

---

95 V. g. *Ishârât*, 146.
96 C'est le thème même du très éclairant article ci-dessus cité, *Avicenne et le point de départ
de Duns Scot*. Voir également *Avicenne en Occident au Moyen Age*, 109-112.— L'expression
"augustinisme avicennisant" proposée par M. Gilson a été discutée. Sans doute n'aurait-elle point
été acceptée par les tenants de ce courant médiéval. Mais en nous reportant aux textes mêmes
d'Ibn Sînâ, et quelles qu'aient été les critiques de Guillaume d'Auvergne contre le *faylasûf*, nous la
croyons, quant à nous, parfaitement justifiée: la plupart des augustiniens et augustinisants
médiévaux empruntèrent à Avicenne les arguments même qui fondaient nombre de leurs thèses
philosophiques, — croyant un peu vite avoir désamorcé son monisme et déterminisme existentiels,
et certaines vues cosmologiques qui y étaient liées.
97 Cf. *Sum. theol.*, II-II, 3, c. — Un rapprochement serait à établir ici avec la foi musulmane,
non avec la *falsafa*.
98 Cf. ibid., 4, c. et *De Veritate*, 12, 5.
99 *Sum. theol.*, ibid., a. 4.
100 Cet intermédiaire angélique, reconnu par les *falâsifa*, est chez eux au point de jonction
d'une double influence, coranique et hellénistique.

souci d'accorder leur vision du monde à la Loi religieuse, les *falâsifa* ne pouvaient pas ne pas la rencontrer. Et cela vaut tout autant pour Ibn Rushd "apologète" que pour Fârâbî ou Ibn Sînâ. Saint Thomas connut certainement le chapitre du *Shifâ'* qui traite du sujet; non moins des textes d'Ibn Rushd et les exposés et discussions de Maïmonide. [101] Or, l'explication donnée par les *falâsifa* comme étant la vraie nature de la prophétie, saint Thomas en fera ce qu'il appelle une "prophétie naturelle"; et c'est à Avicenne qu'il se réfère. — Aucune influence ici sur la notion proprement théologique, mais une sorte d'annexe philosophique, "similitude déficiente" de la prophétie proprement dite.

Il n'est que de comparer les textes mêmes d'Avicenne, [102] et les deux textes majeurs où saint Thomas définit et discute la "prophétie naturelle." [103] L'homme par ses propres forces (et la nature angélique plus encore) peut acquérir une certaine connaissance des choses à venir, non plus en elles-mêmes, comme dans le *lumen propheticum*, mais dans leurs effets: cela, à la mesure de la "perfection de la vertu imaginative et de la clarté de l'intelligence." [104] Or, telles sont, mot pour mot, les deux premières conditions qui, dans le déterminisme existentiel avicennien, feront de tel homme un prophète. Pour les *falâsifa*, cette prophétie, illumination nécessaire de l'Intellect agent reçue dans un intellect possible prédisposé par nature, sera infaillible. Pour saint Thomas, elle est de soi faillible. Pour les *falâsifa*, elle atteint aux vérités suprêmes. Pour saint Thomas, son objet, au contraire de l'objet de la "prophétie divine," ne dépassera jamais les capacités naturelles de la raison, et sera reçu non plus immédiatement, mais par l'intermédiaire de causes secondes. Et les communications des anges déchus n'en sont qu'un exemple privilégié. [105]

Nous avons ici l'un des cas les plus nets d'un emprunt de saint Thomas à la problématique de ses prédécesseurs arabes. Mais cet emprunt en resituant leur pensée dans une synthèse de théologie chrétienne, en est en quelque sorte la réfutation. Aussi bien, les questions du *De Veritate* qui traitent de la nature de l'illumination prophétique se référeront plus d'une fois, elles aussi, aux vues des *falâsifa*: ce sera, en général, pour les discuter ou rectifier. [106]

---

101 Cf. Bruno Decker, *Die Entwicklung der Lehre von der prophetischen Offenbarung von Wilhelm von Auxerre bis zur Thomas von Aquin* (Breslau 1940).

102 Pour nous borner à cette référence: *Shifâ', Illâhiyyât*, II, 441-443 (textes parallèles dans *Najât, Ishârât*, etc.).

103 *De Veritate*, 12, 3 et 4; *Sum. theol.*, II-II, 172, 1 et 2.

104 *Sum. theol.*, ibid., a. 1, c.

105 Ibid., a. 5.

106 *De Veritate*, q. 12, en particulier a. 6 et 7.

3. *Le principe d'individuation.* Nous renvoyons aux études fort bien menées de M. Forest et du P. Roland-Gosselin.[107] Sans revenir sur les détails de l'élaboration thomiste, signalons du moins cet exemple de l'outillage technique que saint Thomas n'hésita pas à emprunter à ses devanciers *falâsifa*; il montre par ailleurs que l'arrivée d'Averroès ne signifia nullement un abandon de ce que pouvait apporter Avicenne.

Avicenne comme Averroès sont fidèles à Aristote en faisant de la matière le principe de l'individuation.[108] Mais le premier précisera[109] *materia signata quantitate determinata*, matière "déterminée" en raison du double principe par lui admis de la "forme de corporéité" et de la "forme spécifique." C'est l'un des points où Averroès s'opposera à son prédécesseur; et l'on sait que pour lui, pour éviter ce recours à une notion platonisante de "forme", le principe d'individuation est la *materia signata quantitate interminata*, selon des dimensions préexistantes en la matière.

Nous avons chez saint Thomas des prises de position successives. Dans le *De Ente et Essentia*, il emprunte à Avicenne sa notion de "quantité déterminée," mais selon une acception qui ne doit plus rien à la "forme spécifique." Dans le *Commentaire des Sentences* et du *De Trinitate* de Boèce, par contre, il adopte la formule d'Ibn Rushd; et, dans le *De Veritate*,[110] mentionne les *dimensiones praeintellectae in materia*. Cependant ces "dimensions indéterminées" qui, au sens d'Ibn Rushd, préexistent réellement dans la matière antérieurement à la forme, sembleront par la suite à saint Thomas compromettre le vrai hylémorphisme de l'unité des formes substantielles. Si bien que dans la *Summa Theologica*, il reviendra, pour expliquer le principe d'individuation, à une matière "déterminée en fonction de la quantité," et qu'il appellera *quantitas dimensiva*.[111]

D'autres exemples de ce très souple procédé d'investigation pourraient être donnés: ainsi la distinction de l'essence et de l'existence dans l'être contingent, réelle comme le voulait Ibn Sînâ (au contraire d'Ibn Rushd), mais non point "extrinsèque" comme l'exigeait le monisme émanatiste avicennien. Rares sont les élaborations philosophiques où n'apparaît point quelque référence, directe ou indirecte, à l'un ou l'autre *faylasûf*. Mais plus rares encore sont les cas où

---

107 A. Forest, op. cit., 234-257; M.-D. Roland-Gosselin, *Le "De Ente et Essentia" de S. Thomas d'Aquin* (Le Saulchoir 1926), 104-117.

108 Au contraire de tout un courant de pensée shî'ite qui, en Islam, explique l'individuation par la forme.

109 V. g. *Ishârât*, 98.

110 5, 9, ad 6.

111 III, 77, 2, c.

la solution adoptée est pleinement conforme à l'enseignement de l'un ou de l'autre. C'est en fonction de vues plus larges, — et plus larges encore que la simple fidélité à Aristote, — que saint Thomas repense et resitue les apports des "Arabes". Ils lui donnèrent à pied d'œuvre des matériaux de toute première importance pour mettre en place son outillage philosophique; ils n'infléchirent jamais les lignes fondamentales de sa synthèse.

CONCLUSION

Nous le disions au début de ces pages: l'analyse exhaustive de ce que put apporter à saint Thomas la pensée philosophique (*falsafa*) et "théologique" (*'ilm al-kalâm*) du monde musulman est à poursuivre. Il est hautement souhaitable que soient menés à bien, patiemment, des travaux analogues à ceux d'A. Forest et C. Vansteenkiste. Un triple *requisit* nous semble devoir les commander.

a) Tout d'abord, une collaboration suivie entre médiévistes et islamisants. Saint Thomas ignora sans doute bien des circonstances socio-culturelles qui commandaient les prises de position du *kalâm* ou de la *falsafa*. Nous croyons cependant que ces circonstances-là ne peuvent qu'éclairer du dedans la portée de l'outillage conceptuel des "philosophes arabes" dont il se servit si volontiers. Son génie sut bien des fois opérer les rectifications nécessaires. Nous avons tout à gagner à en comprendre les conditions et la portée historique, eu égard à la pensée musulmane elle-même.

b) En outre, une telle collaboration médiévistes-islamisants devrait permettre de résoudre certaines difficultés des traductions. Grâce aux travaux patients des érudits, les textes sont ou seront dans un jour prochain à notre disposition. Nous songeons ici, par exemple, aux travaux de Mlle M.-Th.d'Alverny sur l'Avicenne latin,[112] et au texte arabe du *Shifâ'* publié au Caire, en édition critique, sous la direction du Prof. Ibrahim Madkour.[113] Il faut souhaiter qu'un effort analogue (à

---

112 Voir, en particulier, les travaux préparatoires présentés dans la chronique "Avicenna latinus", *Archives d'Hist. doctr. et litt. du Moyen Age*, 1961-1970. Egalement: "Les traductions d'Avicenne (Moyen Age et Renaissance)", *Avicenna nella storia della cultura mediaevale* (Academia dei Lincei, Rome 1957), etc. Grâce à ces travaux, Mlle Simone Van Riet a pu publier le *Liber De anima seu sextus De naturalibus* (Louvain 1968), édition critique de la traduction latine médiévale (psychologie du *Shifâ'*).

113 Par ailleurs, le texte arabe du *De anima* (*Shifâ'*) a été publié à Bratislava (1956) par Jan Bakos, et à Oxford (1959) par M. F. Rahmân; sans oublier les éditions critiques bien connues du P. Bouyges (Beyrouth), qui mirent, entre autres, à la disposition des spécialistes, les grands textes de la querelle des *Tahâfut*.— Mentionnons encore les éditions de textes arabes, *Aristote chez les Arabes* (Le Caire 1947), *Plotin chez les Arabes* (Le Caire 1955), etc., de M. A. Badawî: s'y trouvent et la pseudo-*Théologie d'Aristote* et les *Gloses* d'Avicenne sur la pseudo-*Théologie*, etc.

peine commencé) se poursuive sur les textes arabes et latins des commentaires d'Averroès.

Les traductions médiévales sont précises, mais très littérales. La connaissance directe des texte arabes peut les éclairer. Elle peut permettre aussi d'éviter certains faux-sens. A titre d'exemple: l'arabe philosophique distingue nettement *dhât* (essence) et *mâhiyya* (quiddité). La *mâhiyya*, c'est ce qui répond à la question *mâ* (*quid*), c'est ce qui est "compréhensible" — au sens étymologique — pour la raison humaine, le définissable. Or, si Avicenne a bien dit qu'il n'y a pas de *mâhiyya* en Dieu, il n'a jamais dit que Dieu n'a point de *dhât*. Il a dit avec force que le *dhât* de Dieu, l'Essence divine, est Son être (*mawjûd*): selon une problématique à la fois différente et très proche de celle du *kalâm*, qui fait du *mawjûd* (être, existence) l'"attribut de l'essence" (*sifat al-dhât*).[114]

c) Une troisième exigence nous semble devoir porter sur la spécificité des lumières (*lumen sub quo*) qui commandent respectivement la synthèse thomiste, l'apologie défensive du *kalâm*, la philosophie hellénistique de la *falsafa*. Il faut bien voir ici que des rencontres d'expression, parfois la similitude des problèmes matériellement pris, ne signifient point forcément filières ou emprunts. Les recherches d'Asin Palacios nous ont valu de très précieux relevés de textes, fort éclairants. Mais d'une part, de simples possibilités (ainsi la connaissance que saint Thomas *aurait* pu avoir de l'*Iqtisâd*) ne sauraient constituer des preuves historiques; et d'autre part une non considération de cette spécificité des lumières ne peut que conduire à des affirmations trop rapides de similitudes supposées. Nous songeons à cet "averroïsme théologique" par lequel le savant espagnol voulut expliquer la thèse centrale de saint Thomas sur la révélation.

Enfin — ce n'est plus une exigence, mais un souhait — il conviendrait que les spécialistes de saint Thomas soient attentifs à divers travaux, parallèles aux leurs, qui ont vu le jour en climat musulman. Des chercheurs musulmans s'intéressent, eux aussi, à l'influence du *kalâm* ou de la *falsafa* sur la pensée médiévale latine, spécialement sur l'Aquinate. Ils s'y intéressent en fonction, cette fois, de leur propre passé culturel. C'est ainsi un élargissement des perspectives qu'il nous proposent, et peut-être une voie pour faire aboutir, à travers le temps et l'espace, ce dialogue si bien inauguré aux XIIᵉ-XIIIᵉ siècles. Par la force des choses, il ne pouvait se poursuivre alors que sur des points limités. Il appartient peut-être à notre temps de le reprendre et de l'élargir.

---

114 Autre aporie: *tasdîq*, selon le contexte, veut dire tantôt "jugement" (2° opération de l'esprit), et tantôt adhésion intérieure de foi (par "jugement de véridicité"). Or, les traductions latines ont parfois rendu *tasdîq*-jugement par *fides*.

SAINT THOMAS D'AQUIN
ET LA *MÉTAPHYSIQUE* D'AVICENNE

Georges C. Anawati O.P.

$\mathbf{D}$ANS la mémorable étude qui ouvre les *Archives d'histoire doc-trinale et littéraire du moyen âge,* [1] M. Gilson s'est posé une question à première vue assez étrange. Il se demande, en effet, "Pourquoi saint Thomas a critiqué saint Augustin?"

Quand on connaît la place que S. Augustin occupe dans la tradition chrétienne, il semble en effet étonnant que le Docteur Angélique ait cru devoir critiquer, du point de vue philosophique, le maître par excellence des penseurs chrétiens médiévaux. La raison, M. Gilson l'a mise en évidence, c'est qu'à l'époque de S. Thomas, l'augustinisme avait été compromis précisément par Avicenne et que, dorénavant, opter pour l'évêque d'Hippone, c'était s'engager dans une ligne avicennienne qui compromettait à la fois la doctrine de la connaissance, celle de la causalité et, en fin de compte, les rapports entre Dieu et le monde. C'est dire à la fois la profonde influence de l'auteur du *Shifā'* et les réserves qu'elle suscita chez le plus grand penseur chrétien du moyen âge.

L'étude des rapports de la philosophie d'Avicenne avec celle de s. Thomas d'Aquin remonte déjà à de nombreuses années. Mais depuis un demi-siècle surtout, elle a attiré l'attention d'un certain nombre de chercheurs occidentaux. La place de choix dont jouissait le Docteur Angélique jusqu'à ces dernières années dans la formation des clercs dans l'Eglise catholique a multiplié les travaux sur les sources de sa pensée, le développement de sa doctrine, etc. Très vite on s'est aperçu que les "philosophes arabes," en particulier Avicenne et Averroès, ont joué un grand rôle dans la transmission de la pensée d'Aristote en Occident au moyen âge et que leur étude approfondie n'était pas moins nécessaire que celle de ce dernier pour la pleine compréhension de la pensée des grands penseurs chrétiens du moyen âge. Pour ne citer qu'un témoignage de M. Gilson, voici ce qu'il disait déjà au sixième Congrès international de philosophie en 1926: "On n'obtiendra aucune in-

1   1 (1926), 6-127.

terprétation correcte des philosophies médiévales tant que l'on n'aura pas fait précéder leur étude de celle des philosophies arabes qu'elles réfutent ou dont elles s'inspirent. La pensée arabe et la pensée latine que nous tendons plus ou moins à isoler dans la pratique, ont été en continuité historique et l'étude que nous en faisons doit tenir compte de cette continuité plus qu'il n'a été fait jusqu'ici". Et plus loin: "L'une des tâches les plus urgentes qui s'imposent serait la réédition des traductions latines médiévales des philosophes arabes en général, et d'Avicenne en particulier."[2]

Aussi vit-on une série d'importants travaux consacrés à Avicenne soit à s. Thomas mais où les doctrines des deux grands penseurs étaient confrontées. Pour nous en tenir aux travaux importants consacrés surtout à la *Métaphysique* d'Avicenne, mentionnons les travaux suivants:

Tout d'abord la traduction, en allemand, de cette *Métaphysique* du *Shifâ'*,[3] entreprise en 1907 par Max Horten qui contient en notes de nombreux textes de s. Thomas. Le *Metaphysices Compendium* de Mgr. Nematallah Carame,[4] qui est une traduction latine moderne de la *Métaphysique du Najât*. On sait que ce dernier est un résumé du *Shifâ'* dont il reproduit quelquefois des chapitres entiers.[5] La traduction, exécutée à Rome sur les conseils du P. Gény, professeur à la Grégorienne, est accompagnée de nombreuses notes et références à s. Thomas.

La même année 1926 paraissait une édition critique du *De ente et essentia*, une des premières œuvres de s. Thomas et où l'influence d'Avicenne est prépondérante. L'édition était faite très soigneusement par le P. Roland-Gosselin, un des professeurs du Centre d'Etudes dominicain du Saulchoir où les études historiques concernant la pensée de s. Thomas étaient particulièrement en honneur.[6] A la suite du texte critique, où les renvois à la traduction latine d'Avicenne sont signalés, le savant éditeur a établi une étude historique très précise sur deux

---

2 "L'étude des philosophes arabes et son rôle dans l'interprétation de la scolastique," *Proceedings of the Sixth International Congress of Philosophy* (1927), 596.

3 Max Horten, *Die Metaphysik des Avicenna* (Leipzig 1907). Reproduction photostatique, 1960.

4 N. Carame, *Avicennae Metaphysices Compendium* (Rome 1926). Mgr. Carame était un prélat maronite, établi à Rome qui connaissait admirablement l'arabe, sa langue maternelle. La plus grande partie de l'introduction (pp. xiii-xlvii) à laquelle a collaboré le Prof. Sestili, a pour objet la doctrine d'Avicenne. Cf. C. R. (Chenu) dans *Bulletin thomiste* 2 (1927-29), n. 88, p. (31).

5 En fait le *Najat* (*Salus*) est composé d'*extraits* quasi littéraux du *Shifâ'*. Mlle Goichon, dans son livre *La distinction de l'essence et de l'existence d'après Ibn Sina (Avicenne)* (Paris 1937), 499-503, a donné une table de concordance des textes du traité de l'âme du *Najât* copiés sur le *Shifâ'* avec le texte original de celui-ci et sa traduction médiévale. Les derniers chapitres de la Métaphysique du *Shifâ'* se retrouvent dans la *Najât*.

6 Cf. la collection *Bibliothèque thomiste* fondée par le P. Mandonnet (le directeur actuel est le P. Chenu), qui jusqu'en 1971 avait publié 39 volumes, chez Vrin.

points capitaux de la métaphysique avicennienne: le principe de l'individuation et la distinction réelle entre l'essence et l'existence. Une
enquête soignée était également poursuivie auprès des principaux
philosophes et théologiens du moyen âge.

Presqu'en même temps paraissait le très important article de M.
Gilson, signalé plus haut: "Pourquoi s. Thomas a critiqué s.
Augustin?" où le maître des études philosophiques médiévales mettait
en vif relief l'enjeu de l'option que faisait s. Thomas pour se dégager de
la pensée augustinienne de son époque, compromise par l'avicennisme.
Nul doute que cette très longue étude, très documentée et fortement
pensée, fut le point de départ de nouvelles recherches. Les trois
volumes de Mgr. Masnovo, *De Guglielmo d'Auvergne a s. Tommaso
d'Aquino*,[7] décrivent, en fait, l'influence de l'avicennisme sur la pensée
de ces grands auteurs. Il en est de même de la thèse importante d'Aimé
Forest, consacrée à l'étude de *La structure métaphysique du concret
selon saint Thomas d'Aquin*.[8] C'est surtout par confrontation avec la
pensée avicennienne que l'auteur caractérise la position de s. Thomas.
Cela est si vrai qu'il a jugé indispensable de recueillir le plus grand
nombre de textes de s. Thomas mentionnant explicitement Avicenne et
de les reproduire en appendice à sa thèse (près de 250 textes).[9]

A son tour le P. de Vaux, en 1934, pour fournir à son hypothèse d'un
avicennisme latin une base documentaire, éditait dans ses *Notes et textes sur l'avicennisme latin aux confins du XIᵉ-XIIIᵉ siècles*,[10] contenant,
en particulier, l'édition critique du *De fluxu entis*. Là aussi des comparaisons avec les positions de s. Thomas éclairent utilement le texte.

Continuant son travail directement sur Avicenne et sur ce qu'elle
considère comme l'axe de sa métaphysique, Mˡˡᵉ M.-A. Goichon
publiait en 1937 sa thèse sur *La distinction de l'essence et de l'existence
d'après Ibn Sina (Avicenne)*.[11] Cette fois, comme pour le cas de Mgr.
Carame, Mˡˡᵉ Goichon joignait à la connaissance de la philosophie
scolastique sa science d'arabisante. Sa thèse contient près de quarante
textes de s. Thomas se rapportant à la doctrine d'Avicenne. Quelques
années plus tard elle devait d'ailleurs consacrer trois conférences, faites

---

7 3 vol. (Milan 1945-46).

8 (Paris 1931). Sur cet livre voir le jugement de M. Gilson dans son article "Avicenne en occident au moyen âge", *Archives d'histoire doctrinale et littéraire du moyen âge* 36 (1969) 104, n.
14: "...livre, toujours indispensable"; "ce remarquable travail".

9 331-360. Les œuvres dépouillées sont les suivantes: 4 *Sent.*, *De ente et essentia*, *De principiis
naturae*, *De veritate*, *In Boethium de Trinitate*, *De potentia*, *Summa contra Gentiles*, 8 *Phys.*, *De
generatione et corruptione*, *Metaph.*, *Quodlibeta*, *Summa theol.* (Ia pars seulement), *De virtutibus*,
De spiritualibus creaturis, *De anima*, *De unitate intellectus*, *De substantiis separatis seu De
angelorum natura*.

10 (Paris 1934).

11 (Paris 1937).

à Oxford, à *La philosophie d'Avicenne et son influence en Europe médiévale.* [12]

En 1938 M. Jean Paulus publiait une importante thèse sur *Henri de Gand. Essai sur les tendances de sa métaphysique,* où, de nouveau, la pensée métaphysique d'Avicenne était soulignée avec vigueur et sa comparaison avec celle de s. Thomas établie avec pénétration. [13]

Plus récemment, M. Louis Gardet, fidèle à la méthode de philosophie et de théologie comparées, ne manquait pas, dans *La pensée religieuse d'Avicenne,* [14] d'instituer, sur plus d'un point, une fructueuse confrontation de la pensée avicennienne avec la pensée thomiste.

Il faudrait à côté de ces ouvrages et de ces mémoires, citer un certain nombre d'articles qui ont plus particulièrement étudié Avicenne du point de vue de la pensée thomiste: celui du P. Bouyges, *L'idée génératrice du "De Potentia" de s. Thomas,* [15] qui a essayé de montrer que la question disputée du *De Potentia* de s. Thomas était en fait destinée à réfuter la position émanatiste d'Avicenne. Ce travail servit de point de départ à une thèse plus longue de Mlle Béatrice Zedler dont un important chapitre, "Saint Thomas and Avicenna in the *De Potentia,*" fut publié dans la revue *Traditio.* [16]

De même citons deux études où deux aspects de la métaphysique avicennienne sont comparés à la métaphysique de s. Thomas: l'article de G. Smith, "Avicenna and the Possibles," [17] et celui de J. Collins, "Intentionality in the Philosophy of Avicenna." [18]

Les fêtes du Millénaire d'Avicenne [19] suscitèrent également quelques articles ou communications qui, sur l'un ou l'autre point, confrontaient la pensée métaphysique des deux auteurs: un article de H. D. Dondaine, professeur au Saulchoir, "A propos d'Avicenne et de saint Thomas (de la causalité dispositive à la causalité instrumentale)," [20] et deux communications au congrès de Téhéran, celle de Mlle Goichon, "Un chapitre de l'influence d'Ibn Sina en Occident, le *De Ente et Essentia* de s. Thomas d'Aquin," [21] et celle de l'auteur de ces lignes, "Avicenne et s. Thomas d'Aquin." [22]

---

12   (Paris 1944).
13   (Paris 1938).
14   (Paris 1951). Cf. notre long compte rendu dans *Revue thomiste* (1961) 109-135.
15   *Revue de philosophie* (1931) 113-131, 247-268.
16   6 (1948) 105-149.
17   *New Scholasticism* 17 (1943).
18   *The Modern Schoolman* 21 (1944) 204-215.
19   Sur ce millénaire cf. G. C. Anawati, "L'œuvre scientifique du Congrès d'Avicenne de Téhéran", (21-30 avril 1954), *Mideo* 2 (1955) 351-356; "Chronique avicennienne" 1951-1960, *Revue thomiste* 60 (1960) 613-634.
20   *Revue thomiste* 51 (1951) 441-453.
21   *Le livre du Millénaire d'Avicenne* 4 (Téhéran 1956) 118-131.
22   Ibid. 139-148.

Enfin signalons deux thèses qui ont été dernièrement soutenues et qui portent sur la confrontation de la métaphysique d'Avicenne et celle de s. Thomas: celle de S. Renzi, *La fondazione radicale dell'essere nella metafisica avicenniana,* soutenue à l'Angelicum,[23] et celle de A. G. Judy, "The Use of Avicenna's *Metaphysics* VIII, 4 in the *Summa contra Gentiles.*"[24]

De l'ensemble de ces travaux quelles sont les conclusions que l'on peut tirer en ce qui concerne l'influence de la métaphysique d'Avicenne sur la pensée de s. Thomas d'Aquin? Pour répondre d'une façon précise à cette question, il est indispensable de ne pas perdre de vue les considérations suivantes:

1. L'œuvre de s. Thomas est immense et s'est succédée dans le temps sur une période de près de trente ans. Les travaux des spécialistes de sa doctrine ont montré que, bien que les grandes lignes de cette doctrine soient restées fidèles à ses intuitions de base, il y a eu cependant une maturation, un développement de la pensée et, sur certains points, des rectifications apportées dans les œuvres postérieures. C'est ainsi, par exemple, que, rallié au début à la causalité dispositive d'Avicenne pour l'explication de l'action sacramentelle, il l'abandonne par la suite et adopte la causalité instrumentale. Même évolution au sujet de l'individuation et du problème de la matière indéterminée, de la question du mixte, etc.

---

23 La thèse n'a pas été imprimée mais divers chapitres l'ont été: Stanislao Renzi, "Una fonte della IIIa via: Avicenna," *Freib. Zeit. Phil. Theol.* 13-14 (1966-67) 283-293; "La fondazione radicale dell'essere possibile nell'Avicenna latino", *Aquinas* 9 (1966) 294-313; "L'essere necessario e l'essere possibile in Avicenna", *Aquinas* 10 (1967) 40-52; "La fondazione radicale dell'essere possibile nel'Avicenna latino", *Aquinas* 10 (1967) 153-169; "L'attributo operativo del primo principio degli essere in Avicenna", *Aquinas* 10 (1967) 260-270; "Carattere intellectivo della fondazione radicale dell'essere possibile in Avicenna", *Studi e ricerche di scienze religiose* (Rome 1968) 273-287.

24 Thèse de licence inédite présentée à l'Institut Pontifical d'Etudes Médiévales, Toronto, 1969. On pourrait allonger beaucoup cette liste. Contentons-nous de mentionner les travaux suivants, que nous classons par ordre chronologique. (Ne sont signalés que les travaux où se fait une confrontation entre s. Thomas et la métaphysique d'Avicenne): E. Gilson, *L'être et l'essence* (Paris 1948); *Being and Some Philosophers* (Toronto 1949), (cf. le très long C.R. du P. Isaac dans le *Bulletin thomiste* 8 (1951) 39-59; A. Lobato, "Avicena y santo Tomas," *Est. Filos.* (Las Caldas) 4 (1955) 45-80; 5 (1956) 83-130, 511-551. B. Zedler, "St. Thomas, Interpreter of Avicenna," *The Modern Schoolman* 33 (1955) 1-18. L. de Raeymaeker, "L'être selon Avicenne et selon s. Thomas d'Aquin," *Avicenna Commemoration Volume* (Beruni) A. H. 370 - A. H. 1370 (Calcutta 1956) 119-131; "La esencia avicenista y la esencia tomista," *Sapientia* 11 (1956) 154-165 (cf. le C.R. du P. Geiger dans le *Bulletin thomiste* 10 (1957-59) 163-4). M. de Contenson, "S. Thomas et l'avicennisme latin," *Revue des sciences philosophiques et théologiques* 43 (1958) 3-31. T. O'Shaughnessy, "St. Thomas' Changing Estimate of Avicenna's Teaching on Existence as an Accident," *The Modern Schoolman* 36 (1958-59) 245-60; "St. Thomas and Avicenna on the Nature of the One," *Gregorianum* 41 (1960) 665-79. C. Giacon, "In tema di dipendenze di S. Tommaso da Avicenna," *L'Homme et son destin* (Louvain 1960) 535-544. E. Gilson, "Avicenne et les origines de la notion de cause efficiente," *Atti XII Congr. intern. filos.* 9 (1960) 121-130; "Avicenne en occident au moyen âge," *Archives d'histoire doctrinale et littéraire du moyen âge* 36 (1969) 89-121.

2. S. Thomas a cité abondamment Avicenne, du moins à première vue. Le P. Vansteenkiste a repris le travail de M. Forest et a essayé de relever tous les textes de s. Thomas où il mentionne explicitement Avicenne.[25] Il en a trouvé près de 450. Ce n'est pas négligeable... Evidemment en comparaison des citations d'un s. Augustin ou d'Aristote, le chiffre prend un caractère plus relatif. De plus, beaucoup de textes sont identiques — quant au sens du moins, car souvent s. Thomas semble citer de mémoire — et répétés cinq ou six fois. Il reste cependant que ce nombre est assez révélateur de l'influence, ne serait-ce que matérielle, d'Avicenne sur s. Thomas. Sans compter qu'il y a très probablement des passages qui utilisent implicitement certaines distinctions avicenniennes. A partir du moment où on intègre organiquement une notion ou une distinction, on n'éprouve pas le besoin de dire d'où on l'a empruntée.

Nous devons toutefois faire remarquer, — il y a déjà longtemps que la remarque a été faite, — que les citations d'Avicenne, nombreuses dans les premiers écrits de s. Thomas, se font plus rares par la suite. Beaucoup plus maître de sa propre doctrine, il se dégage de tout ce qui ne concorde pas avec celle.

3. S. Thomas a toujours gardé pour Avicenne un grand respect et le ton à son égard est toujours courtois. Il le considère comme un maître et est heureux de constater, sur certains points, l'accord de sa doctrine avec la foi chrétienne.[26] Souvent ses citations se terminent par un *sicut dixit Avicenna* comme pour apporter un *confirmatur* décisif. Jamais il n'aura à son égard les paroles dures que dans un moment d'indignation il aura pour Averroès, "corrupteur bien plus que commentateur" (*depravator potior quam Commentator*). Quand il refuse de suivre son opinion, il se contente de dire: "Sur ce point, il ne faut pas suivre Avicenne,"[27] ou "c'est à tort (*irrationabiliter*) qu'Avicenne a rejeté l'opinion d'Aristote,"[28] ou bien: "Avicenne fut trompé par..." (*deceptus fuit*),[29] etc. Peut-être l'espèce de respect affectueux que s. Thomas montra toujours pour Platon, même lorsqu'il le critique, rejaillit in-

---

25   C. Vansteenkiste, "Avicenna-Citaten bij S. Thomas", *Tijdschrift voor philosophie* 15 (1953) 457-507. Cf. l'analyse de cet article par E. Gilson dans *Archives d'histoire doctrinale et littéraire du moyen âge* 36 (1969) 104 ff. et n. 14.

26   "Et ideo accipienda est via Avicennae...", *In Boethium de Trinitate*, q. 4, a. 3, c. "Dicendum secundum Avicennam..." 2 *Sent*. d. 13, q. 1, a. 3, ad 4. "Similiter Avicenna istum errorem reprobat satis efficaci ratione..." 2 *Sent*. d. 17, q. 2, a. 2, c. "Alia opinio est Avicennae, quae verior videtur," 4 *Sent*. d. 44, q. 1, a. 1, ql. 2, ad 2.

27   "...in hoc non est standum auctoritate Avicennae", 2 *Sent*. d. 16, q. 1, a. 3, obj. 3. "Dictum Avicennae quantum ad hoc non sustinemus", 4 *Sent*, d. 49, q. 2, a. 1, ad 9; mais il essaie quand même de le sauver: "nisi forte velimus dicere quod Avicenna intelligit..."

28   2 *Phys*. lect. 1.

29   10 *Metaph*. lect. 3.

consciemment sur Avicenne souvent ramené, au point de vue doctrinal, aux positions platoniciennes. [30]

4. Il ne faut pas oublier que, même quand s. Thomas emploie certaines distinctions ou certaines expressions d'Avicenne, il ne le fait pas toujours dans le même sens que ce dernier. Fidèle à sa propre intuition et à la cohérence de sa doctrine, il ne craint pas d'employer le langage de ses adversaires dans son propre sens, de reprendre, par exemple, à son compte une formule d'Avicenne en lui donnant un sens nettement différent.

5. Enfin, et ceci s'adresse surtout aux arabisants qui seraient tentés de s'appuyer trop fortement et trop exclusivement sur le texte arabe d'Avicenne pour prendre en faute s. Thomas critiquant Avicenne, il ne faut pas perdre de vue que l'Avicenne qu'utilise le Docteur Angélique est celui des traductions latines. Et il n'est pas du tout exclus que certains aspects de sa doctrine aient été interprétés dans un sens défavorable à l'auteur du *Shifâ'*, à la suite des critiques acerbes et quelquefois injustifiées adressées par Averroès à son coreligionnaire. Il était difficile pour un s. Thomas ignorant l'arabe et ne connaissant qu'une partie des œuvres d'Avicenne d'échapper complètement aux jugements malveillants que le Philosophe de Cordoue portait contre son collègue de Boukharah.... Cela justifierait la distinction proposée par J. Paulus entre l'Avicenne "fictif" présenté par Averroès et qui n'a pas manqué d'agir fâcheusement sur les scolastiques, et l'Avicenne "réel" que nous découvrent les œuvres d'Avicenne lues objectivement, au besoin en recourant au texte arabe lui-même.

Ces considérations vont nous permettre de présenter d'une façon schématique les rapports de la métaphysique d'Avicenne avec la pensée de s. Thomas. Nous allons dans une première partie signaler les notions, les définitions, les distinctions d'Avicenne que s. Thomas cite et qu'il fait siennes. Dans une deuxième partie nous mentionnerons les points de doctrine où, au contraire, s. Thomas refuse de suivre Avicenne et considère ces positions erronées. Dans cette deuxième partie, nous mettrons aussi les distinctions ou les notions avicenniennes que s. Thomas utilise mais après les avoir redressées selon sa propre doctrine.

---

30 "Quia Platonici et Avicenna..." *De potentia*, q. 5, a. 1, ad 5; "Quidam enim, ut Plato et Avicenna..." *Quodl*. 9, a. 11, c.; "Et sic in hoc Avicenna cum Platone concordat.." *Summa theol.* 1, 84, 4, c.

I. NOTIONS, DÉFINITIONS OU DISTINCTIONS D'AVICENNE APPROUVÉES PAR S. THOMAS

A. *Pour l'enseignement de la métaphysique*

1. Il faut l'apprendre après les sciences naturelles car dans ces sciences il y a beaucoup de notions comme la génération, la corruption, le mouvement dont on a besoin en métaphysique. Egalement après les mathématique: la métaphysique doit en effet étudier les substances séparées et donc connaître le nombre des sphères, leur ordre, etc. Quant aux autres sciences, comme la musique, la morale, etc., elles servent *ad bene esse (In Boethium de Trinitate*, q. 5, a. 1, ad 9).

B. *Genre, espèce, différence. Rapports avec le tout. Nature.*

2. La quiddité de ce qui se trouve dans un genre n'est pas son *esse* (1 *Sent.* d. 19, q. 4, a. 2, c; 2 *Sent.* d. 3, q. 1, ad 1).

3. Le genre est pris des principes matériels, l'espèce des principes formels (2 *Sent.* d. 3, q. 1, a. 5, obj. 4; d. 36, q. 1, a. 5, sed contra).

4. La différence désigne toute la nature de l'espèce, autrement elle ne pourrait pas lui être attribuée, mais elle ne la désigne qu'à partir des principes formels (2 *Sent.* d. 5, q. 1, a. 2, ad 2).

5. Le genre n'est pas intelligé dans la différence comme une partie de son essence mais comme de l'être en dehors de l'essence (*De ente et essentia* 2, ed. Roland-Gosselin, p. 17).

6. La différence ne dit aucune forme qui ne se trouve implicitement dans la nature du genre (2 *Sent.* d. 3, q. 1, a. 6, ad. 1).

7. Le genre signifie le tout mais indistinctement; aussi se rapproche-t-il de la raison de matière (2 *Sent.* d. 18, q. 1, a. 2, c.).

8. La définition de la substance "ce qui n'est pas dans un sujet" n'est pas exacte, car l'être n'est pas un genre. Ni non plus la définition "ce qui existe pas soi." La véritable définition, c'est "ce qui a une quiddité demandant à exister par soi et non dans un autre" (1 *Sent.* d. 8, q. 4, a. 2, ad 2; 2 *Sent.* d. 3, q. 1, a. 5, c.; 4 *Sent.*, d. 12, q. 1, a. 1, q1. 1, ad 2; *De potentia,* q. 7, a. 3, ad 4; *Quodl.* 9, a. 5, ad 2).

9. C'est l'intelligence qui produit l'universalité dans les choses (*De ente et essentia* 3, p. 28).

10. L'universel est perpétuel et incorruptible; il peut être entendu en deux sens (*De veritate*, q. 1, a. 5, ad 14).

11. La considération de la nature est triple: en tant qu'elle existe dans les êtres singuliers, en tant qu'elle existe dans l'intelligence de celui qui

la saisit, en elle-même, abstraction faite de toute considération (*Quodl.* 8, a. 1, c.).

12. Bien que la nature engendre tel homme, elle entend cependant engendrer l'homme (3 *Sent.* d. 8, q. 1, a. 2, obj. 2).

13. La première intention de la nature, c'est l'espèce spécialissime (*Quodl.* 8, a. 2, c.).

C. *Le sujet. L'individuation.*

14. Tout accident est causé par la substance parce que le sujet est ce qui, complet en lui-même, offre à autre chose l'occasion d'exister (*subjectum est quod in se completum, praebens alteri occasionem essendi*) (1 *Sent.* d. 17, q. 1, a. 2, obj. 2.).

15. Dans ses premiers ouvrages, s. Thomas a affirmé que le principe de l'individuation des substances matérielles était la matière. Mais il y a eu hésitation sur la manière dont elle jouait ce rôle. Au début, à la suite d'Avicenne, il admet une "forme de corporéité," qui entraîne nécessairement la quantité en acte et ses dimensions. Cette matière principe d'individuation n'est pas à confrondre avec la matière commune, partie essentielle de la définition. Il affirme dans le *De ente et essentia* (2, pp. 10-11) "Et ideo sciendum est quod materia non quolibet modo accepta sit individuationis principium, sed solum materia signata; et dico materiam signatam quae sub determinatis dimensionibus consideratur."

Dans le commentaire du deuxième livre des *Sentences* (2 *Sent.* d. 3, q. 1, a. 1) reparaît la théorie de la corporéité, forme première et une notion empruntée à Averroès (dans le *De substantia orbis*) de "dimensions indéterminées," antérieures dans la matière aux dimensions déterminées. Dans le commentaire du troisième livre des *Sentences*, il ne mentionne que ce dernier principe comme principe d'individuation.

Dans le commentaire du *De Trinitate,* les dimensions indéterminées sont préférées aux dimensions déterminées à cause des changements continuels qui affectent les déterminations quantitatives de l'individu au cours de sa vie. Mais à partir du *Summa contra Gentiles,* la théorie des "dimensions indéterminées" ne paraît plus jamais.

16. Dans le *De ente et essentia* (2, pp. 12ff) s. Thomas expose et accepte la position d'Avicenne concernant le corps. Celui-ci peut avoir deux acceptions: le corps comme genre; il signifie alors une chose possédant une forme de laquelle peuvent procéder trois dimensions quelle que soit cette forme, qu'une perfection ultérieure puisse en dériver ou non. Dans ce sens le corps sera le genre de l'animal. L'autre acception, c'est le corps signifiant une chose qui a une forme im-

pliquant la détermination des trois dimensions *cum praecisione*, c'est-à-dire à l'exclusion de toute perfection ultérieure. Dans ce dernier cas, le corps sera la partie intégrante et matérielle de l'animal.

D. *L'être; l'essence et l'existence. Les causes.*

17. Le nom *ens* vient de *esse* et celui de *res* de la quiddité (1 *Sent.* d. 25, q. 1, a. 4, obj. 2 et c; 2 *Sent.* d. 37, q. 1, c. etc.).

18. L'être et l'essence, c'est ce que l'intelligence conçoit en premier lieu. Cette assertion capitale est exprimée par s. Thomas sous diverses formes et toujours rapportée à Avicenne au début de sa *Métaphysique*: "Ens est illud quod primo cadit in conceptione humana, ut Avicenna dicit" (*In Boethium de Trinitate*, q. 1, a. 3, obj. 3); "Primum cadens in apprehensione intellectus est ens, ut Avicenna dicit" (1 *Sent.* d. 38, q. 1, a. 4, obj. 4); "Primo in intellectu cadit ens" (1 *Metaph.* lect. 2); "Illud autem quod primo intellectus concipit quasi notissimum, et in quo omnes conceptiones resolvit, est ens, ut Avicenna dicit in principio *Metaphysicae* suae" (*De veritate*, q. 1, a. 1, c.).

19. L'*esse* n'est pas un genre (2 *Sent.* d. 11, q. 1, a. 2, ad 2).

20. Dans tout être créé l'*esse* est autre que l'essence et n'entre pas dans sa définition (*Quodl*, 9, a. 6). Pour la distinction réelle de l'essence et de l'existence, voir Roland-Gosselin, *Le "De ente et essentia" de s. Thomas d'Aquin* (Paris 1948): chez Avicenne, pp. 150-156, chez s. Thomas d'Aquin, pp. 185-199. Sur le rapport des deux, voir surtout pp. 197-198. La distinction est réelle chez les deux. S. Thomas s'inspire d'Avicenne mais le corrige dans le sens de sa doctrine: l'*esse* joue par rapport à l'essence qu'il actualise le rôle d'acte: "Oportet igitur quod ipsum esse comparetur ad essentiam quae est aliud ab ipso, sicut actus ad potentiam" (*Summa theologiae* 1, 3, 4, c.).

21. Division de la cause efficiente en: perfective, dispositive, adjuvante et *consilians* (5 *Metaph.* lect. 2).

22. Posée la cause suffisante, l'effet suit nécessairement, à supposer qu'aucun empêchement ne vienne entraver l'action de la cause, explique s. Thomas (6 *Metaph.* lect. 3; *De veritate* q. 23, a. 5, obj. 1; *De potentia*, q. 3, a. 17, obj. 4). De même la cause disparaissant, l'effet disparaît (1 *Sent.* d. 37, q. 1, c.).

23. L'agent divin donne tout l'*esse* en tant que créateur du monde; l'agent naturel donne seulement le mouvement (1 *Sent.* d. 7, q. 1, a. 1, ad 3; 1 *Sent.* d. 9, q. 2, a. 2, obj. 2).

24. L'agent qui agit par son essence est l'Agent premier (1 *Sent.* d. 3, q. 4, a. 2, sed contra 2).

25. La vérité de l'énonciation se réduit aux premiers principes évidents comme à ses premières causes et en particulier à ce principe:

l'affirmation et la négation ne sont pas vraies en même temps (1 *Sent.* d. 19, q. 5, a. 1, c.).

26. "Veritas cujuslibet rei est proprietas sui esse quod stabilitum est ei" (définition d'Avicenne, *Metaph.* 8, c. 6, Venice, 1508, fol. 100ra), (4 *Sent.* d. 44, q. 1, a. 2, sol. 4; *Summa theol.* 1, 16, 1, c.).

27. Tout vrai n'est tel qu'un vertu de la Vérité première (*De veritate* q. 21, a. 4, obj. 5).

E. *La relation*

28. Elle ne se réfère pas par une autre relation (*De potentia*, q. 3, a. 3, ad 2).

29. Elle n'est pas numériquement identique dans les deux extrêmes (4 *Sent.* d. 27, q. 1, a. 1, obj. 3).

30. Elle n'est pas réelle entre l'être et le non-être (*De potentia,* q. 3, a. 1, ad 7).

31. Les relations de raison peuvent être multipliées (*De veritate*, q. 3, a. 8, ad 4).

F. *Dieu*

32. Dieu n'est pas dans un genre (1 *Sent.* d. 8, q. 4, a. 2, c; *In Boethium de Trinitate*, q. 6, a. 3, c.).

33. En Dieu l'essence est son propre *esse* (1 *Sent.* d. 3, q. 1, a. 2, obj. 4).

34. Dieu est unique: démonstration d'Avicenne: "et haec est via Avicennae" (2 *Sent.* d. 1, q. 1, a. 1, c; *De potentia*, q. 3, a. 5, c.).

35. Dieu est l'Etre nécessaire (*De veritate,* q. 24, a. 10, obj. 4; *De potentia*, q. 2, a. 3, c.).

36. Dieu se connaît (*De veritate,* q. 2, a. 2, c.).

37. La connaissance de Dieu n'est pas évidente ("Deum non esse per se notum"), (1 *Sent.* d. 3, q. 1, a. 2, c.).

38. Dieu est le seul libéral à proprement parler (*Summa contra Gentiles* 1, 93, 7).

39. Dieu agit par son essence (1 *Sent.* d. 42, q. 1, a. 1, obj. 2.).

G. *Création ex nihilo*

40. Même si le monde est éternel, on peut dire qu'il est créé *ex nihilo* (1 *Sent.* d. 5, q. 2, a. 2, c) parce que *ex nihilo* peut indiquer soit un ordre temporel soit un ordre de nature (2 *Sent.* d. 1, q. 1, a. 5, ad 2, sed contra; *De potentia*, q. 3, a. 14, ad 7, sed contra).

H. *Les anges*

41. Les anges sont identifiés aux substances séparées: "Les créatures spirituelles qu'Avicenne et certains autres appellent intelligences et que nous appelons anges" (*Summa theol.* 1, 65, 4, c.). Les anges sont à colloquer dans le prédicament substance (2 *Sent.* d. 3, q. 1, a. 5, c.). S. Thomas rapporte l'assertion d'Avicenne disant que pour les philosophes, les intelligences des sphères représentent ce que le Coran appelle les anges supérieurs comme les Chérubins et les Séraphins, tandis que les âmes des sphères représentent les anges messagers (2 *Sent.* d. 14, q. 1, a. 3, c.).

42. Les substances spirituelles séparées sont simples, absolument dénudées de matière (*De spiritualibus creaturis*, a. 11, obj. 17).

43. Dans les substances simples créées, personne et nature ne diffèrent pas réellement bien qu'en elles l'accident diffère de la substance (3 *Sent.* d. 5, q. 2, a. 1, obj. 4).

44. Dans les substances spirituelles, il y a autant d'individus qu'il y a d'espèces (*De ente et essentia,* 4, p. 34).

45. "Dans les substances simples la quiddité est *simpliciter* la substance même, mais elle en diffère quant au mode de signifier, car la quiddité est signifiée comme forme, tandis que la *res* elle-même est *simpliciter* signifiée comme subsistante" (1 *Sent.* d. 26, q. 1, a. 1, ad 3).

I. *Problème du mal*

46. "Avicenne a fait dans sa *Métaphysique* une très utile division du mal," que s. Thomas résume et synthétise (2 *Sent.* d. 34, q. 1, a. 2, c.).

47. Au-dessus de la sphère de la lune, le mal n'existe pas (*De veritate*, q. 5, a. 9, c.).

II. LA CRITIQUE THOMISTE D'AVICENNE

S. Thomas a donc emprunté à Avicenne un certain nombre de distinctions ou de définitions. Mais, comme nous le signalions plus haut, il garde à son égard le plus entière liberté et, en définitive, si on caractérise avant tout l'avicennisme comme un "essentialisme," i.e. une philosophie des possibles, des essences, celle de s. Thomas en diffère profondément en ce qu'elle se présente comme une philosophie de l'être existant.

De cette position fondamentale découlent un certain nombre d'oppositions faites par s. Thomas à la métaphysique avicennienne. Les principaux reproches qu'il lui fait sont les suivants:

1. *L'extrincésisme de la causalité efficiente*

S. Thomas associe Avicenne à Platon dans le reproche qu'il lui fait d'ôter aux causes secondes leur efficacité. "Et ainsi Platon, et Avicenne qui le suit en certains points, affirmaient que les agents corporels agissent selon les formes accidentales en disposant la matière à la forme substantielle. Mais la perfection ultime obtenue par l'introduction de la forme substantielle, provient du principe immatériel" (*Summa theol.* 1, 115, 1, c.).

Dans le même sens: "D'autres ont dit que les formes provenaient totalement de l'extérieur soit par participation des idées comme le pose Platon soit de l'Intellect Agent comme l'affirme Avicenne et que les agents naturels disposent seulement la matière à la forme (*De virtutibus in communi*, a. 8, c.).

Ailleurs (dans *Summa contra Gentiles*, 2, 74), s. Thomas montre qu'au fond la position d'Avicenne se ramène à celle de Platon car "il n'y a pas de différence entre recevoir la science d'une seule intelligence séparée ou de plusieurs; dans les deux cas cela revient à dire que notre science n'est pas basée sur les données sensibles, ce qui va contre l'expérience; celle-ci montre que celui qui est privé d'un sens est également privé de la science qui correspond à ce sens."

S. Thomas va plus loin: il trouve que la position de Platon est plus logique avec ses prémisses quand il affirme que la connaissance est d'autant plus profonde que l'âme s'éloigne davantage du sensible tandis qu'Avicenne voudrait que plus on retourne aux phantasmes corporels plus on se dispose à recevoir l'influence de l'intellect séparé (Cf. *Summa contra Gentiles*, 2, 74).

Par ailleurs, s. Thomas repousse la théorie avicennienne de l'intellect agent séparé comme s'opposant à l'enseignement religieux: "sequitur aliquid fidei nostra repugnans" (*Q. disp. De Anima*, a. 5, c) et à l'expérience: celle-ci montre que chaque homme peut, quand il veut, abstraire l'universel du particulier et donc le principe qui est à la base de cette abstraction lui est propre (ibid. et *Q. disp. De spiritualibus creaturis*, a. 10, c; *Summa theol.* 1, 79, 4, obj. 4 et Resp.).

2. *La création médiate*

Que la théorie de l'intellect agent séparé aille contre la foi vient de ce que la source de notre illumination est aussi la source de notre béatitude. Et pour la même raison s. Thomas repoussera avec force la théorie avicennienne de la création par intermédiaires car la béatitude de l'homme consiste à rejoindre son principe. A plusieurs reprises s. Thomas réfute cette création médiate par l'intermédiaire des anges, basée sur le principe que de l'Un ne peut venir que l'un. Il montre qu'une telle doctrine: a) mène à l'idolâtrie (2 *Sent.* d. 1, a. 3; d. 18, q. 2, a. 2; 4 *Sent.* q. 1, a. 3, q1. 3; *Contra Gentiles*, 2, 120; *De potentia,* q. 3, a. 4). b) Elle est logiquement liée à des erreurs touchant à la fin de l'homme (2 *Sent.* d. 18, q. 2, a. 2). c) Elle est liée à des erreurs concernant le rôle des anges dans le plan providentiel et leur action sur les volontés humaines (*De veritate*, q. 22, a. 9; q. 5, a. 10). d) Elle porte atteinte à la toute-puissance divine: l'action de Dieu se trouve déterminée à un premier effet unique selon un mode nécessaire (*Contra Gentiles*, 2, 21-22; 1 *Sent.* d. 43, q. 2, a. 1).

3. *La création nécessaire*

Une des affirmations essentielles de la révélation est l'infinie liberté de Dieu. Aussi le déroulement nécessaire du monde à partir de Dieu ne pouvait être accepté d'aucune manière par s. Thomas et il multiplie les arguments pour montrer qu'on ne peut assigner aucune nécessité à cette création: nécessité de nature, de volonté, de justice ou nécessité de science (*De potentia,* q. 3, a. 15). Bien qu'Avicenne ne soit pas visé dans cette dernière réfutation, il n'y a pas cependant de doute que ce soit lui qui est visé. En effet, s. Thomas parle de l'erreur de certains philosophes affirmant "ex hoc quod Deus intelligit, fluit ab eo ipso de necessitate talis rerum dispositio" (*Contra Gentiles*, 2, 26), et donne cinq arguments pour la réfuter, basés principalement sur la toute-puissance divine.

4. *La création éternelle*

Concernant l'éternité du monde, la position de s. Thomas a été toujours très nette. Pour lui le commencement du monde dans le temps est un fait que l'on ne connaît que par la foi. La raison démontre la relation de création qui relie le monde à Dieu mais elle est impuissante à elle seule de démontrer ni que le monde a commencé ni qu'il est éternel. Le Docteur Angélique a recueilli toutes les objections soulevées par les partisans ou les adversaires de l'éternité du monde et il a montré que ni les unes ni les autres n'avaient de valeur apodictique (2 *Sent.* d. 1, q. 1, a. 5, obj. 7 et 12).

Parmi les objections soulevées par les partisans de l'éternité contre un monde ayant commencé dans le temps, certaines sont dues à Avicenne, en particulier celle qui est basée sur la relation nécessaire de l'effet avec la cause efficiente. S. Thomas montre que la cause peut être naturelle ou volontaire (*De potentia*, q. 3, a. 17, ad 4).

5. *Négation du libre-arbitre*

S. Thomas reproche à la théorie avicennienne de l'émanation nécessaire d'aboutir à la négation du libre-arbitre chez l'homme. En effet pour Avicenne, de même que les mouvements des corps sont déterminés par les mouvements des corps célestes, de même les mouvements de leur âme de sorte que notre volonté se trouve causée par la volonté de l'âme céleste. Théorie qui "est absolument fausse" (*omnino falsum*), affirme s. Thomas et qui, de plus, va à l'encontre de la foi chrétienne pour qui Dieu, qui est la fin immédiate de la vie humaine, est aussi celui qui meut librement notre volonté (cf. *De veritate*, q. 5, a. 10; q. 22, a. 9, c; 2 *Sent.* d. 15, q. 1, a. 3, c; *Contra Gentiles*, 3, 87).

6. *La négation de la résurrection des corps*

S. Thomas rapporte dans les *Sentences* (4 *Sent.* d. 44, q. 3, a. 2, sol. 1) l'opinion de certains philosophes dont Avicenne, qui ne croient pas à la résurrection des corps et interprètent métaphoriquement les peines de l'âme. Il rejette cette opinion (cf. également *De veritate*, q. 26, a. 1, c.).[31]

7. *La prophétie naturelle*

Pour s. Thomas, la prophétie proprement dite, prise au sens large (synonyme de révélation divine) soit au sens strict (préconnaissance des futurs contingents) ne peut venir que de Dieu. Elle est surnaturelle et ne requiert aucune disposition ou qualité préalable dans le sujet (accord de la théologie chrétienne avec le kalâm musulman contre les Falâsifa).[32]

Quant à la "prophétie naturelle," elle consiste dans la connaissance des choses non par elles-mêmes mais dans leurs causes; l'homme peut l'acquérir par voie expérimentale, elle est à la mesure de "la perfection de la vertu imaginative et de la clarté de l'intelligence" (*Summa theol.* 2-2, 172, 1 et 3). Mais c'est une prophétie improprement dite, elle n'est qu'une similitude déficiente de la prophétie proprement dite.

8. *Connaissance des singuliers par Dieu*

Voici comment s. Thomas expose et réfute la position d'Avicenne sur ce point:

Certains, comme Avicenne (*Metaph.* 8, ch. 6 vers le milieu) et ces disciples, soutiennent que Dieu connaît chacun des singuliers d'une ma-

---

[31] Cf. notre article, basé sur la *Risâla al-aḍḥawiyya* d'Avicenne, "Un cas typique de l'ésotérisme avicennien: sa doctrine de la résurrection des corps," *Revue du Caire* (1951) 68-94. Depuis ce traité a été édité critiquement et traduit (en italien): Avicenne, *Epistola sulla vita futura* (Padova 1969), par F. Lucchetta.

[32] Cf. F. Rahman, *Prophecy in Islam* (London 1958), et L. Gardet, *La pensée religieuse d'Avicenne* (Paris 1951), ch. 4: Le prophétisme et les vérités religieuses.

nière universelle (*quasi in universali*), du moment qu'il connaît toutes les causes universelles desquelles est produit le singulier, comme si un astronome, s'il connaissait tous les mouvements du ciel et les distances des corps célestes, connaîtrait toute éclipse qui se produirait jusqu'à cent ans. Mais il ne les connaîtrait pas en tant qu'elles sont singulières comme s'il les savait être maintenant ou ne pas être. C'est de cette manière qu'ils ont posé que Dieu connaissait les singuliers non comme s'il regardait leur nature singulière mais par la position des causes universelles.

Mais cette position n'est pas soutenable parce qu'à partir des causes universelles, il ne résulte que des formes universelles s'il n'y a pas quelque chose qui vient individuer les formes. Or quel que soit le nombre des formes universelles réunies ensemble, elles ne constitueront jamais un singulier parce que cette collection de formes peut être intelligée comme existant dans plusieurs ... L'effet universel est proportionné à la cause universelle, l'effet particulier à la cause particulière. (2 *Sent.* d. 3, q. 2, a. 3: 1 *Sent.*, d. 36, q. 1, a. 1; d. 38, q. 1, a. 3; *De veritate,* q. 8, a. 11).

9. *L'unité de la substance concrète et le caractère accidentel de l'existence*

Il reste deux points sur lesquels s. Thomas a constamment fait porter sa critique. A première vue ils peuvent paraître d'importance secondaire mais ils correspondent en fait à des positions entièrement différentes concernant le fondement de la métaphysique.

Le premier est celui de l'unité de la substance concrète. Certains, dit s. Thomas, ont cru que l'un qui se convertit avec l'être est identique à l'un principe du nombre. A partir de là deux erreurs contraires ont pris naissance: Pythagore et Platon voyant que l'un qui se convertit avec l'être n'ajoute rien à celui-ci mais exprime la substance de l'être en tant qu'elle est indivise, s'imaginèrent qu'il en était de même de l'un principe du nombre. Et comme le nombre est composé d'unités, ils pensèrent que les nombres étaient les substances de tous les êtres.

Dans un sens contraire, poursuit s. Thomas, Avicenne, considérant que l'un principe du nombre ajoutait quelque chose à la substance (autrement le nombre composé d'unités ne serait pas une espèce de quantité), crut que l'un qui se convertit avec l'être ajoute quelque chose à la substance de l'être comme le blanc à l'homme. Ce qui, ajoute s. Thomas, est manifestement faux. Car si une chose était une par quelque chose de surajouté à celle de l'être, il faudrait que cette nature accidentelle surajoutée à l'être soit une à son tour, et si elle ne l'est pas par elle-même, on est obligé de reculer jusqu'à l'infini. Aussi faut-il s'arrêter au premier (*Summa theol.* 1, 11, 1, ad 1).[33]

---

33   Cf. T. O'Shaughnessy, "St. Thomas and Avicenna on the Nature of the One", *Gregorianum*

L'autre point important reproché à Avicenne c'est celui de l'accidentalité de l'existence par rapport à l'essence.[34] Que l'essence soit distincte de l'existence dans tout être autre que Dieu, s. Thomas l'admet et ce sera même une des positions centrales de sa métaphysique. Il dira même que l'*esse est adveniens extra* (*De ente et essentia*, 4, p. 34), mais cela "ne signifie pas ici que l'exister s'ajoute du dehors à l'essence, comme ferait un accident, mais qu'il lui vient d'une cause efficiente transcendante à l'essence, donc extérieure à elle, qui est Dieu."[35]

C'est en partant de l'essence qu'Avicenne aboutit forcément à considérer l'*esse* qui l'affecte comme un accident. S. Thomas, au contraire, part de l'être existant et il fait de l'*esse* ce qu'il y a de plus intime et de plus profond dans cet être; le rapport de l'*esse* à l'essence n'est pas le rapport de deux entités du même ordre, d'un accident à une substance, même d'un point de vue logique, mais le rapport d'acte à puissance. Les deux points de vue sont entièrement différents. "Entre l'extrinsécisme avicennien de l'acte d'être," dit M. Gilson, "et l'intrinsécisme thomiste de l'acte d'être, aucune conciliation n'est possible. On ne passe pas de l'un à l'autre par voie d'évolution mais de révolution."[36]
1960.

*

* *

Cette affirmation de M. Gilson, que nous faisons entièrement nôtre, va nous permettre de conclure en quelques mots notre brève étude. S. Thomas s'est profondément assimilé la *Métaphysique* d'Avicenne. Il en a retenu comme valables certains éléments, certaines distinctions qui, au besoin rectifiées, lui ont permis de mettre au point maint outillage conceptuel. Nous avons signalé plus haut cet apport. Mais la façon vigoureuse dont il a réagi contre "l'essentialisme" avicennien et a repoussé son émanatisme déchéant et ses conséquences: création éternelle, nécessaire et par intermédiaires, non-connaissance par Dieu des singuliers, extrinsécisme de la causalité et de l'existence, montre que d'aucune manière on ne peut qualifier d'avicennienne la synthèse théologique thomiste.

---

41 (1960) 665-679. "It may have been that St. Thomas in attributing such teaching to Avicenna was using his name as a convenient label to designate a class of doctrines that made the one univocal....It is likely too that certain errors in Gundissalinus' Latin translation of the *Shifā'* from which Thomas drew his information about Avicenna's doctrine, confirmed his opinion of the Arabian's teaching on the nature of the one". Ibid. 678.

34 Cf. T. O'Shaughnessy, "St. Thomas' Changing Estimate of Avicenna's Teaching on Existence as an Accident," *The Modern Schoolman* 36 (1958-59) 245-260.

35 E. Gilson, *Le thomisme*, 6ᵉ éd. (Paris 1965), p. 180, n. 61.

36 Ibid., p. 181.

MOTION IN A VOID: AQUINAS AND AVERROES

James A. Weisheipl O.P.

T HE concept of the void has attracted the attention of philosophers and scientists since pre-Socratic times. There are, however,
a number of aspects of the void that should be distinguished before
discussing the particular one we are concerned with in this paper. One
generic category for the concept of the void is some kind of space or
"place in which there is nothing."[1] On the Aristotelian hypothesis that
every body is either heavy or light, one might concretize the definition
of the void in the phrase "that in which there is nothing heavy or
light."[2] Aristotle has very little to say about space, but he devotes five
chapters to the nature of "place" and four to the concept of the "void."
The notion of place is a very complex one, involving both the innermost
boundary of the containing body and the formal immobility of the containing body itself, so that bodies can be said to move in and out of
places. It can be defined as "the innermost (immoveable) boundary of
the container."[3] Place thus involves a qualitative environmental container that is somehow immobile relative to the system of the universe.
While the qualitative environmental container is sufficient to explain
the natural movement of bodies for Aristotle, the quantitative immobility of the container need not be taken as something absolute, as I
have tried to show elsewhere.[4] For Aristotle the whole universe is a
plenum. Therefore a void would be some kind of place devoid of every
body. A *locus sine corpore locato* is not a contradiction in terms, as E.
J. Dijksterhuis would have us believe,[5] but an attempt to define and cir-
cumscribe the notion of void.

P. H. Wickstead and F. M. Cornford are undoubtedly correct when
they say that κενόν (void) comes nearer to our "space" than τόπος

---

1 Arist., *Phys.*, IV, 7, 213 b 32-33.
2 Ibid., 214 a 4-5.
3 *Phys.*, IV, 4, 212 a 20-21.
4 *Nature and Gravitation* (River Forest, Ill. 1955) pp. 74-76.
5 *The Mechanization of the World Picture* (Oxford 1961) p. 39.

(place). [6] Space, as such, denotes essentially some kind of dimensionality. This dimensionality can be real and physical, as when we give the extension between two bodies and there is real quantity belonging to another body between them. This is one common usage in all measurements. These dimensions are quantities belonging to the intervening body, but for practical purposes they can be temporarily disregarded. In other words, the intervening dimensions or quantity are not relevant to the case. We simply want to know the space available or the distance to be covered. Even if there were no intervening body with its proper dimensions, we would still speak of dimensions. Thus dimensionality, as such, abstracts from the question whether or not there is a real accident of quantity belonging to any body. Further, there is mathematical space, which is nothing more than a geometrical description of a situation in reference to determined coordinates. In Euclidean geometry there is nothing between a point, line, or figure, and the coordinates. While we do not speak of mathematical space as a void, because there is no advantage is doing so, it can nevertheless suggest the nature of emptiness, non-being, the void. Finally, there is imaginative space, a kind of mental framework, within which objects of imagination are placed. Immanuel Kant was so struck by the natural inevitability of some spatial dimensionality that he thought it must be an a priori condition of the human mind, a condition which makes experience possible. This framework or screen is a kind of absolute space, much like Plato's "matter" or "winnowing basket" within which, or against which, we project images, including mathematical points, lines, and figures. When we speak of "space" beyond the universe, whether this be the Aristotelian universe or our present collection of gallaxies, the kind of space that is required by human philosophy is nothing more than a *quid imaginativum*. [7]

By "void" in this paper we mean an empty space existing outside the mind, a space that has absolutely nothing in it. Even the term "nothing" is to be taken strictly as meaning no objective reality whatever, neither being, nor force, nor resistance. When we ask the more sophisticated question whether there could be a motion of a real body through a void, we grant the existence of such a void as an hypothesis. We wish to know whether there would be movement of a natural body through such a void, if one did exist.

6 *Aristotle, The Physics*, Loeb ed. (London 1963) I, 271.
7 St. Thomas, *In III Phys.*, lect. 7, n. 6; see J. A. Weisheipl, "Space and Gravitation," *The New Scholasticism*, 29 (1955) 175-223.

The question was a serious one in Greek antiquity and it aroused considerable discussion in the Middle Ages, as we shall see. The question is also of interest to modern historians of science, who see in the medieval position on this question one of the fundamental obstacles to the rise of the new physics of the seventeenth century. Anneliese Maier in particular maintains that the universal teaching on the question of motion in a void involved a major obstacle to the rise of modern science. In her paper of 1960[8] she noted that two basic medieval hypotheses may be singled out as the most significant and the most fatal for the birth of classical physics.

The first of these[9] is the theorem that qualities, as such, are independent factors with their own laws in natural processes, quite distinct from quantitative factors. That is, as "intensive magnitudes" they are only parallel to extensive and quantitative magnitudes, presumably susceptible to mathematical treatment, but were not. This aspect of Anneliese Maier's hypothesis will not be considered in this paper.

The second is much more important and relevant to the problem with which we are concerned.[10] Since "omne quod movetur ab alio movetur," according to A. Maier every movement requires a particular mover bound to it and generating motion directly. Moreover, every normal movement of a successive nature requires, over and above the mover, a resistance that opposes the moving force and is overcome by that force, for without resistance there would be no motion (*motus*), but change (*mutatio*), that is, an instantaneous change of place.[11]

This second theorem of the so-called Scholastics is highly complex. Each part must be considered before the implications of the whole can be fully understood. The first part is "Omne quod movetur ab aliquo movetur": every movement requires a particular mover bound to it and generating motion directly. I have presented my views on this point in *Isis* some years ago.[12] Briefly, I argued that practically all historians, and many philosophers interested in medieval thought, have mistranslated and misunderstood the Latin phrase. It does not mean, and never

8 "Ergebnisse der Spätscholastischen Naturphilosophie," *Scholastik,* 35 (1960) 161-187.
9 Ibid., 169-170.
10 Ibid., 170.
11 "Das andere Prinzip ist der Satz 'Omne quod movetur ab aliquo movetur': jede Bewegung erfordert einen partikulären, mit ihr verbundenen und sie unmittelbar erzeugenden Beweger; und jede normal, sukzessiv sich vollziehende Bewegung erfordert überdies einen Widerstand, der sich der vis motrix entgegensetzt und von ihr überwunden wird; denn ohne Widerstand würde sich kein *motus*, sondern eine *mutatio*, d. h. eine in instanti erfolgende Ortsveränderung ergeben." loc. cit.
12 "The Principle *Omne quod movetur ab alio movetur* in Medieval Physics," *Isis,* 56 (1965) 26-45.

did mean, that everything here and now moving needs a mover; for Aristotle this is true only of violent motion. This principle was formulated in antiquity, particularly by Aristotle, as applicable to passive principles of motion. Today it is largely a question of bad grammar, turning the Greek middle or passive voice and the Latin passive into a vernacular active. Even Averroes was misled by the Arabic rendering of the Aristotelian principle, and it was upon this that he built his own natural philosophy. Whatever is to be said of the Arabic formulation, it is not the meaning in Latin or for the Latin Scholastics. St. Thomas Aquinas, Albertus Magnus, and even Siger of Brabant, an ardent Averroist, saw the predicament this would lead to and opposed the Averroist view, but they had few followers in a detail such as this. Ockham also dismissed the necessity of the scholastic principle, but for very different reasons. We must remember that in the fourteenth century there were at least five different philosophical schools: the Averroists, the Thomists, the Scotists, the Nominalists, and a variety of eclectics defending Platonic and Augustinian elements. Therefore care must be taken when speaking of "Scholastic Physics" in the Middle Ages. We must be especially careful not to fall into the Averroist error of thinking that Aristotle was god and that Averroes was his prophet.

In this paper I should like to consider the other elements in Anneliese Maier's "most important and most fatal" hypothesis of the Scholastics: (1) that all motion properly so-called requires a resistance which opposes the moving force, (2) that without resistance there would be no motion (*motus*), strictly so-called, but only change (*mutatio*), and (3) that without resistance, such as in a void, there could be only instantaneous change, that is, without time. Miss Maier goes on to say that "these principles hold for every local motion, inertial movement as it was called later, as well as others that flow from local motion... and which one and all stand in contradiction to classical physics."[13] For A. Maier, as for Averroes before her, motion in a void would be motion without resistance, and therefore it cannot possibly exist. The crucial point for Maier and for Averroes is that resistance is essential to the possibility of motion; without resistance, as would be the case of motion in a void, there cannot be any motion (*motus*, $\varkappa\acute{\iota}\nu\eta\sigma\iota\varsigma$) at all.

*

*   *

13 Loc. cit. 170.

The problem of motion in a void and, indeed, the existence of a void itself, goes back to the dilemma raised by Parmenides, who insisted that only what *is* can be real; whatever does not exist cannot be real.[14] However, a void seems to exist between bodies of whatever kind and between numbers; therefore it would seem that the void is real. But by definition a void is "that which does not exist"; therefore bodies cannot be separated by a void, since a void is non-being and cannot exist. Separation, for Parmenides, is only an illusion. Moreover, local motion also seems to require a void, for bodies can move only into places devoid of bodies. However, since the void is non-being and cannot exist, neither can local motion exist. More important, there cannot be γένεσις or coming-into-being, for every "coming into being" must come from something or nothing. If it comes from something, then it already exists; if it comes from nothing, then it can never begin, for nothing does not exist. Latin philosophers and historians pose the dilemma of Parmenides very simply: a being cannot come into being from nothing, for *ex nihilo nihil fit*; and it cannot come from something already existing, for *quod est, non fit*. Consequently all motion and change is logically impossible; what appears to be multiplicity and movement is only an illusion. They belong to the way of "seeming," or "opinion." The way of "truth" declares that all being exists as one and immobile.[15]

The first serious response to the dilemma of Parmenides came from the Atomists, Leucippus and Democritus. They conceded that real being, ultimate being, namely the atoms, could not be generated or annihilated. However, by making one simple alteration in the philosophy of Parmenides, the appearance of change and motion — even the multiplicity of being — could be preserved. That one simple alteration was the admission that non-being, the void, was just as real as being itself. If this were granted, there could be a multiplicity of atoms, constructs from atoms, and numbers. More important, the possibility of motion — at least local motion — could be preserved.[16] But as for the atoms themselves, they were as ungenerable and indestructible as the single Being of Parmenides.

Even the demonstration by Anaxagoras that air is a body did not deter the Atomists, because even air had to be considered a body insufficient to constitute a void. The Atomists could explain all kinds of motion without admitting the generability of atoms. In other words,

---

14 *Die Fragmente der Vorsokratiker*, ed. H. Diels (7th ed. with additions by W. Kranz) frag. 7-8.

15 See Kirk & Raven, *The Presocratic Philosophers* (Cambridge Univ. Press 1957) 277-282.
16 Ibid. 404-409.

atoms themselves could not be generated or corrupted. The void within bodies could explain condensation and rarefaction, while a void outside bodies could explain local motion, growth, alteration, birth and death. This solution was an alluring one to physicists and to metaphysicians. Even Aristotle commended Democritus for his method and for having brought the study of physics back to respectability.[17] We must remember that for the Atomists the void was not only a condition of motion, but the very cause of motion. It is not a question of whether some vacua exist in the universe, or whether man can produce a vacuum. It is a question of whether the movements we see in the universe are to be explained in terms of bodies and the void. It is not even a question of "nature abhorring a vacuum," or whether the void outside the entire universe is real or not. For Leucippus and Democritus it was simply whether the movements evident in the universe must be explained by postulating a void. "In the acceptance of void (Leucippus) was consciously correcting an Eleatic axiom."[18] "At the same time Leucippus remained faithful to the principles of his probably Ionian background."[19]

Aristotle took the view of the Atomists seriously, even though he deals specifically with the void in only four chapters of his *Physics*, Bk.IV, cc.6-9. His arguments are not always demonstrative. Dealing with the void, he arrives at different conclusions; many are simply arguments contradicting the hypothesis of a void. Because of the complexity of these chapters, many readers of Aristotle have been misled by the apparent variety of conclusions. While Aristotle was aware of the Atomists throughout his works, notably the *Physics* and *De generatione*, we are concerned only with the difficult chapters of Bk.IV, cc.6-9.

After discussing the nature of place (τόπος) in the Fourth Book of the *Physics*, Aristotle turns to the void (κενόν), and says, "The investigation of similar questions about the void, also, must be held to belong to the physicist — namely whether it exists or not, and how it exists or what it is — just as about place" (213 a 11-13). The entire four chapters, 6 to 9, are a kind of disputation in which arguments are given for and against the existence of a void, and finally the limited sense in which it can be said to exist. In the sixth chapter he lists the three previous arguments from the Atomists and two additional arguments from the Pythagoreans, namely, that there must be a void in the heavens to separate the stars, and that there must be a void between numbers to

---

17 Arist., *De gen. et corrup.* 1, 2. 315 a 34-315 b 32; cf. 316 a 14-15; 324 b 35-325 a 2.
18 Kirk & Raven, op. cit. 406.
19 Ibid.

keep them distinct. In the seventh chapter, where he tries to determine the exact meaning of the void, he shows that there is often a confusion between place and void, "void" often serving the function of "space" and "place." In essence, a void is a place devoid of any body whatever (213 b 30-214 a 6).

In a lengthy chapter 8, Aristotle refutes the notion of the void as existing separate from body, using six different arguments leading to different immediate conclusions, but all leading up to the general conclusion that there can be no motion in a void. The first argument (214 b 13-35) considers the vacuum as undifferentiated space. If a natural body were placed in it, the body could not move, for there are no directions. Second (215 a 1-13), if there is no natural motion there can be no unnatural or violent motion. Third (215 a 13-18), if there is no medium, as is required for violent motion, there can be no violent motion. Fourth (215 a 19-23), the void is completely undifferentiated; there is no "up" or "down," and therefore there cannot be motion, but eternal rest, or, if a body were put into motion, it would continue *ad infinitum* until stopped by a weightier body. Fifth (215 a 23-24), the void is postulated because it yields to bodies, but this quality is equally present in every direction; therefore it would have to move in all directions at once, and consequently it would not move at all. Finally (215 a 24-216 a 8), between any two movements there must be a ratio between any two times, as long as both are finite; but there is no ratio of void to full. In other words there is no ratio between zero and any number. Therefore motion would be instantaneous, and hence impossible. Concluding this section, Aristotle says "These are the consequences that result from a difference in media" (216 a 12).

It is relatively clear what might happen according to Aristotle if the motion of bodies had to be explained by a void instead of by natural place. A variety of things might happen, but it would not be the motion we know bodies to have in the world we live in. First, there could be no natural motion of certain bodies "up" and other bodies "down," for in a void there are no preferential environments towards which different bodies are wont to move. Second, there could be no "violent" or compulsory motion, for this presupposes that it is "natural" for light bodies to move up and heavy bodies to move down. Third, in Aristotle's view and in that of Plato, all violent or non-natural motion must be explained in terms of some "medium" as the extrinsic instrumental cause of continued motion.[20] Fourth, a body might be eternally at rest unless

---

[20] For a fuller explanation of this, see J. A. Weisheipl, "Natural and Compulsory Movement," *The New Scholasticism,* 29 (1955) 50-61.

moved by something already in motion, or a body in motion would go on *ad infinitum* in a straight line unless a more powerful body stopped or deflected it. Fifth, there might be no motion at all, or in every direction at once, for the void is equally susceptible to motion in all directions. Sixth, there might be instantaneous motion, which is not true motion at all because there is no medium to be divided, and between zero and any number there must be a ratio such that $S = 1/0$, where S is the speed and the divider is zero, as in the absence of any medium. For Aristotle, all of these arguments, or perhaps any one of them, is sufficient to show that natural motions in the universe cannot be explained by postulating a void distinct from bodies, as the Atomists contend.

In chapter 9, Aristotle considers briefly the interstices in bodies as voids, e.g., when one body absorbs another and when one body expands and occupies more room. If there were no vacuum within bodies, the Atomists say, there could be no contraction and expansion. But if there were no contraction and expansion, either there would be no movement of this kind, such as we see taking place, or the universe would bulge, as Xuthus, the Pythagorean of Croton, said, or air and water must always change into equal amounts. For example, if air has been made out of a cupful of water, then conversely out of an equal amount of air a cupful of water must have been made — or there must be a void within bodies. There is no other way — so the argument of the Atomists goes — for compression and expansion to take place. There are four possibilities, and three of them are absurd; therefore compression and expansion must be explained in terms of a void existing within bodies.

Aristotle answers this briefly. The Atomists want to place little void spaces within the interstices of bodies. But if nothing moves in a void separate from bodies, neither can anything move in the interstices. Aristotle goes on to state his own doctrine of condensation and rarefaction, based on the doctrine of potency and act, which was not considered by the Atomists. "Our statement is based on the assumption that there is a single matter for contraries, hot and cold and other natural contrarieties, and that what exists actually is produced from a potential existent (ἐϰ δυνάμει ὄντος ἐνεϱγεία ὂν γίνεται), and that matter is not separable from the contraries but its being is different, and that a single matter may serve for color and heat and cold" (217 a 22-26). This is Aristotle's own doctrine of alteration, one type of which is condensation and rarefaction, or compression and expansion. Therefore, there is no void outside of bodies or within them, unless one wishes to call the *potential* a void. In this case, the matter of the heavy body is "void" with respect to the natural place downward, just as the matter of light bodies is "void" with respect to their natural place upward. Thus, in locomotion the void is the potential element in the body that needs to be fulfilled. Alteration, on the other hand, has to do with passivity and impassivity, which permit or resist change (217 b 23-27). In this case passivity could be called a void. Aristotle concludes, "So much, then, for the discussion of the void, and of the sense in which it exists and the sense in which it does not exist" (217 b 27-28). Since neither the Atomists nor anyone else use the term "void" to designate the potential principle in moving bodies, it must be said that Aristotle denies the need for postulating a void to explain motion.

Are we to say, then, that Aristotle denies the possibility of motion in a void outside the context of the arguments presented?

The most devastating argument of the Atomists, and the one Aristotle spends most time on, is the sixth one presented above. He seems to argue from the necessity of some resisting medium not only to show that differentiation of speed arises from differentiation of the medium, but also to the absolute necessity of some resisting medium for the possibility of motion at all. His stated principle is that between any two movements there must be a ratio of times (216 a 9); in the absence of a medium "there is no ratio of void to full" (216 a 11). Therefore, the commentators concluded, in a void motion would be instantaneous, for the body would have to be in position A and in position B at the same time, *in instanti*. Aristotle does not say explicitly that motion in a void would be instantaneous, but it is the only conslusion one can draw from his premises.

Most commentators have taken this to be Aristotle's personal position, forgetting that he is arguing from the premises of the Atomists. Thus David Ross says, "(Aristotle) has been misled by thinking of velocity as essentially the overcoming of resistance and not as the traversing of a certain distance in a certain time."[21] E. J. Dijksterhuis also understands this to be Aristotle's personal opinion: "In a void there would be no resistance to motion, and thus, in view of the inverse proportion between the velocity and the density of the medium, the fall would have to proceed instantaneously, i.e., the falling body would have to reach the end-point at the same moment at which the fall starts."[22] For Dijksterhuis, this and the other arguments are "emotional rather than logical in character, an expression of self-assertion rather than a refutation."[23] A. C. Crombie states that "Aristotle's 'law' (that $V = P/R$) expressed his belief that any increase

21 *Aristotle's Physics* (Oxford 1936) 61.
22 *The Mechanization of the World Picture* (Oxford 1961) 40.
23 Ibid.

in velocity in a given medium could be produced only by an increase in motive power. It also followed from the 'law' that in a void bodies would fall with instantaneous velocity; as he regarded this conclusion as absurd, he used it as an argument against the possibility of a void."[24] In like manner all the modern exegetes of Aristotle's arguments against the void presume that the content of each argument, particularly the sixth, is an expression of Aristotle's own doctrine. The number of medieval and modern exegetes who interpret Aristotle in this way is too numerous to list here. They credit Aristotle with the formula $V = F/R$, maintaining that resistance is essential for all motion in such a way that if $R = O$, then motion must be instantaneous.

More attentive exegetes are careful to point out that in the passage on the void Aristotle argues from the position of the Atomists to intrinsic absurdities. Thus, for the Atomists, the void is postulated as the sole source of motion, while for Aristotle the *natural body itself* is the principle of motion and rest; all that is needed is a place to go, namely natural place. After discussing the sixth argument at great length, St. Thomas says, "And so it is better and simpler to say that the argument induced by Aristotle is an argument to contradict a position taken (*ratio ad contradicendum positioni*), and not a demonstrative argument strictly speaking (*simpliciter*)."[25] Those who postulate a void do so that motion would be possible, and so according to them the cause of motion arises on the part of the medium that permits motion. Consequently Aristotle argues against them "as though the whole cause of swiftness and slowness were on the part of the medium."[26] But if "nature" is the cause of velocity, as Aristotle firmly believes, then there is no need to postulate the void. However, Aristotle makes no mention of his own doctrine in this argument, as he does in the first, second, and third, namely the distinction between "natural" and "violent" motion. All that he is saying in the sixth argument is that, if the void is the whole cause of motion and its velocity, then in a void there would be no way to account for obviously different ratios of velocity through it; with the reason for slowness gone, there could be only instantaneous velocity, which is not *motus*. In other words, Aristotle would not admit that the void or the medium is the whole cause of motion. Rather, the cause of motion is the nature of the body itself, moving through some medium that must be divided over some distance in a given time. This is the only interpretation consistent with Aristotle's teaching throughout the

24 *Medieval and Early Modern Science* (New York 1959) II, 48-49.
25 *In IV Phys.*, lect. 12, n. 10.
26 Ibid.

Physics. For him, all natural bodies contain within themselves the principle of motion and rest, i.e., φύσις; the medium can only resist or assist in the traversal of distance in a given time. Since in the sixth argument Aristotle makes no mention of the nature in bodies as the cause of motion, it cannot be taken as an expression of his own doctrine, but only as an argument "to contradict the position" of his adversaries.

In late antiquity John Philoponus (fl. 480-547) objected to Aristotle's sixth argument precisely on the grounds that speed is proportional to the weight of the body, and that the function of a resisting medium is only to retard the body's motion, thereby allowing the possibility of motion in a void.[27] While Philoponus considers this to be contrary to Aristotle's position, it is in fact a principle of Aristotle's own doctrine that he is defending.

In a relatively long comment on text 71 (= 215 a 25-b 20) of *Physics*, Book IV devoted to this matter, the Spanish Moslem, Averroes (1126-1198), preserves an objection of Ibn-Badja (d. 1138), another Spanish Moslem, known to the Christians as Avempace. Ibn-Badja's contention that Aristotle's argument is "false" is based on time and the divisibility of all motion: Aristotelian notions used show that the sixth argument will not hold good on Aristotelian grounds.[28]

Avempace, contends that every motion has a determined natural velocity by virtue of a proportion between the body itself and the cause that generated it. By removing all additional resistances, such as that produced by the medium and friction, there is still left a natural body capable of moving in a natural time. In the Seventh Book of his *Physics* commentary, according to Averroes (*Phys.* IV, comm. 71), Avempace proves this by a visible example and by a rational argument: 1) we see every day that the celestial bodies, whose motion is in no way impeded by resistance, move with a definite velocity according to a definite time, 2) the distance over which all bodies must traverse is divided by *prius* and *posterius*, before and after, from which it follows that motion takes place not in an instant, but in a determined time. It is true, Avempace

---

27 See relevant section in M. R. Cohen and I. Drabkin, *A Source Book in Greek Science* (Cambridge 1958) 217-221; Edward Grant, "Motion in a Void and the Principle of Inertia in the Middle Ages," *Isis*, 55 (1964) 266.

28 The text of Averroes used in this paper is that of the *editio princeps*, Padua 1472, containing the medieval translation of both Aristotle and Averroes. However, this edition has no foliation. For recent discussion of the opposition between Averroes and Avempace, see Pierre Duhem, "Le vide et le mouvement dans le vide," in *Le Système du Monde*, 10 vols. (Paris 1913-1959) 8, 7-120; Avempace is discussed on pp. 10-16. E. A. Moody, "Galileo and Avempace," *Journal of the History of Ideas*, 12 (1951) 163-193, 375-422; abbreviated in *Roots of Scientific Thought*, ed. P. P. Wiener & A. Noland (New York 1957) 176-206. Edward Grant, "Motion in the Void and the Principle of Inertia in the Middle Ages," *Isis*, 55 (1964) 265-292.

says, that one can substract "accidental impediments" such as a medium. But it does not thereby follow that the proportion between speeds of motion is like the proportion of one impediment to another, so that if there is no resisting medium, the motion would be without time, but rather like the proportion of one slowness (or velocity) to the slowness of the other. In other words, there would still be a proportion between the velocity of one body with an "accidental impediment" to another body with no accidental impediment, because their times are proportionate. Thus, for Avempace, all impediments are to be subtracted from the natural velocity of the body; and when all are subtracted, as in a void, there is still left a body moving with natural velocity. Moody expresses this in the modern formula: $V = P-M$.[29] Hence a resisting medium is not at all necessary for motion. At this point we come into conflict with Averroes' entire doctrine of motion and his opposition to Ibn Badja.

Basic to Averroes' concept of motion is the medium. According to Averroes, for all free fall of heavy bodies there must be not only the natural mover (*movens*, or *motor*) attached to the body and generating motion, but there must also be a resisting medium to help the movement downward. The same holds true of light motion upward; there must be a mover moving the body upward and a resisting medium to help it climb. In other words, every body moving must have a mover conjoined to the body, a *motor conjunctus*, here and now moving it. But Averroes knew perfectly well that he could not say that the "form," or mover, *per se* moves the body, for this would be to describe a living body. Living things move themselves *per se* by parts, the living soul being the efficient cause of these parts moving one another. Averroes' ingenious explanation was that the "form," or mover, in inanimate things *per se* moves the resisting medium, which in turn moves the matter. Thus, for Averroes, the substantial form of the body moves the matter only *per accidens* by means of the resisting medium.[30] By allowing form to act in its own right on the resisting medium, instead of acting directly on the matter, Averroes preserves the important distinction between living and non-living movement.

Basically Averroes' doctrine of motion rests on a complete dichotomy between matter and form, body and soul, moved and mover, in a given composite. He believes that form in inanimate bodies can act as a true *efficient* cause of its own motion, instead of being simply an active prin-

---

29 Op. cit., 186.
30 Averroes, *De caelo*, III, comm. 28; cf. St. Thomas, *In III De caelo et mundo*, lect. 7, nn. 8-9; J. A. Weisheipl, "The Principle *Omne quod movetur ab alio movetur* in Medieval Physics," *Isis*, 56 (1965) 26-45.

ciple of natural motions.[31] "Motor est forma et res mota est materia."[32] Such a dichotomy between matter and form is much more than Aristotle would allow between two intrinsic principles of a natural substance that is an *unum per se*. Nevertheless, for Averroes the resistance to motion is an absolutely essential element in every motion. Without resistance there can be no motion.

Averroes gives a lengthy answer to Avempace's argument in favor of natural velocity even in a void. For Averroes, resistance can arise from three sources. First, it can arise from the *position* of the mobile body which is to be moved to another place; in this case resistance arises from the body to be moved. Second, it can arise from the *nature* of the body moved, as in violent motion where nature overcomes the imposed force. Third, it can arise from the *medium* through which the body moves. In celestial bodies there is only resistance arising from position. In living things there is a resistance to the mover both from the body and from the medium. According to Averroes, Avempace's objection applies only to the third kind of resistance, namely the medium. In this case, if the medium were subtracted from the movement of animals, there would still remain the proportion of times to time. But in heavy and light bodies there is no increase in velocity unless this is done by decreasing the resistance. Thus, if all increase of velocity arises solely from the medium, then removing all resistance, such as in a void, the speed would be infinite. Averroes rejects the idea of "subtracting" or adding velocities by adding or subtracting media, for when motion is slower every part of that motion is decreased, while by increasing a line not every part of that line is made greater. Therefore, the speed of motion can be increased not simply by subtracting the medium, but by increasing or decreasing the proportion between mover and body moved. And if the moving force is divided by zero, the velocity can only be instantaneous.[33] The cause of Avempace's error, according to Averroes, is that he thinks that slowness and swiftness are motions to be added or taken away from natural motion, just like a line added to a line. In other words, Averroes claims that velocity arises from the proportion between the moving force and the body moved; for him there must always be some proportion between a moving force and the resistance. If no resistance arises from the body itself, or from the medium, or from the nature of the body, there can be no proportion

---

31 J. A. Weisheipl, "The Concept of Nature," *The New Scholasticism*, 38 (1954) 377-408.
32 Averroes, *Phys.*, IV, comm. 71.
33 "In naturalibus vero diversitas aut equalitas est propter diversitatem aut equalitatem proportionis motoris ad rem motam." Averroes, *Phys.*, IV, comn. 71.

between the velocities of the two motions compared one to the other. If there is no resistance (that is, zero resistance), the body will move instantaneously, that is, without time and without divisibility of that motion.

Averroes answers Avempace's argument about celestial motions by saying that there is indeed resistance between body and the moving force, both of which are *in act*, whereas in natural motions there is no resistance between the form and matter, which is only *potential*. Therefore in natural free fall of bodies motion can arise only from the resistance of the medium.

Thomas Aquinas, in his commentary on the *Physics*, Book IV, lect. 12, rejects Averroes' arguments as *omnino frivola*. He goes on to explain:

> Although the quantity of slowness is not like a continuous quantity, so that motion is added to motion, but rather is like an intensive quantity, as one whiteness is more white than another, nevertheless the quantity of time, from which Aristotle argues, is like a continuous quantity, so that time can be made longer by adding time to time. Hence by subtracting all the time that is added by the resistance, there would still be a natural time for natural speed.

For St. Thomas, what is added and subtracted is not the medium, but time. Even when all resistance is taken away and the additional time taken because of it, there still remains natural velocity in the time necessary to traverse a distance: "Unde subtracto tempore quod additur ex impediente, remanet tempus naturalis velocitatis."[34]

Applying this view to natural motions upward and downward, St. Thomas says,

> If the form, which the generator gave, were removed, there would theoretically remain a quantified body (*corpus quantum*); by the very fact that it has a natural inertia to being moved, it has a resistance to the mover. There is no other way of conceiving resistance in celestial bodies to their movers. Hence not even in heavy and light bodies would the argument of Aristotle follow, according to what he says.[35]

A natural body with its form needs nothing else to move in a void. This should not be taken to imply that, for St. Thomas, the form is in any way the mover, the efficient cause, the *motor* of natural motion downward or upward.[36] The form is nothing more than the active principle of natural motion and rest. Therefore all that is needed is a

---

34 St. Thomas, *In IV Phys.*, lect. 12, n. 10.

35 Ibid.

36 See J. A. Weisheipl, "The Principle *Omne quod movetur ab alio movetur* in Medieval Physics," *Isis*, 56 (1965) 26-45.

natural body with an active principle of movement and the term toward which the motion is destined. The resisting medium in itself contributes nothing to the possibility or impossibility of motion unless it is greater than the moving power, in which case there is no motion at all.

To recapitulate the discussion up to this point, it can be said that the sixth argument of Aristotle against the Atomists is not and never was Aristotle's own doctrine. He takes a position contrary to his own and argues from it to a patent absurdity. On the other hand, Averroes accepts the sixth argument as part of Aristotle's teaching and he makes it a cornerstone of his own doctrine of motion. St. Thomas is fully aware of the difference between Avempace, who claims that Aristotle's argument is false, and Averroes, who insists on its absolute validity. St. Thomas insists that Aristotle's argument is only *ad contradicendum positioni*, and that according to Aristotle's own principles motion in a void is possible.

Aquinas was about 45 when he wrote his commentary on the *Physics* and about 47 when he wrote his unfinished commentary on *De caelo et mundo* in 1272. After a clear and precise recognition of the errors of Averroes, he says,

> ...the motion of heavy and light bodies does not come into being from the generator by means of any other moving principle; it is not even necessary (*neque oportet*) to look for any other resistance in this motion than that which exists between the generator and the body generated. And so it follows that air is not required for natural motion out of necessity, as in violent motion, because that which moves naturally has within itself an innate power (*sibi inditam virtutem*), which is the principle of motion.[37]

In this passage St. Thomas does not discuss the void, but simply rejects Averroes' position demanding a resisting medium for both natural free fall of bodies and for violent motion of heavy bodies upward. In other words, St. Thomas does not recognize any resistance necessary for motion other than exerted by a body being generated in the first place. Once a body is generated, it needs no resistance for it to move upward or downward or any other natural way. This is diametrically contrary to the foundation of Averroes' principles of natural science.

It is interesting to note that when Aquinas was only a young man of about 30, he was already aware of Averroes' rejection of Avempace in text 71. In the fourth Book of the *Sentences*, dist. 44, q. 2, a. 3, ql. 3 ad 2, which was written in 1256, he raises various questions about the resurrected body, among them the possibility of their moving from one

---

37 *In III De caelo*, lect. 8, n. 9.

place to another instantaneously. In the second objection favoring the instantaneous transportation of glorified bodies from place to place, the objector quotes the Philosopher in text 71.[38]

> He argues that...if there is motion in a void, (the body) would have to move in an instant, i. e., without time, because a void does not resist a body at all, while a plenum does. Thus there would be no proportion between motion which takes place in a vacuum and one which takes place in a resisting medium. For two motions to take place in time, there must be proportional velocities, since every time is proportional to time. But no plenum can resist a glorified body, which can co-exist with another body in the same place, however this may take place. Therefore, if (a glorified body) moves, it moves in an instant.

This is the objection. Although the reply is rather long, I shall quote a substantial part of it, since this passage is rarely, if ever, referred to in contemporary literature, and never translated.[39]

> To understand the proof of the Philosopher, as the Commentator expounds it in the same place (comm. 71), it must be noted that one must take the whole as a unit, namely resistance of the body to the moving power, and resistance of the medium through which it moves, and any other resisting force whatever, so that one talks about the *quantitas tarditatis* of the whole motion according to the proportion of resistance of moving power to the body resisting in any way whatever, either *ex se* or *ex alio extrinseco*. For it is necessary that the moving body always resists the mover in some way, because the moving power and the body moved, the agent and the patient, inasmuch as they are such, are contraries. (1) Sometimes the body resists the mover *ex seipso* or because it has the power inclining it to move in the opposite direction, as is evident in violent motions, or at least, because it has a place contrary to the place intended by the mover; this kind of resistance is found in celestial bodies with respect to their movers. (2) Sometimes, however, the body resists the moving force *ex alio tantum* and not *ex seipso*, as is evident in the natural motion of heavy and light bodies, since by their very form they are inclined to such motion, for it is a form impressed by the generator which is the *per se* mover of heavy and light bodies. On the part of matter there is no resistance or power inclining to a contrary motion or to a contrary place, because "place" does not pertain to matter unless it is quantified by dimensions brought about by natural form. Hence there cannot be any resistance except on the part of the medium, which resistance is connatural to their motions. (3) Sometimes resistance arises from both sources, as is evident in the movement of animals. When, therefore, there is no resistance to motion except on the part of the body, as happens in

---

38   The Vives edition of 1874 gives the erroneous source, text 75, and the Parma edition of 1858 refers to text 73. The correct reference is text and comm. 71.

39   The text used for this translation is the Paris, Vives edition of 1874, 11, 332.

celestial bodies, then the time of motion is measured by the proportion of mover to body. In cases such as these, the argument of Aristotle does not apply, because if all media are removed, there would still remain motion in time.

But in those motions where there is resistance only on the part of the medium, one takes the measure of time arising from the impediment of the medium solely. Hence, if one were to subtract the medium altogether, there would remain no impediment. In this case it would either move in an instant or in a time equal to the time it would take to move in empty space and a plenum, because, granting that it would move in time through a void, that time would be proportional to the time it would have if it moved in a plenum.[40] It is possible, however, to imagine another body with the same proportions more subtle than the body by which the place was full, in which, if the other space were equally filled, it would move through that plenum in the same short time as formerly it did in a vacuum, because the more one adds to subtlety, by that much one subtracts from the quantity of time (*quantitate temporis*); and the more subtle the medium, the less it resists. But in other motions in which there is resistance from the mobile body and from the medium, the quantity of time is computed from the proportion of the moving force to the resistance of the body and from the medium together. Hence, granted that the medium is totally subtracted or does not impede, it does not follow that motion would be in an instant, but that the time of motion would be measured only by the resistance of the body. Nothing absurd follows if a body were to move at the same rate of time in a plenum as in a void, if we imagine an extremely subtle body, because the greater the determined subtlety of the medium, the greater is its tendency to diminish the slowness in motion. Hence one can imagine a subtlety so great that it would tend to make less slowness than that slowness which the resistance of the body would have. And so the resistance of the medium would add no slowness to the motion.

It is, therefore, evident that although the medium does not resist glorified bodies inasmuch as it does not prevent two bodies from being in the same place, in no way whatever would their motions be instantaneous, because the very body itself offers resistance to the moving power by the fact that it has a determined position (in place), just as has been said of celestial bodies.

The basic position St. Thomas takes throughout the entire discussion in the *Sentences* is that if all media and all additional forces were taken away, there would still be movement in a void. St. Thomas recognizes only three kinds of resistance: (1) *ex seipso*, that coming from the body itself (a) in coming into being, i. e., the resistance between the body

---

40 All the printed editions consulted have "per vacuum" in this place; but this fails to makes sense. However, the fragment preserved by Capreolus (*Defensiones Theologiae*, II dist. 6, q. 1 ad 7, ed. Tours 1902, 3, 419) reads "per plenum," which is correct.

being generated and the generator, (b) the force of the natural in-clination resisting a contrary motion, as in violent motions, and (c) the internal inertia of bodies being moved in place, as in celestial bodies; (2) *ex alio extrinseco*, that coming from the resisting medium through which the body must pass, as in free fall of bodies; and (3) a com-bination of internal and external resistance, as in the case of animals moving themselves. Once a body has been generated, like water from air, there may or may not be a resisting medium to hinder its natural motion. If there is a medium, the heavier the body is the slower it moves; if there is no medium, the body moves with natural velocity because of the distance to be traversed in a natural time. The basic reason for this is that all bodies and all distances are divisible. Granting this divisibility of the continuum, there follows that time itself is divisible. Therefore a body would move in a void more swiftly than it would in a plenum. But in either case these motions would take time, and time is proportional to time as long as both are finite. Therefore T_1: T_2: :V_1: V_2. For St. Thomas, at least in the commentary on the *Sentences*, it is possible for a body to move in a void with the same time as a body moving in a very subtle medium. In this case the medium would make little or no difference; there is always the natural velocity of a given body, whether there were a medium or not. Thus, unlike Averroes, who demands a medium for the very possibility of motion, St. Thomas holds that the medium is irrelevant to the possibility of motion, and may even be absent altogether, as in a void.

It is important to note that for St. Thomas, as for Aristotle and perhaps for Averroes, the motion under discussion is not only local motion, but also alteration and augmentation. These too can take place in a void, and these too encounter analogously the same kind of resistance.

The position taken by St. Thomas was adopted and maintained by his followers throughout the centuries. Philosophers and theologians, such as John Capreolus,[41] Domingo de Soto,[42] John of St. Thomas,[43] Cosmo Alamanno[44] and many others strongly defended the position of St. Thomas against Averroes. Domingo de Soto, for example, is well aware that he is arguing against "an extremely common position that is being proposed as Aristotle's, which some think can be gotten out of Chapter

41 *Defensiones Theologiae*, II, dist. 6, q. 1 ad 7, ed. C. Paban and T. Pègues (Tours 1902) 3, 418-422.

42 *Super octo libros Physicorum Arist. Quaestiones*, IV, q. 3, a. 2 (Salamanca 1555) fol. 66v-67v. I am grateful to Rev. W. A. Wallace for the use of the text and his translation of the question.

43 *Cursus Philosophicus*: Phil. Nat., I, q. 17, a. 2, ed. B. Reiser (Turin 1933) 365-369.

44 *Summa Philosophiae*: Physica, q. 20, a. 3-4, ed. F. Ehrle (Paris 1885) 197-202.

8, text 71 and the following" *(vulgatissima illa sententia, quae cir-
cumfertur tanquam Aristotelis, quam elici putant ex c. 8, text 71 et infra).* There can be no doubt that the opinion of Averroes, demanding
resistance for every motion, and the correlative notion that in a void a
body would move instantaneously, were common in late medieval
physics. Domingo de Soto refers to Paul of Venice (*In II Sent.*) and
Gregory of Rimini (*In II Sent.*, dist. 6, q. 3, a. 2), "whom practically all
of the Nominalists follow."[45] It was a prevalent opinion when Galileo
was a student and professor at Pisa.

In his early work *De motu*, c. 10, (ca. 1590), Galileo goes to great
lengths[46] to demonstrate, in opposition to Aristotle, that if there were a
void, motion in it would not take place instantaneously, but in time. His
arguments are not so much against Aristotle, as against the Averroist
interpretation of Aristotle. Galileo begins by saying:

> Aristotle, in Book 4 of the *Physics*, in his attempt to deny the existence
> of a void, adduces many arguments. Those that are found beginning with
> text 64[47] are drawn from a consideration of motion. For since he assumes
> that motion cannot take place instantaneously, he tries to show that if a
> void existed, motion in it would take place instantaneously; and, since
> that is impossible, he concludes necessarily that a void is also impossible.
> But, since we are dealing with motion, we have decided to inquire
> whether it is true that, if a void existed, motion in it would take place in-
> stantaneously. And since our conclusion will be that motion in a void
> takes place in time, we shall first examine the contrary view and
> Aristotle's arguments.[48]

It should now be clear that Galileo was not the first to refute the
Averroist interpretation of Aristotle. There was a long tradition on this
subject reaching back to St. Thomas, Avempace and Philoponus.
Galileo was certainly aware of this, for in defending motion in a void,
he explicitly cites "Scotus, Saint Thomas, Philoponus, and others."[49]

*
*   *

By way of conclusion it would be well to summarize the views ex-
plained above. Although the problem is very difficult, and the
Scholastic terms are unfamiliar to many, this is an important subject in
High and Late Scholastic thought. In this paper we have discussed the

---

45 Op. cit., fol. 66vb.
46 *De motu*, trans. and annotated by I. E. Drabkin (Madison 1960) p. 41 f.
47 I. E. Drabkin translates this as "section," but he mistakenly identifies the Bekker numbers;
the reference should be to 214 b 11 ff.
48 Ibid. p. 41.
49 Ibid. p. 49.

opinions of four major figures on the question of motion in a void:
Aristotle, Avempace (Ibn Badja), Averroes, and St. Thomas Aquinas.
Aristotle dealt with the void in the fourth Book of his *Physics*. Having
discussed the problems of place, he felt it also necessary to discuss the
void. The void was a vital problem in pre-Socratic philosophy, because
the Atomists, notably Leucippus and Democritus, tried to explain the
possibility of motion in face of the paradox of Parmenides and his
disciples. The Atomists postulated the void and indivisible atoms as the
only possible explanation of movement witnessed in the real world.
Aristotle tried to revive the concept of φύσις or "nature" to explain
motion, and therefore he postulated natural place and natural motion.
In order to maintain his over-all philosophy of nature, he had to face
the real problem of motion in a void. He presented six difficulties about
motion in a void in order to deny the need of a void in nature. Some of
the arguments against the void postulated by the Atomists presuppose a
distinction between "natural" and "violent" motions. But the sixth and
last argument tried to show that if the void were postulated as the cause
of motion, then it would follow that motion in a void would be instantaneous, that is, without time, for force divided by zero resistance
would be instantaneous.

A great number of commentators thought this expressed Aristotle's
personal view of dynamics, which can be stated in the formula: $V
= F/R$, where V is the velocity, F the moving force, and R the
resistance of a medium. The implication of interpreting Aristotle in this
way is that all motion needs *resistance* in order for bodies to move at
all. In the Latin West, the first to oppose this notion was Avempace, or
Ibn Badja. He claimed that even if all media were removed, as in a
void, there would still be the natural resistance of the body coming into
existence, that is, between mover and moved, and the natural body
would still move in time over a given distance. Avempace argued that if
there were no resistance, such as a medium, the measure of motion
would be the subtraction of all resistance from the natural force of the
body, as in free fall of bodies. His position has been interpreted to mean
$V = F-R$. The crux of the problem discussed is not so much the instantaneous or temporal nature of motion, but the need for resistance in
all motion. This brief passage from Avempace's argument in Book VII
of the *Physics* was reported by Averroes in Book IV, commentary on
text 71.

Averroes, the ardent defender of the very words of Aristotle on all
occasions, opposed Avempace, insisting that all movement, natural or
violent, required a medium. The natural fall of free bodies required a
medium, so that the form could move the matter of the body downward;
for Averroes, "form" was the *per se* mover of the medium and the *per*

accidens cause of the body's movement. Averroes, like Aristotle, had no problem in showing that violent motion needed a medium, for in their view the medium carried "the power to move." Thus both natural and violent motion needed a resisting medium, though in different ways. Without a medium there could be no movement at all under any circumstances. Therefore, Averroes concluded that movement without a medium would have to take place in an instant (*in instanti*), and this is not motion (*motus*) at all, but the simultaneous occupation of two places at once. If the resistance is zero in the formula V = F/R, then motion would be instantaneous.

St. Thomas Aquinas rejected Averroes' arguments as "frivolous," contending that whenever one removes a hindrance, like a resisting medium, the body would move naturally in a given time over a given distance with "natural velocity." This "natural velocity" depends upon the distance to be covered, a magnitude that can be divided, and the time taken to cover that distance, a derived magnitude that can also be divided. Therefore, without resistance, the force of the φύσις itself would move over a given distance in a given time. In other words, St. Thomas denied that motion in a void would be instantaneous. More important, he denied the need for resistance derived from the medium. From this it follows that St. Thomas denied in principle that the formula V = F/R expresses Aristotle's dynamics except for violent or mechanical motion. Although many modern historians of Aristotelian physics accept this formula as authentically Aristotelian, St. Thomas and his followers would not consider it to be an expression of authentic free fall of bodies. For them, once a body is generated it has an innate force to do what comes naturally; it does not move the medium or the "matter," but just moves faster in a void than in a plenum.

What we have tried to show is that the sixth argument in chapter 8 against the void does not represent Aristotle's own view, but is only an argument *ad contradicendum positioni*. The formula V = F/R cannot be derived from Book IV, c. 8, for it neglects the essential element in the whole of Aristotlian physics, namely that φύσις is the principle of motion and rest, and therefore the body moves spontaneously downward if it is a heavy body, and upward if it is a light body. The formula V = F/R is also found by modern historians of science to be implicit in Book VIII, c. 5, of Aristotle's *Physics*. We have not discussed this problem, for it is a different one altogether. In that passage Aristotle gives the example of the "shiphaulers," but here Aristotle is clearly discussing a problem of mechanics, which is not "natural" motion. [50] In

50 See Edward Grant, "Aristotle's 'Shiphaulers' and Medieval Criticisms of His Law of Motion," in *Acts of the Ithaca Congress of the History of Science* (Paris 1962) 587-590.

this paper we have not been concerned with mechanical motion, but only with the free fall of bodies in a void. We have argued that such motion does not need resistance or a medium according to Aristotle and St. Thomas, whereas it does need resistance according to Averroes and his followers.

At the beginning of this paper we noted the view of Anneliese Maier regarding the obstacles in medieval physics that prevented the growth of modern classical physics. She pointed to two basic hypotheses as the most important and the most fatal for the birth of modern classical physics. The more significant of the two was the hypothesis that every movement required a particular mover bound to it and generating it directly, and every normal movement of a successive nature required, besides, a resistance which opposes the moving force and which is overcome by that force, for without resistance there could be no motion (*motus*), but only change (*mutatio*), i. e., and instantaneous change of place. [51]

The first part of this "fatal" hypothesis was discussed in my paper on "Omne quod movetur, ab alio movetur," already cited. In this paper we showed that the view proposed by Maier is Averroist and not universally held in the Middle Ages. The second part of the "fatal" hypothesis was discussed in this paper. We have pointed out that this opinion was also Averroist, and not universally held in medieval physics. There can be no doubt that it was commonly held by Averroists and Nominalists; Domingo de Soto even called it *sententia vulgatissima*. Nevertheless, the notion that "every motion required a resistance which opposes the moving force and which is overcome by that force," and that without this force, as in a void, all motion would take place instantaneously, was rejected by the whole Thomistic and probably Scotistic tradition. Galileo rejected the Averroist hypothesis, and he was well aware that he had precursors in this rejection, namely "Scotus, Saint Thomas, Philoponus, and some others." When there is a strong vital tradition for the opposing view, it is misleading to present the Averroist position as the common "Scholastic teaching."

The teaching of St. Thomas, rejecting both a conjoined mover (*motor conjunctus*) and the need for resistance in all natural motion, is much more compatible with the views of modern classical physics than the Averroist teaching on both points. By this we do not mean that Thomistic natural philosophy prepared the way for classical physics. This would be to claim too much. But it is clear that a specifically Averroist physics did exist in medieval philosophy and that it was vigorously opposed by St. Thomas and others. Only when the Averroist physics was rejected could modern classical physics begin.

51 A. Maier, loc. cit.